SAFEWARE

SAFEWARE

System Safety and Computers

Nancy G. Leveson

University of Washington

ADDISON-WESLEY PUBLISHING COMPANY

Reading, Massachusetts • Menlo Park, California • New York • Don Mills, Ontario
Wokingham, England • Amsterdam • Bonn • Sydney • Singapore
Tokyo • Madrid • San Juan • Milan • Paris

Publishing Partner: Peter Gordon
Associate Editor: Helen Goldstein
Production Coordinator: Marybeth Mooney
Production: Superscript Editorial Production Services
Composition: Windfall Software (Paul C. Anagnostopoulos and Jacqueline Scarlott, using ZzTEX)
Cover Design: Diana C. Coe
Manufacturing Manager: Roy Logan

Library of Congress Cataloging-in-Publication Data

Leveson, Nancy
    Safeware : system safety and computers / Nancy Leveson.
      p. cm.
    Includes bibliographical references and index.
    ISBN 0-201-11972-2
    1. Computer software—Reliability.   2. Electronic digital
computers—Reliability.   3. Industrial safety. I. Title.
QA76.76.R44L48   1995
629.8'9'0289—dc20   94-19779
                                       CIP

Reprinted with corrections September, 1995

Printed in the United States of America.

Text printed on recycled and acid-free paper.

ISBN 0201119722

3 4 5 6 7 8   MA   02 01 00 99

3rd Printing September 1999

There will always be engineering failures. But the worst kind of failures are those that could readily be prevented if only people stayed alert and took reasonable precautions. Engineers, being human, are susceptible to the drowsiness that comes in the absence of crisis. Perhaps one characteristic of a professional is the ability and willingness to stay alert while others doze. Engineering responsibility should not require the stimulation that comes in the wake of catastrophe.

— Samuel C. Florman
The Civilized Engineer

Whoever destroys a single life is as guilty as though he has destroyed the whole world; and whoever rescues a single life earns as much merit as though he had rescued the entire world.

— Sanhedrin 37:a
The Talmud

PREFACE

These days we adopt innovations in large numbers, and put them to extensive use, faster than we can even hope to know their consequences . . . which tragically removes our ability to control the course of events.

—Patrick Lagadec
Major Technological Risk

Although the introduction of new technology has always led to accidents, the pace of technological change is increasing along with the potential consequences of accidents. As the industrialized world has learned to cope with and protect itself from the natural forces that used to cause the majority of accidents, manmade systems have taken their place.

Concerns about the dangers of technological innovation are not new. For example, in the early 1800s, James Watt argued against the use of high-pressure steam engines because of the dangers of boiler explosions. Thomas Edison similarly warned against high-voltage electricity in the 1880s. In the past, however, the consequences of accidents caused by dangerous new technology—such as high-pressure steam or high-voltage electricity—were limited. It was possible to learn from our mistakes and to improve our technology as we found out about its dangers. This situation no longer exists. Today we are building systems—and using computers to control them—that have the potential for large-scale destruction of life and the environment: Even a single accident may be disastrous. We do not have the luxury of learning from experience, but must attempt to anticipate and prevent accidents before they occur.

Goals

This book examines what is currently known about building safe electromechanical systems and looks at the accidents of the past to see what lessons can be applied to new computer-controlled systems. One obvious lesson is that most accidents are not the result of unknown scientific principles but rather of a failure to apply well-known, standard engineering practices. A second lesson is that accidents will not be prevented by technological fixes alone, but will require control of all aspects of the development and operation of the system.

In 1968, Jerome Lederer, then the director of the NASA Manned Space Flight Safety Program for Apollo, wrote

> Systems safety covers the total spectrum of risk management. It goes *beyond the hardware* and associated procedures of systems safety *engineering*. It involves: attitudes and motivation of designers and production people, employee/management rapport, the relation of industrial associations among themselves and with government, human factors in supervision and quality control, documentation on the interfaces of industrial and public safety with design and operations, the interest and attitudes of top management, the effects of the legal system on accident investigations and exchange of information, the certification of critical workers, political considerations, resources, public sentiment and many other non-technical but vital influences on the attainment of an acceptable level of risk control. These non-technical aspects of system safety cannot be ignored [171, p.8].

Most of these issues are addressed in this book.

Mixing social and technical issues in one book is unusual for engineering or computer science. However, considering technology and its social implications separately can limit and distort both and can result in wasted time arguing the wrong questions, as well as tragic mistakes.

Treating technology apart from its impact on society can lead not only to negative social consequences, but also to unrealistic and unusable technology. Engineers and applied mathematicians are not working in a controlled laboratory situation: The application of scientific principles to real problems requires interaction with the messy world outside the laboratory. Furthermore, most technology is based on assumptions that have political or ethical aspects that can never be "proved." We need not only to identify these assumptions, but also to understand their implications and to evaluate their reasonableness.

Conversely, considering social issues without considering what is technically feasible leads to misunderstanding and useless argument. It may, for example, produce conclusions that are overly optimistic about technological improvements or overly defeatist and negative. Social arguments based on incomplete or inaccurate understanding of the associated technology are at best misleading: To be effective, engineers and social scientists need to understand both aspects. Otherwise, they end up arguing at cross-purposes without touching the most appropriate issue: how technical, political, and social decisions should be made considering both the technological and social reality of the time.

Another underlying assumption of this book is that system safety and software safety should not be separated. Safety is a system problem; it cannot be handled in a vacuum. It is rare to find a complex system today that does not include a computer, yet few safety engineering analysis techniques include consideration of computer software, and few software engineering specification and design techniques include specific consideration of system hazards. Most standards and technical approaches to safety involve just "getting the software right" or attempting to increase software reliability to ultrahigh levels. Although in the future it may be possible to construct perfect software, the current reality is that we cannot accomplish this goal for anything but the simplest systems. Moreover, even if the software had no errors, there would be no way to know this with high confidence.

This book attempts to convince the computer science and engineering communities that a different approach is possible and should be tried. The title of the book, *Safeware*, expresses the impossibility of separating the various aspects of the system in dealing with safety issues. The approach advocated here requires a change in attitude and changes in design and development practices. These changes may result not only in safer systems, but in more reliable ones and in cost savings for equal levels of assurance.

Audience

Anyone building or managing the construction of complex, safety-critical systems should find this book helpful. The information provided will be of use to practitioners, regulators, and researchers. In keeping with the basic philosophy that system safety, software safety, and nontechnical issues cannot be separated, all three are intermingled. No assumption of knowledge about system safety is made: The book introduces basic system safety concepts and then demonstrates how they can be extended to include software.

Practitioners will find the information necessary to design a safety program, but a cookbook approach is not provided. One set of procedures that applies to all systems and all organizations does not and cannot exist. By following cookbook solutions, we are very likely to find that we feel satisfied and our jobs are greatly simplified, but risk is not appreciably reduced. The goal of this book is to educate rather than to train—to provide enough information to design safety programs that are tailored to the characteristics of the system being constructed and the organization constructing and operating it.

Those responsible for regulating computer-controlled systems should also find the book useful. A delicate balance between protecting the public and not unduly inhibiting technological progress is difficult to achieve. Any regulation of technology needs to be based on the state of the art in the relevant field and on what is practical versus what is desirable. This book attempts to distinguish between what is currently achievable and what is not. Unfortunately, the information that regulators need for optimal decision making is just not obtainable at this point. Wishing or pretending that the techniques we have work better than they do or that probabilistic risk assessments are possible for software will not make it so. The only option is to do the best possible with what is known and to be flexible enough to change quickly when the state of the art advances.

Researchers will find descriptions of a wealth of open problems on which to focus their attention. To make progress, however, we need to build on what is already known. A goal of this book is to provide the background and information necessary to create new and better solutions to our problems. I have tried to summarize what is known in order to clarify what needs to be done. It will be obvious on reading this book that there is a great deal left to be learned.

Content

Each of the four parts of the book (and most of the chapters) can stand alone. Part 1 examines the nature of risk and the causes of accidents. We must understand the problems we are attempting to solve before we can design effective solutions or select appropriate methodologies. This part provides a foundation for selecting or devising risk reduction strategies.

Part 2 provides the context for the approach to safety taken in this book. To understand a technology, we must understand the basic science that underlies it, along with the social context that provides its purpose, goals, and decision criteria [221]. The foundations of system safety are presented in this part as well as the distinctions between it and other approaches to safety.

Part 3 introduces some terminology in order to enhance communication among engineers and computer scientists, and it describes models of accidents and human error that underlie safety techniques. Using these techniques effectively and making appropriate choices among them requires understanding their underlying models and assumptions.

Using the background provided in the first three parts of the book, Part 4 describes the elements of a safeware program, including management, process, hazard analysis, requirements analysis, design for safety, design of the human–machine interface, and verification. Experienced safety engineers may skip to this part, although they are encouraged to skim the rest of the book. Managers may be primarily interested in Chapters 3, 4, 11, and 12. Chapters 13 and 14 are review for those already familiar with hazard analysis and hazard analysis techniques, but an introduction is included because most software engineers are unfamiliar with them.

Throughout this book, real accidents are used to illustrate the points being made. A mix of applications and types of systems are included. Many of the examples were selected because extensive information about them is available—for example, Three Mile Island, *Challenger*, Bhopal, Chernobyl, Flixborough, and the Therac-25. Oversimplification of the causes of accidents is a common problem; only a few major accidents have been investigated in enough detail to learn what really happened and thus how to prevent future ones. For readers not familiar with the details of these accidents, descriptions are included in the appendices. Some involve computers and some do not. As Kletz has noted, computers do not provide new ways of making errors, but merely new and easier opportunities for making the old errors [158]. A shift to computer control should not require us to relearn old lessons the hard way.

Readers will quickly realize that I have not solved the software safety problem. This book summarizes what is known, evaluates what has been proposed, and points to a path to follow. Technological development will not stop for scientists and engineers to find optimal solutions to complex problems. Systems must be built using the best approaches that we currently have. If these are unsatisfactory, then either we should reconsider whether we should be building these systems using computers, or we should admit that we may be increasing risk but that we believe the additional risk is justified with respect to the benefit the system provides.

Acknowledgements

Engineers at Hughes Aircraft Company—including Marion Moon, Bill Noble, and Pete Goddard—first introduced me to the importance of software safety problems, convinced me I should look more deeply into them, and started my education in system safety. I am indebted to them and to others at Hughes for their assistance and encouragement.

Many people provided comments on early drafts of this book. I would especially like to thank Capt. Oscar Overton of the U.S. Air Force, Michael Brown of the Naval Surface Warfare Center, Grady Lee, Martin Kazubowski, my colleague Prof. David Notkin, Michael DeWalt of the U.S. FAA, Robert Dorsett, Gary Lynn Johnson and Gary Preckshot of Lawrence Livermore National Laboratories, and the University of Washington graduate students who provided feedback, especially Kurt Partridge, Michael Van Hilst, Ross Ortega, and Gail Murphy.

Support for the research described in this book was provided by the NASA/Langley Research Center, the National Science Foundation, the FAA, the California Department of Transportation and the University of California PATH program, Sandia Labs, the University of California Micro program, and private industry. I am particularly grateful to Hughes Aircraft Company and to Dr. David Eckhardt of NASA/Langley Research Center for their continued support over the years.

C O N T E N T S

PART ONE

The Nature of Risk

A life without adventure is likely to be unsatisfying, but a life in which adventure is allowed to take whatever form it will, is likely to be short.

— Bertrand Russell

The first step in solving any problem is to understand it. We often propose solutions to problems that we do not understand and then are surprised when the solutions fail to have the anticipated effect. This section explores the nature of risk and the causes of accidents.

Chapter

1

Risk in Modern Society

Living in a technological society is like riding a bucking bronco. I don't believe we can afford to get off, and I doubt that someone will magically appear who can lead it about on a leash. The question is: how do we become better bronco busters?

—William Ruckelshaus
Risk in a Free Society

Many of the most serious accidents of this century have occurred in the past 15 years. The worst industrial accident in history (in terms of deaths and injuries) took place in 1984, when the release of a highly toxic chemical, methyl isocyanate, at a Union Carbide chemical plant in Bhopal, India, killed between 2,000 and 3,000 people and seriously injured over 200,000. The worst series of accidents in the 35-year history of medical accelerators occurred between 1985 and 1987, when six people were massively overdosed by a computer-based radiation therapy machine called the Therac-25—all died or were seriously injured. In 1979 and 1986, respectively, the accidents at the Three Mile Island and Chernobyl nuclear power plants occupied the world's attention. Before the Chernobyl disaster, it was widely thought that nuclear power plant accidents involving release of significant radioactive materials to the atmosphere were highly improbable, if not virtually impossible. Just three months before Chernobyl, the *Challenger* accident gripped the world's attention. Is new technology making our world riskier?

3

Risk is not a new problem. Humans have always had to face risk from their environment, although the risks have changed as society and the natural environment have changed. In the past (or currently in rural areas of developing countries), the greatest concerns were natural (geological and climatological) disasters such as floods, drought, earthquakes, and tropical storms. Today, industrialization has substituted man-made hazards for those rooted in nature. In the United States, technological hazards account for 15 to 25 percent of human mortality and have significantly surpassed natural hazards in impact, cost, and general importance [87]. Damage to our ecosystem is difficult to assess, but danger signals include a high rate of species extinction and high concentrations of toxic chemicals in the environment.

Although industrialized nations have used technology to control many natural hazards, a strict distinction between natural and man-made disasters is an oversimplification. Human tampering with the environment has exacerbated and sometimes caused natural disasters, such as the destruction of watersheds leading to flooding or the release of chemicals into the atmosphere affecting climate and crops. Flood damage in the United States, for example, has increased as expenditures on flood control have increased [154]. Areas prone to flooding were not developed until we introduced flood prevention measures. When an exceptional flood overwhelms these measures (or they do not achieve their design goals), the damage is much worse than it would have been before prevention measures were introduced.

The number of recorded natural disasters in which people were killed or injured rose, on average, during the 1960s and 1970s. This increase does not reflect a change in geophysical or climatological extremes (abnormalities in the physical environment), which held relatively constant during this time, but rather reflects an increasing risk of casualties resulting from these extremes, partly due to societal and technological changes [30].

Similarly, the amount of damage caused by technological accidents may be affected by natural phenomena: The result of an accidental release of radiation or chemicals, for example, may be dependent on weather factors such as wind direction and strength.

Thus, the distinction between natural and technological hazards is often useful, but is not completely accurate. In fact, all hazards are affected by complex interactions among technological, ecological, sociopolitical, and cultural systems [30, 174, 339]. Attempts to control risk by treating it simply as a technical problem or only as a social issue are doomed to fail or to be less effective than possible.

To discover effective solutions to these problems, we must understand the factors underlying the risks we face. Part 1 of this book delineates these factors and the myriad aspects of the general problem of risk. Parts 2 through 4 examine the foundations of system safety and present an approach to controlling technological risks in the complex systems that characterize modern society, especially those systems that include computers among their components.

1.1 Changing Attitudes toward Risk

All human activity involves risk; there is no such thing as a risk-free life. Safety matches and safety razors, for example, are not *safe*, only *safer* than their alternatives; they present a reduced level of risk while preserving the benefits of the devices they replace. No aircraft could fly, no automobile move, and no ship put out to sea if all hazards had to be eliminated first [106].

Progress demands taking some risks, and despite great advances in technology, we are unable to eliminate risk altogether. However, much more so now than in the past, humans are demanding that risks be known and controlled to the extent possible and practical. Societies are recognizing the right of workers, consumers, and the general public to know what risks they face and are making worker and public safety a responsibility of the employer and manufacturer [97, 172].

The shift from purely personal to organizational or public responsibility for risk is a recent phenomenon. Until the early part of this century, workers were expected to provide their own tools, to understand the risks associated with their trade, and to accept personal responsibility for their own safety. This attitude was justified partly by the fact that workers devoted their entire careers to the manufacturing of one or two products [294]; they could thoroughly understand their jobs and had control over the way they performed their tasks.

Today, workers are more at the mercy of their employers in terms of safety, and, accordingly, responsibility has shifted from the employee to the employer. In most industrialized countries, employers are expected to provide a safe working environment and the necessary tools and equipment to maintain that environment. In addition, changes in legal liability and responsibility have led to product safety programs that are concerned with consumer as well as employee safety.

Clearly, in matters of risk, today's complex, technological society requires that the general public place its trust in "expert knowledge" [30]. Accordingly, responsibility for detection of and protection from hazards has been transferred from the public to the state, corporate management, engineers, safety experts, and other professionals. Complete abdication of personal responsibility, however, is not always wise. In some instances—such as the Bhopal accident—the public has completely trusted others to plan for and respond effectively to an emergency, with tragic results. The Bhopal Union Carbide plant was run in a way that almost guaranteed a serious accident would occur. In addition, emergency and evacuation planning, training, and equipment were inadequate. The surrounding population was not warned of the hazards, nor were they told (either before or during the chemical release) of the simple measures (such as closing their eyes and putting wet cloths over their faces) that could have saved their lives. Such incidents have aroused the public to become more involved in risk issues.

In turn, public involvement in issues that past generations took for granted—such as the hazards related to medicine, transportation, and industry—have led to government regulation and to the creation of public interest groups to control hazards that were previously tolerated [113, 172]. System safety engineers, who used to focus on uncontrolled-energy accidents such as explosions or the inadvertent firing of a weapon, are now being asked to control new hazards such as air and ground pollution and to ensure that the systems we build do not produce, contain, or decompose into hazardous materials [42].

In writing about the Bhopal tragedy, Bogard expresses this new attitude:

> We are not safe from the risks posed by hazardous technologies, and any choice of technology carries with it possible worst case scenarios that we must take into account in any implementation decision. The public has the right to know precisely what these worst case scenarios are and participate in all decisions that directly or indirectly affect their future health and well-being. In many cases, we must accept the fact that the result of employing such criteria may be a decision to forego the implementation of a hazardous technology altogether [30, p.109].

Increased regional and national concern about safety has expanded in the past decade to include international issues. The greenhouse effect, acid rain, and accidents such as the release of radiation at Chernobyl do not recognize national borders. The global economy and the vast potential destructiveness of some of our technological achievements are forcing us to recognize that risk can have international implications and that control of risk requires cooperative approaches.

Because risk reduction can be expensive and often requires tradeoffs with other desirable goals, it is important to consider whether the increased public and governmental concern about technological risk is justified and whether engineers, both hardware and software, should be worrying about these problems at all. Is risk increasing in our modern society as a result of new technological achievements, or are we simply experiencing a new and unjustified form of Luddism?[1]

1.2 Is Increased Concern Justified?

Determining whether technological risk is increasing or not depends on the data used and its interpretation. On the one hand, Harris and colleagues argue that technological hazards, in terms of human mortality, were greater in the earlier, less fully managed stages of industrial development [112]. They cite data from the National Safety Council showing that occupational death and injury rates have declined steadily since the early part of this century [112] and conclude that technological hazard mortality is not currently rising. However, they warn that "the positive effects of technology have for some time reached their maximum effect on human mortality, while the hazards of technology continue partially

---

[1] The Luddite disturbances occurred in England between 1811 and 1816, when workers in the woolen industry tried, through violence, to stem the increasing mechanization of the mills. *Luddism* has become a generic term describing opposition to technological innovation.

unchecked, affecting particularly the chronic causes of death that currently account for 85 percent of mortality in the U.S.A." [112].

On the other hand, examination of the technological accident rate, rather than the occupational death and injury rate, suggests that technological risk *is* increasing. Sixty percent of all the major industrial disasters from 1921 to 1989 occurred after 1975 [30]. Writing in 1989, Bogard argued that 12 of the 19 major industrial accidents in the twentieth century involving 100 or more deaths occurred after 1950. When we include smaller-scale incidents, transportation accidents, dam breaks, and structural collapses, the evidence supporting the hypothesis of increasing risk is even more compelling.

Complicating things further, although the total technological accident rate has been increasing, accident rates in specific *types* of systems have been decreasing. For example, the military aviation accident rate has generally improved over time. This improvement has been attributed to an emphasis on system safety programs and concerted efforts to eliminate and control hazards [88]. Thus, the experience of military aviation seems to support an argument that technological advances need not increase risk if efforts are made to control it. Recently, however, the decrease in military aviation accident rates attributed to the use of system safety techniques has slowed. One explanation for this slowing may simply be the naturally increasing difficulty in finding ways to make large improvements. However, other, less obvious factors may be at work here.

Clearly, we will not find the answer to our question in such ambiguous and contradictory statistical data. In fact, the major changes occurring in the post–World War II era make most long-term historical risk data inapplicable to today's world: Past experience does not allow us to predict the future when the risk factors in the present and future differ from those in the past. Examining these changes will help us understand the problems we face.

1.3 Unique Risk Factors in Industrialized Society

Risk is a combination of the *likelihood* of an accident and the *severity* of the potential consequences. Risk increases if either the likelihood or the magnitude of loss increases (as long as the other component does not decrease proportionally). Different factors may affect these two components of risk. Some factors that are particularly relevant today are the appearance of new hazards and the increasing complexity, exposure, energy, automation, centralization, scale, and pace of technological change in the systems we are attempting to build.

1.3.1 The Appearance of New Hazards

Before the Industrial Revolution, accidents were the result of natural causes or involved a few relatively well-understood, simple technological devices. In the twentieth century, scientific and technological advances have reduced or eliminated many risks that were once commonplace. Modern medicine, for example, has provided cures for previously fatal diseases and eliminated some scourges, such as smallpox, altogether.

At the same time, science and technology have also created new hazards. Misuse and overuse of antibiotics have given rise to resistant microbes. Children no longer work in coal mines or as chimney sweeps, but they are now exposed to man-made chemicals and pesticides in their food or to increased environmental pollution [57]. The harnessing of the atom has increased the potential for death and injury from radiation exposure.

Some of the new hazards are more pervasive and harder to find and eliminate than were the ones eliminated or reduced in the past [57]. In addition, we have no previous experience to guide us in handling these new hazards. Much of what has been learned from past accidents is passed down through codes and standards of practice. But appropriate codes and standards have not yet been developed for many new engineering specializations and technologies. Sometimes lessons learned over centuries are lost when older technologies are replaced by newer ones—for example, when digital computers are substituted for mechanical devices.

Many of the approaches that worked on the simpler technologies of the past—such as replication of components to protect against individual component failure—are ineffective in controlling today's complex risks. Although redundancy provides protection against accidents caused by individual component failure, it is not as effective against hazards that arise from the interactions among components in the increasingly complex and interactive systems being engineered today. In fact, redundancy may increase complexity to the point where the redundancy itself contributes to accidents.

1.3.2 Increasing Complexity

Many of the new hazards are related to increased complexity (both product and process) in the systems we are building. Not only are new hazards created by the complexity, but the complexity makes identifying them more difficult.

Perrow distinguishes between accidents caused by component failures and those, which he calls *system accidents*, that are caused by interactive complexity in the presence of tight coupling [259]. High-technology systems are often made up of networks of closely related subsystems. Conditions leading to hazards emerge in the interfaces between subsystems, and disturbances progress from one component to another. As an example of this increasingly common type of complexity, modern petrochemical plants often combine several separate chemical processes into one continuous production, without the intermediate storage that would decouple the subsystems [274].

In fact, analyses of major industrial accidents invariably reveal highly complex sequences of events leading up to accidents, rather than single component failures. Whereas in the past, component failure was cited as the major factor in accidents, today more accidents result from dangerous design characteristics and interactions among components [108].

The operation of some systems is so complex that it defies the understanding of all but a few experts. Increased complexity and coupling make it difficult for the designer to consider all the hazards, or even the most important ones, or for the operators to handle all normal and abnormal situations and disturbances safely [323].

Not only does functional complexity make the designer's task more difficult, but the complexity and scope of the projects require numerous people and teams to work together. The anonymity of team projects dilutes individual responsibility [172]. Moreover, many new specializations do not have standards of individual responsibility and ethics that are as well developed as those of older professions.

Kletz points out the paradox that people are willing to spend money on complexity but not on simplicity [158]. Consider the following accident that occurred in a British chemical plant. In this plant, a pump and various pipelines had several different uses, which included transferring methanol from a road tanker to storage, charging it to the plant, and moving recovered methanol back from the plant. A computer set the various valves, monitored their positions, and switched the transfer pump on and off.

On this particular occasion, a tank truck was being emptied:

> The pump had been started from the control panel but had been stopped by means of a local button. The next job was to transfer some methanol from storage to the plant. The computer set the valves, but as the pump had been stopped manually it had to be started manually. When the transfer was complete the computer told the pump to stop, but because it had been started manually it did not stop and a spillage occurred [157, p. 225].

In this case, a simpler design—independent pipelines for different functions, which were actually installed after the spill—makes errors much less likely and may not be more expensive over the lifetime of the equipment.

Computers often allow more interactive, tightly coupled, and error-prone designs to be built, and thus may encourage the introduction of unnecessary and dangerous complexity. Kletz has noted, "Programmable electronic systems have not introduced new forms of error, but by increasing the complexity of the processes that can be controlled, they have increased the scope for the introduction of conventional errors" [158]. If we accept Perrow's argument that interactive complexity and coupling are a cause of serious accidents, then the introduction of computers to control dangerous systems may increase risk unless great care is taken to minimize complexity and coupling.

1.3.3 Increasing Exposure

Not only is our *technology* becoming more complex, but our *society* has become more complex, interdependent, and vulnerable [172]. The consequences of an accident depend not only on the hazard itself but also on the exposure of the hazard—that is, the length of time and the environment within which the hazard exists.

More people may be exposed to a given hazard today than were previously. Passenger capacity in aircraft, for example, is increasing to satisfy economic concerns. Siting of dangerous facilities near large populations is increasing as more people move to cities and larger plants need larger workforces within commuting distance. Interdependence and complexity can cause ripple effects beyond the immediate exposure area of the hazard, magnifying the potential consequences of accidents.

1.3.4 Increasing Amounts of Energy

Another factor related to increased risk is the discovery and use of high-energy sources—such as exotic fuels, high-pressure systems, and atomic fission—which have increased the magnitude of the potential losses. Other new systems use more conventional energy sources, but they involve technology that requires larger amounts of energy than was required in the past.

The larger amounts of energy increase both the surrounding area potentially affected by an accident and the amount of damage possible. New hazards that can cause genetic damage and environmental contamination introduce the potential for affecting not only the current generation but our descendants as well.

1.3.5 Increasing Automation of Manual Operations

Although it might seem that automation would decrease the risk of operator error, the truth is that automation does not remove people from systems—it merely moves them to maintenance and repair functions and to higher-level supervisory control and decision making [270]. The effects of human decisions and actions can then be extremely serious. At the same time, the increased system complexity makes the decision-making process more difficult.

Automation often removes the operator from the immediate control of the energies of the system [150]. Consequently, an individual moving within the physical system may find it difficult to anticipate the possible energy flows—for example, the physical behavior of an industrial robot. This difficulty is enhanced in systems that use exotic chemical and physical processes that are not well understood.

In addition, operators in automated systems are often relegated to central control rooms, where they must rely on indirect information about the system state: This information can be misleading. In 1977, New York City had a massive and costly power blackout [259]. When the operator followed prescribed procedures to handle the initial symptoms, the electrical system was brought to a complete halt. The operator did not know that there had been two relay failures—one that would lead to a high flow of current over a line that normally carried little or no current (and thus would have alerted the operator to the real problem) and a second relay failure that blocked the flow over the line, making it appear normal. The operator was unaware of the particular set of circumstances that made the zero-current reading abnormal and treated it as normal. Lack of direct information increases the probability of such faulty hypotheses. Operators then become the scapegoat when accidents are blamed on human error, even though the "error" was induced by features of the automated system.

These problems will only get worse with the current trend toward decentralization of control. Microprocessors embedded in the plant or system are taking over most control functions, with only high-level information being fed back to the central control room or control point. This design limits even further the operator's options and hinders broad comprehension of the system state [259].

A control loop, by its very nature, masks the occurrence and subsequent development of a malfunction precisely because it copes with the immediate effects of the problem, at least for a time [70]. But this masking does not continue indefinitely: When the malfunction is finally discovered, it may by then be more difficult to control, or the symptoms may be hidden or distorted. By the time a human gets involved, the symptoms may be referred forward or backward by the major loops in the overall process. For example,

> In 1985, a China Airlines 747 suffered a slow loss of power from its outer right engine. This would have caused the plane to yaw to the right, but the autopilot compensated, until it finally reached the limit of its compensatory abilities and could no longer keep the plane stable. At that point, the crew did not have enough time to determine the cause of the problem and to take action: the plane rolled and went into a vertical dive of 31,500 feet before it could be recovered. The aircraft was severely damaged and recovery was much in doubt [242, p.138].

The energy-saving systems incorporated in many process plants, particularly during the 1970s, to conserve energy and to improve thermal economy complicate this problem further [70]. For example, heat generated by a process might be recovered through a complex exchange system. As is often the case, multiple goals—in this case safety and economy—lead to conflicts. The energy-saving systems introduce component interactions that make the functioning of the system less transparent to its designers and operators [274]. From the designers' standpoint, systematic analysis and prediction of events that could lead to accidents become increasingly difficult. From the operators' standpoint, the extra complexity makes diagnosis of problems more difficult and again leads to masking and referral of symptoms: The place in the plant where signs of trouble first emerge may not be where the problems occurred [70].

1.3.6 Increasing Centralization and Scale

Increasing automation has been accompanied by centralization of industrial production in very large plants and the potential for great loss and damage to people, equipment, and the environment. For many decades, plant size has been increasing, resulting in a change of scale in production: Devices and whole processes are being extrapolated into untested areas. In nuclear power, for example, Bupp and Derian observed that by 1968, manufacturers were taking orders for plants six times larger than the largest one then in operation. "And this was in an industry which had previously operated on the belief that extrapolations of two to one over operating experience were at the outer boundary of acceptable risk" [46, p.73]. The Browns Ferry Nuclear Power Plant, which was the site of a serious accident in 1975, was 10 times the size of any plant already in operation at the time its construction began in 1966. In fact, it was to become one of the world's largest electrical generating facilities [350].

Ocean shipping is another industry experiencing enormous changes in scale that are alien to its previous caution and conservatism. In order to maximize profits, supertankers are being built without the sound design and redundant systems (such as double hulls) they once had. Mostert writes about these superships:

> The gigantic scale of vessels creates an abstract environment in which crews are far removed from direct experience of the sea's unforgiving qualities and potentially hostile environment. Heavy automation undermines much of the old-fashioned vigilance and induces engineers to lose their occupational instincts—qualities that in earlier days of shipping were an invaluable safety factor [231].

1.3.7 Increasing Pace of Technological Change

A final risk factor is the increasing pace of technological change in this century. The average time required to translate a basic technical discovery into a commercial product has decreased from 30 years during the early part of this century (1880–1919) to 5 or fewer years today. In addition, the number of new products or processes is increasing exponentially [294]. The twentieth century has seen a major acceleration in the growth of new industries stemming from scientific and technological innovation, such as gene splicing. Dangerous substances are being handled on an unprecedented scale, and economic pressures often militate against extensive testing [172].

The increased pace of change lessens opportunity to learn from experience. Small-scale and relatively nonhazardous systems can evolve gradually by trial and error. But learning by trial and error is not possible for many modern products and processes because the pace of change is too fast and the penalties of failure are too great. Design and operating procedures must be right the first time when there is potential for a major fire, explosion, or release of toxic materials. Nuclear energy is just one example. Christopher Hinton, who was in charge of the first British atomic energy installations, said in 1957,

> All other engineering technologies have advanced not on the basis of their successes but on the basis of their failures. The bridges that collapsed . . . have added more to our knowledge of bridge design than the ones which

held; the boilers that exploded more than the ones that had no accidents. . . . Atomic energy, however, must forego this advantage of progressing on the basis of knowledge gained by failure (quoted in [81, p.53]).

As a result, empirical design rules and equipment standards are being replaced by reliance on hazard identification and control or by attempts to build ultrareliable systems that never fail. The feasibility of accomplishing either of these goals and the amount of protection they afford are unknown in comparison to the older methods involving learning by experience and using well-tested standards and guidelines.

Given the difficulty that industry is having in coping with all the changes, it is not surprising that government agencies charged with the licensing and safety monitoring of these industries are also having problems keeping pace. New technology, such as digital computers, requires new standards, regulatory procedures, and expertise that take time to develop and perfect. Industry and society are unwilling to slow progress while these agencies catch up.

1.4 How Safe Is Safe Enough?

We are back where we started—with no real proof that a problem exists but with much supporting evidence. Examining the risk factors described, a strong argument can be made that concern is justified.

Because of the recent changes and unique conditions for which historical experience does not apply, the nonoccurrence of particular types of accidents in the past is no guarantee that they will not occur in the future. In addition, if we must learn from accidents and if failure teaches us more than success (as Petroski [263] and others have argued), then what can we do about systems in which a single accident can have such tragic consequences that the process of learning from accidents is unacceptable to society?

The system safety approach to reducing risk is to anticipate accidents and their causes in before-the-fact hazard analyses (rather than relying on after-the-fact accident investigations) and to eliminate or control hazards as much as possible throughout the life of a system. The goal is to understand and manage risk in order to eliminate accidents or to reduce their consequences. Frola and Miller claim that system safety investment has reduced losses where it has been applied rigorously in military and aerospace programs [88].

Unfortunately, hazards will never be eliminated completely from all systems. In addition to the technical difficulty of anticipating and reducing risks, there is the basic problem of conflicting goals. Desirable qualities tend to conflict with each other, and design tradeoffs between safety, performance, and other goals are required. A large industrial robot arm, for example, carrying a heavy load at high speed cannot be stopped quickly in emergencies without damaging the arm. The longer it takes the arm to stop in response to a deadman switch or other safety device, the less the wear on the arm but also the more likely that the arm will hit something before it stops [252]. Likewise, human–machine interfaces that are designed to be easy to use often are less safe. For example, computer input errors can be reduced if operators are required to repeat operations, but that requires extra time and seemingly wasted effort.

Designing a system to protect against a variety of hazards is clearly possible, but designing a system to protect against all hazards, no matter how perverse or remote, might require making so many compromises in functionality and other goals that the system is not worth building at all [332]. Finding the right balance is difficult.

Wolf suggests that we may be "in the presence of a contradiction of technological culture that can neither prevent potentially disastrous accidents nor accept their consequences" [357]. But even if the number of accidents and their associated losses increase, we are unlikely to abandon the new and risky systems that represent technological progress. The benefits of technology usually come with disadvantages, and society is unwilling to live without many of those benefits. If this assumption is correct, then the process for determining exactly which systems to build and what new technology to introduce into them becomes critical.

Several ways of making this decision have been suggested. At one extreme is an anti-technology stance that blames accidents on new technology alone and concludes that advanced technology should not be used in dangerous systems. Such a simple, negative stance is not the solution to complex engineering and ethical problems. At the opposite extreme is the pro-technology position that all new technology is good: If it can be built, then it should be. Those who hold this position often put the blame for accidents on humans and assume that risks will be reduced by replacing human operators by computers. Again, this position is oversimplistic.

The prevailing position in our society is the utilitarian view that the only reasonable way to make technology and risk decisions is to use risk–benefit analysis. This belief is so widespread that we often accept risk–benefit analysis as the *only* way to make technology and risk decisions, without realizing that there are alternatives.

1.4.1 Risk–Benefit Analysis and the Alternatives

To utilitarians, catastrophic accidents (such as Bhopal) are one of the risks of high technology, which, in the long run, are outweighed by the technology's overall benefits. Decisions can be made by comparing these risks and benefits.

To apply this approach, we must be able to (1) measure risk and (2) choose an appropriate level for decision making. Unfortunately, it is impossible to measure risk accurately, especially before a system is built: Systems must be designed and built while knowledge of their risk is incomplete or nonexistent. Even if past experience could be used, it might not be a valid predictor of future risk unless the system and its environment remain static, which is unlikely. Small changes may substantially alter the risk involved [83].

Risk assessment tries to solve this dilemma. The goal is to quantify risk, including both likelihood and severity of a loss, before historical data is available. The accuracy of such risk assessments is controversial. William Ruckelshaus, former head of the U.S. Environmental Protection Agency, argues that the current use of risk assessment data is a kind of pretense: "To avoid paralysis resulting from waiting for definitive data, we assume we have greater knowledge than scientists actually possess and make decisions based on those assumptions" [303, p.110].

In fact, risk assessment may never be able to provide definitive answers to these types of risk questions. Estimates for extremely unlikely events, such as a serious nuclear reactor accident, can never have the same scientific validity as estimates of events for which there are abundant statistics. Because the required probabilities are so small (such as 10^{-7} per reactor per year), there is no practical possibility of determining this failure rate directly—that is, by building 1,000 reactors, operating them for 10,000 years, and tabulating their operating histories [351].

Instead, probabilities of serious accidents are calculated by constructing models of the interaction of events that can lead to the accident. In practice, the only events included are those that can be measured. At the same time, the causal factors involved in most major accidents (see the appendices for some examples) are almost all unmeasurable. The difficulty of performing risk assessments is discussed in later chapters of this book. In brief, the technique is controversial, and the results are far from universally accepted as meaningful.

Even if risk could be measured, there is still the problem of choosing the level of risk to use in decision making. The most common criterion is that of *acceptable risk*: A threshold level is selected below which risk will be tolerated. But who determines what level of risk is acceptable in comparison to the benefits?

Often, those getting the benefits are not those assuming the risks. The people who are negatively affected are rarely asked their opinion, especially when they are not represented by an influential lobby or trade association [214]. The attitude of some decision makers is reflected in a statement by the director of Electricité de France who explained French secrecy about nuclear power this way: "You don't tell the frogs when you are draining the swamp" [214, p.156]. Hence, along with technical problems, utilitarianism and risk–benefit analysis present many philosophical and ethical dilemmas.

The moral implications of risk–benefit analysis are epitomized by the Ford Pinto gas tank case. Reportedly, Ford knew of the danger of explosion upon impact. But after doing a risk analysis weighing the cost of fixing the gas tank against the incidence of rear-end collisions and the damages usually assessed in wrongful death law suits at that time, the company decided that it would be cheaper to settle lawsuits after explosions than to fix the gas tank design. Here the benefits went to Ford while the (nonmonetary) risks were unknowingly assumed by the drivers and passengers of the Pinto. Admiral Bobby Inman argued in the wake of the *Challenger* accident that "There is a difference between risks taken with the unknown and risks taken to save on costs" [145, p.58]. Perrow suggests that the issue ultimately is not risk but power—the power to impose risks on the many for the benefit of the few [259].

Another moral difficulty with risk–benefit analysis involves selecting a common unit of measurement to compare losses and benefits. Usually, dollars are chosen. This choice raises the question of whether human suffering should simply be regarded as a cost and assigned a dollar value. Moreover, there is the problem of how to do this assignment. The most common approach is to use the amount of money the person would have earned from the point of death to his or her statistical life expectancy. Thus, a young, healthy, high-earning person would be worth more than a young, low-earning person or an older person close to retirement. The moral difficulties with this approach to assigning dollar values to human life are obvious, especially if you consider what dollar value you personally would place on the life of your child or spouse.

Alternatives to the use of acceptable risk have been proposed. *Optimal risk* involves a tradeoff that minimizes the sum of all undesirable consequences [100]. Optimal risk is achieved when the incremental or marginal cost of risk reduction equals the marginal reduction in societal costs—that is, where the sum of the cost of risk abatement and the expected losses from the risk is at a minimum. Estimating expected losses, however, still requires the ability to make probabilistic likelihood estimates of accidents and losses.

In *Normal Accidents* [259], Perrow offers a model for making decisions that attempts both to limit the potential for accidents resulting in large numbers of deaths and to minimize the effects of abandoning high-risk technology. This model uses catastrophic potential (severity) and cost of alternatives, but not probabilistic likelihood. Perrow views accidents as normal and therefore inevitable in complex systems. According to this perspective, we should assume that accidents will occur and make decisions accordingly, rather than assume that accidents will not occur on the basis of low probability estimates.

Perrow divides high-risk systems into three categories. The first category includes those systems with either low catastrophic potential or high-cost alternatives, such as chemical plants, aircraft, air traffic control, dams, mining, and automobiles. These systems should be tolerated and could be further improved with modest effort. The second category includes those technologies with moderate catastrophic potential and moderate-cost alternatives. These are the systems that we are unlikely to be able to do without (such as marine transport) or where the expected benefits are substantial (such as recombinant DNA). Perrow suggests that these systems should be strictly regulated. The final category includes systems with high catastrophic potential and relatively low-cost alternatives. He places nuclear weapons and nuclear power in this group and argues that the systems in this final category should be abandoned and replaced.

One problem with Perrow's approach is that it does not provide any way to make decisions about specific systems; it deals only with large classes of systems. An alternative is to require that accident rates not be increased when new technology is introduced. If, for example, accidents have occurred in a specific type of system at a certain historical rate, then the new technology should only be required to achieve an equivalent rate to be considered acceptable. This approach is based on the belief that if the public currently accepts a technology with a particular accident rate, then they will continue to accept this level of risk.

Aside from the technical problem of how to determine that the accident rate in the new system will be equivalent, difficult moral problems again arise if the new technology has the potential to reduce the accident rate but this reduction requires tradeoffs and increased costs. From an ethical standpoint, equivalent safety in this case may not be adequate. Consider air bags and other improvements in automobile safety: By the "acceptable risk is what has been accepted by the public previously" argument, such safety improvements are unnecessary, since people apparently accept the current risk by their willingness to drive.

The use of computers, in particular, may offer a potential increase in safety, but, at the same time, allow a decrease in safety margins; their use, therefore, provides the possibility of economic or productivity benefits along with the same historic level of safety. Should equivalent risk levels be accepted when reduced risk is possible? Even worse, do computers really reduce risk as much as is assumed when these types of tradeoff decisions are made?

It appears that there are no entirely satisfactory methods for making these decisions. Part of the explanation for this lack of mathematical and engineering solutions is that the decisions involve deep philosophical and moral questions—not simply technical choices.

1.4.2 Trans-Scientific Questions

A basic problem with utilitarian approaches is that they attempt to use scientific methods and arguments to answer what are fundamentally *not* scientific questions. Alvin Weinberg, former head of Oak Ridge National Laboratory, writes,

> Many of the issues that lie between science and politics involve questions that can be stated in scientific terms but that are in principle beyond the proficiency of science to answer. . . . I proposed the term "trans-scientific" for such questions . . . Though they are, epistemologically speaking, questions of fact and can be stated in the language of science, they are unanswerable by science; they transcend science . . . In the current attempts to weigh the benefits of technology against its risks, the protagonists often ask for the impossible: scientific answers to questions that are trans-scientific [351].

Even though scientists cannot provide definitive answers to such risk questions, they still have an important role to play: to provide what scientific information they can about the question at hand and to make clear where science ends and trans-science begins. Weinberg contends that the debate on risks versus benefits would be more fruitful if we recognized those limits.

Making decisions such as how safe is safe enough involves addressing moral, ethical, philosophical, and political questions that cannot be answered fully by algebraic equations or probabilistic evaluations. "Scientific truth is established in the traditional methods of peer review: only what has value in the intellectual marketplace survives. By contrast, where trans-science is involved, wisdom (rather than truth) must be arrived at by some other mechanism" [351].

Although scientists and engineers can legitimately disagree about the extent and reliability of their expertise, they often appear reluctant to concede limits on their ability to answer what are essentially trans-scientific questions. Answering such questions involves moral and aesthetic judgments: they deal not with what is *true* but rather with what is *valuable*. As such, where there is no consensus on these values, the decisions must be made by political processes.

Unfortunately, conflicts of value present special difficulties for the predominantly scientific and technocratic modes of rationality of Western society [56]. Cotgrove argues that beliefs about risk are embedded in complex belief and value systems that constitute distinct cultures: The way individuals see the world and evaluate risk is part of this culture. Until recently, the master value of our industrial society has been wealth creation—the overall goal for society was taken for granted to be maximizing economic growth and the production of goods and services. Today, this dominant value system is starting to be rejected by some members of our society. Table 1.1 outlines some of the features of these competing social paradigms [56].

For groups that hold such different paradigms, communication is nearly impossible: They essentially inhabit different worlds. What is rational and reasonable from one perspective is irrational from another. Each side is unable to comprehend alternative viewpoints, which requires, in Kuhn's terms [166], a paradigm shift. If the goal is maximizing output, for example, then not only are nuclear risks justified, but it would be unreasonable not to take them. From a different perspective about how the world works and what kind of society is desirable, to take even the possibly small—but in practice incalculable—risks for future generations stimulates moral indignation. Perhaps the explanation behind scientists' often-expressed frustration with the "irrational" way many people evaluate risk is just that different groups evaluate it from very different cultural viewpoints, all of which are rational within their different contexts.

Because of the futility of attempting to change deep-rooted cultural beliefs, trans-scientific questions will not be covered in this book. However, it is important to point out which issues are truly scientific and which are trans-scientific so that communication lines can be kept open. We must also realize that decisions about safety will cause legitimate disagreements that cannot be resolved by simple utilitarian arguments. Some opposition to our technological inventions goes beyond questions of measurable risks and economic benefits and instead focuses on social, political, and psychological risk and intangible, unmeasurable risk considerations [56]. According to Weinberg, it is the scientist's duty to inject some order into this often chaotic debate by distinguishing scientific from trans-scientific issues. An attempt is made throughout this book to identify these trans-scientific problems.

TABLE 1.1
Alternative social paradigms

	Dominant technocratic paradigm	Alternative environmental paradigm
Core values	Material (economic growth)	Nonmaterial (self-actualization)
	Natural environment valued as a resource	Natural environment intrinsically valued
	Domination over nature	Harmony with nature
Economy	Market forces	Public interest
	Risk and reward	Safety
	Individual, self-help	Collective, social provision
Form of governing	Authoritarian (experts influential)	Participatory (citizen, worker involvement)
	Hierarchical	Nonhierarchical
Society	Centralized	Decentralized
	Large-scale	Small-scale
	Ordered	Flexible
Nature	Ample reserves	Earth's resources limited
	Nature hostile or neutral	Nature benign
	Environment controllable	Nature delicately balanced
Knowledge	Confidence in science and technology	Limits to science and technology
	Rationality of means	Rationality of ends
	Separation of fact from value, thought from feeling	Integration of fact and value, thought and feeling

Source: Adapted from Stephen Cotgrove. Risk, value conflict, and political legitimacy. In Richard F. Griffiths, editor, *Dealing with Risk: The Planning, Management, and Acceptability of Technical Risk*, Manchester University Press, Manchester, England, 1981, page 129. Reprinted with permission.

2

Computers and Risk

We seem not to trust one another as much as would be desirable. In lieu of trusting each other, are we putting too much trust in our technology? . . . Perhaps we are not educating our children sufficiently well to understand the reasonable uses and limits of technology.

—T.B. Sheridan
Trustworthiness of Command and Control Systems

And they looked upon the software, and saw that it was good. But they just had to add this one other feature . . .

—G.F. McCormick
When Reach Exceeds Grasp

Just as James Watt's invention of the first practical steam engine fueled the Industrial Revolution, the invention of the first practical computer 50 years ago has drastically altered our society. The uniqueness and power of the digital computer over other machines stems from the fact that, for the first time, we have a general-purpose machine (Figure 2.1). We no longer need to build a mechanical or analog autopilot from scratch, for example, but simply to write down the "design" of an autopilot in the form of instructions or steps to accomplish the desired goals.

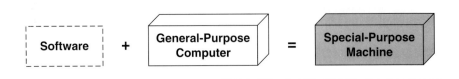

FIGURE 2.1
Software plus a general-purpose computer creates a new special-purpose machine.

These steps are then loaded into the computer, which, while executing the instructions, in effect *becomes* the special-purpose machine (the autopilot). If changes are needed, the instructions can be changed instead of building a different physical machine from scratch.

Machines that previously were physically impossible or impractical to build become feasible, and the design of a machine can be changed quickly without going through an entire retooling and manufacturing process. In essence, the manufacturing phase is eliminated from the lifecycle of these machines: The physical parts of the machine can be reused, leaving only the design and verification phases.[1] The design phase also has changed: Emphasis is placed only on the steps to be achieved without having to worry about how those steps will be realized physically.

The advantages of computers have led to an explosive increase in their use, including their introduction into potentially dangerous systems. This chapter explores the role of computers in accidents, some of the myths related to their use, and why we seem to have so much difficulty with the engineering of software.

2.1 The Role of Computers in Accidents

Few systems today are built without computers to provide control functions, to support design, and sometimes to do both. Computers now control most safety-critical devices, and they often replace traditional hardware safety interlocks and protection systems—sometimes with devastating results. Even if the hardware protection devices are kept, software is often used to control them. Frola and Miller describe the problem of computer-related hazards in military aircraft:

> A relatively new breed of hazards and associated problems has appeared. They appear primarily in flight control systems, armament control systems, navigation systems, and cockpit displays. They add new dimensions to the human-error problem. Some of the hazards are passive until just the right

---

[1] Although duplication of software might be considered to be manufacturing, it is usually a relatively trivial process.

combination of circumstances arrives. . . . Some result from the crew's multitude of choices in aircraft system management, often during prioritization of tasks. Conversely, computer-based systems are supposed to relieve pilot workload, but perhaps too much so in some instances, with resultant complacency and/or lack of situation awareness [88, p.7–13].

Computers can be used in safety-critical loops in several ways. Figure 2.2 shows some of these uses, including:

1. Providing information or advice to a human controller upon request (2.2a)
2. Interpreting data and displaying it to the controller, who makes the control decisions (2.2b)
3. Issuing commands directly, but with a human monitor of the computer's actions providing varying levels of input (2.2c)
4. Eliminating the human from the control loop completely (2.2d).

Even if the human is eliminated from direct control, the computer still needs to be supervised: The computer closes the control loop, but humans may be assigned the role of setting initial parameters, making intermittent adjustments, and receiving information from the computer.

The safety implications of computers exercising direct control over potentially dangerous processes are obvious (Figure 2.3a). Less obvious are the dangers when (as depicted in Figure 2.3b)

1. Software-generated data is used to make safety-critical decisions (such as air traffic control and medical blood analyzers)
2. Software is used in design analysis (such as CAD/CAM)
3. Safety-critical data (such as blood bank data) is stored in computer databases.

The FDA has received reports of software errors in medical instruments that led to mixing up patient names and data, as well as reports of incorrect outputs from laboratory and diagnostic instruments (such as patient monitors, electrocardiogram analyzers, and imaging devices) [20]. In 1979, the discovery of an error in the software used in the design of nuclear reactors and their supporting cooling systems resulted in the Nuclear Regulatory Commission's temporary shutdown of five nuclear power plants that did not satisfy earthquake standards. There is a serious danger of overreliance on the accuracy of computer outputs and databases.

In some cases, companies and government agencies have argued that software that generates data but does not make decisions, such as air traffic control software, is not safety critical or is less so than direct-control software because the human controller makes the ultimate decision, not the computer:

If diagnostic devices produce incorrect results, the errors may be readily noticed or may be inconsistent with other clinical signs. Thus, the risk to the patient is less than in the case of software-driven devices that directly affect patients [141, p.6].

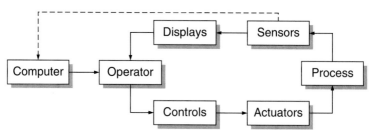

(a) Computer provides information and advice to controller,
     perhaps by reading sensors directly.

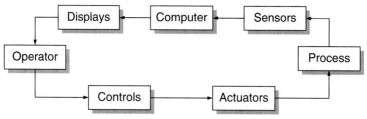

(b) Computer reads and interprets sensor data for operator.

FIGURE 2.2
Alternative uses of computers in control loops.

Although risk *may* be reduced by the use of a human intermediary, this reduction is by no means assured. Often, information from a computer or technological
device is more readily believed than conflicting information that is directly observed. Even more frequently, systems are built that require the operator to rely
on computer-generated information that the human has no independent way to
check. In almost all cases, risk from incorrect computer operation is not eliminated by having a human in the loop, and it may not even be reduced.

Arguments about who makes the ultimate decision and is therefore responsible may be appropriate in a courtroom when affixing blame and determining
financial liability, but not when the goal is to build safer systems. Engineers need
to consider all the contributors to accidents if their efforts to reduce risk are to be
effective. Often the argument that software providing information or advice to humans is not safety critical is used to avoid the difficult task of ensuring the safety
of the software. If system safety truly is to be increased, then all the components
whose operation can *directly* or *indirectly* affect safety must be considered, and
the related hazards must be eliminated or reduced.

In addition to software's direct and indirect contributions to accidents, com-

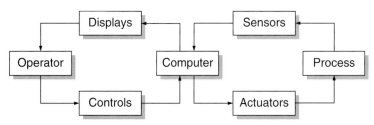

(c) Computer interprets and displays data for operator and issues commands; operator makes varying levels of decisions.

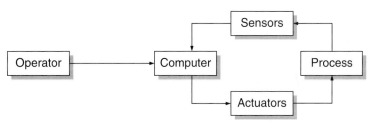

(d) Computer assumes complete control of process with operator providing advice or high-level direction.

FIGURE 2.2 (continued)

puters also add difficulty and cost to accident investigations. New procedures are required because, unlike failures of mechanical devices, "malfunctioning electrons will not be found in the wreckage" [88]. In the case of the Therac-25 medical accelerator, overdoses were first denied and not investigated or were attributed to transient hardware failures. Even if the possibility of software error *is* investigated, subtle errors that cause accidents in well-tested and sometimes long-used systems are not easy to find (or to prove that they may or may not exist). One software error cost millions of dollars to investigate after it caused the loss of an F-14 military aircraft [88].

The widespread use of computers in safety-critical systems is creating new problems for software and system engineers. Methods to ensure the safety of computer-controlled systems have lagged behind the development of these systems. Proven system safety engineering techniques do not include software, and, because of the unique characteristics of this new technology, are not easily adapted to software. In addition, because of the relatively recent introduction of computers to control potentially dangerous systems and the relatively safe nature of the computer itself (in terms of explosion, fire, or other direct hazards), few

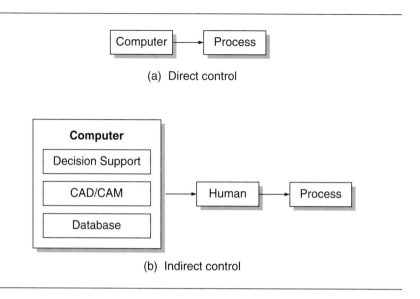

FIGURE 2.3
Direct and indirect control.

software engineering techniques have been developed to cope with safety problems. For the most part, standard software engineering techniques and processes are being used to develop safety-critical software without any consideration of the special factors and unique requirements for enhancing safety.

Communication problems are making efforts to rectify these deficiencies more difficult. System and software engineers have few common models or tools, and even their vocabulary is different. Computer science, by developing separately from engineering, has created its own technical vocabulary—sometimes the two groups use different names for the same things, or they give the same name to different things. Kletz has described the problems operators, engineers, and programmers have in working together:

> Operating and design staff have been known to complain that programmers resent being watched or checked and that they produce programs that are not resistant to mistakes, cannot tolerate plant errors, and are difficult to understand. No doubt programmers make similar remarks about operators and designers [162, p.1].

2.2 Software Myths

If there are problems, why are computers being used so widely? The basic reason is that computers provide a level of power, speed, and control not otherwise possible; they are also relatively light and small. Many other supposed advantages of using computers are myths, however, and usually stem from looking only at the short term. Understanding these myths is important if we are to make competent decisions about using computers to control safety-critical processes.

Myth 1. *The cost of computers is lower than that of analog or electromechanical devices.*

Reality. This myth, like most myths, has some superficial truth: Microcomputer hardware is cheap relative to other electromechanical devices. However, the cost of writing and certifying highly reliable and safe software to make that microprocessor useful, together with the cost of maintaining that software without compromising reliability and safety, can be enormous. The on-board Space Shuttle software, for example, while relatively simple and small (about 400,000 words) compared to more recent control systems, costs NASA approximately $100,000,000 a year to maintain [53].

Designing an electromechanical system is usually much easier and cheaper, especially when standard designs can be used. Of course, software *can* be built cheaply, but then lifetime costs—including the cost of accidents and required changes when errors are found—increase and may become exorbitant.

Myth 2. *Software is easy to change.*

Reality. Again, this myth is superficially true: Changes to software *are* easy to make. Unfortunately, making changes without introducing errors is extremely difficult. And, just as for hardware, the software must be completely reverified and recertified every time a change is made, at what may be an enormous cost. In addition, software quickly becomes more "brittle" as changes are made—the difficulty of making a change without introducing errors may increase over the lifetime of the software.

Myth 3. *Computers provide greater reliability than the devices they replace.*

Reality. Although true in theory—software does not "fail" in the sense this term usually implies in engineering—there is little evidence to show that erroneous behavior by software is not a significant problem in practice.

When systems were made only from electromechanical and human components, engineers always had to worry about mechanical failure and operator or maintenance error. Techniques were developed to reduce greatly (but not eliminate) random wearout failures and human errors and to mitigate their consequences.

Now that computers are being introduced into these systems, a new, completely abstract factor—software—has been added. Since software is pure design, there is no need to worry about the random wearout failures found in physical devices, but system behavior now can be significantly affected by software design errors.

Little hard data is available on the reliability of operational software, especially data that compares software reliability to the reliability of equivalent systems that do not use computers. What is available mixes too many types of software (such as game, business, and control software) to be useful.

A study by the British Royal Signals and Radar Establishment used commercially available tools to examine the number of errors in software written for some highly safety-critical systems [59]. Up to 10 percent of the program modules or individual functions were shown to deviate from the original specification in one or more modes of operation. Discrepancies were found even in software that had undergone extensive checking using sophisticated test platforms. Many of the detected anomalies were too minor to have any perceptible effects—for example, a discrepancy of 1 part in 32,000 in a computation using 16-bit arithmetic. However, about 1 in 20 of the functions found to be faulty (that is, about 1 in 200 of all new modules) contained errors with direct and observable effects on the performance of the system being controlled. For example, potential overflows in integer arithmetic were detected that caused a change in the direction of deflection of an actuator—such as "turn left" when the correct action was "turn right."

On the surface, it seems that the solution to the software reliability problem is simply to get the software right. Although human error is a factor (since software is designed by humans), ample time *appears* to be available to use sophisticated techniques to eliminate any design errors before the software is used. However, accomplishing this goal has turned out to be harder than expected. Very few sophisticated software systems have been fielded that have not contained a significant number of errors.

These are not just "teething" problems that go away after the software is used for a while: Software-related errors usually occur over the entire system lifetime, sometimes after tens or hundreds of thousands of hours of use. The Therac-25 worked correctly thousands of times before the first known overdose, and the accidents were spread out over two and a half years. The Space Shuttle software has been in use since 1980, and NASA has invested an enormous amount of effort and resources in verifying and maintaining this software. Despite this effort, since the Shuttle started operation in 1980, 16 severity-level 1 software errors[2] have been discovered in released software. Eight of those remained in code that was used in flights, but none have been encountered during flight. An additional 12 errors of lower severity have been triggered during flight—none threatened the crew, three threatened the achievement of the mission, and nine were worked

---

[2] Shuttle flight software errors are categorized by the severity of their potential consequences, without regard to the likelihood of their occurrence: severity 1 errors are defined as errors that could produce a loss of the Shuttle or its crew; severity 2 errors could affect the Shuttle's ability to complete its mission objectives; severity 3 errors affect procedures for which alternatives, or workarounds, exist; severity 4 and 5 errors are minor coding or documentation errors.

around. These problems occurred despite NASA having one of the most thorough and sophisticated software development and verification processes in existence.

Although reliability is easily augmented by the use of redundancy for random hardware wearout failures, techniques that provide the equivalent reliability enhancement for software design errors have not been found. For various reasons (described in the next section), including the fact that eliminating failures caused by design errors is inherently much more difficult than predicting and eliminating wearout failures, highly effective techniques are unlikely to be found. Vendors often tout tools or approaches that will lead to "zero-defect" software, but these claims are more sales than science.

Even if the techniques did exist to produce perfect software, there is usually not enough time to accomplish this goal: The ideal conditions—including unlimited funds and time—seldom if ever exist [63]. Instead, there are competing needs to reduce software costs (which already exceed hardware costs in many large systems). Time pressures also become severe, since the time required to develop software often controls the pace of the overall project.

But even if this myth were true—that is, computers are more reliable than other devices—this fact would not necessarily mean that they were *safer* than the devices they replace.

Myth 4. *Increasing software reliability will increase safety.*

Reality. Software reliability can be increased by removing software errors that are unrelated to system safety, thus increasing reliability while not increasing safety at all.

In addition, software reliability is defined as compliance with the requirements specification, while most safety-critical software errors can be traced to errors in the requirements—that is, to misunderstandings about what the software should do. Many software-related accidents have occurred while the software was doing exactly what it was intended to do—the software satisfied its specification and did not "fail." Software can be correct and 100-percent reliable and still be responsible for serious accidents. (Examples are given in later chapters.) Safety is a system property, not a software property.

Safety and reliability, while partially overlapping, are not the same thing: Increased computer or software reliability does not necessarily result in increased system safety.

Myth 5. *Testing software or "proving" (using formal verification techniques) software correct can remove all the errors.*

Reality. The limitations of software testing are well known. Basically, the large number of states of most realistic software makes exhaustive testing impossible; only a relatively small part of the state space can be covered. Although research has resulted in improved testing techniques, no great breakthroughs are on the horizon, and mathematical arguments have been advanced for their impossibility [105].

The use of mathematical techniques to verify the consistency between the software instructions and the specifications is another way to gain assurance. Although not currently practical, mathematical verification of software is likely to be so in the future. Unfortunately, such verification will not solve all our problems. The process requires that the "correct" behavior of the software first be specified in a formal, mathematical language. This task is not easy and may turn out to be as difficult and error-prone as writing the code.

In addition, although the basic computations and algorithms are easily specified and verified, the most important errors may not lie in these aspects of the code. For example, many software-related accidents have involved overload. A recent case occurred in England when a computer that was dispatching emergency ambulance services stopped working because it was unable to handle the number of calls it received [68]. Such sophisticated timing problems are much more difficult, and perhaps impossible, to verify formally because they involve more than just the application software itself.

Most important, as stated earlier, practical experience and empirical studies [200] have shown that most safety-related software errors can be traced to the requirements and not to coding errors (which tend to have less serious consequences in practice). Writing adequate software requirements is a difficult problem. This book presents some techniques that may help, but the problem is far from solved and may remain unsolved for quite some time.

Myth 6. *Reusing software increases safety.*

Reality. Although reuse of proven software components can increase reliability, reuse has little or no effect on safety. In fact, reuse may actually *decrease* safety because of the complacency it engenders and because the specific hazards of the new system were not considered when the software was originally designed and constructed. Examples of safety problems arising from the reuse of software include the following:

□ The Therac-20, parts of which were reused for the Therac-25, contained the same error responsible for at least two deaths in the Therac-25. The error had no serious consequences when encountered in the Therac-20; it resulted only in an occasional blown fuse and not in a massive overdose, and so was never detected and fixed (see Appendix A).

□ Software used successfully for air traffic control for many years in the United States was reused in Great Britain with less success. The American developers had not worried about handling zero degrees longitude (since that was not relevant in the United States); as a result, the software basically folded England along the Greenwich Meridian, plopping Manchester down on top of Warwick [358].

□ Aviation software written for use in the northern hemisphere often creates problems when used in the southern hemisphere [32]. In addition, software written for American F-16s has caused accidents when reused in Israeli aircraft flown over the Dead Sea, where the altitude is less than sea level.

Safety is not a property of the software itself, but rather a combination of the software design and the environment in which the software is used: It is application-, environment- and system-specific. Therefore, software that is safe in one system and environment may be unsafe in another. Reuse is *not* a solution to the safety problem.

Myth 7. *Computers reduce risk over mechanical systems.*

Reality. Computers have the potential to decrease risk, but not all uses of computers achieve this potential. Computers can automate tedious and potentially hazardous jobs such as spray painting and electric arc-welding, thus reducing the risk to workers in these particular jobs. However, other arguments that computers can reduce risk are debatable:

1. *Argument.* Computers allow finer control in that they can check parameters more often, perform complicated computations in real time, and take action quickly.

   Counter-argument. Computers *do* provide finer control computations in real time, and they *can* take action quickly. But finer control allows the process to be operated closer to its optimum, and the safety margins can be cut. The resulting systems have economic benefits, because they will, theoretically, shut down less often, and productivity may be increased by allowing more optimal control. However, any potential safety benefits of the finer control may be negated by the decrease in safety margins—perhaps without the concomitant attainment of the high software reliability on which the arguments for smaller safety margins were based. There is no way to know before extensive use outside the test environment whether high software reliability has been achieved.

2. *Argument.* Automated systems allow operators to work farther away from hazardous areas.

   Counter-argument. Because of lack of familiarity with the hazards, more accidents may occur when operators *do* have to enter hazardous areas. Assumptions that plants controlled by robots will not require operators to intervene physically are usually wrong and can lead to accidents. For example, a computer-controlled robot killed a worker in a plant that the designers had assumed would require a minimum of intervention—they did not include walkways for humans or standard safety devices such as audible warnings that the robot was in motion [90]. After the plant was operational, the operators found that they needed to enter the hazardous areas 15 to 20 times a day to bail out the robots and maintain adequate productivity: The original assumption that all robots (and thus the plant) would be shut down before humans entered hazardous areas became impractical. The designers had overestimated the ability of the plant to work adequately without human intervention and had not foreseen changes that would be required to planned operating procedures to meet productivity goals.

3. *Argument.* By eliminating operators, human errors are eliminated.

Counter-argument. Operator errors are replaced by human design and main-tenance errors: Humans are not removed from the system, they are merely shifted to different jobs. It should not be too much of a surprise that human designers have been found to make the same types of errors as operators (see Chapter 5).

Moreover, as noted in Chapter 1, when humans are removed from direct contact with the system, they lose information that is necessary for correct decision making. Physically removing operators from the processes they supervise may simply lead to new types of errors and hazards.

4. *Argument.* Computers have the potential to provide better information to operators and thus to improve decision making.

Counter-argument. While theoretically true, in reality this potential is very difficult to achieve. The subject is complex, and a detailed discussion is deferred until later. Briefly, computers make it easy to provide too much information to operators and to provide it in a form that is less usable for some purposes than traditional instrumentation.

5. *Argument.* Software does not fail.

Counter-argument. This common belief is true only for a very narrow defi-nition of "failure." Later chapters propose precise definitions of relevant en-gineering terms and their application to software. The important point here is that computers can exhibit incorrect and hazardous behavior, whether we call this behavior failure or not.

One of the results of substituting computers for mechanical devices is a reduced ability to predict failure modes. Most mechanical systems have a limited number of failure modes, and often they can be designed to fail in a safe way—for example, a valve can be designed to fail closed or a relay can be designed to fail with its contacts open. In comparison to software, the limited number of physical failure modes also simplifies (1) the analysis of a system for potentially unsafe behavior, (2) the process of assuring that the design is adequately safe, and (3) the elimination or control of hazards to make the system safer. The unpredictability of software behavior and the potentially large number of incorrect behaviors often preclude the same type of failure-mode analysis and fail-safe design.

In summary, computers have the potential to increase safety, and, surely, this potential will be realized in the future. But we cannot assume that we know enough now to accomplish this goal. In addition, any increased potential may not be realized if those building the systems use it to justify taking more risks.

Computers will not go away: Their use and importance in complex systems is only going to increase. Software engineers, often with little training or expe-rience in safety engineering, are building software for safety-critical systems. At the same time, safety engineers are finding themselves faced with ensuring that computer-dominated control systems are safe. To achieve and ensure safety in these systems, software must be included in the system-safety activities, and the software must be specifically developed to be safe using the results of system hazard analysis. A goal of this book is to provide information and ideas about how to do this.

2.3 Why Software Engineering is Difficult

Why do we have so much trouble engineering software when, for the most part, the software is performing the same functions as the electromechanical devices it is replacing? Shouldn't the same engineering approaches apply since the same type of design errors can be made in both? Shouldn't they be equally hard or easy to construct?

Parnas [253] and Shore [314] have written excellent descriptions of the unique engineering problems in constructing complex software. Much of the following discussion comes from these two sources.

Analog versus Discrete State Systems

In control systems, the computer is usually simulating the behavior of an analog controller. Although the software may be implementing the same functions previously performed by the analog device, the translation of the function from analog to digital form may introduce inaccuracies and complications. Continuous functions can be difficult to translate to discrete functions, and the discrete functions may be much more complex to specify.

In addition, the mathematics of continuous functions is well understood; mathematical analysis often can be used to predict the behavior of physical systems. The same type of analysis does not apply to discrete (software) systems. Software engineering has tried to use mathematical logic to replace continuous functions, but the large number of states and lack of regularity of most software result in extremely complex logical expressions. Moreover, factors such as time, finite-precision arithmetic, and concurrency are difficult to handle. There is progress, but it is very slow, and we are far from being able to handle even small software. Mathematical specifications or proofs of software properties may be the same size as the program, more difficult to construct, and often harder to understand than the program. They are therefore as prone to error as the code itself [94].

Physical continuity in analog systems also makes them easier to test than software. Physical systems usually work over fixed ranges, and they bend before they break. A small change in circumstances results in a small change in behavior: A few tests can be performed at discrete points in the data space, and continuity can be used to fill in the gaps. This approach does not work for software, which can fail in bizarre ways anywhere in the state space of inputs; the failure behavior need not be related in any way to normal behavior [105].

The "Curse of Flexibility"

A computer's behavior can be easily changed by changing its software. In principle, this feature is good—major changes can be made quickly and at seemingly low cost. In reality, the apparent low cost is deceptive, as discussed earlier, and the ease of change encourages major and frequent change, which often increases complexity rapidly and introduces errors.

Flexibility also encourages the redefinition of tasks late in the development process in order to overcome deficiencies found in other parts of the system. During development of the C-17, for example—a project that has run into great difficulties largely because of software problems—the software was changed to cope with structural design errors in the aircraft wings that were discovered during wind tunnel tests. This case is typical. As Shore says, "Software is the resting place of afterthoughts" [314].

With physical machinery, major design modifications are much more difficult to make than minor ones. The properties of the physical materials in which the design is embedded provide natural constraints on modification. The design of a computer application, on the other hand, is stored in electronic bits and presents no physical barriers to manipulation. Thus, while natural constraints enforce discipline on the design, construction, and modification of a physical machine, these constraints do not exist for software.

Shore explains this difference by comparing software with aircraft construction, where feasible designs are governed by mechanical limitations of the design materials and by the laws of aerodynamics. In this way, nature imposes discipline on the design process, which helps to control complexity. In contrast, software has no corresponding physical limitations or natural laws, which makes it too easy to build enormously complex designs. The structure of the typical software system can make a Rube Goldberg design look elegant in comparison (see Figure 2.4). In reality, software is just as brittle as hardware, but the fact that software is logically brittle rather than physically brittle makes it more difficult to see how easily it can be broken and how little flexibility actually exists.

The myth of software flexibility also encourages premature construction, before we fully understand what we need to do. The software medium is so forgiving that it encourages us to begin working with it too soon. Although we often intend to go back and start again after the details are worked out, this iteration process rarely happens in practice, and design decisions made in prototypes and early design efforts usually remain unchanged. Few engineers would start to build an airplane before the designers had finished the detailed plans.

Another trap of software flexibility is the ease with which partial success is attained, often at the expense of unmanaged complexity. The untrained can achieve results that appear to be successful, but are really only partially successful: The software works correctly most of the time, but not all the time. Attempting to get a poorly designed, but partially successful, program to work all of the time is usually futile; once a program's complexity has become unmanageable,

FIGURE 2.4
The simplified pencil sharpener. Open window (A) and fly kite (B). String (C)
lifts small door (D), allowing moths (E) to escape and eat red flannel shirt (F).
As weight of shirt lessens, shoe (G) steps on switch (H), which heats electric
iron (I) and burns hole in pants (J). Smoke (K) enters hole in tree (L), smoking
out opossum (M) which jumps into basket (N), pulling rope (O) and lifting cage
(P), allowing woodpecker (Q) to chew wood from pencil (R), exposing lead.
Emergency knife (S) is always handy in case opossum or the woodpecker
gets sick and can't work. (From *Rube Goldberg vs. The Machine Age* by Rube
Goldberg © 1968 King Features. Edited by Clark Kincaid, New York: Hastings
House Publishers. Reprinted with special permission of King Features Syndicate.)

each change is as likely to hurt as to help. Each new feature may interfere with
several old features, and each attempt to fix an error may create several more.
Thus, although it is extremely difficult to build a large program that works correctly under all required conditions, it is easy to build one that works 90 percent
of the time. Shore notes that it is difficult to build reliable aircraft too, but it is not
particularly easy to build planes that fly 90 percent of the time.

Few people would dare to design an airplane without training or after having
built only model airplanes, but there seem to be few such qualms about attempting to build complex software without appropriate knowledge and experience.
Shore explains,

Like airplane complexity, software complexity can be controlled by an appropriate design discipline. But to reap this benefit, people have to impose
that discipline; nature won't do it. As the name implies, computer software
exploits a "soft" medium, with intrinsic flexibility that is both its strength

and its weakness. Offering so much freedom and so few constraints, computer software has all the advantages of free verse over sonnets; and all the disadvantages [314].

Another type of discipline is also necessary—limiting the functionality of the software. This discipline may be the most difficult of all to impose. Theoretically, a large number of tasks can be accomplished with software, and distinguishing between what *can* be done and what *should* be done is very difficult. Software projects often run into trouble because they try to do too much and end up accomplishing nothing. When we are limited to physical materials, the difficulty or even impossibility of building anything we might think about building limits what we attempt. The flexibility of software, however, encourages us to build much more complex systems than we have the ability to engineer correctly. A common lament on projects that are in trouble is "If we had just stopped with doing *x* and not tried to do more . . . ." McCormick notes that

> A project's specification rapidly becomes a wish list. Additions to the list encounter little or no resistance. We can always justify just one more feature, one more mode, one more gee-whiz capability. And don't worry, it'll be easy—after all, its just software. We can do anything.
>
> In one stroke we are free of nature's constraints. This freedom is software's main attraction, but unbounded freedom lies at the heart of all software difficulty [216].

Complexity and Invisible Interfaces

One way to deal with complexity is to break the complex object into pieces or modules. For very large programs, separating the program into modules can reduce individual component complexity. However, the large number of interfaces created introduce uncontrollable complexity into the design: The more small components there are, the more complex the interface becomes. Errors occur because the human mind is unable to fully comprehend the many conditions that can arise through the interactions of these components [253].

An interface between two programs is comprised of all the assumptions that the programs make about each other. Shore notes that such dependencies can be subtle and almost impossible to detect by studying the programs involved. For example, one program might work properly only if another program can be relied on to finish its job in a specific amount of time. When changes are made, the entire structure collapses.

Finding good software structures has proven to be surprisingly difficult [253]. In the design of physical systems, such as nuclear power plants or cars, the physical separation of the system functions provides a useful guide for effective decomposition into modules. Equally effective decompositions for software are hard to find. In addition, the relatively high cost of the connections between physical modules helps to keep interfaces simple. As Shore points out,

Physical machines such as cars and airplanes are built by dividing the design problems into parts and building a separate unit for each part. The spatial separation of the resulting parts has several advantages: It limits their interactions, it makes their interactions relatively easy to trace, and it makes new interactions difficult to introduce. If I want to modify a car so that the loudness of its horn depends on the car's speed, it can be done, at least in principle. And if I want the car's air conditioner to adjust automatically according to the amount of weight present in the back seat, that too can be done—again in principle. But in practice such changes are hard to make, so they require careful design and detailed planning. The interfaces in hardware systems, from airplanes to computer circuits, tend to be simpler than those in software systems because physical constraints discourage complicated interfaces. The costs are immediate and obvious [314].

In contrast, software has no physical connections, and logical connections are cheap and easy to introduce. Without physical constraints, complex interfaces are as easy to construct as simple ones, perhaps easier. Moreover, the interfaces between software components are often "invisible" or not obvious: It is easy to make anything depend on anything else. Again, discipline and training are required to control these problems, but when the software reaches a certain size (which is often found in control systems today), the complexity can overwhelm even the few tools we have to control it. McCormick suggests, "The underlying premise is suspect, namely that we really can build any system, no matter how complicated. The right tool, the right process will let us do anything, or so the salesmen assure us" [216]. Those waiting for tools to solve our problems are likely to be disappointed:

> Regrettably, humans can cope with very little complexity. Better tools and methods can help us with many of the rote aspects of system development; the tools and methods we use are valuable, even indispensable. But consultants and tool vendors often perpetuate a delusion, the delusion that we can cope with endless complexity, if only we would use a better tool or a different method.
>
> Tools can only be an aid to judgment. Tools cannot substitute for the physical constraints encountered naturally in other disciplines. Without a harsh and uncaring nature forcing us to make hard choices, we tend to rationalize the complexity we see growing before us on each new project. . . . Despite the best intentions of highly skilled people, each new increment of complexity seems entirely plausible on its own. We are willingly seduced.
>
> I submit that the grand failures of big, software-intensive systems have been due primarily to this willing seduction. Post-mortem analysis of such projects routinely reveals a specification that grew in complexity until project cancellation. Natural constraints simply do not apply to software, and nobody knew when to say no. After all, it was only software [216].

Lack of Historical Usage Information

A final difficulty with software not found in hardware systems is that no historical usage information is available to allow measurement, evaluation, and improvement on standard designs. Software is almost always specially constructed, whereas physical systems benefit from the experience gained by the use of standard designs over long periods of time and in varied environments. Consider the difficulty that would ensue if every part of an airplane or car were completely changed for each new model or version and the entire design process started anew. That basically describes the situation for software. To complicate matters further, the features that are most likely to change from one complex system design to another are exactly those that are most likely to be controlled by or embedded within software.

2.4 The Reality We Face

When systems were composed only of electromechanical and human components, engineers knew that random wearout failures and human errors could be reduced and mitigated but never completely eliminated. They accepted the fact that they had to devise ways to build systems that were robust and safe despite random failures. Design errors, on the other hand, could be handled fairly well through testing and reuse of proven designs.

Because software has only design errors, the primary approach used to deal with reliability and safety problems has been simply to get the software correct. Theoretically, the possibility does exist for finding a set of techniques or methodology that will allow us to build perfect software. Much energy has been invested in looking for this methodology and less in finding ways to build software and systems that are robust and safe in the presence of software errors.

In reality, the time to create perfect software is never there, and perhaps it never can be. We may be seeking an impossible goal: software that is free of requirements and implementation flaws and that will always do what is required under all circumstances, no matter what changes occur to it or to the environment in which it operates.

Those who believe that the methodology exists that will allow us to construct such perfect software will find this book quite unsatisfactory. For those who have reached the conclusion that this goal is impossible to achieve—or at least not reachable now or in the immediate future—and that other solutions, perhaps adapted from those developed to cope with similar problems in hardware, are necessary, this book will provide some clues as to what might be done. But to devise and effectively use these solutions, we first need to understand why accidents occur.

Chapter

3

A Hierarchical View of Accidents

We saw that NASA had no system for fixing the [Shuttle O-ring] problem, even though engineers were writing letters like, "HELP!" and "This is a RED ALERT!" Nothing was done.

—Richard P. Feynman
*An Outsider's Inside View
of the Challenger Inquiry*

In order to devise effective ways to prevent accidents, we must first understand what causes them. Determining the cause of an accident is much more complex than is often imagined. Many categories have been suggested: proximate causes, probable causes, root causes, contributing causes, relevant causes, direct causes, indirect causes, significant causes, and so on. Before looking at what causes accidents, we need to clarify just what "cause" means.

3.1 The Concept of Causality

Consider the following recounting of events that appeared in a French newspaper:

> The vessel *Baltic Star*, registered in Panama, ran aground at full speed on the shore of an island in the Stockholm waters on account of thick fog. One of the boilers had broken down, the steering system reacted only slowly, the compass was maladjusted, the captain had gone down into the ship to

telephone, the outlook man on the prow took a coffee break and the pilot had given an erroneous order in English to the sailor who was tending the rudder. The latter was hard of hearing and understood only Greek.[1]

The complexity of conditions and events contributing to this accident is not unusual—the only unusual part is the thorough search for contributory conditions rather than the more usual assignment of one cause (such as fog or human error) without consideration of other factors. Even this rather detailed investigation does not mention larger organizational or sociological factors: The pressure on ship captains to maintain tight schedules is very great, and the money loss in being late to port makes keeping to tight schedules an important component in judging job performance [259]; this pressure may have led to a lack of caution in negotiating the fog-bound waters.

Some accidents are so complex and so permeated with uncertainties that they defy any simple explanation of their cause or even an exhaustive listing of all the factors involved. The accidental release of methyl isocyanate (MIC) at Bhopal, India, in December 1984, for example, in which 2,000 to 3,000 people were killed, 10,000 suffered permanent disabilities (including blindness), and 200,000 were injured, was blamed by management on human error—water entering the MIC storage tank from an improperly cleaned pipe at the plant. Given the operating conditions at the plant, however, it seems that an accident was just waiting to happen regardless of how the water got into the MIC tank:

> However it got in, it would not have caused the severe explosion had the refrigeration unit not been disconnected and drained of freon, or had the gauges been properly working and monitored, or had various steps been taken at the first smell of MIC instead of being put off until after the tea break, or had the scrubber been in service, or had the water sprays been designed to go high enough to douse the emissions, or had the flare tower been working and been of sufficient capacity to handle a large excursion [260, p.349].

Were all these failures of crucial safety mechanisms merely a matter of once-in-a-lifetime coincidence? On the surface, it does appear incredible that the vent scrubber, flare tower, water spouts, refrigeration unit, and various monitoring instruments could all fail simultaneously (Figure 3.1). However, a closer look shows a different picture.

It is not uncommon for a company to turn off passive safety devices, such as refrigeration units, to save money, and gauges at plants are frequently out of service [30]. At the Bhopal facility, there were few alarms or interlock devices in critical locations that might have warned operators of abnormal conditions.

A number of thresholds established for the production of and exposure to MIC were routinely exceeded at the Bhopal plant. Workers said that it was

---

[1] Extract from the protocol of a Swedish maritime tribunal, reprinted in *Le Monde*, November 15, 1979, and translated to English in [168].

Tank 610

Pressure in tank 610 builds up due to chemical reaction. MIC vapor escapes, rupturing safety valve.

Tank 619

Tank 619 was empty but nobody opened the valves between the two tanks to relieve the pressure in 610.

Refrigeration Systems

Turned off so tank 610 could not be cooled down to slow reaction.

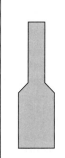
Vent gas scrubber supposed to spray caustic soda on escaping vapors to neutralize them. Scrubber shut down for maintenance. Design inadequate anyway.

Water curtain, which could have neutralized some MIC, designed to reach height of 40 to 50 feet. MIC vapor vented over 100 feet above ground.

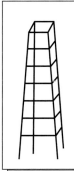
Flare tower could not be used because a length of pipe was corroded and had not been replaced. Design inadequate anyway.

FIGURE 3.1
Some causal factors at Bhopal.

common to leave MIC in the spare tank, which violated standard safety procedures. The operating manual specified that the refrigeration unit *must* be operating whenever MIC was in the system: The chemical has to be maintained at a temperature no higher than 5° Celsius to avoid uncontrolled reactions. A high temperature alarm was to sound if the MIC reached 11°. The refrigeration unit was turned off, however, and the MIC was usually stored at nearly 20°. The plant management adjusted the threshold of the alarm, accordingly, from 11° to 20°, thus eliminating the possibility of an early warning of rising temperatures.

Other protection devices at the plant had inadequate design thresholds. The vent scrubber, had it worked, was designed to neutralize only small quantities of gas at fairly low pressures and temperatures: The pressure of the escaping gas during the accident exceeded the scrubber's design by nearly two and a half times, and the temperature of the escaping gas was at least 80° Celsius more than the scrubber could handle. Similarly, the flare tower (which was supposed to burn off released vapor) was totally inadequate to deal with the estimated 40 tons of MIC that escaped during the accident [30].

Alarms at the plant sounded so often (the siren went off 20 to 30 times a week for various purposes) that an actual alert could not be distinguished from routine events or practice alerts. Ironically, the warning siren was not turned on until two hours after the MIC leak was detected and then was turned off after only five minutes—which was company policy [15]. Moreover, the practice alerts did not seem to be effective in preparing for an emergency: When the danger during the release became known, many employees ran from the contaminated areas of the plant, totally ignoring the buses that were sitting idle ready to evacuate nearby residents. Plant workers had only a bare minimum of emergency equipment—for example, a shortage of oxygen masks was discovered after the accident started—and they had almost no knowledge or training about how to handle nonroutine events.

The police were not notified when the chemical release began; in fact, when called by police and reporters, plant spokesmen first denied the accident and then claimed that MIC was not dangerous. Nor was the surrounding community warned of the dangers, before or during the release, or informed of the simple precautions that could have saved them from lethal exposure, such as putting a wet cloth over their face and closing their eyes. If the community had been alerted and provided with this simple information, many (if not most) lives would have been saved [167].

These are only a few of the factors involved in this catastrophe. Appendix C provides a detailed description of the accident, and other factors are described in Chapter 4, including technical and human errors within the plant, design and management negligence, regulatory deficiencies on the part of the U.S. and Indian governments, and general agricultural and technology transfer policies (which relate to the reason that Union Carbide was making such a dangerous chemical in India in the first place). Any one of these perspectives or "causes" is inadequate by itself to understand the accident and to prevent future accidents.

These examples illustrate some of the complexity in assigning causes to accidents. Philosophers have debated the notion of causality for centuries. A cause must precede a related effect, but a condition or event may precede another event without causing it. Furthermore, a condition may be considered to cause an event without the event happening every time the condition holds. Drunk driving, for example, is said to cause accidents, but being drunk while driving a car does not always lead to an accident. The same type of relationship holds between smoking and lung cancer.

John Stuart Mill (1806–1873) defined a cause as a set of *sufficient conditions*. "The cause is the sum total of the conditions, positive and negative, taken together, the whole of the contingencies of every description, which being realized, the consequence invariably follows" [222].

As an example, combustion requires a flammable material, a source of ignition, and oxygen. Each of these conditions is necessary, but only together are they sufficient. The cause, then, is all three conditions, not one of them alone. The distinction between *sufficient* and *necessary* is important [190]. An event may be caused by five conditions, but conditions 1 and 2 together may be able to produce the effect, while conditions 3, 4, and 5 may also be able to do so. Thus, there are two causes (sets of conditions sufficient for the event to occur); both of the causes have a set of necessary conditions.

In this book, a cause of an event (such as an accident) is composed of a set of conditions, each of which is necessary and which together are sufficient for the event to occur. The individual conditions will be called *causal* or *hazardous conditions* or *factors* to distinguish them from causes.

Interpreting statements about the "cause" of an accident requires some care. The explanation may be based on biased interpretations of the events, or the cause may be oversimplified.

3.2 Subjectivity in Ascribing Causality

Descriptions of accident causes often involve subjectivity and filtering. Rarely are the causes of an accident perceived identically by corporate executives, engineers, union officials, operators, insurers, lawyers, politicians, the press, the state, and the victims. Bogard suggests that "the specification of possible causes will necessarily bear the marks of conflicting interests" [30].

Some conditions may be considered hazardous by one group yet perfectly safe and necessary by another. Such conflicts often occur in situations that involve normative, ethical, and political considerations. In addition, judgments about the cause of an accident may be affected by the threat of litigation.

In fact, each person questioned may attribute an accident to a different cause [175]. One study found that workers who were satisfied with their jobs and who were integrated into and participating in the enterprise attributed accidents mainly to personal causes. In contrast, workers who were not satisfied and who had a low degree of integration and participation more often cited nonpersonal causes that implied that the enterprise was responsible. Another study found differences in the attribution of accident causes among victims, safety managers, and general managers. Other researchers suggest that accidents are attributed to factors in which the individuals are less directly involved. Another factor may be position in the organization. The lower the position in the hierarchy, the greater the tendency to blame accidents on factors linked to the organization; individuals who have a high position in the hierarchy tend to blame workers for accidents [175]. In contrast, data on near-miss (incident) reporting suggest that causes for these events are mainly attributed to technical deviations [76, 149].

After examining the research data, Leplat concluded that causal attribution depends on some characteristics of the victim and of the analyst (hierarchical status, degree of involvement, and job satisfaction) as well as on the relationships between the victim and the analyst and on the severity of the accident [175].

Causal identification may also be influenced by the data collection methods. Data usually is collected in the form of textual descriptions of the sequence of events of the accident, which tend to concentrate on obvious conditions or proximal events (those closely preceding the accident in time). On the one hand, report forms that do not specifically ask for nonproximal events often do not elicit them. On the other hand, more directive report forms may limit the categories of conditions considered [151].

Thus, as one would expect, accident data is often systematically filtered and unreliable. Leplat explains this phenomenon by noting that the analyst's mental representation (model) of the accident may cause him or her to remember or include only those factors that agree with that mental model [176].

Accidents can be described in terms of normal chains of events, goals, or motives. Consider the example, provided by Leplat, of an accident that occurs when a person steps onto a sidewalk and trips on the pavement. This explanation (stepping on the sidewalk and tripping) represents the basic chain of events leading to the accident. An explanation based on goals would include the fact that a car was rapidly approaching and the person wanted to walk on the sidewalk. An explanation based on motive would describe the events as a car rapidly approaching and the person wanting to avoid the car.

While the basic chain of events is usually not subject to interpretation, explanations that include goals and motives will be influenced by the analyst's mental model. Leplat illustrates this process by describing three different motives for the event "The operator sweeps the floor": (1) the floor is dusty, (2) the supervisor is present, or (3) the machine is broken and the operator needs to find other work [176].

In summary, the causal factors selected for a particular accident may involve a great deal of subjectivity and need to be interpreted with care.

3.3 Oversimplification in Determining Causality

A second trap in identifying accident causes is oversimplification. Out of a large number of necessary conditions for the accident, one is often chosen and labeled as *the* cause, even though all the factors involved were equally indispensable to the occurrence of the event. For example, a car skidding in the rain may involve many factors, including a wet road, the driver's lack of knowledge about how to avoid a skid, the driver's lack of attention, and the lack of anti-skid brakes. None of these is sufficient to cause the skid, but one will often be cited as the "cause." A condition may be selected as the cause because it is the last condition to be fulfilled before the effect takes place, its contribution is the most conspicuous, or the selector has some ulterior motive for the selection. Lewycky [190] argues that although we often isolate one condition and call it "the cause" and the other conditions "contributory," the basis for this distinction does not exist.

Oversimplification of the causal factors in accidents can be a hindrance in preventing future accidents. For example, in the crash of an American Airlines DC-10 at Chicago's O'Hare Airport in 1979, the U.S. National Safety Transportation Board (NTSB) blamed only a "maintenance-induced crack," and not also a design error that allowed the slats to retract if the wing was punctured. Because of this omission, McDonnell Douglas was not required to change the design, leading to future accidents related to the same design error [259].

Some common types of oversimplifications include applying legalistic approaches, ascribing accidents to human error or technical failure alone, ignoring organizational factors, and looking for single causes.

3.3.1 The Legal Approach to Causality

Lawyers and insurers often oversimplify the causes of accidents and identify what they call the *proximate* (immediate or direct) cause. They recognize that many factors contribute to an accident, but identify a principal factor for practical and particularly for liability reasons. The goal is to determine which parties in a dispute have the legal liability to pay damages. This determination may be affected by the ability to pay or by public policy considerations.

Usually, however, there is no objective criterion for distinguishing one factor or several factors from other factors that make up the cause of an accident. Although the legal approach to causality may have benefits when establishing guilt and liability, it is of little use from a technical perspective, where the goal is to understand and prevent accidents. It may even be a hindrance because the most relevant factors (in terms of preventing future accidents) may be ignored for nontechnical reasons.

Haddon [103] argues that countermeasures to accidents should not be determined by the relative importance of the accident's causal factors; instead, priority should be given to the measures that will be most effective in reducing losses. Simplistic explanations for accidents often do not provide the information necessary to prevent them, and, except for liability reasons, spending a lot of time determining the relative contributions of causes to accidents is not productive.

3.3.2 Human Error

The most common oversimplification in accident reports is blaming the operator. In any system where humans are involved, a "cause" may always be hypothesized as the failure of the human to step in and prevent the accident: Virtually any accident can be ascribed to human error in this way. Even when human error is more directly involved, considering that alone as a cause and the elimination of humans or of human error as the solution is too limiting to be useful in identifying what to change in order to increase safety most effectively. Coupling accidents on railroads, for example, used to be one of the principal causes of injury and death to railroad workers [108]. Managers claimed that such accidents were due only to worker error and negligence, and therefore nothing could be done aside from telling workers to be more careful. The government finally stepped in and required that automatic couplers be installed. As a result, fatalities dropped sharply.

In general, human error is used much too loosely to describe the cause of accidents; too often, analysis stops there and ignores all the other necessary conditions that must accompany human error for the accident to occur.

> Almost any accident can be said to be due to human error and the use of the phrase discourages constructive thinking about the action needed to prevent it happening again; it is too easy to tell someone to be more careful. . . . Perhaps we should stop asking if human error is the "cause" of an accident and instead ask what action is required to prevent it happening again [160, p.182].

Because an understanding of the role of humans in accidents is so important in reducing risk, it is discussed in depth in Chapters 5 and 6.

3.3.3 Technical Failures

Just as important an oversimplification is concentrating only on technical failures and immediate physical events. This type of overly narrow focus may lead to ignoring some of the most important factors in an accident. For example, an explosion at a chemical plant in Flixborough, Great Britain, in June 1974 resulted in 23 deaths, 53 injuries, and $50 million in damages to property (including 2,450 houses) up to five miles from the site of the plant (see Appendix C).[2] The official accident investigators devoted most of their effort to determining which of two pipes was the first to rupture. The British Court of Inquiry concluded that "The disaster was caused by a coincidence of a number of unlikely errors in the design and installation of a modification," and "such a combination of errors is very unlikely ever to be repeated" [245].

Yet the pipe rupture was only a small part of the cause of this accident. A

---

[2] Many more lives might have been lost had the explosion not occurred on a weekend when only a small shift was at the plant, the wind was light, and many of the nearby residents were away at a Saturday market in a neighboring town.

full explanation and prevention of future such accidents requires an understanding, for example, of the management practices of running the Flixborough plant without a qualified engineer on site and allowing unqualified personnel to make important modifications to the equipment, of making engineering changes without properly evaluating their safety, and of storing large quantities of dangerous chemicals close to potentially hazardous areas of the plant [57]. The British Court of Inquiry investigating the accident amazingly concluded that "there were undoubtedly certain shortcomings in the day to day operations of safety procedures, but none had the least bearing on the disaster or its consequences and we do not take time with them." Fortunately, others did not take this overly narrow viewpoint, and Flixborough led to major changes in the way hazardous facilities were allowed to operate in Britain.

3.3.4 Organizational Factors

Large-scale engineered systems are more than just a collection of technological artifacts: They are a reflection of the structure, management, procedures, and culture of the engineering organization that created them, and they are also, usually, a reflection of the society in which they were created. Accidents are often blamed on operator error or equipment failure without recognition of the industrial, organizational, and managerial factors that made such errors and defects inevitable. The causes of accidents are frequently, if not almost always, rooted in the organization—its culture, management, and structure. These factors are all critical to the eventual safety of the engineered system.

Some support for this hypothesis about the cause of accidents can be found by looking at major accidents of the past. In-depth, independent accident investigations usually point to organizational and managerial deficiencies. For example, the Kemeny Commission's official report on the Three Mile Island (TMI) accident contains 19 pages of recommendations, 2 of which deal with technical matters and 17 of which concern management, training, and institutional shortcomings in the nuclear industry. The commission concluded that the nuclear industry must "dramatically change its attitudes toward safety and regulation" and recommended that the utilities and the suppliers establish appropriate safety standards; systematically gather, review, and analyze operating experiences; plan to make changes with respect to a realistic deadline; integrate management responsibilities; clearly define roles and responsibilities; attract highly qualified personnel; devote more care and attention to plant operating procedures (providing clear and concise wording, clear formats, practical procedures, and so on); and establish deadlines for resolving safety issues [143].

The Rogers Commission study of the Space Shuttle *Challenger* Accident (see Appendix B) concluded that the root of the accident was an accumulation of organizational problems [295]. The commission was critical of management carelessness, bureaucratic interactions, disregard for safety, and flaws in the decision-making process. It cited various communication or organizational failures that affected the critical launch decision on January 28, 1986, including a lack of problem reporting requirements; inadequate trend analysis; misrepresentation of criticality; lack of adequate resources devoted to safety; lack of safety personnel involvement in important discussions and decisions; and inadequate authority, responsibility, and independence of the safety organization.

Similar results were found by a commission investigating the explosion on the Bravo oil rig in the North Sea: Seven main reasons are given for the accident, only one of which concerns a purely technical question. The others refer to organizational and training problems [324].

These are not isolated cases. In most of the major accidents of the past 25 years, technical information on how to prevent the accident was known and often even implemented. But in each case, the technical information and solutions were negated by organizational or managerial flaws.

3.3.5 Multifactorial Explanations of Accidents

In general, any particular condition in a complex technological system is unlikely to be either necessary or sufficient to cause an accident. In most systems, where some care has been taken in their design, accidents or hazards will depend on a multiplicity of causal factors and each event on a complex combination of conditions, including technical, operator, and organizational or societal conditions and actions. For example, design errors in the DC-10 caused accidents only after millions of flight hours. For such accidents to happen, the conditions involved necessarily must be very rare or must be the result of a complex interaction and coincidence of factors; preventing any of these conditions might eliminate the accidents.

The high frequency of accidents having complex causes probably results from the fact that competent engineering and organizational structures eliminate the simpler causes. On the positive side, the very complexity of accident processes means that there may be many opportunities to intervene or interrupt them. Therefore, thorough consideration of the conditions leading to accidents will be more useful than simplistic explanations.

3.4 A Hierarchical Approach to Causality

While it is clear that accidents rarely have single causes, specifying all necessary conditions (including the lack of things to prevent the conditions) may be impractical. The search for causes and causal conditions is obviously influenced by the goal of the investigation. If that goal is to prevent future accidents (which is the goal of this book), then the investigation must be carried out on multiple hierarchical levels including technical, human, organizational, and regulatory perspectives.

Lewycky [190] proposes a three-level model of understanding accidents (see Figure 3.2). In this general organization of causality, the lowest level describes

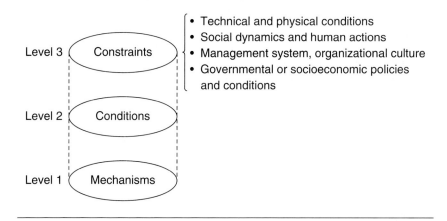

Level 3 — Constraints
- Technical and physical conditions
- Social dynamics and human actions
- Management system, organizational culture
- Governmental or socioeconomic policies and conditions

Level 2 — Conditions

Level 1 — Mechanisms

FIGURE 3.2
Hierarchical model of accident causes.

the mechanism of the accident—the chain of events. For example, the driver hit the brake, the car skidded and hit the tree, the driver was thrown from the car and injured.

The second level of understanding causality includes the conditions or lack of conditions that allowed the events at the first level to occur. For example, the driver does not know how to prevent or stop the skid, the car is not equipped with anti-lock brakes, the driver is driving too fast, the street is wet from rain and thus friction is reduced, an object suddenly appears in front of the car that requires the driver to apply the brakes quickly, the driver is not wearing a seat belt, the seat belt is defective. At this level, the cause or causes may be overspecified; not all conditions may have to be met before the accident will occur.

The third level includes constraints or the lack of constraints that allowed the conditions at the second level to cause the events at the first level, or that allowed the conditions to exist at all. This level includes constraints on technical and physical conditions, social dynamics and human actions, the management system and organizational culture, and governmental or socioeconomic policies.

This third level is often referred to as the "root" causes of an accident. Root causes affect general classes of accidents; they are weaknesses that not only contributed to the accident being investigated but also can affect future accidents. Responses to accidents tend to involve fixing only a specific causal factor while leaving the more general or root causes untouched. Blame is more likely to be placed on operator errors or on specific component failures than on poor training, lack of general hazard controls, or management deficiencies.

Because accidents rarely repeat themselves in exactly the same way, patches to particular parts of the system may be ineffective in preventing future accidents.

For example, if another Space Shuttle accident like that of *Challenger* occurs, it is unlikely to be caused by the exact same type of O-ring problem: An O-ring failure precipitated the accident, but the root causes identified in the accident investigation were related to organizational deficiencies. Preventing accidents in the future requires fixing those deficiencies.

The Therac-25 accidents (Appendix A) were not all the result of the same software flaw or even just software errors; they involved such factors as overconfidence in software and replacing standard mechanical interlocks with computers, lack of followup and investigation of reported incidents and accidents, and risk assessment procedures that ignored software. Each time the Therac-25 overdosed a patient (once the company finally admitted that their machine was responsible), the machine was "fixed" by eliminating the assumed hardware failure mode or software error, and the company claimed that any further accidents were impossible. This sequence continued until the FDA required the company to add mechanical interlocks that significantly reduced the possibility of an overdose no matter what the cause, to change their software development procedures, to perform comprehensive hazard analyses, and so on.

The DC-10 cargo-door saga is another example of the serious consequences of failing to eliminate root causes (see Appendix B). In March 1974, one of the worst accidents in aviation history occurred when a fully loaded Turkish airline DC-10 jumbo jet crashed in the suburbs of Paris, killing 346 people. The crash was attributed to the faulty closing of a cargo door, causing rapid decompression of the cabin and collapse of the cabin floor. The collapse destroyed all the major control cables and hydraulic lines. The inherent flaw in running the cables through the cabin floor was amply demonstrated in advance by a failed pressure test of the aircraft in 1970 that caused the cabin floor to collapse; by a near loss of a DC-10 near Windsor, Ontario, in 1972, which was avoided only by the extraordinary poise and skill of the pilot; and by the warnings of three Dutch engineers in 1968 when the first prototype was being built [309]. In addition, a Failure Mode and Effects Analysis (FMEA) drafted by Convair (the fuselage subcontractor) in 1969 for Douglas identified the lower cargo door system as a hazard that could lead to loss of the aircraft. However, the FMEAs required by the FAA to be submitted by Douglas before certification of an aircraft did not mention this hazard [75].

An internal memorandum by Dan Applegate [75], Convair's senior engineer on the fuselage subcontract, documents that after the failed pressure test, Convair engineers discussed possible corrective actions with Douglas, including blow-out panels in the floor. He argued at the time that these panels would have provided a predictable cabin floor failure mode that would have accommodated the loss of cargo compartment pressure without loss of tail surface and aft center engine control. Applegate wrote, "It seemed to us then prudent that such a change was indicated since 'Murphy's Law' being what it is, cargo doors will come open sometime during the twenty years of use ahead for the DC-10" [75, p.184].

Instead, Douglas tried to fix the cargo doors. The Applegate memorandum claims that this "bandaid fix" not only failed to correct the inherent catastrophic failure mode of cabin floor collapse, but the redesign also further degraded the safety of the original door latch system.

In June 1972, a cargo door latch system in a DC-10 failed over Detroit at 12,000 feet, leading to the collapse of the cabin floor and the disabling of most of the tail controls. Only by chance was the plane not lost. Douglas again studied corrective actions and, according to Applegate, applied more bandaids to the cargo door latching system.

> It might well be asked why not make the cargo door latch system really "foolproof" and leave the cabin floor alone. Assuming it is possible to make the latch "fool-proof" this doesn't solve the fundamental deficiency in the airplane. A cargo compartment can experience explosive decompression from a number of causes such as sabotage, mid-air collision, explosion of combustibles in the compartment and perhaps others, any of which may result in damage which would not be fatal to the DC-10 were it not for the tendency of the cabin floor to collapse [75, p.184].

Applegate ends his memorandum this way: "It seems to me inevitable that, in the twenty years ahead of us, DC-10 cargo doors will come open and I would expect this to usually result in the loss of the airplane" [75, p.185]. The Paris accident proved him to be correct.

The lesson is clear: To reduce the risk of accidents significantly, root causes must be identified and eliminated. If we are unable to eliminate a particular causal factor, we may still be able to provide protection against it leading to an accident. To accomplish this goal we need to know more about the root causes of accidents.

Chapter

4

Root Causes of Accidents

The [FAA] administrator was interviewed for a documentary film on the [Paris DC-10] accident. He was asked how he could still consider the infamous baggage door safe, given the door failure proven in the Paris accident and the precursor accident at Windsor, Ontario. The Administrator replied—and not facetiously either—'Of course it is safe, we certified it.'

—C.O. Miller
*A Comparison of Military and
Civilian Approaches to Aviation Safety*

The root or level-three causes of accidents can be divided into three categories: (1) deficiencies in the safety culture of the industry or organization, (2) flawed organizational structures, and (3) superficial or ineffective technical activities. This chapter examines the influence of these factors on accidents.

4.1 Flaws in the Safety Culture

The *safety culture* in an industry or organization is the general attitude and approach to safety reflected by those who participate in that industry: management, workers, and government regulators. Major accidents often stem from flaws in this culture, especially (1) overconfidence and complacency, (2) a disregard or low priority for safety, or (3) flawed resolution of conflicting goals.

4.1.1 Overconfidence and Complacency

Complacency and overconfidence are common elements in most of the major accidents of our century. In fact, complacency may be one of the most important factors in risk. The Kemeny Commission identified a major contributor to the Three-Mile Island (TMI) accident as a failure by the Nuclear Regulatory Commission (NRC) to believe that a serious accident could happen. One official testified that those involved had developed a "mindset" about the infallibility of the equipment as a result of repeated assurances that the technology was safe [143]. An NRC post-TMI Lessons Learned Task Force noted that the mindset regarding serious accidents was "probably the single most important human factor with which this industry and the NRC has to contend" [3, p.43].

Although the U.S. Atomic Energy Act of 1954 refers repeatedly to the "health and safety of the public," this phrase is never defined. According to a former AEC[1] attorney, Harold Green, "nobody ever thought that safety was a problem. They assumed that if you just wrote the requirement that it be done properly, it would be done properly" [3, p.3].

Sometimes, lessons learned from accidents do not cross national borders. After TMI, the French Prime Minister said that "the scenario that unfolded in the United States couldn't happen in the same way in France. We have in fact safety systems that take the possibility of such accidents into account, and this shelters us from the consequences" [168].

Eight months after the TMI accident, top Soviet government and scientific leaders told a party from the United States that they regarded nuclear safety as a "solved problem" and that the problems raised by the U.S. experience at TMI had been overdramatized. They quoted the head of the Soviet Academy of Sciences as saying that Soviet reactors would soon be so safe that they could be installed in Red Square [169]. Soviet authorities at the Chernobyl plant described the risk of a serious accident as extremely slight a year before it occurred, and only a month before the Chernobyl accident, the British Secretary of State for Energy repeated the often stated belief that "nuclear energy is the safest form of energy yet known to man" [260].

Nuclear energy is not the only area where optimism prevails. After the *Challenger* accident in January 1986, the Report of the Presidential Commission on the Space Shuttle *Challenger* Accident [295] pinpointed two related causes as complacency and a belief that less safety, reliability, and quality-assurance activity was required during "routine" Shuttle operations. Richard Feynman, a member of the commission, wrote an appendix on the reliability of the Shuttle in which he asked, "What is the cause of the management's fantastic faith in the machinery?" and concluded that "for whatever purpose, be it for internal or ex-

---

[1] In 1975, the Atomic Energy Agency (which had been formed in 1946) was broken into two parts in order to separate its two contradictory missions: (1) promotion and development of commercial nuclear power and (2) regulation and licensing. The Nuclear Regulatory Commission assumed the regulatory activities, while promotional activities were assigned to a new agency that eventually became the Department of Energy.

ternal consumption, the management of NASA exaggerates the reliability of its product, to the point of fantasy" [295].

The Bhopal accident is a classic case of events caused by widespread complacency. The accidental release of MIC came as a complete surprise to almost everyone, including Union Carbide's own scientists and risk assessors. They believed that such a catastrophe could not happen with such modern technology, that so many safety devices could not fail simultaneously, and that the Bhopal plant was a model facility [30]. Claims were made that overemphasized or exaggerated the safety of the production. Many employees believed that adequate precautions had been taken and that nothing more could be done to improve safety. Problematic practices were labeled "acceptable" or "necessary" risk.

Employees were apathetic about routine mishaps and about the value of emergency drills. Although several minor accidents and many warnings had preceded the Bhopal disaster, nobody seemed to believe that an accident of the size that occurred was possible. The Union Carbide Bhopal plant works manager, when informed of the accident, said in disbelief: "The gas leak just can't be from my plant. The plant is shut down. Our technology just can't go wrong, we just can't have leaks" [30].

Such disbelief was common before the accident, even though the plant had experienced so many problems with hazard detection instruments that, even when the instruments worked reliably and recorded real changes, these changes were often ignored and assumed to be faulty. One gauge in the MIC unit, right before the MIC release, recorded a fivefold rise in the storage tank's pressure, but it was ignored or disbelieved.

After the Bhopal disaster, both Union Carbide and the U.S. Occupational Safety and Health Administration (OSHA) announced that the same type of accident could not occur at Union Carbide's plant in Institute, West Virginia (which also makes MIC) because of that plant's better equipment, better personnel, and America's generally "higher level of technological culture" [260]. Yet only eight months later, a similar accident occurred at the Institute plant that led to brief hospital stays for approximately 100 people.[2] As in Bhopal, the warning siren at the Institute plant was delayed for some time, and the company was slow in making information available to the public [169].

A few months after the Institute accident, a leak at yet another Union Carbide plant created a toxic gas cloud that traveled to a shopping center. Several people had to be given emergency treatment, but for two days doctors and health officials did not know what the toxic chemical was or where it came from because Union Carbide denied the leak's existence [260]. OSHA fined Union Carbide $1.4 million after the Institute accident, charging "constant, willful, and overt violations" at the plant and a general atmosphere and attitude that "a few accidents here and there are the price of production" [260, p.350].

---

[2] The consequences were less serious in this accident because of such incidental factors as the direction of the wind and the fact that the tank happened to contain a less toxic substance at the time.

In these and many other accidents, complacency seems to play a major role. Examining more carefully the various aspects of complacency will help us to understand it and its contribution to accidents. These aspects include discounting risk, overrelying on redundancy, unrealistic risk assessments, ignoring high-consequence and low-probability events, assuming risk decreases over time, underestimating software-related risks, and ignoring warning signs.

Discounting Risk

One aspect of complacency is a basic human tendency to discount risk. Most accidents in well-designed systems involve two or more low-probability events occurring in the worst possible combination. When people attempt to predict the system risk, they explicitly or implicitly multiply events with low probability—assuming independence—and come out with impossibly small numbers, when, in fact, the events are dependent. Machol calls this phenomenon the *Titanic coincidence* [202].

When the *Titanic* was launched in 1912, it was the largest and safest ship the world had ever known. The fact that it was unsinkable was widely touted and generally accepted. The ship was designed with a double-bottom hull having 16 separate water-tight compartments. Calculations showed that up to four compartments could be ruptured without the ship sinking: In the history of maritime accidents, none had involved the compromise of more than four underwater compartments. The builders had promised an unsinkable hull, and confidence in their claim was so great that one of the ship's officers assured a female passenger that "not even God himself could sink this vessel" [168]. Lloyd's of London issued the *Titanic* a certificate of unsinkability, even though the partitions between the 16 compartments were not high enough to shut every compartment hermetically. In case of trouble, designers thought that there would be time to intervene before the water reached the height where it could spill over into adjacent compartments.

On its maiden voyage, while the owners were trying to break the current speed record, the *Titanic* ran into an iceberg that cut a 300-foot gash in one side of the ship, flooding 5 adjacent compartments. The ship sank with a loss of 1,513 lives.[3] Several telegrams had been received that day warning about the presence of icebergs, but nobody worried. When the *Titanic* hit the iceberg about 95 miles south of Newfoundland, passengers were told that there was no reason for alarm and that they should stay in their cabins. The captain finally ordered an evacuation, but "the evacuation turned into disorder and terror: the classical evacuation exercises had not been carried out, the sailors did not know their assignments" [168].

A number of "coincidences" contributed to the accident and the subsequent loss of life; for example, the captain was going far too fast for existing conditions,

---

[3] In comparison, during the previous 10 years, British ships had transported more than 3.5 million passengers while suffering losses of just 73 people [72].

a proper watch was not kept, the ship was not carrying enough lifeboats,[4] lifeboat drills were not held, the lifeboats were lowered properly but arrangements for manning them were insufficient, and the radio operator on a nearby ship was asleep and so did not hear the distress call. Many of these events or conditions might be considered independent, but appear less so when we consider that over-confidence most likely led to the excessive speed, the lack of proper watch, and the insufficient number of lifeboats and drills. That the collision occurred at night contributed to the iceberg not being easily seen, made abandoning ship more difficult than it would have been during the day, and was a factor in why the nearby ship's radio operator was asleep [214]. Multiplying together the probability of all these conditions would not have provided a good estimate of the probability of the accident occurring. In fact, given these factors, an accident was almost inevitable.

Watt defines a phenomenon he calls the *Titanic effect* to explain the fact that major accidents are often preceded by a belief that they cannot happen. The *Titanic* effect says that the magnitude of disasters decreases to the extent that people believe that disasters are possible and plan to prevent them or to minimize their effects [348]. Taking action in advance to prevent or deal with disasters is usually worthwhile, since the costs of doing so are inconsequential when measured against the losses that may ensue if no action is taken.

Overrelying on Redundancy

Redundancy and diversity are often used in an attempt to avoid failures and increase reliability. For example, a chemical plant protection system might be diverse in that it monitors two independent parameters, such as temperature and pressure, and it might redundantly include multiple channels using majority voting. However, one factor might cause all these components to fail simultaneously, such as an electrical outage or a fire. *Common-cause failures*[5] are failures that are "coincident" in time because of dependencies among conditions leading to the events. Many accidents can be traced to common-cause failures in redundant or diverse systems.

Such an accident occurred at the Browns Ferry Nuclear Power Plant in Alabama, where a fire burned uncontrolled for seven and a half hours in March 1975. All of the emergency safety devices failed totally because the fire destroyed the redundant electrical power and control systems. One of the two nuclear reactors was dangerously out of control for several hours: In the end, it was controlled by some available equipment that was not part of the safety system and that by

---

[4] The *Titanic* was certified to carry 3,547 passengers and crew while providing lifeboat space for 1,178. The rules in effect at the time allowed the ship legally to provide lifeboat space for only a little over 700 people [72]. These regulations were outdated and did not foresee vessels the size of the *Titanic* [310].

[5] In this book, *common-cause* failures are multiple component failures having the same cause, such as failure of a common power supply. *Common-mode* failures denote the failure of multiple components in the same way, such as stuck open or silent. Redundant systems can have failures that are common-cause, common-mode, or both.

chance had emerged from the fire undamaged [350]. Engineers of the Tennessee Valley Authority, the operator of Browns Ferry, stated privately that a potentially catastrophic radiation release was avoided "by sheer luck" [3].

One of the rationales used in deciding to go ahead with the disastrous *Challenger* flight despite engineering warnings was that there was a substantial safety margin (a factor of three) in the O-rings over the previous worst case of Shuttle O-ring erosion. Moreover, even if the primary O-ring did not seal, it was assumed that the secondary one would [295]. During the accident, the failure of the primary O-ring caused conditions that led to the failure of the secondary O-ring.

In November 1961, all of the U.S. Strategic Air Command's (SAC's) special communication lines with early warning radars and with early warning command headquarters (NORAD) suddenly went dead. Commercial phone circuits also were not working. Because the outage could have been caused by enemy action, an emergency alert was sounded at SAC bases across the United States. Later, it was discovered that although redundant communication links had been established between SAC and NORAD, they had been run through a single relay station, despite assurances to the contrary. An overheated motor at that station had cut all communications [307].

At Bhopal, as we have seen, a number of independent safety devices "failed" at the same time. Juechter warns that a poorly designed safety device is worse than no safety device at all, since its presence creates a sense of security that allays natural fears and caution [142]. The Bhopal, *Challenger*, and other accidents are apt examples of common-cause failures in which the common cause may arise out of complacency about the risk of accidents. Thus, a paradox arises: Providing redundancy may lead to the complacency that defeats the redundancy.

Unrealistic Risk Assessment

Unrealistic risk assessments may also lead to complacency and lack of appropriate safety activities. For example, instead of launching an investigation when first informed about possible overdoses by their machine, the manufacturer of the Therac-25 responded that the probabilistic risk assessment showed that accidents were impossible, and no action was taken.

A hazard analysis had been performed on the Therac-25, but software errors were excluded [187]. The possibility of the computer giving an overdose *was* contained in the fault tree, where the event "Computer selects wrong energy" was assigned a probability of 10^{-11} and the event "Computer selects wrong mode" was assigned 4×10^{-9}. No justification for either number was provided. After the accidents and the corrections to the machine were made, the manufacturers performed another safety analysis. This time, they included software in the fault tree, but they assigned a probability of 10^{-4} to every type of software error. This seems to be a popular number to assign to any box in a fault tree that includes the word "software," but there is no justification for such a number, and it is unlikely that all errors would be of equal probability.

Probabilistic safety analysis can be useful in making decisions about the acceptability of a particular design. For example, it can be used to demonstrate that design changes are necessary to reduce risk and to show the rationale for tradeoff decisions. Too often, however, such assessments are misused and lead to overconfidence in the small numbers obtained. The assumptions underlying such assessments, which are usually easily violated, are forgotten, and the numbers are taken at face value.

Numerical assessments measure only what they *can* measure and not necessarily what *needs* to be measured. The unmeasurable factors (such as design flaws and management errors) are ignored—even though they may have a greater influence on safety than those that are measurable. In addition, the underlying assumptions of the assessment—for example, that the plant or system is built according to the design or that certain failures are independent—are often ignored. The belief grows that the numbers actually have some relation to the real risk of accidents, rather than being a way to evaluate specific aspects of the design.

A U.S. Air Force handbook description of an accident in a highly critical system provides a cogent example [5]. The system design includes a relief valve opened by the operator to protect against overpressurization. A secondary valve is installed as backup in case the primary relief valve fails. The operator must know if the first valve did not open so that the second valve can be activated.

On one occasion, a position indicator light and open indicator light both illuminated; however, the primary relief valve was *not* open, and the system exploded. A post-accident examination discovered that the indicator light circuit was wired to indicate *presence of power* at the valve, but it did not indicate valve *position*. Thus, the indicator showed only that the activation button had been pushed, not that the valve had operated.

An extensive quantitative safety analysis of this design had included a low probability of simultaneous failure for the two relief valves, but ignored the possibility of a design error in the electrical wiring; the probability of the design error was not quantifiable.[6] No actual examination of the electrical wiring was made; instead, confidence was established on the basis of the low probability of coincident failure of the two relief valves.

All of the major accidents described in the appendices involved important causal factors that are not quantifiable. In fact, a case can be made that the most important causal factors in terms of accident prevention (the root factors) are often the unmeasurable ones. As just one example, the Bhopal accident involved such unmeasurable factors as the refrigeration being disconnected, an operator ignoring or not believing a recording on a gauge, operators putting off investigating the smell of MIC until after a tea break, the vent scrubbers being turned off, the insufficient design and capacity of the scrubbers and the flare tower, and the failure to inform the community about what to do in case of emergency. Most such

---

[6] This same type of design error was a factor in the TMI accident: An indicator misleadingly showed that a discharge valve had been ordered closed but not that it had actually closed. In fact, the valve was blocked in an open position.

"design" errors, if they are known beforehand, should be fixed rather than measured. A probabilistic risk assessment of the Bhopal facility that included only the usual failure probability of the protection system components could not have predicted this accident.

Another limitation of probabilistic risk assessments is that they frequently change the emphasis in development from making a system safer to proving that the system is safe as designed. Attention is directed away from critical assessment of the design and instead is focused on lowering the numbers in the assessment. In the worst case, such assessments start with a required probability (such as 10^{-9} per year or per use), and then a model is built to justify that number for the existing design—often an exercise in fantasy rather than engineering. Occasionally, the numbers used in risk assessment are chosen in order to make the overall risk assessment match the specified numerical requirement. William Ruckelshaus, two-time head of the U.S. Environmental Protection Agency (EPA), has cautioned that "Risk assessment data can be like the captured spy; if you torture it long enough, it will tell you anything you want to know" [302, p.157].

A final limitation of using numeric goals is that designers may work to achieve that goal only and proceed no further, even where additional corrective action is possible.

These limitations do not mean that quantitative analysis is not useful for some purposes, only that it should be interpreted and used with care. E.A. Ryder of the British Health and Safety Executive has written that the numbers game in risk assessment "should only be played in private between consenting adults as it is too easy to be misinterpreted" [306, p.12].

Ignoring High-Consequence, Low-Probability Events

Complacency often leads to a limited, unsystematic consideration of serious risks. Usually, the most likely hazards are controlled, but hazards with high severity and (assumed) low probability are dismissed as not worth investing resources to prevent: A common discovery after accidents is that the *events involved were recognized before the accident, but were dismissed as incredible.* After the accident occurs, we find that independence of causative events was incorrectly assumed or that probabilistic assessments were unrealistic. Finding examples is easy—most accidents that occur in systems that have safety programs are of this type.

> People generally learn best by experience. People can—and do—learn to behave with reasonable caution so as to avoid accidents of kinds they have personally experienced or seen at first hand. This stimulus-response mechanism for learning caution depends on feedback between accidents and safety-related activities. Study after study reveals that new safety regulations in all countries are adopted largely after major accidents—not in advance of them. Shutting the barn door after the cow escapes seems to be an irremediable human trait. Obviously, this mechanism works best in avoiding repetitions

of small to medium-sized accidents that are reasonably frequent, i.e., they have occurred before. Humans seem to be unwilling to be proportionally more careful to avoid larger but rarer calamities of kinds they have never personally experienced. The fact that a complex system has not (yet) failed massively is perhaps regarded subconsciously as evidence that it is fail-safe. This, in turn, leads to laxity [15, p.36].

A Therac-25 operator, who was involved in two of the overdoses, testified that she had been told the system had so many safety devices that it was impossible for an overdose to occur. The first accident reports were not investigated; instead, those reporting them were told that an accident was impossible on this machine. Proof was provided in terms of the number of safety devices on the equipment and, later, a hardware change that increased the safety of the machine, according to the manufacturer, by five orders of magnitude (10,000,000%).

During the *Apollo 13* emergency, when the spacecraft and crew were almost lost (see Appendix B), the ground-control engineers did not believe what they were seeing on the instruments. The reason for their reluctance was later reported by a NASA engineer: "Nobody thought the spacecraft would lose two fuel cells and two oxygen tanks. It couldn't happen." Jack Swigert, an astronaut, supported this view: "If someone had thrown that at us in the simulator, we'd have said, 'Come on, you're not being realistic'" [31].

It is impractical to require that all hazards, no matter how remote they are judged, be eliminated or controlled. However, independence and other assumptions used in either informal or formal risk assessments should be scrutinized with great skepticism. In addition, the potential for catastrophic accidents of a type not yet experienced should not be casually dismissed.

Assuming Risk Decreases over Time

A common thread in most accidents involving complacency is the belief that a system must be safe because it has operated without an accident for many years. The Therac-25 was operated safely thousands of times before the first accident. Industrial robots operated safely around the world for several million hours before the first fatality [252]. Nitromethane was considered nonexplosive and safe to transport in rail tank wagons for 18 years (between 1940 and 1958), until two tank wagons exploded in separate incidents [154]. Carrying out an operation in a particular way for many years does not guarantee that an accident cannot occur, yet informal risk assessments appear to decrease quickly when there are no serious accidents.

In reality, risk may decrease, remain constant, or even increase over time. Risk can increase for several reasons, including the fact that as time passes without an accident, caution wanes and attempts to build more complex and error-prone systems increase. Tradeoffs between safety and other factors start to be made in the direction of the other factors, and safety margins are cut, giving rise to a rather surprising fact: *As error rates in a system decrease and reliability increases, the risk of accidents may actually be increasing.*

Risk also may increase over time either because the system itself changes as a result of maintenance or evolution, or because the environmental conditions change. In some cases of automation, the introduction of the newly automated device may actually cause the environment to change from what it was assumed to be during design. For example, human operators may change their behavior as they become more familiar with an automated control system. As operators became more familiar with the Therac-25 operation, they started to type faster and triggered a software error that had not surfaced previously. The difficulty of testing more than a small fraction of the possible software states complicates even further the problem of ensuring that hazards will not occur under any plausible environmental conditions.

One dilemma in arguing for safety programs is the impossibility of determining how many accidents a good program has avoided. The ultimate irony is that a successful safety program may lead to complacency when few or no accidents occur and that complacency can then lead to accidents. Thus the more successful an organization is in eliminating accidents, the more likely that complacency will increase risk. The title of a chapter in the Rogers Commission report on the *Challenger* accident, *The Silent Safety Program*, reflects this dilemma. After the 1967 *Apollo* accident—in which three astronauts died in a fire on the launch pad during a test, NASA built one of the best system safety programs in the world and was very successful in avoiding accidents. But that success led to a diminished emphasis on safety, a mindset that success was inevitable, and a shifting of priorities to other goals. The result was the *Challenger* accident.

After the Shuttle became operational in 1980, the workforce and functions of several Shuttle safety, reliability, and quality assurance offices were reduced. A safety committee, the Space Shuttle Program Crew Safety Panel, ceased to exist at that time. The panel had been established to ensure a minimum level of communication about safety among the engineering, project management, and astronaut offices, but NASA expected it to be functional only during the design, development, and flight test phases. After it was disbanded, according to the Rogers Commission, the NASA Shuttle program had no focal point for flight safety.

This belief that system and software safety activities can be phased out once a system becomes operational is incorrect. Many of these systems are highly complex, the requirements are exacting, and changes are bound to occur, especially in software. Such systems usually have little or no history of use: As the system matures and experience changes, careful tracking is required to prevent accidents. As the flight rate of the Shuttle increased, more hardware operations were involved and more total in-flight anomalies occurred.

The Shuttle flight software is continually changing as a result of changes in Shuttle hardware (including an upgrade in the computers used), detection of errors, and decisions to add functionality. These major updates to the software, called operational increments, occur approximately once a year. Between

1980 (when the Shuttle first became operational) and 1991, a total of 14 operational increments involved changing 152,000 words of code (out of approximately 400,000 total words in the flight software) with the largest number of words changed (60,000) in two recent operational increments [53]. Decreasing the level of safety activities when all these changes are being made is bound to lead to problems.

Underestimating Software-Related Risks

With the introduction of computers into the control of complex systems, a new form of complacency appears to be spreading—a belief that software cannot "fail" and that all errors will be removed by testing. Those who are not software professionals, in particular, seem to believe this myth, which leads to complacency and overreliance on software functions. Although it is true that software, unlike hardware, is not subject to random wearout failures, software design errors are much harder to find and eliminate. Furthermore, hardware failure modes are generally much more limited, and therefore it is usually easier to build in protection against them.

The Therac-25 provides a cogent example of the potential result of such complacency. Software was not even included in the original hazard analysis of the machine since they believed (according to the hazard analysis report): "Programming errors have been reduced by extensive testing on a hardware simulator and under field conditions on teletherapy units. Any residual software errors are not included in the analysis. . . . Program software does not degrade due to wear, fatigue, or reproduction process" [187].

When accidents started happening, the software was not investigated; instead, the overdoses were blamed on transient hardware failures. Additional hardware redundancy was added, and inflated claims of increased safety were issued. This unrealistic risk assessment led to even more complacency about the safety of the machine and a continuing lack of accident investigation.

Hardware backups, interlocks, and other safety devices are currently being replaced by software in many different types of systems, including commercial aircraft, nuclear power plants, and weapon systems. Where the hardware interlocks are still used, they are often controlled by software. Many basic mechanical safety devices invented long ago are well tested, cheap, reliable, and fail-safe, and they are based on simple principles of physics. Replacing these with programmable devices, which have few of the desirable properties of the original interlocks and are apt to increase complexity and coupling, seems misguided.

Underestimation of software risks can also be seen in some of the new software standards for civil aircraft and nuclear power plants. Software functions are defined to be safety critical only if they alone can lead to an accident. Because systems are rarely designed so that a single failure or error can cause a catastrophe, little or no software is ever designated as safety critical. An assumption seems to be prevalent that common-cause, common-mode, or coincident failures involving software and other devices, such as monitors, will never occur.

Ignoring Warning Signs

A final aspect of complacency is discounting the warning signs of potential accidents. Accidents are frequently preceded by public warnings or by a series of minor occurrences or other signs. Often, these precursors are ignored because individuals do not believe that a major accident is possible. In fact, there are always more incidents than there are accidents because most systems are designed to handle single failures or errors; the problems usually are corrected before they lead to hazards. Also, hazards may not lead to accidents because the specific environmental conditions necessary for serious losses may not occur while the hazardous condition exists, at least in that particular instance.

For seven years before the Flixborough explosion, the Chief Inspector of Factories in Britain had been warning about the risks involved in the increasing use and amounts of dangerous materials in British factories [113].

At least six serious accidents occurred at the Bhopal plant in the four years before the big one in 1984, including one in 1982 in which a worker was killed. People in key positions were alerted to the potential dangers by a number of sources, including a series of newspaper articles by a journalist, R. K. Keswani, who virtually predicted the accident; however, local authorities and plant managers did nothing [15, 52]. Early warning signs were ignored.

The TMI accident was preceded by records of similar accidents and operator errors, reports predicting such an accident, and evidence of persistent and uncorrected equipment failures. All of these signals were disregarded or dismissed [258]. For example, since 1970, 11 pilot-operated relief valves (PORVs) had stuck open at other such plants (a stuck-open PORV initiated the TMI events).

James Creswell, a reactor inspector for the NRC, noticed incidents at two Babcock and Wilcox (B&W) reactors[7]—Rancho Seco and Davis-Besse—in which the instruments did not give the operators adequate indication of the reactors' true operating conditions [143]. At Davis-Besse, the main feedwater system failed when a pressure-relief valve stuck open, and the operator misinterpreted the water level in the reactor based on indications of the level in the pressurizers. The false information led the operator to shut off the emergency core-cooling pumps mistakenly. This is exactly what happened at TMI, except that Davis-Besse was operating at 9 percent of rated capacity at the time while TMI was operating at 96 percent, and the failure of the relief valve to close was discovered at Davis-Besse after 22 minutes rather than the more than 2 hours it took at TMI.

For over a year before the TMI accident, Creswell tried to tell the NRC, the utility, and B&W about his concerns. Finally, he found two NRC commissioners who were willing to listen; the memo they sent to the NRC staff requesting answers to Creswell's questions was delivered the day after the TMI accident [143].

The 1977 incident at Davis-Besse had caused concern at B&W too, and engineers were sent out to investigate. Some employees tried to get word out to

---

[7] The nuclear power plant at TMI was a B&W reactor.

B&W customers, but were unsuccessful. Internal B&W memos later revealed that the company was aware of reactor defects [214].

There is a final example of the mishandling of prior warnings of the TMI accident. A report to the NRC's Division of System Safety, written in late 1977 by Carlyle Michelson, a senior nuclear engineer at the Tennessee Valley Authority, raised the possibility of a steam bubble forming in a B&W reactor's cooling-water system. The report also mentioned the danger of misreading the reactor coolant level by looking at the pressurizer. According to protocol, the report should have been forwarded to the Division of Operating Reactors, which would have alerted users to the problems. The assistant director of the Division of System Safety later said that he thought the Office of Inspection and Enforcement would have taken action if any was needed. Ten days after the TMI accident, the Advisory Committee on Reactor Safeguards asked the NRC to carry out some of Michelson's recommendations [214].

A fire at London's King's Cross underground station in 1987, in which 31 people were killed and many more injured, was apparently caused by a lighted match dropped by a passenger on an escalator, which set fire to an accumulation of grease and dust on the escalator running track [160]. A metal cleat that should have prevented matches from falling through the space between the treads and the skirting board was missing, and the running tracks had not been cleaned regularly. No water was applied to the fire, which spread for 20 minutes and then suddenly erupted in the ticket hall above the escalator. The water spray system installed under the escalator was not actuated automatically, and the acting inspector on duty walked right past the unlabeled water valves. London Underground employees had little or no training in emergency procedures; their reactions were haphazard and uncoordinated.

Although the combination of a match, grease, and dust was an obvious causal factor in the fire, a (level-three) factor was the view accepted by all concerned, including the highest levels of management, that occasional fires on escalators and other equipment were inevitable and could be extinguished before they caused serious damage or injury [160]. There had been an average of 20 fires per year from 1958 to 1967 (called "smoulderings" to make them seem less serious), but although some had caused damage and passengers had suffered from smoke inhalation, no one had been killed: The view grew that no fire could become serious, and fires were treated almost casually:

> Recommendations after previous fires were not followed up. Yet escalator fires could have been prevented, or reduced in number and size, by replacing wooden escalators by metal ones, by regular cleaning, by using non-flammable grease, by replacing missing cleats, by installing smoke detectors that automatically switched on the water spray, by better training in fire fighting, and by calling the Fire Brigade whenever a fire was detected, not just when it seemed to be getting out of control [160, p.85].

On March 22, 1975, during plant modification at the Browns Ferry Nuclear Power Plant, a candle being used to detect air leaks ignited polyurethane foam (which was used in parts of the electrical system), causing extensive damage to the electrical power and control systems and leading to the common-mode failure described earlier. Before the 1975 fire in Browns Ferry Units 1 and 2, the record shows that "there was extensive official fore-knowledge of safety deficiencies in Browns Ferry and that the very combination of problems responsible for the accident had been identified by Federal safety authorities but left uncorrected" [350].

Weil details prior warnings about the dangers of electrical cable fires arising from poor control of combustible materials, inadequate fire prevention programs, and poor separation of redundant circuitry that go back to 1969 (the Browns Ferry plant went into full operation in August, 1974):

1. The Atomic Energy Commission's Division of Operational Safety warned about the combustibility of polyurethane foam in 1963 (the construction of Browns Ferry began in 1966).

2. A series of fires over several years, starting in 1965, demonstrated that electrical cable fires could cause failures of important safety systems.

3. In 1969, an inspector monitoring the Browns Ferry construction wrote a memo to the AEC in which he noted the need for specific criteria for cable separation.

4. In 1970, five AEC inspectors reported deficiencies in quality control at Browns Ferry involving cable separation.

5. In 1970, an Advisory Committee on Reactor Safeguards subcommittee meeting included a presentation on the poorer aspects of the Indian Point 2 reactor protection and electrical systems (similar to the design at Browns Ferry), including cable separation.

6. In 1971, before Indian Point 2 was in operation, a fire broke out and led to an AEC review that concluded there was an urgent need "to re-evaluate previously approved cable separation criteria for this facility and other facilities."

7. In October 1971, three AEC inspectors warned about safety problems at Browns Ferry.

8. One year later, in 1972, AEC safety reviewers criticized electrical cable separation at Browns Ferry, but deferred improvements to new construction (Unit 3).

9. In November 1973, the AEC's Director of Regulation criticized Browns Ferry officials for serious deficiencies in their quality assurance program, but allowed them to operate during a grace period of several years while they upgraded the program.

10. In March 1974, the supervisor of preoperational testing at Browns Ferry warned AEC headquarters about the plant electrical cable installation (which he had been discussing with AEC officials since 1970), but the plant was allowed to go into full operation anyway.

11. There were numerous small fires at Browns Ferry before the big fire on

March 22, 1975 (two fires occurred just two days before, on March 20). One of these fires was large enough to require the use of dry chemicals to extinguish it. These fires were not reported properly, and no safety review of their significance was conducted.

A good argument can be made that it is unfair to judge too harshly those who have ignored warnings: Too many accident warnings that prove to be unfounded may desensitize those in decision-making positions and result in real warnings being ignored. Hindsight is always perfect. Nevertheless, there is a tendency to disregard events that do not lead to major accidents. If such events were taken more seriously and if lessons were learned from them, accidents might be avoided.

Because people tend to underestimate risks and ignore warnings, one or more serious accidents are often required before action is taken. Similar accidents tend to repeat themselves until one has such enormous impact that it is impossible not to notice or to ignore the problem.

Government, management, and researchers tend to react more strongly to a major disaster than to smaller-scale accidents or incidents, even when the latter are frequent [172]. The loss of the *Titanic*, for example, resulted in recommendations for installation and 24-hour manning of wireless equipment aboard international passenger ships, reliable auxiliary power sources, adequate manning of lifeboats and lifeboat drills for both crew and passengers, more watertight compartments in ocean-going ships, enough lifeboats for all on board, better lookout, and a prohibition against the firing of rockets or Roman candles on the high seas for any purpose other than as a distress signal [72].[8] International regulations also were adopted regarding safety at sea, and an International Iceberg Patrol was established to watch over the North Atlantic [145]. North Atlantic ships are now warned twice a day about the position of icebergs. As a result, no iceberg collision has occurred since 1959 [97].

Two relatively recent accidents that have had far-reaching effects on legislation are the 1974 Flixborough explosion in England and the 1976 release of dioxin at Seveso near Milan, Italy. The Seveso accident resulted in lasting environmental pollution over a wide area (see Appendix C).

Flixborough led to the establishment of various expert committees that provided important reports and to the passing of the British Health and Safety Act, which among other things established a Health and Safety Commission and a Health and Safety Executive. Seveso has resulted in new European Economic Community (EEC) safety standards and legislation. Neither accident was the largest of its decade, but both were accidents that people realized could happen again under existing regulations and in which the potential danger of new industrial processes to life, property, and the environment was seen to be enormous and beyond the damage caused in these particular instances. These accidents also made clear the need to plan for mitigating the effects of an industrial accident on

---

[8] Such signals were used previously for night recognition.

people, property, and services beyond the plant itself and even beyond national boundaries [248].

In addition to legislative initiatives, serious accidents such as TMI, Bhopal, and *Challenger* have led to industry and organizational learning, as well as to advances in research. Kemp suggests, "If it is true that technology advances as much by overcoming failures as it does by achieving successes, then the price of betterment will always include heartbreaks" [145]. Boiler explosions were an impetus to learning more about the nature of steam and the causes of explosions, and they led to the first technological research grant (to the Franklin Institute in 1824) by the U.S. government. The Morrison Inquiry into box-girder bridges, held after failures of such bridges in England, led to research resulting in improvements in design and quality control. Farmer argues that there would have been no inquiry and no sense of urgency if there had been only cracks and traffic limitations on a number of bridges [81]. The Therac-25 accidents led to new U.S. Food and Drug Administration guidelines for medical devices containing software, changes in practices by purchasers and suppliers of such devices, and generally increased awareness of risks by the medical instrumentation community and others—particularly the risks posed by software.

Despite these results, major accidents have arguably been more expensive than the benefits of the lessons learned, especially if we consider that most of the findings on the accidents were known beforehand, but were not taken seriously [346]. Using this information to attempt to predict and prevent accidents before they occur seems reasonable.

4.1.2 Low Priority Assigned to Safety

Even if complacency is not the norm and individuals in an industry or organization are concerned about safety, their efforts will most certainly be ineffective without support from top management. The entire organization must have a high level of commitment to safety in order to prevent accidents, and the lead must come from the top and permeate every organizational level. Employees must believe that they will be supported by the company if they reasonably choose safety over other goals. The informal rules (social processes) as well as the formal rules of the organizational culture must support the overall safety policy.

Exhortation or policy statements alone are not enough. In December 1988, a crowded commuter train ran into the rear of another, stationary train near Clapham Junction in Great Britain. After the initial impact, the first train veered to its right and struck an oncoming train. Thirty-five people died in this accident and nearly 500 were injured, 69 of them seriously. According to the official government report on the accident, there was a sincere concern for safety at all levels of management, but

> The best of intentions regarding safe working practices were permitted to go hand in hand with the worst of inaction in ensuring that such practices were put into effect. The evidence therefore showed the sincerity of the concern

for safety. Sadly, however, it also showed the reality of the failure to carry that concern through into action. It has to be said that a concern for safety which is sincerely held and repeatedly expressed but, nevertheless, is not carried through into action is as much protection from danger as no concern at all [121, p.163].

One way management can demonstrate true commitment to safety goals is through the assignment of resources. The Rogers Commission report on the *Challenger* accident noted that the chief engineer at NASA headquarters, who had overall responsibility for safety, reliability, and quality assurance, had a staff of 20 people of which one person spent 25 percent of his time on Shuttle maintainability, reliability, and quality assurance and another spent 10 percent of his time on these issues. The Rogers Commission concluded that "Limited human resources and an organization that placed reliability and quality assurance functions under the director of Science and Engineering reduced the capability of the 'watch dog' role" [295].

Staff, training, and maintenance at Bhopal had been severely reduced prior to the accident [30]. Top management justified these measures as merely reducing avoidable and wasteful expenditures without affecting overall safety. Although some workers complained about the cost-cutting measures, their complaints were ignored. Union Carbide management stated after the accident that they did not think that reduced spending had resulted in the malfunction of the key safety equipment. Maintenance reductions, however, certainly affected the lack of working safety devices at the time of the accident, and inadequate training contributed to the severity of the accident.

Management's most important actions in preventing accidents involve setting and implementing organizational priorities. Many managers recognize that safety is good business over the long term; others put short-term goals ahead of safety. Government agencies and user or customer groups can force management to take safety seriously. This type of pressure will be exerted only if safety receives societal support and emphasis. In general, user groups are much more effective than government regulatory agencies in building management support for safety activities. Regulatory agencies are viewed as a mere nuisance to work around, while user groups that refuse to buy unsafe products have control over the continued existence of the company. In the aftermath of the Therac-25 accidents, for example, the demands of medical physicist associations and users of the Therac-25 were instrumental in getting the machine fixed and in implementing standards to increase the safety of future linear accelerators. Other alternatives to mandatory government standards include tort and common law, insurance, and voluntary standards-setting organizations.

4.1.3 Flawed Resolution of Conflicting Goals

Safety not only needs to be recognized as a high priority goal, but procedures for resolving goal conflicts need to be established. Desirable qualities tend to conflict with each other, and tradeoffs are necessary in any system design or development process. Attempts to design a system or a development process that satisfies all desirable goals, or to provide standards to ensure several goals without considering the potential conflicts, will result only in failure or in *de facto* (and nonoptimal) decision making.

The *Challenger* accident is a classic case of poorly handled conflicts between safety and schedule, but other, less well-known examples abound. Nichols and Armstrong examined industrial accidents and found a large number that occurred during an interruption of production and while an operator was trying to maintain or restart production [239]. In each case, the dangerous situation was created by a desire to save time and ease operations. And in each case, the company's safety rules were violated:

> The [operators] acted as they did in order to face up to the pressure exercised by the foremen and the management who aimed at maintaining production. This pressure was continuous; the interruptions of the process were rather frequent and equally hasty methods used to deal with them were employed repeatedly.
>
> Why do foremen, no matter how trained in matters of safety and used, like the workers, to hear management speak of the requirements of safety, exercise such pressure? They know where management's fundamental preoccupation lies. They see the man in charge of production burst out of his office like a cannon ball when the conveyor stops. Naturally, from time to time, management and the foremen have preached about safety; there are even some sanctions in case of an accident. But in day-to-day operations one sees clearly what is important [239, p.20].

The best technology can be defeated by such management failures. Often, accidents blamed on operator error or equipment failure can as easily be traced to management placing higher priority on goals other than safety. Howard provides several examples of this from the chemical process industry [129]. One accident in a polymer processing plant occurred after operating management bypassed all the alarms and interlocks in order to increase production by 5 percent; their perception of top management's priorities was maximum production over all other factors. In another accident, a severe ethylene decomposition in a long pipeline resulted in a costly business disruption. The interlocks and alarms had failed (at a normal rate), but this was unknown because management had decided to eliminate regular maintenance checks of the safety-related instrumentation. In a third accident, a holding tank ruptured from an exothermic decomposition of the contents. Management had for many years suspected that the material in the tank could exothermically decompose, but tests to determine the decomposition properties of the material had been postponed because they were "too busy" running the unit and maintaining high production records. In addition, most of the operator training had been eliminated in order to save money, so an untrained operator in charge of the tank was unaware of the significance of a gradual increase in the temperature of the tank contents over several hours.

Safety often suffers in tradeoffs between conflicting goals because of a dearth of hard data on benefits. Cost and schedule are usually the primary drivers of a project, while benefits from investments in system safety show up primarily in the long run and even then are observable only indirectly—as nonaccidents and the avoidance of modifications or retrofits to improve safety [88]. Long-term uncertainties are difficult to quantify, so short-term factors tend to be emphasized in making tradeoffs. Sacrificing a sure productivity gain in favor of preventing a seemingly low-probability accident may not seem like a reasonable course of action.

Belief that safety conflicts with the basic benefits of technology is common. For example, Fischoff and colleagues write:

> Controlling hazards often requires foregoing benefits. The benefits of a technology are the reason for its existence. Customarily the benefits are as clear and tangible as the risks are ambiguous and elusive. Moreover, the sponsors of a technology, workers, and consumers all have a sizable stake in its existence. It is not surprising, therefore, that hazard management is not practiced to the fullest extent possible. For some groups, benefits may outweigh corresponding risks, and thus it often happens that the beneficiaries of technologies are at political loggerheads with hazard managers concerned with the general welfare [83, p.168].

This belief is also a factor in the use of *downstream* protection (adding protection features to a completed design) rather than *upstream* hazard elimination and control (designing safety into the system from the beginning by eliminating or reducing hazards in the original design). For example, Fischoff and colleagues claim that "The importance of benefits also accounts for the paucity of 'upstream' hazard management. Intervention of this type tends to conflict much more fundamentally with benefits than does more conventional 'downstream' management" [83, p.168].

Although it may be true in some cases that increasing safety requires foregoing some of the benefits of technology, this is not a basic law. The truth of the statement depends on what benefits are being considered and how the safety fixes are implemented. Safety can be increased using upstream methods without giving up any of the benefits of the design. Later chapters describe some of these methods.

On the surface, it does seem that the fewest compromises are required if the basic control system is built without concern for safety, and protection devices are added later to detect and ameliorate hazards if they occur. This downstream approach may eliminate the need for some types of design tradeoffs, but it may increase the overall cost of the system and schedule delays while also increasing risk relative to what the upstream approach might have achieved. In contrast, eliminating or controlling hazards in the early design stages and making tradeoffs early (the upstream approach) may result in lower costs during both development and the overall system lifetime, in fewer delays and less need for costly redesign, and in lower risk.

The difficulty in any discussion of cost and tradeoffs with respect to safety, as stated earlier, is that benefits from system safety programs show up only in the long run and even then are observable only indirectly [5, 88, 171]. There is evidence, however, that system safety programs, especially if directed to upstream safety, can save money. It often costs no more to build an inherently safe system, or one in which hazards are controlled, if the system is designed correctly in the first place. In fact, an inherently safe system is often cheaper than one with a lot of overdesign in the form of added-on protection devices [195]. Moreover, designing in safety from the start is much cheaper than making retroactive design changes. And even these costs may be minimal in comparison with the potential costs of a major accident.

Removing hazards makes systems inherently safe so that failures cannot lead to an accident. The best way to eliminate the hazards of a dangerous material, for example, is to substitute a safe material. After the *Apollo 13* accident, modifications were made to the command module and service module systems to eliminate or reduce the potential dangers in spacecraft that use pure oxygen, such as replacing all teflon insulation in the oxygen tanks with stainless steel [31]. Nonflammable materials often may be substituted for flammable ones in the design stage. As Kletz states with respect to the design of chemical plants, "What you don't have, can't leak" [154].

This approach works for electronic and digital systems as well as for mechanical systems. Martin and Schinzinger demonstrate how the introduction of a safety feature at the early design stage may involve a simple rearrangement of functions at no additional expense [214]. Their example, a motor-reversing system, is shown in Figure 4.1. The design in Figure 4.1(a) potentially allows sticky contacts to short out battery B, making B unavailable for further use, even after the contacts are loosened. A rearrangement of wires, as shown in Figure 4.1(b), removes the problem altogether. During a hazard analysis for a computer-based nuclear power plant shutdown system, engineers found that simple coding changes, such as rearranging the order of statements, eliminated certain hazardous failure modes [34].

Even if hazards cannot be eliminated completely, they may be controlled in the design (by, for instance, reducing the amount of hazardous material used or using it at a lower temperature or pressure). For example, chemical plant designers may be able to avoid the need for relief valves and associated flare systems by using stronger vessels.

Eliminating or reducing hazards often results in a simpler design, which may, in itself, reduce risk. The alternative is to add protective equipment to control hazards, which usually adds complexity. The Refrigerator Safety Act was passed because children were being trapped and suffocated while playing in unused refrigerators. Manufacturers had insisted that they could not afford to design safer latches, but when forced to do so, they introduced magnetic latches that permit the door to be opened from the inside without major effort. The new latches not only eliminate the hazard, but also happen to be cheaper than the older type.

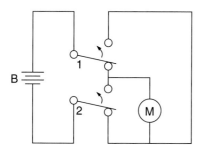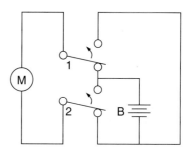

a. Arms 1 and 2 of the switch are both raised by a solenoid (not shown). If either one does not move (for example, a contact sticks) while the other does, there is a short across the battery. The battery will discharge and be useless even after the trouble is detected.

b. By exchanging the position of the battery and motor, a stuck switch will cause no harm to the battery (the motor can be shorted without harm).

FIGURE 4.1
Motor reversing system. (Source: Mike W. Martin and Roland Schinzinger. *Ethics in Engineering*. McGraw-Hill Book Company, New York, 1989. Reprinted with permission of McGraw-Hill, Inc.)

No child has died in a refrigerator that satisfies the design requirements of the act [108, 214].

Using an analogy with the way nuclear and chemical process plants are often built, the protection system approach to the refrigerator problem might have retained the original latch but inserted sensors into the refrigerator to detect a human inside and then sounded an alarm or piped oxygen into the closed space. This admittedly far-fetched solution would have been extremely expensive and less effective than redesign of the latch.

It is widely believed that increasing safety slows operations and decreases performance. In reality, experience has shown that, over a sustained period, a safer operation is generally more efficient and can be accomplished more rapidly. One reason is that stoppages and delays are eliminated [108].

Juechter [142] provides an example involving power presses. Because of a number of serious accidents, OSHA tried to prohibit the use of power presses where employees had to place one or both hands beneath the ram during the production cycle. Preliminary motion studies showed, however, that reduced production would result if all loading and unloading were done with the die out from under the ram. After vehement protests that the expense would be too great in terms of reduced productivity, the requirement was dropped. Some time after OSHA gave up the idea, one manufacturer who used power presses decided, purely as a safety and humanitarian measure, to accept the production penalty. Instead of reducing production, however, the effect was to increase production from 5 to 15 percent, even though the machine cycle was longer.

The belief that safer systems cost more or that building safety in from the beginning necessarily requires unacceptable compromises with other goals is not justified.

4.2 Ineffective Organizational Structure

Many accident investigations uncover a sincere concern for safety in the organization, but find organizational structures in place that were ineffective in implementing that concern. Zebroski [360] examined the causal factors of four major accidents—Bhopal, *Challenger*, Three Mile Island, and Chernobyl—and found similar deficiencies in organizational style and structure, including multilayered hierarchies with diffuse responsibility and poor communication.

Basic management principles apply to safety as well as to any other quality goals: the need for delegation of responsibility, authority, and accountability and the establishment of clearly delineated lines of communication, cooperation, and administration. Nevertheless, some specific issues in organizational structure appear to be related to accidents: diffusion of responsibility and authority for safety along with decision making at the wrong level of management, lack of independence of the safety organization in the management structure, low-level status of safety personnel and exclusion from critical decision making, and limited communication channels for safety-related information.

4.2.1 Diffusion of Responsibility and Authority

Accidents are often associated with a fractured, organizationally dispersed safety staff [140] and with ill-defined responsibility and authority for safety matters. Problems arise especially when responsibility is divided across organizational boundaries: There should be at least one person in the organization with overall responsibility for safety. Interface problems are particularly likely in the building of complex systems that are composites of subsystems and components designed and manufactured by more than one contractor. A central organization is needed to handle the interface issues and to ensure that each subgroup does not assume another group is taking care of safety. As an example, if one subsystem contains ordnance or flammable materials, a central safety organization must make the existence of such materials known to the designers of other subsystems that could provide sources of ignition [208].

With different contractors all making decisions influencing safety, some person or group is required to integrate the information and make sure it is available to all decision makers. For *Challenger*, the responsibility for information about a factor such as safety margins and temperature limits on O-rings was several organizational levels and at least two contractual interfaces away from the people making decisions on schedules and launch. Memoranda and analyses raising concerns about performance and safety issues were subject to many delays in transmittal up the organizational chain and could be edited or stopped from further transmittal by some individual or group along the chain [360]. Accident investigations often reveal that identified risks were accepted at an inappropriately low level, without the knowledge of higher levels of management [140].

A large organizational distance between decision makers and those with technical awareness and competence is, of course, a common problem in engineering organizations, but poor decision making can have especially disastrous results when safety is involved.

4.2.2 Lack of Independence and Low-Level Status of Safety Personnel

Safety is usually viewed as part of the normal activities of the line and project organization, backed by a specialized safety organization. The location of this safety organization in the management structure, and its independence from the project or program management for which it provides oversight or input, is important in terms of both reporting responsibility and funding.

A factor identified by the Rogers Commission as contributing to the ineffectiveness of the *Challenger* safety program was that the safety, reliability, and quality assurance offices were under the supervision of the organizations and activities whose efforts they were to check. This lack of independence reduced their effectiveness as watchdogs. Similarly, one of the criticisms that emerged during the official inquiry into the Flixborough explosion was that there was no engineering organization independent of production-line management responsible for assessing the overall system and ensuring that proper controls were exercised [347].

In addition, serious accidents are often associated with a low status of the safety personnel and their lack of involvement in critical discussions and decision making. The critical teleconference calls between the NASA Marshall Space Center and Morton Thiokol on January 27, 1986, about the *Challenger* launch decision did not include a single safety, reliability, or quality assurance engineer, and no representative of safety was on the management team that made key decisions during the countdown on January 28. (The Rogers Commission itself has been criticized for not including a safety professional, and only one was included on its staff [224].) The status of safety personnel and their involvement in decision making is a clear sign to everyone in the organization of the real (as opposed to professed) emphasis that management places on safety.

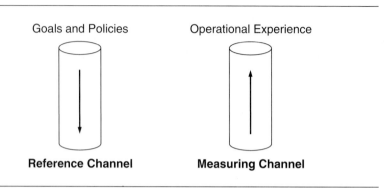

FIGURE 4.2
Information channels.

4.2.3 Limited Communication Channels and Poor Information Flow

An examination of organizational factors in accidents often turns up communication problems. Prior to 1983, the Shuttle program at NASA was required to report all problems, trends, and problem-closeout actions to higher levels of management. After 1983, these requirements were severely cut back, and higher levels lost all insight into safety, operations, and flight schedule issues resulting from lower-level problems [295]. Furthermore, NASA did not have a concise set of problem-reporting requirements for anomalies (unexpected events or unexplained departures from past experience) that occurred during missions. Problems with O-rings during previous flights were not properly documented and reported. For example, a launch constraint had been imposed on the solid rocket booster for the next six Shuttle flights after a serious incident involving erosion of a nozzle O-ring during mission 51-B (the *Challenger* accident occurred in mission 51-L[9]). A launch constraint is issued for a flight safety problem that is serious enough to justify a decision not to launch. Official procedures require that the issuance of a launch constraint be reported up through the proper management chain, but this was not done.

Communication paths and information need to be explicitly defined (Figure 4.2). Two types of information flow are necessary: (1) a *reference channel* that communicates goals and policies downward and (2) a *measuring channel* that communicates the actual state of affairs upward [274].

In the reference channel, the reasons for decisions, procedures, and choices need to be communicated downward along with goals and policies, in order to

---

[9] Space Shuttle flights are designated by two digits and a letter: the first digit indicates the fiscal year of the scheduled launch (such as 5 for 1985), the second digit identifies the launch site (1 for Kennedy and 2 for Vandenberg), and the letter corresponds to the alphabetical sequence for the fiscal year.

avoid undesirable modifications by lower levels and to allow detection and correction of misunderstanding and misinterpretation. In the measuring channel, the feedback from operational experience and communication of technical uncertainties and safety issues up the chain of command are crucial for proper decision making.

In large projects with significant software components, the software development organization is often totally divorced from the safety organization, and information flow is nonexistent or limited. Software development activities tend to go on in relative isolation from system safety and other engineering activities. Serious problems can often be traced to such disconnects.

4.3 Ineffective Technical Activities

A third group of level-three factors related to accidents reflects poor implementation of the specific activities necessary to achieve an acceptable level of safety. These flaws include superficial safety efforts; ineffective risk controls; failure to evaluate changes; and failure to collect, record, and use safety information.

4.3.1 Superficial Safety Efforts

Sometimes safety organizations are caught in the same type of bureaucratic environments as other groups. Paperwork may be completed to meet milestones, irrespective of the quality of that work. This problem is most likely to arise when the system safety engineers become so enmeshed in the project development effort that they lose their objectivity and become defenders of group decisions.

Childs calls this *cosmetic system safety*, which is characterized by superficial safety efforts and perfunctory bookkeeping. Hazard logs may be meticulously kept, with a line item that amazingly supports and justifies each design decision and tradeoff made by the project management and engineers [51].

In some cases, adequate safety analyses are performed, but no follow-up is done to ensure that the hazards are controlled or that the safety devices are maintained and kept in working order. At the Union Carbide plant in Bhopal, a review and audit performed in 1982 noted many of the deficiencies involved in the later accident, but there was no follow-up to ensure that the deficiencies were corrected [360]. A number of hazardous conditions were known and allowed to persist for considerable amounts of time, or inadequate precautions were taken against them.

4.3.2 Ineffective Risk Control

The majority of accidents are not the result of lack of knowledge about how to prevent them but of failure to use that knowledge [154] or to use it effectively. As suggested earlier, the particular causal factors of an accident often are identified, but nothing is done about them because of complacency or underestimating risks. Even with good intentions, the ways to prevent particular hazards, though well understood, may not be known to the people concerned. This education problem is particularly acute when using computers in safety-critical systems, where those actually building the software may know little about basic engineering practices and safeguards.

In some accidents, the hazards are identified and efforts are made to control them, but that control is inadequate. One of the frustrations of those who attempt to reduce risk is that risk reduction often results merely in risk displacement: A risk that appears to be eliminated reappears in a different guise. Workers in the scrap metal industry are exposed to toxic materials originally used to protect metal in bridges or in steel frameworks used for large buildings [208]. X-ray examinations may help diagnose illness, but they may also contribute to future disease. Chemicals introduced to reduce the incidence of particular risks (for example, the use of nitrites and nitrates to counter botulism) are suspected causes of cancer. A flame retardant material (TRIS or dibormopropyl phosphate) used in children's pajamas in the 1960s and early 1970s was found to be a carcinogen. We are very likely to create a new problem while trying to solve an old one.

In fact, technological safety fixes themselves sometimes create accidents. A partial meltdown at the Detroit Fermi nuclear reactor, for example, was caused by the breaking loose of a flow-deflecting zirconium plate that had been installed to *reduce* the likelihood of a core meltdown [89]. The triangular piece of zirconium became detached and blocked the flow of sodium coolant.

In another accident, 72 out of 141 French weather balloons were inadvertently destroyed by a software control program feature originally intended to protect the public from out-of-control balloons [11]. The computer in the French meteorological satellite was supposed to issue a READ instruction to the high-altitude weather balloons, but instead ordered an EMERGENCY SELF-DESTRUCT. [10] In a chemical plant, an error in a watchdog card, installed to protect against errors or failures in another device, opened some valves at the wrong time, and several tons of hot liquid were spilled [158].

To make our technological fixes more effective, we need to understand why they sometimes do not work. Four major factors appear to explain why past efforts to reduce risk have been unsuccessful: (1) patches are used to eliminate the specific causes of past accidents and not the basic design flaws; (2) the design of the safety devices is based on false assumptions; (3) the safety "fixes" increase complexity and cause more accidents than they prevent; and (4) the safety devices are effective in achieving their original goals, but are then used to justify reducing safety margins.

---

[10] It is interesting to ponder why the other 69 balloons did not self-destruct.

Failing to Eliminate Basic Design Flaws

In some cases, technological fixes (safety devices) do not work because they are added to compensate for poor organization or for poor system design, but they do not offset the effect of the organizational or design problems. Referring back to the hierarchical model of accidents in Section 3.4, changes made at level two are unlikely to overcome problems or to make up for a lack of constraints at level three.

The overuse of and reliance on checklists is related to this failure to eliminate basic design flaws. Checklists are often constructed using information from previous accidents. Although checklists are useful in learning from the past and making sure that obvious things are not forgotten, blindly using checklists alone can also limit the factors that are considered. As Johnson writes, one finds triple locks on those doors from which horses have been stolen while other doors are wide open [140].

Basing Safeguards on False Assumptions

A second reason that risk-reduction measures may not be effective is that they are predicated on false assumptions. Kletz relates an example of an attempt to increase safety that actually increased loss and damage [154]. A tank was filled once a day with sufficient raw material to last for 24 hours. An operator was tasked to watch the level and then switch off the filling pump and close the inlet valve when the tank was 90 percent full. The operator performed this task without incident for five years, until one day he allowed his attention to wander, and the tank was overfilled. The spill was small, as the operator soon noticed it and switched off the pump. To prevent another spill, a high-level trip was fitted to the tank to switch off the pump automatically if the level exceeded 90 percent. Everyone was surprised when the tank overflowed again after about a year.

The designer's intention was that the operator would continue to watch the level and that the trip would take over on the rare occasion when the operator forgot to do so. The designer had assumed that the chance of the operator and the trip failing at the same time was negligible. Unfortunately, this assumption was unrealistic. The operator left the control of the level to the trip and turned his attention to other duties, relying on the trip to turn off the pump. Both the manager and the foreman decided that the operator's time was better spent elsewhere. The trip failed, and the tank overfilled. This type of trip is known to have a mean time between failure of two years, so the tank was bound to overflow around that time, but the spill was much greater than before because the operator was doing something else and not paying attention to the level of the tank [157].

This story is not unusual. Often, operators are blamed for an accident when equal blame should be put on the designers who failed to understand the problems in using humans as monitors and who made unrealistic assumptions about the operation of the plant.

Predicating safety devices on assumptions that may not be true (especially assumptions about human behavior) is a serious mistake. One common assumption is independence of events or components. As discussed earlier, safety devices are often defeated by events that, because of dependencies, cause coincidental failures of the safety devices.

Complexity

A third reason why safety devices may not reduce risk is that they may increase system complexity so much that they cause more accidents than they prevent. This increased complexity results more often when safety devices are added as an afterthought than when safety is considered in the original design. If hazards can be identified early in the design process, removing them by a design change may be possible, rather than attempting to control them by adding protective equipment, as discussed earlier in this chapter. Risk may be reduced without increasing complexity or cost and the risk reductive measures may be more effective.

Protection systems are those features added to a standard design in order to restore the system from an unsafe to a safe state or to warn that an unsafe state has been reached. Such systems are usually expensive and are effective only if they exhibit ultrahigh reliability. In one accident, for example, a valve did not reseat and the indicator light to warn the operators about this event failed [259]. If there had been no light to assure them that the valve had closed, the operators would have taken other steps to check the status of the valve.

Techniques to achieve ultrahigh reliability often involve redundancy and diversity in the protection-system design, adding to the complexity of the system and perhaps causing failures themselves. A NASA study of an experimental aircraft found that all of the software problems occurring during flight testing resulted from errors in the redundancy management system and not in the control software itself, which worked perfectly [204].

The seeming ability to add software functions "easily" may unwittingly encourage the addition of functions to computer-based protection systems, such as different types of stop functions, additional inputs reporting the state of the system, or additional status checks of the protection system itself. Complexity may be increased to the point where the increased risk of software errors is greater than the added protection. Adding functions to software is easy; determining whether you *should* do so is much more difficult.

Using Risk Control Devices to Reduce Safety Margins

In some cases, the technological fix does reduce risk, but it then is used to justify the reduction of safety margins—for example, performance is increased by running the system faster or in worse weather or with larger explosives. The net effect may not be reduced risk and may even be greater risk than before the safety device was introduced. As Perrow notes for aviation, "As the technology im-

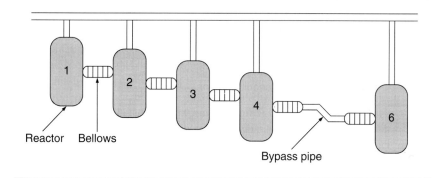

FIGURE 4.3
The temporary change at Flixborough.

proves, the increased safety potential is not fully realized because the demand for speed, altitude, maneuverability, and all-weather operations increases" [259]. As radar and collision avoidance systems are introduced, minimum separation distances between planes may be reduced. The responsibility lies with managers who use the safety devices as an excuse to reduce operating expenses, to increase productivity and profits, to gain time, and to reduce staffing.

4.3.3 Failure to Evaluate Changes

Accidents often involve a failure to reevaluate safety after changes are made. At Flixborough, the process was changed, and the production capacity was tripled without a proper hazard analysis. A temporary pipe was used to replace a reactor that had been removed to repair a crack (see Figure 4.3). The crack was the result of a process modification. The bypass pipe was not properly designed (the only drawing was a sketch on the workshop floor) and was not properly supported (it rested on scaffolding). The pipe failed, and the resulting explosion killed 28 people and destroyed the site. At Seveso, the process was changed to manufacture a different chemical (tricholophenol), which was more dangerous, without a review of the safety measures.

Some members of the chemical industry apparently did not learn the lesson of Flixborough. Many years later, a batch reactor exploded as a result of an exothermic decomposition after a temporary change. Management had decided that it was not cost-effective to connect the high-level interlock from the regular feed-tank pump to a temporary pump for only a month; instead, they instructed the operators to "be careful." An operator overfilled the feed tank, and the reactor overcharge led to the runaway decomposition. Attempts to achieve safety goals by instructing employees not to make mistakes are not going to be effective.

In another accident, a leased crane was being used to lift a $100 million satellite into its shipping container.

> Once the crane started lifting, it could not be stopped. When the hook reached the top of the crane boom, the cable snapped and dropped the satellite 20 feet to the floor. Subsequent investigation showed that the leased crane had been modified and not tested prior to delivery to the contractor. A relay had been installed that was rated for less than 10% of the electrical load it was to carry. When electrical power was applied, the contacts fused so the power could not be shut off [5, p.5-22].

Any change in either hardware or software must be evaluated to determine whether safety has been compromised. Changes in critical hardware or software not only require complete regression testing; they also require system and software safety analysis. In some very dangerous systems, the risk of some proposed changes may be judged as too great relative to the benefits of the changes and the costs of reverification.

One of the requirements for performing an effective change analysis is that the safety-related design decisions have been documented. The system engineers and the original designers of both the hardware and software parts of the system need to specify the constraints and assumptions of the safety assessment and the safety-related design features, so that maintainers do not accidentally violate the assumptions or eliminate the safety features. The decision makers need to know why safety-related decisions have been made so they do not inadvertently undo those decisions.

As an example of what can happen when this documentation does not exist, consider the following accident. In a test of an experimental ballistic missile launch detection satellite, the launch had to occur precisely at 11 A.M., but problems in the launch caused an estimated 30-minute delay. One task took exactly 30 minutes to complete: spinning up the guidance system gyros and physically checking them to be sure that they were all running and functioning properly. An inquiry revealed that no problems had been experienced with these gyros in the last few launches. Against the advice of the guidance-system engineers, the gyro test was deleted to make up the 30 minutes. The missile was launched at precisely 11 A.M., but a pitch gyro did not function; the missile looped and had to be destroyed. The people who made the decision to delete the gyro test did so without knowing that it had been included to control a known hazard; the gyros were due to be replaced by a new model with the deficiency corrected [5].

In another example, a satellite was to be launched with an aged ballistic missile as a booster. During launch preparation, technicians questioned the necessity of installing a cumbersome heater hose into the engine bay. They were told that it was a carryover from the booster's use as a ballistic missile, and they decided to delete the installation. During launch, the engine gearbox coagulated because of the low temperature of an adjacent liquid oxygen (LOX) tank. The gearbox failed, and the booster fell back on the launcher. Again, appropriate documentation of the reason behind a design feature was lacking, and a procedure was deleted without an adequate analysis of its purpose [5].

Safety design decisions must be documented, and this documentation must be used when making decisions.

4.3.4 Information Deficiencies

Feedback of operational experience is one of the most important sources of information in designing, maintaining, and improving safety. Two types of data are important: (1) information about incidents and accidents in other systems and (2) trend and incident data in the system being maintained. This data must be both collected and used.

Information Collection and Recording

The difficulty of systematizing knowledge is an important factor in explaining why similar accidents occur. The large volume of accident case histories is uncollated and often nonexistent in a usable form. Although accident investigations can provide very useful information for improving the design of new systems and for avoiding repetition of similar accidents, information that is detailed enough to be useful is difficult to acquire.

A few accidents have had such disastrous consequences that the government or others have stepped in to conduct a thorough investigation, such as Three Mile Island, *Challenger*, Bhopal, Chernobyl, Therac-25, King's Cross, Clapham Junction, and the *Titanic*. The results of these accident investigations are used frequently throughout this book, as they provide the only substantial information to affirm or disaffirm hypotheses and intuition and to learn the mistakes not to repeat. But the results are useful precisely because the investigations were so thorough and comprehensive. More such investigations are needed along with less oversimplification of accident reports.

Even careful investigations of the causes of accidents are subject to bias and incompleteness, as discussed earlier. Incomplete evaluations, such as those that blame everything on operator error, are worse than useless because they encourage designers to ignore other factors that contribute to accidents. Liability considerations complicate matters further because causal information can be used as a basis for lawsuits—companies may be reluctant to look too hard at an accident—and individuals may not provide complete information because of fears about job security.

Pate-Cornell, writing about safety in offshore oil platforms, observed that learning from experience and transfer of experience are slowed down by some management procedures:

> Management by goals in high-pressure industries encourages an image of super performance and creates a tendency to cover up past mistakes. In such an environment, learning is difficult for the individual and the corporation.

Furthermore, promotions and transfers in the oil industry often occur so fast that people do not have the time to observe the effects of their past actions. These transfers and incentives to remove evidence of past errors make it still more difficult for the engineer who inherits a problem to understand what happened and to learn from it. . . .

Corporate learning requires formal or informal mechanisms to observe, record, and retrieve past collective experience, including mistakes. When appearance of performance is essential to personnel evaluation, protection of identity may be a necessary condition for the disclosure of past errors [254, p.1215].

Pate-Cornell [254] illustrates this problem using an accident at an offshore drilling site. A steel jacket had been designed to be towed to the site and launched from a barge. Buoyancy tanks were placed at the upper face of the top of the jacket. When the jacket was launched, it rotated because of high momentum, the tanks were ineffective in slowing the movement, and the jacket turned upside down and became embedded. This accident was the result of ignorance and the use of a wrong model by the engineer who had designed the system. However, the accident was kept secret, and nothing was learned from it. Two years later, someone else made the same mistake at a different site; this time the accident was reported and the lesson was finally absorbed by the industry.

The official report on the King's Cross fire noted that there was "little exchange of information or ideas between departments and still less cross-fertilisation with other industries and outside organizations" [160].

Trends that should have been apparent in Shuttle O-ring anomalies were not recognized or reported before the *Challenger* accident. Only one field joint O-ring anomaly was found during the first nine flights of the Shuttle. Between the tenth and twenty-fifth missions (the fateful *Challenger* flight), more than half of the flights experienced field joint O-ring blow-by or erosion. "This striking change in performance should have been observed and perhaps traced to a root cause. No such trend analysis was conducted" [295].

Although flight anomalies involving the O-rings received considerable attention from the engineers, the significance of the developing trend went unnoticed; therefore, the changes in procedures that occurred at the time the trend started—and that accounted for the problems—were not discovered until after the accident. The Director of Safety, Reliability and Quality Assurance at Marshall Space Flight Center testified during the hearings on the accident:

I agree with you from my purview in quality, but we had that data. It was a matter of assembling that data and looking at it in the proper fashion. Had we done that, the data just jumps off the page at you [295, p.155].

The final report of the commission concludes:

Development of trend data is a standard and expected function of any reliability and quality assurance program. Even the most cursory examination of failure rate should have indicated that a serious and potentially disastrous situation was developing on all Solid Rocket Booster joints. Not recognizing and reporting this trend can only be described, in NASA terms, as a "quality escape," a failure of the program to preclude an avoidable problem. If the program had functioned properly, the *Challenger* accident might have been avoided. The trend should have been identified and analyzed to discover the physical processes damaging the O-ring and thus jeopardizing the integrity of the joint [295, p.156].

AECL's engineers totally ignored several of the Therac-25 accidents and never launched even a minimal investigation until several people had been massively overdosed. Instead, they repeatedly stated both orally and in writing that an overdose was impossible on their machine.

Software errors or computer failures have caused potentially serious problems for the U.S. military, but learning from them has been diminished because of a failure to disseminate this information. In October 1962, in the midst of the Cuban missile crisis, the radar operators at an early warning site in Moorestown, New Jersey, reported to the national command center (NORAD) in Colorado that a missile had just been launched from Cuba and was about to detonate 18 miles west of Tampa, Florida [307]. NORAD alerted the rest of the command centers and asked the radar operators in New Jersey to recheck their data. The reply confirmed that a missile was coming. The NORAD officers immediately passed the warning information to the Strategic Air Command (SAC) and checked with the bomb alert system (a network of nuclear detection devices placed on telephone poles around cities and military bases in the United States), but were told that no detonation had been reported.

Afterward, they discovered that a software test tape simulating a missile launch from Cuba had been mistakenly loaded into the radar operators' computer. At the same time, an object in space (most likely a satellite) came over the horizon right in the location that a missile launched from Cuba would be. The early warning system included overlapping redundant radars to provide more reliability, but the other radars were not turned on when the incident occurred. In addition, the facility that was supposed to provide advance information about satellites passing overhead had been taken off that function, ironically, to help provide early warning of missiles during the Cuban missile crisis. None of this information was reported in any of the classified after-action reports—it appeared only on the NORAD command post log. Sagan concludes that this reporting failure had very unfortunate consequences: "It ensured that higher authorities would fail to learn from the incident, increasing the likelihood of a later repetition of this particular failure mode in nuclear command and control systems" [307, p.130].

Indeed, seventeen years later it happened again. In November 1979, a realistic display of a Soviet nuclear attack appeared on NORAD and SAC computer screens: A large number of Soviet missiles appeared to have been launched in a full-scale attack on the United States. The air defense interceptor force was launched along with the president's special "doomsday plane" (the National

Emergency Airborne Command Post), but without the president. FAA air traffic controllers were instructed at some locations to order commercial aircraft in their area to prepare to land immediately. "For a few frightening moments, the U.S. military got ready for nuclear war" [307]. After six minutes, the alert was canceled when direct contact with the warning sensors (satellites and radars) indicated that no attack was underway and that the information on the computer displays was false.

Officials later reported to the press and Congress that the incident had been caused by an operator error—which, in fact, was untrue (see Chapter 5)—when an "exercise or training tape" simulating an attack had been mistakenly inserted into the warning system at Cheyenne Mountain. As a result of this incident, stringent test procedures and rules were instituted and an off-site computer testing facility was constructed near Cheyenne Mountain, "reducing the need for software 'test tapes' to be stored near or used on the live computer again" [307].

Other false warning incidents have resulted from computer problems, including one (described in Chapter 16) involving a computer chip fault. Sagan notes significant gaps in NORAD's ability to learn from these incidents:

> In response to public disclosure of false warning events, air force officials quickly began to circle the wagons. Important details about what happened were not reported and the incidents were incorrectly blamed on operator errors or simple computer chip failures, instead of reflecting more serious problems with the way portions of the command system had been designed. Under such conditions, learning would be highly biased.
>
> . . . This 1962 [Moorestown] incident should have served as a permanent and effective reminder of the danger of running simulation tapes on the computers that are operating active warning screens. . . . The October 1962 software testing incident had never been reported even in the classified reports of air force warning operations after the Cuban crisis. All information on the problem was buried in the command post logs and the memories of the individuals involved in the incident [307, p.237].

Sagan concludes, "Better organizational reporting procedures and a more complete learning process might therefore have prevented or at least ameliorated the consequences of the November 1979 incident" [307, p.239].

Information Use

Information not only has to be recorded and available, but it has to be used to be effective in preventing accidents. Section 4.1.1 detailed many instances of warnings that were disregarded or dismissed. Information from such warnings and incidents must not only be taken seriously, but used to construct safeguards against future accidents.

In the Clapham Junction railroad accident (which was blamed on a wiring error by an employee in a relay room), similar wiring errors had been made a few years before but with less serious results, and procedures had not been changed to eliminate this type of error [160].

Operators of nuclear plants in the United States are required to file a licensee event report (LER) with the NRC whenever an irregular event occurs during plant operation. However, although feedback from LERs is available, it has not in the past been adequately utilized [193, 104]. Patrick Haggarty, one of the three engineers who were members of the President's Commission on the Accident at Three Mile Island, argued that better evaluation of the LERs might have prevented the accident ([193]). In fact, before TMI, Babcock and Wilcox did not have any formal procedures to analyze ongoing problems at plants they had built or to review the LER reports on their plants filed with the NRC [214].

The TMI accident sequence started when a pilot-operated relief valve stuck open. Since 1970, 11 of those valves had stuck open at other plants. Haggarty concluded:

> If that kind of incident had been monitored, it would have been recognized as an incident that conceivably could start a sequence that could cause some trouble. . . .
>
> Nobody ever asked: How are we going to use the information that we've got? How are we going to use that to grade the NRC, the industry, and the individual utilities so we achieve some kind of overall quality measure with respect to safety?
>
> When you consider that there are 400 reactor-years of operation now, certainly you would think that the first thing somebody would do would be to stand back and try to arrive at some measure, some statistic or collection of statistics that they'd keep examining to see what the trends were and to control the work required on the plants (quoted in [193, p.55]).

An important use for operational experience is for feedback on the hazard analysis and assessment process. Were the failures or errors not included in the accepted hazards, were the controls ineffective, or were the hazards overlooked? When numerical risk assessment techniques are used, operational experience can provide insight into the accuracy of the models and probabilities used. In various studies of the DC-10 by McDonnell Douglas, the chance of engine power loss with resulting slat damage during takeoff was estimated to be less than one in a billion. However, this highly improbable event occurred four times in DC-10s before changes were made. Even one event should have warned someone that the models used might be incorrect. A device was finally installed in 1982 to prevent slat retraction in such emergencies; this type of locking device is part of the standard design of other jets [259].

A study of the safety information systems of various companies by Kjellan showed that, in general, these systems were inadequate to meet the requirements for systematic accident control. For example, collected data was improperly filtered and thus inaccurate, methods were lacking for the analysis and summarization of causal data, and information was not presented to decision makers in a way that was meaningful to them. As a consequence, learning from previous experience was delayed and fragmentary [150].

An effective system, either formal or informal, for reporting incidents requires delegation of responsibility for reporting; a government, industry, or organizational policy that includes protection and incentives for informants; a system for handling incident reports; procedures for analyzing incidents and identifying causal factors; and procedures for using reports and generating corrective actions [346].

Although software errors are usually reported during testing and maintenance, to be useful for safety analysis the criticality of the errors must be identified. Moreover, the information obtained about these errors should be used to improve the process or to make the software or system safer. All errors (erroneous behavior) in critical software should be monitored for potential safety problems, not only during implementation but during operational use of the software.

Engineers encode experience in standards and checklists. Codes of practice and standards are one of the principal ways that engineers organize lessons learned and effective solutions in a form that can be easily digested and passed forward. Hazard identification techniques also use past experience, but the use of standards and codes helps to avoid hazards that have not been specifically identified and that may be unknown to the designers and hazard analysts.

Unfortunately, software engineering has not had the long experience necessary to develop this type of knowledge sharing and has not yet developed effective means to pass on lessons learned. Neumann [236] has written a book on incidents reported informally to a computer bulletin board, but there is no way to check the accuracy of most of these reports and, for the most part, not enough information is included to be useful in preventing future accidents. With only a few exceptions, thorough investigations of computer-related incidents have not been published or collected.

Most problematic with respect to safety is the tendency to replace electromechanical systems with computer systems without incorporating the knowledge about accident prevention that has been passed down through standard hardware designs and codes of practice. Most of the accidents related to computer control have not involved new hazards or new causes but merely ignorance on the part of the programmer about standard engineering practices or lack of translation of basic engineering design principles to computer software [162].

4.4 Summary

This chapter has looked at the level-three factors that have been implicated in past accidents. Some of these factors relate to deficiencies in the general safety culture of the industry or organization and to general management attitudes: complacency, disregard or low priority for safety, and flaws in procedures for resolving conflicts between goals.

Complacency is a common factor in major accidents. Factors related to complacency include discounting risk; overrelying on redundancy; unrealistic risk assessment; ignoring high-consequence, low-probability events; assuming risk decreases over time; underestimating software-related risks; and ignoring warning signs.

Other flaws in the safety culture relate to problems in resolving conflicting goals. To ensure that conflicts and tradeoffs in system goals are resolved appropriately, an effective system safety program needs the interest and support of management at all levels. Safety needs to be a component of all decision making so that technical achievements are not undone by poor management decisions or by an industrial or organizational culture that puts more emphasis and attention on other goals.

In other cases, a sincere concern for safety existed, but the organizational structure was ineffective for implementing that concern. For example, responsibility and authority for safety were diffused throughout the organization, the safety personnel had a low status or were not independent from the project management, and communication channels were limited.

A final group of factors discussed involve poor implementation of the specific technical activities necessary to achieve an acceptable level of safety: superficial safety efforts, ineffective risk control, a failure to reevaluate safety after changes are made, and deficiencies in the collection, recording, and use of operational information.

In later chapters, information about these causal factors is used to generate and evaluate accident models and to design risk reduction programs. But first, we need to examine the relationship between human error and accidents in more depth.

5

Human Error and Risk

In childhood, falling down may be part of growing up. But do we need the falls of hundreds of "London Bridges," Tacoma Narrows bridges, and Hyatt walkways? Do we need DC-10's to plummet, commercial and private aircraft to collide and devastate a neighborhood, nuclear plants to release radioactive fallout, and other such falls to wake up to the critical importance of human factors in design, analysis, production, installation, maintenance, training, and operation of our products?

—Richard Hornick
Dreams: Design and Destiny

Technological advances, especially computers, have made automation of many manual operations feasible. The potential advantages of automation include increased capacity and productivity, reduction of manual workload and fatigue, relief from and more precise handling of routine operations, and elimination of individual human differences [354].

Economics plays an important role in automation. For example, automation can create potentially enormous savings in energy costs through economical utilization of machinery. In the aviation industry, for instance, fuel consumption can be reduced if flight time is reduced and more fuel-efficient climb and descent patterns are implemented [354].

However, all of these savings are potential and not necessarily completely realizable. *How* one automates will determine the actual savings. In addition, automated equipment is not cheap, additional large maintenance and training costs may be incurred, overall personnel requirements may not be reduced, and the redundancy needed to achieve required reliability levels may add to the cost. From the operational point of view, it is unclear whether overall workload and total operational costs are reduced or increased by automation, and the long-range effects on operators and other personnel are still largely unknown.

Aside from economic considerations, there are technical reasons to automate some manual operations. As control requirements of systems grow more complex, they may exceed human capabilities. In some systems, automated controls are required because humans cannot react fast enough to control the process adequately and safely. The control of the aerodynamic surfaces on unstable aircraft and spacecraft reentry maneuvers are examples of control functions that require automation. Whether such systems can and should be built is a trans-scientific question, as described in Chapter 1, that cannot be answered completely by scientific means. But if they are built, at least partial automation is a necessity.

A third possible reason for automation is to increase safety. Many accidents are attributed to human error. Automation, for example, can eliminate small errors that result from human boredom, inattention, or fatigue. Increasing safety through automation is not usually a simple matter, however, as the introduction of automation may create a risk–risk situation—there may be risk in both the use and nonuse of automated equipment. Aircraft collision avoidance systems, for example, warn pilots about potential collisions, but also may reduce pilot alertness and visual scanning. Ground terrain warning systems reduce terrain-strike accidents, but they have also been denounced for generating frequent false alarms that are annoying and potentially dangerous.

The long-term effects of automation, including complacency resulting from overconfidence in automated equipment, are not well understood. Whether automation increases safety and the role of human errors in accidents are important issues for system designers to understand: The answers have important implications for the design of safer systems.

5.1 Do Humans Cause Most Accidents?

A common assumption, supported by a great deal of data, is that human operators cause the majority of accidents. Certainly, operators are actively involved in many industrial accidents, but this fact is not surprising because they play a fundamental role in the operation of industrial production systems. The real question is whether they cause the accidents or are merely swept up in the events and blamed for them.

A commonly cited statistic is that 85 percent of work accidents are due to unsafe acts by humans rather than unsafe conditions [140]. Heinrich claimed that 88 percent of all accidents are caused primarily by dangerous acts of individual workers [118]. More recent studies of various industries (steel and rolling mills, construction, and railroads) show that 60 to 80 percent of accidents were the direct result of the operator's loss of control of energies in the system [150].

Other studies show similar numbers. This data, however, should not be merely taken at face value, but needs to be examined more closely. Are there other explanations that do not cast so much blame on the operator?

■ *The data may be biased and incomplete.*

Reports of human error as the cause of accidents and incidents have been found to be based on highly subjective judgments by classifiers using questionable definitions. Often these reports are written by supervisors, whose motives may be self-serving. Johnson claims that the less that is known about the accident, the more likely it will be attributed to human error: Thorough investigations of serious accidents almost invariably find unsafe conditions and nonoperator factors [140].

The study cited above that found that 60 to 80 percent of the accidents in various industries were the result of the operators' loss of control also determined that in 75 percent of these cases, various malfunctions of production and safety control systems *preceded* the operator actions. Perrow claims that even in the best of industries, there is rampant attribution of accidents to operator error, to the neglect of errors by designers or management [259]. He cites a U.S. Air Force study of aviation accidents that concludes that the designation of human error, or pilot error, is a convenient classification for mishaps whose real cause is uncertain, complex, or embarrassing to the organization.

After the 1979 crash of a DC-10 into Mount Erebus in Antarctica during a sightseeing flight, the initial report of the New Zealand inquiry board found pilot error as the cause [207]. The conclusions of the report were contested by the pilot's widow and the pilots' union, and a subsequent, more thorough investigation was conducted [206]. The later investigation found that some autopilot headings—used during briefing and simulator training by the crew—had been altered by employees of the airline right before the flight without informing the crew. The controversy over this accident continued with the airline claiming that the airplane was flying too low. The second investigative report noted, however, that the airline advertised the fact that low flights were made to improve sightseeing, and, therefore, the captain was expected to fly low. Similar controversy over pilot culpability continues over the cause of the crash of an A320 during an air show in Habsheim, Germany, in June 1988 and other A320 accidents.

After a false warning of a Soviet nuclear attack appeared on NORAD displays at the Cheyenne Mountain command and control center (see Chapter 4), a government spokesman informed the press and Congress that the November 1979 incident was the result of a simple operator error—mistakenly inserting an "exercise or training tape" that simulated an attack into the operational computer warning system in Cheyenne Mountain. The NORAD commander, General James Hartinger, announced that the false warning was "a 100-percent personnel error" [307].

In fact, Sagan reports, recently declassified internal NORAD documents and congressional investigations confirm that the test data was purposely being run on the computer and that the false warning was not just a matter of an operator erroneously loading the "wrong tape" [307]. At the time of the incident, NORAD was in the process of deploying an upgraded computer system to improve the reliability of the early warning system. During this deployment, some of the software development and testing was being done on the on-line NORAD missile warning network because no other computer system was available for this purpose.

NORAD was unable to determine why the test information appeared on the operational warning displays and was sent to SAC, the Pentagon, and Fort Richie: The command's internal investigation of the incident (as reported in a private letter from one general to another) stated that they were unable to replicate the mode of failure [307]. Blaming the incident on a human operator loading an incorrect tape was apparently more politically acceptable than suggesting that there might be technical problems in the early warning system, that it had been a poor decision to run tests on the same computers responsible for warning about nuclear attacks, or that they could not determine the exact cause of the incident.

In commenting on these events, Sagan warns, "The common tendency to assign blame for accidents on operator errors, and thereby protect the interests of those who designed the system and the leaders of the organization, was also found to increase the likelihood of repeated mistakes. . . . the November 1979 incident did not produce a thorough search for potential failure modes that remained in the system" [307, p.246].

- *Positive actions are usually not recorded.*

One reason why human error reports may be misleading is that human actions are generally reported only when they have a negative effect on safety. A human action with a positive effect, such as restoring normal operation after a technical failure, is usually not reported because it is considered to be normal operational performance. A U.S. Air Force study of 681 in-flight emergencies showed 659 crew recoveries from equipment and maintenance deficiencies, with only 10 pilot errors. The proportion of pilot errors was about 1.5 percent in these incidents, while the proportion of equipment failures was 91 percent.

- *Blame may be based on the premise that operators can overcome every emergency.*

Given the role of human operators in highly automated plants as monitors and supervisors, the major risk often is not that they will cause accidents but that they may not succeed in preventing them [270]. Aviation accident boards have predicated the finding of pilot error on the premise that pilots should be able to and must overcome any emergency. In many instances, pilots were overwhelmed by failures due to causes beyond their control; many of these failures could have been prevented by the incorporation of suitable precautions in the design stage [106].

Almost every accident can be traced to human error of some kind. It appears, however, that the operator who does not prevent accidents caused by design deficiencies or lack of proper design controls is more likely to be blamed than the designer.

■ *Operators often have to intervene at the limits.*

Not only are operators expected to overcome any possible emergency, but they often are required to intervene at the limits of system behavior, when the consequences of not succeeding are likely to be serious. The emergency may involve a situation that the designer never anticipated and that was not covered by the operators' training. Operators not only have to diagnose and respond quickly to the situation, but they must do so using creativity and ingenuity under conditions of extreme stress and perhaps limited information about the state of the system. We should be more amazed at how well humans often do in these circumstances than surprised at the times they fail.

■ *Hindsight is always 20/20.*

Hindsight often allows us to identify a better decision, but detecting and correcting potential errors before they have been made obvious by an accident is far more difficult [346]. In an emergency situation, operators are required to detect a problem, diagnose its cause, and determine an appropriate remedial action—all of which are much easier to do after the fact. Before the accident, the operator cannot always be expected to know what is going on and what should be done when confronted by unexpected failures and interactions among components and working with often limited information. The situation may lead the operators to construct erroneous mental models of the system state, which are obviously incorrect only when after-the-fact knowledge of the real state is considered; they were just as likely to be correct as the real model at the time they were constructed.

The official report of the Clapham Junction railroad accident concluded that "There is almost no human action or decision that cannot be made to look more flawed and less sensible in the misleading light of hindsight. It is essential that the critic should keep himself constantly aware of that fact" [121].

The TMI accident has been widely judged to be the result of operator error. However, examining the factors involved suggests that this judgement is a classic example of the misattribution of an accident to operators and the use of hindsight to label operators' actions as erroneous. The accident sequence was initiated and compounded by equipment failure. The major errors of the operators could only have been seen after the fact; at the time, there was not enough information about what was going on in the plant to make better decisions.

The major operator "error" at TMI was throttling back on two high-pressure injection pumps to decrease water pressure, thus allowing the core to become uncovered and overheat [258]. However, unless the operator knows that an accident involves a loss of coolant to the core (called a *loss of coolant accident* or LOCA), the recommended procedure is to throttle back in order to avoid other kinds of damage. Theodore Taylor, a theoretical physicist from Princeton University, argued at the hearings of the Kemeny Commission on the accident [143] that there was no way for the operators to know what kind of an accident they were experiencing when they cut back on the high-pressure injection: The decision to cut back had to be made *before* anyone could know that it was the wrong thing to do.

There was no direct way at TMI to determine that the core was being uncovered and superheated. A Babcock and Wilcox official testified at the Kemeny hearings that such indicators would be difficult to provide, would be too expensive, and would create other complications. In fact, the readings of the core that are normally used to determine the amount of coolant present indicated that there *was* enough coolant. Although there were several indirect measures that might have shown the true state of the plant, each was faulty or ambiguous. A drain-pipe pressure indicator would have suggested a LOCA, but it was located on the back side of the 7-foot control panel; unaware that they were in a LOCA, the operators had no reason to look at it. The temperatures on a drain pipe would similarly have indicated the problem, but the operators had been discounting these readings prior to the accident because the drain pipe had leaky valves; they assumed that decay heat had caused a particularly high reading.

Knowing that the pressure had dropped in the core would have warned the operators that throttling back on the high-pressure injection was the wrong thing to do. The core pressure indicator was next to the indicator showing a rise in pressure in the pressurizer. These two indicators are supposed to move together, but one dropped as the other rose. The operators believed that the indicator measuring pressure in the pressurizer was more accurate than the indicator measuring pressure in the core because various other factors pointed to that conclusion. They were used to receiving faulty readings—there had been several during the accident—so they relied on those that made sense and discounted or explained away those that did not [258].

The control room quickly filled with managers and engineers, none of whom knew that the problem was a LOCA, either. It was several hours later, and much too late to matter, before even the outside experts realized what had happened:

> Consider the situation: 110 alarms were sounding; key indicators were inaccessible; repair-order tags covered the warning lights of nearby controls; the data printout on the computer was running behind (eventually by an hour and a half); key indicators malfunctioned; the room was filling with experts; and several pieces of equipment were out of service or suddenly inoperative. In view of these facts, a conclusion of "severe deficiency in training" seems overselective and averts our gaze from the inevitability of an accident even if training were appropriate [258, p.178].

According to Richard Hornick, past president of the Human Factors Society, "The chain of events at TMI was not the result of immediate human errors in the usual sense. Rather, it reflected the prior failure of owners, managers, and engineers to appropriately design interactions between humans and machines" [127]. Victor Gilinsky, a Nuclear Regulatory Commission official, argues that "In emphasizing the human failures, and thereby vindicating the equipment, the report does not stress enough that the equipment could have been designed to avoid this kind of trouble" [212]. Finally, Malcolm Brookes, a member of the Kemeny Commission investigating the accident, concludes,

> There were no operator errors as such: the events that occurred seem "inevitable," given existing instrumentation (which is typical to the industry). The events were a direct function of the electro-mechanical system design and detail, e.g., computer update rates, alarming, wrong placement of controls and displays, wrong instrumentation giving the wrong sort of information. The fundamental errors were in systems design (quoted in [357, p.220]).

Operators often are placed in situations where they must make choices between several actions, any of which could turn out to be wrong after the fact. In the unsuccessful attempt to rescue the American hostages in Teheran in 1979, when the pilots inappropriately grounded the helicopters in the desert, changes in atmospheric pressure had triggered a false alarm indicating failure of the rotor blades. This mechanical misdiagnosis presented the pilots with two possibly erroneous actions: (1) they could trust their own instincts and ignore the alarm, thus risking a real emergency, or (2) they could ground the helicopters in perfect running condition. The correct decision could only be known in hindsight [123].

■ *Separating operator error from design error is difficult and perhaps impossible.*

All human activity is affected by the environment in which it takes place. In complex, automated plants, the human operator is often at the mercy of the system design and operational procedures.

Nuclear power plants have been reported to display the following examples of poor design [123, 127, 279]:

- □ Dials measuring the same quantities are calibrated in different scales.
- □ Normal ranges are not uniformly marked.
- □ Irregular scale divisions are used on seemingly identical dials.
- □ The location of critical decimal points is unclear.
- □ Recorders are cluttered with excess information.
- □ Labels and colors are inconsistent and confusing.
- □ The left-hand pair of displays is driven by the right-hand pair of controls.
- □ Panel meters cannot be read from more than several feet away, but controls for these panel meters are located thirty feet away.
- □ Critical displays are located on the back side of a panel, while unimportant displays occupy central, front-panel space.
- □ Two identical (unmarked) scales are placed side by side, one of which the operator must remember differs from the other by a factor of ten.
- □ Labels on alarm enunciators differ from the supposedly corresponding labels in the written procedures.

FIGURE 5.1
Labeling on pumps.

□ Refresher training in emergency procedures uses a control board on which displays and controls are laid out differently from those on the control board the operators will actually use.

In some plants, operators have jury-rigged their own marking systems in order to eliminate some of the confusion, using colored tape, homemade control knobs and supplemental equipment to highlight the logic of the system [258].

The nuclear industry is not the only one with these types of design errors. Kletz describes two accidents in the chemical process industry involving similar human–machine interface design deficiencies. In the first, a row of pumps was labeled as shown in Figure 5.1. Not unreasonably, the operator assumed that number 7 was the last one, and so he did not check the numbers. Hot oil came out of the pump when he dismantled it [157]. In a second accident, a plant had four crystalizers—three old ones and one just installed (Figure 5.2). A worker was asked to repair crystalizer *A*. When he went onto the structure, he found that two were labeled *B* and *C*, but the other two were not labeled. He assumed that *A* was the old unlabeled crystalizer and started work on it. Actually, *A* was the new crystalizer. The original three were called *B*, *C*, and *D*; *A* had been reserved for a possible future addition.

In addition to simple labeling and layout problems, designers may fail to understand fully the system characteristics or to anticipate all the environmental conditions under which the system must operate. The operator can intervene effectively only if the system has been designed to allow the operator to build a complete and accurate mental model of its operational status, including providing the information necessary for the operator to understand the system state and providing it in a form that is understandable under stressful conditions.

Williams examined failures in U.S. nuclear power reactors over a two-year period [104]. He found that in boiling water reactors, slightly over half of the reported occurrences were caused by design deficiencies and one third by human error, whereas in pressurized water reactors, the exact opposite proportions were found—over half were caused by human error or oversight and one third by design errors. Since the classification was done by one person, misclassification does not explain the differences: If human error were independent of design, the percentage of accidents attributed to human error should be constant over

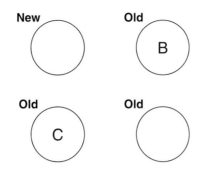

FIGURE 5.2
Labeling on crystalizers.

the different reactor designs. Aerospace studies show that about 80 percent of pilot-error accidents are due to poor training or neglect of human engineering in controls and instruments, not to stupidity or panic [320]. Claims have been made that the same ratio is true for the nuclear industry. The most serious human error may be in not being able to overcome the inadequacies and complexities of the equipment humans must use [258].

By simply blaming accidents on human error and not looking at the design features that might have contributed to those errors, future accidents cannot be reduced. In June 1987, the pilot of a Delta Boeing 767 taking off from LAX accidentally turned off both engines while reaching for a fuel control switch [307]. The plane, originally at 1,700 feet, dropped 1,100 feet before the pilots got the engines started, and the plane leveled off at 600 feet above the ocean. Instead of simply blaming the incident on pilot error, the Federal Aviation Administration (FAA) ordered that a safety guard be placed over the two engine shutdown switches in order to reduce the likelihood that a future "operator error" would inadvertently turn off both engines.

In summary, human actions both prevent and contribute to accidents in high-technology systems. Accidents and incidents occur because of human error, machine failure, poor design, inadequate procedures, social or managerial inadequacies, and the interaction of all these factors. Assignment of blame to operator error alone ignores the multiple causality of accidents and the relationship between human actions and the context in which they occur. It also suggests that little can be done about reducing accidents aside from removing humans from systems. Recognition of other causal factors in the work environment and system design presents more possibilities for improvement.

This conclusion does not imply that humans do not make mistakes, only that ascriptions of blame to humans for accidents in complex systems is often simplistic and may get in the way of reducing risk through improved engineering and management.

But even if humans have been blamed incorrectly for accidents, they certainly have contributed to many of them. The question then becomes why we should not just eliminate humans from systems and replace them with computers.

5.2 The Need for Humans in Automated Systems

Computers and other automated devices are best at trivial, straightforward tasks. An *a priori* response must be determined for every situation: An algorithm provides predetermined rules and procedures to deal only with the set of conditions that have been foreseen. Not all conditions are foreseeable, however, especially those that arise from a combination of events, and even those that can be predicted are programmed by error-prone humans.

As system design becomes more complex and requires coordination and integration of various types of expertise, system behavior and performance become increasingly difficult to understand and anticipate. For example, the designers of the TMI reactor had anticipated a crisis of high pressure in the concrete containment building; in the actual accident, however, the pressure was not high enough to trigger the automatic feedback mechanism. Later in the accident sequence, the pressure was too high to permit activation of an emergency heat removal device. The designers of the system had failed to anticipate and correctly handle the conditions that actually occurred. In addition, because they had assumed that the system was self-regulating, they did not design the system (or train operators) for effective human intervention [123].

It is difficult to anticipate all conditions that might occur in the environment of a system or to anticipate all undesired interactions in the system components. Although designers may work under conditions of less stress than operators, designers also make mistakes. Many of the same limitations of human operators that contribute to accidents are also characteristic of designers. Designers have been found to have (1) difficulty in assessing probabilities of rare events, (2) a bias against considering side effects, (3) a tendency to overlook contingencies, (4) a propensity to control complexity by concentrating only on a few aspects of the system, and (5) a limited capacity to comprehend complex relationships [150]. Designers may fail to understand fully the system characteristics or to anticipate all the environmental conditions under which the system must operate. There will remain events, usually of low probability, against which the automated system does not provide protection because they were unforeseen, they were handled improperly, or their probability was estimated as below the designer's cut-off level [172].

Human operators are included in complex systems because, unlike computers, they are adaptable and flexible. In a computer, the response to each situation is preprogrammed. Humans are able to look at tasks as a whole and to adapt both the goals and the methods used to achieve them. Thus, humans evolve and develop skills and performance patterns that fit the peculiarities of a system very effectively, and they are able to use problem solving and creativity to cope with unusual and unforeseen situations. For example, the pilot of a Boeing 767 made use of his experience as an amateur glider pilot to land his aircraft safely after a series of equipment failures and maintenance errors caused the plane to run out of fuel while in flight over Canada [189]. Humans can exercise judgment and are unsurpassed in recognizing patterns, making associative leaps, and operating in ill-structured, ambiguous situations [300].

Human error is the inevitable side effect of this flexibility and adaptability. The behavior involved when operators take undesirable shortcuts in prescribed procedures is the same behavior that gives them the ability to diagnose problems and find unique paths to goals when unforeseen events occur that were not covered by their training.

Examples abound of operators ignoring prescribed procedures in order to solve a problem, but those instances when the decision was incorrect are more likely to get attention. For instance, a U.S. NRC regulation laid down after the TMI accident required operators to leave the emergency cooling pumps on for at least 20 minutes after a reactor scram. In one incident in 1979, the operators at the North Anna nuclear power plant could see that obeying this regulation would lead to a dangerous temperature shutdown profile. They decided to disobey the regulation and turned off one of the two pumps for four minutes "without knowing precisely what reduction in total output could be expected, and what the net result on pressure and level might be, but it was considered a step in the right direction" [70]. In this case, it turned out to be the correct thing to do.

Other examples of imaginative jury-rigging or deviation from rules occurred in the TMI and Browns Ferry accidents. At TMI, two pumps were put into service to keep the coolant circulating, even though neither was designed for core cooling. Something more complex, but similar, happened at Browns Ferry.

An incident at the Crystal River nuclear power plant would have been much worse if the operator had not stepped in and overridden erroneous computer commands. The trouble began when, for some unknown reason, a short circuit occurred in a section of the control room not related to the reactor controls. The utility believes that the short circuit was caused either by a bent connector pin in the control panel or by some maintenance work being done on an adjacent panel. In any event, the short did not knock out the whole system, but it did distort readings flowing through all the controls.

The coolant in this type of reactor must remain within a relatively narrow temperature band. The computer, which was responsible for controlling the temperature, "thought" that the coolant was growing too cold. It therefore began to accelerate the nuclear reaction in the core by withdrawing control rods. At the same time, the computer reduced the flow of coolant. The reactor overheated, drove the pressure up to the danger level, and then automatically shut down.

The computer then erroneously ordered the pressure relief valve to open and stay open, supposedly because of a "design defect in the electrical system" [345]. The emergency core cooling system began pumping water into the reactor. An alert operator noticed the computer error in opening the relief valve and, several minutes later, plugged the leak by shutting a block valve. Water filled the reactor to the top and then poured out through two safety valves. One of these did not at first reseat properly. Before the incident was over, 43,000 gallons of radioactive water were dumped on the floor.

These and other incidents demonstrate the danger of trying to prescribe regulations, procedures, or algorithms. Human error is often defined as behavior that is inconsistent with normal, programmed patterns and that differs from prescribed procedures [108]. Sometimes, however, deviating from the prescribed procedures is exactly the *right* thing to do to avoid an accident: Accidents have resulted precisely because the operators *did* follow the predetermined instructions that were given to them for a particular situation. Automating those instructions will not solve the problem or make it any easier to design the instructions. Note the chaos that results when workers "work to rule" during a limited job action.[1] Deviation from the rules is the hallmark of experienced people, but it is bound to lead occasionally to human error and related blame after the fact [277].

5.3 Human Error as Human–Task Mismatch

Rasmussen argues that *human error* is not a useful term and should be replaced by considering such events to be *human–task mismatches*. The term human error implies that something can be done to humans in order to improve the state of affairs; however, the "erroneous" behavior is inextricably connected to the same behavior required for successful completion of the task. The tasks in modern automated systems involve problem solving and decision making that in turn require adaptation, experimentation, and optimization of procedures. Rasmussen explains the relationship between these three behaviors and human error using a three-level model based partly on Newell and Simon's general theory of problem solving (GPS) [237].

After analyzing error reports from nuclear power plants, Rasmussen identified three levels of cognitive control (see Figure 5.3): *skill-based behavior*, which is characterized by patterns of movement generated from a dynamic, internal model of the world; *rule-based behavior*, which depends on implicit models of the environment embedded in procedural rules; and *knowledge-based behavior*, which depends on structural models of the environment [275]. Each of the three levels of behavior can be mapped to different types of mental representations of the system and to different activities.

---

[1] Working in accordance with the written rules has become an effective replacement for formal strikes.

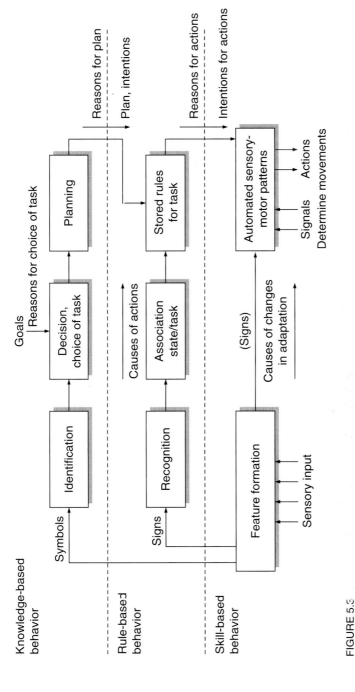

FIGURE 5.3
Rasmussen's model of cognitive control. (Source: Adapted from J. Rasmussen, "What Can Be Learned from Human Error Reports?" in K. Duncan et al., eds., *Changes in Working Life.* New York: John Wiley & Sons, 1980. Reprinted with permission.)

5.3.1 Skill-Based Behavior

Skill-based behavior involves smooth, automated, and highly integrated sensory–motor behavior arising from a statement of intention. Such behavior is characterized by almost unconscious performance of routine tasks, such as driving a car on a familiar road. Performance is based on feedforward control[2] and requires a very flexible and efficient world model and the use of sensory–motor inputs, or *signals*.

Efficiency results from fine-tuning human sensory–motor performance to the features of the task environment. Frequently, however, a mismatch is required before behavior is updated. If the criteria being used to optimize skill are speed and smoothness, operators can only discover an appropriate speed–accuracy tradeoff through the experience gained by occasionally crossing the limits, and the proper limits can only be determined if surpassed occasionally. Some "errors," therefore, have a function in maintaining a skill at its proper level, and they neither can nor should be eliminated if skill is to be maintained.

5.3.2 Rule-Based Behavior

The second level, *rule-based behavior*, involves more conscious solving of familiar problems. At this level, sequences of actions in familiar work situations are controlled by stored rules or procedures (heuristics). The rules may be derived empirically from previous experience, communicated or taught in the form of a set of instructions or recipe, or prepared by conscious problem solving and planning. Performance is goal-oriented, but structured by feedforward control using a stored rule. Often, the goal is not explicitly formulated, but is found implicitly in the situation releasing the rules.

Selection of appropriate rules is controlled by inferences about the current state and events. When interacting with complex systems, operators often do not have direct interaction with the components and thus are controlling more or less invisible processes. They have to infer the state of the world and select the proper action on the basis of a set of physical measurements that are seldom presented in a way that allows perceptual identification of the state.

To avoid the mental effort necessary to determine the state and events from scratch each time the physical measurements change, operators generally use indications that are typical of normal events and states as convenient *signs*. The signs are associated with appropriate rules by training or experience, which allow the operator to interact efficiently with a complex system using a large number of rules along with know-how for linking and updating those rules. This interaction

---

[2] *Feedforward control* attempts to anticipate undesired changes in the process and issue commands to prevent them. As an example, experienced drivers increase pressure on the gas pedal when going up hill in order to maintain speed instead of waiting for the car to slow down and then giving it more gas. In contrast, *feedback control* uses information about the current state of the process to generate corrective actions: The process first develops some undesired characteristic, which is then corrected.

is susceptible to mistakes, however, if the environment changes in a way that does not affect the signs but makes the related behavior inappropriate.

When the environment changes, the rules need to change. Often, the signs or inputs are underspecified and do not discriminate between alternatives for action in the new situation [271]. The operator cannot tell that the same or similar signs should not be relied upon to select appropriate behavior until receiving feedback that they have not worked as expected.

Basic experimentation is necessary to develop and adjust efficient rules and to identify the conditions (signs) under which the rules should be applied. Initially, the rules may be based on rational planning (using knowledge-based behavior) or on a set of procedures supplied by an instructor. In both cases, the process of adapting rules and learning to apply them successfully leads to experiments, some of which are bound to end up as human errors under some environmental conditions.

5.3.3 Knowledge-Based Behavior

During unfamiliar and unanticipated situations, when the controller is faced with an environment for which no know-how or rules for control are available from previous experience, control of performance moves to a higher conceptual level where performance is goal-controlled and *knowledge-based*. In this situation, the goal is explicitly formulated, based on an analysis of the environment and the overall aims, and a plan is constructed. The plan may be formulated (1) by selection, where different plans are considered and their effect is tested against the goal, (2) by physical trial and error, or (3) by a conceptual understanding of the functional properties of the environment and prediction of the effects of the plan being considered.

When operators must adapt their behavior to the requirements of a system in a unique and unfamiliar state and switch to knowledge-based reasoning, they interpret information about the system as *symbols* to be used in symbolic reasoning rather than as signs that trigger rules. Rasmussen suggests that this switch is difficult because the use of signs basically means that information from the system is not actually observed, but is obtained by 'asking questions' that are heavily biased by expectations based on a set of well-known situations. Reasoning at the knowledge-based level requires overcoming those biases.

One of the tools humans use to deal with unusual situations and solve problems at the knowledge-based level of control is experimentation accompanied by hypothesis formation and evaluation. Robert studied human exploratory behavior in learning about a personal computer system. He found that humans try to understand the facts they observe and to find relations between them: "They draw analogies, form hypotheses, run experiments for testing and refining their knowledge, put up explanations, make diagnoses when problems occur, and so on. They are curious, motivated, full of initiative for extracting the secrets of the machine, persevering at finding a solution, sensitive to their environment" [292].

At the same time, humans have the ability to monitor their own performance and devise strategies to recover from errors. In fact, some types of human error could be defined as a lack of recovery from the unacceptable effects of exploratory behavior [277]. Eliminating these types of human error requires eliminating the very same problem-solving ability, creativity, and ingenuity needed to cope with emergencies and the unexpected situations for which automated systems have not been preprogrammed or for which the preprogrammed recovery algorithms are not effective. Emergencies are likely to be caused by subtle combinations of malfunctions and to require diagnostic and problem-solving behavior, not just the skill- and rule-based behavior used for routine tasks. Thus, human errors are the inevitable side effects of human adaptability and creativity and are very different from faults in technical components [189].

5.3.4 The Relationship between Experimentation and Error

At the knowledge-based level, mental models of unfamiliar situations often are not complete enough to test a set of hypotheses entirely conceptually (by "thought" experiments); the results of applying unsupported mental reasoning to a complex causal network may be unreliable [271]. Reliable conclusions may require testing the hypotheses, judging their accuracy by comparing predicted responses from the environment with actual responses, and making corrections when the hypotheses are in error. To accomplish the same task, designers are often supplied with tools such as experimental rigs, simulation programs, and computational aids. In contrast, operators usually have only their heads and the plant itself. Operator actions that appear quite rational and important during a search for information and a test of a hypothesis may be judged as erroneous in hindsight: If the test is successful, the operator is often judged to be clever; if it is not successful, the operator is blamed for making a mistake.

The designer relies most on knowledge-based behavior, but the operator at times will employ all three levels of behavior. During training in a particular task, control moves from the knowledge- or rule-based levels toward skill-based control, as familiarity with the work situation develops. In an unfamiliar situation, knowledge-based behavior may be used first to develop rules or heuristics to accomplish explicit goals. After a while, explicit knowledge and rules will no longer be needed for behavioral control of normal scenarios, and they may eventually deteriorate.

Knowledge needs to be maintained, however, to enable error detection, even though high skill has been developed. Because goals do not explicitly control activity at the skill- and rule-based levels, errors may not be observable until a very late stage—an error in following a recipe may not be evident until someone tastes the finished dish. Early detection of problems depends on an ability to monitor the process using an understanding of the underlying processes.

As control naturally moves downward toward skill-based behavior during training and adaptation, the only information the operator has to judge the proper limits of adaptation and to detect mistakes is occasional mismatches between the behavior and the environment. In this way, conscious as well as subconscious experiments providing feedback are integral to adaptation at all three levels of cognitive control.

In summary, human errors can be considered to be unsuccessful experiments performed in an "unkind" environment, where an unkind work environment is one in which it is not possible for the human to correct the effects of inappropriate variations in performance before they lead to unacceptable consequences. Rasmussen concludes that human performance is a balance between a desire to optimize skills and a willingness to accept the risk of exploratory acts. Attempts to eliminate such behavior by admonishing humans to take more care or by enforcing predefined procedures will have only short-term effects.

Instead, Rasmussen suggests that the ability of the operator to explore should be supported by the system design and that a means for recovery from the effects of errors should be provided. This goal can be achieved by the design of work conditions in which errors are immediately observable and reversible— an approach he calls *design for error tolerance* [276, 274, 271]. Some ways to accomplish this goal, along with other approaches to enhancing safety through human–machine interface design, are described in Chapter 17.

5.4 Conclusions

Human skill needs may be changing in modern systems. With automation increasingly taking over routine tasks, operators will use less skill-based and rule-based behavior and more knowledge-based behavior. Operator training will need to focus less on building skills and rules for action and more on general ability to understand how the system functions and to think flexibly when solving problems. Because effective action may require teams, each worker may need some familiarity with the tasks and skills of other workers. Much current research on work teams suggests that workers with broader knowledge can function much more effectively than workers trained in a single skill [123].

Hirschhorn suggests that managers and engineers in traditional industries are highly reluctant to introduce operators to questions of system design or to train them to think conceptually beyond a limited list of specified responses to anticipated problems:

> Engineers have not learned to design a system that effectively integrates worker intelligence with mechanical processes. They seldom understand that workers even in automated settings must nevertheless make decisions; rather they tend to regard workers as extensions of the machines [123, p.44].

This chapter has laid out some of the reasons why this approach may be exactly the wrong one. TMI and other incidents are exemplars of what can happen in complex systems when operators do not understand how equipment works, do not understand what they are required to do in an emergency, and the system is not designed to provide them with the information necessary to intervene effectively.

The term *human error* is generally used in two different ways: (1) the human did something that he or she should have known was wrong; and (2) the human did something that could not have been known at the time to be wrong but in retrospect was. The distinction is useful only if we are trying to assign blame or guilt rather than reduce accidents.

Several authors have suggested that the whole concept of human error as a cause of accidents is outdated and that the term should be eliminated from use. For one thing, the individual operator in a complex, automated plant will be, to a large extent, at the mercy of the system design [150]. In addition, removing dependence on an operator by installing an automatic device to take over the operator's functions only shifts that dependence onto the humans who design, install, test, and maintain the automatic equipment—who also make mistakes.

Thus, almost any accident can be attributed to human error, and doing so does not provide much help in determining how to prevent it. Indeed, Kletz suggests that the phrase actually discourages constructive thinking about how to prevent future accidents [160]. Outdated scientific concepts such as ether, phlogiston, and protoplasm have been determined to be unnecessary: They do not explain anything that cannot be explained without them or explained better differently—that is, they serve no useful purpose:

> Perhaps the time has come when the concept of human error ought to go the way of phlogiston, the ether, and protoplasm. Perhaps we should let the term "human error" fade from our vocabularies, stop asking if it is the "cause" of an accident, and instead ask what action is required to prevent it happening again. Perhaps "cause" as well as "human error" ought to go the way of phlogiston, ether, and protoplasm.
>
> According to Dewey, "intellectual progress usually occurs through sheer abandonment of questions together with both of the alternatives they assume—an abandonment that results from their decreasing vitality. . . . We do not solve them: we get over them. Old questions are solved by disappearing, evaporating, while new questions corresponding to the changed attitude of endeavour and preference take their place [160, p.181].

The new question may be how to prevent human–machine mismatches and how to design an interaction between human and machine that allows a symbiotic relationship enhancing the natural abilities and advantages of both.

6

The Role of Humans in Automated Systems

The question today is not whether a function can be automated, but whether it should be, due to various human factors issues. It is highly questionable whether total system safety is always enhanced by allocating functions to automatic devices rather than human operators, and there is some reason to believe that flight-deck automation may have already passed its optimum point.

—Earl Weiner and Renwick Curry
Flight-Deck Automation:
Promises and Problems

Human tasks are more and more being taken over by machines. There are several reasons for this change, one of which is the belief that operator errors account for the majority of accidents, as discussed in Chapter 5. Ironically, when designers attempt to eliminate humans from systems, they almost inevitably make the operators' jobs more complex and, perhaps, more accident prone. In fact, the automation of control systems and attempts to eliminate human operators from them have led to *increased* interest in human factors and the human–machine interface.

Automation usually does not eliminate humans, but instead raises their tasks to new levels of complexity. The easy parts of tasks may be eliminated, leaving the difficult parts or increasing the difficulty of the remaining tasks. Operators may be assigned monitoring tasks for which they are not suited or the responsibility for intervening at the extremes. Often, automation merely assigns humans to new functions related to maintenance and moves them to higher levels of supervisory control and decision making. Centralization and advanced automation typically increase the consequences of human decisions and actions; at the same time, the basis for these decisions becomes more obscure because of increased system complexity [270]. In addition, human error will still be a factor in accidents, even if operators are eliminated completely, since automatic devices are designed by humans.

Rasmussen, Duncan, and Leplat [278] have stressed the ethical component of system design: People should not be caught by the irreversible consequences of typical everyday human behavior; instead, systems should be designed that tolerate human error. Volvo, for example, has adopted this approach:

> Our philosophy is that every operator or maintenance mistake that can be made will be made sooner or later. Therefore, we have taken all safety measures against human error. This approach is difficult to develop. It is much more convenient to stick to the idea of negligence [146, p.206].

To take this approach, designers need to have a good knowledge of human behavior. Human factors is the study of the capabilities and limitations of humans relative to the systems they operate. The importance of human factors first gained recognition during World War I; the early work combined research in psychology, physiology, engineering, and education.

Traditionally, human factors research has been concerned with anthropomorphics, which is the study of body measurements and how humans fit the layout of a system—for example, whether the operator can reach the controls and see the console. While these questions are still important, cognitive (versus physical) issues have taken the forefront.

Human factors engineering or ergonomics plays an important role in civil and military aircraft design, but it is often an afterthought in other fields. The inclusion of human factors in engineering design may have been inhibited by a cultural clash between human factors researchers, who typically have a background in psychology, and design engineers, who typically have little educational background in this area [317]. Nevertheless, interest in human cognition and error mechanisms has increased rapidly in the past decade as a result of two factors: (1) accidents—some receiving a great deal of attention (such as Three Mile Island), where humans played an important role—either in preventing or precipitating the accident, and (2) risk analysts' need for data on human error to use in probabilistic risk assessments, particularly for licensing purposes.

The accident at Three Mile Island (TMI) brought a great deal of attention to human factors in engineering design. The TMI accident investigation revealed inadequacies in maintenance, bad design of the console and control room, operator errors of judgment, and inappropriate operator training.

Before the TMI accident, human factors issues were largely ignored in the design of nuclear power plants. A pre-TMI survey of human engineering aspects of reactor control panels found serious deficiencies. The following comment from a designer was cited in the results of the survey as typical: "I have no pride of authorship in the layout of these boards. The client has to live with them. Nobody here cares that much. The NRC is only interested in knowing whether or not there is a certain function covered on the boards—either in front or in back" (quoted in [320, p.63]).

A participant at a symposium sponsored by the Electric Power Research Institute (EPRI) commented, "There is little gut-level appreciation of the fact that plants are indeed man–machine systems. Insufficient attention is given to the human side of such systems, since most designers are hardware-oriented" [320, p.63].

It is now widely recognized that the TMI accident was not the result of operator errors as usually defined, but instead reflected a lack of appropriate design of the interactions between humans and machines, as discussed in Chapter 4. This conclusion implies the need for greater integration of human factors and system safety into general engineering efforts.

If we are to avoid the trap of oversimplifying human error and do not attempt simply to replace humans in systems, then we need to determine their proper role in automated systems. Three roles are possible: as monitors of the automated equipment, as backups to automated equipment, and as partners with machines in the control of the process. Each of these roles presents difficult design problems. Describing these problems requires using the concept of mental models.

6.1 Mental Models

In dealing with complexity, abstraction is one of our most powerful tools. Abstraction allows us to concentrate on the relevant aspects of a problem while ignoring the irrelevant. Without abstraction, humans would be unable to cope with complex natural and man-made systems.

Abstraction involves forming mental models that provide predictive and explanatory power. Because these models contain the most relevant aspects of an individual's interaction with a system, different people may form different models of the same system, depending on their goals, experience, and potential use for the model. Some mental models may be very simple while others may be very elaborate. Carroll suggests that multiple mental models may exist within the same person. DeKeyser has found that even having two contradictory models of the same process does not seem to constitute a problem for people [198].

Because mental models reflect individual goals and experience, the designer's model of a system may differ greatly from the operator's model (see Figure 6.1). The designer's vision of the plant is often based on engineering or mathematical models of a control loop and is appropriate for situations where important decisions need not be made quickly. According to Duncan, the designer's model of a control loop involves taking an output signal to some comparator and maintaining a "set point" by feeding signals to an actuator. At a more detailed level, the designer's model may represent the quality of sensor information, the

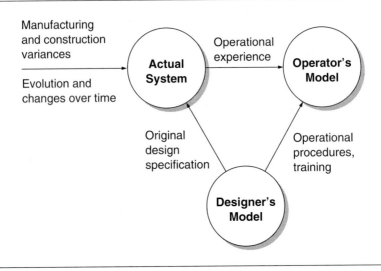

FIGURE 6.1
The relationship between mental models.

power and other response characteristics of the controlled device, and the comparator functions that ensure adequate tracking of the set point to avoid hunting when perturbations occur [71].

Operators' models may be more mechanistic, since their goal is to keep the plant in a particular state. Their models need to be useful for making diagnoses of situations and for determining remedial action easily and often quickly [120]. Wickens and Kessel suggest that the operator's mental model consists of the mapping of a set of expected system outputs to known system inputs, given that the plant is operating normally. Effective monitoring is accomplished by constantly comparing the observed output and inputs with the expected output. If a discrepancy, beyond the margin of error, between the observed and expected output is noted, it is stored, and the discrepancies are then accumulated over time. If this accumulation of differences eventually exceeds some internal limit over a given time interval, a failure is detected [356].

Thus, the operator most likely has some type of model of the physical locations of the points of control in the plant, along with system states, values, and limits, together with a model of the consequences of changes in those states [41].

It is quite natural for the designer's and operator's models to differ. In addition, both may have significant differences from the actual plant as it exists. During design, the designer evolves a model of the plant to the point where it can be built. The designer's model is an idealization formed before the plant is constructed. Significant differences may exist between this ideal model and the actual constructed system. Besides construction problems, the designer always deals with ideals or averages, not with the actual components themselves. Thus, a designer may have a model of a valve with an average closure time, while real valves have closure times that fall somewhere along a continuum of behavior that reflects manufacturing and material differences.

The operator's model will be based partly on formal training and partly on experience with the system. The operator must cope with the system as it is constructed and not as it may have been envisioned. Also, physical systems will change over time and the operator's model must change accordingly.

Humans process data about a system in terms of their model of how that system works. Although an operator may be taught the designer's model, models are adjusted on the basis of experience. When operators receive inputs about the system being controlled, they first try to fit that information into their model and find reasons to exclude information that does not fit. Because operators are continually testing their mental models against reality, the longer a model has been held, the more resistant it will be to change due to conflicting information. Thus, experienced operators may act differently than novices.

Physical environments and systems change, however, and operators do change their models in the face of continued conflicts between the evidence and their perception of what is going on. This ability to change mental models is what makes the human operator so valuable. Based on current inputs, the operators' actual behavior may differ from the prescribed procedures. When the deviation is correct (the designers' models are less accurate than the operators' models at that particular instant in time), then the operators are considered to be doing their job. When the operators' models are incorrect, they are often blamed for any unfortunate results, even though their incorrect mental models may have been reasonable given the information they had at the time.

6.2 The Human as Monitor

With the automation of control systems, the operator's role changes from active control to monitoring: The human becomes responsible for detecting problems and providing a repair capability. A reasonable argument can be made that this change is an improvement: Malfunctions theoretically can be detected rapidly, since the operators are not burdened by mundane (and attention-consuming) control tasks [79]; they can devote all their attention to the monitoring task.

Unfortunately, experience shows that humans make very poor monitors of automatic systems. There are several posited explanations for their poor performance.

■ *The task may be impossible.*

Bainbridge points out the irony that automatic control systems are put in because they can do the job better than a human operator, but a human is then asked to monitor that the automatic system is doing the job effectively [17]. Two problems arise:

1. The human monitor needs to know what the correct behavior of the process should be; however, in complex modes of operation—for example, where the variables in the process have to follow a particular trajectory over time— evaluating whether the automatic control system is performing correctly requires special displays and information that may be available only from the automatic system being monitored.

2. If the decisions can be specified fully, then a computer can make them more quickly and more accurately than a human can. Whitfield and Ord found that air traffic controllers' appreciation of the traffic situation was reduced at the high traffic levels made feasible by using computers [355].

Therefore, there is usually no way for a human to check in real time whether a computer is operating correctly or not. As a result, humans must monitor the automatic control system at some metalevel, deciding whether the computer's decisions are acceptable rather than completely correct. If the computer is being used to make decisions because human judgment and intuition are not satisfactory, then which one should be trusted as the final arbiter?

The same argument applies when a computer is monitoring another computer. Unless there is a different way to make the same decisions that is just as good, the better decision-making algorithm will be employed in the primary system rather than in the monitor. In most cases, identically accurate and efficient algorithms are not available.

■ *The operator is dependent on the information provided; it is easy to provide too much or too little information or to display it poorly.*

Computers provide the means to overload the operators with massive amounts of information. Humans respond more quickly, however, to the minimum amount of information needed to make a correct decision than to a lot of relevant and irrelevant data supplied in an uncoordinated fashion [158]. Kletz writes about an accident in which a computer printed a long list of alarms after a power failure in the plant. The operator did not know what had caused the upset and did nothing. After a few minutes, an explosion occurred. The designer admitted that he had overloaded the operator with too much information, but had presumed that the operator would assume the worst and trip the plant. When people are overloaded with information, however, they tend to do nothing until they have figured out what is going on.

Information often needs to be condensed into a manageable form [37]. At TMI, so many alarms had to be printed that the printer fell behind by as much as two hours in recording them [143]. A current trend is to provide "smart" alarm and warning systems that, among other things, prevent obvious false alarms and assign priorities to alarms [354]. However, the necessarily complex logic of these systems may be too complex for operators to perform validity checks and thus may lead to the operator overrelying on them. It may be difficult to preset appropriate alarm priorities for all situations, and operators may not have the information to recognize when the priorities are incorrect.

Although the automated system may be designed to provide only a certain amount of information to an operator, the operator may try to get more information by manipulating the system to figure out how it works. Such manipulation may lead to serious problems, but it may also be the only way that operators have to get the information they need to form the mental model necessary to operate the system correctly [37]. Miller tells of a test pilot who, having some free time on the flight line, randomly pushed buttons on the computer to see what would happen [223]. We can criticize, but, in fact, the information obtained from this exploratory behavior may be exactly what the pilot will need to handle situations that the designer has not anticipated. Actions that in hindsight are judged as mistakes may merely be reasonable attempts to gain information about the actual state of the system or to learn about how the system works. The designer provides the information necessary to handle a range of anticipated decisions, but the operator is usually given the task of handling the unforeseen decisions, perhaps without the information needed to perform this task.

■ *The information is more indirect with automated systems, which may make it harder for the operator to obtain a clear picture of the state of the system.*

Technology changes not only the amount but also the basic character of the information available to operators. When operators control systems directly, their mental models of the current system state and how the system works develop from direct experience. Central control rooms separate operators from the system—the equipment cannot be seen, heard, or touched. Information about the operation of the system or about abnormal events must be obtained indirectly via remote sensors and instrumentation. Any particular set of indications may not be unique to a particular system state or to the cause of an abnormal event [78].

Brehmer claims that modern technology makes the connection between actions and outcomes opaque. The relationship between the operator and the system being controlled becomes more indirect and abstract:

> Both the information he receives and the outcomes he creates are mediated by complex processes that are hidden from direct view. Work thus becomes mental and abstract, rather than physical and concrete. The problem, then, is how people are able to form those mental models that can help them to make decisions under conditions where they have little insight into the process they want to control [37, p.113].

Thus, to create and update mental models that will help in decision making about unexpected events, operators may need to maintain manual involvement at some level.

In addition, a designer's lack of understanding of the mental models used by operators may limit the operators' monitoring and decision-making ability. In a highly automated system, the information operators receive about the system state through the instrumentation is not reality, but merely a representation of reality [37]. That representation is a model that contains the information designers think operators need for decision making based on the designers' mental models of the system. The operators, however, may require a different type of information to make rational and correct decisions based on their own mental models of the system state. Thus, much of the decision-making power rests with the designers, who, by giving only certain information to the operators, limit the range of possible decisions the operators can make.

At TMI, the instrumentation gave the operators information about the system state that caused them to make the situation worse. For example, the instruments reported that a particular valve had closed when it had not; it took the operators two hours to discover this error. Turbulence and voids in the reactor vessel caused the instrumentation to indicate incorrectly that the vessel was full when, in fact, the control rods were nearly uncovered. The reactor coolant-system water-temperature sensors registered values only between 520° and 620° Fahrenheit. If the actual values fell outside these limits, the devices showed only the limit value; the operators did not know how much above or below these limits the temperature had moved. In addition, temperatures were averaged across the hot and cold poles of the system, which misled the operators; it appeared that the reactor temperature had stabilized at 570° Fahrenheit for 11 hours (which was within limits), but the actual cold temperature of the reactor had far exceeded the cold limits, resulting in damaging temperature differentials [41]. Instruments can be designed to prevent such ambiguous information, but such a design requires extra sensors and increases construction costs. More important, it requires that the designers recognize the need for the information.

Once an operator, because of ambiguous information, interprets a complex situation incorrectly, that mental model will be difficult to change. An observer's pattern matching determines the category into which an input is placed. Expected evidence is much more readily accepted as conclusive than is unexpected evidence [228]. A warning that does not fit our mental model of what is going on can be swamped by the multitude of signals that fit our expectations and thus be discounted as noise in the system [259].

Human observers are often reluctant to accept evidence that requires them to change their hypotheses. Computers complicate this problem by encouraging trust, which leads operators to ignore external cues that suggest a computer error has occurred. In the Air New Zealand accident at Mount Erebus in Antarctica, Green hypothesizes that the crew trusted the inertial navigation computers and were "probably seduced into interpreting external visual information in a way that conformed with the world model generated for them by the aircraft" [101]. Green suggests that because the pilots cannot possibly understand the technology involved in the generation of the display, they are compelled to use the display itself as their mental model of the world instead of creating their own model from the raw data.

The decisions made in these situations are perfectly rational; the decision makers just have the wrong mental models:

Selecting a context ("this can happen only with a small pipe break in the secondary system") is a pre-decision act, made without reflection, almost effortlessly, as a part of a stream of experience and mental processing. We start thinking or making decisions based upon conscious, rational effort only after the context has become defined. And defining the context is a subtle, self-steering process, influenced by long experience with trials and errors. If a situation is ambiguous, without thinking about it or deciding upon it, we sometimes pick what seems to be the most familiar context, and only then do we begin to consciously reason [259, p.318].

Thus, when a control system's behavior conflicts with the operator's experience or training, the operator may ignore information or bypass the control system, assuming that it must be malfunctioning. On the other hand, it *may* be malfunctioning, and in that case, we *do* want the operator to ignore it. To resolve this dilemma, the designer must provide ways for the operator to check the functioning of the instrumentation.

■ *Failures may be silent or masked.*

Automatic control systems are designed to cope with the immediate effects of a deviation in the process—they are feedback loops that attempt to maintain a constant system state, and as such, they mask the occurrence of a problem in its early stages. An operator will be aware of such problems only if adequate information to detect them is provided. That such information is often *not* provided may be the result of the different mental models of the designers and experienced operators, or it may merely reflect financial pressures on designers due to the cost of providing operators with independent information [71].

In some cases, the required information may be impossible to provide: Norman points out [242] that building an automated system with a self-monitoring capability that would allow it to recognize that conditions are changing would require a higher level of awareness—that is, a monitoring of its own monitoring abilities. Although automatic systems that monitor themselves at a metalevel for a few specific conditions could be constructed, the general case is currently unachievable.

As an example, autopilots may fail so gracefully that a decoupling may not be noticed by the crew until the plane is badly out of limits. One example is a PAA B-707 that experienced a graceful autopilot disconnect while cruising at 36,000 feet above the Atlantic. The aircraft went into a steep descending spiral before the crew took action; it lost 30,000 feet before the crew recovered [354]. In another instance, an Eastern Air Lines L-1011 slowly flew into the Florida Everglades after an autopilot became disengaged, and the crew (and air traffic controllers) failed to notice.

Problems with masked or delayed feedback in the monitoring of automated systems may be exacerbated by designs that cause referred symptoms: The place where the signs of trouble first appear may not be the place where the failures have occurred. For example, petrochemical plant design has responded to social and financial pressures, especially in the 1970s, to conserve energy and improve thermal economy. A designer may use heat exchangers to transfer recovered heat to another plant unit that is driven by heat, as described in Chapter 1. This design makes sense, but it introduces diagnostic difficulty because the symptoms of a problem may first appear in an unrelated part of the plant. Duncan asks:

> Do operators always develop a process model that incorporates the 'referred symptoms' complication? If they do, then their model is again different from the designers, which I suspect is very much a heat extraction and transport model. So we have another diagnostic problem for the operator which, as it follows from other sensible plant design considerations, was probably not envisaged by anyone: the problem of symptoms referred forward, or referred back by major loops in the overall process. This problem is a design error, by definition, since we can be reasonably sure that the diagnostic complications were not intended. Moreover, it is a design error resulting rather directly from the designer's model of the plant, which is limited in a way that an experienced operator's model is not [71, p.268].

■ *Tasks that require little active operator behavior may result in lowered alert-ness and vigilance and can lead to complacency and overreliance on auto-mated systems.*

Vigilance studies show that it is impossible for even a highly motivated person to maintain effective visual attention for more than about a half hour to a source of information on which very little happens [17]. This limitation makes it vir-tually impossible for humans to monitor for unlikely abnormalities, since the operator cannot monitor an automatic system effectively if it has been operating acceptably for a long time. Substituting an automatic alarm system only raises the question of who monitors the alarm system to determine when *it* is not work-ing properly. In Chapter 4, an accident was described in which a high-level trip was fitted onto a tank to determine when it was full. The operator stopped watch-ing, and the resulting accident was worse than the accidental spill that led to the automatic trip being installed in the first place.

The higher the reliability of the automatic system, the more likely the oper-ator is to become complacent and less vigilant. An intermediate level of reliability may create an impression of high reliability, and the operator may not be able to handle a failure when it occurs. Ironically, if the equipment is very unreliable, the operator will expect malfunctions and will be adept at handling them.

Ternham [336] reports many examples of pilots relying on automatic flight control systems to such a degree that they become lax in their attention to the primary flight instructions or even revise their priorities.

> □ In an approach under autopilot control, a bend in the glidepath at 500 feet caused a very marked lowering of the nose (pitchdown), resulting in an excessive rate of descent. The pilot, although fully aware of the situation, did not react until the situation was so critical that a very low pullup had to be made.

□ While in navigation mode (where the autopilot is steering the aircraft to maintain a track over the ground), the aircraft turned the wrong way over a checkpoint. Although this behavior was immediately noticed, the aircraft turned more than 45 degrees before the pilot acted.

□ In an approach, the autothrottle became inactive. The speed dropped 15 knots below correct speed before the malfunction was noticed.

□ During descent, the altitude preselect malfunctioned. This malfunction went unnoticed by the pilots and an overshoot (a descent below desired altitude) was made.

□ When leveling off by using the altitude preselect and with the throttles in idle, the speed dropped close to stall before the pilot detected and rectified it by applying power.

Ternham suggests that complacency and inattention may have caused the pilots to react to failures and errors in the automatic controls much more slowly than they should have. Danaher [60] has examined human error in air traffic control incidents and also voices concern about human reliance on automated systems leading to accidents. Experiments have shown that the likelihood of an operator taking over successfully when the automated system fails increases as the operator's subjective assessment of the probability of equipment failure increases [343].

False alarms can lead to operators taking corrective action when, in fact, nothing is wrong with the system (other than the spurious alarm). Weiner and Curry tell of such an error that occurred during the takeoff of a Texas International DC-9 from Denver, when a stall warning spuriously activated [354]. Believing that a stall was imminent, in spite of normal airspeed and pitch attitude indications, the crew aborted the takeoff, resulting in a runway overrun, severe damage to the aircraft, and nonfatal injuries to some passengers. The pilots had both experienced spurious stall warnings on takeoff before, but they probably had little choice but to regard this warning as real. The crew had to choose between aborting the takeoff, with an almost inevitable but perhaps noncatastrophic accident, and continuing the takeoff with a plane that might not be flyable, which could have resulted in a much worse accident [354].

Too many false alarms, in contrast, can lead the operator to ignore an alarm. Indications of a problem at Bhopal, for example, were not taken seriously because so many previous alarms had been spurious.

DeVille cites experience supporting the view that challenging tasks are performed extremely well and, in the vast majority of cases, without accidents: Accidents are more likely on less challenging tasks [66]. DeVille's basic premise is that awareness or lack of awareness of the elevated risk of a procedure provides a better measure of accident potential than does an evaluation of the risk level itself: As awareness increases, accident potential decreases. If a distraction (such as an unplanned event) occurs during the more difficult operations—those that require planning and preparation and have high visibility with management—accident potential is relatively low. When the normal or routine elements of a job are performed with standard levels of visibility and interest and an identical unplanned event occurs—causing loss of the same amount of awareness—accident potential is high.

A classic method for enforcing operator attention is to require entries in a log; unfortunately, people can write down numbers without noticing what they are [17]. Various studies have attempted to determine appropriate operator workload levels. These results along with potential solutions to alertness and complacency problems (such as introducing challenges into routine tasks) are discussed in Chapter 17. Weiner has suggested that "the burning question of the near future will not be how much work a man can do safely, but how little" [353].

6.3 The Human as Backup

A second role an operator may be required to perform in an automated system is backup in the event of an emergency. Again, poorly designed automation may make this role more difficult.

■ *A poorly designed human–machine interface may leave operators with lowered proficiency and increased reluctance to intervene.*

Operators need both manual and cognitive skills, but both decline in the absence of practice. An experienced operator performs the minimum number of actions while controlling a process, with the process moving smoothly and quickly to the desired level of operation. With an inexperienced operator, the process is likely to oscillate around the target value. Physical skills deteriorate when not used, which means that the skills of an experienced operator who has been relegated to monitoring may degrade to the level of an inexperienced operator:

> If he takes over he may set the process into oscillation. He may have to wait until feedback, rather than controlling by open-loop, and it will be difficult for him to interpret whether the feedback shows that there is something wrong with the system or more simply that he has misjudged his control action. He will need to take action to counteract his ineffective control, which will add to his workload. When manual takeover is needed, there is likely to be something wrong with the process, so that unusual actions will be needed to control it, and one can argue that the operator needs to be more rather than less skilled, and less rather than more loaded, than average [17, p.272].

> Cognitive skills also decline. The efficient retrieval of knowledge from long-term memory depends on frequency of use and on feedback about the effectiveness of that knowledge [17]. If operators assume the role of problem solver and decision maker only when things go wrong, they will have little experience to go on when they *do* need to take over. And, again, the mental models necessary for correct decision making will be inaccurate or incomplete. Therefore, theoretical

instruction must be accompanied by practical exercises and associated with re-trieval strategies that are integrated with the other parts of the task. Simulation provides a partial solution to these problems, but it is not obvious how to provide effective simulation facilities.

A common but mistaken belief is that automated systems require less skilled users. A counterexample can be found in computer-aided design systems, which tend to work well with the original builders and users of the system, who are often very skilled designers. As time passes, less skilled users may be substituted or skills may decline from nonuse. As a result, flawed outputs sometimes are not detected by the less skilled staff until product flaws show up much later [345].

Lack of control experience or declining skills may lead to a reluctance to intervene in an emergency. The investigation of a productivity problem in a strip-rolling steel mill in the Netherlands found that the operators did not always know when to step in and take over for the computer [345]. The operators became so unsure of themselves that they sometimes left the control panels unattended. They also had difficulty in observing the process. The designers had enclosed the steel strips being rolled, which seriously lessened the ability of the staff to determine whether the computer was controlling the operation effectively.

The investigation also found that the operators did not fully understand the control theory used in the control software, and this lack of understanding rein-forced their reluctance to intervene except when things were very clearly going awry. By intervening late, the operators let productivity drop below that of plants using traditional (not computer-based) control systems. In this case, automation had led both to lower productivity and to operator alienation.

Proficiency seems to be important to operators. In one automated plant, man-agement had to be present during the night shift or the operators would switch the process to manual [17]. Many pilots regularly turn off the autopilot or other au-tomated systems in order to retain their manual flying skills. Proficiency allows operators to be confident that they can take over if required to do so. Bainbridge notes that the worst type of job is one that is boring yet requires assuming great responsibility without the opportunity to acquire or maintain the skills necessary to handle that responsibility [17].

■ *Fault-intolerant systems may lead to even larger errors.*

Sometimes designers are so sure that their systems are self-regulating that they do not include appropriate means for human intervention. For example, in aircraft inertial navigation systems, the latitude and longitude of the initial position of the aircraft and a series of checkpoints (waypoints) defining the desired track across the earth are loaded into the computer by keyboard before the flight. During one initial setup, the crew loaded their position with a northern latitude rather than the southern latitude of their actual position. This error was detected neither by the computer nor by the crew until after takeoff. The aircraft had to return to the departure point because the navigation computer could not be reset in flight [354].

Hirschhorn argues that automatic systems do not eliminate failures—they merely raise them to a new level of complexity [123]. The system may fail in ways that the designer did not anticipate, and unless the designer provided appropriate means for the operator to intervene, serious problems can result.

- *The design of the automated system may make the system harder to manage during a crisis.*

Systems may respond reasonably in a calm atmosphere, but they may add to frustration and errors during a crisis. The semiautomatic system may require the operator to make too many decisions in a short time. Some nuclear reactors, for example, use computers to make split-second judgments and adjustments because a human operator cannot be expected to respond quickly enough when the reactor's equilibrium is disturbed. The operator may have a grace period of only 30 to 60 seconds after a loss of coolant before the reactor blows dry. In contrast, other reactors typically allow 30 to 60 minutes for the same thing. This unforgiving quality of the reactor design greatly magnifies the demand placed on human capabilities when something unexpected happens, as was the case at TMI, or when the computer makes an error, as was the case at Crystal River [213].

Computer-based systems may provide the operator with many more choices during a crisis, but, at the same time, may provide inadequate information to make a decision among the choices. In addition, the human operator who has to take over quickly may be disoriented and may need a significant warm-up period to change effectively from passive monitor to active controller; in an emergency, that time may not be available. Automated systems have made some operator workload (such as that for pilots) nonuniform, with long periods of inactivity and short bursts of intense activity [259]. Long periods of passive monitoring make operators unprepared to act in emergencies.

Control decisions are made on the basis of the operator's knowledge of the current state of the process. This knowledge is accumulated by making predictions and decisions about the process, which are validated by feedback. Obviously, this knowledge takes time to build up. Manual operators often arrive at the control room 15 to 30 minutes before they are due to take control so they can get a feel for what the process is doing [17]. In aircraft, this feel is often referred to as *situational awareness*. Without this awareness, it may be very difficult for the operator to make decisions quickly with minimum information.

Norman notes that the crew in modern automated aircraft are isolated both physically and mentally from the moment-to-moment activities of the aircraft and of the controls because the automatic equipment provides the crew with little or no trace of its operations [242]. When problems arise and the operators need to take over, they may not be sufficiently in touch with the current state of the system to diagnose the problems in a reasonable amount of time. He argues that the culprit is not automation but rather the lack of continual feedback and interaction.

The situation may be further complicated by disorientation resulting from the sudden appearance of many alarms. In an incident from CHIRP, a British confidential incident-reporting service, a pilot wrote:

I was flying in a Jetstream at night when my peaceful reverie was shattered by the stall audio warning, the stick shaker, and several warning lights. The effect was exactly what was *not* intended; I was frightened numb for several seconds and drawn off instruments trying to work out how to cancel the audio/visual assault rather than taking what should be instinctive actions. The combined assault is so loud and bright that it is impossible to talk to the other crew member, and action is invariably taken to cancel the cacophony before getting on with the actual problem (quoted in [257, p.37]).

In summary, automation can change the role of a human operator from an active controller of the process to a passive monitor and occasional backup controller during emergencies. In addition, computers allows systems to be built that are naturally unstable and more difficult to control, requiring more complex and faster control maneuvers. Thus, at the same time that the opportunities for learning and practicing skills are decreasing, the demands for those skills (on the rare occasion when they are needed) may be growing because of the steadily increasing complexity of the processes being controlled.

6.4 The Human as Partner

In a third type of human–machine interaction, the human and the automated system may both be assigned control tasks. However, unless this partnership is carefully planned, the operator may simply end up with the tasks that the designer cannot figure out how to automate. The number of tasks that the operator must perform is reduced, but, surprisingly, the error potential may be increased. There are several possible explanations for this increase:

1. The operator may simply be assigned the tasks that the designer cannot figure out how to automate. The operator is then left with an arbitrary collection of tasks for which little thought was given to providing support.
2. The remaining tasks may be significantly more complex, and new tasks may be added, such as maintenance and monitoring. Partial automation may not eliminate or even reduce the operator workload but may merely change the type of demands on the operator.
3. By taking away the easy parts of the operator's job, automation may make the more difficult parts even harder [17]. The importance of the operator's mental model in controlling a system has been described. Eliminating some tasks may make it more difficult or impossible for the operator to receive the feedback necessary to maintain an accurate model of the system.

An interesting experiment by Allnutt and colleagues [8] on the effects of sleep deprivation in operators compared performance on a battery of cognitive tests and performance on a simulator. The simulator tasks were stimulating and varied, provided good feedback, and required the active involvement of the subjects in most operations. Relatively few of the simulator activities involved either passive or repetitive action—the designers deliberately resisted pressures to remove human error by automation except to help overcome operator overload. The results of the experiment showed the usual deterioration from sleep deprivation on the battery of cognitive tests, but performance held up remarkably well on the simulator.

Some of the issues in the automation of functions currently performed by humans are exemplified by the automation of air traffic control. The FAA is investigating the possibility of eliminating human control over minute-to-minute traffic decisions. The human role would change from controller of every aircraft to a manager who handles exceptions while the computer takes care of routine commands to aircraft.

Doubts about this goal have been raised in a Rand Corporation report commissioned by the FAA, which characterizes the program as potentially jeopardizing the safety of the system [178]. The Rand report cites two principal drawbacks to the proposal:

1. The design would not really allow a human backup in case the computer failed to handle a given situation correctly. The volume of traffic handled by each control station would be about double that handled today, so the controller probably would not have time to check the computer's assessment of possible conflicts.

2. Even if controllers had the time to handle conflicts, their passive role in the system would over time tend to make them unreliable monitors. They would lose touch and skill in dealing with traffic.

The Rand report also questioned whether any software could handle the job because of unexpected situations such as military aircraft flying outside prescribed routes, pilots making errors in their flight paths, contingencies, and so on. The FAA responded that the system would have two independent backups: (1) central computers would have a separate checking algorithm that would monitor all flight paths for conflicts independently of the main algorithm and (2) TCAS (an airborne collision avoidance system) would alert both the pilots and controllers if the other two systems were wrong.

The Rand report proposed an alternative concept, called shared control, in which primary responsibility for air traffic control would rest with human controllers, but the automated system would assist them by continually checking and monitoring their work and proposing alternative plans. In high-traffic periods, controllers could turn increasing portions of the planning over to the automated system. Thus, they could keep their own workloads relatively constant, neither overtaxed in high-traffic periods nor underused in low-traffic periods. The most routine functions requiring the least intellectual ability, such as monitoring plans for deviations from agreed flight paths, would be the only functions fully automated.

In a shared control system, controllers could use any module of the automated system to assist them. The automated system could perform the automatic monitoring, trajectory projection, and conflict resolution functions of the FAA proposal, but in this design, these functions would be requested by the controller instead of being preassigned to the computer.

FAA officials argue that the Rand shared-control concept would be unprofitable, since only marginal productivity gains could be realized until the responsibility for maintaining aircraft separation was passed from the human controller to the machine. Only at that point could productivity gains of as much as 100 percent be achieved [178]. The European approach to the same problem, which appears to have a philosophy similar to that expressed in the Rand report, is a partnership between computer and human that is superior in effect to either of them working alone [345].

How that partnership should be defined is an open question that highlights important technical problems. For example, task allocation can be dynamic, with either the computer or the human in charge; tasks can be partitioned statically (preassigned) between the two partners; or one partner can assist the other in performing a task. The best way to make this allocation is still unknown.

In addition, a partnership of human and computer requires some means of communication between the two:

> But what should be the nature of the communication? If communication is explicit, there is less uncertainty as to what is being communicated, but the human must invest resources in receiving and transmitting information. This resource demand may be less if communication is implicit, but there may be less certainty as to what is communicated. There may also be a need for the human to invest resources into determining what the computer is doing [229, p.67].

Designing a partnership ventures into the trans-scientific domain. Margulies argues that economic as well as social, ethical, and humanitarian reasons dictate that man should be dominant in this partnership, using most modern machines as supporting tools: Robots would take over the heavy, hazardous work, and other machines would do the boring and monotonous work [210]. Humans would not be left to fill in the gaps left by automation or to be laid off. Instead, system designs would allow operators to apply their own discretion, skills, and creativity while the machine handles the unintelligent, repetitive, and routine parts of a job.

> This crucial relationship must not stop at making man and machine equally important parts of the system or at trying to find an optimal order of precedence between man and machine; it will rather have to clearly subordinate the machine to the interests, requirements, and strivings of man. The human–machine system of the future will have to offer to its users an improvement of working and living conditions, greater individual freedom for action and decision-making, and a wider scope to apply their skills and creativity [210, p.11].

In summary, automation allows almost unlimited freedom in the design of the human–machine interface—designers can either enhance the difficulty of the operator's task by a poor human–machine interface design or simplify the operator's task by matching tasks and data to human abilities and preferences. The human–machine interface becomes especially critical in an emergency, when the operator is under stress or is tired. Much more attention to the design of the human–machine interface is needed if we are to reduce accidents in automated systems.

6.5 Conclusions

If the alternatives are considered, the unique abilities of human operators seem to outweigh any disadvantages of including them in complex systems. The goal of human–machine interface design should be to preserve the human capability to intervene positively while making harmful intervention as difficult as possible [114]. The risk with respect to human operators may not be that they will cause accidents but that they may not succeed in preventing them [270].

> What we need is a procedure of design that begins by considering the operator. In designing a system, the focus should be on its operation, not its function. This approach calls for a dramatic change in engineering attitude. Rather than engineering a layout to show temperature, pressure, flow, and so on, it is much more relevant to ask "What is it that the operator needs to know in order to maintain the temperature values within their limits?" and "What is it that we must give to the operator in order that he or she can control the system within those limits?" [41, p.160].

Unfortunately, in too many cases, the operator is not considered part of the system throughout the entire design process, but instead is tacked on when the design is nearly complete. One way to solve this problem is to involve operators in safety analysis and design decisions throughout development. The solution to our problem may be to involve humans more, not less.

PART TWO

Introduction to System Safety

It is an easy task to formulate a plan of accident-preventing devices after the harm is done, but the wiser engineer foresees the possible weakness, as well as the dangers ahead, which are involved in his new enterprise, and at once embodies all the necessary means of safety in his original design.

—John H. Cooper, 1891

The Safeware program described in this book is based on the system safety approach to preventing accidents in complex systems. This section describes the development and scientific foundations of this historically American approach to safety, which grew out of the needs of the U.S. defense and aerospace industries. Comparisons are made with related areas such as industrial safety and reliability engineering.

Chapter

7

Foundations of System Safety

*Underlying every technology is at least one basic science, although
the technology may be well developed long before the science
emerges. Overlying every technical or civil system is a social system
that provides purpose, goals, and decision criteria.*

—Ralph F. Miles, Jr.
*Systems Concepts: Lectures on
Contemporary Approaches to Systems*

Truly understanding a technology requires understanding its history, scientific basis, and cultural and social milieu. System safety has its roots in industrial safety engineering, which dates back to the last century. But the relatively new discipline of system safety is a response to conditions arising after World War II, when its "parent" disciplines—systems engineering and systems analysis—were developed to cope with new and complex engineering problems. The scientific basis for all these new developments in engineering lies in systems theory, whose development, starting in the 1930s, laid the foundation for a new way of dealing with complex systems.

7.1 Safety Engineering Before World War II

Humans have always been concerned about their safety. Prior to the industrial age, natural disasters provided the biggest challenge, but things started to change during the early part of the Industrial Revolution in Europe and the United States. Workers in the factories were considered expendable and were often treated worse than slaves: Slaves cost a great deal of money and owners wanted to protect their investment, but workers cost nothing to hire or replace [97]. The prevailing attitude was that when people accepted employment, they also accepted the risks involved in the job and should be smart enough to avoid danger. At the same time, factories were filled with hazards, such as unguarded machines, open holes, flying shuttles, and open belt drives. There were no fire escapes, and the lighting was inadequate. Hardly a day went by without some worker being maimed or killed [97].

Without workers' compensation laws, employees had to sue and collect damages for injuries under common law. In the United States, the employer almost could not lose, since common law precedents established that an employer did not have to pay injured employees if

1. The employee contributed at all to the cause of the accident (*contributory negligence* held that if the employee was responsible or even partly responsible for an accident, the employer was not liable)
2. Another employee contributed to the accident (the *fellow-servant* doctrine held that an employer was not responsible if an employee's injury resulted from the negligence of a co-worker)
3. The employee knew of the hazards involved in the accident before the injury and still agreed to work in the conditions for pay (the *assumption-of-risk* doctrine held that an injured employee presumably knew of and accepted the risks associated with the job before accepting the position).

A nonemployee fared somewhat better, since a stranger presumably had no knowledge of the potential hazards in the plant. However, under the doctrine of *respondeat superior*, the employer was not responsible for an injury to a third party caused by an employee, and the employee usually did not have the means to compensate the injured party [261, 97].

The horrible working conditions existing at this time led to social revolt by activists and union leaders. Miners, railroaders, and other workers became concerned about the hazards of their jobs and began to agitate for better conditions. Voluntary safety organizations, such as the American Public Health Association, the National Fire Protection Association, and Underwriters Laboratories, were formed in the late nineteenth century and were active in setting standards. The first efforts focused on health rather than safety; accidents were seen as fortuitous events over which we had little control [82].

Concern in Europe over worker safety preceded that in the United States. Otto von Bismarck established workers' compensation and security insurance, paid for by the employees, in Germany during the 1880s. Bismarck sought to undercut the socialists by demonstrating to the German working class that its government was in favor of social reform [97]. Soon, most other countries in Europe followed Bismarck's lead.

Other types of safety legislation were also passed in Europe. For example, the Factory and Workshop Act of 1844 in Great Britain was the first legislation for protection from accidents involving shafts, belts, pulleys, and gears used to transmit power from a water wheel or a stationary steam engine throughout the factory. Later, laws setting standards for equipment such as high-pressure steam engines and high-voltage electrical devices were enacted.

The textile industry was one of the first to become mechanized and also contributed more than its share of injuries to workers. The abuses in the mills led to protective legislation and codes in many countries by the end of the nineteenth century. The same was true for industries that employed metal and woodworking machines. Unfortunately, many safety devices, added only grudgingly, were poorly designed or ineffective [293].

In the United States, employers remained indifferent to the many workers being killed and maimed on the job. Eventually, social revolt and agitation by unions against poor working conditions led to social reform and government intervention to protect employees and the public.

Individual state laws preceded federal legislation. For example, in 1869 the Pennsylvania legislature passed a mine safety act for "better regulation and ventilation of the mines" [97]. The first factory inspection law, passed by the Massachusetts legislature in 1877, required the guarding of machines, floor openings, and shafts; good housekeeping; and fire safety. Eight other industrial states followed the lead of Massachusetts during the 1870s and passed similar laws.

The main concern of labor unions at that time was the safety and health of their members, and they demanded federal occupational safety and health legislation, which did not come until the 1900s. The first successful regulatory legislation in the U.S. was enacted in 1852, when Congress passed a law to regulate steamboat boilers. This law resulted from public pressure plus a series of marine disasters that had killed thousands of people. Little other safety legislation was passed until Theodore Roosevelt led the way toward federal involvement in unsafe and unhealthy working conditions [82].

In 1908, the state of New York passed the first workers' compensation law, which, in effect, required management to pay for injuries that occurred on the job regardless of fault. The New York law was held to be unconstitutional, but a similar law passed in Wisconsin in 1911 withstood judicial scrutiny. All other states have now provided similar laws, with the last being enacted in 1947.

When management found that it had to pay for injuries on the job, effort was put into preventing such injuries, and the organized industrial safety movement was born. Owners and managers also began to realize that accidents cost money in terms of lower productivity and started to take safety seriously. The first industrial safety department in a company was established in the early 1900s. The heavy industries, such as steel, in which workplace accidents occurred frequently, began to set safety standards. In the early 1900s, the president of the United States Steel Corporation wrote, "The Corporation expects its subsidiary companies to make every effort practicable to prevent injury to its employees. Expenditures necessary for such purposes will be authorized. Nothing which will add to the protection of the workmen should be neglected" [140, p.220].

A few engineers had recognized the need to prevent hazards early in the industrial era, when the machines they were designing and building began to kill people. James Watt had warned about the dangers of high-pressure steam engines in the early 1800s. The Davy Safety Lamp, invented about the same time, helped decrease some of the danger of methane gas explosions in mines. In 1869, George Westinghouse developed a brake based on compressed air, which made railroad travel vastly safer for riders and crew. In 1868, the first patent was granted by the U.S. Patent Office for a machine safety device—an interlocking guard used in a machine for filling bottles with carbonated water. Other patents later appeared for guards for printing presses, two-hand controls, and circular saws and other woodworking machines [293].

Near the end of the nineteenth century, engineers began to consider safety, as well as functionality, in their designs instead of simply trying to add it on in the form of guards. One of the first organizations to study accidents was the Society for the Prevention of Accidents in Factories (also called the Mulhouse Society), which was founded in the town of Mulhouse in Alsace-Lorraine. The Mulhouse Society held annual meetings to exchange ideas about safety improvements in factories and published an encyclopedia of techniques for injury prevention in 1889 and 1895 [315]. By the early part of the twentieth century, a German engineering society was established for the prevention of accidents [293].

About the same time, the engineering technical literature started to acknowledge that safety should be built into a design [293]. The first paper dealing with the safe design of machinery was presented to the American Society of Mechanical Engineers by John H. Cooper in 1891:

> It is an easy task to formulate a plan of accident-preventing devices after the harm is done, but the wiser engineer foresees the possible weakness, as well as the dangers ahead, which are involved in his new enterprise, and at once embodies all the necessary means of safety in his original design [55, p.250].

In 1899, John Calder published a book in England, *The Prevention of Factory Accidents*, which provided accident statistics and described safety devices in detail. The book emphasized the need for anticipating accidents and building in safety and argued that legislation to compel manufacturers to provide safe products would probably not be necessary; free market forces would provide a stronger incentive:

> Safeguarding by the user, of some kind, can in the long run be compelled by statute, but the author's experience is that, in the case of the multitude of occupiers of small factories, with no mechanical facilities or aptitude, nothing can take the place of good fencing fitted by the makers, and all accidents thereby *prevented* by being anticipated (quoted in [293, p.89]).

Calder later moved to the United States and changed his mind: By 1911, he was calling for legislation to force manufacturers to provide safe products [47].

Trade journals started to editorialize about the need for designers to eliminate hazards from machinery. An excerpt from a 1910 editorial stated

We reiterate that the time to safeguard machinery is when it is on the drawing board; and designers should awaken fully to a sense of their responsibility in this respect. They should consider safety as of equal importance with operating efficiency, for if the machines, unprotected, are not safe to work, they are failures, no matter how efficient they may be as producers (quoted in [293, p.90]).

The first American technical journal devoted solely to accident prevention, *The Journal of Industrial Safety*, began publication in 1911, and individual states started to hold safety conferences. The first American National Safety Congress, organized by the Association of Iron and Steel Electrical Engineers, was held in Milwaukee in 1912.

In 1914 the first safety standards published in the United States, the Universal Safety Standards, were compiled under the direction of Carl M. Hansen [109]. These standards required first defining hazards and then finding ways to eliminate them by design, which is similar to the system safety approach developed much later. According to these standards, a safeguard should

1. Afford all possible safety to the operator and surrounding workmen
2. Be automatic in its action, application, or operation (if possible)
3. Be an integral part of the machine itself (if possible)
4. Not materially diminish the output or efficiency of the machine to which it is applied.

Engineers and others started to study safety as an independent topic. In 1929, H.W. Heinrich published a study of 50,000 industrial accidents, concluding that for every serious injury that occurred after exposure to a hazard, there were 29 minor injuries and 300 incidents involving no reportable injury. He also suggested that thousands of near misses were occurring as well. This hypothesis became known as Heinrich's pyramid and established a statistical basis for eliminating hazards even though no serious injuries had yet occurred.

Another study around the same time examined the widely held conviction that safer machines with guards were inefficient and resulted in reduced production. This study, conducted by a group that included the major engineering societies, involved employees of 20 industries and 60 product groups who had a combined exposure of over 50 billion hours. The final report confirmed the hypothesis that *production increased as safety increased*—a lesson still to be learned by many people today.

The study also explained the historical increase in accidents despite industrial safety efforts to reduce them. The increase was found to be related to the tremendous increase in the rate at which American industry was becoming mechanized. Mechanization affected safety in three ways: (1) it displaced the use of hand tools, (2) it increased the exposure of maintenance personnel to machine hazards, and (3) it allowed increased operating and material-feed speeds. The primary conclusion of the study was, "While . . . there has been this recent increase in the hazard of industry per man-hour, production per man-hour has increased so much more rapidly that the hazard in terms of production has decreased" [293].

In the early years of the safety movement, emphasis was concentrated on hazardous physical conditions. Correcting these conditions produced remarkable results during the first 20 years. As the improvements started to decline, other explanations were sought. In 1931, Heinrich published a book, *Industrial Accident Prevention*, in which he maintained that accidents result from unsafe actions and unsafe conditions and suggested that people cause far more accidents than do unsafe conditions [118]. This assertion became the basis for much future argument.

Citing Heinrich's hypothesis, opponents of mechanical solutions to safety began to direct attention away from unsafe machinery and toward unsafe user acts. Claims were made that accident-prone workers and carelessness were responsible for 85 to 90 percent of all industrial accidents. These claims were based on the fact that accidents occurred despite the use of machine guards; however, they ignored the fact that accidents such as slips and falls or injuries from falling objects or from lifting were not machine-related and thus could not be prevented by any type of guarding [293]. More recent data shows that humans are more likely to be blamed for accidents than are unsafe conditions even when unsafe conditions make human error almost inevitable. The issue is a complex one, as was discussed in Chapter 5.

But the argument may be moot in this case. A more important question than blame or cause may be how to eliminate accidents in the future. Hansen, back in 1915, had written

> Forgetfulness, for example, is not a crime deserving of capital punishment; it is one of the universal frailties of humanity. The problem is, therefore, to destroy as far as possible the interrelationship between safety and the universal human shortcomings, which can be done by designing the safeguards on machines and equipment so that if a man's acts are essential to safety, it becomes mechanically necessary for him to perform this act before proceeding with his task [110, p.141].

Heinrich was also the first to provide a conceptual model upon which to build a theoretical framework for industrial safety. He proposed a "domino theory" for accident causation that now appears somewhat simplistic compared to later models (see Chapter 10), but this theory of accident causation was the beginning of safety theory.

The Depression, followed by World War II, temporarily diverted attention away from designing safety as well as function into products. In the long run, however, World War II led to even greater safety efforts than had previously been attempted. Along with the vastly increased war manufacturing—the greatest manufacturing effort of all time—came a tremendous increase in accident and injury rates. The rates were so bad that the Allies were actually in danger of losing the war because of them. Statistics show that more people were killed in industrial accidents than on the battlefield. As Ferry writes,

Not so well known is that for a while, accidents in the workplace were nearly negating the increased production. We were losing twice as many aircraft to training accidents as in combat, worldwide. In nearly all theaters of operation, ground and air accidents were three times those of the combat losses [82].

With the realization that accidents at home were hurting our military efforts, an enormous safety and health program was initiated and thousands of people were trained for industrial safety work. The armed services learned that most accidents could be prevented and belatedly took appropriate action. When the war ended, so, too, did many of the health and safety activities—they no longer had a high priority and safety records worsened again. As normal times and prosperity returned to the country, the safety and health activities also returned. The majority of businesses and industry learned that safety was good business, and the accident and injury rates decreased again dramatically [82].

The post-war period also gave rise to a new approach to safety based on systems engineering principles. Despite the efforts by some engineers to foster the idea of building safety into products and industrial processes, most safety programs had been established on an *a posteriori* philosophy: After an accident, an investigation was conducted to determine how to prevent a similar accident in the future. Since most industry had operated on a relatively small scale, development of new products and processes was slow enough for accident prevention to be based upon learning from mistakes. But these factors were changing. The increased complexity and cost of new products made it uneconomical to follow the accident–investigate–fix philosophy [294]. Discovery and use of high-energy sources, such as exotic fuels, high-pressure systems, and atomic fission, increased the potential effects of an accident. In the case of some industries, such as atomic power, even one accident was considered unacceptable. At the same time, the rapid expansion of technology following World War II caused American industry to begin to think in terms of *systems*.

7.2 Systems Theory

Systems theory dates from the thirties and forties and was a response to certain limitations of science in coping with complexity. Two early proponents of this approach were Norbert Weiner in control and communications engineering and Ludwig von Bertalanffy in biology. Bertalanffy insisted that the emerging ideas in various fields could be combined into a general theory of systems, and he is recognized as the movement's founder [49].

Systems theory is a complementary approach and reaction to scientific reductionism. Reduction, repeatability, and refutation together form the basis of the scientific method. Descartes is usually credited with first elucidating the principle of analytic reduction, where problems are divided into distinct parts and the parts are examined separately.

The principle of reductionism makes three important assumptions [49].

1. The division into parts will not distort the phenomenon being studied.
2. The components of the whole are the same when examined singly as when they are playing their part in the whole.
3. The principles governing the assembling of the components into the whole are straightforward.

These are reasonable assumptions for many of the physical regularities of the universe, that is, for systems that may be described as exhibiting *organized simplicity* [352]. In these systems, the precise nature of the interactions is known and component interactions can be examined pairwise, so that the number of interactions to consider together is limited. Thus, systems can be separated into non-interacting subsystems for analysis purposes without distorting the results. In physics, this approach has been highly effective and is embodied in structural mechanics.

Other types of systems display what systems theorists have labeled *unorganized complexity*—that is, they lack the underlying structure that allows reductionism to be effective. These systems, however, can often be treated as aggregates: They are complex but regular and random enough in their behavior that they can be studied statistically. Their study is simplified by treating them as a structureless mass and interchangeable units and then describing them in terms of averages. The basis of this approach is the *law of large numbers*: The larger the population, the more likely that observed values are close to the predicted average values. In physics, this approach is embodied in statistical mechanics.

A third type of system exhibits what system theorists call *organized complexity*. These systems are too complex for complete analysis and too organized for statistics; the averages are deranged by the underlying structure [352]. It is this type of system, which describes many of the complex engineered systems of the post–World War II era as well as biological systems and social systems, that is the subject of systems theory. Organized complexity also represents particularly well the problems that are faced by those attempting to build complex software.

The systems approach focuses on systems taken as a whole, not on their parts taken separately. It assumes that some properties of systems can only be treated adequately in their entirety, taking into account all facets and all variables and relating the social to the technical aspects [268]. These system properties derive from the relationships between the parts of systems: how the parts interact and fit together [1]. Thus, the systems approach concentrates on the analysis and design of the whole as distinct from the components or the parts.

Systems theory starts from some basic definitions. A *system* is a set of components that act together as a whole to achieve some common goal, objective, or end. The components are all interrelated and either directly or indirectly connected to each other. This concept of a system relies on the assumptions that the

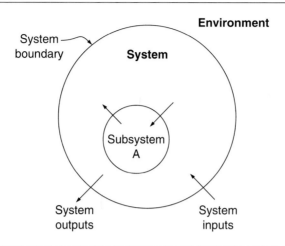

FIGURE 7.1
Definition of a system.

system goals can be defined and that systems are atomistic, that is, capable of being separated into component entities such that their interactive behavior mechanisms can be described [220].

The system *state* at any point in time is the set of relevant properties describing the system at that time. The system *environment* is a set of components (and their properties) that are not part of the system but whose behavior can affect the system state. The existence of a boundary between the system and its environment implicitly defines as *inputs* or *outputs* anything that crosses that boundary (Figure 7.1). And, of course, any set of components that is considered to be a system is, in general, at least potentially part of a hierarchy of systems: A system may contain subsystems and may also be part of a larger system.

It is important to remember that a system is always a model—an *abstraction conceived by the analyst*. For the same system, an observer may see a different purpose than the designer (assuming the system is man-made) and may also focus on different relevant properties. Thus, the designer or observer defines (1) the system boundary, (2) the inputs and outputs, (3) the components, (4) the structure, (5) the relevant interactions between components and the means by which the system retains its integrity, and (6) the purpose or goal of the system that makes it reasonable to consider it to be a coherent entity.

Starting from these basic definitions, systems theory provides a means for studying systems exhibiting organized complexity. The foundation of systems theory is composed of two pairs of ideas: *emergence* and *hierarchy*, and *communication* and *control* [49].

7.2.1 Emergence and Hierarchy

A general model of organized complexity can be expressed in terms of a *hierarchy* of levels of organization, each more complex than the one below, where a level is characterized by having *emergent* properties. Emergent properties do not exist at lower levels; they are meaningless in the language appropriate to those levels. The shape of an apple, although eventually explainable in terms of the cells of the apple, has no meaning at that lower level of description. Thus, the operation of the processes at the lower levels of complexity result in a higher level of complexity—that of the whole apple itself—that has emergent properties, one of them being the apple's shape [49]. The concept of emergence is the idea that at a given level of complexity, some properties characteristic of that level (emergent at that level) are irreducible.

Hierarchy theory deals with the fundamental differences between one level of complexity and another. Its ultimate aim is to explain the relationships between different levels: what generates the levels, what separates them, and what links them. Emergent properties associated with a set of components at one level in a hierarchy are related to constraints upon the degree of freedom of those components. Describing the emergent properties resulting from the imposition of constraints requires a language at a higher level (a metalevel) than that describing the components themselves. Thus, different languages of description are required at different levels.

Relating these concepts to the topic of this book, it is clear that safety is an emergent property of systems. Determining whether a plant is acceptably safe is not possible by examining a single valve in the plant. In fact, statements about the "safety of the valve" (or the safety of the software) without information about the context in which that valve (or software) is used, are meaningless. Conclusions can be reached, however, about the reliability of the valve, where reliability is defined as the probability that the behavior of the valve will satisfy its specification over time and under given conditions. This is one of the basic distinctions between safety and reliability. Safety can only be determined by the relationship between the valve and the other plant components—that is, in the context of the whole.

The hierarchical model of accidents presented in Chapter 3 adopts the basic systems theory idea of hierarchical levels where constraints or lack of constraints at the higher levels control or allow lower-level behavior.

7.2.2 Communication and Control

The second major pair of ideas in systems theory is *communication* and *control*. The imposition of constraints upon the activity at one level of a hierarchy, which define the "laws of behavior" at that level that yield activity meaningful at a higher level, is an example of regulatory or *control* action. Hierarchies are characterized by control processes operating at the interfaces between levels [49]. The link between control mechanisms studied in natural systems and those engineered in man-made systems is provided by a part of systems theory known as cybernetics. Checkland writes,

> Control is always associated with the imposition of constraints, and an account of a control process necessarily requires our taking into account at least two hierarchical levels. At a given level, it is often possible to describe the level by writing dynamical equations, on the assumption that one particle is representative of the collection and that the forces at other levels do not interfere. But any description of a control process entails an upper level imposing constraints upon the lower. The upper level is a source of an alternative (simpler) description of the lower level in terms of specific functions that are emergent as a result of the imposition of constraints [49, p.87].

Control in open systems (those that have inputs and outputs from their environment) implies the need for *communication*. Bertalanffy distinguished between *closed systems*, in which unchanging components settle into a state of equilibrium, and *open systems*, which can be thrown out of equilibrium by exchanges with their environment. He pointed out that organisms (representing open systems) can achieve a steady state that depends upon continuous exchanges with an environment.

The same concepts apply to man-made systems, such as a factory, as well as to biological systems: The designer of a factory must consider not only the individual components or devices that make up the plant but also the plant as a whole. The plant's overall performance has to be controlled in order to produce the desired product while satisfying cost and quality constraints. The plant controller obtains information about the process state from measured variables (feedback) and uses this information to initiate action by manipulating *control variables* to keep the process operating within predefined limits (set points) despite disturbances to the process (Figure 7.2). In general, the maintenance of any open-system hierarchy (either biological or man-made) will require a set of processes in which there is communication of information for regulation or control [49].

7.3 Systems Engineering

The emerging theory of systems, along with various historical factors, gave rise after World War II to a new emphasis in engineering, eventually called systems engineering. During and after the war, technology expanded rapidly and engineers were faced with designing and building more complex systems than had been attempted previously. These systems had the following characteristics [203, 221]:

- □ *Large* in number of parts, replication of identical parts, functions performed, and cost

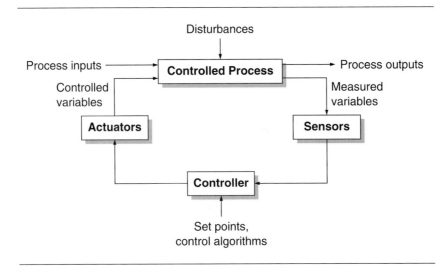

FIGURE 7.2
A standard control loop.

- □ *Complex*, in terms of a change in one variable affecting many other variables, usually in a nonlinear fashion
- □ *Semi-automatic* with a human–machine interface, where machines perform some functions while humans perform others
- □ *Unpredictable* (random) in terms of the inputs, the rate of inputs, or other environmental disturbances.

Although the term *systems engineering* was used first shortly after World War II by the Bell Telephone Company, much of the early impetus for the creation of systems engineering as a discipline arose from aerospace programs such as the intercontinental ballistic missile (ICBM) systems of the 1950s and 1960s. *Apollo*, which involved many of the same engineers and companies that built the ICBMs, was the first major nonmilitary government program in which systems engineering was recognized from the beginning as an essential function [33]. The increasing complexity of the projects attempted was accompanied by an increase in the systems engineering component: Early aerospace projects employed no more than a handful of people who could be called systems engineers, whereas current systems often involve hundreds of them.

Systems theory provides a theoretical foundation and approach for systems engineering, which is concerned with optimizing the design and development of an overall system as opposed to optimizing the components. Although many of the techniques were developed and were being used before the creation of the formal discipline and the underlying theory, the development of systems engineering as a discipline enabled the solution of enormously more complex and difficult technological problems than before [221], and the discipline has evolved during a series of major (primarily aerospace) programs.

Many of the elements of systems engineering can be viewed merely as good engineering: It is more a shift in emphasis than a change in content. More emphasis is placed on

1. Defining goals and relating system performance to these goals
2. Establishing and using decision criteria
3. Developing alternatives
4. Modeling systems for analysis
5. Controlling and managing implementation and operation [221].

While much of engineering is based on technology and science, systems engineering is equally concerned with overall management of the engineering process.

Systems engineering views each system as an integrated whole even though it is composed of diverse, specialized components. The objective is to integrate the subsystems into the most effective system possible to achieve the overall objectives. Complicating matters is the fact that a system may have multiple objectives and some of these may partially conflict—for example, the goal of safe operation may conflict with other objectives such as ease of operation and maintenance or low initial cost. A goal of systems engineering is to optimize the system operation according to prioritized design criteria.

Underlying any approach to achieving this goal is the basic assumption of systems engineering that optimization of individual components or subsystems will not lead in general to a system optimum; in fact, improvement of a particular subsystem actually may worsen the overall system. Since every system is merely a subsystem of some larger system, this principle presents a difficult, if not unsolvable, problem—one that is always present in any major system design effort [203].

The systems approach provides a logical structure for problem solving (Figure 7.3). First, a need or problem is specified in terms of objectives that the system must satisfy and criteria that can be used to rank alternative designs. Then, a process of system synthesis takes place that results in a set of alternative designs. Each of these alternatives is analyzed and evaluated in terms of the stated objectives and design criteria, and one alternative is selected to be implemented. In practice, the process is highly iterative: The results from later stages are fed back to early stages to modify objectives, criteria, design alternatives, and so on.

Systems engineers need not be experts in all the aspects of the system, but they must understand the subsystems and the various phenomena involved in them well enough to describe and model their characteristics. As a result, system engineering often requires a team effort. Some of the basic components of this process are

□ *Needs analysis:* The starting point of any system design project is a perceived need. This need must first be established with enough confidence to

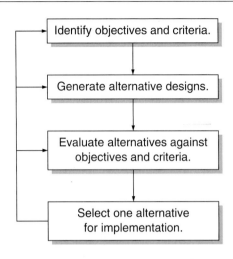

FIGURE 7.3
The problem-solving model for systems engineering.

justify the commitment of resources to satisfy it and understood well enough to allow appropriate solutions to be generated. Design criteria must be established to provide a means to evaluate both the evolving and final system. These criteria may include safety design criteria if safety is a perceived need for the project.

☐ *Feasibility studies:* The goal of this step in the design process is to generate a set of realistic designs. This goal is accomplished by (1) identifying the principal constraints—including safety constraints—and design criteria for the specific problem being addressed; (2) generating plausible solutions to the problem; and (3) selecting potential solutions on the basis of physical and economic feasibility.

☐ *Trade studies:* This step in the process evaluates the alternative feasible designs with respect to various design criteria. A hazard might be controlled by any one of several safeguards: A trade study would determine the relative desirability of each safeguard with respect to effectiveness, cost, weight, size, and any other relevant criteria. For example, substitution of one material for another may reduce the risk of fire or explosion, but also may reduce reliability or efficiency. Each alternative design may have its own set of hazards and other qualities that need to be assessed. Although, ideally, decisions should be based upon mathematical analysis, quantification of many of the key factors is often difficult, if not impossible, and subjective judgment often has to be used.

☐ *System architecture development and analysis:* In this step, the systems engineers break down the system into a set of subsystems, together with the

functions and constraints imposed upon the individual subsystem designs, the major system interfaces, and the subsystem interface topology. These aspects are analyzed with respect to desired system performance characteristics and constraints—again including safety constraints—and the process is iterated until an acceptable system design results. The preliminary design at the end of this process must be described in sufficient detail that subsystem implementation can proceed independently.

□ *Interface analysis:* The interfaces define the functional boundaries of the system components. From a management standpoint, interfaces must (1) optimize visibility and control and (2) isolate components that can be implemented independently and for which authority and responsibility can be delegated [265]. From an engineering standpoint, interfaces must be designed to separate independent functions and to facilitate the integration, testing, and operation of the overall system. Because interfaces tend to be particularly susceptible to design error and are implicated in the majority of accidents, a paramount goal of interface design is simplicity. Simplicity aids in ensuring that the interface can be adequately designed and tested prior to integration and that interface responsibilities can be clearly understood.

7.4 Systems Analysis

During the 1950s, at the same time that systems engineering concepts were evolving, the RAND Corporation developed a methodology called systems analysis to provide a rational way to evaluate the alternatives facing a decision maker. Briefly, systems analysis is a method for broad economic appraisal of the costs and consequences of the various ways to satisfy a particular goal. Systems analysis is related to operations research, but systems analysis is more comprehensive, less quantitative, and more oriented toward broad strategic and policy questions [49].

In most cases, all elements of uncertainty cannot be eliminated from the decision process because all the relevant information will not be obtainable. Therefore, the consequences of a particular course of action cannot be determined completely. However, systems analysis provides an organized process for the acquisition and investigation of specific information pertinent to a given decision.

Systems engineering and systems analysis have merged over the years, with systems engineering coming to mean the overall process of creating a complex human–machine system and systems analysis providing (1) the data for the decision-making aspects of that process and (2) an organized way to select the best among the alternative designs. These two disciplines provide the foundation for system safety.

Chapter

8

Fundamentals of System Safety

My company has had a safety program for 150 years. The program was instituted as a result of a French law requiring an explosives manufacturer to live on the premises with his family.

—Crawford Greenwalt
Former president of Dupont[1]

After World War II, system safety developed in parallel with and in conjunction with systems engineering, although its roots go back much further. As seen in the previous chapter, the concern about industrial safety dates back at least to the turn of the century, and many of the basic concepts of system safety, such as anticipating hazards and accidents and building in safety, predate the post–World War II period. In addition, as with general systems engineering concepts, individuals developed and practiced system safety approaches and techniques before system safety became a recognized discipline.

8.1 Historical Development

Much of the early development of system safety as a separate discipline began with flight engineers immediately after World War II. The Air Force had long had problems with aircraft accidents. For example, from 1952 to 1966, it lost 7715 aircraft, in which 8547 persons, including 3822 pilots, were killed [108]. Most of

---

[1] Quoted in [140].

these accidents were blamed on pilots. Many industry flight engineers, however, did not believe the cause was so simple: They argued that safety must be designed and built into aircraft just as are performance, stability, and structural integrity [223, 319].

Seminars were conducted by the Flight Safety Foundation, headed by Jerome Lederer (who would later head the NASA Apollo safety program), that brought together engineering, operations, and management personnel. It was in 1954, at one of these seminars, that the term "system safety" may have first been used—in a paper by one of the aviation safety pioneers, C.O. Miller, titled "Applying Lessons Learned from Accident Investigations to Design Through a Systems Safety Concept." Around the same time, the Air Force began holding symposiums that fostered a professional approach to safety in propulsion, electrical, flight control, and other aircraft subsystems, but they did not at first treat safety as a system problem.

When the Air Force began to develop intercontinental ballistic missiles (ICBMs), there were no pilots to blame for accidents, yet the liquid-propellant missiles blew up frequently and with devastating results. The missiles used cryogenic liquids with temperatures down to $-320°$ F and pressurized gases at 6000 pounds per square inch, and the potential safety problems could not be ignored—the highly toxic and reactive propellants were sometimes more lethal than the poison gases used in World War II, more violently destructive than many explosives, and more corrosive than most materials used in industrial processes [108]. The Department of Defense and the Atomic Energy Commission were also facing the problems of building and handling nuclear weapons and finding it necessary to establish rigid controls and requirements on nuclear materials and weapon design.

In that same period, the AEC (and later the NRC) was engaged in a public debate about the safety of nuclear power. Similarly, civil aviation was attempting to reduce accidents in order to convince a skeptical public to fly, and the chemical industry was coping with larger plants and increasingly lethal chemicals. These parallel activities resulted in different approaches to handling safety issues. These approaches are described in Appendices B and D.

System safety itself arose out of the ballistic missile programs. In the fifties, when the Atlas and Titan ICBMs were being developed, intense political pressure was focused on building a nuclear warhead with delivery capability as a deterrent to nuclear war. In an attempt to shorten the time between initial concept definition and operational status, a concurrent engineering approach was developed and adopted. In this approach, the missiles and the facilities in which they were to be maintained ready for launch were built at the same time that tests of the missiles and training of personnel were proceeding. The Air Force recognized that this approach would lead to many modifications and retrofits that would cost more money, but, with nuclear war as an alternative, they concluded that additional money was a cheap way to buy time. A tremendous effort was exerted to make the concurrent approach work [294].

On these first missile projects, system safety was not identified and assigned as a specific responsibility. Instead, as was usual at the time, each designer, manager, and engineer was assigned responsibility for safety. These projects, however, involved advanced technology and much greater complexity than had previously been attempted, and the drawbacks of the standard approach to safety became clear when many interface problems went unnoticed until it was too late.

Within 18 months after the fleet of 71 Atlas F missiles became operational, four blew up in their silos during operational testing. The missiles also had an extremely low launch success rate. An Air Force manual describes several of these accidents:

> An ICBM silo was destroyed because the counterweights, used to balance the silo elevator on the way up and down in the silo, were designed with consideration only to raising a fueled missile to the surface for firing. There was no consideration that, when you were not firing in anger, you had to bring the fueled missile back down to defuel. The first operation with a fueled missile was nearly successful. The drive mechanism held it for all but the last five feet when gravity took over and the missile dropped back. Very suddenly, the 40-foot diameter silo was altered to about 100-foot diameter.
>
> During operational tests on another silo, the decision was made to continue a test against the safety engineer's advice when all indications were that, because of high oxygen concentrations in the silo, a catastrophe was imminent. The resulting fire destroyed a missile and caused extensive silo damage. In another accident, five people were killed when a single-point failure in a hydraulic system caused a 120-ton door to fall.
>
> Launch failures were caused by reversed gyros, reversed electrical plugs, bypass of procedural steps, and by management decisions to continue, in spite of contrary indications, because of schedule pressures. [5, p.1-1].

Not only were the losses themselves costly, but the resulting investigations detected serious safety deficiencies in the system that would require extensive modifications to correct. In fact, the cost of the modifications would have been so high that a decision was made to retire the entire weapon system and accelerate deployment of the Minuteman missile system. Thus, a major weapon system, originally designed to be used for a minimum of ten years, was in service for less than two years primarily because of safety deficiencies [294].

When the early aerospace accidents were investigated, it became apparent that the causes of a large percentage of them could be traced to deficiencies in design, operations, and management. The previous "fly–fix–fly" approach was clearly not adequate. In this approach, investigations were conducted to reconstruct the causes of accidents, action was taken to prevent or minimize the recurrence of accidents with the same cause, and eventually these preventive actions were incorporated into standards, codes of practice, and regulations. Although the fly–fix–fly approach was effective in reducing the repetition of accidents with identical causes, it became clear to the Department of Defense (DoD), and later to others, that it was too costly and, in the case of nuclear weapons, unacceptable.

This realization led to the adoption of system safety approaches to try to prevent accidents before they occur the first time.

The first military specification on system safety was published by the Air Force (Ballistic Systems Division) in 1962, and the Minuteman ICBM became the first weapon system to have a contractual, formal, disciplined system safety program. From that time on, system safety received increasing attention, especially in Air Force missile programs where testing was limited and accident consequences serious. In fact, the United States was so concerned about inadvertent launch of a ballistic missile—including those pointed at us—that the DoD exported the developing system safety techniques to the Soviet Union and recommended that they apply them [42]. The Army soon adopted system safety programs because of the many personnel it was losing in helicopter accidents, and the Navy followed suit. In 1966, the DoD issued a single directive requiring system safety programs on all development or modification contracts.

At first, there were few techniques that could be used on these complex systems. But, step by step, the specialized safety engineering and operational safety practices that had evolved over the years were integrated with scientific, technical, and management techniques that were newly developed or adapted from other activities. Particular emphasis was placed on hazard analysis techniques, such as fault trees, which were first developed to cope with complex programs such as Minuteman.

The first system safety specification was a document created by the Air Force in 1966 (MIL-S-38130A). In June 1969, this became MIL-STD-882 (*System Safety Program for Systems and Associated Subsystems and Equipment: Requirements for*), and a system safety program became mandatory on all DoD-procured products and systems. This first standard stated that

> The contractor shall establish and maintain an effective system safety program that is planned and integrated into all phases of system development, production, and operation. The system safety program shall provide a disciplined approach to methodically control safety aspects and evaluate the system's design: identify hazards and prescribe corrective action in a timely, cost effective manner. The system safety program activities shall be specified in a formal plan which must describe an integrated effort within the total program. . . . The system safety program objectives are to ensure that:
>
> a. Safety, consistent with mission requirements, is designed into the system.
>
> b. Hazards associated with each system, subsystems, and equipment are identified and evaluated and eliminated or controlled to an acceptable level.
>
> c. Control over hazards that cannot be eliminated is established to protect personnel, equipment, and property.
>
> d. Minimum risk is involved in the acceptance and use of new materials and new production and testing techniques.

e. Retrofit actions required to improve safety are minimized through the timely inclusion of safety factors during the acquisition of a system.

f. The historical safety data generated by similar system programs are considered and used where appropriate.

Many of the later system safety requirements and programs in other agencies and in industry are based on this standard. In 1977, an updated version, MIL-STD-882A, was adopted, and software was incorporated in 1984 in MIL-STD-882B. In parallel, the Air Force developed its own standard (MIL-STD-1574A: *System Safety Standard for Space and Military Systems*). These two documents were consolidated in 1993 into the current version, MIL-STD-882C, which has eliminated the separation of software tasks from other safety tasks and has better integrated software into the entire process.

The space program was the second major application area to apply system safety approaches in a disciplined fashion. Until the *Apollo 204* fire in 1967 at Cape Kennedy, in which three astronauts were killed, NASA safety efforts had focused on industrial worker safety. The accident alerted NASA, and they commissioned the General Electric Company at Daytona Beach, among others, to develop policies and procedures that became models for civilian aerospace safety activities [224]. Jerome Lederer was hired to head manned space-flight safety and, later, all NASA safety efforts. Through his leadership, an extensive program of system safety was set up for space projects, much of it patterned after the Air Force and DoD programs. Many of the same engineers and companies that had established formal system safety programs for DoD contracts also were involved in space programs, and the technology and management activities were transferred to this new application.

As computers became increasingly important components of complex systems, concern about the safety aspects of software began to emerge in DoD and NASA programs. Some of the earliest software safety activities were attempted on the Space Transportation System (Space Shuttle) program in the 1970s. For example, in 1979 TRW was under contract to NASA to provide a Software Hazard Analysis for critical functions of the Space Shuttle ascent and re-entry software. The DoD, again led by the Air Force, started to integrate software into system safety programs in the early 1980s. An extensive set of tasks for safety analysis of software was incorporated into MIL-STD-882B (Notice 1) in July 1987. For some reason, NASA's efforts to integrate software into their system safety programs dwindled in the 1980s, whereas the military programs continued to advance.

Slowly, commercial industry either adopted the system safety programs pioneered by the military and NASA, or they independently developed programs of their own as they found themselves faced with the same problems—manufacturing plants and products that were becoming increasingly complex, dangerous, and expensive to construct. Waiting for accidents to occur and then eliminating the causes became uneconomical as modification, retrofit, and replacement costs soared and liability concerns were raised.

Building many of today's complex systems requires integrating parts built by separate contractors or organizational entities. Even if each contractor or group takes steps to build quality into its own component, combining subsystems into a system introduces new failure modes and hazards that are not apparent when viewing the parts separately. It became evident in many industries that designing safety into a plant or product could reduce overall life-cycle costs and that a system safety approach was required to achieve acceptable levels of safety.

8.2 Basic Concepts

System safety uses systems theory and systems engineering approaches to prevent foreseeable accidents and to minimize the result of unforeseen ones. Losses in general, not just human death or injury, are considered. Such losses may include destruction of property, loss of mission, and environmental harm. The key point is that the loss is considered serious enough that time, effort, and resources will be put into preventing it. How much of an investment is considered worthwhile to avoid the accident or its effects will depend upon social, political, and economic factors.

The primary concern of system safety is the management of hazards: their identification, evaluation, elimination, and control through analysis, design and management procedures. Mueller, in 1968, described the then new discipline of system safety engineering as "organized common sense" [171]. It is a planned, disciplined, and systematic approach to identifying, analyzing, and controlling hazards throughout the life cycle of a system in order to prevent or reduce accidents.

System safety activities start in the earliest concept development stages of a project and continue through design, production, testing, operational use, and disposal. One aspect that distinguishes system safety from other approaches to safety is its primary emphasis on the early identification and classification of hazards so that corrective action can be taken to eliminate or minimize those hazards before final design decisions are made.

Although system safety is a relatively new discipline and still evolving, some general principles are constant throughout its various manifestations and distinguish it from other approaches to safety and risk management.

- *System safety emphasizes building in safety, not adding it on to a completed design.*

Safety considerations must be part of the initial stage of concept development and requirements definition: From 70 to 90 percent of the design decisions that affect safety will be made in these early project phases [140]. The degree to which it is economically feasible to eliminate a hazard rather than to control it depends upon the stage in system development at which the hazard is identified and considered. Early integration of safety considerations into the system development process allows maximum safety with minimal negative impact. The alternative is to design the plant, identify the hazards, and then add on protective equipment to control the hazards when they occur—which may be more expensive and less effective.

■ *System safety deals with systems as a whole rather than with subsystems or components.*

Safety is an emergent property of systems, not a component property. One of the principle responsibilities of system safety is to evaluate the interfaces between the system components and determine the effects of component interaction, where the set of components includes humans, machines, and the environment.

■ *System safety takes a larger view of hazards than just failures.*

Hazards are not always caused by failures, and all failures do not cause hazards. Serious accidents have occurred while system components were all functioning exactly as specified—that is, without failure. If failures only are considered in a safety analysis, many potential accidents will be missed. In addition, the engineering approaches to preventing failures (increasing reliability) and preventing hazards (increasing safety) are different and sometimes conflict.

■ *System safety emphasizes analysis rather than past experience and standards.*

Standards and codes of practice incorporate experience and knowledge about how to reduce hazards, usually accumulated over long periods of time and resulting from previous mistakes. While such standards and learning from experience are essential in all aspects of engineering, including safety, the pace of change today does not always allow for such experience to accumulate and for proven designs to be used. System safety analysis attempts to anticipate and prevent accidents and near-accidents *before* they occur.

■ *System safety emphasizes qualitative rather than quantitative approaches.*

System safety places major emphasis on identifying hazards as early as possible in the design stage and then designing to eliminate or control those hazards. At these early stages, quantitative information usually does not exist. Although such quantitative information would be useful in prioritizing hazards, subjective judgments about the likelihood of a hazard are usually adequate and all that is possible at the time that design decisions must be made.

The accuracy of quantitative analyses is also questionable. The majority of safety aspects cannot be evaluated in numerical terms, and those that can often receive undue weighting in decisions based on absolute measures. Quantitative evaluations usually are based on unrealistic assumptions, often unstated, such as that accidents are caused by failures; failures are random; testing is perfect;

failures and errors are statistically independent; and the system is designed, constructed, operated, maintained, and managed according to good engineering standards. In addition, some components of high technology systems may be new or may not have been produced and used in sufficient quantity to provide an accurate probabilistic history of failure.

Although such quantitative analyses may be useful for comparisons of the failure properties of particular designs, using absolute probability figures to make decisions about which hazards to eliminate or whether a particular system provides acceptable safety is problematic.

- *System safety recognizes the importance of tradeoffs and conflicts in system design.*

Nothing is absolutely safe, and safety is not the only, and is rarely the primary, goal in building systems. Most of the time, safety acts as a constraint on the possible system designs and may conflict with other design goals such as operational effectiveness, performance, ease of use, time, and cost. System safety techniques and approaches focus on providing information for decision making about risk management tradeoffs.

- *System safety is more than just system engineering.*

System safety engineering is an important part of system safety, but the concerns of system safety extend beyond the traditional boundaries of engineering to include such things as political and social processes; the interests and attitudes of management; attitudes and motivations of designers and operators; human factors and cognitive psychology; the effects of the legal system on accident investigations and free exchange of information; certification and licensing of critical employees and systems; and public sentiment [171].

Using these general principles, system safety attempts to manage hazards through analysis, design, and management procedures.

8.2.1 Hazard Analysis

Hazard analysis investigates factors related to accidents. Such analyses have been used

1. In *development* to identify and assess potential hazards, and the conditions that can lead to them, so that the hazards can be eliminated or controlled
2. In *operations* to examine an existing system to improve its safety and to formulate policy and operational procedures
3. In *licensing* to examine a planned or existing system to demonstrate acceptable safety to a regulatory authority.

The type of analysis performed will vary with the purpose of the analysis. One approach might be used to make something safer; another to convince a government licenser that it already is safe. Emphasis in this book is on the former, that is, techniques to engineer safer systems, but the latter, usually called risk assessment, is discussed briefly. Many good books are available on risk assessment; fewer have been written on risk reduction.

System safety analyses, as defined originally in the defense projects in which they were developed, are divided into four stages, based on when they are performed and their various goals.

Preliminary Hazard Analysis (PHA) is used in the early life cycle stages to identify critical system functions and broad system hazards. The identified hazards are often assessed and prioritized, and safety design criteria and requirements may be identified. The PHA is started early in the concept exploration phase or in the earliest life-cycle phases of the program so that safety considerations are included in tradeoff studies and design alternatives. The process is iterative, with the PHA being updated as more information about the design is obtained and as changes are made. The results serve as a baseline for later analysis and may be used in developing system safety requirements and in preparing performance and design specifications.

Because PHA starts at the concept formation stage of a project, little detail is available, and assessments of hazard and risk levels are necessarily qualitative and limited.

System Hazard Analysis (SHA) begins as the design matures (around preliminary design review) and continues as the design is updated and changes are made. SHA involves detailed studies of possible hazards created in the interfaces between subsystems or by the system operating as a whole, including potential human errors.

Specifically, SHA examines subsystem interfaces for (1) compliance with safety criteria in the system requirements specification; (2) degradation of safety resulting from normal operation of the system and subsystems; and (3) possible combinations of independent, dependent, and simultaneous hazardous events or failures, including erroneous behavior of safety controls and devices, that could cause hazards.

The purpose of SHA is to recommend changes and controls and evaluate design responses to safety requirements.

Subsystem Hazard Analysis (SSHA) is started as soon as the subsystems are designed in sufficient detail, and it is updated as the design matures. As in SHA, design changes are evaluated to determine whether system safety is affected. The purpose of SSHA is to identify hazards associated with the design of the subsystems, including operating modes, critical inputs and outputs, and hazards resulting from functional relationships between the components and equipment comprising each subsystem. Software Hazard Analysis is a type of SSHA.

SSHA examines each subsystem or component and identifies hazards associated with normal operating or failure modes, including normal performance, performance degradation, functional failure, or inadvertent functioning. It also identifies necessary actions to determine how to eliminate or reduce the risk of identified hazards and evaluates the design response to the safety requirements of the subsystem specification.

SHA and SSHA are accomplished in similar ways, but the goals are different. SSHA examines how *individual* component operation or failure affects the overall safety of the system, whereas SHA determines how normal and failure modes of the components *operating together* can affect system safety.

Operating and Support Hazard Analysis (OSHA) identifies hazards and risk reduction procedures during all phases of system use and maintenance. It especially examines hazards created by the human–machine interface.

Hazard analysis is discussed in depth in later chapters. In general, the process used may be formal or informal and ranges from the use of design reviews and walkthroughs, checklists, and informal worksheets and tabular layouts of information to formal, mathematical modeling and analysis.

8.2.2 Design for Safety

Once hazards have been identified, the highest priority should be assigned to eliminating them. System safety has a widely accepted precedence for dealing with hazards [106]:

1. Hazard elimination (intrinsic safety)
2. Hazard reduction
3. Hazard control
4. Damage reduction.

The precedence does not mean that only one of these approaches should be taken, only that the higher levels are more desirable. In fact, a design very likely will include features at several levels.

An intrinsically safe design is one that is incapable, under either normal or abnormal conditions, of (1) generating sufficient energy to cause an accident or (2) producing harmful exposures. Although all hazards usually cannot be eliminated, many can.

If a hazard cannot be completely eliminated, the next best choice is to prevent or minimize its occurrence by designing in hazard reduction measures, such as lockouts, lockins, or interlocks, to prevent or minimize conditions that could lead to the hazard.

Next in the accepted order of precedence are devices to control a hazard (mitigate its effects) once it has occurred. For example, a pressure relief valve can be used to relieve overpressurization when this possibility cannot be completely eliminated. Controls may be passive or active.

The most effective control devices are passive and rely on basic physical principles, for example, gravity. *Passive* control measures do not require a positive action to be effective. An example of a passive device is a railway semaphore that uses weights to ensure that if the cable (controlling the semaphore) breaks, the arm will automatically drop into the STOP position.

Active control devices are less desirable; they require some action to prevent or mitigate the hazard's effects. These actions include hazard detection and recovery or fail-safe procedures. Examples of active devices for a fire hazard are smoke detectors and sprinkler systems.

A design should always provide for damage minimization in case the hazard control measures are ineffective or an unidentified hazard occurs. Damage minimization may take the form of (1) warning devices, training, and procedures to use in the event of an emergency, or (2) isolation of the hazardous system from population centers. Contingency measures, including emergency and fail-safe procedures (to put the system into a less dangerous state), must be planned and prepared before the system is put into operation: When an emergency arises, sufficient time may not remain after hazard detection to assess the situation, diagnose the problem, and determine and implement corrective actions.

System safety also has a precedence for selecting specific safeguards: (1) eliminate the hazard, (2) use safety devices to preclude its occurrence, (3) provide warning devices to alert the operator and other personnel, and (4) provide training.

8.2.3 Management

The most important aspects of system safety in terms of accident prevention may be management procedures. Effective management of safety includes setting policy and defining goals; planning tasks and procedures; defining responsibility, granting authority, and fixing accountability; documenting and tracking hazards and their resolution (establishing audit trails); maintaining safety information systems and documentation; establishing reporting and information channels; and so on.

System safety is responsible for system-level safety efforts, including analysis of component interfaces. Component-level safety activities, such as ensuring the safety of a missile launch system or the safety of on-board avionics, may be part of the general system safety responsibility or, on large and complex projects, part of the component engineering efforts. Further division of responsibility for limited hazard domains, such as fire, nuclear, and explosive safety, may be warranted. Even if safety efforts are subdivided, system safety engineers are still responsible for integrating the component safety activities and information. System safety also has obvious interfaces with related disciplines such as reliability engineering, quality assurance, and human factors.

The actual process and tasks implemented will be project specific and will depend on the size of the project and the level of risk associated with the system. Safety management issues and specific tasks for both large and small projects are described in Chapters 11 and 12.

8.3 Software System Safety

The increased use of computers in safety-critical applications presents new problems. Methods for handling the software aspects of system safety have not yet been developed to the extent necessary to ensure safety in these systems. System safety engineers often are not trained in software engineering, and software engineers often do not have adequate training in basic engineering fundamentals and in system safety.

The result is often a chasm or disconnect between software engineering and system or safety engineering. System safety engineers for the most part ignore software or treat the computer as a black box. At the same time, software engineers treat the computer as a stimulus–response system—a stimulus is received and a response is supplied. Software engineers seldom look beyond the computer; they usually construct the software with little or no consideration of system hazards and the effect of the software on system safety. System-level tools and techniques that include the computer are lacking, and communication between safety engineers and software personnel is often limited, at best.

The computer serves a control function in many systems. Not only does it have the usual interfaces with other components, but often it is responsible for controlling the behavior of electromechanical components and the interactions among these components. Since most accidents arise in the interfaces and interactions among components, software plays a direct and important role in system safety and must be an integral part of the system safety efforts.

> **Definition.** *Software system safety* implies that the software will execute within a system context without contributing to hazards.

Software can affect system safety in two ways: (1) it can exhibit behavior in terms of output values and timing that contribute to the system reaching a hazardous state, or (2) it can fail to recognize or handle hardware failures that it is required to control or to respond to in some way. Both of these software safety issues must be handled in an effective system safety program.

> **Definition.** *Safety-critical software* is any software that can directly or indirectly contribute to the occurrence of a hazardous system state.

> **Definition.** *Safety-critical functions* are those system functions whose correct operation, incorrect operation (including correct operation at the wrong time), or lack of operation could contribute to a system hazard.

> **Definition.** *Safety-critical software functions* are those software functions that can directly or indirectly, in consort with other system component behavior or environmental conditions, contribute to the existence of a hazardous state.

Software does not exhibit random wearout failures as does hardware; it is an abstraction, and its "failures" are therefore due to logic or design errors. As noted in Chapter 2, however, once loaded and executed on a computer, the software becomes essentially the design of a special-purpose machine, into which the general-purpose computer has been temporarily transformed. Software is merely the *design of a machine*; it is an abstraction—like an architect's plans or an electrical engineer's circuit diagrams—and has no physical reality. When the software design is executed on a general-purpose computer, the special-purpose machine (as reflected in the software) ceases to be an abstraction alone and becomes a concrete machine. Software, therefore, can and must be evaluated both as an abstract design *and* as a concrete machine. Looking at the abstract design alone (pure static analysis) can never be adequate.

As with any other machine, a computer's hardware components may fail. In comparison with mechanical devices, however, reliability of computer hardware is quite good. Engineering techniques to cope with random failures and design error in digital computer hardware can be and usually are implemented in its design. Checks to detect certain types of hardware failure can sometimes also be implemented in software. These hardware reliability-enhancing techniques, however, have no effect on errors in the software design, which must be treated separately.

Firmware is just software; it is a layer of abstraction that has been inserted between the digital hardware and the application software. Therefore, firmware must be treated the same as software—it is simply software (instructions) that controls the operation of a general-purpose machine.

In addition to hardware faults and failures, a computer can behave incorrectly because of logic errors in the software—that is, the design of the special-purpose machine. These logic errors are of two types:

□ The software is written from incorrect requirements (the code matches the requirements, but the behavior specified in the requirements is not desired from a system perspective)

□ The implementation of the requirements in a programming language does not match or satisfy the requirements (coding errors)

Both types of errors must be considered when attempting to increase software reliability and safety. The majority, by far, of the existing software engineering techniques deal only with the second problem. The first, being at the intersection of software engineering and system engineering, suffers from the lack of communication between these two disciplines and the tendency for software engineers to work in isolation from the rest of the system developers. This fact is especially unfortunate from a safety standpoint, since empirical evidence seems to validate the commonly stated hypothesis that the majority of safety problems arise from software requirements errors and not coding errors. For example, Lutz examined 387 software errors uncovered during integration and system testing of the Voyager and Galileo spacecraft. Safety-related software errors were found to arise most often from (1) discrepancies between the documented requirements speci-fications and the requirements needed for correct functioning of the system, and (2) misunderstandings about the software's interface with the rest of the system [200].

There are three ways to deal with software errors. The first, and most obvi-ous, is just to get the requirements and code "correct." This approach is enticing, since it is theoretically possible compared to the impossibility of eliminating ran-dom or wearout errors in hardware devices. Many people have realized, however, that although perfect software can be constructed theoretically, it is impossible from a practical standpoint. It requires building software that will make the com-puter do exactly what it should under all conditions, no matter what changes occur in the other components of the system (including failures), in the environ-ment, and in the software itself. Of course, getting correct software is an appropri-ate and important goal. However, engineers—software, system, and safety—need to consider what will happen if this goal is not achieved.

A second approach to dealing with logic errors in software is to enhance software reliability by attempting to make the software fault tolerant through var-ious types of redundancy. Even were this approach to work, it would provide protection only against coding errors (errors in translating the requirements and algorithms into a programming language), which may have the least effect on safety. And even this gain may be limited: Experiments with general software fault-tolerance techniques based on redundancy have shown that programmers often make the same mistakes and that independently coded software does not necessarily fail independently [39, 73, 163, 164, 181]. In addition mathemati-cal analysis and models have demonstrated limitations in the actual amount of reliability improvement possible using this approach [74]. These limitations are discussed in more depth later. Even if software redundancy was effective, there is another problem with this approach: Reliability and safety are sometimes at odds with respect to critical functions. Redundancy designed to increase reliabil-ity may decrease safety and vice versa.

The previous two approaches attempt to increase safety by increasing oper-ational software reliability. Although this goal is appropriate, merely increasing reliability may not be adequate to ensure safety. Software-related accidents have occurred when the software satisfied its specification and when the operational reliability of the software was very high. In these cases, either

□ The software correctly implements the requirements, but the requirements specify behavior that is not safe from a system perspective

□ The requirements do not specify some particular behavior that is required for system safety

□ The software has unintended (and unsafe) behavior beyond what is specified in the requirements.

Software testing and operational reliability measurement techniques determine whether the software matches the specified required behavior—they do not determine whether that behavior is safe, whether something has been left out, or whether additional, unspecified behavior is possible.

A way out of this dilemma is to recognize that systems can be made safe despite the occurrence of errors and failures and despite a relatively low reliability level of individual components. Instead of merely attempting to increase software reliability, the third approach to dealing with software errors is to apply standard system safety techniques. The particular software behaviors that can lead to system hazards are identified and are eliminated or controlled in the software and system requirements and design. For example, some hazardous software behavior can be identified and eliminated through special safety analyses of the software requirements and code. Other hazardous software behavior can be controlled by adding hardware interlocks or human controls to the system design. In addition, special protection can be built into the software itself in the form of software interlocks, fail-safe software, and software monitoring or self-checking mechanisms. This third approach, based on system safety concepts, is the *Safeware* approach to software system safety.

8.4 Cost and Effectiveness of System Safety

To be practical, system safety approaches must be effective and have a comparatively reasonable cost. Military aviation has implemented some of the most sophisticated system safety programs and has demonstrated that large investments are not necessary for programs to be cost-effective. U.S. military aviation accidents (over 200 aircraft are lost each year) and modification programs to correct safety problems discovered after accidents cost over $1 billion annually. A typical aviation system safety program, on the other hand, costs about $5 to $10 million for a major project [88]. Another common estimate of the cost of a comprehensive system safety program is 5 to 7 percent of the cost of the entire program [5]. The contractor part of the F-14 system safety program was less than one-third the cost of an airplane today. Obviously, the investment in an aviation safety program is worthwhile if it prevents the loss of a single aircraft (which is, for example, $15 million for the AH-64, $25 million for the F-18, $200 million for the B-1B and over $2 billion for the B-2), not to mention the loss of human lives. The same ratios apply to other industries.

The payoff occurs, of course, only if accidents are prevented. The evidence for effectiveness of system safety programs is harder to obtain: Measuring something that does not happen is difficult. However, the military aviation accident rate has generally decreased over time, and this improvement has been attributed to the emphasis placed on system safety programs and concerted efforts to eliminate and control hazards [88].

One indirect measure of effectiveness, although not entirely satisfactory because of lack of controlled comparisons, is to compare systems with and without safety programs [88]. Through 1981, the F-4 and F-14 aircraft had somewhat similar missions in the Navy. The F-4 did not have a formal system safety program, but the F-14 did. Cumulative material failure accidents for the F-4 occurred at a rate of 9.52/100,000 hours. The comparable F-14 rate was 5.77/100,000 hours. The difference in accident rates between the two aircraft was even greater during initial fleet operations. While unique features of the two programs, unrelated to system safety, could partly explain the difference in accident rates, the comparative data provides strong support for the effectiveness of system safety approaches.

Another way of examining effectiveness is to look at the many hazards that system safety personnel corrected before accidents occurred and well before the problem would have been identified otherwise. Frola and Miller provide the following examples [88]:

□ During the design of the F-18, an increased fire hazard was avoided when a system safety engineer convinced program decision makers that a proposed increase in allowable bleed air-duct temperature was dangerous. A way to avoid a similar hazard was also noted—ensuring that the bleed air shutoff valve closed when power was removed. The system was changed.

□ During a modification to the B-52, a system safety engineer noticed that if the front lugs of the Air-Launched Cruise Missile retracted but the rear ones did not, parts of the pylon would tear from the wing and, together with the missile, would cause severe structural damage to the wing and possibly to the horizontal stabilizer. The system was redesigned.

□ The CH-47D originally had a single-point hook for load lifting. To improve load retention, a three-point attachment was designed. The system safety engineer discovered that if one hook were to hang up with the others open, it was quite probable that the aircraft could not be controlled and cables might contact rotor blades. The redesign assured that either all hooks opened or none of them did.

□ A system safety engineer found that loss of voltage in a radar circuit of the PAVE LOW helicopter system would cause a command to the aircraft to fly at zero altitude with no warning to the pilot. The safety engineer also checked with personnel on the RF-4C and A7D programs, knowing that they used the same system. All aircraft were immediately prohibited from flying certain low-level missions until the systems were corrected.

A third way of assessing the effectiveness of system safety programs is to examine cases where system safety recommendations were not followed and an accident occurred. Again, Frola and Miller [88] provide examples. In one case, a project manager decided to save money by eliminating a "roll-over" fuel valve in a helicopter crashworthy fuel system. The valve was reincorporated after an accident demonstrated the need for it. Similarly, other changes to aircraft made for economic reasons, without system safety approval, have caused accidents. The

F-18 is an example of a major program where specific safety recommendations were made, ignored, and later had to be retrofitted.

Sagan recounts an example involving the B-52 [307]. After investigating the breakup of a B-52 in midair in 1961, both the Air Force Directorate of Flight Safety and the National Bureau of Standards concluded that small fatigue cracks were developing in B-52 wings and recommended immediate corrections on the entire B-52 fleet. The Strategic Air Command ignored this recommendation, instead insisting that severe air turbulence had caused the accident. Only after two more B-52s crashed for identical reasons two years later did the command finally agree to modify the wings.

A strong testimonial for system safety programs is found in their use by some aerospace contractors, even though the programs were not funded directly under their contracts, because they believed the upfront expenditures would save them money in the long run [88]. Of course, the effectiveness of any system safety program, and thus any potential cost savings and risk reduction, depends on how program management implements the safety program, but past experience seems to support the hypothesis that hazards can be identified and eliminated at a reasonable cost using system safety techniques.

8.5 Other Approaches to Safety

Industrial (or operational) safety and reliability engineering are related to, but differ from, system safety; the relationships and differences are important in understanding system safety and the approach to increasing safety taken in this book.

8.5.1 Industrial Safety

Industrial, or occupational, safety has been called the "hard hat and safety shoe" philosophy; it tries primarily to control injuries to employees on the job. The industrial safety engineer usually is dealing with a fixed manufacturing design and hazards that have existed for a long time, many of which are accepted as necessary for operations. More emphasis is placed on teaching employees to work within this environment than on removing the hazards.

Industrial safety engineers collect data during the operational life of the system and eliminate or control unacceptable hazards if possible or practical. When accidents occur, they are investigated and action is taken to reduce the likelihood of a recurrence—either changing the plant or changing employee work rules and training. The hazards associated with high-energy or dangerous processes are usually controlled either (1) by disturbance control algorithms implemented by operators or an automated control system or (2) by transferring the plant to a safe state using a separate protection system.

Safety reviews and audits are conducted by industrial safety divisions within the company or by safety committees to ensure that unsafe conditions in the plant are corrected and that employees are following the work rules specified in manuals and instructions. Lessons learned from accidents are incorporated into standards, and much of the emphasis in the design of new plants and work rules is on implementing these standards. Often, the standards are enforced by the government through occupational safety and health legislation.

In contrast, system safety is concerned primarily with new systems. The concept of loss is treated much more broadly: Relevant losses may include injury to nonemployees; damage to equipment, property, or the environment; and loss of mission. As has been seen, instead of making changes as a result of operational experience with the system, system safety attempts to identify potential hazards before the system is designed, to define and incorporate safety design criteria, and to build safety into the design before the system becomes operational. Although standards are used in system safety, reliance on standards is often inadequate for new types of systems, and more emphasis is placed on upfront analysis and designing for safety.

There have been a few attempts to incorporate system safety techniques and approaches into traditional industrial safety programs, especially when new plants and processes are being built. Although system safety techniques are considered "overkill" for many industrial safety problems [140], larger plants and increasingly dangerous processes have raised concern about injuries to people outside the plant and have made system safety approaches more relevant. Furthermore, with the increase in size and cost of plant equipment, changes and retrofits to increase safety are costly and may require discontinuing operations for a period of time.

From the other side, system safety is increasingly considering issues that have been traditionally thought to be industrial safety concerns. In some cases, the neglect of these issues has caused serious losses:

> Over a period of two years, a contractor experienced 26 satellite damaging mishaps during manufacturing! Twice they hit it with a forklift. Twice more they hit it with a crane hook. Wrenches were dropped into the satellite. Makeshift workstands failed. It appeared as if there were forces bent on destroying the satellite before it got to the launch site. Investigation revealed that the System Safety activity never had addressed the manufacturing phase of the program because the phase was covered by existing industrial safety activities [5, p.5-22].

In summary, industrial safety activities are designed to protect workers in an industrial environment; extensive standards are imposed by federal codes or regulations providing for a safe workplace. However, few, if any, of these codes apply to protection of the product being manufactured. With the relatively recent introduction of robots into the manufacturing environment, the traditional concerns of industrial safety and system safety, along with new concerns about software and computers, have become intertwined.

8.5.2 Reliability Engineering

In the years following World War II, the growth in military electronics gave rise to reliability engineering. One study in the late 1940s revealed that only one-third of U.S. military electronic equipment was available at any given time—the remaining two thirds was under repair [337]. Electronic reliability improved greatly in the 1950s when vacuum tubes were replaced by transistors, and this trend has continued. Reliability was also important to NASA and our space efforts, as evidenced by the high failure rate of space missions in the late 1950s and early 1960s.

> **Definition.** *Reliability* is the characteristic of an item expressed by the probability that it will perform its required function in the specified manner over a given time period and under specified or assumed conditions.

Reliability engineering is concerned primarily with failures and failure rate reduction [108]. The reliability engineering approach to safety thus concentrates on failure as the cause of accidents.

Reliability engineers use a variety of techniques to minimize component failures and thereby the failures of complex systems caused by component failure. Some reliability engineering design techniques are discussed further in later chapters; briefly these techniques include

- □ **Parallel redundancy:** The same functions are performed by two or more components at the same time, often with some type of voting mechanism to determine which output to use. If one unit fails, the function can still be performed by the remaining unit or units.

- □ **Standby sparing:** Inoperative or idling standby units take over if an operating unit fails. In this form of series redundancy, failure detection and switchover devices are usually needed to activate the standby unit at the proper time.

- □ **Safety factors and margins:** An item is designed to be several times stronger than is necessary to withstand the expected stress. This type of overdesign is most appropriate for reducing structural failures and mechanical equipment failures.

- □ **Derating:** The maximum operational stress ratings of components are reduced. Failures occur in electronic components under specific conditions and stresses; reducing the stress level under which components are used will reduce their failure rates. This approach is the equivalent for electronic equipment of the safety factors approach used for structures and mechanical equipment.

- □ **Screening:** Components are eliminated that pass operating tests for certain parameters but with indications that they will fail within an unacceptable time.

- □ **Timed replacements:** Components are replaced before they wear out.

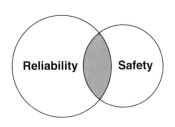

FIGURE 8.1
Safety and reliability are overlapping, but are not identical.

While these techniques are often effective in increasing reliability, they do not necessarily increase safety. In fact, their use under some conditions may actually reduce safety. For example, increasing the burst-pressure to working-pressure ratio of a tank often introduces new dangers of an explosion or chemical reaction in the event of a rupture [296]. System safety hazard analyses look at these interactions and not just at failures or engineering strengths.

Reliability engineers often assume that reliability and safety are synonymous, but this assumption is true only in special cases. In general, safety has a broader scope than failures, and failures may not compromise safety. There is obviously an overlap between reliability and safety (Figure 8.1), but many accidents occur without any component failure—the individual components were operating exactly as specified or intended, that is, without failure. The opposite is also true—components may fail without a resulting accident.

Accidents may be caused by equipment operation outside the parameters and time limits upon which the reliability analyses are based. Therefore, a system may have high reliability and still have accidents. In addition, generalized probabilities and reliability analyses may not apply to specific, localized areas: The probability of a bird strike causing an aircraft accident, for example, is much higher at Midway Island than at most other places. Most important, accidents are often not the result of a simple combination of component failures.

Safety is an emergent property that arises at the system level when components are operating together. The events leading to an accident may be a complex combination of equipment failure, faulty maintenance, instrumentation and control problems, human actions, and design errors. Reliability analysis considers only the possibility of accidents related to failures; it does not investigate potential damage that could result from *successful* operation of the individual components.

Consider an accident that occurred in a batch chemical reactor in England [162]. The design of this system is shown in Figure 8.2. The computer was responsible for controlling the flow of catalyst into the reactor and also the flow of water into the reflux condenser to cool off the reaction. Additionally, sensor in-

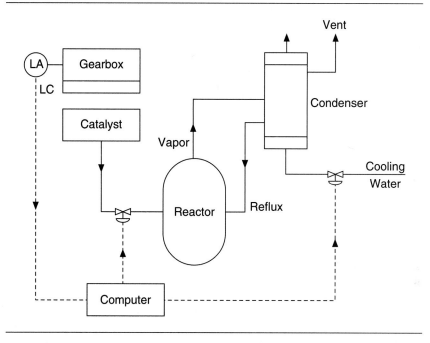

FIGURE 8.2
A chemical reactor design. (Source: Trevor Kletz, Human problems with computer control, *Plant/Operations Progress*, 1(4), October 1982. Reproduced by permission of the American Institute of Chemical Engineers. ©1982 AIChE. All rights reserved.)

puts to the computer were supposed to warn of any problems in various parts of the plant. The programmers were told that if a fault occurred in the plant, they were to leave all controlled variables as they were and to sound an alarm. On one occasion, the computer received a signal telling it that there was a low oil level in a gearbox. The computer reacted as the requirements specified: It sounded an alarm and left the controls as they were. By coincidence, a catalyst had just been added to the reactor, and the computer had just started to increase the cooling-water flow to the reflux condenser; the flow was therefore kept at a low rate. The reactor overheated, the relief valve lifted, and the contents of the reactor were discharged into the atmosphere.

This accident was a result of a sequence of events, none of which involved a component failure. The individual components worked as specified, but together they created a hazardous system state. Reliability uses a bottom-up approach to evaluate the effect of component failures on system function, while safety requires a top-down approach that evaluates how hazardous states can occur from a combination of both incorrect and correct component behavior, such as proper behavior of a component at an improper time or under the wrong environmental conditions.

Hammer provides another example that involves a nonpropulsive attachment (NPA) once used on the U.S. Navy's Sidewinder missile [108]. The NPA was made to fit on the end of the missile's rocket motor: it looked like an automobile piston with four equidistant holes bored around its side. If the motor accidentally ignited while the missile was in storage, being transported, or being installed on an aircraft, the NPA would direct the exhaust gases out at right angles rather than straight back, making the missile unmovable. The NPA had almost perfect reliability; it never failed to work. Unfortunately, sometimes the ordnance personnel forgot to remove the NPAs after they had hung the missiles under the wing of the launch aircraft. When the pilots tried to launch the missiles in flight, "the hot gas discharge hit the wings and caused damage so severe that the planes had to be abandoned" [108, p.79]. After the third aircraft was lost this way, the Navy eliminated the use of the NPA.

Reliability engineering has an important role to play in reducing random failures in hardware. But these techniques will not necessarily increase safety unless they are specifically applied to reduce the likelihood of the component failures that lead to hazards. And sometimes measures taken to increase individual component reliability will reduce safety, that is, the qualities may conflict.

A pistol is a common example of a highly reliable but frequently unsafe product. Another example of a conflict between reliability and safety are missile launch mechanisms where increased reliability may increase the probability of an inadvertent launch. Weaver notes that the more reliable a channel configuration is for its intended purpose, the more likely is its spurious operation [349]. In some cases, spurious activation may be as dangerous as a failure of the system to function. The Ranger 6 mission failure is an example of this phenomenon.

The purpose of the Ranger moon missions in the 1960s was to take high-resolution photographs of potential landing sites for the Apollo missions. Redundancy was used in the television cameras, but this redundancy was not effective unless there were also redundant power supplies and triggering circuits to turn on the power supplies. Ranger 6 had a spurious activation during takeoff, caused by plasma shorting out pins in a test circuit of the triggering device for the television's command circuit. As a result of this spurious activation, the power supplies were depleted by the time Ranger 6 reached the moon and pictures could not be taken. This failure was caused by the redundancy in the design [349].

But while reliability engineering cannot replace system safety, it can supplement it. In these circumstances, it must be used with a clear understanding that the goal is to improve a system's tolerance to hazardous random failures. While many accidents are not caused by such failures, they do contribute to some accidents. It is, of course, better to design the system so that individual random failures cannot lead to an accident even if they do occur, but this is not always possible.

In addition, care needs to be taken when applying reliability assessment techniques to safety. Since accidents are not necessarily caused by events that can be measured this way, it should not be used as a measure of risk. Reliability

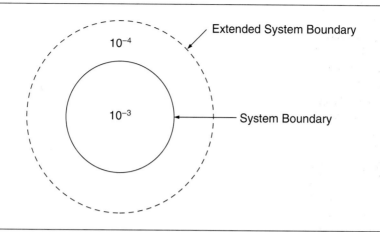

FIGURE 8.3
The bounding and resolution problem in system modeling. (Source: W. E. Veseley, F. F. Goldberg, N. H. Roberts, and D. F. Haasl. *Fault Tree Handbook*, Technical Report NUREG-0492, U.S. Nuclear Regulatory Commission, Washington, D.C., 1981, pages I–7.)

assessment measures the probability of random failures—not the probability of hazards or accidents. Also, if a design error is found in a system, safety will be more effectively enhanced by removing the design error than by measuring it in order to convince someone that it will never cause an accident. In the case of the batch reactor, if the scenario that unfolded had been known and therefore could have been included in a system reliability assessment, then the engineers would simply have changed the design to require opening the water valve before the catalyst valve, rather than attempting to measure its probability. High reliability numbers do not guarantee safety, and safety need not require ultrahigh reliability.

The major drawbacks in reliability models are often not what they include but what they do *not* include. Vesely and his co-authors provide an example of the bounding and resolution problem in reliability modeling (Figure 8.3):

> The solid inner circle represents our system boundary inside of which we are considering events whose probabilities of occurrence are, say, of order 10^{-3} or greater. If the system boundaries were extended (dotted circle), we include, in addition, events whose probabilities of occurrence were, say of order 10^{-4} or greater. By designing two-fold redundancy into our restricted system (solid circle) we could reduce event probabilities there to the order of $(10^{-3})(10^{-3}) = 10^{-6}$ but then the probabilities of events that we are ignoring become overriding, and we are suffering under the delusion that our system is two orders of magnitude safer or more reliable than it actually is.

When due consideration is not devoted to matters such as this, the naive reliability calculator will often produce such absurd numbers as 10^{-16} or 10^{-18}. The low numbers simply say that the system is not going to fail by the ways considered but instead is going to fail at a much higher probability in a way not considered [344, pp. I-7].

As a concrete example, the failure frequency of a fuse is approximately 10^{-6} or 10^{-7} per year. However, the fuse can be poorly calibrated or replaced by a copper wire that relieves the operator from having to replace it. The frequency of this latter error has been estimated as 10^{-3}. Concentrating only on the failure rates of the fuse will give an unrealistic estimate of the risk [168].

Absurd risk estimates based on failure rates are not uncommon. Until recently, the record appeared to be a risk assessment in a liquified natural gas study that came up with an accident probability of 10^{-53} [341]. This record was broken when a study of a nuclear weapon safety problem (the inadvertent delivery of a unique signal over a communication line) calculated the probability of this event at 2.8×10^{-397} [133]. Considering that the probability of being struck by a falling plane is 10^{-7} to 10^{-8} [341], the absurdity of these computations become obvious.

> In my view, risk analysis of the type considered here is to safety what the merry-go-round is to transport. We can spend a lot of time and money on it, only to go round and round in circles without really getting anywhere [195, p.250].

These limitations do not mean that reliability assessments are not useful—treating all events as equally unlikely can lead to a nonoptimal allocation of resources. Reliability assessments based on hardware failure rates provide information about which random events are most likely and therefore where failure reduction resources should be applied to reduce hazardous random hardware failures. But assessing failure rates should not be confused with assessing hazards or risk of accidents. One of the founders of system safety, C.O. Miller, cautioned that "distinguishing hazards from failures is implicit in understanding the difference between safety and reliability" [223]. Chapter 9 carefully defines and differentiates these and other basic concepts in system safety.

PART THREE

Definitions and Models

"When I use a word," Humpty Dumpty said, in rather a scornful tone, "it means just exactly what I choose it to mean—neither more nor less."

—Lewis Carroll
Through the Looking Glass

Solutions to problems are based on definitions and underlying models of the problem and its causes. To select solutions and to develop new ones, we must understand these underlying concepts. This third part of the book attempts to provide a basic set of terms to help us communicate and to examine the models of accidents and human error that are the basis of proposed approaches and techniques for reducing accidents.

Terminology

Defining concepts is frequently treated by scientists as an annoying necessity to be completed as quickly and thoughtlessly as possible. A consequence of this disinclination to define is often research carried out like surgery performed with dull instruments. The surgeon has to work harder, the patient to suffer more, and the chances for success are decreased.

—Russell L. Ackoff
Towards a System of Systems Concepts

As in most new fields, terms in system safety are not used consistently. Differences exist among countries and industries. The confusion is compounded by the use of the same terms, but with different definitions, by engineering, computer science, and natural language. The goal of this chapter is to establish the definitions of a few basic terms that are used in this book—*failure, accident, hazard, risk*, and *safety*—and to differentiate safety from related qualities.

An attempt is made in this book to be consistent with engineering terminology even though the definitions may conflict with computer science usage; the goal of this book is to enhance communication and to deal with systems in general, including those containing computers. When computer scientists redefine standard engineering terms, a great deal of confusion and misunderstanding often results, which can lead indirectly to accidents or to ineffective procedures to increase safety.

9.1 Failure and Error

> **Definition.** *Reliability* is the probability that a piece of equipment or component will perform its intended function satisfactorily for a prescribed time and under stipulated environmental conditions.

Unreliability is the probability of failure. Therefore,

> **Definition.** *Failure* is the nonperformance or inability of the system or component to perform its intended function for a specified time under specified environmental conditions.

A distinction is often made between two causes of failure in physical devices. A failure may be caused by design flaws—the intended, designed and constructed behavior does not satisfy the system goal. This type of failure is sometimes called a *systemic failure*. Alternatively, a failure may result from a deviation from the originally designed behavior—the operation does not follow the original design, perhaps because of environmental disturbances or changes in the structure or design such as wear-out or degradation over time. Both of these types will be categorized as failures here and qualified (normally by denoting the mechanism behind the failure) if necessary.

> **Definition.** An *error* is a design flaw or deviation from a desired or intended state.

Note that a failure is defined as an event (a behavior) while an error is a static condition (a state).[1] A failure occurs at a particular instant in time; an error remains until removed, usually through some sort of human intervention. Abstractions, models, designs, diagrams, programs, and other things that do not operate (but have states) can be erroneous, but they do not fail. Failures occur when designs are realized in concrete devices and the devices are operated. An error or erroneous state may lead to an operational failure (inability of the system to perform its expected function). A failure, in turn, may lead to an erroneous system state.

Software itself does not fail; it is a design for a machine, not a machine or a physical device. However, the computer on which the software is executing may fail, either because of problems in the computer hardware or errors in the software being executed on that hardware. Computer hardware failures may, in turn, be wear-out failures or systemic failures (resulting from computer hardware design errors). Software-related computer failures are always systemic.

Engineers distinguish between a *fault* and a *failure*, but they use the term *fault* differently than it is used in computer science. In engineering, failures are

---

[1] The one intentional exception to this distinction here is the use of the term *human error*. This term is too ingrained in our language and in psychology to try to make it match the engineering definition of error.

basic abnormal occurrences such as a burned-out bearing in a pump or a short circuit in an amplifier [344]. If a relay fails to close properly when a voltage is impressed across its terminals, then this event is a relay failure. Faults, on the other hand, are higher-order events. If the relay closes at the wrong time due to the improper functioning of some upstream component, then the relay has not failed but untimely relay operation may well cause the entire circuit to enter an unsatisfactory state—this event is called a fault. In general, *all failures are faults, but not all faults are failures*. For example, the relay closing when it should not is a fault. If the fault was caused by a problem within the relay itself, it is also a failure. If the valve fault was due to a spurious signal from a shorted amplifier, then this fault does not involve a failure of the valve (although the amplifier did fail).

Vesely and colleagues [344] provide another example taken from one of the earliest battles of the American Civil War. General Beauregard sent a message to one of his officers via mounted messenger #1. Some time later, the overall situation changed, and he sent out an amended message via mounted messenger #2. Still later, he sent a further amended message via mounted messenger #3. All messengers arrived, but in the wrong order. No failure occurred, but the events had a deleterious effect on the progress of the battle. This is an example of a fault that does not involve a failure.

Frequently, a distinction is also made between primary faults, secondary faults, and command faults [217]. In a *primary fault* (and failure), a component fails within the design envelope or environment. This type of failure occurs in an environment and under a loading for which the component is qualified—such as a pressure vessel bursting at less than the design pressure. Most often, this type of failure is caused by defective design, manufacture, or construction. It may also be caused by excessive or unanticipated wear or by improper maintenance and replacement policy.

Secondary faults (and failures) occur when components fail because of excessive environmental stresses that exceed the requirements specification or design environment. They occur in an environment or under a loading for which the component is not qualified—such as a pressure vessel failing because of excessive pressure for which it was not designed. Such failures occur randomly and are characterized by constant failure rates.

Command faults involve the inadvertent operation of the component because of a failure of a control element—the component operates correctly, but at the wrong time or place [217]. For example, the pressure vessel might lose pressure through the inadvertent opening of a relief valve, even though there is no excessive pressure. If the valve opened because of an erroneous signal, there was a command fault.

These types of failures and faults can be interpreted in the same way for computers. If the computer fault or failure is due to problems with the underlying hardware, then the analogies are obvious. If the computer fault is related to the software, then primary faults occur when software errors result in the computer output not meeting its specification; secondary faults occur when the computer

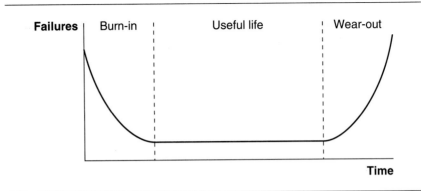

FIGURE 9.1
"Bathtub" model of reliability for electronic components, so-called because of its shape. Mechanical components tend not to exhibit the same type of constant failure rates over most of their lifetime and thus are more V-shaped.

gets inputs that differ from what was anticipated and designed for; and command faults occur when the computer responds to erroneous inputs that are expected but occur at the wrong time or in the wrong order.

A third and final distinction is often made among three different types of equipment failures (Figure 9.1):

- **Early failures** occur during a *debugging* or *burn-in* period and are due to poor assemblies or to weak, substandard components that fail soon after system startup. These failures are gradually eliminated, with a resulting decrease in failure rate until the failure rate reaches a fairly constant level. Software-related computer failures also exhibit early high failure rates, which decrease after testing and use in an operational environment. Early failure patterns may recur when the software is modified. Early software-related computer faults or failures are often due to incorrect assumptions about the operating environment.

- **Random** or **chance failures** result from complex, uncontrollable, and sometimes unknown causes. The period during which malfunctions are due primarily to random failures is the *useful life* of the component or system. The failure rate during this time is often assumed to be constant. The application of hardware reliability models to computers in order to measure operational software reliability assumes that random failures exist for software too. This assumption is based on the argument that inputs leading to computer failures or faults are encountered randomly in the input space. Note that the application of these models to the software alone makes no sense: Reliability measurement applies only when the software is executed on a particular computer; for example, differences in computer hardware can change timing and other performance characteristics.

□ **Wearout failures** begin when the components are past their useful life: The malfunction rate increases sharply in old age. This type of failure does occur in computers, but it is due primarily to hardware failures. Some computer scientists argue that software modification and maintenance cause the computer failure rate to increase after a while, but this mechanism is not what engineers describe as wearout; instead, software maintenance errors are more closely related to early failures in hardware. In fact, every time software is modified, it can be thought of as having a new design that must undergo another burn-in period. Frequently modified software may never get beyond exhibiting early failure behavior.

9.2 Accident and Incident

Definition. An *accident* is an undesired and unplanned (but not necessarily unexpected) event that results in (at least) a specified level of loss.

There are several important aspects of this definition. First, an accident is *undesired*, and because it is undesired, it is also *unplanned* or *unintentional*, although it may or may not be foreseen: What is possibly planned are prevention and remedial measures. Natural language usage of the term *accident* does sometimes imply something that is unforeseen, but engineering usage does not. We can foresee or expect automobile accidents, but they are not planned or desired. In natural language, the term *accident* can also mean something that is unavoidable, although again this meaning is not used in engineering. Many accidents are avoidable, although they may not be avoided for various reasons. The use of the qualifier *unplanned* excludes events caused by hostile action (such as sabotage).

Second, an accident results in a *specified level of loss*, which implies that there must be some type of damage to life, property, or the environment. The damage may be immediate, or it may be long term and only affect future generations. What level of loss is significant enough to be labeled an accident is subjective. Thus, what is an accident for a particular system must be defined, just as correct or expected behavior must be defined. Sometimes the definition of a specific type and level of loss is provided by the government; at other times, it is provided by the commissioner, builder, or user of the system. Sometimes distinctions are made between different levels of loss, such as catastrophic accidents, serious accidents, and minor accidents.

Finally, an accident is defined as a *loss event*, without placing limits on the type of event. Occasionally, an accident is defined in terms of causal mechanisms (for example, as a loss of control of an energy source) or a limited type of event (such as an unwanted or uncontrolled release of energy). In providing definitions of engineering terms, it is important not to limit the possible solution space of a problem by the definition itself. By defining an accident in terms of uncontrolled energy, certain types of events are excluded, such as energy deficiencies (suffocation) or toxic exposures. To include harmful exposures, the Department of Defense uses *mishap* instead of *accident*. But this new term just substitutes a different model—it defines an accident as an unwanted or uncontrolled release of energy or a toxic exposure while excluding other types of accidents that are not necessarily of concern in military systems. Accident models are discussed further in the next chapter.

The definition of an accident event is important because it influences the approach taken to increase safety. For example, if an accident is defined as an unwanted or uncontrolled release of energy, then prevention measures should focus on energy controls and barriers between the possibly harmful energy flow and the things that can be damaged by it. If the accident is defined in terms of a different underlying mechanism or model, then other approaches to preventing losses are viable. To avoid limiting solutions by the definition, an accident is defined here without any limitation on the type of loss event considered.

An incident can be differentiated from an accident.

Definition. A *near miss* or *incident* is an event that involves no loss (or only minor loss) but with the potential for loss under different circumstances.

For example, a release of a toxic substance that dissipates in the air causing no harm is an incident, not an accident. It might have led to an accident given different circumstances, such as people being in the vicinity or different wind or weather conditions. Natural language is fairly imprecise about this distinction, but it is important in engineering and leads to the concept of a hazard.

9.3 Hazard

To prevent accidents, something must be known about their precursors, and these precursors must be under the control of the system designer. To satisfy these requirements, system safety uses the concept of a *hazard*.

A hazard has been defined in various ways. Some define it as an inherent property of an object, substance, or system that has the potential to cause harm—such as chlorine or a falling rock. Others note that the substance itself is not the hazard; rather the hazard is a set of conditions (a state) associated with that substance. Chlorine, for example, is not harmful if it is properly contained, but it may become harmful if it is released in significant quantity into the air. Similarly, water is not a hazard, but it is easy to think of combinations of conditions in which it could lead to death by drowning, scalding, or automobile accident [194].

Occasionally, a hazard is defined as an event (such as an explosion), but for various technical reasons, it will be defined as a state here. There is no significant difference, since states can be thought of as leading to events, which in turn create new states. Thus, there is no important difference in defining the hazard as, say, the system exploding or as the system having explosive energy.

The problem with the usual definition of a hazard—something that has the potential to do harm or that can lead to an accident—is that most every state, given certain conditions, has the potential to do harm or can lead to an accident. An airplane that is in the air is in a hazardous state, but there is little that the designer of an air traffic control system, for example, can do about designing a system where planes never leave the ground.

Considering these factors, the definition to be used here is

> **Definition.** A *hazard* is a state or set of conditions of a system (or an object) that, together with other conditions in the environment of the system (or object), will lead inevitably to an accident (loss event).

There are some things to note about this definition.

■ *A hazard is defined with respect to the environment of the system or component.*

In most cases, accidents involve the environment within which a component or system exists. As an example, the release of toxic material or explosive energy will cause a loss only if there are people or structures in the vicinity. Weather conditions may also affect whether a loss occurs in the case of a toxic release. If the appropriate environmental conditions do not exist, then there is no loss and, by definition, no accident.

The only exception is a physical system where the boundaries have been drawn such that they include the object that is damaged plus all the conditions necessary for the loss. Note that, by definition, the latter case cannot happen for software since it is not a physical object, only an abstraction. Thus, software by itself is not safe or unsafe, although it could theoretically become unsafe when executed on a computer. But even then, there are few hazards that are inherent in the computer system itself since computers do little besides generate electronic signals. They can catch fire or fall on someone, but these hazards normally have nothing to do with the software design. Thus, we can only talk about the safety of software and its hazards in the context of the particular system design within which it is being used. Otherwise, the hazards associated with software do not exist. That there are no inherent software hazards is one of the reasons that many system safety engineers prefer the term *software system safety* to *software safety*.

■ *What constitutes a hazard depends upon where the boundaries of the system are drawn.*

A system is an abstraction, and therefore the boundaries of the system can be drawn anywhere the person who is defining the system wants. The boundaries, in turn, determine which conditions are considered part of the hazard and which are considered part of the environment. Since this choice is arbitrary, it is most useful to define the boundaries (and thus the hazard) in such a way that safeguards can be implemented within the constraints of also achieving the basic mission and other system goals: The system boundaries should be drawn to include the conditions related to an accident over which the system designer has some control. At the extreme, they can be drawn to include all conditions involved in the accident, but drawing the boundaries in this way would serve no purpose since many of these conditions are not controllable by the designer. Normally, we try to define a system we are building in such a way that we have control over the states.

Sometimes, an accident is defined as the non-accomplishment of the system mission or the loss of the system itself, such as the loss of a spacecraft. Even in these cases, the loss may involve environmental variables (for example, electromagnetic particles) over which the designer has little control beyond attempting to shield the system against them.

As an example of how to define hazards and system boundaries, consider an air traffic control system. If an accident is defined as a collision between two aircraft, then an appropriate hazard is the lack of minimum separation between aircraft. The designer of a collision avoidance system or a more general air traffic control system theoretically has control over the separation between aircraft, but may not have control over other factors that determine whether two aircraft that get close together actually collide (such as the weather conditions or the state of mind or attentiveness of the pilots). As noted earlier, a hazard can be defined as two planes being in the same air space, but this definition is not useful as the state is inevitable and cannot be avoided. For practical reasons, we need to define hazards as the states we want to avoid.

As another example, for flammable mixtures to catch fire or explode, there must be both air and a source of ignition. Kletz argues that when flammable gases or vapors are handled on an industrial scale and mixed with air in flammable concentrations, experience shows that sources of ignition are likely to turn up [154]. Therefore, the only safe rule is to assume that mixtures of flammable vapor in air in the explosive range will sooner or later catch fire or explode and should never be deliberately permitted, except under carefully defined circumstances where the risk is accepted. Using this argument, the hazard might be defined as a mixture of vapor in air (and not the ignition source), since those are the only two of the three necessary conditions over which control can be exercised.

In summary, the definition of a hazard is arbitrary, and one of the first steps in designing a system is to decide what conditions will be considered to be hazards that need to be eliminated or controlled.

Occasionally, it is useful to classify hazards as *endogenous* or *exogenous* [208]. An endogenous hazard is caused by defects in design, material, workmanship, or operating procedures—that is, by factors inherent in the system or device itself. In contrast, an exogenous hazard is brought about by phenomena external to the system, such as lightning or cosmic radiation.

A hazard has two important characteristics: (1) *severity* (sometimes called *damage*) and (2) *likelihood* of occurrence. Hazard *severity* is defined as the worst possible accident that could result from the hazard given the environment in its most unfavorable state.

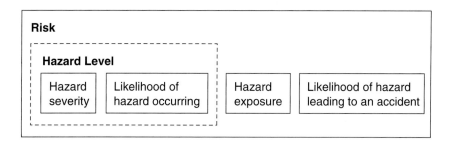

FIGURE 9.2
The components of risk.

The hazard *likelihood* of occurrence can be specified either qualitatively or quantitatively. Unfortunately, when the system is being designed and hazards are being evaluated for potential tradeoffs and ranked as to which should be eliminated first, the information needed to evaluate the likelihood accurately is almost never available. For a few hazards associated with standard designs, historical data is available. For the rest, qualitative evaluation of likelihood is usually the best that can be done.

The combination of severity and likelihood of occurrence is often called the *hazard level*. Hazard level, along with two other factors related to hazards, are used in the definition of risk.

9.4 Risk

Definition. *Risk* is the *hazard level* combined with (1) the likelihood of the hazard leading to an accident (sometimes called *danger*) and (2) hazard exposure or duration (sometimes called *latency*).

Sometimes risk is limited to the relationship between the hazard and the accident (the likelihood of the hazard leading to an accident but not the likelihood of the hazard occurring). In this book, the more inclusive definition is used (Figure 9.2).

Exposure or *duration* of a hazard is a component of risk: Since an accident involves a coincidence of conditions, of which the hazard is just one, the longer the hazardous state exists, the greater the chance that the other prerequisite conditions will occur. The coincidence of conditions necessary for an accident may be a statistically low-probability event, but the probability of coincidence can be dramatically increased if the hazard is present over long periods [274].

As an example of the definition of risk, if a computer has a control function, such as controlling the movement of a robot, a very simple model [61] defines risk as a function of the

1. Probability the computer causes a spurious or unexpected machine movement
2. Probability a human is in the field of movement
3. Probability the human has no time to move or will fail to diagnose the robot failure
4. Severity of worst-case consequences

If the computer has a continuous protective or monitoring function, along with a requirement to initiate some safety function upon detection of a potentially hazardous condition, then another example risk definition is a function of the

1. Probability of a dangerous plant condition arising
2. Probability of the computer not detecting it
3. Probability of the computer not initiating its safety function
4. Probability of the safety function not preventing the hazard
5. Probability of conditions occurring that will cause the hazard to lead to an accident
6. Worst-case severity of the accident

If it is assumed that all of these events are independent, the probabilities could be multiplied together, but this assumption is normally not realistic and a more complex relationship and computation are required. For example, the probability of a person being in the field of movement of a robot may be higher if the robot is behaving strangely—the operator may have approached in order to investigate. A more sophisticated model also would include such factors as the exposure time of the hazard (the average time to detection and repair).

In almost all cases, the correct way to combine the elements of the risk function is unknown, as are the values of the parameters of the function. In addition, agreement has not been reached on how to combine probability and severity and other nonprobabilistic factors such as exposure time. Finally, how can an event that is catastrophic but very unlikely be compared with another event that is much more likely but less serious? Ad hoc quantitative methods could be devised to make this comparison, but, in the end, the process must necessarily involve qualitative judgment and personal values and is therefore trans-scientific.

Sometimes the terms *risk analysis* and *hazard analysis* are used interchangeably, but an important distinction exists. *Hazard analysis* (as defined here) involves only the identification of hazards and the assessment of hazard level, while *risk analysis* adds the identification and assessment of the environmental conditions along with exposure or duration. Thus, hazard analysis is a subset of risk analysis.

As has been discussed earlier, risk (or safety) is sometimes confused with reliability, and reliability measurement is often used incorrectly as a measure of risk. Reliability is a component property, whereas safety or risk cannot be defined or measured without considering the environment. As an example, we can talk about the reliability of a pistol (the probability that it will fire when the trigger is pulled), but to talk about the "risk of the pistol" is meaningless by itself. Consider a pistol being fired in the middle of an uninhabited forest versus being fired in the middle of a crowded shopping mall. The reliability in each situation has not changed and neither has the pistol, but the risk or safety of the two situations is very different. In fact, if the reliability of the pistol is relatively high (as it usually is), it becomes an almost inconsequential factor in assessing the risk in these two situations; reliability, in this case, is swamped by the other factors involved in calculating the risk of injury.

While it is indisputably true that reliability is a factor in safety or risk and thus should be included in risk assessments, other factors may be equally or even more important. However, because component failure is the most convenient thing to measure, we often use it as *the* measure of risk or assign it too much importance in risk assessments. Most accidents in complex systems involve factors other than single component failure.

9.5 Safety

Safety is defined in this book in an absolute sense:

Definition. *Safety* is freedom from accidents or losses.

Some people have argued that there is no such thing as absolute safety, and therefore safety should be defined in terms of acceptable loss. William Lowrance is usually credited with originating this alternative definition: "We will define safety as a judgment of the acceptability of risk, and risk, in turn, as a measure of the probability and severity of harm to human health. A thing is safe if its attendant risks are judged to be acceptable" [197].

Lowrance himself raises questions about this definition: What is meant by "acceptable" risk? To whom is the risk posed? By whom is it judged acceptable? A condition that is acceptable to an employer may not be acceptable to the employee and vice versa. These questions lead to endless arguments about what level or type of loss is "acceptable."

One can envision safety, like other qualities, along a continuum, with one end being freedom from losses and the continuum stretching toward increasing loss (Figure 9.3). If "safe" is not at the left end of the continuum, then where should it be? That question is trans-scientific, as argued in Chapter 1, and, in general, definitions of engineering terms should not involve trans-scientific concepts. To avoid the hopeless quagmire of arguments about acceptability, it is simplest to put safety at the left end of the continuum and then determine how close one comes to that ideal.

In fact, many qualities are ideals that can only be approached asymptotically. There is no such thing as a totally secure system; anything can be compromised.

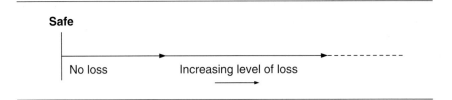

FIGURE 9.3
Safety as a continuum.

Nevertheless, that does not keep us from defining security in absolute terms. The same is true for reliability—nearly everything will break or wear out over time or under some conditions. We deal with this dilemma by defining reliability very narrowly—that is, by restricting the conditions and time under which we evaluate reliability in a particular system. The same could be done for safety; we could restrict the definition to identified hazards and conditions. But those who suffer losses are unlikely to accept that an accident did not happen (the system was safe) despite the loss, just because the specified conditions or time were exceeded or an unidentified hazard was involved.

A relative definition of safety also implies that hazards cannot be eliminated, when they often can. While, in most instances, *all* hazards cannot be eliminated, this book describes many ways that specific hazards can be totally eliminated from a product or system. Often, hazard elimination requires sacrificing some other goals or requires more knowledge and effort, especially up-front design effort, but it is not impossible. Thus, it *does* make sense to talk about absolute safety from a particular hazard. By accepting a relative definition of safety, it is possible to ignore design alternatives that eliminate or greatly reduce particular hazards but require compromises with respect to other goals.

9.6 Safety and Security

Arguments have been advanced that safety is a subset of reliability or a subset of security or a part of human engineering—usually by people in these fields. Although there are some commonalities and interactions, safety is a distinct quality and should be treated separately from other qualities, or the tradeoffs, which are often required, will be hidden from view.

Safety and security, however, are closely related, and their similarities can be used to the advantage of both in terms of borrowing effective techniques from each to deal with the other. Both qualities deal with threats or risks—one with threats to life or property and the other with threats to privacy or national security. Both often involve negative requirements or *constraints* that may conflict with some important system goals. Both involve protection against losses, although the types of losses involved may be different. Both involve global system properties that are difficult to deal with outside of a system context. Both involve requirements that are considered of supreme importance (in relation to other requirements) in deciding whether the system can and should be used—that is, particularly high levels of assurance may be needed, and testing alone is insufficient to establish those levels [170]. In fact, a higher level of assurance that a system is safe or secure may be needed than that the system performs its intended function. Finally, both qualities involve aspects of a system that are regulated by government agencies or licensing bureaus (such as the National Security Agency and the Nuclear Regulatory Commission), where approval is based on factors other than whether the system does anything useful or is economically profitable.

These shared characteristics lead to other similarities. Both may benefit from using technologies that are too costly to be applied to the system as a whole, such as formal verification, but that may be cost-effective for these limited subsets of the requirements. Both also involve problems and techniques that apply specifically to them and not to other, more general functional requirements or constraints.

Some of the techniques applicable to one are applicable to the other. For example, both can benefit from the use of barriers. For security, barriers are used to prevent malicious incursions rather than accidental ones, but the technique is the same. Other security techniques do not seem to apply to safety—for example, the use of traps to encourage attacks against hidden defenses or the randomization of limited defensive resources to reduce the expected success of planned attacks [98].

There are also important differences between safety and security. Security focuses on malicious actions, whereas safety is also concerned with well-intended actions. In addition, the primary emphasis in security traditionally has been on preventing unauthorized access to classified information, as opposed to preventing more general malicious activities. Note, however, that if an accident or loss event is defined to include unauthorized disclosure, modification, and withholding of data, then security becomes a subset of safety.

The definition of safety or security could be extended to include both qualities, but nothing appears to be gained by making this extension, while important differences become obscured. Separation of qualities to better control and understand them, to allocate limited resources, and to enforce priorities is an appropriate goal. However, attempts to integrate several qualities into one abstraction (like *dependability*, which has been proposed as a combined measure of reliability, safety, security, availability and just about every other quality) seem misguided. These global abstractions have only disadvantages, since they inhibit understanding and control. Often qualities conflict, and *de facto* tradeoffs are lost in global abstractions or measurements. For example, it is possible to increase dependability while decreasing safety without it being at all apparent that this increase in risk has occurred.

9.7 Summary

This chapter has tried to clarify some basic concepts and establish workable definitions. Agreeing on terminology is always a difficult process, but it is important for communication and progress in finding solutions to our problems: Definitions can have powerful effects on the way we express our problems and therefore how we go about solving them. Establishing a common terminology is always painful but is worth the effort in the long run.

Chapter

10

Accident and Human Error Models

Accidents on the whole are becoming less and less attributable to a single cause, more to a number of contributory factors. This is the result of the skill of the designers in anticipating trouble, but it means that when trouble does occur, it is inevitably complicated.

—DeHavilland and Walker
(after reviewing failures
of the Comet aircraft)[1]

Models provide a means of understanding complex phenomena and recording that understanding in a way that can be communicated to others. All models are abstractions—they simplify our world by abstracting away irrelevant details and focusing on the features that are assumed to be the most relevant.

The design and analysis methods used for safety-critical systems are based on particular underlying models of the accident process and of human errors. How effective our procedures are depends, to a large extent, on how accurate our models are—that is, how well they reflect the features of the environment to which they are applied. To design an effective safety program and select an appropriate set of procedures and techniques, we need to understand the models that underlie our options and the assumptions about accidents and human errors they embody.

---

[1] Quoted in [339].

185

10.1 Accident Models

Various accident models have been devised to reduce the description of an accident to a set of events and conditions that account for the outcome. The models have been used for two purposes: to understand past accidents and to learn how to prevent future ones.

Models are used in accident investigations to help identify the salient factors to be considered. The models impose patterns on an accident and thus will influence what factors are identified as causative. A model may be used as a filter in the collection of data to narrow down the investigation, or as a way to expand the investigation by forcing consideration of factors that are often omitted. In general, models are a way to organize data and set priorities in accident investigations.

A second use for models is for accident prediction—to determine what factors might be involved in future accidents so that they can be eliminated or controlled. This use assumes that there are common patterns in accidents, which the models help us to understand. In essence, predictive modeling can be thought of as investigating an accident that has not yet occurred in order to determine how to prevent it.

Because accident models influence what cause is ascribed to an accident and the countermeasures taken to prevent future accidents, the power and features of the model used will greatly affect our ability to identify and control hazards and thus prevent accidents. A very large number of models have been proposed, many of them differing only slightly. One way of understanding and comparing these models is to examine the underlying accident mechanism, the types of causal factors, and the relationship among the causal factors.

10.1.1 Basic Energy Models

The oldest and most pervasive model views accidents as the result of an uncontrolled and undesired release of energy (Figure 10.1). The energy might be ionizing or non-ionizing radiation or kinetic, chemical, thermal, electrical, acoustic, or biological energy. The type of energy is an important variable in predicting or explaining expected hazard or accident consequences and in designing safety measures.

If accidents are the result of uncontrolled energy flows, then the obvious way to reduce them is to use barriers or other flow control mechanisms. In this way, accidents are prevented by altering or controlling the path (on which the energy flows) between the energy source and the at-risk object (the potential victim). This simple model, however, does not account for many types of accidents, such as those involving suffocation.

MacFarland extended the basic energy model and described accidents as resulting either (1) from the application of specific forms of energy in amounts exceeding the resistance of the structures on which they impinge or (2) from

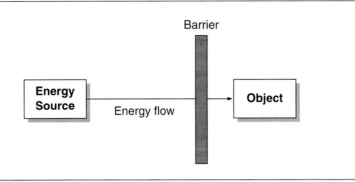

FIGURE 10.1
Simple energy model of accidents.

interference in the normal exchange of energy between an organism and its environment (including lack of oxygen and exposure to the elements) [140].

Energy can take a large number of forms and has an even larger number of potential carriers, but the energy constitutes the direct cause of injuries in this model. Accidents can be prevented by controlling the source of the energy or the carrier through which the energy reaches the body (such as bullets, boiling water, or sharp blades).

The mechanisms described so far are sufficient for accidents involving human injury but not for accidents involving property damage. A more general energy model divides accidents into two types: energy transformation and energy deficiency [119].

An *energy transformation accident* occurs when a stable or controlled form of energy is transformed in a way that damages property or injures people. For example, a fire might result when the chemical energy of gasoline is transformed into thermal energy through some form of combustion. An energy transformation accident requires both an energy source and an associated energy transformation mechanism. The mechanisms for transmitting or altering the energy may be either passive or active. Prevention of such accidents requires controlling the sources or the mechanisms of energy transformation or both.

An *energy deficiency accident* occurs when the energy needed to perform a vital function, such as powering the engines in an airplane, is not available and damage to property or injury to humans results. The energy deficiency may be either a direct or indirect cause of the accident. This type of accident requires both a need for some type of energy to perform a function essential for safety (such as brake fluid in an automobile) and an event or condition that makes the available energy insufficient to perform the function (such as a leak of brake fluid).

A final energy model divides systems into two types: those that produce energy (action systems) and those that constrain energy (nonaction systems, such as pressure vessels, buildings, and support structures) [5]. A complex system will usually consist of both action and nonaction components. Action components contribute directly to the switching and modification of energy or the operation of the system; nonaction components do not contribute to system operation but only to the support or containment of energy. The action components may include safety devices, such as relief valves or fuses, that control the buildup of energy that could exceed minimum design allowances and thus affect the nonaction components.

Hazards in action systems are controlled by imposing limitations on the operation of the system. Hazards in nonaction systems are controlled by the application of a fixed standard, design allowance, or minimum safety factor.

In all these energy models, software cannot directly cause an accident, since it does not contain energy; however, it may contribute to the release of energy when it controls or monitors the condition or state of hardware components. Two types of software may be involved: (1) command and control software that can command the hardware into a hazardous state, fail to detect the occurrence of a hazard, or even mask the occurrence of a hazard so that other monitors (such as operators) do not detect it; and (2) information systems that provide data or information used by other system components (including humans) to make safety-critical decisions.

The drawback to all of the energy models is that their scope is limited to energy processes and flows, and so may not include accidents involving nonphysical losses caused by logical errors in operation. If accidents are defined as including loss of mission, then energy models will not be sufficient. No simple mechanism can be defined for this very general definition of loss; more sophisticated models of *causal factors* are needed.

Causal factor models are useful even when the underlying mechanism is energy flow: They expand the possibilities for preventive action, beyond simply controlling the energy (or lack of energy) directly, to dealing with the conditions and events leading to the loss of energy control. Although many categorizations are possible, the following sections divide these models into single event and domino models, chain-of-events models, and models based on systems theory.

10.1.2 Domino and Single Event Models

The earliest accident models come from industrial safety and reflect the factors inherent in protecting workers against industrial accidents. From the first, hazardous conditions were recognized as causing accidents. The early focus in industrial safety on unsafe conditions (such as open blades and unprotected belts) was very successful in reducing industrial injuries. Later, the emphasis shifted from unsafe conditions to unsafe human acts. Accidents were regarded as someone's fault rather than as an event that could have been prevented by some change in the system.

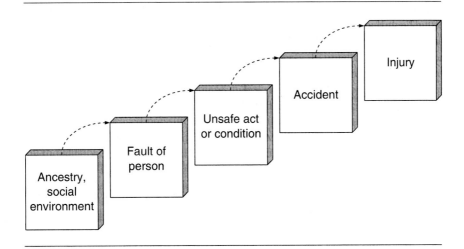

FIGURE 10.2
Heinrich's Domino Model of accidents.

Domino Models

Heinrich was one of the first to emphasize unsafe acts over unsafe conditions. In 1931, he proposed the first real accident model, in which he hypothesized that people, not things, were the cause of accidents:

> The occurrence of an injury invariably results from a completed sequence of factors, the last one of these being the injury itself. The accident which caused the injury is in turn invariably caused or permitted directly by the unsafe act of a person and/or a mechanical or physical hazard [118].

Heinrich compared the general accident sequence to five dominoes, standing on end in a line; hence, his model has become known as the domino theory of accident causation (Figure 10.2). The dominoes are labeled

1. Ancestry or social environment, leading to
2. Fault of a person, which is the proximate reason for
3. An unsafe act or condition (mechanical or physical hazard), which results in
4. An accident, which leads to
5. An injury.

When the first domino falls, it automatically knocks down its neighbor and so on until the injury occurs. Removing any of the dominoes will break the sequence and prevent the injury, but Heinrich argued that the easiest and most effective domino to remove was the third one, representing an unsafe act or condition. Heinrich's model has been very influential, and accident investigators often look for the one unsafe act or condition that caused the accident in order to remove it and, hopefully, prevent future accidents.

To see the problem with the domino theory, consider the following simple industrial accident [261]. A worker climbs on a ladder, which breaks, and the worker falls. The unsafe act here would be identified as climbing the ladder, and the unsafe condition would be a defective ladder. A solution might be to get rid of the defective ladder. However, limiting the identified causal factors limits the potential solutions. Symptoms may be removed while root (level three) causes remain. Petersen suggests that, in the ladder example, an investigator should go beyond identifying an unsafe act or condition and ask why the defective ladder was not found during normal inspections, why the supervisor allowed its use, why the injured worker did not know he or she should not use the ladder, and so on. Answers to such questions might lead to improved inspection procedures, improved training, and a better definition of responsibilities.[2]

Bird and Loftus extended Heinrich's domino theory to include management decisions as a factor in accidents [28]. The modified sequence of events becomes

1. Lack of control by management, permitting
2. Basic causes (personal and job factors) that lead to
3. Immediate causes (substandard practices/conditions/errors), which are the proximate cause of
4. An accident or incident, which results in
5. A loss.

In this model, the four major elements of a business operation—people, equipment, materials, and environment—individually or in combination are the factors involved in a particular accident.

Adams suggested a modified and more general management model [2] that included:

1. Management structure (objectives, organization, and operations)
2. Operational errors (management or supervisor behavior)
3. Tactical errors (caused by employee behavior and work conditions)
4. Accident or incident
5. Injury or damage to persons or property

The National Safety Council Model

In the 1950s, the National Safety Council developed a relatively sophisticated model of accidents in the home that includes background factors, initiating factors, intermediate factors, and measurable (recognizable) results (Figure 10.3) [140].

---

[2] Note that merely computing the historic probability of ladder failures might be useful for purchasing insurance, but it is not particularly useful in designing safeguards or fixing the problems associated with a particular accident or factory.

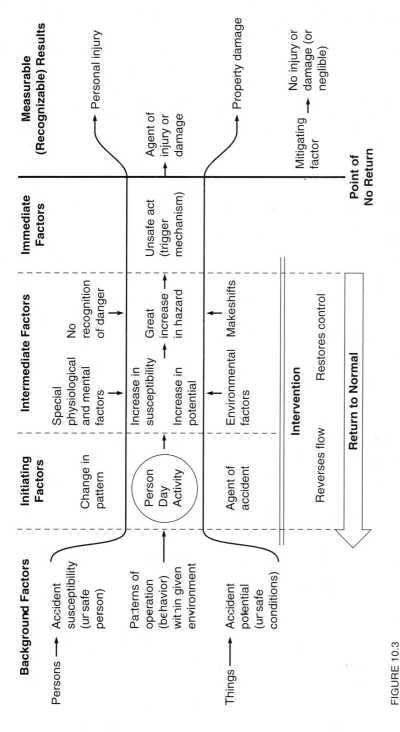

FIGURE 10.3
National Safety Council model of home accidents. (Source: Adapted from National Safety Council. *Journal of Safety Research*, June 1973. Copyright 1973, with kind permission from Elsevier Science Ltd., The Boulevard, Langford Lane, Kidlington OX5 1GB UK.)

Background factors include (1) *accident susceptibility factors* (an unsafe person), such as individual training, experience, and judgment; physiological and mental factors; intelligence; sight; hearing; health; coordination; and impairments; and (2) *accident potential factors* (unsafe conditions), such as equipment, goods, appliances, material, and automatic controls. Accident susceptibility and accident potential combine with patterns of operation (behavior) in the given environment—such as operating with or without knowledge and skill, paying attention or not paying attention, practicing good housekeeping, and operating with or without supervision.

Initiating factors include both the *agent* of the accident (such as a gas leak, grease on the floor, a flammable mixture, a curled-up rug, hot liquid, a mop on the stairs) and a *change in pattern* (such as a loud noise, a machine breakdown, a baby crying, a telephone ringing, or other distractions).

Intermediate factors include special *physiological* and *mental factors* (such as illness, emotional upset, alcohol and drugs), *environmental factors* (such as darkness or an explosive gas–air mixture), *nonrecognition of danger*, and *makeshifts*. Physiological factors, according to this model, increase susceptibility, while environmental factors increase potential.

Immediate factors are *unsafe acts* or trigger mechanisms, such as lighting a match, tripping, slipping, or spilling hot liquid. Once all these factors have combined and no intervention has occurred to reverse the flow, restore control, or return to normal procedures, the point of no return is reached. The damage may involve personal injury or property damage, and may be serious or negligible depending on various *mitigating factors* (conditions or actions that reduce or eliminate the damage or injury, such as grabbing a handrail or having someone there to catch the potential victim).

Epidemiological Models

John Gordon, in the 1940s, was one of the first to stress the multifactorial nature of accidents. He and others suggested that accidents should be viewed as a public health problem that can be handled using an epidemiological approach. In these models, accidents can be described in terms of the agent (physical energy), the environment, and the host (victim). Accidents, then, are the result of complex and random interactions between these three things and cannot be explained by consideration of only one of the three.

Two types of epidemiology have been applied [338]:

- **Descriptive epidemiology:** The general distribution of injuries in the population is described by determining the incidence, prevalence, and mortality rates for accidents in large population groups according to characteristics such as age, sex, and geographical area.
- **Investigative epidemiology:** The specific data on the causes of injuries is collected in order to devise feasible countermeasures.

The epidemiological approach assumes that some common factors are present in accidents and that these can be determined by statistical evaluation of accident data. Because specific relationships between factors are not assumed, previously unrecognized relationships can be discovered. Also, determinant as opposed to chance relationships can be distinguished [209, 25].

The validity of the conclusions from such studies relies on the quality of the database and the statistical significance of the anomalies found in the sample [126]. The data used, which is that reported by accident investigators, may be limited or filtered. Also, the sequencing and timing relationship between events and conditions is not captured in a purely statistical approach.

10.1.3 Chain-of-Events Models

The earliest accident models hypothesized a single unsafe act or condition as the cause of an accident, but these models have been discredited. The models described in the previous section include multiple causal factors and relationships among them, but not multiple events. A third type of model organizes causal factors into chains of events—for example, the driver hit the brakes, the car skidded, the car hit the tree. If the chain can be broken, then the accident will not happen. Prevention measures using this model concentrate on eliminating particular events or intervening between the events in the chain. In the example of a tank rupture shown in Figure 10.4, use of a desiccant may keep moisture out of the tank, or a mesh screen can be used to trap projected fragments.

In these models, events are often chained together into chronological sequences, with various events or conditions labeled as proximate, primary, basic, contributory, systemic, root, and so on. Unsafe acts and conditions are identified only as a starting point to learn why they were allowed to happen. The problem with this approach is that there is no real stopping point when tracing events back from an accident, yet many of the preceding events are not relevant to designing prevention procedures. For example, if the worker in the ladder example had not come to work that day, he or she would not have fallen off the ladder. In general, the selection of particular events to include is subjective.

Simple chain-of-events models have been expanded to include the relationships among events and conditions in accident sequences. Converging chains (logic trees) connected by AND/OR relationships (see Figure 10.4) are often used to describe the accident process. Countermeasures based on these accident models involve either removing the events or conditions or adding enough AND gates (required simultaneous conditions or events) that the probability of the chaining factors being realized is very low.

The Perturbation Theory of Accidents

Benner [25, 26] argues that a logic tree does not include the timing or duration of interactions in the accident process and does not provide a systematic way to

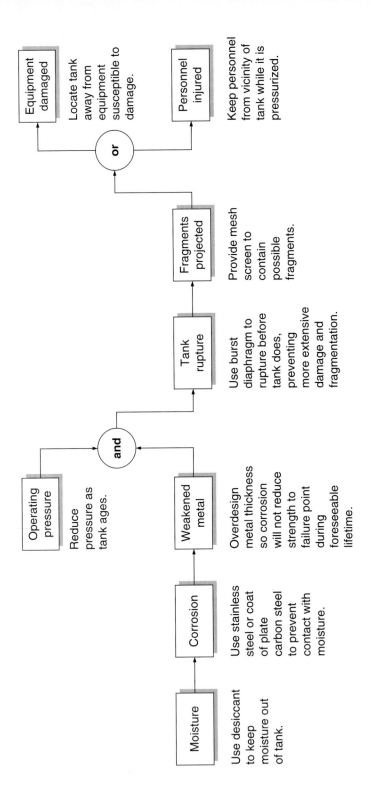

FIGURE 10.4
A model of the chain of events leading to the rupture of a pressurized tank. (Source: Adapted from Willie Hammer. *Product Safety Management and Engineering*, page 203. Englewood Cliffs, N.J.: Prentice-Hall, 1980. Reprinted with permission of Mrs. W. Hammer.)

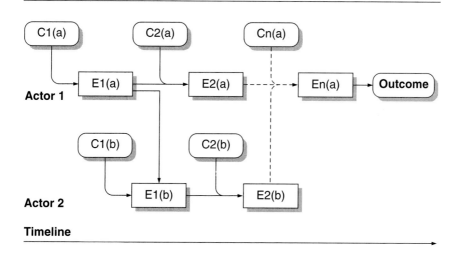

FIGURE 10.5
Multilinear Events Sequence model. (Source: Ludwig Benner, Jr. Accident investigations: Multilinear events sequencing methods. *Journal of Safety Research*, 7(2), June 1975, page 71. Copyright 1975, with kind permission from Elsevier Science Ltd., The Boulevard, Langford Lane, Kidlington, OX5 1GB UK.)

trace either (1) the behavior of each actor involved in determining the outcome of the phenomenon or (2) the relationship of that actor's actions to the actions of the other actors. In his Multilinear Events Sequence model, Benner describes accidents in terms of a succession of events, where an event is defined as one actor plus one action (Figure 10.5) [24]. He explains the accident process in terms of specific interacting actors, each acting in a sequential order with discrete temporal and spatial relationships. Accidents are modeled using parallel horizontal event tracks (with a track for each actor) with cross links to show relationships, all of which are shown above a timeline. This model can be likened to the display of performance data from an aircraft flight recorder.

The successive events require adaptive behavior or adaptive learning by the actors in order to progress toward the intended outcome in the face of varying external influences. Benner calls the external influences *perturbations* when they vary from what is usual or expected. As long as the actors adapt to the perturbations without being stressed beyond their capability to adapt or recover, stability is maintained and an accident does not result. If one of the actors fails or is unable to adapt, the perturbation initiates an accident sequence (Figure 10.6). From that event onward, the event sequence may overstress an actor, causing injury or damage, which in turn may initiate other changes or energy releases that overstress subsequently exposed actors, resulting in cascading injury or damage. Until the actors are able to accommodate the stresses without further harm, the accident

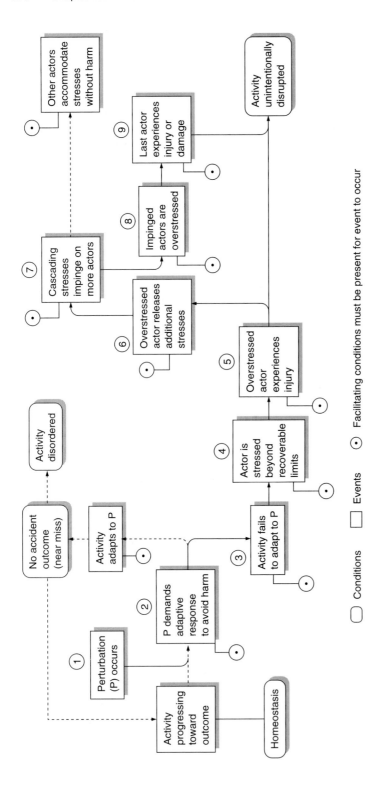

FIGURE 10.6

The Perturbation (P) model of accidents. (Source: Ludwig Benner, Jr. Accident investigations: Multilinear events sequencing methods, *Journal of Safety Research*, 7(2), June 1975, page 69. Copyright 1975 with kind permission from Elsevier Science Ltd., The Boulevard, Langford Lane, Kidlington OX5 1GB UK.)

continues toward its outcome, governed by the condition of the actors, the events, and the laws of nature. If the actors adapt to the perturbation at any time before injury occurs, there will be no accident, even though the activity may be "disordered." Benner calls this model the P (for *perturbation*) theory of accidents.

According to Benner, this model enhances the ability to select countermeasures, since it supplements the principle of intervening between events in a sequence (used for the chain-of-events models) with other possibilities, such as reordering the time relationships between events or retiming relationships among events by different actors engaged in the activity.

The INRS Model

Another chain-of-events model, called INRS, also emphasizes the importance of change. In this model, deviations or changes are classified in terms of (1) the individual (operator), (2) the machine being operated, (3) the surrounding environment, and (4) the task (the interaction between the operator and the machine). Accidents and incidents are viewed as the consequence of chains of events released or conditioned by a number of variations in normally successful performance [177]. In this model, accident causes are not identified in order to collect data on their frequency, to find a way to remove them, or to find someone to blame. Instead, accidents are mapped as a tree of variations, and points are identified that are sensitive to future improvements (rather than the causes of past events). Emphasis is placed on finding ways to break the accident sequence rather than on removing the cause. Basically, this approach amounts to finding critical decision points where conditions for existing decisions or acts can be improved or new decisions introduced.

Since accidents in the INRS model originate in changes or variations (also called variation antecedents), changes are first identified and their interrelationships are defined. The variation antecedents are diagrammed using event chains to show two types of relationships. *Event chain relationships* indicate that if X event had not occurred, Y event would not have occurred. *Confluence relationships* indicate that in the absence of two independent events (X1 and X2), Y would not have occurred [174, 177]. Figure 10.7 shows an example of an INRS diagram of an accident.

The National Transportation Safety Board Model of Accidents

A problem with most of the chain-of-event models is that factors other than simple events and conditions are difficult to incorporate. Important systemic factors might include structural deficiencies in the organization or factors related to the safety culture in the industry. In the seventies, the National Transportation Safety Board introduced a model and sequencing method that described accidents as patterns of direct events and causal factors arising from contributory factors, which in turn arise from systemic factors (Figures 10.8 and 10.9). This model is similar to Lewycky's hierarchical model introduced in Chapter 3.

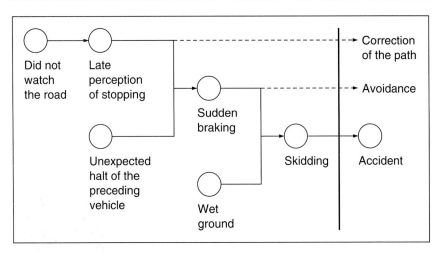

X ——→ Y   Event chain relationship

$$\left.\begin{array}{c} X1 \\ X2 \end{array}\right\}\!\!\!→Y$$ Confluence relationship

(Dashed lines show possible consequences of these actions, if they succeed.)

FIGURE 10.7
An INRS diagram of an accident. (Source: Adapted from Jacques Leplat,
Accidents and incidents production: Methods of analysis. In Jens Rasmussen,
Keith Duncan, and Jacques Leplat, editors, *New Technology and Human Error*,
page 138, New York: John Wiley & Sons, 1987. Reprinted with permission.)

Johnson's MORT Model

Johnson argues that simple chain-of-events models fail to recognize the role of
purpose, goal, performance, and supervisory control and intervention, and thus
are not appropriate for occupational accidents [140]. He developed a model for
the Nuclear Regulatory Commission based on a logic diagram (fault trees) that
he calls Management Oversight and Risk Tree (MORT). MORT is actually a
very detailed checklist for accident investigation, in which the factors involved
in an accident are arranged in a tree connected by logical (AND/OR) gates and
accompanied by lists of criteria used to evaluate the performance of the steps
necessary to complete a process. Over 1,500 basic events or factors are included
in the MORT tree; these factors are related to 98 generic problems.

Johnson's model is based on the belief that all accidental losses are caused
by unwanted transfers of energy due to a lack of barriers or controls. He takes
the basic energy model further, however, by suggesting that accidents result from
lengthy sequences of planning and operational errors that fail to adjust to hu-

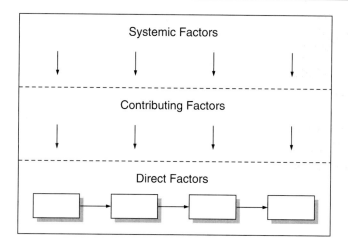

FIGURE 10.8
The National Transportation Safety Board model of accidents.

man or environmental changes. Losses arise from two sources: (1) specific job oversights and omissions and (2) the management system that controls the job (Figure 10.10). Johnson stresses the role of change in accidents, particularly a nonroutine operating mode, such as trials and tests (Chernobyl), maintenance and inspection (TMI), changeover or repair (Flixborough), starting or stopping, special jobs, troubleshooting, and incipient problems (rather than routine operations).

Because accidents tend to have many causal factors with lengthy sequences of errors and changes, MORT provides a method for breaking down the accident sequence into individual events. It considers such factors as the technical information system, design and planning, maintenance, inspection, immediate supervision and high-level management, barriers, unwanted energy flows, policy, and the management system [209].

10.1.4 Models Based on Systems Theory

With the rise of system safety, accidents have begun to be viewed in terms of the interactions among humans, machines, and the environment. The components of a system are interrelated—each part affects the others either directly or indirectly. In the most general case, the relationship between causal factors can be seen (according to Leplat) as a complex net, with the factors at different distances from the accident along a proximal–distal axis [175]. An accident is then the

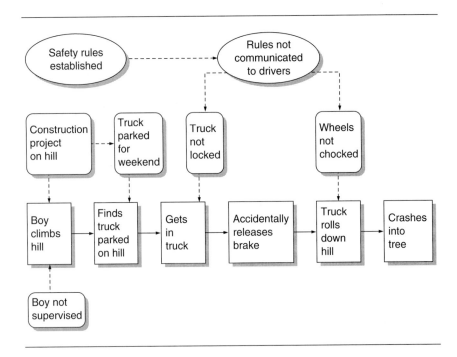

FIGURE 10.9
Example of the National Transportation Safety Board model of accidents. (Source: Adapted from William G. Johnson. *MORT Safety Assurance Systems.* Marcel Dekker, Inc., New York, 1980. Reprinted by permission of Marcel Dekker, Inc.)

coincidence of factors related to each other through this network and stemming from multiple, independent events.

Systems theory models usually do not specify single variables or factors that account for accidents [175]. Whereas industrial safety models focus on unsafe acts or conditions, systems engineering models instead look at what went wrong with the system's operation or organization to allow the accident to take place.

Models based on systems theory consider accidents as arising from the interactions between components of a system. In this approach, safety is an emergent property that arises when the system components interact within an environment. Emergent properties are controlled or enforced by a set of constraints related to the behavior of the system components. Accidents result from interactions among components that violate these constraints—in other words, from a lack of appropriate constraints on the interactions. Since software often acts as a controller in such systems, it embodies or enforces the constraints as it controls the component interactions. Software, then, can contribute to an accident by not enforcing the appropriate constraints on behavior or by commanding behavior that violates the constraints.

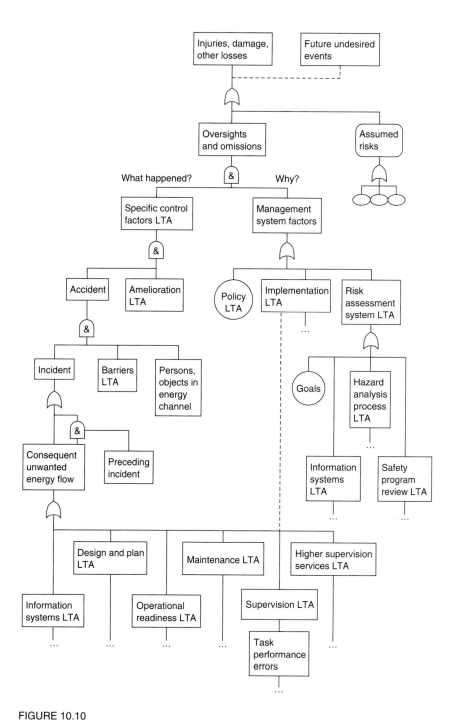

FIGURE 10.10
Top part of the MORT model. Each of the leaf nodes is expanded in further tree structures and each has a checklist associated with it. LTA stands for "less than adequate." (Source: Adapted from William G. Johnson. *MORT Safety Assurance Systems*, Marcel Dekker, Inc., New York, 1980, p.160. Reprinted by permission of Marcel Dekker, Inc.)

A system is merely an abstraction, so different types and levels of subsystems can be identified in these accident models. Industrial engineering models divide the system into appropriate categories of production subsystems. For example, Johansson describes a production system as four subsystems—physical, human, information, and management. The physical subsystem includes the inanimate objects: equipment, facilities, and materials. The human subsystem controls the physical subsystem. The information subsystem provides flow and exchange of information that authorizes activity, guides effort, evaluates performance, and provides overall direction. The organizational and management subsystem establishes goals and objectives for the organization and its functional parts, allocates authority and responsibility, and generally guides activities for the entire organization and its parts [323]. Other models divide the system into an organizational level, a socio-technical level, and an elementary human–machine level [175] or into physical, human (production workers), environmental, and managerial subsystems [299].

Systems models describe accidents in terms of dysfunctional interactions, control theory, or deviations and determining factors.

Dysfunctional Interactions

If accidents are seen as arising from the interactions between components or subsystems, they can be eliminated by controlling dysfunctional interactions, defined as those interactions that lead to hazardous states. The factors related to accidents, then, can be classified in terms of the type of dysfunctional interaction. Leplat divides these interactions into two types: (1) deficiencies in the articulation of subsystems and (2) lack of linkup between elements of a system [175].

Leplat's first type of dysfunctional interaction suggests that accidents arise from problems in articulating and coordinating subsystems. The operation of the entire system depends not only on the operation of the subsystems, but also on the way in which the subsystem operations are coordinated to meet the aims of the system as a whole. He identifies three problem types[175]:

1. *Boundary areas as zones of insecurity*: The functions of the boundary areas between subsystems are often poorly defined. For example, in an iron and steel plant, frequent accidents occurred at the boundary of the blast furnace department and the transport department. One conflict arose when a signal informing transport workers of the state of the blast furnace did not work and was not repaired because each department was waiting for the other to fix it. Faverge suggests that the dysfunctioning can be related to the number of management levels separating the workers in the departments from a common manager: The greater the distance, the more difficult the communication, and thus the greater the uncertainty and insecurity.

2. *Zones of overlap as zones of insecurity*: When a function is achieved by the cooperation of two subsystems or when two subsystems exert influence on the same object, conflicts can arise. A study of the steel industry found that

67 percent of technical incidents with material damage occurred in zones of co-activity, although these represented only a small percentage of the total zones of activity.

3. *Asynchronous evolution of subsystems*: Changes to subsystems may be carefully designed, but consideration of their effects on other parts of the system may be neglected. Another type of asynchronous evolution occurs when one part of a properly designed system deteriorates. In these cases, the erroneous expectations of users or other system components about the behavior of the degraded subsystem may lead to accidents.

Leplat defines a second type of dysfunctional interaction as a lack of linkup between system elements. Examples include poor circulation of information within a group, lack of correspondence between individual capacity and the task requirements, and incompatibility between the system operation and the mental models or expectations of its users.

Control Theory Models

A different type of system model, based on control theory, views safety as a control problem. In these models, systems are viewed as interrelated components that are kept in a state of dynamic equilibrium by feedback loops of information and control. Accidents occur when disturbances are not adequately handled by the control system. From a control point of view, safety presents special problems because the control variable of interest (safety) is not directly measurable and must be inferred by a systematic and analytic prediction of the target state from indirect evidence [274]. Rather than focusing on energy flows, control models focus on changes—which can have unforeseen consequences in a complex system because of incomplete understanding of the system.

Deviations and Determining Factors

Systems theory accident models often emphasize the role of deviations in accidents [151]. A *deviation* occurs when the value of a system variable falls outside a norm, where the norm is defined with respect to the planned, expected, or intended production process. According to Kjellan, accidents occur as a result of maladaptive response to deviations. Deviations may occur in human actions, material, information and instructions, technical equipment, the environment, energy barriers, and relations among activities [150].

The OARU model examines the contribution of deviations and determining factors to the accident process. *Deviations* are as defined above. The *determining factors* are relatively stable properties of the production system that vary little over time and were created primarily when the system was established. They might include features of the design or the operating procedures. Although a deviation does not necessarily lead to a hazard in this model, a deviation, a determining factor, or a combination of these is necessary for the hazard occurrence [323].

The models presented so far handle human error only superficially. Humans, however, play an important role in both causing and preventing accidents. Thus, while the foregoing accident models may provide some help in understanding accidents and in designing many aspects of systems, the design of a safer human–machine interface requires a better understanding of human behavior. For that we need to look to cognitive psychology.

10.2 Human Task and Error Models

Human errors arise in design and in operations. To reduce accidents, we need to consider both these sources of error. Reason differentiates two ways in which humans contribute to the breakdown of complex systems: (1) *active failures* that have an immediate adverse effect, such as an operator pushing a wrong button, and (2) *latent failures* that may lie dormant for a long time and only become evident when they combine with local triggering conditions [285]. The triggering conditions include active failures, technical faults, or unusual system conditions.

Latent failures are present within the system long before the start of a recognizable accident sequence. Rather than being the main instigators of accidents, operators often are the inheritors of system defects created by poor design, conflicting goals, defective organization, and bad management decisions. The conditions under which the latent failures could reveal themselves actually were created by people far removed in time and space from the direct human–machine interface: designers, high-level decision makers, regulators, managers, and maintenance staff. Note the similarity of Reason's active and latent failures to the deviations and determining factors of the system theory accident models described in the previous section.

The design of better human–machine interfaces requires that we understand these types of human failures better. Various types of models of human error have been proposed; unfortunately, no single model captures all of the complexity of human behavior in control situations.

One simple and common approach is to categorize human errors by their external manifestations—such as omission (not performing a function), commission (performing a function that should not have been performed), not recognizing a hazardous situation, making a wrong decision in response to a problem, responding inadequately to a situation, and poor timing (responding too early or too late). When errors are classified according to such externally visible behavior, however, the search for complex and hazardous scenarios quickly leads to combinatorial explosion [274]. More important, this classification provides little understanding of human error or help in eliminating it.

Alternative approaches classify human error according to task characteristics, human cognitive mechanisms, or social factors. Each of these three types of models is useful in understanding different aspects of a very complex problem.

10.2.1 Task and Environment Models

Classical human factors theory is concerned with the effects of equipment design, environment, and task structure on the probability of human errors. These models consider *performance-shaping factors* such as task structure and workload, physical and psychological stress, and design of displays and controls. The basic organizing principle behind these models is the task, where tasks can be categorized by the activity or by the types of human behavior involved.

The first way of categorizing tasks is by activity, such as coordinating, executing procedures, scanning, recognizing, problem solving, regulating, steering, communicating, planning, recording, and maintaining. Rouse [301] surveys human error models that have been devised for each of these activities on the basis of operating experience and laboratory experiment.

One problem with these models is that humans rarely perform just one task, and performance on a task may be affected by other tasks. For example, sequentially moving among regulation, steering, recognition, and problem-solving may degrade performance compared to doing just one of these tasks at a time. A possible interference factor might be mental or physical switching time or setup cost [301]. On the other hand, different tasks may be complementary in the sense that performing one may make performing the other easier. One factor, in this case, may be a natural relationship between the information requirements of particular tasks.

A second way to categorize tasks is by the general types of behavior involved. Lees identifies five types: (1) simple, (2) vigilance, (3) emergency response, (4) complex, and (5) control [172].

Simple tasks are composed of relatively uncomplicated sequences of operations involving little decision making. A large body of work exists on the performance of simple tasks, as they are easy to study in the laboratory. Error rates are affected by the level of presumed psychological stress, the quality of human engineering of controls and displays, the quality of training and practice, the presence and quality of written instructions and methods of use, the coupling of human actions (loose or tight), and personnel redundancy (checking or inspection of one person's work by another).

Vigilance tasks involve the detection of signals. Again, there is a large body of research on this type of task. Some of the factors that affect performance are sensory modality (such as sight or hearing), nature of signal (a simple Go/No-Go or a complex pattern), strength of signal (strong and noise-free or weak and noisy), frequency of signal, expectedness of signal, length of watch, motivation, and action required on receipt of a signal. In general, auditory signals are superior to visual signals for simple Go/No-Go signals such as alarms. The probability of detection also varies greatly with signal frequency—detection is much more likely for frequent than for infrequent signals. Performance tends to fall off with time—error depends very much on the response time allowed.

Emergency response tasks are much less well-defined than simple or vigilance tasks, and their complexity can vary greatly. A common factor in emergency tasks is stress. Low stress can lead to carelessness and lack of attention, but high stress also can degrade performance: Medium stress is required for optimal human performance. It is easy to build systems that behave reasonably during low-stress conditions, but that add to frustration and lead to poor decisions in a crisis [345]. Behavior under stress can be improved by the use of easily understandable procedures for all anticipated situations and frequent training on emergency procedures, preferably with simulators that model realistic conditions [189].

Two types of behavior are common under emergency conditions [189]. The first is the *incredulity response*, in which the operator is more likely to believe that the instruments or alarms are producing incorrect or spurious signals than to believe a serious problem has occurred. This belief is especially likely when operators have been subjected to a substantial number of false alarms.

A second type of emergency response behavior is to *revert to stereotype*, even though recent training has been to the contrary. The obvious solution is not to violate cultural stereotypes in the design of displays and controls; for example, "up" means turning a light switch on in the United States and the opposite in Europe. Once a mistake is made, such as placing a switch in the wrong position, an operator under stress is likely to repeat the mistake rather than think through the problem.

Complex tasks are fairly well-defined sequences of operations that involve some decision making. Although these tasks make up a large proportion of most operators' jobs, relatively little is known about them from a human factors standpoint. The same is true of **control tasks**, where the activities are not completely specified by discrete and vigilance tasks, but also include general responsibility for determining whether a control intervention is required and, if so, carrying it out.

In general, task models provide little help on several dimensions: accounting for interactions among tasks; determining error modes and probabilities for the more complex decision tasks used in control and involved in emergencies; and analyzing or designing new types of tasks and work environments (interface designs) for which past experience is not available. Thus they provide only limited help in designing better human–machine interfaces in the highly automated systems being designed today: Simple tasks are being automated, and humans are increasingly responsible for the complex tasks and decision making not included in these models. An alternative is to build models that look beyond the task and environment and incorporate human cognitive processes.

10.2.2 Models Based on Cognitive Mechanisms

Instead of focusing on task and environment characteristics, cognitive models of human error consider the psychological mechanisms used by the operator in performing the tasks—the interaction of psychological factors with the features of the work environment. Human errors are defined in terms of the reasons or underlying psychological mechanisms from which they stem.

These cognitive models assume that the seemingly large variety of human errors reflects the complexity of the environment rather than the complexity of the psychological mechanisms involved. One argument for the cognitive models is that multifaceted taxonomies can be used to make fine distinctions among error situations using only a limited number of categories on each dimension of the taxonomy [278]. Thus, in comparison to models based on *external* tasks, useful models of the *internal task* components and the psychological mechanisms associated with them can be based on a more limited number of basic concepts—that is, they explain a large number of behaviors using a small number of psychological mechanisms.

There are many human error models in cognitive psychology, and no attempt is made here to be comprehensive; rather the goal is simply to illustrate such models using a few well-known ones. Each is based on Bartlett's concept of *schemas*. This classic model assumes a knowledge base with an apparently limitless number of specialized theories or internal representations of the regularities of the world, as well as our routine dealings with it. Each schema deals with a particular aspect of the world through one or a variety of cognitive domains (such as perception, action, memory retrieval, thought, and judgment). Together, our schemas constitute a richly interconnected, immensely powerful, labor-saving device for governing the largely predictable and routine activities of life [289].

Reason's model of human error exemplifies a classic cognitive psychology error model.

Reason's Model of Human Errors

In Reason's classification of human error [286], basic error tendencies, such as resource limitations, interact with information processing domains, such as recognition, to produce primary error groupings. Examples of primary error groupings are inaccurate or blocked recall and unintended words or actions. Reason proposes eight primary error groupings defined by the influence of five basic error tendencies on eight information-processing domains (see Figure 10.11). He stresses that although human errors can be placed in a few classes, the number and variety of contextual determinates remain large.

According to Reason, the five basic error tendencies constitute the fundamental root of most, if not all, of the systematic varieties of human error. Each is also necessary for normal psychological functioning, which explains their power to induce systematic error.

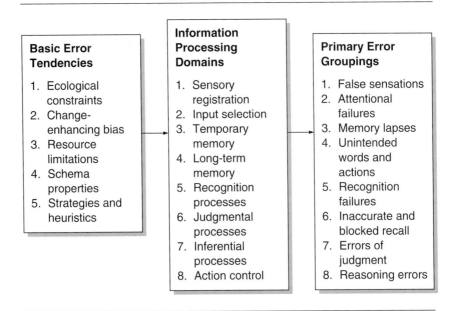

FIGURE 10.11
Reason's primary error groupings arise from the interaction of basic error tendencies and information processing domains.

1. *Ecological constraints* are a product of generations of evolutionary adjustment to a particular environment. Today, many of these behaviors—based on previous environments in which active locomotion was more common—continue even though they may be obsolete and even dangerous.

2. *Change-enhancing biases* arise from the fact that the nervous system is essentially a change detector. Psychological mechanisms change systematically in order to adapt to varying circumstances.

3. *Resource limitations* result from human processing limitations. Limited processing ensures that only a restricted number of cognitive structures will be maximally active at any one time. Without this limitation, it would be impossible to derive meaning from sensory data or to arrange our thoughts, speech, and actions into coherent, goal-directed sequences.

4. *Schema properties* cause a tendency to err in the direction of the familiar and the expected. Errors take the form of "default assignments," which can arise from (a) fitting the data to the wrong schema; (b) employing the correct schema, but filling in gaps in a stimulus configuration with best guesses rather than available sensory data; or (c) relying too heavily upon active or salient schemas. Such errors are most likely at times of change, when existing routines are no longer appropriate for new circumstances or revised goals.

5. *Strategies and heuristics* are both governed by and carried out in relation to schematic knowledge. Most people have a large number of schemas, but also have limited human processing resources. Strategies help to overcome these resource limitations when processing schemas, but inadequate and overused strategies and heuristics (rules of thumb) lead to errors.

In Reason's model, primary errors arise from the influence of these five error tendencies on the basic stages or operations in human information processing— (1) sensory registration, (2) input selection, (3) temporary memory, (4) long-term memory, (5) recognition processes, (6) judgmental processes, (7) inferential processes, and (8) action control. Secondary errors are less certain interactions or are dependent on some primary effect at an earlier stage of information processing.

Reason identifies eight primary error groups:

1. *False sensations* represent a lack of correspondence between our subjective experience of the world and the objective reality. They may arise because aspects of the physical world have been distorted or misrepresented by our senses.

2. *Attentional failures* arise when (a) coping with distraction; (b) processing simultaneous inputs; (c) focusing attention upon one of two concurrent messages; (d) dividing attention between the performance of two concurrent tasks; (e) performing tasks that provide limited opportunity for the appropriate combination of object features; and (f) performing monitoring, custodial, and verification tasks.

3. *Memory lapses* include (a) forgetting list items, (b) forgetting intentions, and (c) losing track of previous actions.

4. *Unintended words and actions* include absent-minded deviations of words, signs, and actions from what was intended. The deviations arise from failures of execution rather than inadequate plans, such as slips of the tongue and Freudian slips.

5. *Recognition failures* are misperceptions of sensory data, such as wrongly identifying something that is not actually present or not recognizing something that is in fact there. These erroneous cognitive interpretations of the data occur most often when the sensory evidence is incomplete and when there is a strong schema-based expectation to perceive either the presence or the absence of a particular stimulus.

6. *Inaccurate and blocked recall* includes misremembering or not remembering sentences, stories, places, faces, or events. Blocked recall is related to memory lapses, but also may be related to schematic bias.

7. *Errors of judgment* include psychophysical and temporal misjudgments, misconceptions of chance and covariation, misjudgments of risk, misdiagnoses, fallacies in probability judgments, and erroneous social assessments.

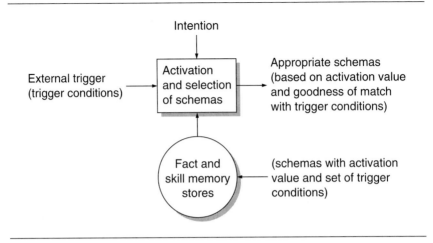

FIGURE 10.12
Norman's Activation Trigger Schema model.

8. *Reasoning errors* include errors in deductive and propositional reasoning, reasoning with positive and negative instances, and reasoning with abstract and concrete instances; errors in concept formation; and errors in hypothesis testing [286].

These eight primary error groupings have been abstracted into two general types of errors—slips and mistakes—and examined further by Norman and Reason. A desired action in their models is called an *intention*. The intention may result from conscious decision making or from subconscious processing. Either way, it starts a chain of processing activities that usually results in its achievement. An error in the intention is called a *mistake*; an error in carrying out the intention is called a *slip*. Thus, mistakes occur in the planning of an action sequence while slips occur during its execution.

Norman's Model of Slips

In Norman's Activation Trigger Schema (ATS) model, a *schema* is defined as an organized structure of knowledge from either fact or skill memory stores (see Figure 10.12) [243, 244]. An intention causes a number of schemas to become active, each with an activation value and a set of trigger conditions. An external trigger leads to internal activation and selection of the appropriate schemas based on the need to satisfy trigger conditions. A particular schema controls behavior whenever the combination of its activation value and the goodness of match of its trigger conditions reaches an appropriate level.

Norman classifies slips into three general types (Figure 10.13), according to their presumed source: slips in the formation of intentions, slips resulting

SLIPS IN THE FORMATION OF INTENTION

Mode Errors: Erroneous classification of the situation.
Description Errors: Ambiguous or incomplete specification of the intention.

SLIPS RESULTING FROM FAULTY ACTIVATION OF A SCHEMA

Unintended Activation: When schemas not part of a current action sequence become activated for extraneous reasons, then become triggered and lead to slips.

Capture Errors	When a frequent or better learned sequence, similar to the sequence being performed, captures control.
Data-Driven Activation	When external events cause activation of schemas.
Associative Activation	When currently active schemas activate others with which they are associated.

Loss of Activation: When schemas that have been activated lose activation, thereby losing effectiveness to control behavior.

Forgetting an intention (but continuing with the action sequence)

Misordering the components of an action sequence

Skipping steps in an action sequence

Repeating steps in an action sequence

SLIPS RESULTING FROM FAULTY TRIGGERING OF SCHEMAS

False Triggering: A properly activated schema is triggered at an inappropriate time.

Spoonerisms	Reversal of event components.
Blends	Combinations of components from two competing schemas.
Thoughts Leading to Actions	Triggering of schemas meant only to be thought, not to govern action.
Premature Triggering	

Failure in Triggering: When an active schema is never invoked because (a) the action was preempted by a competing schema; (b) there was insufficient activation, either as a result of forgetting or because the initial level was too low; or (c) there was a failure of the trigger condition to match, either because the triggering conditions were badly specified or the match botwoon occurring conditions and the required conditions was never sufficiently close.

FIGURE 10.13
Norman's categorization of slips.

from faulty activation of schemas, and slips resulting from faulty triggering of schemas.

■ *Slips that arise during the formation of an intention.*

Slips while forming an intention are categorized as mode errors or description errors. **Mode errors** occur when a situation is incorrectly classified—the resulting action is intended and appropriate for the *assumed* environment but inappropriate for the actual situation. These errors may have serious consequences as the meaning of visual displays or commands may depend on the mode that the system is in; failing to identify the mode correctly can lead to erroneous interpretation of the display or erroneous action. In mode errors, the intentions, the specification of the action, and the actions are all proper; the fault lies in the interpretation of the system state: The actions are entirely appropriate for the assumed state but not the real state.

Mode errors occur frequently in systems that do not provide clear feedback of their current state. Norman suggests that commercial aircraft autopilots provide numerous possibilities for mode errors. An incident in which an Aero Mexico DC-10 stalled, was badly buffeted, and lost the tips of both elevators appears to have occurred because of a mode error in the crew's use of the autopilot [244].

Description errors occur when either (1) not all the relevant information needed to form the appropriate intention is available or (2) an appropriate intention has been formed, but the description of the desired action is insufficient. In the second case, incomplete description leads to ambiguity in selecting information from memory and thus to an erroneous action. In general, description errors occur when different actions have similar descriptions, either in the specification of the actions or in the class of arguments.

Description errors are relatively common in the throwing of switches or the operation of controls, especially when the operations are similar (such as the setting of altimeters, radio frequencies, and transponder codes in aircraft) [244]. Such errors are likely whenever control panels are designed without clear enough distinctions among controls. Norman suggests that this problem is especially bad in the design of nuclear power plant control rooms, where switches and controls are laid out in neat rows. Such designs invite errors in which the right operation is performed but on the wrong device. The middle lights in a row of lights are easily confused, especially when the user is rushed or under stress or views them with peripheral vision, resulting in the potential for reading the wrong instruments or operating the wrong controls.

■ *Slips resulting from faulty activation of a schema.*

A schema may be unintentionally activated (causing an action to intrude when it is not expected), or it may lose its activation before its appropriate time to control behavior (leading to omission of its components in the action sequence).

Unintended activation of a schema can occur because of the mode and description errors described and also because of errors resulting from capture, data-driven activations, or associations. *Capture errors* occur when a familiar habit substitutes itself for the intended action sequence. If a habit is strong enough, even partial matches from the situation are apt to activate and trigger the schema, and a more common or better-learned action is substituted for an infrequent one.

Data-driven activation errors occur when the environment causes the activation of the wrong schema—the environment forces an intrusion in the actions performed. An example from psychology experiments is the Stroop phenomenon, in which the names of colors (such as blue) are printed in colors that are different from the name (such as the word blue printed in red ink), and the subject is asked to look at the word and say the name of the color in which it is printed. The difficulty in this task stems from the intrusion of the printed names. Both capture errors and data-driven association errors involve inappropriate actions, but capture errors result from the intrusion of familiar habits (similarities in action sequences), while data-driven activations are caused by environmental intrusions. This type of error might occur when external events or conditions interfere with the operator's analysis or interpretation of the immediate environment or state of the system.

Associative activation is similar to capture activations, except that there need not be any formal similarity between the action sequences involved, merely a strong association. The intention activates the proper schema, which then activates other schemas with which it is associated.

Loss of activation, a second type of faulty activation of schemas, occurs when appropriate actions are omitted because of memory failure or interference. In memory failure, events intercede between the time an intention is prepared and the time the action should take place, so that the original intention or action sequence is forgotten. Loss of activation or interference can also result in misordering actions, skipping steps, or repeating steps. Skipped steps are a frequent cause of aircraft accidents [244].

- *Slips resulting from the faulty triggering of schemas.*

A schema may be properly selected and activated, but lead to a slip because it is triggered improperly—either at the wrong time or not at all. Examples of triggering at the wrong time include spoonerisms (reversals of event components), blends (combinations of components from two competing schemas), thoughts leading to unintended actions, and premature triggering of schemas.

Schemas may never get invoked when they should, perhaps because they are pre-empted by competing schemas or because the person confuses thought with deeds. Slips that result from failure to perform some action are more difficult to detect than errors that result from a falsely or improperly executed action.

Mistakes or Human Errors in Planning

While Norman's model examines slips or errors in executing action sequences, Reason has looked carefully at *mistakes* or errors in the planning of actions. The planning process can be divided into four parts: (1) the setting of objectives, (2) the search for alternative courses of action, (3) comparison and evaluation

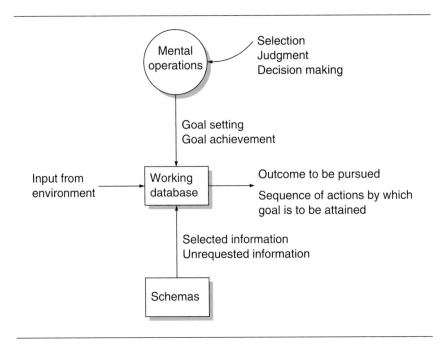

FIGURE 10.14
Reason's basic model of the psychological processes involved in planning.

of alternatives, and (4) decisions about appropriate action. This division is, of course, idealized; usually, planning occurs in the context of ongoing behavior in which the feedback generated by actions requires continual reassessment of the plan [289].

A human error, according to Reason, is simply an act that is counterproductive to the person's intentions or goals. He starts from a simple model of the psychological processes involved in planning (Figure 10.14) [289]:

- A *working database:* the information currently being used in the planning process. This database is limited in capacity and continuously changing in content. At least three kinds of information are likely to be present within it: information derived directly from the environment via the input functions; information intentionally called up from the schema base; and information spontaneously thrown up by active, though not necessarily relevant, schemas.

- The *mental operations:* selection, judgment, and decision making. There are two types of judgments:

    Goal setting: Various desired outcomes are considered and then assigned weightings according to the judged likelihood of their attainability.

   Goal achievement: A similar set of judgments is applied to the alternative means by which these outcomes could be achieved.
Decisions are made on the basis of these judgments as to the outcome to be pursued and the sequence of future actions to achieve that outcome.

□ The *schemas:* Schemas contribute both selected (plan-relevant) and unrequested information to the working database. Unrequested information may take the form of conscious fragments (images and words) thrown up by highly activated schemas: emotionally charged material, stored information triggered by the environmental context or associated with the plan elements, or outputs from recently or frequently used schemas. The mental operations manipulate the schemas and produce a formulated plan that consists of a sequence of schematically controlled operations.

Using this classic model of psychological mechanisms, Reason identifies various types of planning mistakes that people make, associating them with sources of bias within each of these three components of the planning process [288, 289]. Combining what is known about the heuristics of judgment, the limits of human information processing, and agreed on characteristics of schema function, he predicts when and how distortions or mistakes will be introduced.

Some of these distortions stem from features of the working database:

□ At any time, it will contain only a small fraction of all information potentially available and relevant to the plan being considered.

□ No more than two or three factors (variables) relevant to the planning process are likely to be in the database at any one time. This limitation tends to restrict searches and limit the ability to consider all alternatives.

□ The contents of the database will be continually changing.

□ Planning is shaped more by past experience than is appropriate, given the possible variability of future events.

□ Information called into the working store from the schema store will be biased toward availability rather than relevance. Emotionally charged material, contextually relevant information (whether or not it is plan relevant), and recently or frequently used information will have privileged access to the working database, regardless of its bearing on the plan. This feature restricts potentially profitable explorations of the solution space.

□ The contents of the database will be biased toward past successes rather than past failures: Plans are likely to include operations that have proved successful in the past but which may have dubious utility in the present situation.

□ Information in the working database may be cued by local environmental factors. The more vivid and attention grabbing this information is, the more likely it is to be incorporated into the planning process, irrespective of its objective relevance.

Distortions also arise from features of the other two parts of the planning process—mental operations and schemas:

- ☐ Planners will plan for fewer contingencies than are likely to occur because they are guided primarily by past events and will underestimate the likelihood of unexpected or chance intervention.
- ☐ Planners will give priority to information in proportion to its vividness or emotional impact over its objective value in the planning process.
- ☐ Planners will unconsciously fill in missing details in the available evidence that fit their theories (schemas). Later, they will be unable to distinguish between the data that was actually present and that supplied by the schemas.
- ☐ Planners are not good at assessing population parameters on the basis of data samples. They have little appreciation of the unreliability of small samples, the undue influence of available instances, and the effects of bias in the sampling procedures.
- ☐ Planners are poor at detecting many types of covariation.
- ☐ Planners are subject to the *halo effect:* They show a predilection for single orderings and an aversion to discrepant orderings. They have difficulty independently processing two separate orderings of the same people or objects, so they reduce them to a single ordering by merit.
- ☐ Planners tend to have a simplistic view of causality: They are likely to judge it on the basis of perceived similarity between cause and effect. This tendency is compounded by the mistaken belief that a given event can have only one sufficient cause. Planners are also likely to suffer from hindsight bias: Knowledge of the outcome of a past event increases the perceived likelihood of that outcome. This perception may also lead planners to overestimate their ability to influence future events.
- ☐ Planners are likely to be overconfident of the correctness of their knowledge. They tend to justify their chosen course of action by focusing on evidence that favors it and disregarding contradictory signs.
- ☐ Planners are likely to perform poorly when predicting future events, partly because of their failure to understand statistical principles, notably, regression. They also tend to match the features of present evidence with those of a possible outcome and predict that the evidence will lead to the outcome to the extent that the features of the evidence resemble those of the outcome.
- ☐ Planners have an overwhelming urge to make sense of all information, whether internally or externally generated. This *effort after meaning* is so overwhelming that they are prepared to be wrong in particular instances as long as they can preserve order within the world at large.
- ☐ Planners often choose short-term over long-term objectives and choose objectives that are merely adequate rather than ideal.
- ☐ Planners' use of schemas may lead to applying procedures that are too

rigid, rule-bound, and conservative, or to applying contextually inappropriate heuristics.

Once the plan is formulated, planners seek confirmatory evidence for its validity and are unable to assimilate additional information that suggests that the
plan might fail. This resistance of the completed plan to modification is likely to
be greatest when (1) the plan is very elaborate, involving the detailed intermesh-
ing of several different action sequences (the plan represents a complex theory);
(2) the plan is the product of considerable effort and emotional investment and its
completion is associated with a marked reduction in tension or anxiety; (3) the
time interval separating the plan's completion from its intended execution is relatively long; (4) the plan is the brainchild of many people; and (5) the plan has
hidden objectives (it is conceived, either consciously or subconsciously, to satisfy
a number of different needs or motives).

In summary, various sources of distortion are likely to lead to an inadequate
database, unrealistic goal setting, erroneous judgments of the likely consequences
of actions, and an unwarranted confidence in the efficacy of the resulting plan.
Note again, however, that the same human characteristics described by Reason
as distortions can also be described (somewhat differently) as *positive* features
of the human planning process. For example, the bias toward using information
from the past regardless of its relevance to the present or future circumstances,
and the inability to predict the irregularities of the future, can be restated as the
remarkable ability of humans to model the regularities of the past and apply them
to the future. In most instances, this ability allows humans to predict the future
very well. Similarly, the bias to make sense of information in terms of theories
can be restated as the advantage of possessing a virtually limitless long-term
memory that allows humans to process information effortlessly, and in parallel,
in terms of theories. What is human error in one circumstance may be human
ingenuity in another. If we eliminate planning "biases" and distortions, we may
also eliminate the human ability to solve problems. However, understanding these
biases can aid in designing human–machine interactions that help us to overcome
their negative aspects while retaining their positive ones.

Reason and Norman explain human error in terms of classical psychological concepts such as short- and long-term memory and Bartlett's schemas. Rasmussen's models (described in the next section) also use these concepts, but
are influenced by the systems engineering ideas of information processing and
control.

Human–Task Mismatch

Rasmussen [270, 273, 276] argues that "errors" are an integral part of the learning
process, as discussed in Chapter 5, and should be regarded as human–task or
human–system mismatches. He proposes a model (Figure 10.15) based on the
factors necessary to explain the human behavior that precedes an accident. These
factors are found by backtracking along the causal course of events.

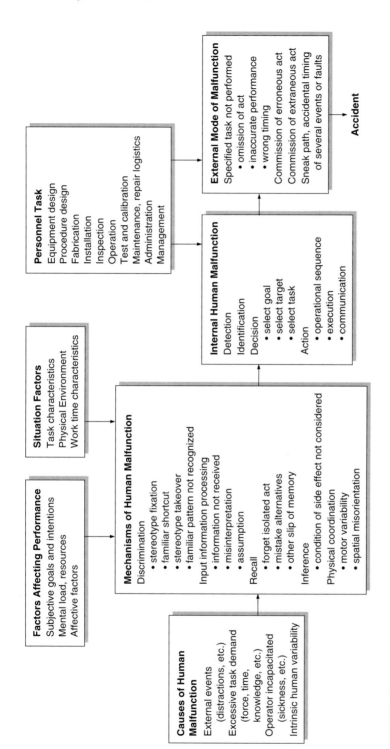

FIGURE 10.15

Rasmussen's model of human–task mismatch. (Source: From Jens Rasmussen, "Human Errors: A taxonomy for describing human malfunction in industrial installaions," Occupational Accident, 4 (2–4), pp. 311–335, 1982. Elsevier Scintific Publishers. Reprinted with permission.)

External Model of Malfunction. The first element of a human–system mismatch found when backtracking from an accident is an unacceptable state of a physical object or component due to a human act. The features of the mismatch are described in terms of inappropriate task performance. Rasmussen labels this part of the model the *External Mode of Human Malfunction* to avoid the term "human error" with its flavor of guilt. In this category, mismatch is expressed in terms of the omission of acts in procedural sequences, acts on wrong components, reversals in a sequence, wrong timing, and so on.

Rasmussen claims that data from this category will be sufficient for the design of work conditions when applying a technology and tools very similar to the environment from which data is collected, such as during a period of slow technological change. When new technology is introduced (such as computers), data is needed that relates mismatches also to psychological mechanisms.

Internal Mode of Malfunction. According to Rasmussen, the first step in the human–machine interface design process should be to characterize the mental task. This cognitive task analysis identifies the *internal mode of malfunction*, that is, the element of the cognitive decision-making process that was involved, either by being improperly performed or by being improperly bypassed by a habitual shortcut. Such human malfunctions involve problems in detection, identification, decisions (selection of a goal, a target, or a task) and action (operational sequence, execution, or communication).

Mechanisms of Human Malfunction. To characterize an event with reference to psychological mechanisms, as is done in the category *Mechanisms of Human Malfunction* in Figure 10.15, a model of cognitive control that can explain the mismatch is needed. Rasmussen proposes the use of the Skill–Rule–Knowledge model described in Chapter 5 and shown in Figure 10.16.

Skill-Based Level. At the skill-based behavior level, human variability during familiar tasks may be the result of

- □ *Motor variability*: The time-space precision of sensory-motor control may not be adequate for the task at hand, leading to occasional mismatches.
- □ *Topographic misorientation*: The internal model becomes unsynchronized with the external world.
- □ *Stereotype takeover*: There is systematic interference between the schema needed for the intended action and other, typically highly trained schema, which take over and lead to what Norman calls *capture errors*. In this case, a single conscious statement of intention may activate a schema, after which attention may be directed toward planning future activities or monitoring the past. Current, unmonitored schema will then be sensitive to interference in which another schema takes over control. The schema that takes over may be a frequently used one that contains part of the current action sequence or, alternatively, it may be related to the new focus of the operator's wandering attention.

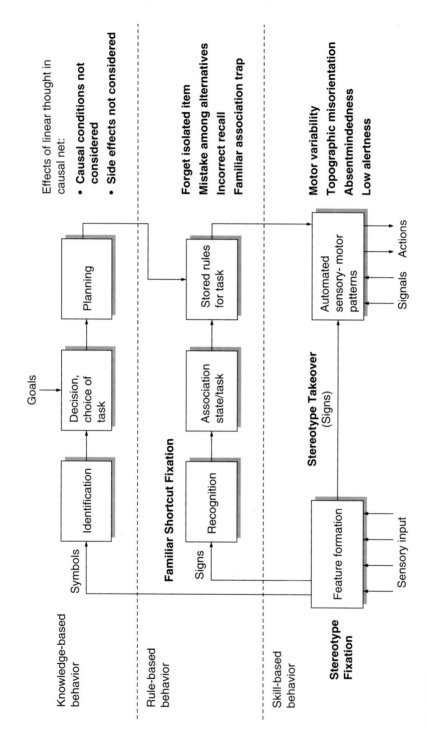

FIGURE 10.16
Skill–Rule–Knowledge model and associated errors. (Source: Adapted from Jens Rasmussen, "What can be learned from human error reports?" In K. Duncan et al., edsl *Changes in Working Life*. New York: John Wiley & Sons, 1980. Reprinted with permission.)

Rule-Based Level. Human variability during the performance of normal, familiar tasks at the rule-based level most often involves incorrect recall of rules and know-how. One typical problem is omitting or forgetting an isolated item that is not a necessary part of the main task sequence, such as forgetting to restore normal operations after repair or calibrations (which accounted for 60 to 70 percent of the test and calibration errors that Rasmussen found in the nuclear power plant incidents he analyzed). Another typical problem is the incorrect recall of isolated items, such as numbers. Variability at this level may also involve an incorrect choice among possible alternatives, such as left or right, up or down, and + or −.

A second type of mismatch at the rule-based level arises from improper adaptation to system changes. Changes in the environment often lead to conscious or subconscious updating of the current schema. Frequently, this update will not take place until a mismatch has occurred. Updating of sensory-motor schemas basically depends upon mismatch occurrences for optimal adjustments: The proper limits for fine tuning can only be found if surpassed once in a while. Rasmussen argues that mismatches, therefore, cannot—and should not—be avoided; instead, the system must be tolerant and not respond irreversibly.

Stereotype fixation and *stereotype takeover* are two additional mismatch mechanisms related to the improper activation of rules. Stereotype fixation occurs when a sensory-motor schema is activated in an improper context and the person, in hindsight, knows what should have been done. In stereotype takeover, people realize the need to use special procedures, but relapse into familiar routines—the stereotype takes over because of overlapping sequence elements (as occurs also at the skill-based level).

When humans interact with complex industrial systems, they are controlling more or less invisible processes. They have to infer the state of the process they are controlling and select appropriate control actions from a set of physical measurements that provide only cues about the state. These cues usually only *correlate* with particular states; they are not attributes that completely define them. Operators ordinarily use indications that are typical for the normal events, including informal signals such as motor or relay noise, as convenient signs for familiar states in the system. This strategy is effective and mentally economical during normal and familiar situations, but it leads the operator into traps if the state changes in a way that does not affect the measurements (signs) but makes the related actions inappropriate. For example, operators may decide that an abnormal instrument reading is due to a lack of calibration (a common occurrence) when it may actually be due to a leak (a less common occurrence).

To perform a proper diagnosis or to adapt performance to the requirements of a system in a unique and unfamiliar state—perhaps caused by a technical fault—the operator must switch from rule-based behavior to knowledge-based reasoning and interpret information not as signs but as symbols. This switch, according to Rasmussen, appears to be very difficult, since the use of signs basically means that information from the system is not observed; instead, it is obtained by asking questions that are heavily biased by expectations based on a set of well-known situations. Thus, highly skilled operators with a large repertoire of convenient signs and related know-how are very likely not to switch to analytical reasoning when required if they find a familiar subset of data during their reading of instruments. They will instead run into a *procedural trap* and be caught by a *familiar association shortcut* [275].

Examples of rule-based mistakes that operators commonly make with industrial robots include assuming that if the arm is not moving, it is not going to move; assuming that if the arm is repeating one pattern of motions, it will continue to repeat that pattern; assuming that if the arm is moving slowly, it will continue to move slowly; and assuming that if they tell the arm to move, it will move the way they want it to move [252].

Knowledge-Based Level. At the skill-based and rule-based levels, behavior is controlled by sensory-motor schemas and rules, goals are implicitly specified, and error mechanisms can be described in terms related to behaviorally normal action sequences. At the knowledge-based level, however, the sequence of reasoning an operator will use during problem solving cannot be described in general terms; the goal to pursue must be explicitly considered, and the actual choice of goals and actions depends on subjective and situation-dependent features. Thus, typical error modes can be described only in very general terms, such as lack of consideration of latent conditions or side effects. General types of mismatch situations that may occur include the following:

1. Adaptation is not possible, because of (a) a need for knowledge about system properties that is not available, (b) a need for data that is not presented, or (c) excessive time or workload requirements.

2. Adaptation is possible but unsuccessful because of inappropriate decisions that result in actions not conforming with requirements. These actions are errors only if they are not corrected in time. In fact, actions not conforming with system requirements can be an important element of problem solving.

For the second category, in which adaptation is possible but unsuccessful, mismatches can occur during any of the necessary phases of decision making, such as identification of the system state, evaluation and choice of ultimate goals, and planning of proper action sequences. The mismatches may be due to

□ Human cognitive variability, memory lapses, mistakes, interference from familiar lines of reasoning, and so on. When the problem-solving process is as unconstrained as it is in a real-life control room task, it is difficult to identify all possible types of human variability or to use them for prediction.

□ Errors caused by the difficulty of keeping track of sequential reasoning in a causal structure that is, in fact, a complex network unsuited for linear reasoning. The mental workload involved in such reasoning may lead to adoption of premature hypotheses through the influence of factors such as the *way of least resistance* and the *point of no return*. The adoption of premature hypotheses leads to a failure to consider important conditions or unacceptable side effects of the ultimate decision.

□ Actions not conforming with system requirements. Such actions may not be related to the ultimate result of erroneous decision making, but may be a reasonable way to test a hypothesis or to get information. However, they may bring the system into a more complex and less controllable state.

□ Familiar or proceduralized relationships serving goals that are not relevant in the present situation. Rasmussen argues that decision errors during complex disturbances are not stochastic events, but often are reasonable mistakes caused by interference.

Causes of Human Malfunction. The errors of the skill–rule–knowledge model (labeled in Figure 10.15 as *Mechanisms of Human Malfunction*) are due to inherent human variability. Frequently, the human–system mismatch is not due to variability alone, but may also result from precursor events in the environment. These events are characterized in the taxonomy as *Causes of Human Malfunction*, and the causal backtracking is continued upstream from the human.

Performance-Affecting Factors. In Rasmussen's taxonomy, only events recognizable at distinct locations in time are considered causal factors (such as a telephone call or a burst of noise). More persistent conditions, such as stressful work environments, bad ergonomic designs, inadequate instruction, and so on, are labeled *Performance-Affecting Factors* and are considered separately. The inclusion of these dimensions of the taxonomy is required because human–system interaction cannot be described adequately by considering only cognitive, information-processing factors; other factors that must be considered are anatomical properties (such as physical workload and injuries), physiological functions (such as inappropriate climate and shift arrangements), and subjective value formation (such as situation, policy, social climate, and management attitudes). Note that these considerations bring us back to the factors included in the general accident models and that this human error model can be embedded within the larger framework of those models. They also bring us to social psychology perspectives.

10.2.3 Social Psychology Models

Human error cannot be thoroughly understood in isolation from the environment in which it occurs. Pure engineering approaches that look at human behavior in terms of tasks or even psychological views that relate human cognition to performance will be inadequate if other social psychology factors are not considered. Reason, while emphasizing the need to understand the formal properties of human error, acknowledges its varied origins in specific conditions of particular environments and in conditions of the human actors. The origins of error in a human include transitory influences—such as moods—as well as more lasting one, such as beliefs, values, and temperaments. "We can no more ignore these influences than we can ignore temporary states of the weather or the persisting trends of climates" [278, p.4].

Taylor [331] has stressed the importance of such factors as individual value systems and feelings of responsibility when trying to understand or account for operator behavior. He argues that human error or behavior, as seen from the outside of a person, can be only partly understood unless it is possible to map the meaning of the acts to the individual value systems and sense of personal responsibility of the person concerned. Safeguards to prevent human error that do not consider these factors will be limited in effectiveness.

10.3 Summary

This chapter has examined a variety of accident models and some well-known human error models. These models of causality are the foundation of approaches to design that attempt to reduce accidents. The sheer number and conflicting nature of these models provides some insight as to why so many design approaches exist and why safety is far from a solved problem. Nevertheless, the models do provide guidance in our search for solutions, and their influence can be seen in the current approaches to building safer systems described in Part 4.

PART FOUR

Elements of a Safeware Program

Accidents are not due to lack of knowledge, but failure to use the knowledge we have.

—Trevor Kletz
What Went Wrong?

With the basic understanding of the problem presented in Part One, information about the foundations of system safety and how it differs from other approaches to risk reduction presented in Part Two, and models and definitions upon which to build described in Part Three, we are now ready to examine potential solutions. Any solution must encompass all aspects of the problem and not just focus on one thing, such as preventing technical failures or improving management awareness.

The success of any safety program will hinge on the ability of everyone involved in the design and operation of the system—application, software, human factors, and safety engineers and operations personnel—to cooperate: Safety is a system problem that will not be solved by any one group working alone. Reducing risk requires basic education about safety and an open-minded attitude toward learning new techniques and incorporating them into the procedures with which people are more familiar and comfortable.

Part Four provides information about how to implement a comprehensive safety program, particularly for systems with computers in the critical loops. Rather than one cookbook procedure that will probably fit no project well, enough information is given here about the options available, and how to make decisions about using these options, to enable designing a safety program that fits the requirements of a particular project.

11

Managing Safety

. . . Management systems must ensure that there is in being a regime which will preserve the first place of safety in the running of the railway. It is not enough to talk in terms of "absolute safety" and of "zero accidents." There must also be proper organisation and management to ensure that actions live up to words.

. . . Sadly, although the sincerity of the beliefs of those in BR [British Rail] at the time of the Clapham Junction accident who uttered such words cannot for a moment be doubted, there was a distressing lack of organisation and management on the part of some whose duty it was to put those words into practice. The result was that the true position in relation to safety lagged frighteningly far behind the idealism of the words.

—British Department of Transport
*Investigation into the Clapham
Junction Railway Accident*

System safety engineers have found that the degree of safety achieved is directly dependent upon the emphasis given to it in the organization. Management plays a crucial role in determining whether accidents occur. Roles must be carefully defined as must the organizational structure, the information gathering and documentation procedures, and the specific process to be followed in system development and operation. All but the last of these topics are covered in this chapter. Process and task requirements are described in Chapter 12, along with real-life examples.

11.1 The Role of General Management

The goals of system safety can be achieved only with the support of management: A sincere commitment to safety by management is perhaps the most important factor in achieving it. Employees need to feel that they will be supported if they exhibit a reasonable concern for safety in their work and if they put safety ahead of other goals such as schedule and costs. Subcontractors in larger projects need the same assurances.

An Air Force study of system safety concluded, "Air Force top management support of system safety has not gone unnoticed by contractors. They now seem more than willing to include system safety tasks, not as 'window dressing' but as a meaningful activity" [88, p.5-11]. An example of how this result was accomplished is the B-1B program, in which the Program Manager or Deputy Manager chaired the meetings of the group where safety decisions were made. "An unmistaken image of the importance of system safety in the program was conveyed to the contractors" [88, p.5-5]. A manager's open concern for safety in everyday dealings with personnel can have a major impact on the reception given to safety issues [261].

Three studies summarized by Cohen found top management's participation in safety issues to be the most effective way to control and reduce accidents [140]. Support for safety is shown by personal involvement (such as direct line orders, regular meetings, and an obvious concern demonstrated in daily tasks), by assigning capable people and giving them appropriate objectives and resources, by setting up appropriate organizational structures, and by responding to initiatives by others.

The presence of senior managers, scientists, and engineers with appropriate expertise and knowledge on high-level peer committees is one measure of the quality of and commitment to a safety program. As one example of such a committee, NASA and Congress set up an Aerospace Safety Advisory Panel after the Apollo command module fire in January 1967 to act as a senior advisory committee to NASA. The panel's charter includes the following:

> The panel shall review safety studies and operations plans referred to it and shall make reports thereon, shall advise the Administrator with respect to the hazards of proposed operations and with respect to the adequacy of proposed or existing safety standards, and shall perform such other duties as the Administrator may request (quoted in [298]).

The panel is set by congressional statute at no more than nine members, with up to four from NASA itself; the NASA Chief Engineer is an ex-officio member. The panel provides independent review and an open forum for NASA and contractor personnel to air technical strengths and weaknesses to a group that reports directly to the NASA Administrator and Congress. It reviews the results of its activities with the appropriate people as soon as they are available in order to provide closure and a feeling that concerns will be acted upon. To ensure cooperation and trust, the panel maintains an atmosphere of teamwork and does not point fingers. Instead, safety improvements are accomplished quietly and unobtrusively and at the lowest appropriate level of the program involved.

> Obviously there are a number of safety, reliability, and quality assurance organizations of all sizes and at different levels at NASA sites and their contractors. The Panel does *not* supercede any of these organizations. The Panel does *not* do their work and it does *not* interfere with them. The Panel *does* add great weight to management's emphasis on safety that is not obtainable in any other way. This is because of the Panel's position in the organizational matrix, the members' individual and collective expertise, their independence, and the true image of 'no axe to grind' [298, p.IX-C-5].

Such a panel provides benefits in addition to those provided by the ongoing safety efforts: independence and lack of involvement in internal politics; additional confidence that nothing falls through the cracks from a safety viewpoint; accountability to management, the stockholders, and the public; and an open forum and expanded communications for all levels and types of technical and administrative personnel.

Other special-purpose and ongoing committees and boards can be used to improve safety understanding and attitudes within managerial, scientific, and engineering groups and to resolve important safety issues. Education about safety is important. Childs suggests that a system safety effort cannot be successful unless all of the people involved have an appreciation of the need for the system safety process and the end results of that process [51].

In general, management is responsible for setting safety policy and defining goals; defining responsibility, fixing accountability, and granting authority; establishing communication channels; and setting up a system safety organization.

11.1.1 Setting Policy and Defining Goals

Management can have its greatest influence on safety by setting safety policy and goals, defining priorities between conflicting goals, establishing procedures for detecting and settling goal conflicts, and setting up incentive structures.

A policy is a written statement of the wisdom, intentions, philosophy, experience, and belief of an organization's senior managers that guides attainment of stated goals [140]. A safety policy should define the relationship of safety to other organizational goals and provide the scope for discretion, initiative, and judgment in deciding what should be done in specific situations.

In England, such a policy is required by law. The British Health and Safety at Work Act of 1974, passed after the Flixborough accident, requires every employer to prepare a written policy statement that includes the organization and arrangements for carrying out the policy. The act also requires that the policy be brought to the attention of all employees.

A safety policy contains such things as the goals of the safety program; a set of criteria for assessing the short- and long-term success of that program with respect to the goals; the values to be used in trade-off decisions; and a clear statement of responsibilities, authority, accountability, and scope of activities. Procedures must exist for reporting back to the policymakers any problems in carrying out the policy.

A safety policy may be broken into two parts: (1) a document that concisely states general policy and organization and (2) a more detailed document or set of documents including standards, manuals, and handbooks describing rules and procedures [172]. Detailed standards have both advantages and disadvantages: They ensure a minimum level of practice, but they also can inhibit flexibility and optimization for particular circumstances. Allowing standards to be tailored while ensuring appropriate oversight on that tailoring is a reasonable compromise.

Not only must a safety policy be defined, it must be disseminated and followed. Management needs to ensure that safety receives appropriate attention in decision making. Progress in achieving goals should be monitored and improvements identified, prioritized, and implemented [346]. The flexibility to respond to safety problems needs to be built into the organizational procedures. For example, schedules should be adaptable to allow for uncertainties and possibilities of delay due to legitimate safety concerns, and production or productivity goals must be reasonable.

Perhaps most important, there must be incentives and reward structures that encourage the proper handling of tradeoffs between safety and other goals. Not only the formal rewards and rules but also the informal rules (social processes) of the organizational culture must support the overall safety policy. London [194] suggests that a practical test of the safety policy is whether managers and supervisors believe they will be supported by the company if they choose safety over the demands of production.

When conflicting goals exist, proper tradeoffs can be ensured using two management approaches: (1) establish strict and detailed guidelines, which sacrifices flexibility, or (2) leave the decisions to employees, which allows more opportunity for major errors of judgment [254]. A compromise strategy between the two extremes leaves much of the decision-making authority in the hands of employees, but also establishes incentives for following general organizational safety policies. For this compromise strategy to work, employees need to feel that they will be supported by management when they make reasonable decisions in favor of safety over alternative goals.

11.1.2 Responsibility, Accountability, and Authority

Responsibility, accountability, and authority for safety within the organization must be clearly defined by management. Authority implies the right to command and determine a course of action, while accountability implies assessment or measurement of the results of that action. Basic management theory holds that the three must go together: If people are assigned responsibility for safety but not held accountable for the results, they will put their efforts into those goals for which they *are* being assessed and measured. Likewise, if people are assigned responsibility for safety and are held accountable for the results, they must be given the authority to do what is necessary to ensure success, and the organization must establish means for measuring performance.

In most cases, responsibility for safety rests with the program manager, who must clearly delineate lines of authority, cooperation, and administration with respect to safety issues throughout the program organization. The system safety manager is responsible for providing the support and information necessary for the program manager to make decisions. Because of the frequent conflicts between safety and other goals, independence of the safety group is important, and responsibility for achieving safety should be separate from responsibility for achieving other goals.

In safety-critical, software-intensive programs, it is rare to find anyone in the software development organization with responsibility for the safety of the software in relation to system safety. The relationship between the software development and system safety groups is often tenuous, although safety may be specified as part of the software development responsibility. Without close ties between the two, however, it is difficult to understand how anything more than software reliability can be evaluated or emphasized.

The U.S. Air Force is a good example of responsibility assignments in large programs. The responsibility for preventing an accident in an Air Force program belongs to the program manager—this responsibility cannot be delegated. The role of the system safety manager is to be sure that when decisions are made, the program manager and other decision makers are fully aware of the risks they accept by their decisions. To implement this role, the system safety manager is responsible for the primary control, direction, supervision, and management of the technical safety aspects of the program, including direct authority over those performing tasks under his or her supervision and guidance, as well as surveillance over those performing tasks under the supervision of others. The system safety manager is directly accountable to the program manager for the conduct and effectiveness of the safety effort for the entire program and must have the appropriate authority.

11.1.3 Establishing Communication Channels

Decision makers need information. A set of channels for information dissemination and feedback needs to be established that includes a means for comparing actual performance with desired performance and ensuring that required action is taken.

Managers are often surprised after accidents, even though the underlying causes were sometimes known in the organization [140]. Problem reports move up slowly and sometimes not at all. Although most safety programs provide centralized hazard monitoring and auditing, information must get to the people who need it. This communication may require redundant channels and cross-checking at successive levels of the organization.

Software development groups are often isolated from the main system safety effort. As a result, the software frequently does not reflect system safety concerns and vice versa. Software developers are then forced to consider only software reliability or conformance with functional requirements in designing and evaluating the quality of their product. Much better two-way communication channels are needed than is commonly found today.

11.1.4 Setting up a System Safety Organization

An effective safety program requires a systematic method and organizational controls. A report by the International Study Group on Risk Analysis, a group of European safety experts, notes that industrial history is full of examples in which the knowledge to prevent a loss existed but, in the absence of an organization to identify and control hazards, the knowledge was not available to the people who could have avoided the accident [196].

Duties and Responsibilities

To be effective, the safety organization must have a high-level, independent role in the organization. That role may include:

- Participation in the formulation and implementation of the safety policy
- Documentation and tracking of hazards and their resolution
- Education and promotion
- Adoption and development of standards
- Conduct of or participation in hazard analysis and other system safety procedures
- Trend analysis and maintenance of safety documentation
- Planning and monitoring of testing and operations for safety issues
- Participation in program reviews and milestones
- Liaison between other safety groups
- Accident investigation and analysis

Software safety management and personnel should participate in the early planning of the safety program, engage in continual interaction with the system safety group, and participate in all aspects of software development activities to ensure that software hazards are eliminated or controlled to an acceptable level.

Personnel Qualifications

The system safety job involves extensive meetings, analysis, and negotiation: Communication skills are extremely important. Personnel need to be trained in system engineering techniques and should have extensive knowledge of and experience with the application involved or a quick capacity to learn. In general, the more experience the safety engineer has with the particular type of system or component being developed, the more thorough, accurate, and useful the safety analysis will be throughout the program [294].

System safety managers in the United States usually are registered as professional engineers and certified as system safety professionals (CSPs).[1] Because of their extensive interaction with almost every activity in the organization and their need to be influential with management, technical competence, experience, and ability to communicate are all important.

Although software safety engineers are rare, a few companies have established this job category, which requires a good knowledge of both hardware and software and the ability to communicate with both groups. The software safety engineer should have overall responsibility for software safety analyses and for software inputs to system safety analyses; participate in software design reviews and configuration board activities; establish and oversee audit trails for identified software hazards; and implement two-way communication between software development and the system hazard auditing process.

For practical reasons, training a software engineer in system safety may be more successful than training a safety engineer in software engineering. In any case, the qualifications of all safety personnel, including education, experience, and certification, should be specified in the organization's policy documents.

As an example of such qualifications, the U.S. Air Force Space and Missile Division (in MIL-STD-1574) requires that the contractor system safety manager have at least a Bachelor of Science degree in engineering or applied science and be registered as a professional engineer in one of the states or territories or certified as a system safety professional. Advanced study or experience in systems management is considered desirable. The system safety manager must have been assigned as a system safety engineer for a minimum of four years and have experience in at least three of six functional areas—system safety management, system safety analysis, system safety design, system safety research, system safety operations, and mishap investigation. Under certain conditions, professional safety experience can be substituted for the education or certification requirements. A new British standard for safety-critical software has similar requirements, including a science or engineering degree, registration as a Chartered Engineer, and minimum experience and training classes or special certification.

Subcontracting

In a large program, where subcomponents are contracted to separate companies or organizations, the tasks and scope of the system safety program should be completely specified in the contracting documents. However, specific analysis

---

[1] In the United States, the Board of Certified Safety Professionals (BCSP) offers a number of specialty exams, including one in system safety that, if completed successfully, confers the title of Certified Safety Professional (CSP).

methods should not be specified, as this may relieve the contractor of any consequent responsibility for an accident if the method is ineffective. Instead, contractors should be required to develop system and software safety program plans that fit their organizations and products. The problem of overspecifying analysis methods seems to be especially relevant to systems containing software. Many techniques sold as providing software safety—and sometimes required in contracts or regulatory standards—are nearly worthless and usually a waste of time and resources.

An exception may be some extremely dangerous systems, such as nuclear systems, where extensive requirements for specific analyses and reviews are common and may be appropriate. However, any required techniques must be state of the art, and the requirements must be constantly evaluated and modified as feedback about effectiveness and new knowledge is obtained. This evaluation is especially important for software, where most of the state-of-the-art techniques have never been scientifically assessed for effectiveness and many of the arguments for their use in safety-critical systems appear to be based primarily on wishful thinking.

Working Groups

In large military programs, system and software safety working groups or committees have proved to be extremely effective in coordinating safety efforts. The System Safety or Software Safety Working Group is a functional organization that provides an interface between the agency's safety efforts and its contractors and subcontractors. Members of the working group are usually the agency safety manager, the integration contractor safety manager, representatives from appropriate offices within the agency, and the safety managers from the contractors and subcontractors. Members of the group are responsible for coordinating the efforts within their respective organizations and reporting the status of unresolved issues.

System Safety in Small Organizations

The system safety organization in large and small programs will, of course, differ. Most small organizations cannot afford a full-time safety engineer, and safety responsibility must be assigned to the design engineering department. Even in this situation, responsibility for safety should be assigned to specific engineers, and written reports and formal presentations should be a part of the product documentation and management review process. Hazard files should be maintained containing all analyses and action taken to eliminate or control the hazards associated with the product.

A belief prevalent in small companies is that any good engineer can write software. This belief has caused some of the worst software-related accidents. Competent software engineering, especially for safety-critical systems, requires expertise and advanced training.

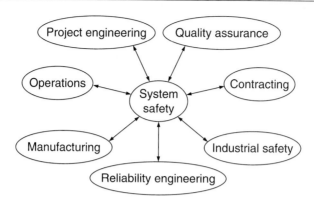

FIGURE 11.1
System safety needs direct communication paths to most parts of the
organization.

11.2 Place in the Organizational Structure

Organizations are all different, so the ideal place for the safety function in each
organization will vary. Some general requirements hold, however:

- The system safety manager needs a *direct link to decision makers*. If critical
  information has to float up a chain of command, it may be lost or modified
  either deliberately, because of schedule or budget pressures, or inadvertently.
  Decision makers often need fast access to information.

- The system safety function needs *independence* in order to provide an external review divorced from other project management concerns. System safety
  also functions best when it is independent of other supporting disciplines
  such as reliability and quality assurance.

- System safety must have *direct communication channels* to most parts of the
  organization (see Figure 11.1). At one time or another, system safety will
  interact with nearly every program or activity, since it provides a continual
  overview of the technical, planning, and operational aspects of the organization. The safety group must be in a position where it can obtain information
  directly from a wide variety of sources to ensure that information is received
  in a timely manner and without being changed by being filtered through
  groups with potential conflicting interests. For example, system safety interacts with engineering activities to check that standards are being applied,
  to certify safety requirements and design features, to obtain information for
  hazard analyses, to review testing and verification activities, and to evaluate
  the effectiveness of current standards. The interface with quality assurance

provides input to system safety about identified problems that are safety related; at the same time, quality assurance receives information from system safety that may help to focus quality assurance activities on the most critical aspects of the system. Reliability and maintainability provide data for hazard analyses. System safety will also need to interact with contracting, industrial safety, manufacturing, operations, and so on.

□ System safety must have *influence on decision making*. At some time or another, the system safety manager may need to exert influence on every department head and therefore must report to a person with influence and to be seen as having the support of senior management.

□ Safety activities must have *focus and coordination*. Although safety issues permeate every part of the development and operations of a complex system, a common methodology and approach will strengthen the individual disciplines. Also, interface issues and communication are important; sometimes safety-motivated changes in one subsystem affects another subsystem and the system as a whole. It is important that system safety efforts do not end up fragmented and uncoordinated. While one could argue that safety staff support should be integrated into one unit rather than scattered in several places, an equally valid argument could be made for the advantages of distribution. But if the effort is distributed, a clear focus and coordinating body are needed.

These requirements suggest some basic principles for locating the safety function within an organization—and some conflicts. To influence decision making, system safety managers should report directly to the executive with ultimate program responsibility for that function. However, to ensure an independent review, system safety managers should report above the program manager. The U.S. Air Force assigns the system safety specialist directly to the program manager, while the Army and Navy do not. NASA and others resolve this conflict by having system safety managers report to the program managers, but with higher-level boards and review groups and established information channels between levels (the NASA structure is described in Chapter 12).

Corporate Level

In a large corporation, system safety at the corporate level can define and enforce corporate safety policy and ensure that safe design and review are applied consistently throughout the various divisions and projects. In some organizations that build extremely hazardous systems, a group at the corporate or headquarters level certifies these systems. For example, the U.S. Navy has a Weapons System Explosives Safety Review Board that assures the incorporation of explosives safety criteria in all weapon systems by reviews conducted throughout all the system's life cycle phases. This board reviews system and software safety analyses and test programs, including

- Identification of generic safety design requirements from general documents and lessons learned
- Identification of hazards
- Development of safety design requirements
- Tracing of safety design requirements
- Identification of causal links to software
- Identification of safety-critical computer software components and units
- Identification and analysis of critical source code and methodology chosen
- Review of results of detailed safety analyses of critical functions
- Analysis of design change recommendations for potential safety impacts
- Final assessment of safety issues

A Software Systems Safety Technical Review Board supports the Weapons Review Board in the review of software system safety. Both boards are independent of the individual weapon system programs.

Lower Levels

At each level below the corporate or headquarters level, the safety manager usually reports to the division or program manager. Thus, a safety group is located at each level, with its function dependent on the level. There should be a system safety engineering group within systems engineering and a software safety group within software development, but tight coordination between these groups must be established. Although arguments could be made that the software safety engineer should be independent of the software development group, it is unlikely that such an independent person would have adequate influence on software development. This dilemma of needing both independence and integration may be solved either by a matrix organization or by separating the control function from the review function—the control function is integrated into the planning and development group to influence decision making, while the review function remains independent.

Coordination

To provide coordination and independent channels for safety information, a coordinating committee or working group is often created, as described earlier. This group assures comprehensive and unified planning and action, and allows for independent review. The working groups may be on different levels; for example, a corporate-level working group may be composed of the safety managers for the different divisions or programs, and a program-level working group may be composed of the system and subsystem safety managers (system engineering, software development, hardware design, and so on) or the subcontractor safety managers.

Putting the subsystem (component) safety engineers within their own groups (such as the software safety engineer within the software development group) has advantages, but they will need close interaction with other groups such as system engineering, testing, and quality assurance. A system safety working group within a project can implement this interaction. In very large projects, with separate software contractors or software development efforts, a software safety working group may be needed to coordinate software safety efforts.

Small Organizations

A small organization may have only one full-time safety engineer or perhaps none, and safety responsibilities must be assigned to the design engineers. Nevertheless, safety analyses, reports, and presentations will still need to be a part of product documentation and management review. Someone needs to be responsible for safety and needs to provide an outside, independent review of the product. Alternatively, an independent organization may contract to provide the safety review. In either case, direct access to top management must be provided.

Examples

These general rules and guidelines (and attempts by others to prescribe one organizational structure as the best) must be tempered by the fact that each system safety effort should be tailored to the management system and philosophy in the organization and to the specific requirements and characteristics of the project and its personnel, such as experience and attitudes, the mix of disciplines, the structural organization, and the difficulty of the development and operations. What will be most effective within one situation may not be effective in another.

Childs provides two examples of similar project developments that have very different project management systems and radically different approaches to system safety organization and management [51]. Both projects have effective system safety efforts.

The first project has no in-line system safety personnel, but has a rigid, well-understood set of system safety requirements imposed by a parent organization. This higher-level organization requires the project to meet specific safety standards, to conduct and document hazard analyses and assessments, and to conduct rigorous safety reviews at critical points in development. The reviews are managed by a small system safety staff within the parent organization. Childs claims this structure works because the project personnel are well educated in the system safety discipline. Each engineer knows his or her part in the safety analysis process and has the added advantage of knowing the system well. The project manager is intimately familiar with the process and knows that he is personally responsible to the parent organization's safety review group. In turn, the small system safety staff reporting to the parent organization has excellent system engineers with extensive backgrounds in project engineering and safety management. In addition, the parent organization safety reviews draw on the most knowledgeable experts in the engineering disciplines critical to safety either as consultants or participants in the formal reviews.

The second project has only very general system safety requirements imposed by its parent organization. Several well-qualified system safety engineers are matrixed (but co-located) from the parent organization's safety staff. The project personnel are familiar with system safety procedures; they furnish engineering support for the hazard analyses and assessments, which are conducted by the system safety professionals. Detailed safety reviews are made a part of the project review process, with summary safety items part of the parent organization reviews. Objectivity is maintained by the co-located system safety personnel's ties to the parent organization's safety staff. As in the first project, liberal use is made of independent experts to pinpoint safety-critical deficiencies in the system.

Surprisingly, the total number of in-line project personnel plus safety personnel in the two projects is comparable. The big difference is in the basic organizational management philosophies. Childs concludes,

> The important point is that each system safety effort is efficiently tailored (albeit in a different way) to its management system. Neither has settled at an extreme of "getting into bed" with the project and losing objectivity or backing off too far and losing insight. This is vitally important for each extreme can, and usually does, result in cosmetic system safety at its worst [51].

11.3 Documentation

There are three major types of documentation in system safety: planning documents, information systems, and reports.

11.3.1 Program Plans

The *system safety program plan* (SSPP) is a management document that describes the system safety objectives and how they will be achieved. It provides a regulatory agency, contracting agency, or manager with a baseline (a basis of understanding among multiple groups and within a single group over time) with which to evaluate compliance and progress. Specifying a plan should be the first step in any safety-critical project.

Plans for subsystem safety should be part of the SSPP rather than in separate documents. Safety is a system—not a subsystem—quality, and separate documents for the subsystems appears to have only disadvantages. Thus planning for software safety should be included within the overall system safety plan; it should not be a separate and hence potentially inconsistent or unintegrated process. Software development too often is separated from the overall system engineering process, with unfortunate results. However, the subsystem development groups should have major input into the SSPP, or compliance may be difficult to achieve.

Many standards exist for program plans—each is a little different, but all contain similar information. Devising a general plan for everyone is not practical, however: Each plan needs to be tailored to its project and goals and to fit the corporate personality and management system.

Although one plan will not suffice for all types of projects, the following information might be included in a comprehensive plan:

I. General Considerations
- A. Introduction
- B. Scope and Purpose
- C. Objectives
- D. Applicable Standards
- E. Progress Reporting
- F. Documentation and Reports

II. System Safety Organization
- A. Personnel Qualifications and Duties
- B. Functional Organization
- C. Staffing and Manpower
- D. Communication Channels
- E. Responsibility, Authority, and Accountability
- F. Subcontractor Responsibilities
- G. Coordination
- H. System Safety Groups/System Safety Working Groups
- I. Safety Program Interfaces with Other Disciplines
    - Reliability
    - Maintainability
    - Design and System Engineering
    - Software Development
    - Configuration Management
    - Quality Assurance
    - Human Factors
    - Test
    - Industrial Safety

III. System Safety Program Schedule
- A. Critical Checkpoints and Milestones
- B. Start and Completion Dates of Tasks, Reports, Reviews
- C. Review Procedures and Participants

IV. System Safety Criteria
- A. Definitions
- B. Identification and Dissemination
- C. Classification/Ranking of Hazards
    - Hazard Severity Categories
    - Hazard Probability Levels
    - Risk Assessment
- D. System Safety Precedence

   E. Safety Design Criteria
       Hardware
       Software
   F. Special Contractual Requirements
V. Safety Data
   A. Data Requirements
       Deliverable
       Non-deliverable
   B. Hazard Tracking and Reporting System
   C. Requirements and Use of Safety Data
       Hazard Data Collection
       Lessons Learned
       Documentation and Files (Safety Data Library)
       Records Retention
VI. Hazard Analyses (Types, Documentation, and Expected Uses)
   A. Preliminary Hazard Analysis
   B. System Hazard Analyses
   C. Subsystem Hazard Analyses (including Software Hazard Analyses)
   D. Operating System Hazard Analyses
   E. Integration of Subcontractor Analyses with Overall System Hazard Analyses
   F. Tracing of System Hazards into Subsystems
VII. Verification
   A. Safety-Related Testing
   B. Special Demonstrations
   C. Review and Feedback Procedures
VIII. Audit Program
IX. Operations
   A. Emergency and Contingency Procedures
   B. Configuration Control Activities
   C. Training
X. Hazard and Incident Reporting and Investigation During Operations
XI. Special Safety Activities
   A. Range Safety
   B. Facility Safety
   C. Explosives Safety
   D. Nuclear Safety
   E. Chemical and Biological Safety

11.3.2 Safety Information System

Although setting up a comprehensive and usable information system can be time consuming and costly, such a system is crucial to the success of safety efforts, and resources invested in it will be well spent. After studying organizations and accidents, Kjellan concluded that an effective safety information system ranked second only to top management concern about safety in discriminating between safe and unsafe companies matched on other variables [151].

Control of any activity requires information. Documenting and tracking hazards and their resolution are basic requirements for any effective safety program. All hazards need to be recorded, not just the most critical; otherwise, there is no record that a particular condition has already been evaluated. Because the hazard list may become quite large, hazard or problem priority lists summarizing the most significant information on complex programs can be useful for reviews and management oversight. The complete hazard log and audit trail will show what was done and how and why decisions were made.

An organization's system safety information system will contain such information as an updated System Safety Program Plan and the status of the activities included, results of hazard analyses, tracking and status information on all known hazards, incident and accident information including corrective action, trend analysis data, and so on. Interfaces with various project databases, such as the software configuration control database, should be well defined.

A crucial aspect of any management system is the feedback of information on which to base future decisions. Information can be used to describe, to diagnose, to compare, to evaluate, and to improve. For example, a safety information system can provide the information necessary (1) to detect trends and deviations that presage an accident, (2) to evaluate the effectiveness of safety controls and standards, (3) to compare models and risk assessments with actual behavior, and (4) to identify and control hazards and to improve designs and standards.

Information can be collected by a company or by an industry. The sharing of information within an industry can add to the general knowledge about hazards and about effective and ineffective control measures. Within a company, an information system can provide valuable feedback about the analysis process and about the need for additional controls or modifications.

An effective information system must consider not only accidents, but also incidents or near-misses. An accident usually occurs only when the complete set of necessary conditions exist; a near miss or incident results when only some of these conditions exist. Whether all or some of the causal conditions exist at any time is often a matter of luck—usually the ratio of incidents to accidents is several orders of magnitude [172]. Examination and understanding of near misses can warn of an impending accident and also provide important information about what conditions need to be controlled. Civil aviation and the nuclear industry are examples of fields that require reporting near misses.

No matter how the information is collected, understanding its limitations and inaccuracies is important. Simply collecting information is not enough—the information must be accurate and timely, and it must be disseminated to the appropriate people in a useful form. Three factors are involved: information collection, analysis, and dissemination.

Collection

Various types of information can be collected: performance and operational data; accident and incident investigations; results of studies and evaluations; technical information such as standards, manuals, and professional literature; and so on. Operational data, obviously, is the most difficult to accumulate; only a limited sample of operational data may be available for a particular hazard. Collection of such data for a single company or organization may be very expensive and require a large quality control group working over an extensive period of time. Industry-wide efforts may be more practical, but it is difficult to obtain comparable data from multiple sources in an unbiased and systematic manner.

Data may be seriously distorted by the way it is collected. The two main problems in collecting data are systematic filtering or suppression and unreliability. Data usually must be obtained from written descriptions of events in a report about an accident or near miss. Such reports tend to identify only the proximal events (events closest in time) and not events that are early in the sequence or causal factors that are at a higher level in the causal framework such as management problems or organizational deficiencies (see Chapter 3).

Studies have shown that data from near-miss reporting by operators are filtered and mainly concern technical failures [151]. Reports by management are similarly filtered and primarily point to operator error as the cause of the incident or accident [140]. General safety inspections also tend to identify limited categories of conditions. Accident reports are usually made after an event, often by witnesses who were confused and disturbed by it [57]: They may not have been paying much attention until the accident itself and thus find it difficult to recreate preceding events.

Hazards, by their nature, involve relatively rare and unpredictable events, and these events are therefore difficult to describe. Data collection is more reliable for accidents that are similar to those that have occurred in the past than for accidents in new types of systems where past experience on hazards and causal factors are less well understood. Software errors and computer problems are often omitted or misdescribed because of lack of knowledge, lack of accepted and consistent categorizations for such errors, or failure to consider them seriously as a causal factor.

Experience has shown that it is difficult to maintain reliable reporting of incidents over an extended period [151]; therefore, this data is not very useful for estimating probabilities of events or their potential consequences. In some industries, up to three-quarters of accidents may be unreported [57]. Sometimes, information is involved that the company wishes to keep secret or that those making the reports may worry will be used against them in job performance evaluations. Potential legal liability may be affected by the reporting of accidents or near misses.

Various research studies have shown that it is possible to improve the comprehensiveness and reliability of data collection [151]. Some measures introduced to improve the process are checklists, special training of data collectors, feedback of results to the data collectors, and fixed routines. Near-miss reporting has been improved through anonymous reporting, directive reporting, and reporting during a limited time period. Those making such reports must be convinced that the information will be used for constructive improvements in safety and not as a basis for criticism or disciplinary action [126].

The *Critical Incident Technique* is a means of collecting information about hazards, near misses, and unsafe conditions and practices from operationally experienced personnel, who are asked to describe all near misses or accidents they can recall. Use of this technique has shown that there is 1 accident for approximately every 400 near misses [108]. Van Horn [342] claims that the Critical Incident Technique generates more relevant and useful information than any other monitoring technique, and it identifies more seemingly minor errors or deficiencies and near misses.

Model accident analysis forms encourage the inclusion of multiple factors and events. The forms may request both advance warnings and preventive factors that might be used to prevent recurrences, and thus they generate practical recommendations [172]. However, care must be taken in the design of the forms not to limit the factors considered.

Automated monitoring can greatly improve the accuracy and completeness of data collection. Instrumentation can provide information on deviations and trends of selected variables and alarms. The great success of black box aircraft monitoring systems lies in the fact that the parameters to be recorded are standard, correct flying behavior is well defined, and an authority exists to analyze the data. Such monitoring systems can be of use in other situations where the data to be recorded can be determined *a priori*, the instruments can be maintained in working order, and the system can be protected against the effects of an accident (for example, fire or explosion) [172].

Analysis

Data, once collected, needs to be analyzed and summarized. Systematizing and consolidating a large mass of data into a form useful for learning is difficult. Raw quantitative data can be misleading and should always be tested for statistical significance. Remember, however, that statistical analysis alone is not enough—it too can be misleading and can leave out important information for hazard control.

Analysis is at the heart of any system safety program: Because of its importance, it is covered in depth in Chapters 13, 14, and 15.

Dissemination

Dissemination of information in a useful form may be the most difficult aspect of maintaining an information system. If information is not presented to decision makers in a meaningful way, learning from the data is inhibited. Traditionally, information has been disseminated in checklists, standards, and codes of practice.

Information about hazards has been distributed also in manuals, such as the *Dow Index* in the chemical industry (see Chapter 14). Books that describe and categorize accidents and their causal factors, such as those by Trevor Kletz on the chemical industry [157, 161], are extremely useful for training and information dissemination.

Accidents are often repeated, and accident/incident files are one of the most important information sources for hazard analysis and control. However, the information needs to be presented in a form that people can learn from, apply to their daily jobs, and use throughout the life cycle of projects, not just in the conceptual design stage. Accidents are frequently the result of risk decisions that were changed by default when operations changed or are due to insufficient updates to the hazard analysis when engineering modifications were made [51].

Much is still being learned about how to integrate and use automated information systems in organizations. The method of presenting the information should be adapted to the cognitive styles and models of the users, and the dissemination of information should be integrated into the environment in which safety-related decisions are made [150]—for example, computer-assisted design (CAD), planning, scheduling, and resource allocation systems.

An Example Information System: The ASRS

The Air Safety Reporting System (ASRS) was established in 1975 and receives over 4,000 reports a year on safety-related incidents and near misses [259]. The U.S. FAA originally sponsored a similar program in the 1960s, which was ostensibly nonpunitive, but pilots and controllers did not support it. The FAA tried again with the ASRS, but this time the program was supervised by NASA and run by the Battelle Memorial Institute, which insured considerable independence from the FAA.

Controllers, pilots, or others can report a dangerous situation in writing or orally. Often, they report errors they made themselves. Names and identification are removed from reports almost immediately (usually in less than four days) after verification contacts with the person who submitted the report. Once the identification has been removed, the report becomes part of the public record.

The FAA cannot penalize pilots who report errors even if they broke federal rules or laws (unless criminal activity is involved); however, pilots are still subject to discipline by their airlines. This immunity, of course, opened the system to abuse, and it was difficult for the FAA to agree to it. However, extensive experience with the system indicates that the limited waiver of disciplinary action compromises or hinders disciplinary action in less than 10 percent of the cases of known violations.

The program seems to be extremely successful. Reported unsafe airport conditions are quickly corrected. Changes in air traffic control and other types of procedures have been made on the basis of ASRS reports. The information in the individual reports is collated by a staff of experts into a series of summary reports on topics such as controlled flight into terrain, distractions, inflight emergencies, and communication problems. From the ASRS reports alone, it has been discovered that there are two potential collisions every day involving air carriers. Perrow writes, "The extent of *mea culpa* in the reports is striking, as is the objectivity of the analysis" [259, p.169].

Similar programs have been implemented in other countries. For example, CHIRP (Confidential Human Factors Incident Reporting Program) in Great Britain, was initiated and is sponsored by the Civil Aviation Authority and operated by the Royal Air Force Institute of Aviation Medicine. Like the ASRS, this reporting system allows any commercial pilot or air traffic controller to report errors in complete confidence, although not anonymously. Each year, about 200 people report errors to CHIRP and why they believe they made them [101]. Europe has a similar reporting system called EUCARE (The European Confidential Safety Reporting Network).

11.3.3 Safety Reports

Although every organization or industry has different names for reports, there are actually only a few types: hazard reporting forms, design documentation, hazard analysis reports, and safety assessment reports. Formats are often specified in great detail by the customer or by a government licensing authority. There are too many formats to review them all, but the basic information is common to most of them.

The *hazard report* contains a description of the potential problem and what is being done about it. These reports are compiled into the hazard catalog or log to form the basis for the hazard auditing and tracking system. As each hazard is identified, it should be documented on a uniquely numbered hazard report form and tracked through closure.

The hazard report form includes, at least, a description and classification of the hazard, a history of action taken, and some verification that the action has been taken. It might also include the system or subsystem involved, the operational phase, the cause(s) and possible effects, and corrective or preventive measures. Figure 11.2 shows a sample hazard reporting form used by the U.S. Air Force. A common mistake is to list causal factors instead of the hazard itself [5]. The causal factors are the types or classes of events or conditions that can lead to the identified hazard.

In the normal design documentation, a section should be included that describes the basis on which safety-related design decisions were made and any special design features that were incorporated for safety reasons. This information is essential for safety reviews and also for maintenance so that safety features are not inadvertently eliminated because the reasons they were included are not known. It can also be useful in writing operating and maintenance procedures, safety manuals, and training manuals.

The various hazard analyses used in a program generate *hazard analysis re-*

System _____	Hazard Level _____
Subsystem _____	Date _____
Operation/Phase _____	Closure _____

Hazard

Causal Factors/Assumptions

Hazard Controls	Status	Reference

Verification Methods	Status	Reference

Remarks

Closure Concurrence

Project Safety Engineer _____   Date _____

Project Manager _____   Date _____

SSWG Chairman _____   Date _____

FIGURE 11.2
A sample hazard reporting form.

ports on the procedures used and the results. These reports usually are combined into one *safety assessment report* that integrates all system, hardware, and software analyses. Special reports, for example on nuclear safety analysis, may focus on just one type of hazard.

At the end of a project, a *final safety assessment report* may be produced, which is used (1) to determine compliance with the program safety requirements and (2) to provide system users and operators with a comprehensive description of the system hazards and the hazardous subsystems and operations associated with the system. This report might contain some or all of the following:

- □ General or detailed system and subsystem descriptions and operating characteristics
- □ Documentation on each hazard—including potential causes, implemented controls, results of the verification activities, closeout status, and any waivers or deviations from requirements
- □ Risk assessments
- □ Summaries of all hazard analysis and verification activities—including a description of the methods used, the sources of any basic data used, and simplifications and assumptions made in the analysis and their potential influence on the results
- □ Safety-related design or operating limits
- □ Hazardous materials
- □ Contingency/emergency procedures
- □ Incident/accident record—a record of all safety-related failures or incidents during development, previous use, or other programs using similar hardware or software, along with all corrective action taken to prevent recurrence.

Once the management system is in place, the next step is to define a process tailored for the particular project and its participants. The components of such a process are described in the next chapter.

Chapter

12

The System and Software Safety Process

For us, the indisputable lesson of Chernobyl lies in this: the principles regulating the further development of the scientific-technological revolution must be safety, discipline, order, and organization. Everywhere and in all respects, we must operate according to the strictest standards.

—Mikhail Gorbachev[1]

Each project is different: System safety processes and tasks need to be tailored to the criticality of the potential hazards; the particular organizational culture, structure, and personnel; the particular industry and application; and so on. The size of the company and project will also affect the design of the system safety process.

In this chapter, a generic process is outlined that may be mapped onto existing standards or used to design specific processes for new standards or for specific projects and companies. System safety tasks have been described in many books and are often specified in government standards, although the standards do not always agree with each other. Less documentation exists about the relationship of software development to these tasks. System and software safety tasks often are defined separately, but they are defined together here to demonstrate that they cannot really be separated: The software safety process is just a subset of the overall system safety process.

The definition of specific milestones, reports, and reviews is a crucial part of any process description, but these items are very project specific. Safety reviews

---

[1] Quoted in [132, p.177]

and reports usually correspond to system development milestones and consist of various types of intermediate reports along with final documentation of the results. Often on large projects, the customer will require the contractors to report periodically on the status of the system safety program. This feedback may take the form of brief reports or complete reviews. As with any process, reviews are valuable ways to assure the quality of the safety program by creating a sense of responsibility and professionalism. According to Johnson [140], teams performing hazard analyses do a better job when they know that there will be a review and that criteria have been established for the review.

Government certification requirements are also specific, this time to the country and application. Licensing agencies will often review and approve the initial safety plan and may review the status of the project and the safety efforts at various stages of the program. The earlier this review is done, the easier it will be to make required changes.

12.1 The General Tasks

System safety can be thought of as an integrating function—it ensures that specific safety considerations are introduced into the program early in the life cycle, that they are integrated into overall system design and development, and that efforts continue throughout the system's existence. Frola and Miller describe the role of system safety as comparable to project management in relation to the safety aspects of the project [88]. System safety has its own body of knowledge and tasks and, at the same time, plays a safety coordinating role with respect to the entire program.

The tasks involved in system safety differ in the various phases of a project, although many merely begin in different phases but then continue, perhaps in slightly different forms, throughout the system life cycle. An engineering project can be divided into five stages: conceptual development, design (demonstration and validation), full-scale development, production and deployment (pre-startup), and operation. The next sections describe the primary system safety activities during each of these phases. These general task descriptions are followed by several examples of safety programs.

12.1.1 Conceptual Development Tasks

At this early stage of system development, essential groundwork must be established for the entire project safety effort.

■ *Develop the system safety program plan.*

As described in Chapter 11, this plan defines how the safety effort will be carried out. Although the program plan is started in this early stage, changes are likely to be required throughout the development process as more is learned about the system and its hazards.

In order to ensure that a coherent and complete plan is derived, as noted earlier, there should *not* be separate plans for software or other parts of the safety effort: All facets of the safety program should be documented in the overall system safety planning document. Software is an integral part of the development and operations process, and the software safety tasks to be implemented must be included, like everything else, in the system safety plan. Including software in the system plan does not mean, however, that the plan should be written only by system safety personnel. It is important that each group that will be responsible for carrying out parts of the plan participate in the planning process to make sure that everyone has bought into the plan from the beginning. If not, compliance by the various development groups with the overall safety efforts and goals will be more difficult to achieve.

The general safety process applied to software development is similar to that applied to any component, especially control components. The basic software system safety tasks include the following:

1. Trace identified system hazards to the software–hardware interface. Translate the identified software-related hazards into requirements and constraints on software behavior.
2. Show the consistency of the software system safety constraints with the software requirements specification. Demonstrate completeness of the software requirements with respect to system safety properties.
3. Develop system-specific software design criteria and requirements, testing requirements, and computer–human interface requirements based on the identified software system safety constraints.
4. Trace safety requirements and constraints to the code.
5. Identify the parts of the software that control safety-critical operations and concentrate safety analysis and test efforts on those functions and on the safety-critical path that leads to their execution.
6. Identify safety-critical components and variables to code developers, including critical inputs and outputs (the interface).
7. Develop a tracking system within the software and system configuration control structure to ensure traceability of safety requirements and their flow through documentation.
8. Develop safety-related software test plans, test descriptions, test procedures, and test case requirements and additional analysis requirements.
9. Perform any special safety analyses such as computer–human interface analysis, software fault tree analysis, or analysis of the interface between critical and noncritical software components.
10. Review test results for safety issues. Trace identified safety-related software problems back to the system level.

11. Assemble safety-related information (such as caution and warning notes) for inclusion in design documentation, user manuals, and other documentation.

■ *Establish the safety information and documentation files.*

The safety information system will contain the current version of the system safety program plan and an account of all analyses and action taken by the system safety office and the other subcomponent safety groups. This information is used to monitor the safety program in order to detect risks and deviations from safety plans quickly, to document information about hazards and corrective measures taken, and to provide prompt and adequate feedback on performance.

■ *Establish the hazard auditing and log file. Develop a tracking system within configuration control (both system and subsystem, including software) for tracing hazards and their resolution.*

The hazard tracking system documents and tracks all identified hazards until their ultimate resolution, including corrective actions, waivers, and verification efforts. The tracking system needs to be established at the start of the hazard identification process.

■ *Review lessons learned and applicable documents.*

At this time, the foundations of hazard identification and control are laid, including the review of applicable lessons learned and successful (and unsuccessful) designs of similar systems along with a review of applicable standards, codes of practice, and guidelines.

■ *Establish certification and training requirements for personnel involved in the development, test, and operation of the system.*

These requirements may already have been defined in the general company safety policy, but special certification and training requirements may be necessary for specific projects.

■ *Participate in system concept formation.*

At the earliest stages of system development, system safety personnel need to participate in all concept formation meetings to ensure that system hazards are given due consideration in the decision-making process. Many potential hazards can be identified and eliminated or controlled at minimal cost during this phase.

System safety provides input to trade studies and other system engineering activities. At this point in the development process, the main focus is on determining the general safety requirements and design constraints and the required level of safety for the various concepts and alternatives under consideration. The system safety analysis results, along with recommendations for each alternative system concept under consideration, must be documented.

Because of the special role that software often plays in a system, software personnel should be included in the overall system engineering and system safety process at this stage to ensure that concerns about software capabilities and limitations are included in the system design. Sometimes, impossible tasks are assigned to software, and it is wise to find this out as soon as possible.

■ *Delineate the scope of the analyses.*

One of the first steps in the hazard analysis process is defining the scope of the analyses. Early in the process, the boundaries and assumptions of the safety analyses need to be established along with the data and information sources and documents to be used. This information is not only necessary to guide the safety process during system development, but is also necessary for proper control of safety during operational use of the system. The assumptions about the construction and operation of the system should be used to manage safety during operation, both (1) as a basis for training, instructions, inspections, and tests, and (2) as a means of evaluating incidents and events to determine whether the assumptions and the resulting hazard analyses were realistic.

In general, the description of assumptions about work procedures and organization underlying the hazard analyses and safety design features will define the limits of freedom of action for management during operational use of the system: The assumptions of the hazard analysis become the preconditions for operation. This scope definition step, along with careful documentation of the models and assumptions of the ongoing hazard analysis, is crucial for success.

In planning the hazard-analysis process, the following aspects should be defined and recorded [126]:

1. The objective of the analysis
2. The basis for the analysis
3. Hazard and cause types to be considered in the analysis
4. Required standards of detail and certainty
5. Standards for approval of the analysis (criteria for acceptability)

The defined process, of course, also needs to allow for unforeseen hazards or changes in priorities.

■ *Identify hazards and safety requirements.*

The first efforts should begin at this time to identify system hazards, hazard levels, criteria for determining priority and limits of hazard resolution, safety design criteria, and verification requirements. Because little is known about the design, system safety requirements will be based partly on past experience with similar systems. Safety requirements will probably change during the system life cycle, and it is helpful (if possible) to identify those requirements most likely to change.

■ *Identify design, analysis, and verification requirements, possible safety-interface problems, including the human–machine interface, and operating support requirements.*

This is also the time to start identifying any system safety design, analysis, test, demonstration, and validation requirements, possible safety interface requirements, and operating support requirements. Verification methods should be considered from the earliest project stages. Otherwise, the project may commit to a particular type of hazard control and then find that it is impossible or very costly to verify (by test, analysis, demonstration, or inspection) that the control is effective and has been implemented correctly.

■ *Establish working groups and other special structures.*

For major programs, special organizational structures that are needed but do not already exist must be established at this time. For example, safety working groups may be formed and start meeting.

12.1.2 System Design Tasks

■ *Update analyses.*

At the design (and every other) stage, all the safety-related analysis, decisions, and documentation must be updated as more information about the system is derived. As the design is developed, causal factors related to the hazards can be identified. System safety personnel will need to examine the interfaces of all subsystems and determine how their interactions may affect the overall system safety. Analysis of the hazards associated with the environment, personnel procedures, and equipment will begin. As the design develops, there needs to be documentation of compliance with contractually imposed safety regulations, standards, and laws: For low-risk programs and standard designs, these steps may be all that is required in terms of safety analysis.

■ *Participate in system tradeoff studies.*

System safety personnel need to participate in any design decisions and design tradeoff studies to ensure that safety design constraints are properly reflected in them. System design changes may be recommended based on the studies to assure that desired safety is achieved, consistent with performance and system requirements.

■ *Ensure that safety requirements are incorporated into system and subsystem specifications, including human–machine interface requirements.*

As early as possible in the design process, system hazards should be traced to the subsystems and components so that specifications and design decisions can reflect system safety concerns.

■ *Ensure that identified hazards are being eliminated or controlled in the evolving design.*

To accomplish this task, the detailed system and subsystem requirements specifications must be evaluated. System safety may recommend corrective action appropriate for the stage of the project. System safety must ensure that the system is protected against unexpected software behavior and that the software is designed to handle unexpected hardware behavior.

■ *Identify safety-critical components.*

System safety will need to closely interact with quality assurance personnel in identifying safety-critical components and functions that will require special quality assurance attention and in developing safety inspection and verification tests.

■ *Trace system hazards into components. Identify subsystem (including software) safety requirements and constraints on subsystem functionality, design, and verification. Identify the parts of the software that control safety-critical operations.*

This is the time when the software safety efforts begin. Software development personnel need to be informed of any software behavior that can contribute to system hazards so that these concerns can be incorporated into the software requirements specification and other documentation. System hazards must be traced into the software requirements and high-level design to order to identify those portions of the software that control safety-critical operations and to identify specific behavior of the software that could contribute in some way to system hazards (critical software inputs and outputs). The resulting software safety requirements and constraints (design criteria) will aid in software design for safety and in concentrating and focusing software analysis and test efforts. Safety requirements and constraints for the computer–operator interface should be included.

A hazard tracking system needs to be established within the software development and software configuration control activities. Its purpose is to implement traceability of safety requirements and constraints into the software and to provide documentation and communication channels back from the software development and verification activities to system safety activities. The initial steps in defining safety-related software test plans, test descriptions, test procedures, and test case requirements start now.

As the hardware and software development paths start to diverge, a minor change in hardware may result in significant potential hazards due to software control (or lack of control) of the system [43]. Safety engineering personnel must maintain the system engineering viewpoint for the safety analysis of the systems and subsystems, and assure the consistency between hardware and software development with respect to hazard analysis and safety requirements. To accomplish this goal, an auditing procedure may need to be established. In addition, top-level safety analyses must be continually updated with new information and constantly reviewed by the safety engineering teams in both the hardware and software analysis and development groups [43].

- *Review general test and evaluation procedures. Start planning system and subsystem safety testing and evaluation procedures. Develop test plans, test descriptions, test procedures, and test case requirements.*

At this stage, system test and evaluation procedures need to be reviewed from a system safety perspective to ensure that no hazards are introduced by test procedures. Planning for specific safety testing and evaluation should begin and criteria should be established for verifying that the safety constraints and requirements have been met.

- *Review training and operations plans.*

Safety personnel should establish or review training plans, logistics and operational procedures, and support and maintenance plans for their consistency with safety requirements.

- *Evaluate design changes for safety impact.*

Because the design will be in flux at this stage and requirements and constraints will change as more information is obtained, system safety must ensure that new safety requirements and constraints are incorporated in the system specifications based on updated system safety studies, analyses, and tests. Design changes must be evaluated for their safety impact, and the design and its documentation must be updated.

- *Document all safety decisions and maintain safety information.*

The information gleaned from safety analyses and tests must not only be incorporated into the evolving design, but it must also be added to the safety information files and hazard logs. All safety decisions must be documented and any changes in the safety program plan included in the overall safety information system.

12.1.3 Full-Scale Development Tasks

- *Review and update the hazard analyses. Perform interface analyses, including interfaces within subsystems (such as between safety-critical and non-safety-critical software components).*

Hazard analyses must again be reviewed and updated. If there are multiple contractors or subcontractors, an integrated safety analysis is needed to coordinate the system safety efforts. All the various safety analyses may need updating, since this phase of the project provides the first chance to analyze the actual hardware and software and their interfaces (as opposed to what was planned or documented in the design specifications).

- *Ensure that safety requirements and constraints are incorporated into the subsystem (including software) safety requirements and constraints.*

As the detailed designs of the subcomponents are developed, the hazards associated with the design of each subsystem can be analyzed in depth. The system hazards that were previously traced to particular components can now be traced through the evolving component designs. Similarly, the results from analyses of specific components to evaluate their impact on system safety must be traced back to the system level. The hardware and software development projects have taken divergent paths by this time, and it is imperative that system safety continue to provide coordination and a system-level approach to the safety analyses.

- *Ensure that the software engineers and code developers understand software-related system safety requirements and constraints.*

Software developers must understand not only the software-related hazards, but also any role that software plays in implementing interlocks and other system safety design features and how these features should work. This understanding requires, in turn, that software developers be informed about system safety design constraints and procedures so that they do not inadvertently disable or override system safety features or implement interlocks and other software-controlled safety design features incorrectly. Merely including the functional requirements in the software documentation is not adequate. Software developers need to understand in detail the reason for and desired operation of any system-level safety features that are controlled or implemented in software (see Chapter 16) or can be affected by software.

- *Trace software safety requirements and constraints through to the code. Identify safety-critical software components and variables to the code developers.*

As the software design evolves, the software safety requirements and constraints should be traced through to the code modules. Critical software requirements, constraints, components, and variables should be identified to the code developers. An interface analysis may be used to evaluate the interaction between safety-critical and non-safety-critical software components. Safety-related software design decisions and design rationales must be included in the software documentation and communicated to those writing maintenance, operator, and user manuals so this information can be included there too.

- *Review engineering designs and design documents. Ensure that safety requirements and constraints are incorporated into subsystem designs and documentation.*

As the system design and documentation continues to evolve, safety personnel must review engineering designs to verify incorporation of safety requirements and design constraints and correction of any previously identified hazards. They must also verify that safety design considerations and design decision rationales (the basis on which design decisions affecting safety have been made) are included in the design documents so that this information can be used during reviews, during future maintenance and upgrade, and in accident and incident analysis during system operation.

■ *Update testing and verification requirements.*

As in the previous stages, testing and verification requirements must be elaborated and updated. Since software usually serves an integration function for virtually every part of the system, the safety of the software must be verified at the system level as well as at the software level: Software system safety considerations must be included in both software and system integration testing (see Chapter 18).

■ *Review both system and subsystem test results. Trace back results to system hazards.*

All tests conducted during this phase need to be reviewed to ensure that no further hazards have developed and that the system is ready for production. The components and subcomponents that have been identified as safety critical, along with other identified safety-critical items, can be used to trigger safety review of the test results. For example, safety personnel may need to review all software test error reports that relate to safety-critical components or variables. The results of the component safety efforts need to be reported back to system safety and incorporated into the system safety information files and the hazard auditing and tracking procedures.

■ *Evaluate changes for their impact on safety.*

Once again, engineering changes need to be evaluated for their safety impact, and redesign or design changes initiated to ensure that the maximum degree of safety is built into the final system. A safety representative should be an active member of the system configuration control board and of the software or other subcomponent configuration control boards. All proposed changes to the system must include a review by safety to assess their potential impact to determine if corrected hazards remain corrected, if new hazards will be introduced, or if the risk assumed is still acceptable.

Each change must be evaluated as to how far back to go in the process, and then the safety process must be repeated from that step. For example, repeated or new analysis and testing may be required. Similarly, changes to the software, or changes to the system that may affect the software, must be incorporated into the entire software safety process—starting from the assessment of the need for and impact on the software safety requirements and constraints, through the tracing of the safety requirements and constraints into the software design and the identification of safety-critical components and items, and finally into the software analysis and testing phases.

■ *Design and evaluate training and operational procedures.*

In the development stage, safety personnel will also need to continue the evaluation and design of the evolving training and operational procedures.

- *Perform final evaluation of product design.*

At the end of the design stage, a final evaluation of the safety of the product or system design must be performed, using all the information gathered to this point, so that necessary changes can be identified prior to production.

12.1.4 System Production and Deployment Tasks

- *Update hazard analyses.*

Hazard analyses continue to be reviewed and updated with respect to known and newly identified hazards during the production and deployment stage.

- *Perform safety evaluation and verification at the system and subsystem levels.*

Various final tests and demonstrations, which were planned in earlier steps, are now performed.

- *Perform safety inspections.*

Safety personnel need to implement controls and to inspect the production process and operations in order to detect and correct any additional hazards.

- *Ensure that safety-related information is incorporated into user and maintenance documents.*

Safety-related information should be incorporated into the system documentation as it is developed. A final review should be done to verify that all the necessary information has been included.

- *Review change proposals for safety impact.*

Engineering change proposals need to be reviewed in the same way as previously.

- *Perform a final evaluation of the produced and deployed system.*

When production is completed, safety engineering is responsible for a final evaluation of the completed system. Besides the information obtained during the previous stages of the life cycle, new information obtained during production and deployment must be incorporated, such as the results of regular testing and "flight" tests (tests performed in a realistic environment), training programs, operational procedures testing, and feedback on deployment experiences. Few if any new hazards should be found in this evaluation if the previous steps were carried out effectively. If serious hazards are found at this stage, they may require significant costs or startup delays, and options for their correction are usually limited and less effective than those implemented earlier.

12.1.5 System Operation Tasks

■ *Update procedures.*

Operational use of a system will invariably identify new and unexpected hazardous modes of operation and point out the need for updating operational procedures or for creating new ones.

■ *Maintain an information feedback system. Review and analyze accidents and incidents.*

In order to make sure that safety is handled adequately during this stage of the life cycle, information feedback is mandatory. Accidents, incidents, and failures must be reviewed for their safety implications and appropriate corrective action taken to eliminate or minimize the likelihood of recurrence. Trend analysis should be ongoing to detect problems before they lead to major accidents.

■ *Conduct safety audits.*

Safety personnel must conduct safety audits to verify that the desired operational level of safety is maintained. The entire process should be reviewed regularly to assess the impact of minor changes in the system, operations, or the environment that may have occurred since the last formal hazard assessment. These audits are usually scheduled on a periodic basis (such as every two or three years): Extremely hazardous systems may need to be reviewed more frequently than others, and specific areas of concern may require continual auditing. The audits will use the documented assumptions, limitations, and models used in the hazard analysis along with documented design decisions to evaluate whether the system, as operated, conforms to the system evaluated in the development stage. Any discrepancies should trigger a reevaluation of safety to make sure that risk has not degraded below that considered acceptable.

Although periodic audits are important, procedures should also be in place that allow for triggering investigations upon need. For example, changes in the environment should be detected and used to trigger analyses of their safety implications: Waiting for a periodic audit may not be wise in all cases. Continual tests and feedback mechanisms might be established that test for the assumptions and preconditions upon which the safety analysis was based and the assumptions or predictions about the operation of the environment used during development. In addition, the safety analyses themselves must be periodically reviewed in the light of accidents, incidents, and other types of feedback to determine whether unrealistic assumptions were made or conditions were overlooked.

■ *Review changes and maintenance procedures.*

Throughout the life of the system, proposed changes to the system and its operation must be evaluated to ensure that new hazards are not introduced or hazard mitigation procedures invalidated. Documentation must be kept up to date, including the safety information system and the hazard auditing and logging files.

12.2 Examples

Although each process must be tailored to a particular system and organization, examples of processes and organizational structures can be useful in understanding the options available. Three examples are provided in this section. The first is a European underground rail station. Although computers were not involved in this project, software considerations could easily be incorporated within the same overall process. The next two examples are military and space projects that, because of their larger scale, required a much different and more elaborate organizational structure.

12.2.1 An Underground Rail Station

Zogg has described the safety process used during the design, construction, and operation of an underground rail station in Zurich [361]. Somewhat surprisingly (since system safety approaches are much more pervasive in the United States than in Europe, where engineering projects are much more likely to depend on reliability engineering techniques), this development is an excellent example of a well-planned system safety process for a relatively small project.

The underground station is part of the existing main station of an electric rail system run by the Swiss Federal Railway. The box-like structure is partially underneath the main station and partially underneath a busy downtown street with road and streetcar traffic. The platform and tracks had to be deep enough to allow a freeway and a greatly fluctuating river to cross the structure and another navigable river to pass over it. A subterranean shopping mall, which is cut in two by the freeway and the river, is above the platform level of the rail station, and a multistory office building is also over part of the station structure.

Trains access the station by a ramp from ground level on one side and through a tunnel under the navigable river on the other side. The vertical connections between platform level and shopping mall are through stairs, escalators, and elevators, while connections from the shopping mall to the ground level are through stairs and ramps. Utilities, such as electricity, water, and sewage, also pass through the station.

This building project had to deal with the interdisciplinary nature of such a structure. The safety process had to be flexible throughout the various life cycle phases and accommodate changing needs. Figure 12.1 shows the process, along with the participants, inputs, and outputs of each step. With each project phase, the depth and extent of the analysis was optimized using the information available and the time and cost framework provided. Hazard analysis expertise was provided by an insurance company.

When safety problems were uncovered, an effort was made to eliminate or reduce them quickly. In the early phases of the project, the need to consider particular problems further could often be eliminated by obtaining more information

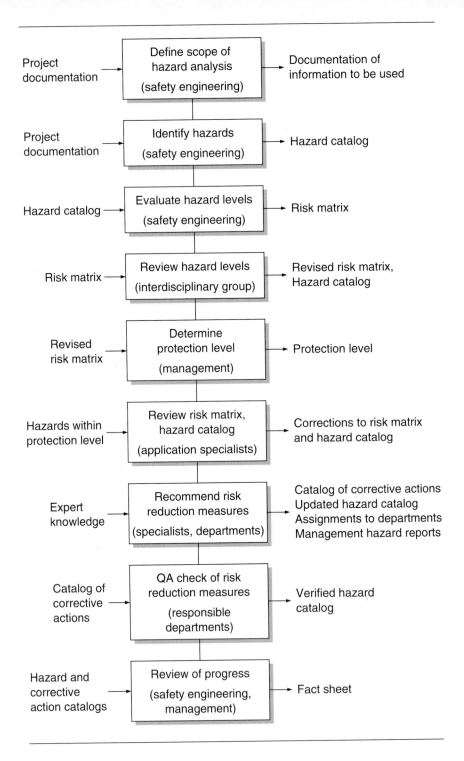

FIGURE 12.1
The process steps in the underground rail project.

about the problem or by sensitizing the relevant design engineers to the potential threat and generating alternative design solutions.

At this early stage, resolution of potential safety problems was relatively simple and seldom called for additional expenditures. As the project and analysis progressed, additional information became available. The increased information led to more detailed analysis, which in turn uncovered new safety concerns and eliminated old ones. When considered necessary, special analyses, to the maximum extent and depth possible, were conducted for problem areas of limited scope but of a complex or interdisciplinary nature. These in-depth analyses required specialized knowledge and were performed by teams of experts on the various aspects of the project.

The hazard analysis was continually updated. For each new concern identified and every corrective action taken, the entire process and scope of the analysis was reiterated.

Definition of Scope

Before starting the preliminary hazard analysis, the safety personnel carefully defined its scope, considering the information and time available and the possible results. Because too ambitious a scope could have jeopardized the project, they decided it was better to start with a limited but achievable analysis and then extend it into other problem areas.

The system to be analyzed was defined in terms of the track length and width and the lowest and highest level of the structure. In this way, a three-dimensional frame was drawn around the project. Various levels of information were available about the different project components. The access ramp and the station–shopping mall layout and construction, for example, were already reasonably defined, whereas the tunnel under the navigable river was only defined as to cross section required, level to be reached, and grade required—the type of structure and construction method were undetermined.

Once the scope was defined, the safety personnel documented the information to be used such as drawings (with their revision status) and findings from ongoing research (qualified and dated).

Hazard Identification and Assessment

Hazards were identified by first considering the hazardous characteristics of the system. Then potential threats from malfunctions were considered, along with environmental influences on system operation. The entire life cycle, including disposal, was included. A list of questions, called a *tickler list*, was used to help uncover hazards.

The initial hazard identification included the hazard, causes, level, effect, and category in a fairly standard way, and was done by a small group of system safety engineers without consulting project specialists. The first step was

Hazard Assessment					Page	of
Company					By/Date	/
Product						
No.	Hazard	Cause	Level	Effect		Category

FIGURE 12.2
Hazard identification form.

to list hazards, potential causes, and possible effects in a hazard catalog (Figure 12.2). While considering causes and effects, further hazards were identified.

The next step was to assign a hazard level from among six levels representing the relative probability of the occurrence of a potential cause: frequent, moderate, occasional, remote, unlikely, and practically impossible. They decided that the less reliable the information about the likelihood, the more conservatively the hazard-cause level would be judged. Similarly, the relative severity of a possible effect was judged using four categories: catastrophic, critical, marginal, and negligible. The most severe possible effect for a hazard was used.

The hazard assessment was first performed by the same system safety engineers involved in the hazard identification. To get expanded input, a large, interdisciplinary group of specialists was brought together and they were sensitized as to the safety aspects of the project in general and to the related problems of other specialists. The hazard catalog was completed by this group of experts, who checked the assessments that had been made. The result was an extended and revised hazard catalog, which was used for the next step in the process.

The hazard level was determined by using a standard matrix, as shown in Figure 12.3, to combine hazard severity and hazard probability. The hazard level was used to allocate resources for hazard control by establishing priorities for identified hazards. The numbers in the boxes represent the criticality. A line was drawn in the matrix representing an arbitrary breakpoint called the protection level. Risk reduction efforts were concentrated on the hazards above the desired protection level. Unlike many similar techniques, the protection level in this project differentiated between voluntary and involuntary risks. They decided that

Hazard Effect Category

	I Catastrophic	II Critical	III Marginal	IV Negligible
A Frequent	I-A	II-A	III-A	IV-A
B Moderate	I-B	II-B	III-B	IV-B
C Occasional	I-C	II-C	III-C	IV-C
D Remote	I-D	II-D	III-D	IV-D
E Unlikely	I-E	II-E	III-E	IV-E
F Impossible	I-F	II-F	III-F	IV-F

Hazard Cause Level (row label, left of table)

FIGURE 12.3
A typical hazard level matrix.

users would accept a higher risk if their involvement in the system was voluntary, the risk was known, or no alternatives were available.

The protection level was determined at a meeting of management by examining the current protection level in other parts of the public transportation system. The managers assumed that the present users of such systems were satisfied with the current safety standard, thus indicating the level of risk acceptance by the public. (The reasonableness of this decision is, again, a trans-scientific question that is beyond the scope of this book.) Using the current level of risk along with predicted safety demands of future users and experience from other countries, a protection level was set.

With the additional information about protection level added to the risk matrix, the complete hazard catalog and risk matrix were sent to the members of the specialist group to double check the assessment of all hazards that appeared below the established protection level. The specialists were told that these hazards would not be pursued further for the time being if they agreed that the hazards had been assessed correctly.

Risk Reduction

The standard system safety precedence (see Chapter 8) was used for risk reduction, with attempts first being made to prevent a hazardous condition. If prevention was not possible within the cost–benefit framework, an effort was made to protect against the possible hazardous conditions or events.

Risk Reduction Company Product				Page of	
				By/Date /	
Risk Profile Location	No.	Hazard	Corrective Action		By/Date

FIGURE 12.4
Risk reduction form.

Information about each hazard above the protection level was documented, and then the hazards were assigned to the specialists or departments that might be able to contribute to the risk reduction. One hazard could go to several departments.

Recommended risk reduction measures were collected and assembled into a catalog of corrective actions that included the hazard, corrective action, and a signoff (name and date) (Figure 12.4). If interdisciplinary measures were needed, small meetings were held with representatives of the affected disciplines, and risk reduction measures were coordinated. The catalog of corrective actions was changed accordingly, and each measure was assigned to the responsible department.

A quality assurance check of the updated catalog was performed by asking all involved departments to double check their assignments. The reassessment was completed after their corrective actions were provided. Zogg claims that this interactive process proved extremely fruitful, and progress became visible in the periodically updated risk profile and risk reduction catalog. Hazards that could not be sufficiently improved to be within the minimum protection level or those that required expenditures for additional improvements were analyzed further and in more detail.

At times during the project, a fact sheet was issued that provided condensed information on a particular subject for those not familiar with it. The goal was to create a need for action by providing additional knowledge.

Because system safety efforts were started early in the project life cycle, risk reduction was possible without additional expenditures for quite some time into project development. Corrective actions requiring expenditures within the authority of the contributing department or project management were usually made on the spot and entered into the risk reduction catalog. Corrective actions that exceeded such authority were documented in management hazard reports and sent to upper management for a decision. These reports usually included the potential cause, the potential effect, the corrective action or actions possible within the means available, the resulting gain, and the associated cost. When the decision was made, appropriate feedback was provided to the work teams and also entered in the risk reduction catalog. Improvements in the corresponding assessment were entered in the related documents.

Each corrective action taken was crossed off in the catalog and the person or department responsible for this action noted. Corrective actions that were dropped, perhaps because of an available alternative, were also crossed off. Each corrective action usually resulted in an improved assessment, and this was entered in the appropriate documents. In this way, open items were clearly visible, and it was possible to check at any time who had taken responsibility for which actions and which actions were dropped altogether.

Although Zogg wrote about this project before it was completed, he concluded that the system safety process followed had already proved its worth. Generally, all participants were sensitized to safety issues, and system safety thinking became an integral part of each individual's daily work. Safety issues were resolved at an early stage through impromptu consultations between the members of the analysis team. Zogg attributes this time- and cost-conscious way of working to the interdisciplinary interactions and contributions required by the analysis methodology.

The hazard catalog, risk profile, and risk reduction catalog provided high visibility of safety issues throughout the project. Any change, additional information, or reconsideration could flow back into the analysis in an integrated way. Zogg claims that "organ pipe'" solutions were eliminated, corrective actions were "concerted and fitting," and a well-balanced system safety concept, including all disciplines involved, emerged [361].

12.2.2 A Combat Weapon System

The next two examples involve much larger projects. Although the technical procedures are similar to those used for the underground rail station, the much greater scale of these projects makes the interactions more complex and difficult to implement. The structural organization and communication flow mechanisms are also more difficult to design and implement and play a much more important role in the success of the safety efforts. A major difference also stems from the fact that the customers in the following two examples (the U.S. Navy and NASA) play a larger role in the development and safety process.

Defense systems are developed using a safety standard, MIL-STD-882,[2] which describes a set of tasks that may be required in any particular contract. Organizational structures and requirements in addition to MIL-STD-882 are sometimes imposed by the individual services.

The Navy, for which this system was developed, has a project-independent board, the Navy Weapons System Explosives Safety Review Board[3] (WSESRB) and an affiliated Software Systems Safety Technical Review Board to assure the incorporation of explosives safety criteria in all weapon systems, as described in Chapter 11. Similarly, a Navy Safety Study Group is responsible for the study and evaluation of all nuclear weapon systems. An important feature of these groups is that they are separate from the programs and thus allow an independent evaluation and certification of safety.

The system being considered here is a U.S. Navy cruiser and destroyer combat system, built in the 1980s, that includes nuclear weapons. This project was very large and had a prime contractor, associate contractors, and subcontractors. The safety effort was coordinated among all these groups by means of a System Safety Working Group (SSWG), which was chaired by the Navy Principal for Safety. The permanent members included the prime contractor system safety engineer and representatives from various Navy offices. Contractor representatives attended working group meetings as required. Members of the group were responsible for coordinating safety efforts within their respective organizations and for reporting the status of outstanding safety issues. They provided information about the system to the WSESRB.

Systems that include nuclear weapons are subject to different and more stringent standards than are nonnuclear systems. For this particular system, a Nuclear Safety Advisory Group (NSAG) was established as an adjunct to the System Safety Working Group. Its members were similar to those of the SSWG and were responsible for all technical matters related to nuclear weapons. They supported the nuclear weapons safety studies and evaluation performed by the Safety Study Group (just as the SSWG supported the activities of the WSESRB). The NSAG

- Provided information on nuclear weapons or support equipment that could affect nuclear weapon safety.
- Prepared, disseminated, and reviewed information related to the prevention of nuclear weapon accidents and incidents.
- Provided technical assistance to Navy groups.
- Participated in safety studies.

The prime contractor led the safety engineering efforts. In this company, system safety engineering (SSE) is part of system engineering. SSE reviewed specifi-

---

[2] This standard is updated periodically, the current version being 882C. The particular version under which a specific system is developed depends on the date when the contracting process is started. This system was developed using MIL-STD-882A.

[3] A similar function is performed for the U.S. Air Force by the Non-Nuclear Munitions Safety Board.

cations and generated safety products early in the definition phase of the program. One of these products was the Preliminary Hazard Analysis (PHA), which was then distributed to the design engineering groups and to other engineering disciplines such as reliability, maintainability, and human factors engineering.

The functional disciplines used the PHA for their own design tradeoffs and provided feedback to SSE to be used in updates to the PHA and in the development of later analyses. These results were then used by the various engineering functions to modify design requirements for any safety deficiencies that had been identified by the analyses.

Throughout the program, the prime contractor's safety engineering group participated in component and system design reviews in order to ensure that safety was implemented at all the stages of system design and development. The results of maintenance and operational analyses were coordinated with appropriate engineering functions in order to avoid system or personnel hazards from changes in layouts, requirements, or design. The Integrated Logistics Support Group was notified when procedural or training requirements were identified in the safety analyses.

SSE also worked closely with configuration management and system interface engineers, reviewing changes to existing hardware or software designs to ensure that safety was not compromised.

Tasks

The overall system safety effort consisted of three major functions: (1) establishment of a safety baseline, (2) identification and elimination or control of hazards, and (3) safety verification.

The baseline function included evaluating the safety of new design features using design reviews and equipment safety histories in Navy safety data files. The procurement documentation provided by the Navy defined the safety data and process requirements as specified by MIL-STD-882A. In this group of baseline functions, SSE

- ☐ Prepared the PHA.
- ☐ Prepared and evaluated hazard reports.
- ☐ Defined the safety requirements for the specifications.
- ☐ Started the system hazard analysis.

The second function, hazard control, used various analyses to track identified hazards through elimination, control, or procedural precautions. With the baseline established, the system safety program plan was modified to prescribe a plan of action for the resolution of all open safety issues. Subfunctions in this grouping included

- ☐ Updating the PHA.
- ☐ Continuing the system hazard analysis.
- ☐ Participating in the SSWG and NSAG activities.

☐ Performing various other types of required hazard analyses.

☐ Completing the Safety Summary Report (SSR), which is the reporting mechanism for all safety activities in Navy programs.

Safety analyses provided by the contractors on their components were reviewed for adequacy and used in the system hazard analysis and other required system-level analyses.

The third function, verification, included a combination of inspections, demonstrations, tests, and data analyses to determine whether all system components could be operated and maintained without risk to personnel or equipment. Necessary tests were identified using the various safety analyses. Controls were implemented to ensure the feedback of test information to the reviews and analyses that were used in design modifications. Safety test results were summarized in the SSR and used to update the system-level analyses.

Types of Hazard Analyses

A relatively large number of hazard analyses were performed on this program:

☐ *Preliminary Hazard Analysis* (PHA) addressed each element of the combat system and identified hazards related to radiation (ionizing and non-ionizing), acoustic noise, electrical energy, moving parts, pressure, temperature, walk or work surfaces, weapon firing, inadvertent launch or fire, no-point no-fire zones, weapon selection, destruct, jettison, misfire and dud, blast protection, toxic fumes, and battleshort.[4] The PHA was continually updated and was maintained in the prime contractor's safety files.

☐ *System Hazard Analysis* (SHA), building upon the PHA as a foundation, involved detailed studies of the possible hazards created by the interfaces between system components. The analysis identified the potential impact of such hazards, recommended corrective actions, and (eventually) documented the actual corrective actions taken.

☐ *Operating Hazard Analysis* (OHA) reviewed operating procedures and sequences to determine hazards created by human–machine interfaces. The OHA specified certification and training requirements and provided safety inputs to technical manuals, warning signs, emergency procedures, and emergency equipment. Typical subjects addressed were dud and misfire procedures, missile identification procedures, launch operations, weapon firing procedures, and emergency procedures.

☐ *Maintenance Hazard Analysis* (MHA) examined the potential hazards involved in the removal, adjustment, alignment, and repair of equipment. The MHA provided recommendations for warning notices, special tools or han-

---

[4] The battleshort function allows safety features to be turned off during engagements or battles.

dling equipment, protective equipment, and electrical and mechanical hazard safeguards.

- □ *Computer Program Safety Analysis* (CPSA) identified computer software safety requirements and traced these requirements through the Combat System Specifications, the Prime Item Development Specifications, the Program Performance Specifications, the Program Design Specifications, and the Interface Design Specifications. Safety-critical functions were identified and documented. This task included evaluations, analyses, and tests used to determine if corrective action was required.

- □ *Subsystem Hazard Analysis* (SSHA) used qualitative fault trees and failure-modes-and-effects analyses for each subsystem to examine hazards created by the subsystems.

- □ *Radiation Hazard Analysis* (RHA) identified areas in which electromagnetic and ionizing radiation posed hazards to personnel. The analysis was conducted using theoretical computations of all ionizing and non-ionizing radiation transmitters based on the current design specifications. The report was updated after design specification changes and when operational test results became available.

- □ *Nuclear Safety Analysis* (NSA) included such topics as positive weapon identification, prevention of inadvertent or deliberate and unauthorized nuclear weapon firing, security of authorization codes, physical security, and identification of critical nuclear weapon control circuits. This analysis, required for all nuclear weapons projects, assesses how the combat system satisfies the four DoD nuclear safety standards:
  1. There shall be positive measures to prevent nuclear weapons involved in accidents or incidents, or jettisoned weapons, from producing a nuclear yield.
  2. There shall be positive measures to prevent deliberate prearming, arming, launching, firing, or releasing of nuclear weapons except upon execution of emergency war orders or when directed by competent authority.
  3. There shall be positive measures to prevent inadvertent prearming, arming, launching, firing, or releasing of nuclear weapons.
  4. There shall be positive measures to ensure adequate security of nuclear weapons.

- □ *Inadvertent Launch Analysis* (ILA) addressed valid generation of engagement orders (such as positive identification of hostile targets and security of threat criteria), weapon control (such as warhead identification, missile readiness assessment, launch prerequisites, inadvertent or premature launch, flight control, and friendly force protection), prevention of unauthorized launch, and simulation and training modes. The analysis used qualitative fault tree analysis.

- □ *Weapon Control Interface Analysis* (WCIA) used qualitative fault tree analysis to address isolation, priority of launches, and missile interference.

TABLE 12.1
Hazard probability ranking.

Rank	Level	Description
Frequent	A	Likely to occur frequently
Probable	B	Will occur several times in unit life
Occasional	C	Likely to occur sometime in unit life
Remote	D	Unlikely to occur in unit life, but possible
Improbable	E	Extremely unlikely to occur
Impossible	F	Equal to a probability of zero

Safety Criteria

The prime contractor's safety engineering group was responsible for establishing qualitative probability rankings of hazard occurrences, hazard consequences, and frequency of exposure. Table 12.1 shows the hazard probability ranking used. Figure 12.5 shows the hazard criticality index matrix used by this project to combine hazard severity and hazard probability. The numbers in the boxes represent the criticality. The heavy dark line in the matrix represents the breakpoint, to the right of which hazards are considered acceptable. Hazards associated with nuclear weapons were all given the highest priority. For all hazards, the goal was to ensure compliance with the four DoD nuclear safety standards (listed above) and to reduce the criticality level below the breakpoint (increase the criticality index to 9 or more) through changes in design, inclusion of safety or warning devices, or use of operational procedures [227].

Reports

The reports used for this system included

- Safety test reports (test results and evaluation of safety test data)
- System hazard alert reports (reports of identified hazards)
- A general safety analysis summary report (a semi-annual submission describing all the analyses and corrective action taken and summarizing all safety issues, safety tests, and plans for each subsequent reporting period)
- A combat system safety statement (a formal, comprehensive safety report on the final design of the combat system that identified all system safety features, inherent design and procedures hazards, and procedures or precautions to circumvent the hazards)
- A nuclear safety analysis report (an overview of the known nuclear safety features of applicable components of the combat system and analyses and assessments supporting the four nuclear safety standards)
- Various nondeliverable reports, memoranda, and analyses generated during

	A Frequent	B Probable	C Occasional	D Remote	E Improbable	F Impossible
Catastrophic I	Design action required to eliminate or control hazard — 1	Design action required to eliminate or control hazard — 2	Design action required to eliminate or control hazard — 3	Hazard must be controlled or hazard probability reduced — 4	9	12
Critical II	Design action required to eliminate or control hazard — 3	Design action required to eliminate or control hazard — 4	Hazard must be controlled or hazard probability reduced — 6	Hazard control desirable if cost effective — 7	Assume will not occur — 12	Impossible occurrence — 12
Marginal III	Design action required to eliminate or control hazard — 5	Hazard must be controlled or hazard probability reduced — 6	Hazard control desirable if cost effective — 8	Normally not cost effective — 10	12	12
Negligible IV	10	11	Negligible hazard — 12	12	12	12

FIGURE 12.5
Hazard criticality index matrix.

the development and use of the system, which were maintained in a central file by the prime contractor.

Safety Hazard Reporting Procedures

Anyone observing or encountering a condition through analysis, inspection, test, observation, or demonstration that in his or her opinion presented a hazard, was required to report it to the prime contractor SSE office within one working day and to document any immediate action. The type of the action taken by the individual observing the hazard depended on the severity of the hazard and could involve filling out a hazard alerter form, installing warning labels, providing a temporary fix, or removing the system from service.

Figure 12.6 shows the controls and procedures for handling safety hazard alerter reports (SHARs). As can be seen, the process needed for a project of this size and complexity is much more elaborate than for a project the size of the underground rail station. System safety engineering contacts the originator of the safety hazard alerter form, identifies the responsible agent, and informs the System Safety Working Group. Reported hazards are summarized and reported by monthly safety hazard alerter summary reports until final corrective action has been demonstrated to be effective or the hazard is closed out by the Systems Safety Working Group.

This combat system, which has been in operation for many years, was involved in a major accident. The causes of the accident were related more to the implementation of the process (and the design of the human–machine interface) than to flaws in the process itself. Perhaps this event demonstrates that having a reasonable and well-defined process is not enough and also that accidents are very difficult to prevent in very complex systems.

12.2.3 The NASA Space Shuttle Project

This project is the size and scope of the combat weapon system project, but it is nonmilitary and nonnuclear and thus places different requirements and constraints on the process. The Shuttle Project may seem to be a strange choice for an example, given the *Challenger* accident and the criticisms of the process in the resulting investigation. Examples of processes that did not work well, however, may be as valuable or more valuable than those that have not experienced problems. In addition, some of the problems that led to the *Challenger* accident involved failures in carrying out the process rather than flaws in the process itself, and they also reflect outside political pressures.

In the following, criticisms of the process that surfaced during the investigation of the *Challenger* accident are included, along with changes that were made to the process after the accident and more recent evaluations of current practices. The more critical nature of this section compared to the descriptions of the two previous examples is due only to the careful examination of the NASA process in the aftermath of the *Challenger* accident. An examination as detailed in the wake of the serious accident in the combat system in the previous section might have turned up even more serious flaws in that process. The Space Shuttle is one of the most complex engineering projects ever attempted, and NASA should be commended for its open attitude toward public examination of its process and its willingness to make changes when problems are found. It is from this type of openness that we learn and improve.

Emphasis in the following is on the process being followed in the operational phase of the National Space Transportation System (NSTS) Program (the official name of the Space Shuttle project) rather than on the development process, which started over 20 years ago. It provides a contrast with the two previous examples, which described development processes.

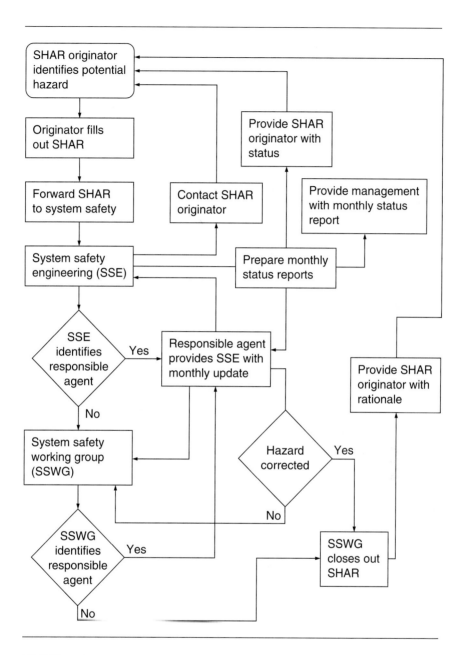

FIGURE 12.6
Safety hazard correction procedure.

Overall NASA Safety Policy

Much of the following description of the NASA process is taken from a National Research Council (NRC) report [247] issued in January 1988 as a follow-up to a Rogers' Commission recommendation for NASA to review certain aspects of the STS risk assessment effort and for the NRC to audit the adequacy of that effort.

Basic NASA safety policy is issued at the Administrator level and implemented by descending levels of management throughout NASA headquarters, the NASA field centers, and contractors involved in the Space Transportation System (STS) development and operation. Various organizations within NASA have different and overlapping responsibilities with respect to the safety of the STS. NASA safety activities since the *Challenger* accident have centered on analyses of the STS system configuration and function and on the required engineering changes that the analyses have identified [247].

The basic NASA policy on safety is to

1. Avoid loss of life, injury of personnel, damage, and property loss.
2. Instill a safety awareness in all NASA employees and contractors.
3. Assure that an organized and systematic approach is utilized to identify safety hazards and that safety is fully considered from conception to completion of all agency activities.
4. Review and evaluate plans, systems, and activities related to establishing and meeting safety requirements both by contractors and by NASA installations to ensure that desired objectives are effectively achieved.

The way this policy is to be carried out is described in an accompanying NASA handbook (NHB 1700.1 [IV]) that states

> . . . the steps necessary to achieve safety of operations begin with initial planning and extend through every facet of NASA's activities. Under this concept, every manager throughout the organization is responsible for systematically identifying risks, hazards, or unsafe situations or practices, and for taking steps to assure adequate safety in the activities and products under his supervision.

Management Structure

Prior to the *Challenger* accident, the NSTS program was managed out of the Johnson Space Center (JSC) in Houston. After the accident, the NSTS Program Director was brought to NASA headquarters (Level I) to manage the program from a location closer to top agency officials and at a level that has oversight of the three field centers. The Deputy Director remained at JSC and the Deputy Director of Operations at Kennedy Space Center in Florida. Various changes and moves have occurred since then.

The program draws on resources from three field centers: (1) JSC, which is responsible for the orbiter component of the STS as well as the integration of all STS components; (2) Marshall Space Flight Center (MSFC) in Alabama, which is responsible for the STS propulsion elements (the main engine, the solid rocket booster and motor, and the external tank); and (3) Kennedy Space Center (KSC) in Florida, which is responsible for major ground support equipment and for launch and landing operations.

Project managers at each NASA center are responsible for particular components and subsystems. They are in a matrix organization and report functionally to the NSTS Program Director as well as organizationally to the center management. Various subsystem managers, who are responsible for the engineering on their subsystems, report to the project managers.

The hierarchy of management levels within the NSTS program is shown in Figure 12.7. Basically, Level I is headquarters and is primarily concerned with policy and broad program formulation and management. Level II is major program management and resides at JSC and KSC. Level III is project management and is dispersed across all the participating NASA centers.

Each management level has one or more associated boards or panels that review and approve or disapprove the actions proposed by technical and other groups at the levels below it. Figure 12.8 shows some of these boards. The most important boards are the two Program Requirements Control Boards, one at Level I and one at Level II, which review the results of the failure-modes-and-effects analysis. The Program Requirements Control Boards, the Configuration Control Boards, and associated panels that support them have the authority to decide upon or recommend changes to documentation, hardware, and software to the extent that the change does not conflict with requirements, schedules, budgets, or other program features established by a higher-level board. A large number of Level II and III multilayered boards are responsible for reviewing specific technical and managerial aspects of STS design, development, and operation. All of them report ultimately to the Level I and II Program Requirements Control Boards, which are the highest boards for configuration and control.

Figure 12.9 shows the review groups associated with the safety processes. Additional NASA boards review design requirements and certification, software, and various operations activities. The many panels and boards play an important role in providing coordination, resolving problems and technical conflicts, and reviewing and recommending actions. They allow the different interests and skill groups to provide input and contribute knowledge to minimize the risk that a proposed action will negatively affect some aspect of the STS.

This structure has been criticized, however, for having lines of authority and responsibility in the flight readiness review decision-making chain that had become vague by the time of the *Challenger* accident. The NRC audit committee contrasted the NSTS system with that of the U.S. Air Force, in which the board (including its chair) makes recommendations to a decision maker instead of the

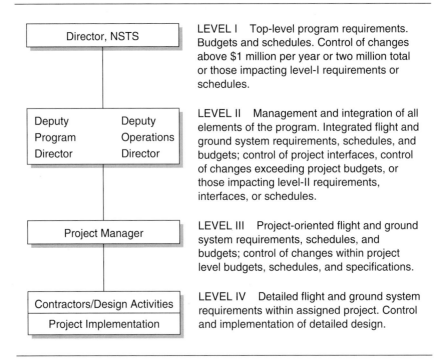

Director, NSTS	LEVEL I Top-level program requirements. Budgets and schedules. Control of changes above $1 million per year or two million total or those impacting level-I requirements or schedules.
Deputy Program Director Deputy Operations Director	LEVEL II Management and integration of all elements of the program. Integrated flight and ground system requirements, schedules, and budgets; control of project interfaces, control of changes exceeding project budgets, or those impacting level-II requirements, interfaces, or schedules.
Project Manager	LEVEL III Project-oriented flight and ground system requirements, schedules, and budgets; control of changes within project level budgets, schedules, and specifications.
Contractors/Design Activities Project Implementation	LEVEL IV Detailed flight and ground system requirements within assigned project. Control and implementation of detailed design.

FIGURE 12.7
National Space Transportation System program management relationships.
(Source: Reprinted with permission from *Post-Challenger Evaluation of Space
Shuttle Risk Assessment Management*, 1988. Courtesy of the National Academy
Press. Washington, D.C.)

board *being* the decision maker. The NASA approach risks diluting and obscuring individual responsibility, but a positive aspect is that the chair (who is the designated decision maker) is required to listen publicly to all dissenting views.

Organizational Roles

In theory, safety, in all its forms, is equally the responsibility of all NASA managers, workers, and contractors. In practice, however, roles and responsibilities are necessarily defined and allocated across various functional organizations:

1. The engineering organizations within the project offices
2. A Safety, Reliability, Maintainability, and Quality Assurance organization at headquarters and corresponding to the Safety, Reliability, and Quality Assurance organizations at each of the centers

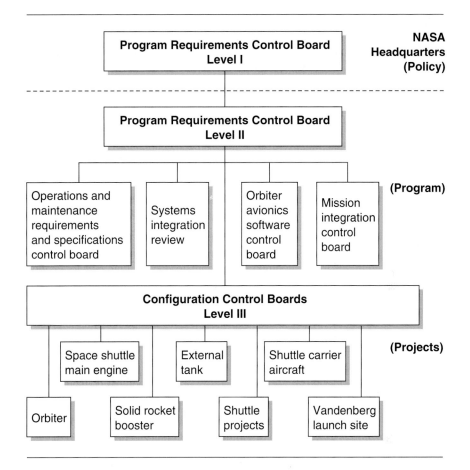

FIGURE 12.8
Structure of NSTS Program Requirements Control Boards and Configuration Control Boards. (Source: Reprinted with permission from *Post-Challenger Evaluation of Space Shuttle Risk Assessment Management*, 1988. Courtesy of the National Academy Press. Washington, D.C.)

3. The Engineering Integration Office

4. The operations organizations

NASA engineers within the Engineering Project offices have primary responsibility for carrying out the failure-modes-and-effects analyses (FMEAs) and for establishing the rationale for retaining critical items identified in those analyses. The argument for this arrangement is that the engineers have the greatest ability to understand and anticipate the ways in which the unit or system might

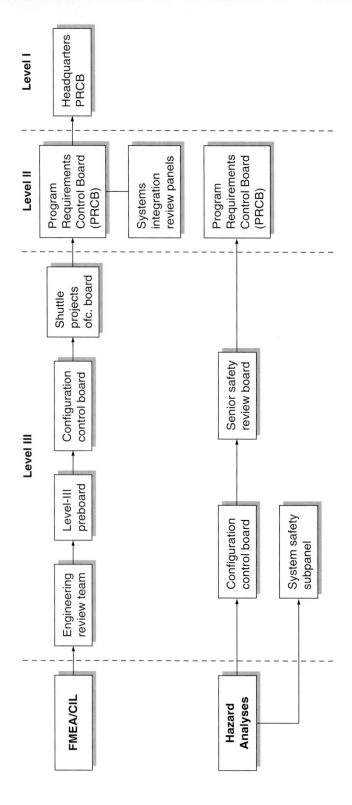

FIGURE 12.9
NASA relies on a multilayered system of panels and boards for decisions on engineering design and safety matters. (Source: Reprinted with permission from *Post-Challenger Evaluation of Space Shuttle Risk Assessment Management*, 1988. Courtesy of the National Academy Press. Washington, D.C.)

fail. However, few of the engineers have any formal grounding in safety engineering techniques and methodologies. This system differs from that used in the previous two case studies, where primary responsibility for all safety-related analyses was given to the system safety engineers who were assisted by the project engineers.

The role of the center's safety, reliability, and quality assurance staff is to oversee the engineering design and development activities and to advise the Project Manager and the various configuration control boards on safety and other relevant aspects of the systems under review. They are also responsible for keeping records on problems and anomalies encountered in the development and operation of the STS and for performing hazard analyses other than the FMEAs.

After the *Challenger* accident, a new safety office was established at headquarters, as recommended by the Rogers' Commission report. This group is supposed to provide broad oversight, but their authority is limited and reporting relationships from the centers are vague [53].

The Engineering Integration Office is located at JSC and is responsible for systems integration and interface design between STS components, Shuttle avionics and ascent flight systems, analyses of integrated structural loads and thermal effects, software requirements and configuration control, and ground systems and operations requirements.

The Engineering Integration office has separate review structures for systems integration and for software. The Systems Integration Review Board is a Level II board that supports the Level II and Level I Program Requirements Control Board in all the integration areas, including ascent and entry, flight control, and thermal design. The Shuttle Avionics Software Control Board is the controlling authority for avionics software. In addition, the Mission Integration Control Board controls changes to mission integration requirements. The Engineering Integration Office is also responsible for carrying out a series of Element Interface Functional Analyses.

Safety-Related Analyses

The FMEA and Critical Items List (CIL) are at the heart of NASA's effort to ensure reliability and safety. FMEAs are performed on all STS hardware and ground support equipment that interfaces with flight hardware at the launch sites. NASA does not perform FMEAs on software. The goal is to identify hardware items that are critical to the performance and safety of the vehicle and the mission, and to identify items that do not meet design requirements. FMEAs are performed by contractor personnel.

The FMEA starts by determining the potential failure modes for the functional units of each component. Each potential failure mode is then analyzed to determine the resulting performance of the system and the worst-case effect of a failure in that mode. All the identified items are categorized according to this worst-case effect using the criticality categories shown in Table 12.2.

TABLE 12.2
NASA criticality categories.

1	Loss of life or vehicle
1R	Redundant hardware element, failure of which could cause loss of vehicle
2	Loss of mission
2R	Redundant hardware element, failure of which could cause loss of mission
3	All others
For ground support equipment only:	
1S	Failure of a safety or hazard monitoring system to detect, combat, or operate when required and could allow loss of life or vehicle
2S	Loss of vehicle system

Items assigned one of the top four categories—Criticality 1, 1R, 2, and 2R—are put on the Critical Items List (CIL) (see Figure 12.10 for an example). In addition to single-point failures, the CIL includes items that could fail in one mode and result in loss of the capability of redundant (backup) systems; items whose operational status is not readily detectable in flight; and redundant systems in which a single failure under certain conditions may result in total loss of the system capability.

Items on the CIL must have design improvements or corrective action to meet the fail-safe and redundancy requirements before the Shuttle can fly with them present. If that is not feasible, a waiver request must be submitted to the appropriate review boards.

FMEAs only consider failures of individual items. Element Interface Functional Analysis is used to examine functional failure modes at the interface of two components resulting from a hardware failure in either component.

All the analyses described so far are reliability analyses. Hazard analyses are also used that consider not only the failures identified in the FMEA process but other potential threats posed by the environment, crew–machine interfaces, and mission activities. The analyses performed include the standard Preliminary Hazard Analysis (Figure 12.11), System Hazard Analysis, Subsystem Hazard Analysis, and Operations Hazard Analysis.

A closed-loop tracking system for hazard documentation, resolution, and approval is maintained by the Safety, Reliability, and Quality Assurance offices. Software hazard analysis is not performed (although an attempt to identify some software hazards for the Shuttle avionics software was started in the late 1970s and later abandoned). This disconnect between the system safety program and the software development and maintenance activities has been criticized in a recent

---

Shuttle Critical Items List—Orbiter

Subsystem: FMEA No.:   Revision:
Assembly: Abort.:   Crit. Func.:
P/N RI: Crit. Hdw.:
                          Vehicle:
P/N Vendor:
Quantity: Effectivity:
                     Phase:
                     Redundancy Screen:

Prepared by: Approved by: Approved by
Item: (NASA):

Function:

Failure Mode:

Cause(s):

Effect(s) on (A) Subsystem (B) Interfaces (C) Mission (D) Crew/Vehicle

Disposition and Rationale:

FIGURE 12.10
A Critical Items List form.

National Research Council report assessing the Shuttle flight software development processes [53].

Data Collection and Reports

NASA uses a number of special reports and reporting systems to collect and integrate data from tests, preflight checkout, postflight inspections, and inflight

PHA No. _ORBI-024_

Space Shuttle Preliminary Hazard Analysis

Mission Phase _Prelaunch Through Landing_   Engineer _J. Railsback_

Subsystem or Operation _Environmental/Consumables_   Date _07/15/86_

Effectivity _All Flights_   Sheet _1_ of _3_

Hazardous Condition	Hazard Cause	Hazard Effect	Hazard Level	Safety Requirements	Hazard Control
Loss of electrical power (total loss of space shuttle power)	Contamination of H_2 or O_2 system	Loss of crew and shuttle	CA	1. The cryogenic system is to be verified clean during acceptance and reverified each time system is opened for maintenance. ...	1. Fuel cells were certified to operate at a specified level of purity during qualification testing. 2. Preload sampling of cryogenic... ...

FIGURE 12.11
Excerpt from a sample Space Shuttle Preliminary Hazard Analysis report.(Source: Reprinted with permission from *Post-Challenger Evaluation of Space Shuttle Risk Assessment Management*, 1988. Courtesy of the National Academy Press. Washington, D.C.)

operational experience. These include problem reports, discrepancy reports (for software), unsatisfactory condition reports, and failure reports.

The Problem Reporting and Corrective Action (PRACA) system is a large, distributed database (one for each STS component and one for ground support equipment at Kennedy Space Center) that contains all of the data from the reports along with information on corrective actions taken. NASA is also developing a central database to integrate a number of existing information systems and sources across the NSTS to provide an integrated view of the status of problems, including trends, anomalies and deviations, and closure information. One problem noted by the most recent evaluation of the program is the proliferation of databases containing software problem reports and their resolution, and the lack of consistency between these databases.

Post-Challenger Changes and Recommendations.

In the wake of *Challenger*, all FMEA/CILs and hazard analyses were reevaluated, but software still seems to be ignored. Other changes were noted above.

The report of the President's Commission Investigating the Space Shuttle Challenger Accident noted many deficiencies in the Shuttle safety program (see Chapter 4), many of which were related to communication and reporting problems, reduction in system safety efforts once the Shuttle became operational, and lack of independence of the safety organizations.

The followup 1988 NRC audit report on Shuttle risk management [247] noted that many of the earlier problems had been fixed but that there was still a need for

□ Looking at multiple-event failures instead of focusing primarily on single-event failures

□ Independence of the oversight activities (including independent software verification and validation) from the organizational elements responsible for design and construction

□ A review of the waiver process

□ Consideration of human factors as the cause of failure modes in the FMEAs

□ Clearer assignment of responsibility and authority

□ The inclusion of software considerations in the various safety analyses

□ Better central direction and integration of the procedures used by the various centers

□ The establishment of a focused, agency-wide systems safety engineering function at both headquarters and the centers.

A more recent report, focusing on the Shuttle software process, echoed many of these recommendations with respect to software [53] and made additional recommendations for improved software oversight (verification and validation), a rigorous software safety program, and various improved or clarified organizational roles and responsibilities.

Chapter

13

Hazard Analysis

The argument that the same risk was flown before without failure is often accepted as an argument for the safety of accepting it again. Because of this, obvious weaknesses are accepted again and again, sometimes without a sufficiently serious attempt to remedy them, or to delay a flight because of their continued presence.

—Richard Feynman
Personal Observations on Reliability of Shuttle [1]

Unfortunately, everyone had forgotten why the branch came off the top of the main and nobody realized that this was important.

—Trevor Kletz
What Went Wrong?

Hazard analysis is at the heart of any effective safety program, providing visibility and coordination (see Figure 13.1). Information flows both outward from and back into the hazard analysis. The outward information, for example, helps designers perform trade studies and eliminate or mitigate hazards and helps quality assurance identify quality categories, acceptance tests, required inspections, and components that need special care. Any changes or additional information must flow back through the analysis so that (1) solutions or corrections can be integrated into the design and (2) the overall conceptual system model and approach to safety is maintained.

Although hazard analysis alone cannot ensure safety, it is a necessary first

---

[1] Appendix F of the Rogers Commission report [295]

FIGURE 13.1
Hazard analysis provides visibility and coordination.

step before hazards can be eliminated or controlled through design or operational procedures. Simply knowing that a hazard exists may provide sufficient information to eliminate or control it, even without in-depth analyses of its causes. Often, general safeguards can be provided even if little is known about the hazard's precursors. A larger number of options for elimination and control usually exist, however, if more is known about the hazard and the conditions and events leading to it. Condition-specific or event-specific safeguards are frequently more effective and less costly in terms of the tradeoffs required.

Hazard analysis is not just performed at the beginning of a project or at fixed stages, but should be continuous throughout the life of the system, with increasing depth and extent as more information is obtained about the system design. As the project progresses, the uses of hazard analysis will vary—such as identifying hazards, testing basic assumptions and various scenarios about the system operation, specifying operational and maintenance tasks, planning training programs, evaluating potential changes, and evaluating the assumptions and foundations of the models as the system is used and feedback is obtained. In an operational system, analyses and their assumptions act as preconditions for safe operation and as constraints on management and operational procedures.

Just as the purpose of and the information available for hazard analyses change with time, so do the analysis requirements and the appropriate analysis methods. There is no one perfect method for every goal, but many that can and should be used. The various techniques provide formalisms for systematizing knowledge, draw attention to gaps in knowledge, help prevent important considerations from being missed, and aid in reasoning about systems and determining where improvements are most likely to be effective.

For many hazards and systems, analysis may consist merely of comparing the design with various standards and codes that have been developed over time to deal with known hazards. Standards and codes provide a means of encoding historical information derived from accidents and near accidents so that safety reviews and analyses need not start from scratch each time. They help us encapsulate and learn from experience.

Nevertheless, as new technology is developed and systems are scaled up in size, new hazards arise and the possibility of introducing hazards increases. Systems with new and complex designs may require sophisticated, formal, documented analytical procedures.

In some countries or industries, the particular hazards to be analyzed and the depth and types of analysis may be established by regulatory authorities or by legislation. In others, these decisions must be made by the safety engineers early in project development. This chapter presents the information used in making such decisions.

13.1 The Hazard Analysis Process

The process chosen depends on the goals or purpose of the hazard analysis. Different goals will require very different processes. Once the goals are defined, the steps to be taken can be determined.

13.1.1 Goals of Hazard Analysis

The goals of safety analysis are related to three general tasks [323, 327]:

1. **Development**: the examination of a new system to identify and assess potential hazards and eliminate or control them.
2. **Operational management**: the examination of an existing system to identify and assess hazards in order to improve the level of safety, to formulate a safety management policy, to train personnel, and to increase motivation for efficiency and safety of operation.
3. **Certification**: the examination of a planned or existing system to demonstrate its level of safety and to be accepted by the authorities or the public.

The first two tasks have a common goal of *making the system safer*, while the third has the goal of convincing management or government that an existing design or system *is safe*. These three broad tasks can be divided into subtasks:

□ **Development** and **operational management**
  1. Identify hazards that singly or in combination could cause an accident.
  2. Show that specific hazards are not present and that safeguards are not needed.
  3. Determine the possible damaging effects resulting from system hazards.

   4. Evaluate the causal factors related to the hazards:
   (a) Determine how hazards could occur, their nature, and their possible consequences.
   (b) Examine the interrelationships among causal factors.
   5. Identify safety design criteria, safety devices, or procedures that will eliminate or minimize and control the identified hazards.
   6. Find ways to avoid or eliminate specific hazards.
   7. Determine how to control hazards that cannot be eliminated and how to incorporate these controls into the design.
   8. Evaluate the adequacy of the hazard controls.
   9. Provide information for quality assurance—quality categories, required acceptance tests and inspections, and items needing special care.
   10. Evaluate planned modifications.
   11. Investigate accidents and near-miss reports. Determine whether they have validity and, if they do, the cause of the problem.

 □ **Certification**
   1. Demonstrate the level of safety achieved by the design.
   2. Evaluate the threat to society from the hazards that cannot be eliminated or avoided.

   Each of these subtasks implies very different types of analysis. The goals and subtasks need to be clarified and documented at the start of any hazard analysis process.

13.1.2 Qualitative versus Quantitative Analyses

Safety analysis ranges from relatively simple qualitative methods to advanced quantitative methods in which numerical values for risk are derived. Even if quantitative methods are used, qualitative analyses must precede them—hazards and their causal factors must be identified before numerical values can be assigned to them. Thus, the quality of the quantitative analysis depends on how good the qualitative one was.

   Often, the analysis can stop with the qualitative aspects. Knowing the causal factors and using best-guess estimates of relative hazard rankings are adequate for most purposes during the system development phase, when few accurate numerical values are available anyway. The most effective and accurate quantitative analyses use operational data from a working system to determine achieved reliability and to identify trends and changes that might affect safety. Quantitative analysis may also be useful in comparing the reliability of alternative features of an emerging design that uses standard parts with established failure rates.

   The use of probabilistic risk assessment has been debated widely. The arguments in its favor are usually based on the technique's ability to provide input for decision making. Identifying hazards alone does not determine how funds should be allocated to reduce hazards. Comparative probability data can be useful in such decisions. Decision making in the certification of plant designs is also eased by the use of such numbers.

However, many important factors—design deficiencies, for example—cannot be easily or reasonably quantified. Because equipment failures are the most easily assessed probabilistically, many quantitative risk assessments have been criticized for placing more emphasis on these failures than on less easily predicted and quantified factors such as design errors, construction deficiencies, operator actions, maintenance errors, and management deficiencies. For example, some probabilistic assessments have emphasized failure probabilities of devices that are in the range of 10^{-7} or 10^{-8} while ignoring installation errors or maintenance errors of those same devices with probabilities in the range of 10^{-2} or 10^{-3}. Quantifying only what can easily be quantified does not provide a realistic estimate of risk. In the space program, where probabilistic risk assessment based on fault tree analysis and failure modes and effects analysis was used extensively, almost 35 percent of the actual in-flight malfunctions were not identified by the method as "credible" [205].

Care also has to be taken that quantification does not divert attention away from risk reduction measures. The danger exists that system safety analysts and managers will become so enamored with the statistics that simpler and more meaningful engineering processes are ignored.

Follensbee cites several recent commercial aircraft accidents caused by events that had been calculated to have a probability of 10^{-9} or less (one was calculated as 10^{-12}) using accepted techniques. In all of these cases, incorrect assumptions about the behavior of the pilots or the equipment led to underestimated failure or risk figures [86]. In several cases, the need for compliance with standard aircraft fail-safe design standards—which might have prevented these accidents—was judged unnecessary based upon the calculations [86].

The Union of Concerned Scientists and others have warned against a disproportionate emphasis on meeting predicted quantitative levels of safety rather than on consideration of technical problems and implementation of engineering fixes [3]. The same may be true for human error. Hornick, past president of the Human Factors Society, has suggested that "the general nuclear power community is couching a cavalier attitude towards human factors in the (false?) comfort of risk-assessment statistics" [127, p.114].

Quantitative risk assessment of a completed design sometimes is required by certification agencies or used in public arguments about the safety of a controversial technology such as nuclear power. The emphasis of this chapter (and this book), however, is on qualitative rather than quantitative hazard analysis.

13.1.3   Role and Qualifications of the Analyst

In general, the role of the safety analyst should be to generate alternatives as well as to eliminate them. A U.S. Air Force acquisition handbook suggests that pointing out new alternatives may be much more valuable to a program than exhaustive analysis of given approaches [5]. The early selection of a single approach can be detrimental to the overall safety program when there are less expensive alternatives that yield equal or better safety or there are alternatives that require fewer tradeoffs with other system goals. Therefore, the job of the system safety analyst is to dig deeply into the design and suggest designs that will yield eventual system operation that is satisfactory from both a safety and performance standpoint.

Successful hazard analysis requires an understanding of the system under consideration. Hazard analysis does not remove the need for engineering expertise and judgment: Standardized analysis approaches and terminology simply help to clarify the problems in order to provide a context for expert judgment and to enhance interdisciplinary communication. The process usually requires a team of people with a wide variety of knowledge and skill. System safety engineers provide expertise in safety analysis, while other team members bring expertise in specific engineering disciplines along with alternative viewpoints. The approaches to solving a problem suggested by system engineers, subsystem engineers, reliability engineers, safety engineers, application experts, operators, and management may be entirely different, but all contribute significantly to finding a satisfactory solution [5]. When humans and computers play important roles in system operation, operators and software engineers should also be involved in the hazard analysis and in the design of hazard reduction measures.

13.1.4 General Features of an Effective Hazard Analysis Process

The hazard analysis process is both *continual* and *iterative* (see Figure 13.2). Hazard identification and analysis begin at the conceptual stage of the project and continue through decommissioning. Starting early is imperative if safety considerations are to be incorporated into trade studies and early design decisions, when hazards can be most effectively and cheaply handled. Planning for hazard elimination and control should begin as soon as safety problems are uncovered— preferably before unsafe features become firmly embedded in the design.

The forms of analysis will be different as the system matures, but all are part of a single analysis process. Each stage of analysis acts as a baseline upon which later steps build. The stages reflect the quality of information available, with analysis depth and breadth increasing as more information is obtained. In the early project phases, hazard resolution may involve simply getting more information about the hazard or generating alternative design solutions. As the project progresses and the design is elaborated, more detailed analyses and tests may uncover new hazards or eliminate old ones from consideration.

If a hazard cannot be resolved at a particular stage, follow-up evaluation and review may be necessary. Organizational controls, such as audit trails and tracking systems, must be installed to ensure that this follow-up occurs.

The operational safety achieved depends on the accuracy of the assumptions and models underlying the design process. The system must be monitored to ensure (1) that it is constructed, operated, and maintained in the manner assumed

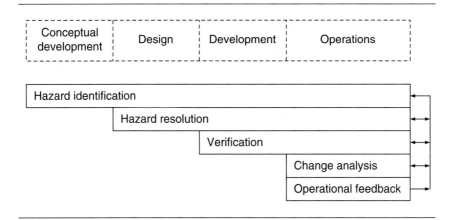

FIGURE 13.2
The hazard analysis process is continual and iterative.

by the designers; (2) that the models and assumptions used during initial decision making and design were correct; and (3) that the models and assumptions are not violated by changes in the system, such as workarounds or unauthorized changes in procedures, or by changes in its environment. Operational feedback on trends, incidents, and accidents should trigger reanalysis.

If a change is proposed to a baseline or completed design, or an unplanned change is detected during operation, it must be analyzed for its potential effect on safety. The process involves reviewing previously generated analyses to identify the impact of the proposed change, updating the analyses and documentation to reflect the changes, and identifying new hazards and hazard causes. The reanalysis must start at the highest level of system design at which the change becomes visible and show that the change does not create a new hazard, affect a hazard that has already been resolved, or increase the severity level of a currently existing hazard.

13.1.5 Steps in the Process

A hazard analysis consists of the following steps:

1. Definition of objectives.
2. Definition of scope.
3. Definition and description of the system, system boundaries, and information to be used in the analysis.
4. Identification of hazards.
5. Collection of data (such as historical data, related standards and codes of practice, scientific tests and experimental results).

6. Qualitative ranking of hazards based on their potential effects (immediate or protracted) and perhaps their likelihood (qualitative or quantitative).

7. Identification of causal factors.

8. Identification of preventive or corrective measures and general design criteria and controls.

9. Evaluation of preventive or corrective measures, including estimates of cost. Relative cost rankings may be adequate.

10. Verification that controls have been implemented correctly and are effective.

11. Quantification of selected, unresolved hazards, including probability of occurrence, economic impact, potential losses, and costs of preventive or corrective measures.

12. Quantification of residual risk.

13. Feedback and evaluation of operational experience.

Each step requires documentation of the results and of any underlying assumptions and models. The purpose of the hazard analysis process is to use the results as a reference for judgment [274] in design, maintenance, and management decisions. Accomplishing this goal requires an explicit formulation of the models, premises, and assumptions underlying the safety analysis and the design features used to eliminate or control hazards. There must also be an explicit description of the assumptions about work procedures and organizational structures that will constrain management's freedom of action.

Not all of the steps may need to be performed for every system and for every hazard. For standard designs with well-established risk mitigation features (perhaps included in standards and codes), only the first 5 steps (plus step 13) may be needed. For new designs, usually the first 10 steps are necessary. Step 11 may be needed when risk control measures require tradeoffs with critical functions or constraints (such as weight or space), or hazards are expensive to resolve. Step 12 may be required for certification or licensing of systems by government agencies when the potential consequences of a hazard are catastrophic. Completely eliminating or controlling hazards may not be possible or practical due to political factors, lack of time, potential cost, or the magnitude or nature of the hazard; quantification of the residual risk provides an estimate of the risk assumed in operating the completed system. Step 13 always needs to be done.

Because, as has been widely noted, what can go wrong probably will, all foreseeable uses and modes of the system over its entire lifetime need to be examined. At various times in its operational life, a system will be exposed to different environments, processes, conditions, and loads, and the effects will differ according to when the stress or condition occurs.

Hazard analysis can be divided into three basic functions: (1) identifying hazards, (2) identifying and evaluating the hazard causal factors, and (3) evaluating risk. Although names such as *Preliminary Hazard Analysis* and *Subsystem Hazard Analysis* are often applied to these functions, these are merely phases, as noted earlier, in a continuing and iterative process rather than disjoint sets of analyses.

13.1.6 Hazard Identification

Hazard identification starts early in the concept formation stages of the project, and hazard lists are continually updated with new hazards and information about previously identified hazards throughout the entire lifetime of the system.

Hazard identification in the earliest stages of a program, often called Preliminary Hazard Analysis (PHA), involves

1. Determining what hazards might exist during operation of the system and their relative magnitude.
2. Developing guidelines, specifications, and criteria to be followed in system design.
3. Initiating actions for the control of particular hazards.
4. Identifying management and technical responsibilities for action and risk acceptance and assuring that effective control is exercised over the hazards.
5. Determining the magnitude and complexity of the safety problems in the program (how much management and engineering attention is required to minimize and control hazards).

The output of the hazard identification process is used in developing system safety requirements, preparing performance and design specifications, test planning, preparing operational instructions, and management planning. The results serve as a framework or baseline for later analyses and as a checklist to ensure that management and technical responsibilities for safety tasks are carried out.

The first step is to identify the system, system boundaries, and the limits of resolution, as described in earlier chapters. If multiple subsystems or systems are involved, the boundaries must be consistent. For simple or well-understood products or systems, the hazards may already be known and the analyst can skip to the next step.

For some special systems regulated by government agencies, hazards or hazard categories may be mandated. For example, the U.S. Department of Defense (DoD) identifies four hazards (see Section 12.2.2) that must be considered when constructing nuclear weapon systems. Special processes, such as Nuclear Safety Cross Check Analysis (NSCCA) and Software Nuclear Safety Analysis (SNSA) may be required on such programs to ensure that the software cannot contribute to any of these four hazards. NSCCA and SNSA are not specific analysis techniques but rather rigorous independent verification and validation procedures; they are described briefly in Chapter 18.

In most systems, however, the hazards are not immediately known or subject to government mandate and need to be determined. Childs warns that the analyst should not just list every conceivable hazard, including those without any clear-cut relationship to the system being studied [51].

A few techniques for identifying hazards have been developed. They are essentially structured ways to stimulate a group of people to apply their personal knowledge to the task—for example, by raising a series of *what-if* questions guided by a model of the system.

Most hazard identification involves less structured procedures, but various activities can be helpful:

- □ Review pertinent historical safety experience, lessons learned, trouble reports, and accident and incident files.
- □ Use published lists and checklists of hazards (Table 13.1 is an example from [232]). Investigate standards and codes of practice; these often reflect known hazards that have caused accidents in the past.
- □ Examine the basic energy sources, energy flows, and high-energy items in the system and provisions for their control.
- □ Consider hazardous materials such as fuels, propellants, lasers, explosives, toxic substances, and pressure systems.
- □ Look at potential interface problems such as material incompatibilities, possibilities for inadvertent activation, contamination, and adverse environmental scenarios.
- □ Examine hazard analyses on previous systems.
- □ Review the mission and basic performance requirements, including the environments in which operations will take place. Look at all possible system uses, all modes of operation, all possible environments, and all times during operation. Stresses and effects of particular conditions will differ as a system is exposed to varying environments, processes, conditions, and loads.
- □ Take advantage of the general engineering experience and personal experience of safety and application experts. *Tiger team attacks*, which are essentially brainstorming sessions, are a standard security technique that might be useful for safety.
- □ Examine the human–machine interface and the interaction between the operators and the automated equipment.
- □ Look particularly at transition phases—changes in the system, changes in the technical and social environment, and changes between modes of operation in the system. Accidents often occur during non-routine operating modes: startup, restart, shutdown, testing, trials of new methods, breakdown, maintenance, repair, inspection, troubleshooting, modifications, changeovers, adjacent system change, nonstandard input, stresses (including budget, schedule, delays, and catch-up), and adverse conditions.
- □ Use scientific investigation of physical, chemical, and other properties of the system, which may involve theoretical studies and small-scale tests.
- □ Think through the entire process, step by step, anticipating what might go wrong, how to prepare for it, and what to do if the worst happens.

As hazards are identified, information about them needs to be recorded.

TABLE 13.1
Generic hazards for the Space Shuttle.

Generic hazards	Generic hazard type	
Contamination/corrosion	Chemical disassociation	Oxidation
	Chemical replacement/combination	Organic (fungus/bacterial, etc.)
	Moisture	Particulate
Electrical discharge/shock	External shock	Corona
	Internal shock	Short
	Static discharge	
Environment/weather	Fog	Radiation
	Fungus/bacterial	Sand/dust
	Lightning	Vacuum
	Precipitation (fog, rain, snow, sleet, hail)	Wind
		Temperature extremes
Fire/explosion	Chemical change (exothermic/endothermic)	Pressure release/implosion
		High heat source
	Fuel and oxydizer in presence of fuel and ignition source	
Impact/collision	Acceleration (including gravity)	Meteoroids/meteorites
	Detached equipment	Moving/rotating equipment
	Mechanical shock/vibration/acoustical	
Loss of habitable environment	Contamination	Toxicity
	High pressure	Low temperature
	Low oxygen pressure	High temperature
	Low pressure	
Pathological/physiological/psychological	Acceleration/shock/impact/vibration	Sharp edges
		Lack of sleep
	Atmospheric pressure (high, low, rapid change)	Visibility (glare, window/helmet fogging)
	Humidity	Temperature
	Illness	Excessive workload
	Noise	
Radiation	Electromagnetic	Thermal/infrared
	Ionizing	Ultraviolet
Temperature extremes	High	
	Low	
	Variations	

Often tabular forms are used. The most effective and efficient way to record hazard information is to use one form, filling it in as the analysis progresses through the various stages. At the beginning, only parts of the form will be completed, but by the end of the project development, all of the information should be available. An example of such a form is shown in Figure 12.11.

The form may include some or all of the following information:

- System, subsystem, unit (equipment grouping where the potential hazard exists).
- Hazard description.
- Hazard cause.
- Possible effects on the system and the environment.
- Category (hazard level).
- Corrective or preventive measures (compensation and control), possible safeguards, recommended action, and design criteria.
- Operational phase when hazardous.
- Organizations responsible for ensuring that safeguards are provided for the specific hazard.
- Verification methods (tests, demonstrations, analysis, inspection) to verify that the hazard is effectively controlled.
- Other proposed and necessary actions.
- Remarks and status of the hazard resolution process. The hazard is closed when it has been verified that the recommended actions have been implemented and are effective.

Hazard Level.   The *hazard category* or *level* is defined by likelihood and severity and often specified in the form of a matrix to aid in prioritization. Example matrices are shown in Figures 12.3 and 12.5. Since the depth of the analysis usually depends upon the severity of the hazard, the worst-case consequences must be determined early. The evaluation of susceptibility to a hazard should consider duration and exposure—how many people are exposed for how long. The warning time (the interval between identification of the problem and the occurrence of injury or damage) may also be important.

Hazard severity categories reflect worst possible consequences. The categories used are specific to the industry and sometimes the system. For example, the DoD (MIL-STD-882B: System Safety Program Requirements) uses these categories:

Category I: Catastrophic; may cause death or system loss.

Category II: Critical; may cause severe injury, severe occupational illness, or major system damage.

Category III: Marginal; may cause minor injury, minor occupational illness, or minor system damage.

Category IV: Negligible; will not result in injury, occupational illness, or system damage.

In contrast, a NASA document (NHB 5300.4) lists NASA hazard categories as:

Category 1: Loss of life or vehicle (includes loss or injury to the public).

Category 2: Loss of mission (includes postlaunch abort and launch delay sufficient to cause mission scrub).

Category 3: All others.

As a final example, a Department of Energy standard (DOE 5481.1) for nuclear systems defines three categories of hazard severity:

High: Hazards with potential for major onsite or offsite impacts to people or the environment.

Moderate: Hazards that present considerable potential onsite impacts to people or environment but at most only minor offsite impacts.

Low: Hazards that present minor onsite and negligible offsite impacts to people or the environment.

The other component of hazard level, likelihood, is commonly divided into discrete categories, such as

Frequent: Likely to occur frequently to an individual item, continuously experienced throughout the fleet or inventory.

Probable: Will occur several times during the life of an individual item, frequently throughout the fleet or inventory.

Occasional: Likely to occur sometime during the life of an individual item, several times throughout the fleet or inventory.

Remote: Unlikely to occur but possible during the life of an individual item; unlikely but reasonably expected to occur in a fleet or inventory.

Improbable: Extremely unlikely to occur to an individual item; possible for a fleet or inventory.

Physically Impossible: Cannot occur to an item or in a fleet or inventory.

Quantitative probability assessment, if used, is stated in terms of likelihood of occurrence of the hazard per unit of time, events, population, items, or activity, such as 10^{-7} per year.

Design Criteria. These broad concepts state *what* has to be achieved, leaving the designer free to use ingenuity in deciding *how* the goal may best be achieved. A design criterion for a collision avoidance system, for example, is that maneuvers should be avoided that require the objects to cross paths. A typical criterion for a pressure system is that all pressure tanks have a relief valve of sufficient size to reduce the tank pressure when the pressure exceeds a specific amount above

TABLE 13.2
The relationship between hazards and design criteria for the doors in a rapid transit system.

Hazard	Design criterion
Train starts with door open.	Train must not be capable of moving with any door open.
Door opens while train is in motion.	Doors must remain closed while train is in motion.
Door opens while improperly aligned with station platform.	Door must be capable of opening only after train is stopped and properly aligned with platform unless emergency exists (see below).
Door closes while someone is in doorway.	Door areas must be clear before door closing begins.
Door that closes on an obstruction does not reopen, or reopened door does not reclose.	An obstructed door must reopen to permit removal of obstruction and then automatically reclose.
Doors cannot be opened for emergency evacuation.	Means must be provided to open doors for emergency evacuation when the train is stopped anywhere.

Source: Adapted from Willie Hammer. *Product Safety Management and Engineering*. Prentice-Hall, Inc., Englewood Cliffs, N.J., 1980, page 207.

normal operating pressure. Table 13.2 shows the relationship between system hazards and system design criteria for the door control in a rapid transit system [108].

Design criteria are not requirements (which are much more specific in nature and apply to a particular design), but rather are used to derive the design requirements. Design criteria are general in nature and can be applied to many different systems and designs.

Operational Phase. Whether an accident actually occurs as a result of a hazard and the severity of the hazard may depend upon the operational phase—the system and environmental conditions—in which the hazard occurs. Therefore, the phase must also be documented for each hazard. Failure of a missile launch system during launch might simply leave the missile sitting on the pad, whereas failure right after launch might result in a fallback and total destruction. Similarly, loss of control of a missile immediately after liftoff might result in more damage (since the missile is filled with propellant) than loss of control far down range [106].

13.1.7 Hazard Causal Analysis

After the hazards are identified, the next step is to determine the causes and effects associated with each hazardous condition. The hazards can be analyzed in greater detail as specific system design features are elaborated during development. Information about the causes of hazards is helpful in specifying the safety requirements and design constraints needed to minimize or control hazards to an acceptable level.

Each hazard can have several potential causes, and each cause can have several potential consequences or effects. The factors considered and the process of identifying them will depend on the underlying accident model used (see Chapter 10), either consciously or subconsciously, by the analyst.

When examining complex systems, the analyst may need to consider conditions or events involving several components or the interfaces among components. For such systems, a model of some type and an analysis method defined for it are often useful in tracing the effects of conditions or events either backward or forward. Sensitivity analysis may be used to determine the most important factors.

Causal analysis can be divided into system (whole) and subsystem (unit or part) analyses. These two types of analysis are merely different parts of a total process and different ways of looking at the system. Both are usually performed, since each contributes important information.

System Hazard Analysis. This analysis considers the system as a whole and identifies how the system operation, the interfaces between the system components, and the interfaces between the system and its operators can contribute to hazards. As stated earlier, segmenting the system operation into sequences of events and actions (operational phases) by considering the mission and goals is often useful. The time at which a condition is critical varies with the system configuration, its location, and the time that an event occurs.

Subsystem Hazard Analysis. This type of analysis looks at individual subsystems and determines the effect of their operating or failure modes on system hazards. Typical subsystems include power, structural, control, sensor, operator, communications, propulsion, and environmental control. This type of analysis identifies the impact on overall safety of component failure modes, critical erroneous human inputs, and operating or failure modes of the subsystem related to performance, operational degradation, functional failure, unintended function, and inadvertent function (proper function but at the wrong time or in the wrong order).

Software Hazard Analysis. Software is just like any other component, especially various types of control or monitoring components, and thus will be included in the system hazard analysis as well as the focus of a subsystem hazard analysis (sometimes called *Software Hazard Analysis*). The computer's behavior and its interfaces to the rest of the system must be evaluated for potential contribution to system hazards. When such critical behavior is identified, it can be traced into the software design and code to identify parts of the software that require special design features or that need to be analyzed in depth.

Later, the software is evaluated to determine if the system design criteria have been satisfied in the software specifications and if the software implementation has impaired or degraded system safety or introduced new hazards. Because of the difficulty of these tasks, normally each part of the software development process is evaluated rather than just waiting until the software is complete.

All software, including commercial off-the-shelf software (COTS), needs to be analyzed to the level necessary to determine any impact or influence on the identified system hazards. In addition, changes to the software must be evaluated for potential impact on hazards.

Operational Hazard Analysis.   A separate analysis of the risk controls that have been assigned to operational procedures, called *Operational Hazard Analysis*, may also be performed. Often this analysis is left until the design is complete. The process, however, is no different than the other analyses, and there is no good reason to separate it or to leave it until the end. Instead, the operational use of the system should be considered from the very beginning (like the other analyses) and should be an integral part of the system and subsystem analyses. Otherwise, hazardous conditions may be left for procedural control that are impossible, unwise, or could have been handled more easily and safely in the design.

In addition, the information uncovered in the analysis of operator procedures should be used in the human–machine interface design and thus needs to be available early. This approach implies a very different design process than is often applied: The operational procedures are defined in concert with the automated systems and do not consist merely of functions that the designers did not know how to automate.

Operational analysis, like the other subsystem analyses, looks at all the ways that the operators can contribute to system hazards if they follow defined procedures (the system operates as it was designed to operate) or if they do not. Typically, operational procedures are divided into phases or tasks (as is done for the other analyses), which are analyzed in detail for their potential contribution to hazards, including proper and improper sequencing of actions.

13.1.8 Risk Assessment and Acceptance Analysis

Once design and development are complete, the system design can be evaluated. The goal here is not to guide the design process but to evaluate the final product. The results may be used internally or for independent certification to determine the residual risk and whether the system is acceptable for use.

The acceptance analysis should include more than just estimates of the probability and consequences of hazards and accidents. Each hazard should be documented to show its potential causes, the implemented controls and tracing of the hazard into the detailed design, and the results of the verification efforts. Basically, this assessment is a description of the potential problem and what is being done about it. The documentation should allow the assessor or reviewer to follow the analyst's reasoning in order to check the correctness of the results [299]. For very critical systems, the informal reasoning may be augmented by formal (and perhaps mathematical) reasoning and argument. The assumptions underlying any formal models or methods used need to be verified.

The acceptance analysis may also include a probabilistic risk assessment, in which the probabilities and severity of accidents are evaluated in addition to the hazard level. A risk assessment alone is not adequate, but it can augment the other information provided. The accuracy of probabilistic risk assessment is quite controversial, however. Briefly, the major limitations lie in the inaccuracies of the available failure and human error data, in the consequence models (such as dispersion of heavy gas and explosions), and in the toxicity data. Some studies have shown widely varying results for parallel assessments performed on the same system by different analysts or analysis teams. The variations seem to be caused by different initial assumptions, different restrictions of the object under study, the particular failure data used, and different analyses of the hazard consequences [299].

Typically, worst-case effects of hazards are all that is needed for hazard analysis and assessment, and these are relatively easily determined. Risk assessment, however, requires elaborate quantitative analyses. Unfortunately, obtaining probabilistic data about the harmful consequences of some hazards and about human errors is quite difficult and perhaps the most error-prone part of any quantitative risk assessment.

Assessing Harmful Consequences. Probabilistic risk assessments have been performed primarily on chemical or radiation hazards. The main physical effects of plant or equipment failure arise from escaping gases or liquids catching fire or exploding [126], or from toxicity. To assess the magnitude of an accident, the analyst first needs to determine (1) how much material is likely to escape, (2) what is likely to happen to it over time and distance (the physical consequences), and (3) the effect on people. Chemical engineering models exist to calculate some of these factors, but the accuracy of the models for some factors, such as gas dispersion, is poor. Considerable simplifying assumptions are needed to make the models manageable since the effects of a release depend on the physical state of the released material, its release rate, natural topography, intervening structure, atmospheric conditions, homogeneity of the gas cloud, ignition sources, and so on. The translation of structural damage into human casualties "is so speculative that in practice it can be no more than a statistical assumption, which in any given case may be orders of magnitude wrong" [126].

The accuracy of consequence assessment not involving release of material, such as the probability that two planes violating minimum separation standards actually collide, depends on the hazard and system involved. Usually, the number of uncontrolled variables makes prediction very difficult.

Assessing Human Error.   A second controversial aspect of probabilistic risk assessment is the accuracy of human error data. Most systems do not provide enough data on human error to be useful for probabilistic modeling. The alternatives are to use laboratory studies or to use numbers collected over a long time and over many types of systems.

The difficulty in extrapolating from laboratory studies stems from the significant differences between the laboratory and industrial settings [269]. Laboratory tasks tend to have (1) a well-defined goal, (2) stable requirements, (3) specific instructions, (4) artificial and low-valued payoffs, and (5) the subject controlled by the task. In contrast,

> In "real" tasks only a (sometimes vague) overall performance criterion is given and the detailed goal structure must be inferred by the operator. . . . The task may vary as the demands of the system vary in real time. Operating conditions and the system itself are liable to change. Costs and benefits may have enormous values. There is a hierarchy of performance goals. The operator is usually highly trained, and largely controls the task, being allowed to use what strategies he will. Risk is occurred in ways which can never be simulated in the laboratory [269].

The other alternative, using historical data from a large number of systems, has two main drawbacks: (1) the data and tasks from one system may not apply to a different system, and (2) data collection is often biased, incomplete, or inaccurate. Case studies and incidents do not represent all the errors that operators make, but merely those that are reported. Unreported errors tend to be those that the operator is able to correct before damage occurs. Monitoring is one way to collect data, but human behavior may be abnormal if the person being monitored is aware of the monitoring.

Human error data also suffers from the difficulty of classifying errors, such as determining whether an error was an operating error or a design error. The variety of classification schemes makes use of data in a different environment unreliable.

Given the discussion of the relationship between human behavior, psychological mechanisms, and task characteristics in Chapter 10, it seems misleading to collect empirical data about human errors without also noting subtle differences in the environment and system design when those errors occurred. There can be wide variation in the environmental situations and physical aspects of the tasks, including stress factors such as noise, temperature, emotional stress, and vibration. For example, collecting probabilistic data about humans misreading a particular type of dial in poor lighting and then applying the "probability of misreading a dial" to systems with a different dial design and better lighting may be unjustified; noting in the database all conditions under which every error was made is probably impossible, and the number of instances is not large enough for such differences to become unimportant. Errors on particular tasks may also depend on the other tasks the operator is performing. Thus, the context of the task is extremely important, further limiting the situations in which historical data applies.

Besides the problems in collecting it, human numerical error rate data also suffers from various other kinds of uncertainty. Human performance exhibits considerable natural variability based on skiil, experience, and personal characteristics [189]. Not only do people differ in their innate capabilities, but the performance of any one individual will vary over time. Some of these variations are unpredictable, while others seem to be circadian. Performance variations over a 24-hour day arise from fluctuations in the work situation and also from modifications in human capabilities [276]. Historically, safety and productivity are low at night. The fact that we are a diurnal species may explain why many of the major industrial accidents involving human error have occurred at night [85]. Variability in performance may also arise from interactions with an unstable environment, from stress, and from interactions with other workers.

Specific methods for assessing human error rates and including them in hazard analysis and risk assessment have been proposed despite these problems. They are discussed in the next chapter.

13.2 Types of System Models

Every hazard analysis requires some type of model of the system, which may range from a fuzzy idea in the analyst's mind to a complex and carefully specified mathematical model. The model may also range from a high-level abstraction to a low-level and detailed prototype. Nevertheless, information about the system must exist in some form, and that constitutes the system model upon which the analysis is performed.

A model is a representation of a system that can be manipulated in order to obtain information about the system itself. Models can be categorized along different dimensions [50]:

- *Material* models (which represent a complex system by another physical system that is simpler yet similar in important respects) versus *symbolic* or *formal* models (which represent the structural properties of a system in terms of assertions or logical statements).
- *Dynamic* models (where the features of the model vary perceptibly with time) versus *static* models.
- *Stochastic* models (containing intrinsic probabilistic or random elements that affect the outcome or response of the model) versus *deterministic* models.
- *Iconic* models (those that pictorially or visually represent aspects of the system), *analog* models (those that employ one set of properties to represent

another set), and *symbolic* models (those that use mathematical or logical operations to predict the behavior of the original system).

Particular models may be categorized along all of these dimensions, with the most useful model being that which provides the information needed most efficiently.

Modeling any system requires a description of the following [50]:

- □ *Structure*: the interrelationships of the parts along some dimension(s) such as space, time, relative importance, and logic or decision-making properties.
- □ *Distinguishing qualities*: a qualitative description of the particular variables and parameters that characterize the system and distinguish it from similar structures.
- □ *Magnitude, probability, and time*: a description of the variables and parameters associated with the distinguishing qualities in terms of their magnitude or frequency over time and their degree of certainty for the situations or conditions of interest.

This information can be stored or displayed in various ways, ranging from simple tables or bubble charts (which provide a way of storing or organizing information but no formal manipulation or analysis methods) to formal structures such as trees or graphs, state machines (which show the states of the system and the events that cause state changes), and full unsteady-state models comprised of algebraic and differential equations. Some of these structures can be combined: Safety models, for example, often employ tree structures to show logical relationships and tables to describe additional information.

Selection of the model will determine what information can be specified and what can be derived from the model through analysis. For example, a particular model may not include any mechanism for showing changes over time, or it may have no way of representing dependencies between the system components being modeled. The better a representation of the original system and the better the match between the properties of the model and the properties of interest in the analysis, the more useful the model will be in providing information about system behavior.

When using any model, it is important to specify the boundaries of the system being modeled and what is not included, assumptions about the system (such as independence of components), and what assumptions are most likely to be incorrect or invalidated by changes and thus need to be checked periodically.

13.3 General Types of Analysis

Different types of models allow for various types of analysis or manipulation of the model to learn more about a system. A model and its associated analysis methods may focus on logical and functional structure of a technical system to evaluate the propagation of events and conditions, or it may include a detailed description of work or tasks to evaluate the effect of various human operations on the system state. The models and analysis techniques also imply different underlying accident and human error models, which influence the hazards and causes that will be identified and considered.

There is often a tradeoff between the difficulty of building and analyzing the model and the quality of information that can be derived from it. In order to make modeling and analysis practical, simplification of complex system behavior may be required. For example, process variables are intrinsically continuous, but for many models and analysis techniques, they are treated as having a discrete and small number of values. Thus, flow may be characterized as *normal*, *high*, or *low*, or the state of a valve may be limited to *normal movement*, *stuck open*, or *stuck closed*.

No one model or analysis technique is useful for all purposes, and more than one type may be required on a project. A relatively simple system with only a few, well-understood hazards may require only simple comparisons with checklists or codes of practice. On the other hand, when what could happen or has happened involves complex sequences or combinations of conditions or events, then formal, documented analysis procedures may be necessary [119].

Analysis techniques can be differentiated by their goals, whether they are quantitative, the phase in the life cycle when they are used (such as pre- or post-design), the depth of analysis, the domain upon which they are defined (such as the structure and function of a technical system, the description of work or tasks, or the structure and function of an organization [323]), and the search methods used.

Analysis techniques usually involve searching. The search strategy will depend upon the type of structure being searched, including the basic elements of the underlying model (such as physical or logical components, events, conditions, or tasks) and the relationship between those elements. Typical relationships are temporal (time or sequence related) and structural (whole–part). For example, if the relationship is temporal, the search may identify prior or succeeding events (that may or may not be causally related to the original event). If the relationship is structural, the search may involve refining the event into constituent events.

Search techniques can be classified as (1) forward and backward, (2) top-down and bottom-up, or (3) combinations of these two.

13.3.1 Forward and Backward Searches

Forward (sometimes called *inductive*) and *backward* (also called *deductive*) searches are useful when the underlying structure is temporal and the elements are events, conditions, or tasks. A forward search takes an initiating event (or condition) and traces it forward in time. The result is a set of states (where a state is a set of conditions) that represent the effects of the initiating event. An example of such a search is determining how the loss of a particular control surface will affect the flight of an aircraft.

The purpose of a forward search is to look at the effect on the system state

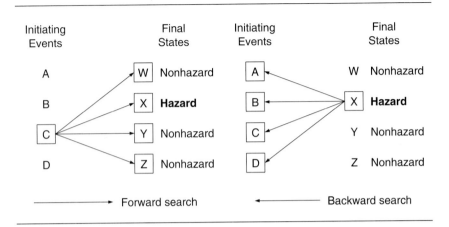

FIGURE 13.3
The states found in a forward search and in a backward search will probably not be the same.

of both (1) an initiating event and (2) later events that are not necessarily caused by the initiating event. In fact, causal independence is often assumed.

Tracing an event forward can generate a large number of states, and the problem of determining all reachable states from an initial state may be unsolvable using a reasonable set of resources. For this reason, forward analysis is often limited to only a small set of temporally ordered events.

In a backward or deductive search, the analyst starts with a final event or state and determines the preceding events or states. This type of search can be likened to Sherlock Holmes reconstructing the events that led up to a crime. Backward search methods fit well with chain-of-event accident models, where the goal is to determine the paths (sets of states or events in temporal ordering) that can lead to a particular hazard or accident. They are useful in accident investigations and in eliminating hazards by installing controls to eliminate predecessor events.

The results of forward and backward searches are not necessarily the same. Tracing an initiating event forward will most likely result in multiple final states, not all of which represent hazards or accidents: There is one initiating state and multiple final states (Figure 13.3).

Tracing backward from a particular hazard or accident to its succeeding states or events may uncover multiple initiating events. Forward searches could, of course, consider multiple events, but combinatorial explosion usually makes this goal impractical and so the number of initiating events that can be considered is usually limited. It is easy to see that if the goal is to explore the precursors of a specific hazard or accident, the most efficient method is a backward search procedure. On the other hand, if the goal is to determine the effects of a specific failure, a forward search is most efficient.

13.3.2 Top-Down and Bottom-Up Searches

A second categorization of search methods is top-down or bottom-up. Here the relationship being investigated is structural (whole–part): Higher-level abstractions are refined or broken down into their constituent parts. A basic event, set, task, or system may be broken up into more basic events, conditions, tasks, or subsystems in a top-down search. When the search is bottom-up, subcomponents are put together in different ways to determine the result. An example of a top-down search is identification of all the ways that power can be lost. A bottom-up search might examine the effect of an individual battery failure on the system as a whole.

As with forward and backward searches, the results of top-down and bottom-up searches are not the same. For example, examining only the effects of individual component failures on the overall behavior of the system (a bottom-up search) misses hazardous system behavior that results from combinations of subsystem failures or from combinations of nonfailure (correct) behavior of several subsystems. As in forward searches, considering the effects at the system level of all possible combinations of component behavior is not practical. Top-down searches that start from a hazardous system behavior will be more practical in this case. On the other hand, determining the effect of a particular component failure on system behavior is, theoretically, most efficiently accomplished using a bottom-up search. Determining the effect of a component failure at the system level using a bottom-up approach, however, is often very difficult for complex systems.

13.3.3 Combined Searches

Some search strategies do not fit into one of these categories. Instead, the search starts with some event or deviation and goes forward and backward or top-down and bottom-up to find paths between hazards (or accidents) and their causes or effects. The search may start with deviations, failures, changes, and so on.

13.4 Limitations and Criticisms of Hazard Analysis

Hazard analysis serves as the basis of judgment for many aspects of system safety. Therefore, understanding its limitations and common problems is important. Since qualitative analysis always precedes quantitative analysis, all limitations of the former apply to the latter. Quantitative techniques have additional limitations, however.

Hazard analyses, along with their underlying accident and system models, may not match reality. They often make unrealistic assumptions, such as assuming that (1) the system is designed, operated, and maintained according to good engineering standards; (2) quality control procedures will ensure that all equipment conforms to the design specifications and is inspected, calibrated, maintained, repaired, and tested at suitable intervals; (3) testing is perfect and repair time is negligible; (4) operators and users are experienced and trained; (5) operational procedures are clearly defined; (6) the system operates perfectly from the beginning; and (7) key events are independent and random.

Phenomena unknown to the analysts obviously cannot be covered in the analysis, and discrepancies between the written documentation and the real system mean that important accident contributors may not be considered [327]. Sometimes, the boundaries of the analysis are drawn incorrectly and relevant subsystems, activities, or hazards are excluded.

Even if all the assumptions are right to begin with, conditions change and the models may not accurately reflect the current system. In general, there is no way to assure completeness—that is, that all factors have been considered.

Kletz claims that, in practice, the majority of errors in hazard analyses result from faults in the model or failure to foresee hazards and not from errors in the data:

> The mistake made by many hazard analysts is to quantify (with ever greater accuracy) the particular hazards that they have thought of and fail to foresee that there are other hazards of much more importance. This means that so-called confidence limits have a very restricted meaning. They are telling you the error that can arise because of the sample size of the data, but they do not tell you that errors can arise because the analyst did not realize that there was some other way in which the hazard can occur [113].

Hope and colleagues suggest that the general nature of some of the methodologies can easily lead to misinterpretation and misuse of the results [126].

The limitations discussed so far relate to the particular models constructed. A second group of limitations relates to simplifications in the modeling techniques themselves. Examples include requiring that continuous variables be specified as discrete variables, not allowing consideration of certain timing factors such as time delays or the ordering of events, and assuming independence so that common-cause failures are not handled.

Simplifications may stem from the inability to represent particular aspects of the system or to evaluate them in the analysis. Policy and principles of management are rarely included, for example, nor are the safety culture of the organization, organizational structure, training factors, and the safety engineering process employed. Models that require assigning numbers to everything may omit important factors because they are not easily quantified. In addition, there may be limitations in the search patterns, the system models, or the underlying accident models that restrict the factors that can be considered. A few evaluations of specific hazard analysis methods and models have been performed (see Section 14.14), but their validity is largely unknown.

Some of the oversimplifications stem from limitations in knowledge. All the data used in the analysis must be relevant to the situation being analyzed, but in practice data are scarce, incomplete, and often not directly applicable [126]. Sometimes assumptions about infrequent events have to be based on extremely limited data with necessarily low confidence levels: It is difficult to collect statistically sufficient data on component behavior that includes different operating conditions, component types, failure modes and distributions, common cause failures, and so on.

Not only are there inaccuracies in failure data, but the information required for consequence modeling and human error data is often unknown or inaccurate, as discussed earlier.

Other limitations of hazard analysis stem not from the techniques themselves but from the fact that they must be used by humans. To varying degrees, the analysis represents the analyst's interpretation of the system; the analyst may inadvertently introduce bias, especially when the system being analyzed is complex. In addition, many of the techniques are complicated and demand appreciable specialist manpower and time that may not be available. Automation of the analysis does not completely solve the human limitation problems—it merely shifts them to the computer programmer, who, in effect, becomes the analyst. Automated analyses also usually require a manually constructed system model, with all its inherent limitations.

With this information about the hazard analysis process and its general limitations in mind, we are ready to examine specific hazard analysis models and techniques.

Chapter

14

Hazard Analysis Models and Techniques

Before a wise man ventures into a pit, he lowers a ladder—so he can climb out.

—Rabbi Samuel Ha-Levi Ben Joseph Ibm Nagrela
Ben Mishle

Many different types of hazard analysis have been proposed and are in use. Some differ primarily in their names, whereas others truly have unique and important characteristics. One of the greatest problems in performing hazard analysis may be in selecting appropriate models and techniques that match the project's goals, tasks, and skills. Because the methods have different coverage and validity, several may be required during the life of the project. No one method is superior to all others for every objective or even applicable to all types of systems. Perhaps the most important fact to keep in mind is that very little validation of any of these techniques has been done, and so all results should be treated with appropriate skepticism. That does not mean that the techniques are not useful, only that they must be used carefully and combined with a large dose of engineering judgment and expertise.

The resources and time for any analysis are limited. Not all resources should be put into one single method or into one single phase of the analysis process. In planning the analysis and selecting appropriate procedures, consideration should be given to its purpose, who will use the results and what kind of information is expected, the seriousness of the potential hazards, the complexity of the system, the nature of the project and the uniqueness of its design and technology, the degree of automation, the types of hazards to be considered, and the role of humans

313

and computers in the system [299]. Only a few of the techniques described can handle software in any reasonable way.

In addition to the analysis techniques presented here, some of the accident models described in Chapter 10, along with appropriate analysis techniques, can be (and are) used in accident investigations and occasionally in predictive analyses.

In this chapter, each technique is first described in terms of its basic features and the life cycle phase to which it applies, and then it is evaluated. The final section of the chapter describes the small amount of experimental validation of techniques that has been carried out.

14.1 Checklists

Description

There is a tremendous amount of hard-earned experience in engineering, and checklists are one way to pass on this experience so that each project need not relearn the lessons of the past and start each hazard analysis from scratch. As the repository of mistakes made and lessons learned, checklists provide feedback to the engineering process.

When checklists are dynamically updated within an organization, they may become uniquely tailored to that organization's procedures and practices. They may also be derived from standards and codes of good engineering practice. Checklists are most useful in the design of well-understood systems, for which standard design features and knowledge have been developed over time.

Checklists are included as an analysis technique here because they guide thinking. In fact, many of the other analysis techniques incorporate some form of checklist in their procedures. Basic checklists are simply lists of hazards or specific design features. Others stimulate thought and enquiry with questions that are open ended rather than requiring only a "yes" or "no" answer or a check in a box. For example, instead of asking "Is the system protected against electromagnetic interference?" the list might instead ask "How is the system protected against EMI?"

Life-Cycle Phase

Checklists are commonly used in all life-cycle phases, and in fact are most useful when oriented toward a specific phase. For hazard identification, they provide information about known hazards or high-risk conditions, helping to make sure that hazards are not overlooked. For a design, they ensure conformance to existing codes and standards of practice. Design checklists often use a series of *what-if* questions like those in design reviews. During operations, checklists may be used for periodic audits or to ensure that steps in procedures are not forgotten (the checklists used by pilots, for example). Information gained during the hazard analysis process for the project should be used to design operations checklists.

Evaluation

Checklists are an excellent way to pass on lessons learned, especially for hazard identification. For designers, they help to ensure good engineering design practices and compliance with standards, codes, and specifications; for reviewers, they help to verify that prohibited or bad practices have been avoided and that requirements have been satisfied.

On the negative side, checklists may encourage users to rely on them too much and thus to overlook items not on the list. Also, to be comprehensive, checklists may have to include a large number of questions, and, as experience reveals problems, more will be added. They can then become large and difficult to use, and users may be lulled into thinking that all issues that should be considered have been included. Checklists often induce false confidence—a belief that if everything is checked off, the system is safe. In addition, most do not allow relative ranking of hazards or include information about relative effectiveness of alternative safeguards [126].

Another problem arises when the lists are used without giving careful thought to the specific situation being considered. Ozog and Bendixen provide an example from the process industry: A checklist might reasonably require flame arrestors in vents from flammable liquid storage tanks, but if the vapors are susceptible to polymerization, venting directly to the atmosphere might be safer [250]. In this case, relying on the checklist without considering special circumstances might create a more hazardous situation.

While checklists may be useful, more sophisticated analyses for all but the simplest systems are essential to an effective safety program.

14.2 Hazard Indices

Description

Hazard indices measure loss potential due to fire, explosion, and chemical reactivity hazards in the process industries. They were originally developed primarily for insurance purposes and to aid in the selection of fire protection methods, but they can be useful in general hazard identification, in assessing hazard level for certain well-understood hazards, in the selection of hazard reduction design features for the hazards reflected in the index, and in auditing an existing plant.

The oldest and most widely used index was developed by the Dow Chemical Company. The *Dow Chemical Company Fire and Explosion Index Hazard Classification Guide* (usually abbreviated as the *Dow Index*) was first published in 1964 and was originally the basis for calculating a Fire and Explosion Index. Later, it was expanded to calculate the maximum probable property damage and the maximum probable days outage. Any operation where a flammable, combustible, or reactive material is stored, handled, or processed can be evaluated with the *Dow Index*. Auxiliary plant, such as power generation equipment, office buildings, control rooms, or water systems, is not covered.

The *Dow Index* first requires dividing the plant into units, a unit being a part of a plant that can be readily and locally characterized as a separate entity. Generally, a unit consists of a segment of the overall process: In some cases, it may be a part that is separated by distance or by walls; in others, it may be an area in which a particular hazard exists [196, 126].

The Fire and Explosion Index indicates the fire and explosion hazard level of a particular unit. The calculation of this index uses a measure, called the *Material Factor* (MF), of the energy potential of the most hazardous material or materials in the unit in sufficient quantity to present a hazard. This measure is a number from 1 to 40 and is calculated on the basis of flammability and reactivity. For some properties, the MF can be found in a table; for others, it must be calculated (Lees [172] explains how). General and special hazards (including factors such as properties of the materials, quantities involved, the type of process and whether it is difficult to control, process conditions, and construction materials) are treated as penalties applied against the MF. A Toxicity Index can also be calculated to evaluate the exposure level of toxicity hazards.

Basically, these calculations combine a number of empirical hazard factors that reflect the properties of the materials being processed, the nature of the process, the spacing of equipment, and the judgment of the analyst about them [126]. The index is then used to determine the fire protection required. Basic fire protection design features, including minimum separation distances, are recommended in the *Dow Index*.

Attempts have been made to improve on this index or to come up with alternative indices, but most alternatives have not found widespread acceptance outside the organizations in which they were developed [249]. One that has been used in the chemical industry, called the *Mond Index*, was proposed in 1979. It expands the *Dow Index* to include additional factors related to the effects of toxic materials and layout features (such as spacing, access, height, and drainage) on the hazard level.

Evaluation

Hazard indices provide a quantitative indication of the potential for hazards associated with a given design. They work well in the process industry, where designs and equipment are standard and change little, but are less useful for systems where designs are unique and technology changes rapidly. Lowe and Solomon [196] claim that the *Dow Index* and others are particularly useful in the early stages of hazard assessment, since they require a minimum of process and design data and can graphically demonstrate which areas within the plant require more attention. The indices can also help to identify which of several competing process designs contain the fewest inherent hazards, and they provide information useful for site selection and plant layout [250].

The indices only consider a limited set of hazards, and even for these, they determine only hazard level. No attempt is made to define specific causal factors, which are necessary to develop hazard elimination or reduction measures beyond the standard equipment information provided in tables. Thus, the indices do not provide a complete picture and are useful primarily to supplement other hazard analysis methods.

14.3 Fault Tree Analysis

Description

Fault Tree Analysis (FTA) is widely used in the aerospace, electronics, and nuclear industries. It was originally developed in 1961 by H. A. Watson at Bell Telephone Laboratories to evaluate the Minuteman Launch Control System for an unauthorized (inadvertent) missile launch. Boolean logic methods had been used at Bell Labs for communications equipment, and these were adapted to FTA. Engineers and mathematicians at the Boeing Company developed the procedure further and became its foremost proponents.

FTA is primarily a means for analyzing causes of hazards, not identifying hazards. The top event in the tree must have been foreseen and thus identified first by other techniques. FTA uses Boolean logic to describe the combinations of individual faults that can constitute a hazardous event. Each level in the tree lists the more basic events that are necessary and sufficient to cause the problem shown in the level above it.

FTA is a top-down search method. Backward or forward search techniques are chronological orderings of events over time, but each level of the fault tree merely shows the same thing in more detail. The intermediate events (events between the top event and the leaf nodes in the tree) are pseudoevents (abstractions of real events)—they are simply combinations or sets of the basic or primary events and are usually removed during the formal analysis of the tree (Figure 14.1).

Once the tree is constructed, it can be written as a Boolean expression and simplified to show the specific combinations of identified basic events sufficient to cause the undesired top event. If a quantitative analysis is desired and feasible (the individual probabilities for all the basic events are known), the frequency of the top event can be calculated.

Fault Tree Analysis has four basic steps: (1) system definition, (2) fault tree construction, (3) qualitative analysis, and (4) quantitative analysis.

System Definition. This is often the most difficult part of the FTA task; it requires determining the top event, initial conditions, existing events, and impermissible events. The selection of top events is crucial, since the assessment of

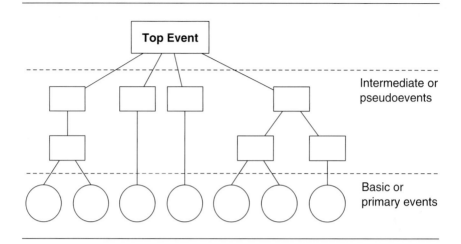

FIGURE 14.1
The leaf nodes of a fault tree represent the basic or primary events.

hazards in the system will not be comprehensive unless fault trees are drawn for all significant top events.

A thorough understanding and definition of the system and its interrelationships is essential for this step and all other steps in FTA. The analyst may use system functional diagrams, flow diagrams, logic diagrams, or other design representations, or may rely on his or her knowledge of the system. The physical system boundaries must be carefully defined.

For any component that has more than one possible state, the analyst must decide upon the system state (initial state) to be analyzed for the occurrence of the top event. If the top event is an inadvertent weapon release from an aircraft, for example, the events in the tree will be very different depending on whether the aircraft is on the ground, in flight and cruising to target, or over the target but not in proper position for the release [296]. Similarly, the fault tree for the collision of two automobiles will depend upon traffic speed and density.

Fault Tree Construction.   Once the system has been defined, the next step is fault tree construction. Briefly, the analyst first assumes a particular system state and a top event and then writes down the causal events related to the top event and the logical relations between them, using logic symbols to describe the relations. Figure 14.2 shows the symbols used for fault trees, of which the most frequently used are AND and OR gates. The output of an AND gate exists only if all the inputs exist (it represents combinations of events); the output of an OR gate exists provided at least one of the inputs exists (it shows single-input events that can cause the output event). The input events to an OR gate do not cause the event above the gate, but are simply re-expressions of the output event. In contrast, the

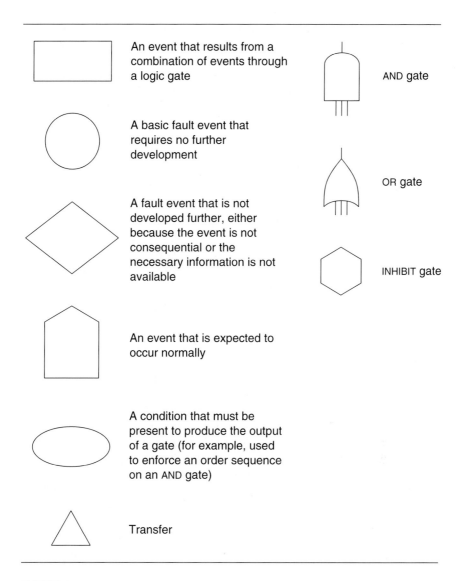

An event that results from a combination of events through a logic gate

A basic fault event that requires no further development

A fault event that is not developed further, either because the event is not consequential or the necessary information is not available

An event that is expected to occur normally

A condition that must be present to produce the output of a gate (for example, used to enforce an order sequence on an AND gate)

Transfer

AND gate

OR gate

INHIBIT gate

FIGURE 14.2
Fault tree symbols.

events attached to the AND gate are the causes of the event above the gate [344]. This causal relationship is what differentiates an AND gate from an OR gate.

Inhibit (NOT) gates can also be used, but are less common. They may be needed in a situation where there are two flows, X and Y, and the top event occurs if there is either no X flow or no Y flow. The simple OR gate is inclusive—it states that the top event occurs if there is a failure of X flow, Y flow, or both. If the goal is to specify that the top event does not occur if there is a failure of *both* X and Y flows (exclusive OR), then the simple OR gate will not suffice and an INHIBIT or other type of gate is needed.

The relationships between the events shown in the fault tree are just standard logical relations and therefore can be expressed using any of the alternative forms of Boolean algebra or truth tables. The tree format, however, seems to have advantages in terms of readability.

The process continues, with each level of the tree considered in turn until basic or primary events are reached. These are completely arbitrary, and the analyst must determine the stopping rule for the analysis, or, in other words, the resolution limit of the analysis. The events considered to be basic in the analysis will depend on its purpose, scope (a first estimate or a fully detailed analysis), and intended users; the available knowledge about the causes of events; and the availability of statistical data if a quantitative analysis is desired. Figure 14.3 is an example of a fault tree.

Qualitative Analysis.   After the tree is constructed, qualitative analysis can begin. The purpose, basically, is to reduce the tree to a logically equivalent form showing the specific combinations (intersections) of basic events sufficient to cause the top event. In essence, the intermediate pseudoevents are removed and only relationships between the top event and the primary events are described. These are called *cut sets*. The goal of the analysis is to find the *minimal cut sets*, which represent the basic events that will cause the top event and which cannot be reduced in number—that is, a cut set that does not contain another cut set. Cut sets are defined such that if even one event in the cut set does not occur, the top event will not take place.

The minimal cut set representation as a tree corresponds to one OR gate with all the minimal cut sets as descendants. The same primary events usually will occur in more than one of the minimal cut sets; thus, the minimal cut sets are generally not independent of each other. A medium-sized fault tree can have millions of minimal cut sets, so computer programs have been developed to calculate them. The procedures for reducing the tree to a logically equivalent form are beyond the scope of this book; the interested reader is referred to one of the many books on this subject. In general, the procedures employ Boolean algebra or numerical techniques, for example using the logical structure of the tree as a model for trial and error testing of the effects of selected combinations of primary events.

Minimal cut sets provide information that helps identify weaknesses in the system. For example, they determine the importance or ranking of each event with respect to the top event. A number of measures of importance have been

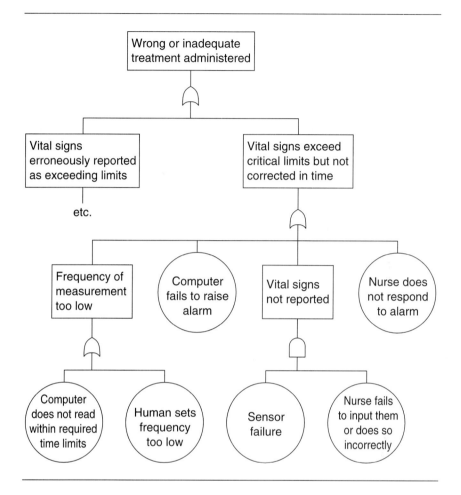

FIGURE 14.3
Portion of a fault tree for a patient monitoring system.

defined; some rely solely on structural considerations, while others require prob-abilistic information [172].

Quantitative Analysis.   The probability of the output of a logical gate is equal to the probability of the corresponding function of the input events—both charac-terize the same event. Quantitative analysis of fault trees uses the minimal cut sets to calculate the probability of occurrence of the top event from the probability of occurrence of the basic events. The probability of the top event will be the sum of the probabilities of all the cut sets if they are all statistically independent (the same event is not present in two or more cut sets). If there is any replication of events in any cut set, independence is compromised and the replication must be taken into account in any quantitative analysis. The probabilities of each cut set are determined by multiplying together the probability of the basic events.

According to Ozog and Bendixen [250], a common mistake in quantifying fault trees is multiplying two or more frequencies together, yielding meaningless results. To help avoid this mistake, they have changed the tree symbols to clarify which events are frequencies and which are probabilities.

If the probabilities of the basic events are given by a probability density function (the range of probabilities over which the event can occur) rather than by a point probability value, then the probability of the top event also must be expressed as a density function. Monte Carlo simulation can be used to determine these functions [126].

Automatic Synthesis. Several procedures for automatic synthesis of fault trees have been proposed, but these work only for systems consisting purely of hardware elements. Basically, a model of the hardware, such as a circuit diagram, is used to generate the tree [7, 10, 172]. Taylor's technique, which is typical, takes the components of the hardware model and describes them as transfer statements [335]. Each statement describes how an output event from the component can result from the combination of an internal change in the component and an input event. Such statements can also describe how the component state changes in response to input events. In general, the transfer statement will be conditional on the previous component state. Together, the transfer statements form the transfer function for the component.

Both the normal and failure properties of the component are described, and each transfer statement is represented as a small fragment of a fault tree or mini-fault tree. The synthesis process consists of building the fault tree by matching the inputs and outputs of the mini-fault trees. The same type of analysis can be done using state-machine models (see Section 14.12).

Software FTA. Fault tree analysis can be applied to software, as described in Chapter 18. With software, the analysis is used for verification, as the code must already have been written to generate the trees. FTA might be applied to software design representations to locate problems early, but the design specification would have to be very detailed in its description of the software logic. Once the code is generated, not only is building the tree difficult, but so is changing the software in any significant way. Software fault trees can be partially generated automatically; however, if loops are used in the code (which is true for virtually all software), the tree generation requires human assistance.

Probabilistic analysis is not applicable when software logic is described by fault trees; assigning a probability to a software statement is basically meaningless. In addition, if design errors are found in the tree through this process, they should be fixed rather than left in the code and assigned a probability.

Life-Cycle Phase

Although generic fault trees can be constructed before the details of design and construction are known, they are of limited usefulness. To be most effective, FTA requires a completed system design and a thorough understanding of the system and its behavior in all operating modes. Information is usually too incomplete to perform detailed fault tree analysis at the preliminary design stage [5], although a few features of alternative designs may be compared. In addition, fault trees can be used early in the design process to identify where interlocks are required and will be most effective, but they are not the most efficient model for this process [42].

FTA may also be applied to completed or existing systems to prove that the system is safe. The quantitative fault tree procedures are most useful for this purpose.

Evaluation

Although FTA was originally developed to calculate quantitative probabilities, it is more commonly used qualitatively. Simply developing the tree, without analyzing it, forces system-level examination beyond the context of a single component or subsystem. The graphical format provides a pictorial display of the relationships between events and helps both in understanding the system and in detecting problems or omissions in the analysis. Problems are also found because the analyst has to think about the system in great detail during tree construction.

Fault trees can help the analyst identify scenarios leading to hazards and can suggest possibilities for hazard elimination or control even before any analysis is performed on the tree. When software is part of the system, drawing the fault tree down to the software interface with other system components will identify safety-critical interfaces and potentially hazardous software behavior.

Knowing the minimum cut sets for a particular fault tree can provide valuable insight into potential weak points of a complex system, even when it is not possible to calculate the probability that either a particular cut set or the top event will occur. Lewis describes three useful qualitative considerations [189]. First, the ranking of minimal cut sets by the number of primary events required allows emphasizing the elimination of cut sets corresponding to small numbers of events. Single-point failures (where the occurrence of a single event could cause a hazard) can be uncovered and eliminated (they appear as a cut set containing a single event).

Second, events or components that appear in several minimum cut sets for a particular top event are likely to have an important effect on the occurrence of that event. In addition, if events or components appear only in minimum cut sets requiring several independent events, their importance with respect to the top event is likely to be small. The result of assessing importance in this way is a prioritized list of events that should be considered in reducing risk.

The independence of the events must be determined, and this determination is the third use for qualitative analysis—to focus common-cause failure analysis on particular cut sets and events. The events can be examined for susceptibility to common influencing factors such as weather or temperature extremes, vibration, corrosion, and environmental conditions such as dust or humidity. Even so, potential common-cause failures are not always obvious from the FTA process unless the analyst is very experienced and knowledgeable.

Most methods to handle common-cause failures in fault trees are qualitative only, but identification is more important than quantification anyway. Once a common-cause failure mode is identified, usually it can be eliminated completely—if there is enough information to measure it, there is usually enough information to eliminate it. A different type of common-cause failure, which occurs by fault propagation (domino effects), is also possible, but there appears to be no way of treating this type of failure in fault trees. Common-cause failures are important because, in very high reliability systems, they can become a dominant factor in system reliability and in accidents [172].

The extra work of a quantitative analysis may be cost effective when there are very subtle differences between several alternative designs [51] and when the causal factors involved have well established and accurate probabilities. The impact of the alternatives on the top-event frequency is calculated to determine the impact of the design decisions and the safety or reliability tradeoffs involved.

Fault Tree Analysis has several limitations. The most useful fault trees can be constructed only after the product has been designed; they require detailed knowledge of the design, construction, and operation of the system. A good safety program, however, requires concentration on the early stages of the system life cycle. Generic fault trees can be built early, but they may provide only information that is well known and already part of the project standards and design criteria. Hammer says that it may be better to spend time ensuring that the design criteria have been incorporated than building fault trees [108]. Childs notes that sometimes fault tree analysis finds only what is intuitively obvious [51]. One use for FTA in the design stage is to trace system hazards to individual components— such as software—in order to identify hazardous component behavior.

Fault tree analysis shows cause and effect relationships but little more. Additional analysis and information is usually required for an effective safety program. Moreover, reliability analysts usually concentrate only on failure events in fault trees whereas hazard analysis (as opposed to reliability analysis using fault trees) requires a broader scope. Thus, the use of fault trees by reliability analysts may differ from their use by system safety analysts. Applications of fault tree analysis that focus primarily on failures are essentially just reliability analyses.

A fault tree, like any other model, is a simplified representation of a generally very complex process: Its relative simplicity can be deceptive [172]. Much of the work on FTA is concerned with correcting the oversimplifications, but the problems might be better overcome by using different types of models and analyses to handle these factors directly rather than trying to forcefit everything into one (perhaps inappropriate) analysis framework. For example, the technique is particularly suited to discrete events, such as a valve opening or closing, but time- and rate-dependent events, such as changes in critical process variables, degrees of failure (partial failure), and dynamic behavior are not so easily represented [126].

Simple AND and OR gates do not convey any notion of time ordering or time delay; the fault tree is a snapshot of the state of the system at one point in time. In some cases, time spans or chronological ordering of events may need to be specified. Other types of gates, such as DELAY and INHIBIT, allow some treatment of time in fault trees and in the tree reduction process [255]. They complicate the evaluation of the tree, however, and somewhat negate one important advantage of FTA—the ease with which the trees can be read and understood and thus reviewed by experts and used by designers. If chronology is important, using a model and analysis technique that involves backward or forward search may be more appropriate than forcefitting this into a hierarchical, top-down modeling technique.

Transitions between states are not represented in fault trees, which deal best with binary states: Partial failures and multiple failures can cause difficulties [62]. Because system states rather than sequences of states are shown, fault trees are used less often in studies of batch systems and plants (where sequence is important) than in continuous systems. Nonaction or static systems (such as pressure vessels) are also difficult to handle, since their state depends primarily on environmental events or event combinations rather than on the component state itself [5].

Problems also occur in the analysis of *phased-mission* systems, which pass through more than one phase of operation [172]. Typically in these systems, the same equipment is used at different times and in different configurations for different tasks, and thus a separate fault tree is needed for each phase. While it is possible to think of this type of system as essentially an OR gate under the top event, where the inputs to the OR gate represent the different phases of the mission, the standard OR will not suffice because the inputs are separated in time. Although phased-mission systems can be handled by constructing several fault trees, problems can occur at the phase boundaries that are not easily resolved [172].

Additional criticisms of fault tree analysis relate to its quantitative aspects. As mentioned, common-cause failures cause problems and can lead to orders-of-magnitude errors in the calculated failure probability [217].

As with any technique that tries to quantify factors in complex systems probabilistically, data may not be available for the most important factors, such as operator work conditions, the management system, design errors, human errors of various kinds, and nonrandom failures and events. Either these factors are left out because they cannot be quantified, or probabilities are assigned that are unrealistic or have very large uncertainties. Combining reliabilities of parts containing five or six significant figures with human error probabilities having significant uncertainties does not produce very useful conclusions. Misleading results can also be obtained by using data that is not applicable because conditions are not similar to those under which the data was obtained or by averaging widely different data (one can drown in a lake with an average depth of six inches) [156].

Actually, most errors in hazard analysis are not due to errors in the data but to the failure to foresee all the ways in which the hazard could occur. According to Kletz, "time is usually better spent looking for all the sources of hazard than in quantifying with ever greater precision those we have already found" [156]. MacKenzie notes that because it is not possible to identify all accident sequences, the absolute values of the calculated risks have large uncertainties. In the space program, where quantitative Fault Tree Analysis (and Failure Modes and Effects Analysis) was used extensively, almost 35 percent of the actual in-flight malfunctions had not been identified by the technique as "credible" [205], as noted earlier.

14.4 Management Oversight and Risk Tree Analysis

Description

Management Oversight and Risk Tree analysis (MORT), developed by Johnson in the 1970s for the U.S. Nuclear Regulatory Agency, was discussed in Chapter 10 as an accident model. It can also be used as an accident investigation or hazard analysis technique. The underlying accident model assumes that accidents are caused by uncontrolled energy released by mishandled changes in the system.

Basically, MORT is a standard fault tree augmented by an analysis of managerial functions, human behavior, and environmental factors. Its aim is to identify problems, defects, and oversights that create hazards or prevent their early identification by poor planning, inadequate operational checks, or limited information exchange within the organization.

The method uses an extensive checklist of 1,500 basic events or factors that facilitates finding those safety problems included in the list. Figure 10.10 shows an example of MORT [140].

Evaluation

MORT has the advantages and disadvantages of any checklist-based analysis. An advantage over most of the other analysis methods described in this chapter is its consideration of factors related to the organization, information system, management practices, and principles and goals of the enterprise. Relatively little emphasis, in practice, has been placed on management and human factors (aside from trying to measure human errors so numbers can be attached to basic events in fault trees) compared to the emphasis on the reliability analysis of engineered systems [322].

Suokas suggests that, in his experience, MORT analysis yields detailed information useful in the planning and coordination of activities involving several departments, a more precise definition of important tasks and responsibilities, the development of planning and operating procedures, and training in professional abilities and safety matters [324]. MORT is not used very often, perhaps, as suggested by Suokas and Kakko, because of its complexity.

14.5 Event Tree Analysis

Description

FTA is the most widely used method for the quantification of system failures, but it becomes very difficult to apply in complicated systems. WASH-1400 was a complex, probabilistic risk assessment of nuclear power plants in the early 1970s. The study team (see Chapter 8.5.2) first attempted to draw a fault tree for nuclear reactors starting with the top event, "accidental release of radioactivity," but they gave up when this led to a hopelessly complicated fault tree [281]. Instead, they adapted the general decision tree formalism, widely used for business and economic analysis, to break up the problem into smaller parts to which FTA could be applied.

This decision tree technique, called Event Tree Analysis when used in this way, uses forward search to identify the various possible outcomes of a given initiating event, such as the rupture of a pipe, by determining all sequences of events that could follow it. The initiating event might be a failure of a system component or some event external to the system. The problem in any forward search, of course, is knowing where to start. In nuclear power plants (the principle application of this method), an accident is defined as any failure of the operating system that might result in the release of radioactivity. Thus, the starting point for listing the initiating events to be considered is the potential failures previously identified and defined by many years of safety analysis and by the licensing process for commercial nuclear power plants.

The states in the forward search are determined by the success or failure of other components or pieces of equipment. In nuclear power or other applications, where the stress is on protection systems, all the protection systems that can be used after the accident are first defined and then structured as headings for the event tree. The engineered protection functions are listed left to right in chronological order after the initiating event. The ordering of the headings on the event tree is important.

The event tree is then drawn from left to right, with branches under each heading corresponding to two alternatives: (1) successful performance of the protection system (the upper branch) and (2) failure of the protection system (the lower branch). After the tree is drawn, paths through it can be traced by choosing a branch under each successive heading, where each path corresponds to an accident sequence.

An example from the WASH-1400 report is shown in Figure 14.4. Here, the headings are pipe break, electric power, emergency core cooling system (ECCS), fission product removal, and containment integrity. Each of these systems is assumed either to succeed or fail in its specified function. The expression at the

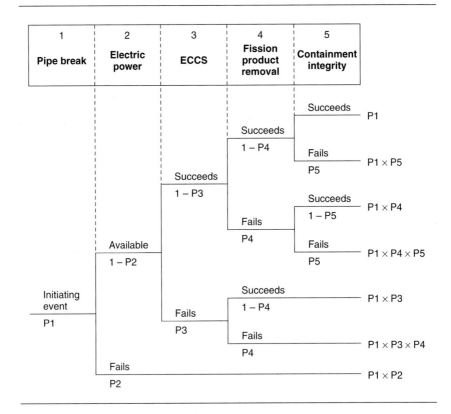

FIGURE 14.4
A reduced event tree for a loss of coolant accident. (Source: *Reactor Safety Study*, U.S. Nuclear Regulatory Commission, WASH-1400, NUREG 75/014, October 1974.)

right of each path is the probability for that path. Because the probability of failure is assumed to be very small, the probability of success is always close to 1. Therefore, the probability associated with the upper (success) branches of the tree is assumed to be 1.

Event trees tend to get quite large. They are reduced by eliminating sequences whose functional and operational relationships are illogical or meaningless. Since the system states on a given branch of the tree are conditional on the previous states having already occurred, another way to prune an event tree is to eliminate all branches that have a zero conditional probability for at least one event.

A path's total probability is found by multiplying together the probabilities at the various branches of the path, and the total risk of an accident is found by combining the path probabilities for all paths leading to an accident. The initial event is expressed as a frequency (events per year), while the other, secondary events are probabilities (failures per demand). The probabilities for protection system failures (secondary events) are often determined using fault trees.

Event Tree Analysis is usually applied using a binary state system, as explained above, where each branch of the tree has one failure state and one success state. If a greater number of discrete states are defined for each branch (for example, if partial failures are included), then a branch must be included for each state. A problem is the possible explosion in the number of paths—for a sequence of N events, there will be 2^N branches of a binary tree. The number can be reduced by eliminating impossible branches, as described, but a large number of paths can still result.

Usually, a finite number of branches is defined at each node, but there is no conceptual problem with introducing a continuous random variable in an event tree [255]. Graphically, the spectrum of possible values of the continuous variable is represented by a fan originating at the event node. The analysis, in this case, uses a continuous conditional probability density and provides continuous joint distributions. In practice, a discrete variable may be more convenient, but in theory a continuous variable could be used [255].

Timing issues can cause problems in event tree construction. In some cases, failure logic changes depending on when the events take place. This happens, for example, in the operation of emergency core cooling systems in nuclear power plants [217]. As with fault trees, phased-mission analysis techniques are then needed to model the system changes during the accident sequence, even though the protection system does not change.

Another consideration is possible dependencies between the various probabilities arising from common-cause failures. In the nuclear reactor example, the value of the probability of ECCS function failure may depend in some way upon the conditions created by the pipe break itself. Such dependencies must be identified and assessed in the analysis, or the results can be distorted [5].

Life-Cycle Stage

Like Fault Tree Analysis, ETA is appropriate only after most of the design is complete. Thus, it has been used primarily to evaluate existing plants or designs. Note that by definition, and by the use of protection systems as the headings for the event tree, a decision is made in advance that the solution to the problem of safety will be to use protection systems. ETA does not require these headings, but it is difficult to determine which events to use for the headings otherwise. A general forward analysis of this type that did not drastically limit the events to be considered would be potentially enormous.

Evaluation

Fault trees lay out relationships between events: They are snapshots of the system state. Event trees, in contrast, display relationships between juxtaposed events (sequences of events) linked by conditional probabilities. As a result, at least in theory, event trees are better at handling notions of continuity (logical, temporal, and physical), while fault trees are more powerful in identifying and simplifying event scenarios. Event trees allow the direct introduction of time factors and continuous random variables, but they are more than fault trees because of the potentially large number of branches. Combinations of events can be more concisely represented in fault trees using logical functions. Figure 14.5 shows the same event represented by a fault tree and an event tree. The accident modeled is described in Section 4.1.1; here, a computer has been added to the original design. Notice that a top-down search model like a fault tree loses the information about the ordering of relief valve operation (although it could be added by adding more complex types of tree structures), while the forward-search event tree model does not include detailed evaluation of the individual events.

Event trees are useful within the scope for which they were devised—probabilistically evaluating the effects of protection system functioning and failure in an accident sequence, particularly when events can be ordered in time. They are practical when the chronology of events is stable and the events are independent of each other [173].

Event trees can be helpful in (1) identifying the protection system features that contribute most to the probability of an accident, so that steps can be taken to reduce their failure probability; (2) identifying top events for subsequent fault tree analysis; and (3) displaying various accident scenarios that may result from a single initiating event.

Like all the analysis techniques discussed in this chapter, event trees have many limitations. For one, they can become exceedingly complex, especially when a number of time-ordered system interactions are involved [58]. A complete risk analysis of a complex plant, using a combination of event trees and fault trees, will require many person-years of effort along with a number of simplifying assumptions. In addition, the use of FTA to determine the probabilities for many of the event tree branches may make it more difficult to identify common causes of failures [250].

A separate tree is required for each initiating event, making it difficult to represent interactions between event states in the separate trees or to consider the effects of multiple initiating events. In addition, while the event tree enumerates all possible combinations of component states related to an initiating event, it offers no help in determining whether the component failure combinations (paths) lead to system failure. Either the system is simple enough and the mapping can be done for each failure scenario without more formal analysis, or the system is more complex and fault trees have to be used to identify the failure modes [255].

The usefulness of event trees depends on being able to define the set of initiating events that will produce all the important accident sequences. For nuclear power plants, where all the risk is associated with one hazard (serious overheating of the fuel) and designs are fairly standard, defining this set of hazards may be easier than for other systems. Whether it can be done completely, even for nuclear power plants, is still undetermined. Similarly, defining the functions across

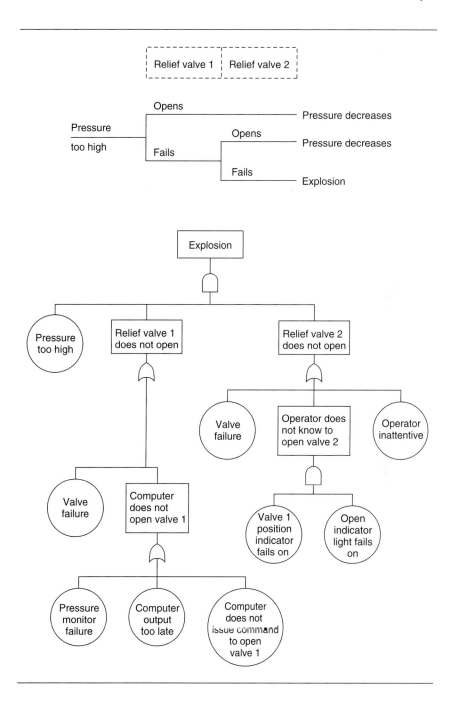

FIGURE 14.5
A fault tree and event tree comparison.

the top of the event tree and their order is difficult. Again, in nuclear power plants, where responsibility for safety is vested in a specific set of protection systems, the events to use are more obvious than in other systems, although the problem of ordering is still there. Order is important when the performance of one system affects the performance of another. To solve the ordering problem, the analyst needs a detailed understanding of all plant systems, how they operate, and how they interact with one another [281]. As in most of these analysis techniques, building the model requires the interaction of analysts with different areas of expertise.

Finally, as with fault trees, continuous, nonaction systems such as dams are not appropriate for event tree analysis.

14.6 Cause–Consequence Analysis

Description

Cause–Consequence Analysis (CCA) is a relatively new technique developed by Nielson in the 1970s that combines several search modes [240]. CCA starts with a *critical event* and determines the causes of the event (using top-down or backward search) and the consequences that could result from it (forward search). The cause–consequence diagram shows both time dependency and causal relationships among events.

The procedure starts with the selection of a critical event, which is followed by a search for factors that constitute the critical event and by a propagation of the potential effects of the event. Finally, the interrelationships of the factors are described by a graphical model (see Figure 14.6).

Several cause charts may be attached to a consequence chart. The cause charts describe the alternative prior event sequences that can lead to the critical event and the conditions under which these sequences can occur. According to Nielson, the initiating events should be traced back to spontaneous events covered by statistical data [240]. Other cause charts attached to the consequence chart may be conventional fault trees, which show the combination of conditions under which a certain event sequence in the consequence chart can take place.

A table of symbols used in CCA is shown in Figure 14.7. The event and condition symbols describe the type of event or condition. The logic symbols include *gates* to describe the relations between cause events, and *vertices* to describe the relations between consequences. Standard AND and OR relations are the main logic gates and vertices. Another useful vertex is EITHER/OR, or the decision box, which specifies the effect of an event or condition on the paths the system takes. If the NO output from the decision box is the result of an abnormal condition, then the fault tree for this condition is derived. Thus, fault trees are used in the diagram not only for the critical event but also for abnormal conditions [172]

Taylor has shown how cause–consequence diagrams can be formalized to provide a semi-automatic analysis method [333]. The plant is represented by a

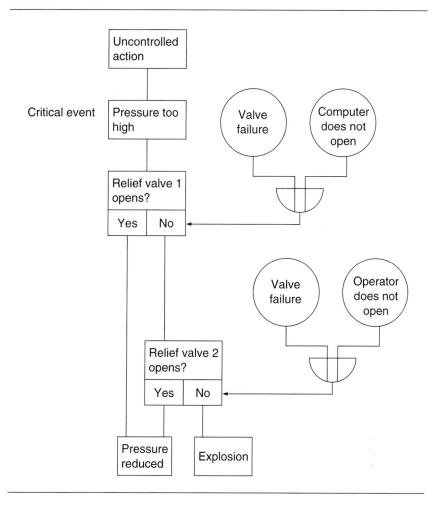

FIGURE 14.6
A cause–consequence diagram.

block diagram, where the arcs represent causal links. The blocks are described by arithmetic or transfer functions, as described earlier. A *condition* is a predicate that restricts the possible states of a system—usually by restricting the range of values of a single system variable—while an *event* is described by a pair of pre- and post-conditions (predicates true before and after the event, respectively). Event sequences can be traced through the block diagram to deduce the next event at each block.

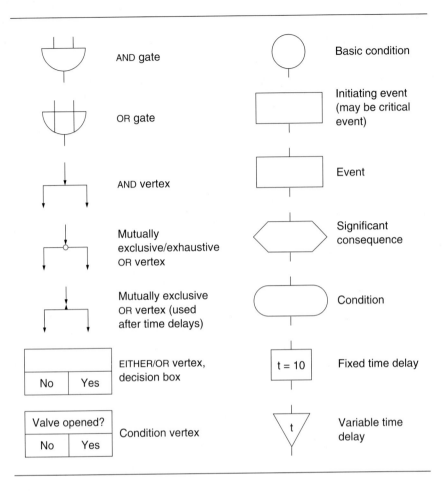

FIGURE 14.7
Cause–consequence diagram symbols.

Evaluation

Compared to fault trees, CCA shows the sequence of events explicitly, which makes the diagrams especially useful in studying startup, shutdown, and other sequential control problems. A systematic technique exists for constructing the diagrams (and also fault trees) from a block or wiring diagram of the plant.

Cause–consequence diagrams have the advantage over event trees of allowing the representation of time delays, alternative consequence paths, and combinations of events. They also take account of external conditions and the temporal ordering of events, where these factors are significant. Like the other techniques, CCA may be used for quantitative assessment.

On the negative side, the diagrams can become unwieldy, separate diagrams are required for each initiating event, and outcomes are related only to the cause being analyzed, although they could be caused by other initiating events [62]. CCA seems to be used more in Europe than in the United States.

14.7 Hazards and Operability Analysis

Description

Hazards and Operability Analysis (HAZOP) was developed by Imperial Chemical Industries in England in the early 1960s and later improved upon and published by the Chemical Industries Association in London. According to Ozog, about half the chemical process industry now uses HAZOP for all new facilities [249]. As the name suggests, the technique focuses not only on safety but also on efficient operations. Although it is usually applied to fixed plants, Kletz describes an application to tank trucks, in which several previously undetected hazards were identified and eliminated or controlled [161].

HAZOP is based on a systems theory model of accidents that assumes accidents are caused by deviations from the design or operating intentions—such as no flow or backward flow when there should be a forward flow. Basically, the technique encourages creative thinking about all the possible ways in which hazards or operating problems might arise. To reduce the chance that anything is forgotten, HAZOP is performed systematically, considering each process unit in the plant (such as pipelines, tanks, and reactors) and each hazard in turn. Questions are generated about the design by a small team of experts. Although prompted by a list of guidewords, the questions arise creatively out of the interaction of the team members [161].

HAZOP is a qualitative technique whose purpose is to identify all possible deviations from the design's expected operation and all hazards associated with these deviations. In comparison with hazard identification techniques like checklists, HAZOP is able to elicit hazards in new designs and hazards that have not been considered previously. It differs from some of the other techniques described in this chapter in that most of the others require that the hazards be identified before the analysis.

Using a description of the proposed process plant, a HAZOP team (composed of experts on different aspects of the system along with an independent team leader who is an expert on the technique itself) will consider

1. The design intention of the plant
2. The potential deviations from the design intention
3. The causes of these deviations from the design intention
4. The consequences of such deviations

TABLE 14.1
Guidewords for HAZOP.

Guidewords	Meaning
NO, NOT, NONE	The intended result is not achieved, but nothing else happens (such as no forward flow when there should be).
MORE	More of any relevant physical property than there should be (such as higher pressure, higher temperature, higher flow, or higher viscosity).
LESS	Less of a relevant physical property than there should be.
AS WELL AS	An activity occurs in addition to what was intended, or more components are present in the system than there should be (such as extra vapors or solids or impurities, including air, water, acids, corrosive products).
PART OF	Only some of the design intentions are achieved (such as only one of two components in a mixture).
REVERSE	The logical opposite of what was intended occurs (such as backflow instead of forward flow).
OTHER THAN	No part of the intended result is achieved, and something completely different happens (such as the flow of the wrong material).

The guidewords used in this process are shown in Table 14.1. They are applied to any variables of interest such as flow, temperature, pressure, level of composition, and time. Each line in a line drawing of the plant is examined in turn and the guidewords are applied. As each process deviation is generated, the members of the team consider every potential cause (such as a valve closed in error or a filter blocked) and its effect on the system as a whole (such as a pump overheating, a runaway reaction, or a loss of output). Questions are generated from the guidewords. The application of the guideword NONE to flow, for example, which means there should be forward flow, but there is no flow or there is reverse flow, might generate these questions:

- □ Could there be no flow?
- □ If so, how could it arise?
- □ How will the operators know that there is no flow?
- □ Are the consequences hazardous, or do they prevent efficient operations?
- □ If so, can we prevent no flow (or protect against the consequences) by changing the design or method of operation?
- □ If so, does the size of the hazard or problem justify the extra expense?

Figure 14.8 shows a detailed flow chart of the HAZOP process [155] while Table 14.2 shows a typical entry in the table that might result.

The procedure differs for continuous and batch processes. In the HAZOP for a continuous plant, the process is as described above. In addition to normal

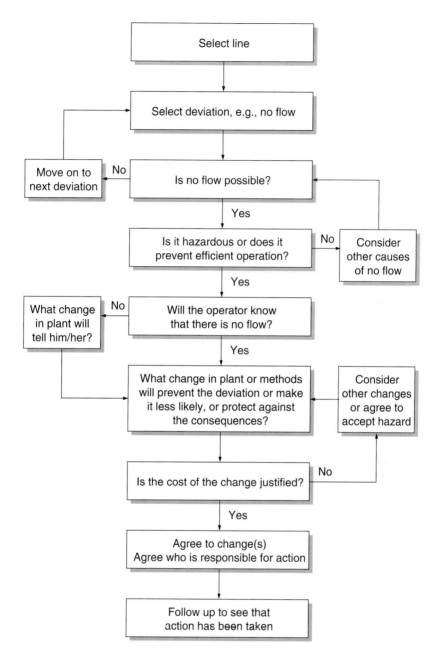

FIGURE 14.8
A flowchart of the HAZOP process. (Source: Trevor A. Kletz, "*Hazop and Hazan—Notes on the Identification and Assessment of Hazards,*" Institution of Chemical Engineers, Rugby, U.K., 1983. Reprinted with permission of Trevor Kletz.)

TABLE 14.2
Entry in a HAZOP report.

Guide Word	Deviation	Possible Causes	Possible Consequences
NONE	No flow	1. Pump failure	1. Overheating in heat exchanger
		2. Pump suction filter blocked	2. Loss of feed to reactor
		3. Pump isolation valve closed	

processing, the study should include operability and safety during commissioning of the plant and during regular startup and shutdown.

For a batch plant, not only the flow diagrams but also the operating procedures are examined. The guidewords are applied to the instructions (whether written for operators or executed by a computer) as well as to the pipelines. If computer instructions will be examined, a software engineer should be part of the HAZOP team. Time is important in batch operations: In applying the guidewords to time, such factors as duration, frequency, absolute time, and sequence may be relevant.

Reese has devised an automated variant of HAZOP, called Deviation Analysis, that can be applied to a software requirements specification [290].

Life-Cycle Phase

HAZOP uses process descriptions; flowsheets; control logic diagrams; piping and instrumentation diagrams; a plant layout; draft operating, maintenance, and emergency procedures; safety and training manuals; and data on the chemical, physical, and toxicological properties of all materials, intermediates, and products. By the time this much information is available, it is usually too late to make major changes in the design if hazards are identified. Therefore, hazards are usually controlled by the addition of protection devices rather than removed by design changes [155].

For this reason, many companies conduct preliminary HAZOPs on conceptual flowcharts and preliminary layout diagrams (noting only safety aspects, not operability problems). At this stage, for example, it is possible to replace a flammable piece of equipment with a nonflammable one. At a later stage, when the design is almost complete, it may only be possible to reduce the risk by adding fire insulation, leak detectors, emergency isolation valves, and so on [155]. A full HAZOP usually is conducted later in the design process even if a preliminary HAZOP has been done.

Evaluation

HAZOP does not attempt to provide quantitative results, but instead systematizes a qualitative approach. In most situations, once a hazard is identified, engineering experience or a code of practice is adequate to determine how far to go to remove it. "There is no need, and we do not have the resources, to quantify every hazard on every plant" [161]. In situations where uncertainty remains about the hazard, however, numerical analysis may help to clarify priorities and provide guidance for decision making. In the chemical process industry, the term HAZAN (for HAZard ANalysis) denotes numerical methods.

The strength of the method lies in its simplicity and ease of application and in the early identification of design problems. It does not concentrate only on failures, but has the potential to find more complex types of hazardous events and causes. Reductions of at least an order of magnitude in the number of hazards and problems encountered in operation have been claimed to result from the use of this technique [172].

Although HAZOP is closely connected with the chemical industry, the basic idea could be adapted to other industries (and perhaps has been). HAZOP has the advantage over checklists of being applicable to new designs and design features and of not limiting consideration to previously identified hazards. Complex, potentially dangerous plants with which there is as yet relatively little experience and procedures that occur infrequently (such as commissioning a new plant) are especially good subjects for this type of study [341].

In addition to its open-ended approach to identifying potential problems, a fundamental strength of HAZOP is the encouragement of cross-fertilization of ideas among members of the study team. People from different disciplines working together often find problems that are overlooked by functional groups working in isolation [155]. HAZOP's success, however, depends on the degree of cooperation between individuals, their experience and competence, and the commitment of the team as a whole. Except for the team leader, who is an expert on HAZOP, the members of the team must be experts on the process: The HAZOP procedures allow their knowledge and experience to be applied systematically.

The drawbacks of the technique are the time and effort required—it is labor-intensive—and the limitations imposed by the search pattern. HAZOP relies very heavily on the judgment of the engineers performing the assessment [337]. For example, the extent to which the guideword AS WELL AS is applied will restrict the number of simultaneous faults that can be considered, and evaluation is done by human reasoning alone. Again, all the methods described have these limitations.

Each of the methods has its own search pattern, limiting the factors that will be considered. HAZOP covers hazards caused by process deviations, which is certainly more comprehensive and inclusive than considering failures only, but it still leaves out hazards having more stable determining factors as the only contributors (see Chapter 10) [326]. Examples of causes covered well are failures of the main operating equipment (such as pumps, compressors, heat exchangers, critical valves, and instrumentation) and human errors in manual operations that involve the main process equipment and its functions (such as opening or closing valves and starting or stopping pumps).

Suokas says that it is unusual for HAZOP to consider deviations or determining factors related to organizational factors such as the information or management systems [327]. On the other hand, an argument can be made that causes related to these factors will be reflected in the process units as a change from the normal state or from acceptable values of the operating parameters, and that tracing back to the causes can reveal management factors. The problem may be more that this type of causal analysis is not encouraged by the technique; the process stops when more proximal factors such as a pump failure are uncovered without necessarily tracing the failure back to a maintenance error and perhaps back from that to a management problem.

14.8 Interface Analyses

Description

Various analysis methods are used to evaluate connections and relationships between components, including incompatibilities and the possibilities for common-cause or common-mode failure. In general, the relationships examined can be categorized as physical, functional, or flow [108]. These analysis methods generally use structured walkthroughs to examine the interface between components and to determine whether a connection provides a path for failure propagation. The types of problems and effects that are examined include

- ☐ No output from the unit or interconnection failures that cause the receiving unit not to receive the output of the upstream unit.
- ☐ Degraded output or partial failures of the unit or interconnection.
- ☐ Erratic output (intermittent or unstable operation).
- ☐ Excessive output.
- ☐ Unprogrammed output (inadvertent operation or erroneous output).
- ☐ Undesired side effects (programmed outputs are within specified limits, but additional damaging outputs are produced), such as a unit generating heat that can shorten the lives of nearby units.

Any such analysis should include connections between components that go through the software.

Noble has defined a specialized version of interface analysis that considers the potential for common-mode failures to affect redundant hardware components. His hardware and software common-mode failure analysis examines each connection between redundant components (including connections through software) to determine whether the connection provides a path for failure propagation [241].

Evaluation

Interface analyses are similar to HAZOP, but generalized somewhat, so they have the same benefits and limitations. Effectiveness depends upon the procedures used and the thoroughness with which the analysis is applied.

14.9 Failure Modes and Effects Analysis

Description

Failure Modes and Effects Analysis (FMEA) was developed by reliability engineers to permit them to predict equipment reliability. As such, it is a form of reliability analysis that emphasizes successful functioning rather than hazards and risk. The goal is to establish the overall probability that the product will operate without a failure for a specific length of time or, alternatively, that the product will operate a certain length of time between failures.

Like event trees, FMEAs use forward search based on an underlying chain-of-events model, where the initiating events are failures of individual components. The first step in an FMEA is to identify and list all components and their failure modes, considering all possible operating modes. For each failure mode, the effects on all other system components are determined along with the effect on the overall system. Then the probabilities and seriousness of the results of each failure mode are calculated.

Component failure rates are predicted from generic rates that have been developed from experience and are often published. Information centers collect and collate such information, and manufacturers usually have this data for their own products. Care must be taken that the environment in which the component will be working is identical to the one for which the statistics were collected. Probabilities are based on averages collected over large samples, but individual components may differ greatly from the average, perhaps because of substandard manufacturing or extreme environments. Confidence levels and error bounds are often omitted from FMEAs, but should be included.

The results are documented in a table with column headings such as component, failure probability, failure mode, percent failures by mode, and effect (which may be broken down into critical and noncritical or any other categories desired).

Figure 14.9 shows a simple FMEA for two amplifiers in parallel [344]. This example assumes that an amplifier failing short or in some other mode causes the system to fail while an amplifier failing open does not. The probabilities in the

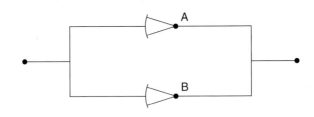

Critical	Failure probability	Failure mode	% failures by mode	Effects	
				Critical	Noncritical
A	1×10^{-3}	Open	90		X
		Short	5	5×10^{-5}	
		Other	5	5×10^{-5}	
B	1×10^{-3}	Open	90		X
		Short	5	5×10^{-5}	
		Other	5	5×10^{-5}	

FIGURE 14.9
FMEA for a system of two amplifiers in parallel. (Source: W. E. Vesely, F. F. Goldberg, N. H. Roberts, and D. F. Haasl, *Fault Tree Handbook*, NUREG-0492, U.S. Nuclear Regulatory Commission, Washington, D.C., 1981, page II-3)

column labeled *critical effects* (that is, they cause system failure) are added to get a failure probability for the entire system.

Life-Cycle Phase

FMEAs are appropriate when a design has progressed to the point where hardware items may be easily identified on engineering drawings and functional diagrams. The analyst needs a detailed design that includes schematics, functional diagrams, and information about the interrelationships between component assemblies.

Evaluation

FMEA is effective for analyzing single units or single failures to enhance individual item integrity. It can be used to identify redundancy and fail-safe design requirements, single-point failure modes, and inspection points and spare part requirements. It is also useful in determining how often the system must be serviced and how components and designs must be improved in order to extend the operational life of a product.

The strength of the technique is its completeness, but that means it is also very time consuming and can become tedious and costly if applied to all parts of a complex design.

All the significant failure modes must be known in advance, so FMEA is most appropriate for standard parts with few and well-known failure modes. The technique itself does not provide any systematic approach for identifying failure modes or for determining their effects and no real means for discriminating between alternate courses of improvement or mitigation. In fact, for systems that exhibit any degree of complexity, identifying all possible component failure modes—both singly and in combination—becomes simply impossible [344].

FMEA does not normally consider effects of multiple failures; each failure is treated as an independent occurrence with no relation to other failures in the system except for the subsequent effects it might produce. By limiting the analysis to single units and not considering multiple- or common-cause failures, the technique becomes simple to apply and the examination is very orderly, but the results may be of limited use if time sequences and the interrelationships among the elements of a complex system are not considered. Studies of product failures have shown that a much greater number are the result of connector problems than of failures in the components themselves [108].

Hammer points out that, as usually applied, FMEAs pay little attention to human errors in operating procedures, hazardous characteristics of the equipment, or adverse environments [106]. Although environmental conditions are considered in identifying the stresses that could cause hardware to fail, the probabilities of occurrence of such environmental stresses are rarely used. Instead, a usage factor is incorporated for the type of system application, such as shipboard, aircraft, or missile use, and another factor is applied for reduction of theoretical reliability that could result from substandard manufacture or assembly. This latter factor is extremely rough, even over a large sample. "Oddly enough," Hammer says, "in spite of all those factors affecting a system but whose probability of occurrence can only be estimated imprecisely, reliability engineers carry out their calculations to six or seven significant figures."

Because they establish the end effects of failures, FMEAs are sometimes used in safety analyses. If the limitations are understood, there is no problem with this. Not all failures result in accidents, however, so analyzing all parts, the ways each part can fail, and the resultant effects is generally a time-consuming and inefficient way to obtain safety-related information. In addition, the technique provides only a small part of the information needed, since the probability of damage determined by an FMEA is related to individual failures only; it rarely involves investigating damage or injury that could arise if multiple components fail or if the components operate successfully.

14.10 Failure Modes, Effects, and Criticality Analysis

Description

Failure Modes, Effects, and Criticality Analysis (FMECA) is basically just an FMEA with a more detailed analysis of the criticality of the failure. Two additional steps (and usually columns) are added to the FMEA: (1) the means of control already present or proposed are determined, and (2) the findings are modified with respect to these control procedures (such as modifying the chance of failure or adding an indication of whether or not further control is necessary). An example is shown in Figure 14.10.

Criticality rankings are generally expressed as probabilities or frequencies, such as the number of failures of a specific type expected during each 1 million operations performed in a critical mode. Rankings may also be ordered in categories from 1 to 10, or assigned letters starting from the beginning of the alphabet [108], to show the principal items that generate problems.

Along with the ranking, a description is provided of the preventive and corrective measures that should be taken and the safeguards to be incorporated.

Sometimes a Critical Items List (CIL) is generated from the results of the FMEA or FMECA. This list might include item, list of possible failure modes, failure probability (for each mode), effect on the mission (such as abort, degradations of performance, or damage) and criticality ranking within the subsystem (perhaps using a numerical scale).

Evaluation

Since this technique is simply an FMEA with two columns added, the same evaluation applies, with the exception that the FMECA does include a description of the means of controlling the failure. Even more effort is now required, though, and it still does not consider one aspect of criticality—possible damage. Hammer [108] suggests various ways that damage could be incorporated.

14.11 Fault Hazard Analysis

Description

Fault Hazard Analysis (FHA) was developed about the same time as FTA and was also used on the Minuteman missile system [344]. It is basically a FMEA or FMECA with both a broader and more limited scope. The scope is broadened by considering human error, procedural deficiencies, environmental conditions, and other events that might result in a hazard caused by normal operations at an undesired time [69]. At the same time, its scope is more restricted than that of a FMEA or FMECA, since supposedly only failures that could result in accidents

Failure Modes and Effects Criticality Analysis

Subsystem _____   Prepared by _____   Date _____

Item	Failure Modes	Cause of Failure	Possible Effects	Prob.	Level	Possible Action to Reduce Failure Rate or Effects
Motor Case	Rupture	a. Poor workmanship b. Defective materials c. Damage during transportation d. Damage during handling e. Overpressurization	Destruction of missile	0.0006	Critical	Close control of manufacturing processes to ensure that workmanship meets prescribed standards. Rigid quality control of basic materials to eliminate defectives. Inspection and pressure testing of completed cases. Provision of suitable packaging to protect motor during transportation.

FIGURE 14.10
A sample FMECA.

are considered, although it is difficult to understand how a forward analysis of this type can be done without all failures being considered first.

Two new pieces of information are added about upstream and downstream effects: (1) upstream components that could command or initiate the fault in question and (2) factors that could lead to secondary failures. The effects on the system are briefly stated in terms of associated damage or malfunction. The column headings may include component, failure probability, failure modes, percent failure by mode, effect of failure (traced to some relevant interface), upstream components that could command or initiate the failure or fault, and factors that could cause secondary failures.

Evaluation

Like FMEAs and FMECAs, FHA primarily provides guidance on what information to obtain, but it provides no help in actually getting that information. And again, in use FHA tends to concentrate primarily on single events or failures.

The technique was developed as a special tool for use on projects involving many organizations, one of which acts as an integrator. Hammer says that FHA is useful in considering faults that cross organizational interfaces. Others consider the technique to have little use.

14.12 State Machine Hazard Analysis

Description

A state machine is a model of the states of a system and the transitions between them. Figure 14.11 shows a simple state machine model of a level control. The model has three states (represented by circles): water level low, water level high, and water level at the set point. The arrows represent transitions between states. Each arrow has the condition for changing state and an output action attached to it. When a condition on a transition from a state becomes true and the machine is in that state, the machine changes to the new state and takes the output action. In the example, depending on the sensor reading of the water level and the current state of the machine, the machine will activate the pump, turn off the pump, open the drain, or close the drain.

State machine models are used often in computer science. One of the problems with using them for complex systems is the large number of states that these systems have and thus must be specified. One way to avoid this problem is to use models that abstract away from all the states to a smaller number of higher-level states, from which the entire state machine can be generated. The complete "state space" may never be generated (and it may be infeasible to do so), but many properties of the state space can be inferred from the higher-level model.

With respect to safety, if a model of the system to be built were created and its entire state space generated, it would be possible to determine if the state

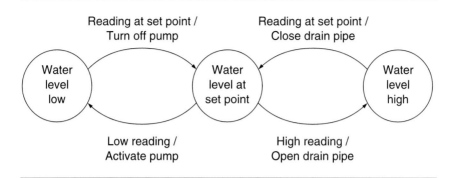

FIGURE 14.11
A state machine model of a water level control.

space contained any hazardous states. Basically, this approach involves a forward search that starts from the initial state of the system, generates all possible paths from that state, and determines whether any of them are hazardous. Unfortunately, for most realistic systems, the computational effort involved makes this approach impractical, even if computers are used.

Backward and top-down search in the general sense is also impractical. It would entail starting with the hazardous states and working backward from each to see if the initial state is reached. If so, then the hazardous state is reachable and the model is unsafe. If not, then the hazardous state is not reachable. The number of backward paths is still enormous for real systems, even if only those ending in hazardous states are considered.

A practical solution is to start from the hazardous state and only work far enough back along the paths to determine how to change the model to make the hazardous state unreachable [186]. Only a small number of the states will need to be generated in most cases. The drawback, although not a serious one, is that the hazardous states eliminated from the design might not actually have been reachable, so more hazards may be eliminated than were actually present. This algorithm was first demonstrated using a Petri-net model,[1] but the procedure can be adapted for any state machine model. Any parts of the system that can be modeled using state machines can be included in the hazard analysis. If faults and failures are included in the model, their effect on the system behavior can be determined.

---

[1] A Petri net is a mathematical representation of a discrete event system that is especially appropriate for representing systems with interacting, concurrent components. Petri nets model discrete state systems in terms of conditions and events and the relationship between them. Algorithms exist for generating the reachable states from a Petri-net model, although this procedure may not be practical for all systems. See Peterson [262] for a complete description of Petri nets.

State Machine Hazard Analysis (SMHA) was first developed to identify software-related hazards [186]. Software and other component behavior is modeled at a high level of abstraction, and faults and failures are modeled at the interfaces between the software and the hardware; thus, the procedure can be performed early in the system and software development process.

SMHA can be used to analyze a design for safety and fault tolerance, to determine software safety requirements (including timing requirements if the model includes timing) directly from the system design, to identify safety-critical software functions, and to help in the design of failure detection and recovery procedures and fail-safe requirements. Since the model used is formal (that is, it has a mathematical definition), the analysis procedures can be implemented on a computer.

Life-Cycle Phase

SMHA works on a model, not the design itself. Therefore, it can theoretically be used at any stage of the life cycle, including early in the conceptual stage, to evaluate alternative designs and design features. The procedure is most effective if performed before the detailed design of the system components begins.

Evaluation

SMHA can be carried out before detailed design of the system is finished, although the partitioning of functions to components must be at least tentatively complete. Since the analysis is performed on a formal, written model, it can be automated and does not depend on the analyst's mental model of how the system works. The model is explicitly specified and can be checked for correctness by expert review and sometimes for various desirable properties by additional automated procedures. Often, the state machine model itself can be executed using test data and simulators.

SMHA's most important limitation is that a model must be built, which may be difficult and time consuming. State machine models have been built for parts of systems and for relatively small systems, but are often impractical for systems that are large or complex. Petri nets, on which the algorithms were first defined, are not a practical modeling language for most real systems. Recent advances in state machine modeling languages have overcome this problem somewhat by defining new types of higher-level abstractions [111]. These abstractions have been incorporated into several languages, one of which, Requirements State Machine Language (RSML), was adopted by the FAA to model the system requirements for TCAS II, an airborne collision avoidance system required on most aircraft in the United States [360].

The SMHA analysis algorithms have been adapted for the RSML language and are being applied experimentally to real systems. Work is also proceeding on automatically generating fault trees and additional standard hazard analysis models from the RSML specification. Other new state machine models could be, but have not been, used for safety analysis, nor have safety analysis procedures been defined for them.

Some of the effort in building the model is justified by the fact that it can be used as the system requirements specification. To be used for this purpose, the specification must be readable by people without advanced mathematical education. The mathematical model analyzed by the SMHA algorithms is actually generated from the high-level RSML specification language, which is readable by application experts with very little training. RSML was developed while specifying the system requirements for TCAS II, which had to be easily readable and reviewable by engineers, pilots, airline representatives, and others in its function as the FAA system specification. The RSML specification can also be simulated (both general and application-specific simulators have been built) so the model can be executed, and test data (for the later software implementation of the specification) can be generated from it. The practicality of the SMHA analysis procedures for RSML has yet to be verified, however, and though the analysis procedures have been experimentally applied to the TCAS II specification, they have not yet been used on other projects.

A second limitation of SMHA is that the analysis is performed on a model, not on the system itself—it will apply to the as-built system only if the system matches the model. This limitation holds, of course, for any analysis that is performed early in the life cycle, but appropriate design and verification procedures must be used to ensure that the implemented system matches the model on which the analysis was originally performed.

Other types of mathematical models, such as logic or algebraic models of software or systems, also could be used for hazard analysis by using mathematical proof methods to show that the models satisfy the safety requirements [137, 283]. Many logic and algebraic models and modeling languages have been proposed for software. Unfortunately, most have been tried only on very small examples, and it is not at all clear that they will scale up to realistic systems. In addition, writing down the model may not be as much of a problem as the effort involved in mathematically proving the safety properties of the system and the inability of reviewers to understand those proofs.

The most important limitation of these algebraic and logic languages is that they are usually very hard to learn and use (including performing proofs on them) without an advanced degree in mathematics. This factor by itself is not necessarily a problem, as people with such training exist or the training can be provided, but the resulting models and proofs cannot readily be understood or checked by engineers and application experts who do not have this training. One of the most important uses of any hazard analysis is as an aid for designers and as a representation of the problem and what is being done about it so that open discussion can be stimulated and supported. If the analysis cannot be audited and understood by application experts, confidence in the results is undermined.

In addition, the models and languages used must match the way that engineers think about the systems they are building, or the translation between the engineer's or expert's mental model and the written formal model will be error prone. The advantage of state machine models is that they seem to match the internal models many people use in trying to understand complex systems.

14.13 Task and Human Error Analysis Techniques

14.13.1 Qualitative Techniques

Much more emphasis in hazard analysis has been on equipment failures than on human errors. Some analysis methods for human error have been suggested, however, including Procedure (Task) Analysis, Operator Task Analysis, Work Safety Analysis, and Action Error Analysis.

A procedure is an ordered set of instructions or actions to accomplish a task. *Procedure* or *Task Analysis* [106] reviews procedures to verify that they are effective and safe within the context of the mission tasks, the equipment that must be operated, and the environment in which the personnel must work. Such analyses involve determination of the required tasks, exposures to hazards, criticality of each task and procedural step, equipment characteristics, and mental and physical demands. As with FMEAs, the results of the analysis are entered on a form with columns labeled Task, Danger, Effects, Causes, Corrective Measures, and so on. Possible results include recommendations for corrective or preventive measures to minimize the possibilities that an error will result in a hazard, changes or improvements in hardware or procedures, warning and caution notes, special training, and special equipment (including protective clothing).

Operator Task Analysis [172] appears to be another name for Procedure Analysis. The operator's task is broken down into separate operations, and the analysis looks for difficulties in executing either the individual operations or the overall plan. Neither of these first two analyses (Procedure Analysis and Operator Task Analysis) seems to have a specific procedure associated with it, and they may simply be generic terms for the goals involved.

Action Error Analysis (AEA) [323, 326] uses a forward search strategy to identify potential deviations in human performance. The analysis consists of a systematic description of the operation, task, and maintenance procedures along with an investigation of the potential for performance deviations (such as forgetting a step, wrong ordering of steps, and taking too long for a step). Internal phases of data processing associated with an operator's tasks are usually excluded; instead, only the external outcomes of the error modes in different steps are studied. Some information about physical malfunctions may result from the analysis, since it includes the effects of human malfunctions on the physical equipment. This method is very similar to FMEA, but is applied to the steps in human procedures rather than to hardware components or parts. The results are entered in a table, this time with columns labeled Work Step, Action Error, Primary Consequences, Secondary Consequences, Detection, and Measures.

Work Safety Analysis (WSA) [323, 342] was developed by Suokas and Rouhiainen in Finland in the early 1980s. It is similar to HAZOP, but the search process is applied to work steps. The goal is to identify hazards and their causes. The search starts, as in the other methods, by breaking a task down into a sequence of steps. Each of the steps is examined with respect to a list of general hazards and examples of their causes (deviations and determining factors). All types of system functions and states, including normal states, are considered. The analyst examines the consequences of (1) forgetting a work step, (2) performing a step too early or too late or too long, and (3) unavailability of the usual equipment. Because of the nature of the search pattern, certain types of hazards will not be identified, such as those related to management procedures or those related indirectly to the operator's task but not to the task being analyzed (for example, contact with chemicals or an explosion in the proximity of the operator) [326].

14.13.2 Quantitative Techniques

All the human error analysis methods described so far focus on the operator's task. The goal is to obtain the information necessary to design a human–machine interface that reduces human behavior leading to accidents and improves the operators' ability to intervene successfully to prevent accidents. Human error is not considered inevitable, but a result of human–task mismatches and poor interface or operating procedures design. When the focus is design, qualitative or semi-quantitative results are usually adequate to achieve the goals.

Probabilistic assessment of human error, on the other hand, necessarily accepts the inevitability of human error. Despite its limited usefulness in improving the human–machine interface, the application of reliability engineering, which focuses on numerical assessment, to process control systems (especially nuclear power plants) has led to a demand for assessing the reliability of the process operator in order to assess risk for the system as a whole. The assignment of probabilities to human error is especially important in system risk assessment because of the large proportion of accidents that are attributed to human error.

Simply having a need is not enough to guarantee that the need can be satisfied. Probabilistic assessment of human error is not very advanced. Some of the problems in collecting and classifying human error data were discussed in Chapter 13. This rest of this section describes the current state of the art; readers can determine for themselves how much confidence they want to place on the resulting numbers.

Most of the numerical data and assessment are based on task analysis and task models of errors rather than on cognitive models. Following Lees' classification (see Chapter 10), tasks are divided into simple, vigilance, and complex.

Simple and Vigilance Tasks

Simple tasks are relatively simple sequences of operations involving little decision making. Some of these tasks or suboperations may involve the detection of signals (vigilance).

The most common way to assign probabilities to these tasks is to break a task down into its constituent parts, assign a reliability to the execution of each part, and then estimate the reliability of the entire task by combining the reliability estimates of the parts using a structural model of their interaction. The most common models involve either series relationships (and thus use product laws) or tree relationships (and use Boolean evaluation methods). The accuracy of the method depends upon the accuracy of the individual part reliabilities and the appropriateness of the structural model.

The sophistication of the quantitative reliability estimates varies greatly [172]. The simplest approaches often use an average task error rate of 0.01. This number is based on the assumption that the average error rate of the constituent task components is 0.001 and that there are, on average, 10 components per task.

A second approach to assigning human error rates uses human experts to rank tasks in order of their error likeliness and then uses ranking techniques to obtain error rates. Sophisticated statistical methods, such as paired comparisons, can be used to produce a ranking [130].

The techniques described so far rely on human judgment to assign error rates to tasks, or they make very simple assumptions. Other approaches collect and use empirical and experimental data evaluated with respect to performance-shaping factors. *Data Store* was developed by the American Institute for Research in 1962 to predict operator performance in the use of controls and displays [108]. The data indicates the probability of successful performance of a task, the time required to operate particular instruments, and the features that degrade performance. To analyze a task using Data Store, the task components are identified and assigned probabilities using tables for standardized tasks. The reliabilities are then multiplied to determine a task reliability.

Data Store and similar techniques assume that the discrete task components are independent. THERP (Technique for Human Error Rate Prediction), developed by Swain at Sandia National Laboratories, relaxes this assumption. Bell and Swain describe a methodology for Human Reliability Analysis (HRA) that encompasses both task analysis and THERP [22].

Most of the errors identified and analyzed in HRA involve not following written, oral, or standard procedures. Only occasionally are actions that are outside the scope of the specified operations (such as extraneous acts) considered.

The first part of HRA (and of most similar methods) involves task analysis, where a task is defined by Bell and Swain as a quantity of activity or performance that the operator views as a unit, either because of its performance characteristics or because the activity is required as a whole to accomplish some part of a system goal. The correct procedure for accomplishing an operation is identified and then broken down into individual units of physical or mental performance. For example, the tasks involved in pressurizing a tank to a prescribed level from a high-pressure source [106] include

1. Opening the shutoff valve to the tank
2. Opening the high-pressure regulator from the source

TABLE 14.3
Typical human error data.

Probability	Activity
10^{-2}	General human error of omission where there is no display in the control room of the status of the item omitted, such as failure to return a manually operated test valve to the proper position after maintenance.
3×10^{-3}	Error of omission where the items being omitted are embedded in a procedure rather than at the end.
3×10^{-2}	General human error of commission, such as misreading a label and therefore selecting the wrong switch.
3×10^{-2}	Simple arithmetic error with self-checking, but without repeating the calculation by redoing it on another piece of paper.
10^{-1}	Monitor or inspector failure to recognize an initial error by operator.
10^{-1}	Personnel on different workshift fail to check the condition of hardware unless required by a checklist or written directive.

   3. Observing the pressure gauge downstream from the regulator until the pre-scribed level is reached in the tank

   4. Shutting off the high-pressure regulator

   5. Shutting the valve to the tank

   Next, specific potential errors (human actions or their absence) are identified for each unit of behavior in the task analysis. Acts of commission and omission are considered errors if they have the potential for reducing the probability of some desired system event or condition. In the above example, the operator could forget to open the high-pressure regulator from the source (step 2), open the wrong valve (step 1), or execute the actions out of proper sequence. The actions actually considered are limited. For example, if the error being examined is the manipulation of a wrong switch, perhaps because of the control panel layout, the analysis does not usually try to predict which other switch will be chosen, nor does it deal with the system effects of the operator selecting a specific incorrect switch.

   The next step in HRA is to determine the likelihood of specific event se-quences using event trees. Each error defined in the task analysis is entered on the tree as a binary event. If order matters, then the events need to be ordered chronologically. Care must be taken to consider all alternatives, including "no ac-tion taken." Other logical models, such as fault trees, can also be used.

   Probabilities are assigned to each of the events in the tree, using handbooks or tables of human error probabilities. If an exact match of errors is not possible, similar tasks are used and extrapolations are made. Table 14.3 is a small example of this type of table [172].

   The data in the THERP handbook is based on a set of assumptions that limit the applicability of the data [22]:

- ☐ The operator's stress level is optimal.
- ☐ No protective clothing is worn.
- ☐ The level of administrative control is average for the industry.
- ☐ The personnel are qualified and experienced.
- ☐ The environment in the control room is not adverse.
- ☐ All personnel act in a manner they believe to be in the best interests of the plant (malevolent action is not considered).

Because these assumptions may not hold and because of natural variability in human performance, environmental factors, and task aspects, the THERP handbook gives a best estimate along with uncertainty bounds. The uncertainty bounds represent the middle 90 percent range of behavior expected under all possible scenarios for a particular action; they are based on subjective judgment rather than empirical data. The analyst is expected to modify the probabilities used in HRA to reflect the actual situation. Examples of performance shaping factors that can affect error rates are

- ☐ Level of presumed psychological stress
- ☐ Quality of human engineering of controls and displays
- ☐ Quality of training and practice
- ☐ Presence and quality of written instructions and methods of use
- ☐ Coupling of human actions
- ☐ Personnel redundancy (such as the use of inspectors)

Bell and Swain [22] suggest that if, for example, the labeling scheme at a particular plant is very poor compared to labeling at other plants, the probabilities should be increased toward the upper uncertainty bound;[2] if the tagging is particularly good, the probabilities for certain errors might be decreased. These performance shaping factors either affect the whole task or affect certain types of errors regardless of the types of tasks in which they occur. Other factors may have an overriding influence on the probability of occurrence of all types of errors under all conditions.

Dependencies or coupling may exist between pairs of tasks or between the performance of two or more operators. The dependencies in the specific situation need to be assessed and estimates made of the conditional probabilities of success and failure.

Once all these steps have been accomplished, the end point of each path through the event tree can be labeled a success or a failure, and the probability of each path can be computed by multiplying the probabilities associated with each path segment. Then the success and failure probabilities of all the paths are combined to determine the total system success and failure probabilities. The results of HRA are often used as input to fault trees and other system hazard

---

[2] The system safety engineer might suggest instead that the labeling at the plant be improved.

TABLE 14.4
Typical error rates used for emergency situations.

Probability	Activity
0.2 − 0.3	The general error rate given very high stress levels where dangerous activities are occurring rapidly.
1.0	Operator fails to act correctly in first 60 seconds after the onset of an extremely high stress condition.
9×10^{-1}	Operator fails to act correctly in the first 5 minutes after the onset of an extremely high stress condition.
10^{-1}	Operator fails to act correctly in the first 30 minutes of an extreme stress condition.
10^{-2}	Operator fails to act correctly in the first several hours of a high stress condition.

analyses, although care must be taken that the limitations and assumptions are not violated.

Humans make errors, but they also often detect their errors and correct them before they have a negative effect on the system state. If it is possible to recover from an error in this way, the actual error rate for the task may be reduced by orders of magnitude from the computed rate [172]. The probability of recovery depends greatly on the cues available to the operator from the displays and controls and from the plant in general. Bell and Swain suggest that the effects of recovery factors in a sequence of actions not be considered until after the total system success and failure probabilities are determined. These may be sufficiently low, without considering the effects of recovery, so that the sequence does not represent a dominant failure mode. Sensitivity analyses (manipulating a particular parameter to determine how changes to its value affect the final value) can also be performed to identify errors that have a very large or very small effect on system reliability.

Most of these probabilities do not apply to tasks under emergency conditions, where stress is likely to be high. Analyses usually assume that the probability of ineffective behavior during emergencies is much greater than during normal processing. In general, error probability goes down with greater response time. For short response times, very little credit is normally given for operator action in an emergency. Table 14.4 shows some typical error rates used for emergency situations [172].

One other factor needs to be considered when computing or using these numbers, and that is sabotage or deliberate damaging actions by the operator, including suicide. Most of the available data on human behavior assumes that the operator is not acting malevolently; instead it assumes that any intentional deviation from standard operating procedures is made because employees believe their method of operation to be safer, more economical, or more efficient, or because they believe the procedure is unnecessary [22]. Ablitt, in a UK Atomic

Energy Authority publication discusses the possibility of suicide by destruction of a nuclear power plant:

> The probability per annum that a responsible officer will deliberately attempt to drop a fuel element into the reactor is taken as 10^{-3} since in about 1000 reactor operator years, there have been two known cases of suicide by reactor operators and at least one case in which suicide by reactor explosion was a suspected possibility. The typical suicide rate for the public in general is about 10^{-4} per year although it does vary somewhat between countries (quoted in [172, p.411]).

Other human reliability estimation techniques have been proposed, although THERP is probably the most widely used. A weakness of all these techniques, as noted, is that they do not apply to emergency situations (very little data on human errors in emergencies is available). If one accepts Rasmussen's Skill–Rule–Knowledge model, the error mechanisms embedded in a familiar, frequent task and in an infrequent task will differ because the person's internal control of the task will be different [270]. Therefore, error rates obtained from general error reports will not apply for infrequent responses.

Another weakness is that the techniques cannot cope with human decisions and tasks that involve technical judgment. Factors other than immediate task and environmental factors are also ignored.

Embrey [77] has suggested an approach to investigating human mistakes linked to organizational weaknesses. His *Goal Method* relates the goals of an operator responsible for specific equipment to the goals of the plant as a whole. Hope and colleagues [126] say that this approach is helpful in training operating teams, particularly for emergency situations.

Many of these human reliability assessment techniques were proposed and the data collected before plants became highly automated, especially by computers. We are automating exactly those tasks that can be measured and leaving operators with the tasks that cannot. Therefore, measurement of this type is bound to be of diminishing importance.

Complex Control Tasks

The measurement approaches described in the previous section consider human performance as a concatenation of standard actions and routines for which error characteristics can be specified and frequencies determined by observing similar activities in other settings. In such analyses, the task is modeled rather than the person. Rasmussen and others argue that such an approach may succeed when the rate of technological change is slow, but is inadequate under the current conditions of rapid technological change [278].

Computers and other modern technology are removing repetitive tasks from humans, leaving them with supervisory, diagnostic, and backup roles. Tasks can no longer be broken down into simple actions; humans are more often engaged in decision making and complex problem solving for which several different paths may lead to the same result. Only the goal serves as a reference point when judging the quality of performance—task sequence is flexible and very situation and person specific. Analysis, therefore, needs to be performed in terms of the cognitive information processing activities related to diagnosis, goal evaluation, priority setting, and planning—that is, in the knowledge-based domain.

From this viewpoint, performance on a task can no longer be assumed to be at a relatively stable level of training. Learning and adaptation during performance will have a significant impact on human behavior. If the models of behavior used do not merely consider external characteristics of the task but have a significant cognitive component, then measurement (and, of course, design) needs to be related to internal psychological mechanisms in terms of capabilities and limitations [274]. If, as Rasmussen recommends, the concept of human error is replaced by human–task mismatch, then task actions cannot be separated from their context. Rasmussen suggests that a FMEA can serve as a basis for analysis of a human–task mismatch. Numbers for these models do not exist and deriving them will be difficult, however, as the cognitive activities involved in complex and emergency situations cannot easily be identified in incident reports. Top-down analysis can also be used (and seems more promising) to relate critical operator errors to cognitive human error models.

14.14 Evaluations of Hazard Analysis Techniques

Given the widespread use of hazard analysis techniques, the small amount of careful evaluation is surprising. The techniques are often criticized as incomplete and inaccurate, but this criticism is based on logical argument rather than on scientific evaluation. Only a few critical evaluations of hazard analysis methods have been performed, and most simply evaluate the structure of the methods. Taylor, Suokas, and Rouhiainen, however, have actually performed empirical evaluations.

Taylor applied HAZOP and AEA to two plants and compared the results with problems found during commissioning and a short operating period. HAZOP found 22 percent and 80 percent of the hazards, while the corresponding results for AEA were 60 percent and 20 percent for the two analyses evaluated [322].

Suokas compared HAZOP to AEA, WSA, and accident investigations for two gas storage and loading–unloading systems. HAZOP identified 77 contributors to a gas release. AEA and WSA found 23 additional factors not found by HAZOP. When the results were quantified with fault trees, the contributors identified only by AEA increased the total frequency of gas release by 28 percent in one system and by 38 percent in the other [327].

Suokas and Pyy evaluated four methods—HAZOP, FMEA, AEA, and MORT—by collecting incident and accident information in seven process plants and one accident database. They defined the search patterns and types of factors covered by the methods, and three groups evaluated which of the causal factors the methods could have identified. HAZOP was the best, identifying 36 percent of the contributors. However, only 55 percent of the contributors were expected to be covered by the four methods [323, 322]. This result is particularly poor given that the analysis involved only determining which factors *could* potentially be identified by the methods—the number actually identified in any application would be expected to be lower.

Many evaluations of the predictive accuracy of reliability estimates have been done for individual instruments and components; these studies vary widely in their results. In a reliability benchmark exercise, 10 teams from 17 organizations and from 9 European countries performed parallel reliability analyses on a nuclear power plant primary cooling system. The purpose was to determine the effect of differences in modeling and data. The ratio between the highest and lowest frequencies calculated for the top event of the different fault trees was 36. When a unified fault tree was quantified by different teams using what each considered to be the best data, the corresponding ratio was reduced to 9.

14.15 Conclusions

Many different hazard analysis techniques have been proposed and are used, but all have serious limitations and only a few are useful for software. But whether these techniques or more ad hoc techniques are used, we need to identify the software behaviors that can contribute to system hazards. Information about these hazardous behaviors is the input to the software requirements, design, and verification activities described in the rest of this book.

15

Software Hazard and Requirements Analysis

Computers do not produce new sorts of errors. They merely provide new and easier opportunities for making the old errors.

—Trevor Kletz
Wise After the Event

The vast majority of accidents in which software was involved can be traced to requirements flaws and, more specifically, to incompleteness in the specified and implemented software behavior—that is, incomplete or wrong assumptions about the operation of the controlled system or required operation of the computer and unhandled controlled-system states and environmental conditions. Although coding errors often get the most attention, they have more of an effect on reliability and other qualities than on safety [80, 200].

This chapter describes completeness and safety criteria for software requirements specifications. The criteria were developed both from experience in building such systems and from theoretical considerations [135, 136] and, in essence, are the equivalent of a requirements safety checklist for software. They can be used to develop informal or formal inspection procedures or tools for automated analysis of specifications. The criteria are general and apply to all systems, unlike the application-specific safety requirements identified in a system hazard analysis. Both application-specific hazards and general criteria need to be checked—in fact, one of the general criteria requires checking the application-specific hazards.

Lutz applied the criteria experimentally in checklist form to 192 safety-critical requirements errors in the Voyager and Galileo spacecraft software. These errors had not been discovered until late integration and system test, and therefore they had escaped the usual requirements verification and software testing process [201]. The criteria identified 149 of the errors.[1] Any after-the-fact experiment of this sort is always suspect, of course; no proof is offered that these errors would have been found if the criteria had been applied to the requirements originally, but the fact that they were related to so many real, safety-critical requirements deficiencies is encouraging. It is not necessarily surprising, however, since most of the criteria were developed using experience with critical errors, incidents, and accidents in real systems.

Jaffe and colleagues have related the original criteria to a general state machine model of process control systems [136] that can be used to derive formal, automated safety analysis procedures for specification languages based on state machines. This chapter describes additional criteria that were not included in earlier papers. The criteria are described only informally here; readers are referred to the research papers for a formal treatment.

15.1 Process Considerations

The software hazard analysis process will be influenced by the underlying accident model being used and its assumptions about the contribution of computers to accidents. Computers contribute to system hazards by controlling the actions of other components (including humans) either directly or indirectly. Humans are controlled to some degree by providing the information to operators or designers on which they base their decisions.

In an energy or chain-of-events model of accidents, software contributes to hazards through computer control of the energy sources, the release or flow of energy, the barriers, or the events that lead to accidents. In a systems theory model that assumes accidents arise from the interactions among components, software contributes directly to safety through computer control of these interactions.

The tasks of the software safety process defined in Section 12.1.1 that relate to software hazard analysis include:

1. Trace identified system hazards to the software–hardware interface. Translate the identified software-related hazards into requirements and constraints on software behavior.

2. Show the consistency of the software safety constraints with the software requirements specification. Demonstrate the completeness of the software

---

[1] Most of the unidentified errors involved design and thus were not the focus of the checklist.

requirements, including the human–computer interface requirements, with respect to system safety properties.

The most direct way to accomplish the first step is with a top-down hazard analysis that traces system hazards down to and into the subsystems. In this type of analysis, the software-related hazards are identified and traced into the software requirements and design. Currently, this goal is often accomplished by a fault tree analysis down to the software interface.

In addition, because software can do more than what is specified in the requirements (the problem of *unintended function*), the code itself must be analyzed to ensure that it cannot exhibit hazardous behavior—that the code satisfies its requirements (even if the required behavior is shown to be safe) is not enough. This chapter looks at requirements analysis, while design and code analysis are described in later chapters.

Software may also be the focus of a bottom-up subsystem hazard analysis. The practicality of this analysis is limited by the large number of ways that computers can contribute to system hazards. For example, a valve that has only two or three relevant discrete states (such as open, closed, or partially open) can be examined for the potential effects of these states on the system state. Computers, however, can assume so many states, exhibit so many visible and potentially important behaviors, and have such a complex effect on the system that complete bottom-up system analyses are, in most cases, impractical.

Bottom-up analyses may have some uses for software, but probably not for identifying software hazards. For example, some specific types of computer failure and incorrect behavior can be analyzed in a bottom-up manner for their effects on the system. In addition, forward analysis can examine (to some degree) a specification of software behavior to make sure that the behavior cannot lead to an identified hazard. To accomplish the latter, the software behavior must be specified completely, and the specification language should have a rigorously and unambiguously defined semantics and be readable by application experts and the user community. If the specification and analysis is not readable and reviewable by system safety and application experts, confidence in the results will be lessened.

Readability and reviewability will be enhanced by using languages that allow building models that are semantically close to the user's mental model of the system. That is, the *semantic distance* between the model in the expert's mind and the specification model should be minimized. In addition, reading the specification or reviewing the results of an analysis should not require training in advanced mathematics. Ideally, the specification language should reflect the way that engineers and application experts think about the system, not the way mathematicians do.

The second step of the process is to document the identified software behavioral requirements and constraints and to show that the software requirements specification satisfies them. This step also includes demonstrating the completeness of the software requirements specification with respect to general system safety properties.

Most current software hazard and requirements analyses are done in an ad hoc manner. Some more systematic approaches have been proposed in research papers, but they have not been validated in practice on real projects. We do not know at this point which ones, if any, will turn out to be useful and including them here would make this book obsolete almost immediately. Instead, this chapter examines what needs to be accomplished in such an analysis.

15.2 Requirements Specification Components

Requirements specifications have three components: (1) a basic function or objective, (2) constraints on operating conditions, and (3) prioritized quality goals to help make tradeoff decisions.

The *constraints* define the range of conditions within which the system may operate while achieving its objectives. They are not part of the objectives; instead, they limit the set of acceptable designs to achieve the objectives. Constraints arise from quality considerations (including safety), physical limitations of the equipment, equipment performance considerations (such as avoiding overload of equipment in order to reduce maintenance), and process characteristics (such as limiting process variables to minimize production of byproducts).

Safety may be and often is involved in both functionality requirements and constraints. In an airborne collision avoidance system, for example, the basic mission—to maintain a minimum physical separation between aircraft—obviously involves safety. There are also safety-related constraints—for example, the surveillance part of the system must not in any way interfere with the radars and message communication used by the ground-based air traffic control (ATC) system; the system must operate with an acceptably low level of unwanted alarms (advisories to the pilot); and the deviation of the aircraft from their ATC-assigned tracks must be minimized. These constraints are not part of the system mission; in fact, they could most easily be accomplished by not building the system at all. Rather, they are limitations on how such a collision avoidance system may be realized.

Goals and constraints often conflict. Early in the development process, tradeoffs among functional goals and constraints must be identified and resolved according to priorities assigned to each. We are most interested in the conflicts and tradeoffs involving safety goals and constraints and in how adequately these goals and constraints are realized in the actual requirements. Goals are just that—they may not be completely achievable. Part of the safety process is to identify not only conflicts, but safety-related goals for the software that cannot be completely achieved. Decisions can then be made about how to protect the system using means other than the software or about the acceptability of the risks if no other means exist. There is no formal or automated technique for this process; it requires the cooperation and joint efforts of the system and software engineers in applying their own expertise and judgment.

15.3 Completeness in Requirements Specifications

The most important property of the requirements specification with respect to safety is completeness or lack of ambiguity. The desired software behavior must have been specified in sufficient detail to distinguish it from any undesired program that might be designed. If a requirements document contains insufficient information for the designers to distinguish between observably distinct behavioral patterns that represent desired and undesired (or safe and unsafe) behavior, then the specification is ambiguous or incomplete [135, 136].

The term "completeness" here is not used in the mathematical sense, but rather in the sense of a lack of ambiguity from the application perspective: The specification is incomplete if the system or software behavior is not specified precisely enough because the required behavior for some events or conditions is omitted or is ambiguous (is subject to more than one interpretation).

If the behavioral difference between two programs that satisfy the same requirements is not significant for a subset of the requirements or constraints, such as those related to safety, then the ambiguity or incompleteness may not matter, at least for that subset: The specification is *sufficiently* complete. A set of requirements may be sufficiently complete with respect to safety without being absolutely complete: The requirement specification must simply be complete enough that it specifies *safe* behavior in all circumstances in which the system is to operate. Absolute completeness may be unnecessary and uneconomical for many situations.

Sufficient completeness, as defined here, holds only for a particular system and environment. The same specification that is sufficiently complete for one system may not be sufficiently complete for another. Therefore, software built from a sufficiently complete, but not absolutely complete, requirements specification may not be safe when reused in a different system. If the software is to be reused, either the specification must be absolutely complete (probably impossible in most cases) or a further requirements analysis is necessary.

The rest of this chapter defines criteria for completeness of software requirements specifications. Software requirements for the human–computer interface are no different than other requirements and are included in the completeness criteria described here. The criteria themselves (especially those for the human–computer interface) are not complete themselves and do not constitute the only checks that should be made. But they are useful in detecting incompleteness that is associated with hazards and accidents. In a sense, they represent a starting point for a safety checklist for requirements specification to which additions may be made as we discover the necessity.

Many types of incompleteness are application dependent and must be identified using system hazard analysis or top-down analysis. Jaffe notes that in any application, at any given point in time, there is a set of *kernel* requirements that derive from current knowledge of the needs and environment of the application itself [135]. These kernel requirements are analytically independent of one another—the need for the existence of any one of them cannot be determined from the existence of the others. For example, an autopilot program may or may not control the throttle along with the aerodynamic surfaces.

Without knowledge of the intent of the application, there can be no way to ascertain whether a particular requirements specification has a complete set of kernel requirements. This type of incompleteness must be identified by system engineering techniques that include modeling and analysis of the entire system with respect to various desired properties (such as safety). In other words, any safety implications of such incompleteness must be identified using system hazard analysis (as described, for example, in Section 14.12) rather than the type of subsystem hazard analysis described in this chapter.

On the other hand, subsystem hazard analysis applied to requirements *can* detect *incompletely specified* kernel requirements. In addition, this type of analysis, involving rigorous examination of the specified software behavior, may also be able to detect some genuine functionality inadvertently omitted during the system engineering process. For example, a specification that includes a requirement to generate an alert condition to tell an air traffic controller that an aircraft is too low is probably incomplete unless it also includes another requirement to inform the controller that an aircraft previously noted as too low is now back at a safe altitude [135]. Safety and robustness considerations can be exploited to develop application-independent criteria for detecting such incompleteness.

15.4 Completeness Criteria for Requirements Analysis

A requirements specification describes the required black-box behavior of the component. Although design information is sometimes included in software requirements specifications, the safety analysis described here is concerned only with the black-box behavior of the software, which is the only aspect of the specification that can directly affect system hazards. Design analysis is covered in later chapters.

The requirements specification defines the function to be implemented by the computer. A description of any process control function uses as inputs

- The current process state inferred from measurements of the controlled process variables
- Past process states that were measured and inferred
- Past corrective actions (outputs) that were issued by the controller
- Prediction of future states of the controlled process

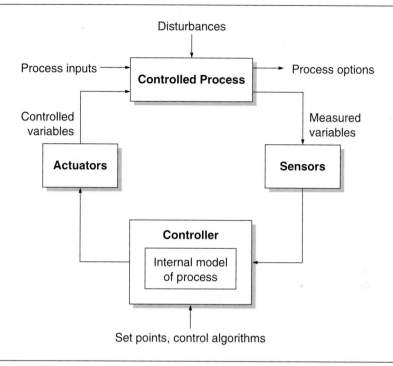

Disturbances

Process inputs ⟶ **Controlled Process** ⟶ Process options

Controlled variables

Measured variables

Actuators

Sensors

Controller

Internal model of process

Set points, control algorithms

FIGURE 15.1
A black-box requirements specification captures the controller's internal model of the process. Accidents occur when the internal model does not accurately reflect the state of the controlled process.

and produces the corrective actions (or current outputs) needed to achieve the process goals while satisfying the constraints on its behavior.

In this chapter, the control function is described using a state machine model. State machines are convenient models for describing computer behavior, and many specification languages use these models. The criteria are described here in terms of the components of a state machine model, but they could be translated to other models or applied to informal requirements specifications.

A state machine is simply a model that describes a system in terms of states and the transitions between the states. State machines are defined in Section 14.12 and an example is shown in Figure 14.11. The controller outputs to actuators are associated with state changes in the model, which are triggered by measurements of process variables (see Figure 15.1).

Theoretical control laws are defined using the *true* values of the process state. At any time, however, the controller has only *measured* values, which may be subject to time lags[2] or measurement inaccuracies. The controller must use these measured values to infer the true state of the process and to determine the corrective actions necessary to maintain certain desirable properties in the controlled system. Considering the problems of measurement error and time lags is essential in developing safe control software.

A state machine model is an abstraction. As used here, it models the view of the process maintained by the computer (the internal model of the process), which is necessarily incomplete (Figure 15.1). Hazards and accidents can result from mismatches between the software view of the process and the actual state of the process—that is, the model of the process used by the software gets out of synch with the real process. For example, the software does not think the tank is full and therefore does not stop the flow into the tank, or it does not know that the plane is on the ground and raises the landing gear.

The mismatch occurs because the internal model is incorrect or incomplete or the computer does not have accurate information about the process state. For example, the model may not include a check for the proper process conditions before doing something hazardous—a check for weight on wheels is not included on the state transition associated with the output to raise the landing gear. Alternatively, the check may be included, but the computer may not have correct information about the current state of the plane.

Safety then depends on the completeness and accuracy of the software (internal) model of the process. A state machine specification of requirements explicitly describes this model and the functions performed by the software. The goal of completeness analysis basically is to ensure that the model of the process used by the software is sufficiently complete and accurate that hazardous process states do not occur. Completeness criteria are defined for each of the state machine parts: the states, the transition (triggering) events, the inputs and outputs, and the relationship between the transition events and their related outputs.

Completeness requires that both the characteristics of the outputs and the assumptions about their triggering events be specified:

$$trigger \implies output$$

In response to a single occurrence of the given stimulus or trigger, the program must produce only a single output set. A black-box statement of behavior allows statements and observations to be made only in terms of outputs and the externally observable conditions or events that stimulate or trigger them (the *triggers* for short). In terms of the state machine, this restriction means that both the states and the events on the transitions must be externally observable.

Not only must the output be produced given a particular trigger, but it must *not* be produced without the trigger:

$$trigger \impliedby output$$

---

[2] Time lags are delays in the system caused by sensor polling intervals or by the reaction time of the sensors, actuators, and the actual process.

A complete trigger specification must include all conditions that trigger the output, that is, the set of conditions that can be inferred from the existence of an output. Such conditions represent assumptions about the environment in which the program or system is to execute.

The next sections informally describe what is required for a complete specification of the triggers and outputs and the other parts of a black-box state machine model of software behavior. Most of this discussion is taken from Jaffe [135].

15.4.1 Human–Computer Interface Criteria

The human–computer interface has many possible completeness criteria. These criteria can be framed in terms of high-level abstractions applicable to this interface. Jaffe suggests that an *alert queue*, for example, is an abstraction with completeness criteria related to alert review and disposal, automatic reprioritization, and deletion [135]. An alert queue is an abstraction external to the computer and thus appropriate for a black-box requirements specification. Some appropriate human–computer abstractions and completeness criteria are presented in this chapter, but the essential requirements needed for other such abstractions can and should be developed.

For human–computer interface queues in general, the requirements specification will include

- Specification of the events to be queued
- Specification of the type and number of queues to be provided (such as alert or routine)
- Ordering scheme within the queue (priority versus time of arrival)
- Operator notification mechanism for items inserted in the queue
- Operator review and disposal commands for queue entries
- Queue entry deletion

A second important abstraction for the human–computer interface is a *transaction*, which may have multiple events associated with it. Multiple-event transactions require additional completeness criteria such as those to deal with preemption in the middle of a transaction.

Often, requirements are needed for the deletion of requested information. An air traffic controller, for example, may request certain graphic information such as the projected path of a trial maneuver for a controlled aircraft. A complete requirements specification needs to state when the trial maneuver graphics should disappear. Some actions by the operator should leave this trial maneuver display untouched (such as retrieving information from the aircraft's flight plan to evaluate the trial maneuver) while other actions should delete the transient information without requiring a separate clearing action (such as operator signoff).

In general, Jaffe identifies three questions that must be answered in the requirements specification for every data item displayable to a human:

1. What events cause this item to be displayed?
2. Can and should the display of this item ever be updated once it is displayed? If so, what events should cause the update? Events that trigger updates may be
   - External observables
   - The passage of time
   - Actions taken by the viewing operator
   - Actions taken by other operators (in multiperson systems)
3. What events should cause this data display to disappear?

In addition to data, the computer may control the labels (such as menus or software-labeled keys or buttons) associated with operator actions. Not only can these labels change, but the software may be responsible for such things as highlighting a recommended action or deleting labels for actions that are unavailable or prohibited under current conditions. Failure to specify all circumstances under which data items or operator-action entry labels should change is a common cause of specification incompleteness for the human–computer interface and a potential source of hazards.

Specific criteria for these human–computer interface requirements are integrated into appropriate sections of this chapter.

15.4.2 State Completeness

The operational states will, of course, be specific to the system. But in general, these states can be separated into normal and non-normal processing modes (where modes are just groups of states having a common characteristic), and completeness criteria can be applied to the transitions between these modes.

□ *The system and software must start in a safe state. Interlocks should be initialized or checked to be operational at system startup, including startup after temporarily overriding interlocks.*

Transitions from normal operation to non-normal operation are often associated with accidents. In particular, when computers are involved, many accidents and failures stem from incompleteness in the way the software deals with startup and with transitions between normal processing and various types of partial or total shutdown.

□ *The internal software model of the process must be updated to reflect the actual process state at initial startup and after temporary shutdown.*

Unlike other types of software, such as data processing software, an important consideration when developing software for process control is that the process continues to change state even when the computer is not executing. The correct behavior of the computer may depend on input that arrived before startup; what to do about this input must be included in the specification. Serious accidents have occurred because software designers did not consider state changes while the system was in a manual mode and the computer was temporarily off-line. In one such accident in a chemical plant, described in Chapter 1, the computer was controlling the valves on pipes carrying methanol between the plant and a tanker, and a pump was stopped manually without the computer knowing it. A similar accident occurred in a batch chemical reactor when a computer was taken off-line to modify the software [158]. At the time the computer was shut down, it was counting the revolutions on a metering pump that was feeding the reactor. When the computer came back on-line, it continued counting where it had left off, which resulted in the reactor being overcharged.

□ *All system and local variables must be properly initialized upon startup, including clocks.*

There are two startup situations: (1) initial startup after complete process shutdown and (2) startup after the software has been temporarily off-line but the process has continued under manual control. In both the initial startup and after temporary computer shutdown, the internal clock as well as other system and local variables will need to be initialized. In addition, the second case (where only the computer has been shut down) requires that the internal model of the process used by the software be updated to reflect the actual process state; the variables and status of the process, including time, will probably have changed since the computer was last operational.

A number of techniques are used for this resynchronization. Message serialization (numbering the inputs), for example, is a commonly used technique that can detect "lost" information and indicate potential discontinuities in software operations. Another technique often used involves checking elapsed time between apparently successive inputs by means of a self-contained timestamp in each input (requiring clock synchronization) or via reference to a time-of-day clock upon the receipt of each input.

□ *The behavior of the software with respect to inputs received before startup, after shutdown, or when the computer is temporarily disconnected from the process (off-line) must be specified, or it must be determined that this information can be safely ignored, and this conclusion must be documented.*

If the hardware can retain a signal indicating the existence of an input after computer shutdown and prior to startup, the program has two startup states—the input is present or is not present—and at least two separate requirements must be specified: one for startup when there is indication of a prior input signal and one when there is not.

In the case of inputs that occur before program startup, the time of that input or the number of inputs is not observable by the software, but one or some of the inputs may be available to the computer after startup. Which inputs are retained is hardware dependent: Some hardware may retain the first input that arrived, some the most recent, and so on. To avoid errors, systems where the ordering of incoming data is important must include requirements to handle pre-startup inputs.

☐ *The maximum time the computer waits before the first input must be specified.*

Any specification for a real-time system should also include requirements to detect a possible disconnect occurring prior to program startup between the computer and the sensors or the process. After program startup, there should be some finite limit on how long the program waits for an input before it tries various alternative strategies—such as alerting an operator or shifting to an open-loop control mechanism that does not use the absent input. This criterion is very similar to a maximum-time-between-events criterion (discussed later), but it applies to the absence of even the first input of a given type. Even if the maximum time between events is checked, the special case of the first such interval after startup is often omitted or handled incorrectly. There may (and in general will) be a series of intervals $d_1, d_2, \ldots$ during which the program is required to attempt various ways of dealing with the lack of input from the environment. Eventually, however, there must be some period after which, in the absence of input, the conclusion must be that a malfunction has occurred.

☐ *Paths from fail-safe (partial or total shutdown) states must be specified. The time in a safe but reduced-function state should be minimized.*

☐ *Interlock failures should result in the halting of hazardous functions.*

The software may have additional non-normal processing modes such as partial shutdown or degraded operation. More completeness criteria for some of these mode transitions are described later.

The normal processing states may also be divided into subsets or modes of operation, such as an aircraft taking off, in transit, or landing. For safety analysis, the states may be partitioned into hazardous and nonhazardous modes with different completeness criteria applied to each.

☐ *There must be a response specified for the arrival of an input in any state, including indeterminate states.*

Completeness considerations require that there be a software response to the arrival of an input in any state, including the arrival of unexpected inputs for that state. For example, if an output is triggered by the receipt of a particular input when a device is in state ON, the specification must also handle the case where that input is received and the device is in state OFF. In addition, not being in state ON is not equivalent to being in state OFF, since the state of the device may be indeterminate (to the computer) if no information is available about its state. Therefore, a requirement is needed also to deal with the case when the input is received and the computer does not know if the device is ON or OFF.

Many software problems arise from incomplete specification of state assumptions. As an example, Melliar-Smith reports a problem detected during an operational simulation of the Space Shuttle software. The astronauts attempted to abort the mission during a particular orbit, changed their minds and canceled the abort attempt, and then decided to abort the mission after all on the next orbit. The software got into an infinite loop that appears to have occurred because the designers had not anticipated that anyone would ever want to abort twice on the same flight [235]. Another example involves an aircraft weapons management system that attempts to keep the load even and the plane flying level by balanced dispersal of weapons and empty fuel tanks [235]. One of the early problems was that even if the plane was flying upside down, the computer would still drop a bomb or a fuel tank which then dented the wing and rolled off. In yet another incident, an aircraft was damaged when the computer raised the landing gear in response to a test pilot's command while the aircraft was standing on the runway [235].

In some cases, there really is no requirement to respond to a given input except in a subset of the states. But an input arriving unexpectedly is often an indication of a disconnect between the computer and the other components of the system that should not be ignored. For example, a target detection report from a radar that previously was sent a message to shut down is an indication that the radar did not do so, perhaps because its detection logic is malfunctioning. If, in fact, the unexpected input is of no significance, the requirements specification should still document the fact that all cases have been considered and that this case truly can be ignored (perhaps by specifying a "do nothing" response to the input).

15.4.3 Input and Output Variable Completeness

The inputs and outputs represent the information the sensors can provide to the software (the controlled variables) and the commands that the software can provide to the actuators (to change the manipulated variables). These input and output variables and commands must be rigorously defined in the documentation.

At the black-box boundary, *only* time and value are observable by the software. Therefore, the triggers and outputs must be defined only as constants or as the value and time of observable events or conditions. Events include program inputs, prior program outputs, program startup (a unique observable event for each execution of a given program), and hardware-dependent events such as power-out-of-tolerance interrupts. Conditions may be expressed in terms of the value of hardware-dependent attributes accessible by the software such as time-of-day clocks or sense switches.

> □ *All information from the sensors should be used somewhere in the specification.*

If information from the sensors is not used in the requirements, there is very likely to be an important omission from the specification. In other words, if an input can be sent to the computer, there should be some specification of what should be done with it.

> □ *Legal output values that are never produced should be checked for potential specification incompleteness.*

As with inputs, an important requirement for software behavior may have been forgotten if there is a legal value for an output that is never produced.

For example, if an output can have values *open* and *close* and the requirements specify when to generate an OPEN command but not when to generate CLOSE, the specification is almost certainly incomplete. Checking for this property may help to locate specification omissions.

15.4.4 Trigger Event Completeness

The behavior of the control subsystem (in our case, the computer) is defined with respect to assumptions about the behavior of the other parts of the system—the conditions in the other parts of the control loop or in the environment in which the controller operates. A *robust* system will detect and respond appropriately to violations of these assumptions (such as unexpected inputs). By definition, then, the robustness of the software built from the specification depends upon the completeness of the specification of the environmental assumptions—there should be no observable events that leave the program's behavior indeterminate. These events can be observed by the software only in terms of trigger events, and thus completeness of the environmental assumptions is related to the completeness of the specification of the trigger events and the response of the computer to any potential inputs.

Documenting all environmental assumptions and checking them at runtime may seem expensive and unnecessary. Many assumptions are based on the physical characteristics of input devices and cannot be falsified even by unexpected physical conditions and failures. For example, an input line connected to a 1200-baud modem cannot fail in a way that causes the data rate to exceed 1200 baud. The interrupt signal may stick high (on), but for most modern hardware, that will stop data transfer, not accelerate it. If the environment in which the program executes ever changes, however, the assumption may no longer be valid; the 1200-baud modem may be upgraded to 9600 baud, for example. Similarly, if the software is ever reused, the environment for the new program may differ from that of the earlier use. Examples were provided in Chapter 2 of problems arising from the reuse of software in environments different from that for which it was originally built.

In addition to being documented, critical assumptions—those where the improper performance of the software can have severe consequences—should be checked at runtime. Examples abound of accidents resulting from incomplete requirements and nonrobust software. For example, an accident occurred when a military aircraft flight control system was intentionally limited in the range of control (travel) by the software because it was (incorrectly) assumed that the aircraft could not get into certain attitudes.

Even when real-time response is not required, it is important that the software or hardware log violations of assumptions for off-line analysis. A hole in the ozone layer at the South Pole was not detected for six years because the ozone depletion was so severe that a computer analyzing the data had been suppressing it, having been programmed to assume that deviations so extreme must be sensor errors [96]. Detecting errors early, before they lead to accidents, is obviously a desirable goal.

15.4.4.1 Robustness Criteria

☐ *To be robust, the events that trigger state changes must satisfy the following:*
  1. *Every state must have a behavior (transition) defined for every possible input.*
  2. *The logical* OR *of the conditions on every transition out of any state must form a tautology.*
  3. *Every state must have a software behavior (transition) defined in case there is no input for a given period of time (a timeout).*

A tautology is a logically complete expression. For example, if there is a requirement on a transition that the value of an input be greater than 7, then a tautologically complete specification would also include transitions from that state when the input is less than 7 and equal to 7.

These three criteria together guarantee that if there is a trigger condition for a state to handle inputs within a range, there will some transition defined to handle data that is out of range. There will also be a requirement for a timeout that specifies what to do if no input occurs at all.

The use of an OTHERWISE clause (in specification languages that permit this) is not appropriate for safety-critical systems. Jaffe writes:

> It was always tempting to guarantee the appropriate level of completeness at any given point by just adding an "otherwise, do nothing" requirement. But the more complex the situation, the more likely it is that there will be some interesting case concealed within the "otherwise." It is better to explicitly delineate exactly what cases provide the "otherwise" condition and then check for tautological completeness [135].

15.4.4.2 Nondeterminism

Another restriction can be placed on the transition events to require deterministic behavior:

☐ *The behavior of the state machine should be deterministic (only one possible transition out of a state is applicable at any time).*

Consider the case where the conditions on two transitions are that (1) the value of the input is greater than zero and (2) the value of the input is less than 2. If the input value is 1, then both transitions could be taken, leading to nondeterministic behavior of the software with respect to the requirements. The problem is eliminated by forcing all transitions out of a state to be disjoint (two transition conditions can never be true at the same time).

Although a specification does not have to be deterministic to be safe, nondeterminism greatly complicates safety analysis and may make it impractical to perform thoroughly. Moreover, software to control the operation of many hazardous systems should be repeatable and predictable. Deterministic behavior aids in guaranteeing hard real-time deadlines; in analyzing and predicting the behavior of software; in testing the software; in debugging and troubleshooting, including reproducing test conditions and replicating operational events; and in allowing the human operator to rely on consistent behavior (an important factor in the design of the human–machine interface).

15.4.4.3 Value and Timing Assumptions

Ensuring that the triggers in the requirements specification satisfy the previous four criteria is necessary, but it is not sufficient for trigger event completeness. The criteria ensure that there is always exactly one transition that can be taken out of every state, but they do not guarantee that all assumptions about the environment have been specified or that there is a defined response for all possible input conditions the environment can produce. Completeness depends upon the *amount* and *type* of information (restrictions and assumptions such as legal range) that is included in the triggers. The more assumptions about the triggers included, the more likely that the four above criteria will ensure that the requirements include responses to unplanned events.

Many assumptions and conditions are application dependent, but some types of assumptions are essential and should always be specified for all inputs to safety-critical systems. In real-time systems, the times of inputs and outputs are as important as the values. Digital flight control commands to ailerons, for example, may be dangerous if they do not arrive at exactly the right time: Flutter and instability (which can and do lead to the loss of the aircraft) result from improperly timed control movements, where the difference between proper and improper timing can be a matter of milliseconds [135]. Therefore, both value and time are required in the characterization of the environmental assumptions (triggers) and in the outputs.

Essential Value Assumptions

Value assumptions state the values or range of values of the trigger variables and events. An input may not require a specification of its possible values. A hardwired hardware interrupt, for example, has no value, but it may still trigger an output. When the value of an input is used to determine the value or time of an output, the acceptable characteristics of the input must be specified, such as range of acceptable values, set of acceptable values, or parity of acceptable values.

> □ *All incoming values should be checked and a response specified in the event of an out-of-range or unexpected value.*

As noted earlier, even where an assumption is not essential, it should be specified and checked whenever possible (whenever it is known) because the receipt of an input with an unexpected value is a sign that something in the environment is not behaving as the designer anticipated. Checking simple value assumptions on inputs is comparatively inexpensive. Since failure of such assumptions is an indication of various reasonably common hardware malfunctions or of misunderstanding about software requirements, it is difficult to envision an application where the specification should not require robustness in this regard— incoming values should have their values checked, *and* there should be a specified response in the event an unexpected value is received.

Some input values represent information about safety interlocks. These *always* need to be checked for values that may indicate failure and appropriate action taken.

Essential Timing Assumptions

The need for and importance of specifying timing assumptions in the software requirements stem from the nature and importance of timing in process control, where timing problems are a common cause of runtime failures. Timing is often inadequately specified for software. Two different timing assumptions are essential in the requirements specification of triggers: timing intervals and capacity or load.[3]

Timing Intervals. While the specification of the value of an event is usual but optional, a timing specification is *always* required: The mere existence of an observable event (with no timing specification) in and of itself is never sufficient—at the least, inputs must be required to arrive after program startup (or to be handled as described previously).

□ *All inputs must be fully bounded in time, and the proper behavior specified in case the limits are violated or an expected input does not arrive.*

Trigger specifications include either the occurrence of an observable signal (or signals) or the specification of a duration of time without a specific signal. Both cases need to be fully bounded in time or a capacity requirement is necessary.

The arrival of an input at the black-box boundary has to include a lower bound on the time of arrival and will, in general, include an upper bound on the interval in which the input is to be accepted. Requirements dealing with input arriving outside the time interval and the nonexistence of an input during a given interval (a duration of time without the expected signal) also have to be defined. The robustness criteria will ensure that a behavior is specified in case the time limits are violated.

The acceptable interval will always be bounded from below by the time of the event that brought the machine to the current state. Some other lower bound may be desirable, but the limit must always be expressed in terms of previous, observable events.

---

[3] *Load* here refers to a rate, whereas *capacity* refers to the ability to handle that rate.

Even requirements such as "The event I shall occur at 11:00 A.M." are ambiguous. The value of the time of I is the value of the reference clock observed "simultaneously" with the occurrence of I. Conceptually, the clock is ticking at the rate of one tick per unit of temporal precision. In general, I will occur between two ticks of *any* clock, no matter how frequent the ticks. Therefore, to say that it must occur *exactly* at 11:00 A.M. is meaningless unless the specification also states what clock is to be used. Even then, the time cannot be known more precisely than the granularity of the clock. Concrete discussion of specific clocks should be avoided in a software requirements specification; all that is really necessary to know is the required precision of the clock. Translating this precision into an attribute of the input results in a requirement with bounding inequalities rather than an equality, such as 10:59 A.M. $< time(I) <$ 11:01 A.M. (commonly written as $time(I) = 11:00$ A.M. $\pm$ 1 min), which specifies an accuracy of plus or minus a minute on the timing.

□ *A trigger involving the nonexistence of an input must be fully bounded in time.*

For requirements that involve the *non*existence of a signal during a given interval, both ends of the interval must be either bound by or calculable from observable events. Informally, there must be an upper bound on the time the program waits before responding to the lack of a signal. There must also be a specific time to start timing the lack of inputs or an infinite number of intervals (and thus outputs) will be specified. For example, a requirement of the type "If there is no input I for 10 seconds, then produce output O" is not bound at the lower end of the interval and is therefore ambiguous. Should the nonexistence interval start at time t, at $t + \epsilon$, $t + 2\epsilon$, . . . ? An example of a complete specification might be "If there is no input I_1 for 10 seconds after the receipt of the previous input I_2, then produce output O." The observable event need not occur at either end of the interval—the ends need only be calculable from that event, such as "There is no input for 5 sec preceding or following event E."

Capacity or Load. In an interrupt-driven system, the count of unmasked input interrupts received over a given period partitions the computer state space into at least two states: normal and overloaded. The required response to an input will differ in the two states, so both cases must be specified.

Failures of critical systems due to incorrectly handled overload conditions are not unusual. A bank in Australia reportedly lost money from the omission of proper behavior to handle excessive load in an automated teller machine (ATM) [266]. When the central computer was unable to cope with the load, the ATMs dispensed cash whether or not the customer had adequate funds to cover the withdrawal. Failure to handle the actual load, although annoying to customers, would not by itself have caused as much damage as that resulting from the lack of an explicit (and reasonable) overload response behavior. Much more serious consequences resulted from the failure of a London ambulance dispatching system in 1992 under an overload condition [68]. According to reports, neither of these systems had been tested under a full load, and each, obviously, had inadequate responses to a violation of the load assumptions.

Although inputs from human operators or other slow system components may normally be incapable of overloading a computer, various malfunctions can cause excessive, spurious inputs and so they also need a load limit specified. In one accident, an aircraft went out of control and crashed when a mechanical malfunction in a fly-by-wire flight control system caused an accelerated environment that the flight control computer was not programmed to handle [88]. Robustness requires specifying how to handle excessive inputs and specifying a load limit for such inputs as a means of detecting possible external malfunctions.

□ *A minimum and maximum load assumption must be specified for every interrupt-signaled event whose arrival rate is not dominated (limited) by another type of event.*

In general, inputs to process control systems should have both minimum and maximum load assumptions for all interrupt-signalled events whose arrival rate is not dominated by another type of event. If interrupts cannot be disabled (locked out) on a given port, then there will always be some arrival rate for an interrupt signaling an input that will overload the physical machine. Either the machine will run out of CPU resources as it spends execution cycles responding to the interrupts, or it will run out of memory when it stores the data for future processing. Both hardware selection and software design require an assumption about the maximum number of inputs N signaled within an interval of time d, so this information should be in the requirements specification.

Multiple load assumptions are meaningful although not necessarily required in any given case. For example, the load could be 4 per second but not more than 7 in any two seconds nor more than 13 in four seconds, and so on. One load assumption is required; multiple assumptions may derive from application-specific considerations. Multiple loads can also be assumed for a given input based on additional data characteristics, such as not more than 4 inputs per second when the value of input I is greater than 8, but not more than 3 per second when I is greater than 20.

□ *A minimum-arrival-rate check by the software should be required for each physically distinct communication path. Software should have the capacity to query its environment with respect to inactivity over a given communication path.*

A load assumption with N equal to 1 is the same as an assumption on the minimum time between successive inputs. Robustness requires the specification of a minimum arrival rate assumption for most, if not all, possible inputs since indefinite, total inactivity by any real-world process is unlikely. Robust software should be able to query its environment about inactivity over a given communication path. Requirements of this type lead to the use of sanity and health checks in the software, as described in Chapter 16.

Where interrupts can be masked or disabled, the situation is more complicated. If disabling the interrupt can result in a "lost" event (depending on the hardware, the duration of the lockout, and the characteristics of the device at the other end of the channel), the need for a load assumption will depend on how the input is used. If the number of inputs I is completely dominated by (dependent on) the number of inputs of a different type, then a load assumption for I is not needed.

Even if a particular statistical distribution of arrivals over time is assumed and specified, a load limit assumption is still required. Assuming that the arrival distribution fits a Poisson distribution, for example, does not preclude the possibility, no matter how improbable, of it exceeding a given capacity. If capacity is exceeded, there must be some specification of the ways that the system can acceptably fail soft or fail safe.

> □ *The response to excessive inputs (violations of load assumptions) must be specified.*

The requirements for dealing with overload generally fall into one of five classes:

1. Requirements to generate warning messages.
2. Requirements to generate outputs to reduce the load (messages to external systems to "slow down").
3. Requirements to lock out interrupt signals for the overloaded channels.
4. Requirements to produce outputs (up to some higher load limit) that have reduced accuracy or response time requirements or some other characteristic that will allow the CPU to continue to cope with the higher load.
5. Requirements to reduce the functionality of the software or, in extreme cases, to shut down the computer or the process.

The first three classes are handled in an obvious way. The behavior in the fourth and fifth classes (commonly called performance degradation and function shedding) should be graceful—that is, predictable and not abrupt.

> □ *If the desired response to an overload condition is performance degradation, the specified degradation should be graceful and operators should be informed.*

Abrupt or random (although bounded) degradation often needs to be avoided. Certainly for operator feedback, predictability is preferable to variability, at least within limits, even if the cost is a slight increase in average response time [84]. For safety considerations, however, as discussed in Chapters 6 and 17, when the program changes to a degraded performance mode or the computer is compensating for extreme or non-normal conditions, the operator should always be informed. Additional action may be required, such as disabling or requesting resets of busy interfaces or recording critical parameters for subsequent analysis.

□ *If function shedding or reconfiguration is used, a hysteresis delay and other checks must be included in the conditions required to return to normal processing load.*

Once a state of degraded performance has been entered, a specification of the conditions required to return to a normal processing mode, including a *hysteresis delay*, is necessary. After detecting a capacity violation, the system must not attempt to return to the normal state too quickly; the exact same set of circumstances that caused it to leave may still exist. For example, assume that the event that caused the state to change is the receipt of the nth occurrence of input I within a period d, where the load is specified as limited to $n - 1$. Then, if the system attempts to return to normal within a period $x \ll d$, the very next occurrence of an I might cause the state to change again to the overload state. The system could thus ping-pong back and forth. A hysteresis factor simply ensures that the transition to normal operation is not too close in time to the inputs that caused the overload.[4]

Besides a hysteresis delay, system robustness requires specification of a series of checks on the temporal history of mode exit and resumption activities to avoid constant ping-ponging.

15.4.5 Output Specification Completeness

As with trigger events, the complete specification of the behavior of an output event requires both its value and its time.

□ *Safety-critical outputs should be checked for reasonableness and for hazardous values and timing.*

Checking to make sure that output values are legal or reasonable is straightforward and helpful in detecting software or other errors. In general, this should *always* be done for safety-critical outputs and may be desirable for other outputs. Hazardous values can be determined by a top-down hazard analysis that traces system hazards to the software, as described previously.

There is no limit to the complexity of timing specifications for outputs, but, at the least, specification of bounds and minimum and maximum time between outputs is required, as it is for inputs. In addition, there are some special requirements for the specification of the outputs: environmental capacity, data age, and latency.

Environmental Capacity Considerations

The rate at which the sensors produce data and send it to the computer is the concern in input capacity. Output capacity, on the other hand, defines the rate at

---

[4] Hysteresis intervals are also useful for specifying conditions other than timing that cause transitions between states, especially transitions to non-normal processing modes.

which the actuators can accept and react to data produced by the computer. If the sensors can generate inputs at a faster rate than the output environments can "absorb" or process outputs, an output overload might occur.

□ *For the largest interval in which both input and output loads are assumed and specified, the absorption rate of the output environment must equal or exceed the input arrival rate.*

Output load limitations may be required because of physical limitations in the actuators (such as a limit on the number of adjustments a valve can make per second), constraints on process behavior (excessive wear on actuators might increase maintenance costs), or safety considerations (such as a restriction on how often a catalyst can be safely added to a chemical process).

Differences in input and output capacity result in the need to handle three cases:

1. The input and output rates are both within limits, and the "normal" response can be generated.
2. The input rate is within limits, but the output rate will be exceeded if a normally timed output is produced, in which case some sort of special action is required.
3. The input rate is excessive, in which case some abnormal response is necessary (graceful degradation).

When input and output capacities differ, there must be multiple periods for which discrete load assumptions are specified. For example, the output capacity might be 10 per second but only 40 per minute, while the input sensor might have a peak rate of 12 per second but a sustained rate of only 36 per minute.

□ *Contingency action must be specified when the output absorption rate limit will be exceeded.*

Over the short term, the program can buffer or shield the output environment from excessive outputs. Over the long term, however, the program might never catch up unless, for the largest interval in which both input and output capacities are assumed and specified, the absorption rate of the output environment equals or exceeds the input arrival rate. Contingency action must be specified for cases where these assumptions do not hold.

□ *Update timing requirements or other solutions to potential overload problems, such as operator event queues, need to be specified.*

When the human–machine interface is synchronous—that is, each computer response is matched to a human action—the operator cannot be overloaded, and he or she is never in doubt about which response pertains to which action. Even when the interaction is asynchronous, operator overload may not be a problem. In some displays, such as an air traffic controller's situation display, much of the data can be added, deleted, or changed in parallel with other human–machine interface activities without interfering with operator performance. In this case, the human monitors the display for patterns and relationships and determines what is significant and what constitutes an event requiring operator attention.

In other asynchronous interactions, however, the human–machine interface may need to make operators explicitly aware of events rather than merely highlight potentially interesting data on a parallel display. Examples of such events include alarms and orders or requests from other operators. This type of asynchronous interaction can result in operator overload, but putting load limits on the outputs may not be practical. A general solution to the discrete event overload problem is an *event bucket*—generally, one or more queues of event data waiting for operator review and acknowledgment. The information defining the event may be inserted into the event queue and a standard signal used to signify that an event has been detected and queued. A particular operator position may have several predefined and operator-defined events that can be added to its queues.

    □ *Automatic update and deletion requirements for information in the human–computer interface must be specified.*

Events placed in queues may be negated by subsequent events. The requirements specification should include the conditions under which such entries may be automatically updated or deleted from a queue. Some entries should be deleted only upon explicit operator request; however, workload may be such that the entries must be queued until the operator can acknowledge them. For example, when an air traffic control operator asks for the count of aircraft whose velocity exceeds a certain speed, the response may be queued and should not disappear until the operator acknowledges receipt.

Some queued events may become irrelevant to the operator, such as information about a warning to an air traffic controller that an aircraft is too close to the ground or to ground-based hazards such as tall antennas (called a minimum safe altitude warning or MSAW). The warning itself may be shown on the situation display, but additional information that cannot be displayed may be put into a queue. If the portion of the queue that contains the MSAW-related information is not currently visible to the operator, it may be removed from the queue automatically when the MSAW is removed from the situation display. If that portion of the queue *is* currently visible, the queued information should not be removed: Operators generally find it distressing when information disappears while they are looking at it or while they are temporarily glancing away.

There could be safety implications as well. Suppose that there are MSAWs for two separate aircraft, but the queue display can accommodate only one event at a time. The operator might glance back at the display, not realizing that the first event has been removed and replaced by the second. The operator would then read the recommended course for the second aircraft and transmit it to the first aircraft, not realizing that the event data he or she is reading is not the same data seen a second or two before.

□ *The required disposition for obsolete queue events must include specifica-*
tion of what to do when the event is currently being displayed and when it
is not.

In general, obsolete event data currently being displayed cannot be automatically deleted or replaced. It may be modified to show obsolescence and removed
when the operator indicates to do so or when the overall display is modified in
such a way that the obsolete event display becomes invisible (for example, the
queue is advanced and the obsolete information is scrolled off the display).

Data Age

Another important aspect of the specification of output timing involves data obsolescence. In practical terms, few, if any, input values are valid forever. Even
if nothing else happens and the entire program is idle, the mere passage of time
renders much data of dubious validity eventually. Although the computer is idle,
the real world in which the computer is embedded (the process the computer is
controlling) is unlikely to be. Control decisions must be based on data from the
current state of the system, not on obsolete information.

□ *All inputs used in specifying output events must be properly limited in the*
time they can be used (data age). Output commands that may not be able to
be executed immediately must be limited in the time they are valid.

Data obsolescence considerations require that all input and output events
be properly bounded in time: The input is only valid to trigger an output O if
it occurred within a preceding duration of time D. As an example of the possible implementation implications of such a requirement, MARS, a distributed
fault-tolerant system for real-time applications, includes a validity time for every
message in the system after which the message is discarded [165].

Frola and Miller [88] describe an accident related to the omission of a data
age factor. A computer issued a CLOSE WEAPONS BAY DOOR command on a B-1A
aircraft at a time when a mechanical inhibit had been put on the door. The CLOSE
command was generated when someone in the cockpit pushed the *close door*
switch on the control panel during a test. The command was not executed (because of the mechanical inhibit), but remained active. Several hours later, when
the maintenance was completed and the inhibit removed, the door unexpectedly
closed. The situation had never been considered in the requirements definition
phase; it was fixed by putting a time limit on all output commands.

The information used in response to queries from operators may also become obsolete before the operator can receive it. The requirements specification
needs to state if a query response sitting in the operator's queue should be automatically updated as the situation changes or flagged as possibly obsolete.

□ *Incomplete hazardous action sequences (transactions) should have a finite*
time specified after which the software should be required to cancel the
sequence automatically and inform the operator.

Data age requirements also apply to human–computer interface action sequences. Some transactions require multiple actions, for example, a FIRE command that is followed by a CONFIRM MISSILE LAUNCH request from the computer and then a CONFIRM action from the operator. Once the FIRE command has been issued, some limit should be imposed on how long it remains active (before it is automatically canceled) without confirmation from the operator. Such a time limit may be important if the incomplete control sequence places the system in a higher risk state: Once such a sequence is started, it may take fewer actions or failures to create a hazard, and thus the exposure should be minimized or at least controlled.

□ *Revocation of a partially completed action sequence may require (1) specification of multiple times and conditions under which varying automatic cancellation or postponement actions are taken without operator confirmation and (2) specification of operator warnings to be issued in the event of such revocation.*

In some cases, the partially completed sequence should not be discarded without a warning to the operator. In other cases, a partially completed complex transaction should be set aside for subsequent, manual reactivation that is simpler than complete reinitialization. The "safing" sequence and the time periods allowed may themselves vary with the current state. On combat aircraft, for example, weapon selection or activation actions that are a prerequisite for weapon launch should not be automatically revoked easily. On the one hand, when pilots are busy in combat, they should not be further burdened with alarms notifying them that their preliminary weapon selection will be revoked automatically in x seconds unless overridden. On the other hand, partial selection and activation states should not be allowed to continue indefinitely. A compromise is to let the times vary as a function of conditions detectable by the computer. If the operator is clearly present and engaged in combat activities, the automatic revocation sequence might be postponed indefinitely until conditions change. A *wheels down and engine idle or off* condition might be the basis for a much shorter delay.

Latency

Since a computer is not arbitrarily fast, there is a time interval during which the receipt of new information cannot change an output even though it arrives prior to the actual output action. The duration of this latency interval is influenced by both the hardware and the software design. An executive or operating system that permits the use of interrupts to signal data arrival may have a shorter latency interval than one that uses periodic polling, but underlying hardware constraints prevent the latency from being eliminated completely. Thus, the latency interval can be made quite small, but it can never be reduced to zero.

The acceptable length of the latency interval is determined by the process that the software is controlling. In chemical process control, a relatively long latency period might be acceptable, while an aircraft may require a much shorter one. The choice of operating system, interrupt logic, scheduling priority, and system design parameters will be influenced by the latency requirements. Also, behavioral analysis of the requirements to determine consistency with process functional requirements and constraints may not be correct unless the value of this behavioral parameter is known and specified for the software. Therefore, the requirements specification must include the allowable latency factor.

□ *A latency factor must be included when an output is triggered by an interval of time without a specified input and the upper bound on the interval is not a simple, observable event.*

Triggering an output on an interval of time without a specified event occurring always requires the specification of a latency factor between the end of the interval and the occurrence of the output. Where the upper bound on the interval is a simple, observable event, latency is not an issue. However, where the intent is to signal the nonoccurrence of an input after some other event, a latency specification is required.

□ *Contingency action may need to be specified to handle events that occur within the latency period.*

Additional requirements may need to be specified to handle the case where an event is observed within the latency period. For example, if an action is taken based on the assumption that some input never arrived and if it is later discovered that the input actually did arrive but too late to affect the output, it may then be necessary to take corrective action.

□ *A latency factor must be specified for changeable human–computer interface data displays used for critical decision making. Appropriate contingency action must be specified for data affecting the display that arrives within the latency period.*

Latency considerations also affect specification of the human–computer interface. Whenever a data display changes just prior to an operator basing a critical decision on it, the computer may need to query the operator as to whether the change was noted before action selection. The display might involve, for example, showing a set of operator options, including a recommended option and several indications of poor ones. If the arrival of asynchronous data results in a change to the recommended action, then whether the operator had sufficient opportunity to observe that change will affect the required human–computer interface behavior. As another example, an operator decision to fire a missile at a target that has just had its displayed threat value reduced (but not completely eliminated) may warrant extra interaction between the program and the operator.

□ *A hysteresis delay action must be specified for human–computer interface data to allow time for meaningful human interpretation. Requirements may also be needed that state what to do if data should have been changed during the hysteresis period.*

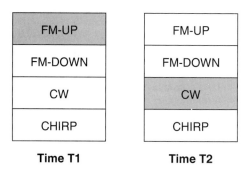

FIGURE 15.2
Two consecutive snapshots of an operation action menu with the recommended action highlighted. The recommendation must be constant long enough for meaningful human interpretation. Requirements are also needed to deal with latency problems when the recommended action changes.

Variable data, such as a computer-recommended operator action, must be constant long enough for meaningful human interpretation, which leads to a requirement for a hysteresis delay (Figure 15.2). An additional requirement will then be needed to cope with situations where the action is selected after the occurrence of an event that should have changed the displayed data but did not because it occurred before the expiration of the hysteresis delay from the previous change.

15.4.6 Output to Trigger Event Relationships

Some criteria for analyzing requirements specifications relate not to input or output specifications alone but to the relationship between them. Although, in general, the relationship depends on the control function being specified, basic process control concepts can be used to generate criteria that apply to all process control systems, such as feedback and stability requirements.

Responsiveness and spontaneity deal with the actual behavior of the controlled process and how it reacts (or does not react) to output produced by the controller. In particular, does a given output cause the process to change, and if so, is that change detectable by means of some input? Basic process control models include feedback to provide information about expected responses to changes in the manipulated variables and information about state changes caused by disturbances in the process.

□ *Basic feedback loops, as defined by the process control function, must be included in the software requirements. That is, there should be an input that the software can use to detect the effect of any output on the process. The requirements must include appropriate checks on these inputs in order to detect internal or external failures or errors.*

Feedback is a basic property of almost all process control systems: If feedback information is not used by the software, the requirements specification is probably deficient. Basic feedback loops need to be included in the software requirements, while missing feedback loops provide clues as to incompleteness in the specification.

As an example, an accident occurred when a steel plant furnace was returned to production after being shut down for repair [16]. A power supply had burned out in a digital thermometer during power-up so that the thermometer continually registered a low constant temperature. The controller, knowing it was a cold start, ordered 100 percent power to the gas tubes. The furnace should have reached operating temperature within one hour, but the computer failed to check (and thus detect) that the thermometer inputs were not increasing as they should have been. After four hours, the furnace had burned itself out, and major repairs were required.

This situation could easily have been avoided if information about the characteristics of the process had been used to predict and check for the expected behavior of the system. In this case, the only information needed to avoid the accident was that the temperature should increase if the burners are on.

If the process does not respond to an output as expected and within a given time period, there is presumably something wrong and the software should be required to act accordingly—perhaps by trying a different output, by alerting a human operator, or, at the least, by logging the abnormality for future, off-line analysis.

Ideally, process control systems should be designed such that the effects of every output affecting a manipulated variable in the system can be detected by some input provided by the feedback loop. The situation is not always that simple, however. Disturbances interfering with the process can cause changes that are not initiated by the computer or can inhibit changes that the computer has commanded.

□ *Every output to which a detectable input is expected must have associated with it: (1) a requirement to handle the normal response and (2) requirements to handle a response that is missing, too late, too early, or has an unexpected value.*

Every output to which a detectable response is expected within a given time period induces at least two requirements: The "normal" response requirement and a requirement to deal with a failure of the process to produce the expected response. The failure could involve the response having an erroneous or unreasonable value, the response arriving at the wrong time, or the expected response might be missing entirely.

□ *Spontaneous receipt of a nonspontaneous input must be detected and responded to as an abnormal condition.*

If the environment responds *too* quickly, coincidence rather than appropriate stimulus-response behavior may be responsible. Most processes do not react instantaneously, but only after a delay (time lag). Thus, the specification of a latency factor is required. A value-based handshake protocol can be used to eliminate the need for the latency factor: Some field of the input *I* identifies it as a unique response to some specific output *O*.

Some inputs are spontaneous—they may be triggered by environmental factors not necessarily caused by some prior output. However, an input that is supposed to be nonspontaneous (it is only supposed to arrive in response to some prior system output) induces yet another requirement to respond to a presumably erroneous (spontaneous) input.

□ *Stability requirements must be specified when the process is potentially unstable.*

In addition to feedback requirements, stability requirements, such as a phase margin of at least 45 degrees and a gain margin of at least 3 decibels, may need to be specified for one or more operating states. The stability requirements apply to the process-control function, which is described by a control law or a transfer function relating output to input [23].

15.4.7 Specification of Transitions Between States

Requirements analysis may involve examining not only the triggers and outputs associated with each state and the relationship between them, but also the paths between states. These paths are uniquely defined by the sequence of trigger events along the path. Transitions between modes are particularly hazardous and susceptible to incomplete specification, and they should be carefully checked.

Reachability

□ *All specified states must be reachable from the initial state.*

Informally, a state is said to be *reachable* from another state if there is a path from the first to the second. In most systems, all states must be reachable from the initial state. If a state is unreachable, there are two possibilities: (1) either the state has no function and can be eliminated from the specification, or (2) the state should be reachable and the requirements document is incorrect and must be modified accordingly.

Most state-based models include techniques for reachability analysis. In complex systems, complete reachability analysis is often impractical, but it may be possible in some cases to devise algorithms that reduce the necessary state space search by focusing on a few properties. The backward-reachability hazard analysis techniques for state machine models described in Chapter 14 are examples of algorithms that limit the amount of the reachability graph that must be generated to get enough information to eliminate hazardous states from the requirements specification.

Recurrent Behavior

Most process control software is cyclic—it is not designed to terminate under normal operation. Its purpose is to control and monitor a physical environment; the nature of the application usually calls for it to repeat one single task continuously, to alternate between a finite set of distinct tasks, or to repeat a sequence of tasks while in a given mode. Most systems, however, include some states with noncyclic behavior such as temporary or permanent shutdown states or those where the software changes to a different operating mode.

□ *Desired recurrent behavior must be part of at least one cycle. Required sequences of events must be implemented in and limited by the specified transitions.*

The specification should be analyzed to verify that desired behavior is repeatable. To be repeatable, the behavior must be part of at least one cycle, but in many cases checking this behavior alone will not be sufficient; more complex sequences of events may need to be identified. An output to turn on a piece of equipment, for example, may be inappropriate unless the last output turned the equipment off. Consider an output to start a piece of equipment. The equipment may need to be started more than once, but it could be damaged if two START commands are issued without an intermediate STOP command. To prevent this hazard, every cycle that includes a START also has to include a STOP.

□ *States should not inhibit the production of later required outputs.*

An *inhibiting state* for an output is a state from which the output cannot be generated. If every state from which the output can be generated is unreachable from an inhibiting state, then the output cannot be generated again once the inhibiting state is reached. Whether or not this condition represents an incompleteness depends upon the application.

Reversibility

In a process control system, a command issued to an actuator often can be canceled or reversed by some other command or combination of commands. This capability is referred to as *reversibility*.

□ *Output commands should usually be reversible.*

Outputs will usually require reversing commands. Therefore, outputs should be reviewed and classified as to their reversibility. For an ON command to be reversible, the state in which the canceling OFF command is issued must be reachable from the state in which the ON command was issued. For example, an alert condition to an operator (such as a below-minimum-safe-altitude warning to an air traffic controller) should be reversible when the condition no longer holds (the aircraft is now at a safe altitude).

□ *If x is to be reversible by y, there must be a path between the state where x is issued and a state where y is issued.*

There will usually be several different classes of the reversing outputs. The appropriate reversing output, for example, may depend on whether the controller has acknowledged the receipt of the original alert, is in the process of reviewing the alert, or has taken positive action to ameliorate the alert condition. The human–computer interface in particular is full of complex classes of reversible phenomena [135].

Preemption

When the same physical resource, such as a data entry device or display, must be used in distinct multistep actions at the human–computer interface, requirements will be needed to deal with preemption logic. In addition, some actions may have to be prohibited until others are completed. An action to recompute estimated time of arrival might be prohibited until an in-progress, manual navigational update is completed or explicitly canceled.

□ *Preemption requirements must be specified for any multistep transactions in conjunction with all other possible control activations.*

In general, there are three possible system responses to an operator action from a parallel-entry source prior to completion of a transaction initiated by some previous control activation: (1) normal processing in parallel with the uncompleted transaction, (2) refusal to accept the new action, and (3) preemption of the partially completed transaction.

If preemption is possible, then the attempted activation of a multistep sequence requiring the use of a resource already involved in another incomplete transaction provides the following three choices:

1. The new request could completely cancel the previous, incomplete transaction, clearing or replacing any displays associated with it.
2. The new request could preempt the shared resources, but the displayed state could be preserved and restored upon completion of the new transaction.
3. The operator could be prompted and required to indicate the disposition of the incomplete transaction, in which case there will in general be four alternatives:
   a. Cancel the incomplete transaction and start the newly requested one.
   b. Complete the old transaction and then proceed automatically with the new request.
   c. Cancel the new request and continue with the old, incomplete transaction.
   d. Defer but do not cancel the old, incomplete transaction.

If any transactions are deferred and restored, obsolete information must be identified, as discussed previously.

Path Robustness

For most safety-critical, process-control software, there are concerns beyond pure reachability: Even if a state fulfills all reachability requirements, there is still the question of the *robustness* of the path, or paths, affecting a particular state.

Consider an output that has the possible values of UP and DOWN. Suppose that every possible path from a state where an UP command is issued to any state where a DOWN command is issued includes the arrival of input *I*. Then if the computer's ability to receive *I* is ever lost (perhaps because of sensor failure), there are circumstances under which it will not be able to issue a DOWN command. Thus, the loss of the ability to receive *I* can be said to be a *soft failure mode*, since it *could* inhibit the software from providing an output with the value DOWN.

If the receipt of input *I* occurs in every path expression from *all* states that produce UP commands to *all* states that produce DOWN commands, the loss of the ability to receive *I* is now said to be a *hard failure mode*, since it *will* inhibit the software from producing a DOWN command.

 □ *Soft and hard failure modes should be eliminated for all hazard-reducing outputs. Hazard-increasing outputs should have both soft and hard failure modes.*

The more failure modes the requirements state machine specification has, whether soft or hard, the less robust with respect to external disturbances will be the software that is correctly built to that specification. Robustness, in this case, may conflict with safety. A fail-safe system should have no soft failure modes, much less hard ones, on paths between dangerous states and safe states. At the same time, hard failure modes are desirable on the paths from safe to hazardous (but unavoidable) states. An unsafe state, where a hazardous output such as a command to launch a weapon can be produced, should have at least one, and possibly several, hard failure modes for the production of the output command: No input received from the proper authority, no weapons launch.

 □ *Multiple paths should be provided for state changes that maintain or enhance safety. Multiple inputs or triggers should be required for paths from safe to hazardous states.*

In general, operators should be provided with multiple logical ways to issue the commands needed to maintain the safety of the system so that a single hardware failure cannot prevent the operator from taking action to avoid a hazard. On the other hand, multiple interlocks and checks should be associated with potentially hazardous human actions—such as a requirement for two independent inputs or triggers before a potentially hazardous command is executed by the computer.

15.5 Constraint Analysis

In addition to satisfying general completeness criteria, the requirements must also be shown to include the identified, system-specific safety requirements and to be consistent with the identified software system safety constraints.

☐ *Transitions must satisfy software system safety requirements and constraints.*

In a system hazard analysis, hazards are traced to the software–system interface. Such hazards involve specific software behavior expressed in terms of the value and timing of outputs (or lack of outputs). In general, software-related hazards involve

☐ Failing to perform a required function: The function is never executed or no answer is produced.

☐ Performing an unintended (unrequired) function, getting the wrong answer, issuing the wrong control instruction, or doing the right thing but under inappropriate conditions (such as activating an actuator inadvertently, too early or too late, or failing to cease an operation at a prescribed time).

☐ Performing functions at the wrong time or in the wrong order (such as failing to ensure that two things happen at the same time, at different times, or in a particular order).

☐ Failing to recognize a hazardous condition requiring corrective action.

☐ Producing the wrong response to a hazardous condition.

Constraint analysis on the software requirements specification includes a reachability analysis to determine whether the software, as specified, could reach the identified hazardous states.

☐ *Reachable hazardous states should be eliminated or, if that is not possible (they are needed to achieve the goals of the system), their frequency and duration reduced.*

It is not always possible to enforce a requirement that the software cannot reach hazardous states—sometimes a hazardous state is unavoidable. But this possibility should be known so that steps can be taken to minimize the risk associated with the hazard, such as minimizing the exposure or adding system safeguards to protect the system against such states.

The type of analysis required to guarantee consistency between the software requirements specification and the safety constraints depends upon the type of constraints involved. The presence of constraints can potentially affect most of the criteria that have been described in this chapter. Some types of constraints can be ensured by the criteria already described; others require additional analysis. For example, basic reachability analysis can verify that only safe states are reachable.

Basic reachability analysis may need to be extended, however, to consider additional constraints on the sequence of events. To illustrate, consider a simple control system to move the control rods in a reactor up and down. The output actions to move the rods may be properly reachable and the paths robust. In addition, a constraint may require that a rod not be allowed to move within 30 seconds of its previous movement. To guarantee this constraint, all transitions where a MOVE ROD1 command can be issued must first be identified. Path analysis can then be used to find the sequences of events that will make the software issue two consecutive MOVE ROD1 commands. By showing that all possible paths described by these sequences will take at least 30 seconds to traverse, the constraint is guaranteed to be satisfied. If all the criteria described in this chapter for complete specification of timing requirements are satisfied, this analysis should be theoretically possible for a state-machine specification.

More generally, the specification may be checked for a general *safety policy* that is defined for the particular system. This process is very similar to checking that a specification satisfies a particular security policy [180]. The following is an example of a general safety policy for which the specification could be checked:

1. *There must be no paths to unplanned hazardous states.*

    The computer never initiates a control action (output) that will move the process from a safe to an unplanned hazardous state.

2. *Every hazardous state must have a path to a safe state. All paths from the hazardous state must lead to safe states. Time in the hazardous state must be minimized, and contingency action may be necessary to reduce risk while in the hazardous state.*

    If the system gets into a hazardous state (by an unplanned transition that is not initiated by the computer such as component failures, human error, or environmental stress), then the computer controller will transform the hazardous state into a safe state (every path from a hazardous state leads to a safe state). The time in the hazardous state will be minimized to reduce the likelihood of an accident.

    There may be several possible safe states, depending on the type of hazard or on conditions in the environment. For example, the action to be taken if there is a failure in a flight-control system may depend on whether the aircraft is in level flight or is landing.

3. *If a safe state cannot be reached from a hazardous state, all paths from that state must lead to a minimum risk state. At least one such path must exist.*

    If a system gets into a hazardous state and there is no possible path to a safe state, then the computer will transform the state into one with the minimum risk possible given the hazard and the environmental conditions, and it will do so such that the system is in a hazardous state for the minimum amount of time possible.

It may not be possible to build a completely safe system—that is, to avoid all hazardous states or to get from every hazardous state to a safe state. In that event, the system must be redesigned or abandoned, or some risk must be accepted. This risk can be reduced by providing procedures to minimize the probability of the hazardous state leading to an accident or to minimize the effects of an accident. For example, activation of a carbon dioxide firefighting system in what may be an occupied space may kill any occupants, but it may be necessary to prevent the loss of an entire ship. Such difficult decisions obviously must be considered and specified carefully.

15.6 Checking the Specification Against the Criteria

The actual procedures that can be used to analyze a particular requirements specification will depend on the form of that specification. The criteria for completeness of states, inputs and outputs, and the relationship between inputs and outputs are easily checked for any type of specification. Criteria for the transitions between states will be checkable to a greater or lesser extent depending on the formality of the specification, the size of the specification, and the availability of software tools to help with the checking.

Heimdahl has automated the checking of the robustness and nondeterminism criteria (Sections 15.4.4.1 and 15.4.4.2) for specifications written in RSML, and validated his tools on an avionics collision avoidance system [116, 117]. Additional tools are being created for safety analysis of RSML requirements specifications.

Some criteria can be enforced simply by using a specification language that incorporates enforcement in its syntax. For example, a language that requires specifying value and time intervals for all inputs and data age limits on all outputs will not require additional analysis. Even if the language syntax does not require specifying a particular characteristic of the inputs or outputs, a syntax that makes omissions immediately apparent will be helpful in locating them.

On many projects, requirements are not complete before software development begins. In addition, changes are often made as the design of the other parts of the system becomes more detailed and problems are found that necessitate changes in the desired software behavior. It is therefore unlikely that the analysis will be completed before software design begins. To avoid costly redesign and recoding, the requirements specification and analysis should be as complete as possible as early as possible. Realistically, however, some of the analysis may need to be put off or redone as the software and system development proceeds.

16

Designing for Safety

Engineers should recognize that reducing risk is not an impossible task, even under financial and time constraints. All it takes in many cases is a different perspective on the design problem.

> —Mike Martin and Roland Schinzinger
> *Ethics in Engineering*

Software temptations are virtually irresistible. The apparent ease of creating arbitrary behavior makes us arrogant. We become sorceror's apprentices, foolishly believing that we can control any amount of complexity. Our systems will dance for us in ever more complicated ways. We don't know when to stop. . . . We would be better off if we learned how and when to say no.

> —G.F. McCormick
> *When Reach Exceeds Grasp*

Safety must be designed into a system. Identifying and assessing hazards is not enough to make a system safe; the information obtained in the hazard analysis needs to be *used* in the design. As discussed earlier, most accidents are not the result of lack of knowledge about hazards and their causes but of the lack of effective use of that knowledge by the organization.

Safeguards may be designed into the product, or they may be designed into the procedures that operators are given for specific situations. Often, the most complex and tricky problems are left to the operators, who are then blamed when they are unsuccessful and accidents occur. Now that operators are being replaced by computer software that is supposed to carry out the same procedures, the onus will be on the software.

Simple design features often can improve safety without increasing complexity or cost, but this requires considering safety early in the design process. An illustration of this idea is the motor-reversing system described in Chapter 4, where the simple rearrangement of two functions, at no additional cost, eliminates a potential battery shorting problem [214]. Other real-life examples are magnetic refrigerator door latches (to prevent children from being trapped inside), deadman switches (which ensure that a system is powered only so long as pressure is exerted on a handle or footpedal), and old-fashioned railroad semaphores (gravity and weight-operated devices that lowered and automatically assumed the STOP position if the cable broke). Many of these simple and safe devices are now being replaced by computers that may not provide an equivalent level of safety. In some cases, similar approaches can be applied to software, but little information about designing such safety mechanisms into software has been compiled and codified.

We need to be careful though: Poorly designed risk reduction measures can actually increase risk and cause accidents. Chapter 4 discussed some of the reasons for this phenomenon. Such designs, for example, can increase system complexity. Adding unnecessary complexity is common when safety is not considered early in design but is instead added on at the end, often in the form of simple redundancy or protection systems. In addition, predicating designs on false assumptions about human behavior or independence between components may defeat attempts to reduce risk while allowing the elimination of other, more effective measures or allowing the reduction of safety margins.

In some cases, safety mechanisms are an attempt to compensate for a poor basic system design. Operators may come to rely on them and take fewer precautions; when they fail, serious accidents may result. System design should make it possible to work in the vicinity of machines without disturbing production unnecessarily. A poorly designed safety device that slows down production or makes it more difficult will encourage operators to bypass or trick it. "It is a much better strategy to design a practical safety system than one that cannot be tricked" [328].

Both software and system design are affected by the introduction of computers into safety-critical systems. Software now controls dangerous systems, and system-safety functions are commonly being implemented in software. Software engineers need to understand the basic principles behind safe system design so they can include them in the software design. It is not enough simply to check the software requirements for consistency with system safety goals and then to implement those requirements: Not everything can be written down in requirements specifications, and software developers must understand enough about system safety that they do not inadvertently contribute to hazards. In turn, software engineers have a great deal of knowledge to contribute to system-safety efforts.

The use of computers also introduces new possibilities for system safety in terms of increased functionality and more powerful protection mechanisms. In a chemical plant, for example, a rapid rise in the temperature in a reactor vessel can indicate a runaway reaction long before the temperature actually reaches a dangerous level; a computer can monitor the temperature and the rate of increase and provide warning early enough to avoid a hazard [158].

At the same time, the system must be protected against software errors. Many hardware backups and safety devices are now being replaced or controlled by software, eliminating protection against software errors and making safety almost totally dependent on the software being perfect. However, assuming that software will be correct when first used and that all errors will be removed by testing is unrealistic, as argued in Chapter 2. Virtually no nontrivial software exists that will function as desired under all conditions, no matter what changes occur in the other components of the system. Therefore, all system designs need to consider the consequences of software errors and build in protection against them.

Unfortunately, protecting against software errors may be more difficult than protecting against hardware failures. Failure modes of electro-mechanical systems are well understood, and components can often be built to fail in a particular way. For example, a mechanical relay can be designed to fail with its contacts open or a pneumatic control valve can be designed to fail closed or open. Those components can then be used to design the system to fail into a safe state, such as shutting down a dangerous machine. It is difficult, however, to plan for software errors, since they are unpredictable. Many computer hardware failures and some software errors can be detected and handled, but doing so requires a great deal of planning and effort.

Although clever ways to design software to enhance safety have been devised for specific projects, little has been published or is widely known. This chapter describes standard system safety design approaches and some of their applications to software design. The safe software design techniques described are far from exhaustive; hopefully they will start people thinking about additional ways to apply standard safety engineering approaches to software design.

16.1 The Design Process

There are two basic approaches to safe design: (1) applying standards and codes of practice that reflect lessons learned from previous accidents and (2) guiding design by hazard analysis. These approaches are complementary and both should be used.

16.1.1 Standards, Codes of Practice, and Checklists

For hardware, general safety design principles have been incorporated into standards, codes of practice, and checklists in order to pass on lessons learned from accidents. For example, the proper use of pressure relief valves is specified in standards for pressure vessels in order to avoid explosions, while the use of electrical standards and codes reduces the probability of fires. There are no equivalent

TABLE 16.1
Checklist Examples

Mechanical Hazards Checklist (incomplete)

1. How are pinchpoints, rotating components, or other moving parts guarded?
2. Have sharp points, sharp edges, and ragged surfaces not required for the function of the product been eliminated?
3. How have bumpers, shock absorbers, springs, or other devices been used to lessen the effect of impacts?
4. Are openings small enough to keep people from inserting fingers into dangerous places?
5. Do slide assemblies for drawers in cabinets have limit stops to prevent them from being pulled out too far?
6. If a product or assembly must be in a particular position, how is this guaranteed? Is it marked with a warning and a directional arrow?
7. How are hinged covers or access panels secured in their open positions against accidental closure?
8. How are the rated load capacities enforced? Is the equipment at least posted with rated load capacities?

Pressure Checklist (incomplete)

1. How have connectors, hoses, and fittings been secured to prevent whipping if there is a failure?
2. Is there any way to accidentally connect the system to a source of pressure higher than that for which the system or any of its components was designed?
3. Is there a relief valve, vent, or burst diaphragm?
4. How will the exhaust from the relieving device be conducted away safely for disposal?
5. How can the system be depressurized without endangering a person who will work on it?
6. Do any components or assemblies have to be installed in a specific way? If so, what means are used to prevent a reversed installation or connection?

standards for safe software. Many of the software design features suggested in various standards are aimed at reliability, maintainability, readability and so on—although little scientific, empirical evaluation of these features has ever taken place. When these qualities coincide with safety requirements in a particular system, they may make the software safer; when they conflict with safety or have little to do with the particular system hazards, they may have little effect on safety and may even increase risk.

Design checklists are another way to systematize and pass on engineering experience and knowledge. Safety checklists identify design features or criteria found to be useful for specific hazards. Table 16.1 gives examples of partial checklists for mechanical hazards and pressure systems.

Although a large number of design errors are possible in hardware, the checklists usually focus on those that lead to known hazards. Checklists are often also used in software design reviews, although they are much less well developed than for hardware and are oriented toward coding errors in general and not toward safety in particular. Since software is not by itself hazardous, there are no generic software *hazards* to consider in design checklists, but checklists could be constructed that included safe software design features (as opposed to common coding errors) from the design features described in this chapter and other sources.

With the introduction of computers into safety-critical systems, many of the lessons learned and incorporated into hardware standards and codes are being lost—either because of a lack of knowledge on the part of the software engineers or because the principles are not translated into the language of the new medium or into the different and sometimes more complex designs possible using computers. Some design principles may not hold when computers replace electromechanical systems, but most do, and these must be incorporated into system and software designs to avoid needless repetition of past accidents.

16.1.2 Design Guided by Hazard Analysis

Although checklists and standards are extremely important, their use alone often is not adequate to prevent accidents, especially in complex systems or in systems where computers allow new features that are not necessarily handled by proven designs and standards. Therefore, the design must also eliminate or control the specific hazards identified for a particular system.

The software tasks identified in Chapter 12 related to software design were:

- Develop system-specific software design criteria and requirements, testing requirements, and computer–human interface requirements based on the identified software safety constraints and software-related hazards.
- Trace safety requirements and constraints to the code; identify those parts that control safety-critical functions and any safety-critical paths that lead to their execution. Design to control the identified hazards.

The system hazard analysis identifies software-related safety requirements and constraints, which are used to validate the software requirements, as described in Chapter 15. These safety-related requirements and constraints should also be identified to the developers and used to guide design. They need to be traced into the design to identify the parts of the software that control safety-critical operations so that analysis, special design efforts, and special verification can then be focused on those functions.

The first step in using hazard analysis information in design is to generate design criteria and general design principles for the software. Some of these criteria may be the same as or related to the system design criteria identified during system hazard analysis (see Section 13.1.6). They should state what is to be achieved rather than how to achieve it so that the designer has the freedom to decide how the goals can best be accomplished. A criterion might be that the software must fail into a safe state if events A, B, or C occur; that the software must not generate avoidance maneuvers that cause unnecessary crossing of paths in a collision avoidance system; or that the software must not issue instructions for the robot to move without receiving proper operator inputs.

Too often, careful consideration in design and testing is focused on the normal (or nominal) operation of a system, but much less attention is paid to erroneous or unexpected (off-nominal) states. Software especially suffers from this problem: Much of it is not designed to be robust against unexpected inputs and environments or to protect against coding or requirements errors.

From the start, testability and analyzability of the design—which often demand simplicity—should receive serious consideration in decision making. Certification and verification of safety are extremely costly procedures and may be impossible or impractical for some large systems unless the design is specifically tailored to be certifiable. The design should leverage the certification effort by minimizing the verification required and simplifying the certification procedures.

The high-level software design process usually identifies the basic modules and the interactions among them, including a set of data flows. Cha [48] has shown how to identify safety-critical modules and data and how to derive formal safety constraints on the modules using a representation of the design as a directed graph. The nodes of the graph represent the functions that the modules compute, and the edges denote the data dependency among the modules. Some of the same goals can be achieved by applying informal techniques to standard data flow and control flow specifications.

Like any requirements, a traceability matrix and tracking procedures within the configuration control system need to be established to ensure traceability of safety requirements and their flow through the documentation.

Conditions change, and decisions need to be reviewed periodically. The system design and software will change over time as well. The design specification should include a record of safety-related design decisions (including both general design principles and criteria and detailed design decisions), the assumptions underlying these decisions, and why the decisions were made. Without such documentation, design decisions can easily be undone accidentally. Finally, incidents that occur during the life of the system can be used to determine whether the design decisions were well founded and allow for learning from experience.

16.2 Types of Design Techniques and Precedence

The idea of designing safety into a product is not new. As shown in Chapter 7, it was advocated by John Cooper and Carl Hansen in the last century. With the development of system safety and reliability engineering has come an increased emphasis on preventing accidents instead of the more standard engineering reliance on learning from our failures. The basic system safety design goal is to eliminate identified hazards or, if that is not possible, to reduce the associated risk to an acceptable level.

Risk is a function of (1) the likelihood of a hazard occurring, (2) the likelihood of the hazard leading to an accident (including duration and exposure), and (3) the severity or consequences of the accident (see Chapter 9). A design can be made safer by reducing any or all of these three factors. System safety guidelines suggest that risk reduction procedures be applied with the following precedence:

1. **Hazard elimination:** Designs are made intrinsically safe by eliminating hazards. Hazards can be eliminated either by eliminating the hazardous state itself from system operation or by eliminating the negative consequences (losses) associated with that state, and thus eliminating the hazard by definition (if a state does not lead to any potential losses, it is not a hazard).

2. **Hazard reduction**: The occurrence of hazards is reduced. Accidents are less likely if the hazards that precede and contribute to them are less likely. For example, if two aircraft do not violate minimum separation standards (the standard hazard in air traffic control), they will not collide. Similarly, if the conditions that lead to a hazard are less likely to occur, the hazard likelihood is reduced.

3. **Hazard control**: If a hazard occurs, the likelihood of it leading to an accident is reduced. One type of hazard control is to detect the hazard and transfer to a safe state as soon as possible. Accidents do not necessarily follow from a hazard; usually, other conditions must be present in the environment of the system that, together with the hazard, lead to losses. Reducing the probability of an accident involves minimizing the duration and exposure of the hazard in the hope of reducing the probability that those other conditions will develop and an accident will occur.

4. **Damage minimization**: The consequences or losses of the accident are reduced. Losses from an accident often cannot be eliminated by the system design alone because the accident occurs outside the boundary of the system. But designers can provide warnings and contingency actions, and governments or other outside forces often have options available to them to reduce potential losses.

The design precedence does not imply that just one of these approaches should be taken. All are necessary because not all hazards will be foreseen, the costs of eliminating or reducing hazards may be too great (in terms of money or required tradeoffs with other objectives), and mistakes will be made.

The higher in the precedence, the more likely the measures are to be successful in avoiding losses; if a hazard is eliminated or its occurrence reduced, for example, there needs to be less reliance on control measures (including humans who may make mistakes or protection devices that may fail, may not be properly maintained, may be turned off or not functioning, or may be ignored in an emergency). Also, as has been stressed repeatedly in this book, it is easier and

Hazard Elimination

Substitution
Simplification
Decoupling
Elimination of specific human errors
Reduction of hazardous materials or conditions

Hazard Reduction

Design for controllability
Barriers
    Lockouts
    Lockins
    Interlocks
Failure minimization
    Safety factors and safety margins
    Redundancy

Hazard Control

Reducing exposure
Isolation and containment
Protection systems and fail-safe design

Damage Reduction

FIGURE 16.1
Safe design techniques in order of their precedence.

cheaper to build safety in than to add it on. An inherently safe process will often be cheaper than a hazardous one with many "add-on" safety devices [195].

Figure 16.1 shows the basic system safety design techniques and their precedence within the general categories. The specific design features chosen to prevent hazards will often depend upon the accident model used and thus upon the types and causes of hazards that are hypothesized. As seen in Chapter 10, many different models of accidents have been proposed.

For example, if accidents are defined as loss of control of energy, then basic accident prevention strategies will often include the use of controls on the energy and the use of barriers or physical separations between it and humans or property. Energy model hazard control measures include such design goals as limiting the energy used in the process, safe energy release in the event of containment failure, automatic control devices to maintain control over energy sources, barriers, strengthening targets, and manual backups to maintain safe energy flow if there are control system failures. The effectiveness of barriers, such as containment vessels and safety zones, depend only on their reliable operation rather than on any particular hypothesized chain of events or causal factors. Accordingly, safe design in energy containment systems often involves the use of design allowances and safety factors rather than hazard analysis.

As has been seen, the energy model is only one possible accident model. A model that focuses on safety as a control problem will emphasize appropriate monitoring and controls and perhaps shutdown systems if the controls fail. A chain-of-events model may try to eliminate the identified events leading to the hazard. A system model that focuses on component interactions will suggest design features that limit interactions and that eliminate hazardous states from the system design.

The specific design features applied will therefore depend upon the accident model selected. The rest of the chapter describes some of these design features. The next chapter presents approaches to design of the human–machine interface.

16.3 Hazard Elimination

The most effective way to deal with a hazard is to eliminate it or to eliminate all possibility that it will lead to an accident (which, by definition, eliminates the hazard).

> If the meat of lions was good to eat, farmers would find ways of farming lions. Cages and other protective equipment would be required to keep them under control and only occasionally, as at Flixborough, would the lions break loose. But why keep lions when lambs will do instead? [154, p.66]

In the energy model of accidents, an intrinsically safe design is one that is incapable of generating or releasing sufficient energy or causing harmful exposures, under normal or abnormal conditions (including outside forces and environmental failures), to cause a hazard, given that the equipment and personnel are in their most vulnerable condition. In a more general systems model, an intrinsically safe design is one in which hazardous states or conditions cannot be reached under any conditions. Of course, philosophically speaking, nothing is impossible. Theoretically, you could be hit by a meteorite while reading this book. But from a practical engineering standpoint, the occurrence of some physical conditions or events is so remote that their consideration is not reasonable.

Several techniques can be used to achieve an intrinsically safe design: substitution, simplification, decoupling, elimination of the potential for human errors, and reduction of hazardous materials or conditions.

16.3.1 Substitution

One way of eliminating hazards is to substitute safe or safer conditions or materials for them, such as substituting nonflammable materials for combustible materials or nontoxins for toxins. Of course, substitution may introduce other hazards, but the goal is for these new hazards to be minor. For example, using pneumatic or hydraulic systems instead of electrical systems may eliminate the possibility of fatal injuries from an electrical hazard, but not the more minor hazards associated with compressed air. Some examples of substitution follow:

- In the chemical industry, water or oils with high boiling points have been substituted for flammable oils as heat transfer agents; silicious materials have been eliminated from scouring powders; flammable refrigerants have been replaced by fluorinated hydrocarbons [154]; and hydraulic instead of pneumatic systems have been used to avoid violent ruptures of pressure vessels that could generate shock waves [108]. Similarly, pressure vessels are generally tested with water or other liquids and not with gas because the rupture of a vessel containing pressurized gas can generate a shock wave and damage similar to that caused by a high explosive. A liquid will not expand the way a gas will when pressure is released, and therefore no shock waves will be created after rupture [107].
- Some missiles have used hybrid propulsion systems, containing both a solid fuel and liquid oxidizer, which eliminate the possibility of combustion and explosion as long as the two are separated. They also eliminate the possibility of uncontrolled combustion due to cracks, voids, and other separations in the solid propellant [106].
- Kletz [152] tells of a plant where a chlorine blower was to be made from titanium, a material suitable for use with wet chlorine but which "burns" in dry chlorine. The chlorine passes through a water scrubber before reaching the blower, and an elaborate trip system was designed to make sure that the chance of dry gas reaching the blower would be small. Following a study of the design, the complex trip system was scrapped and a rubber-covered blower installed instead. Although this blower was less reliable than the titanium one, it eliminated the hazard resulting from the blower coming into contact with dry chlorine.
- After the Apollo 13 near accident (see Appendix B), a review board recommended replacement of Teflon insulation in the oxygen tanks of the command and service module system with stainless steel [108].
- In the nuclear industry, pressurized water reactors depend on engineered

cooling systems. If the normal cooling system fails, emergency systems are needed to prevent overheating. In contrast,

> Advanced gas cooled reactors are cooled to a substantial extent by con-vection if forced circulation is lost. Fast breeder reactors and other de-signs still under development (such as the high temperature gas reactor and the PIUS (process inherent ultimate safety) cannot overheat even if all cooling systems fail completely. In the PIUS design, a water cooled reactor is immersed in a vessel containing borate solution. If coolant pressure is lost, the reactor is flooded by the solution which stops the reaction and cools the reactor [191].

In some extremely critical cases, using very simple hardware protection mechanisms may be safer than introducing computers and the necessarily greater complexity inherent in implementing an analog function on a digital computer. For example, a simple access door or panel that breaks a circuit on high-voltage equipment when opened is much safer than sophisticated electronic devices that detect a human entering an area and send the information to a computer, which then must send a command to an actuator to shut down the equipment. There is no technological imperative that says we *must* use computers to control hazardous functions.

16.3.2 Simplification

One of the most important aspects of safe design is simplicity. A simple design tends to minimize the number of parts, functional modes, and interfaces, and it has a small number of unknowns in terms of interactions with the system and with system operations [265].

Perrow has examined a large number of accidents in many types of sys-tems and concludes that interactive complexity and tight coupling are the major common factors in these accidents [259]. William Pickering, a director of the Jet Propulsion Laboratory, credits the success of early U.S. lunar and planetary spacecraft to simplicity and a conservative approach:

> The most conservative designs capable of fulfilling the mission requirements must be considered. Conservative design involves, wherever possible, the use of flight-proven hardware and, for new designs, the application of state-of-the-art technology, thereby minimizing the numbers of unknowns present in the design. New designs and new technologies are utilized, but only when already existing flight-proven designs cannot satisfy the mission require-ments, and only when the new designs have been extensively tested on the ground [265, p.136].

New technology and new applications of existing technology often introduce "unknown unknowns" (sometimes referred to as UNK-UNKs). Brown notes that after an accident investigation, discussions of these are generally prefaced by "Who would have thought . . . " [42].

Simpler systems provide fewer opportunities for error and failure. The existence of many parts is usually no great problem for designers or operators if their interactions are expected and obvious. But when the interactions reach a level of complexity where they cannot be thoroughly planned, understood, anticipated, and guarded against, accidents occur [259].

Interfaces are a particular problem in safety: Design errors are often found in the transfer of functions across interfaces. Simple interfaces help to minimize such errors and to make the designs more testable.

As argued in Chapter 2, it is easier to design and build complex interfaces with software than with physical devices. Normally, increasing the complexity of physical interfaces greatly increases the difficulty of design and construction. The same rule of thumb is not true for software, which can be used relatively easily to implement complex physical interfaces or complex interfaces within the computer hardware and software itself. Building a *reliable* and *error-free* complex interface using software is extremely difficult, of course, but this lesson seems not to have been learned yet by many engineers.

Reducing and simplifying interfaces will reduce risk. Interface problems often lie in the control systems; thus, a basic design principle is that control systems not be split into pieces [344]. Contrary to this basic engineering design principle, a current trend in complex systems is to break up control systems and implement them on multiple microprocessors, thus increasing the number of interfaces. Where obvious and natural interfaces exist, this separation is reasonable. But sometimes more interfaces are created than necessary, leading to accidents. For example, in one modern military aircraft, the weapons management system was originally implemented on one microprocessor, which both launched the weapon and issued a weapon release message to the pilot. Pilots quickly learned the timing relationships between messages and weapon release, and they timed their maneuvers accordingly. For some reason, the two functions were later divided up and put on separate computers, changing this timing relationship. An accident resulted when a pilot, after seeing the weapon release message, dove and the plane was hit with its own missile.

Kletz has written extensively about simplifying chemical plant designs. Most of the serious accidents that occur in the oil and chemical industries result from a leak of hazardous material [152]. Leaks can be eliminated or reduced by designs with fewer leakage points, such as substituting continuous, one-piece lines for lines with connectors [106]. If equipment does leak, design features can ensure that it does so at a low rate that is easy to stop or control.

Major chemical plant items, such as pressure vessels, do not often fail unless they are used well outside their design limits or are poorly constructed. Instead, most failures occur in subsidiary equipment—pumps, valves, pipe flanges, and so on. Designs can be changed to eliminate as many of these subsidiary devices as possible. For example, using stronger vessels may avoid the need for relief valves and the associated flare system [291]. As another example, adipic acid used to be made in a reactor fitted with external coolers. Now it is made in an internally cooled reactor, which eliminates pump, cooler, and pipelines; mixing is achieved by using the gas produced as a byproduct.

According to Kletz [152], some of the reasons for complexity in system design are

- ☐ The need to add on complicated equipment to control hazards: If the design is made intrinsically safe by eliminating or reducing hazards, less added-on equipment will be necessary. If hazards are not identified early, when it is still possible to change the design to avoid them, the only alternative is to add complex equipment to control them.
- ☐ A desire for flexibility: Multistream plants with numerous crossovers and valves (so that any item can be used on any stream) are flexible but have numerous leakage points, and mistakes in valve settings are easy to make.
- ☐ The use of some types of redundancy to increase reliability: These increase complexity and may decrease safety.

Adding computers to the control of systems often results in increased complexity. Adding new functions to a system using computers is relatively easy: Engineers are finding that they can add functions that before were impossible or impractical, and they are finding it difficult to practice restraint without the experience of long years of failures in these attempts (although we are quickly building up that experience). Even when there are failures, they are often attributed to factors other than the inherent complexity of the projects attempted.

The seeming ease with which complexity can be added both to a system through software and to the software itself is seductive and misleading. As in any system, complexity in software design leads to errors. The complexity of the design in the Therac-25 software added myriad possibilities for unplanned interactions and was an important factor in the accidents. In contrast, the Honeywell JA37B autopilot, the first full-authority fly-by-wire system ever deployed, flew for more than 15 years without an in-flight anomaly [29]. Boebert, one of its designers, attributes its success to the purposeful simplification of the design. Using what they called a *rate structure*, the design rules allowed no interrupts and no back branches in the code; the control flow was "unwound" into one loop that was executed at a fixed rate. This design is an example of simplifying control flow at the expense of data flow:

> Since there were no subroutines, all modules had to communicate by "hiding a note under a rock" and having the recipient look under the rock for it. One bit flags abounded; but this turned out to be a testing advantage because you could build special hardware to "snapshot" the flag vector every cycle and therefore trace the essential state as the thing flew [29].

Many software designs are unnecessarily complex. The nondeterminism in many popular software design techniques is inherently unsafe because of the impossibility of completely testing or understanding all of the interactions and states the software can get into. Nondeterminism also makes diagnosing problems more difficult because it makes software errors look like transient hardware faults: If the software is executed again after a failure, it is likely to work because internal timings will have changed. By eliminating some forms of nondeterminism and multitasking, many of the problems associated with synchronization and possible race conditions are eliminated.

In many real-time process control applications (such as aircraft controls), users, tasks, and communication are known in advance. All processing and communication among system components can be determined at design time, which creates the opportunity for significant reductions in operating system complexity. Sundstrom argues that effective and safe pilot interfaces require a predictable, repeatable system response and thus software that is repeatable in operation and predictable in performance.

The need for deterministic software execution stems from (1) the need for time periodicity in control systems, (2) the need to analyze and predict algorithm behavior, (3) the need to test software and to reproduce test conditions and replicate events, and (4) the need of the human operator to rely on consistency. Since providing time predictability is a major consideration in safe design, it may be better not to allow software to request input and output or to schedule other tasks. Sundstrom recommends some additional ways of achieving deterministic software behavior, including: (1) *a priori* scheduling, (2) exclusive mode definitions, and (3) state transition tables (using only the current state to make control decisions). These features together lead to predictable, repeatable system response and behavior.

Boebert provides one explanation for the overuse of complex designs in software control systems:

> I laid full blame for this circumstance on CS [Computer Science] faculty who either knew nothing other than operating systems or held OS designs up as the ultimate paradigm of software. So CS students and new grad software engineers came out thinking that an autopilot should look like Unix [29].

The explanation may also be that computer science students normally write operating systems and compilers, but probably will never write a control program while in school. Thus, the reason for much unnecessary design complexity may simply be educational and curricular.

A complex software design is usually easier to build than a simple one, and the materials, being abstractions, contain almost unlimited flexibility. Constructing a simple software design for a nontrivial problem usually requires discipline, creativity, restraint, and time.

Software engineers do not yet agree on what features a simple design should have. Defining the criteria such features should satisfy is easier:

- The design should be testable, which means that the number of states is limited, implying the use of determinism over nondeterminism, single-tasking over multitasking, and polling over interrupts.
- The design should be easily understood and readable; the sequence of events

during execution, for example, should be readily observable by reading the listing or design document.

- □ Interactions between components should be limited and straightforward.
- □ Worst-case timing should be determinable by looking at the code.
- □ The code should include only the minimum features and capabilities required by the system and should not contain unnecessary or undocumented features or unused executable code.

The software design should also eliminate hazardous effects of common hardware failures on the software. For example, critical decisions (such as the decision to launch a missile) should not be made on the values often taken by failed components (such as all ones or all zeros). As suggested by Brown,

> Safety-critical functions shall not employ a logic 1 or 0 to denote the safe and armed (potentially hazardous) states. The armed and safe states shall be represented by at least a four bit unique pattern. The safe state shall be a pattern that cannot, as a result of a one or two bit error, represent the armed pattern. If a pattern other than these two unique codes is detected, the software shall flag the errors, revert to a safe state, and notify the operator [45, p.11].

Messages can be designed in ways that eliminate the possibility of computer hardware failures having hazardous consequences. In June 1980, for example, warnings were received at U.S. command and control headquarters that a major nuclear missile attack had been launched against the United States [307]. The military commands prepared for retaliation, but the officers at Cheyenne Mountain were able to ascertain from direct contact with the warning sensors that no incoming missiles had been detected and the alert was canceled. Three days later, the same thing happened again. The false alerts were caused by the failure of a computer chip in a multiplexor system that formats messages sent out continuously to command posts indicating that communication circuits are operating properly. This message was designed to report that there were 000 ICBMs and 000 SLBMs detected; instead, the integrated circuit failure caused some of the zeros to be replaced with twos. After the problem was diagnosed, the message formats were changed to report only the status of the communication system (and nothing about detecting ballistic missiles), thus eliminating the hazard.

The design of software to control a turbine provides an example of the elimination of many potentially dangerous software design features [122]. The safety requirements for the generator are that (1) the governor must always be able to close the steam valves within a few hundred milliseconds if overstressing or even catastrophic destruction of the turbine is to be avoided, and (2) under no circumstances can the steam valves open spuriously, whatever the nature of the internal or external fault.

The software to control the turbine is designed as a two-level structure, with the top level responsible for the less important control functions and for supervisory, coordination, and management functions. Loss of the upper level cannot endanger the turbine and does not cause it to shut down. The upper level uses conventional hardware and software and resides on a processor separate from the safety-critical base-level software processor.

The base level is a secure software kernel that can detect significant failures of the hardware that surrounds it. It includes self-checks to decide whether incoming signals are sensible and whether the processor itself is functioning correctly. A failure of a self-check causes reversion of the output to a safe state through the action of fail-safe hardware.

There are two potential safety problems: (1) the code responsible for self-checking, validating incoming and outgoing signals, and commanding the fail-safe shutdown must be effectively error free; and (2) spurious corruption of this vital code must not cause a hazardous condition or allow a dormant error to be manifested.

The base-level software is held as firmware and written in assembler for speed. No interrupts are allowed in this code other than the one nonmaskable interrupt used to stop the processor in case of a fatal store fault. The avoidance of interrupts means that the timing and sequencing of processor operation can be defined for any particular state at any time, allowing more rigorous and exhaustive testing. It also means that polling must be used. A simple design in which all messages are unidirectional and in which no contention or recovery protocols are required helps ensure a higher level of predictability in the operation of the base-level software.

The organization of the base-level functional tasks is controlled by a comprehensive state table that, in addition to defining the scheduling of tasks, determines the various self-check criteria that are appropriate under particular conditions. The ability to predict the scheduling of the processes accurately means that precise timing criteria can be applied to the execution time of the most important code, such as the self-check and watchdog routines. Finally, the store is continuously checked for faults.

16.3.3 Decoupling

A tightly coupled system is highly interdependent: Each part is linked to many other parts, so that a failure or unplanned behavior in one can rapidly affect the status of others. A malfunctioning part in a tightly coupled system cannot be easily isolated, either because there is insufficient time to close it off or because its failure affects too many other parts, even if the failure does not happen quickly. Tightly coupled systems [259] are more rigid, with an overall design that includes

- More time-dependent processes that cannot wait or stand by until they are attended to.
- Sequences that are invariant (such as the requirements that event B follow event A).
- Only one way to reach a production goal.

□ Little slack (quantities must be precise and resources cannot be substituted for each other).

Accidents in tightly coupled systems are a result of unplanned interactions. These interactions can cause domino effects that eventually lead to a hazardous system state. Coupling exacerbates these problems because of the increased number of interfaces and potential interactions: Small failures propagate unexpectedly.

Two simple examples of the use of decoupling to eliminate hazards are (1) firebreaks to restrict the spread of fire and (2) overpasses and underpasses at highway intersections and railway crossings to avoid collisions.

Why not just decouple all systems? Complex and tightly coupled systems are more efficient (in terms of production) than loosely coupled ones. There is less slack, less underutilized space, and more multifunction components [259]. In addition, transformation systems (which include computers) require many nonlinear interactions.

Computers tend to increase coupling in systems since they usually control multiple system components; in fact, they become the coupling agent unless steps are taken in the system design to avoid it. If Perrow's hypothesis is correct—that complexity and coupling are the causes of what he calls *system accidents* [259]—then adding computers to potentially dangerous systems is likely to increase accidents unless extra thought is put into the design of the system and the software to prevent them.

The principle of decoupling can be applied to software as well as system design. Modularization is used to control complexity, but how the software is split up is crucial in determining the effects and may depend on the particular quality that the designer is trying to maximize. In general, the goal of modularization is to minimize, order, and make explicit the connections between modules. The basic principle of information hiding is that every module encapsulates design decisions that it hides from all other modules; communication is allowed only through explicit function calls and parameters. Besides basic information hiding, some of the principles of software coupling and cohesion [359] also can be used to decouple modules.

When the highest design goal is safety, modularization may involve grouping together the safety-critical functions and reducing the number of such modules (and thus the number of interfaces) as much as possible. An additional advantage of isolating the safety-critical parts of the code is that the most difficult and costly verification techniques can be focused on these components.

After safety-critical functions are separated from noncritical functions, the designer needs to ensure that errors in the noncritical modules cannot impede the operation of the safety-critical functions. Adequate protection of the safety-critical functions will need to be verified.

A common design technique to enhance security is to build the software around a *security kernel*—a relatively small and simple component whose correctness is sufficient to ensure the security of the software. Similarly, a *safety kernel* might consist of a protected set of safety-critical functions, or it might contain operating system functions that protect the safety-critical modules.

Design analysis procedures can be used to identify safety-critical modules and data, which can then be protected by *firewalls*. Firewalls may be physical, such as in the turbine design described earlier where the critical code is executed on a separate computer, or they may be logical. In a logical firewall, a virtual computer is created for each program by making the computer act as if a set of programs or files is the only set of objects in the system, even though other objects may be present. Even when the computer is dedicated to one program, the application code still needs to be protected against the operating system: Usually, barriers between the operating system and the application programs are designed to protect the operating system from the application, but not vice versa.

Logical separation is enforced by providing barriers between programs or modules. To implement a firewall, the design must somehow prevent unauthorized or inadvertent access to or modification of the code or data. This form of protection obviously includes preventing self-modifying code. It also includes reducing coupling through hardware features, such as not using the same input–output registers and ports for both safety-critical and non–safety-critical functions. Additional access control techniques (mostly derived from the security community) are described in Section 16.4.2.

In some systems, critical code or data can be protected physically from unintentional mutilation by being placed in permanent (read-only) or semi-permanent (restricted write) memories.

16.3.4 Elimination of Specific Human Errors

Human error is often implicated in accidents. One way to eliminate operator and maintenance error is to design so that there are few opportunities for error in the operation and support of the system. For example, the design can make incorrect assembly impossible or difficult. In the aircraft industry, it is common to use different sizes and types of electrical connectors on similar or adjacent lines where misconnection could lead to a hazard. If incorrect assembly cannot be made impossible, then the design should make it immediately clear that the component has been assembled or installed incorrectly, perhaps by color coding.

Other human factors issues apply here, such as making instruments readable or making the status of a component clear (whether a valve is open or closed, for example). This topic, including the implications for the design of the software–operator interface, is covered in more depth in Chapter 17.

According to Horning, the design of a programming language can affect human errors in several ways: masterability, fault proneness, understandability, maintainability, and checkability [128]. Not only must a language be simple, but it must encourage the production of simple and understandable programs. Although careful experimental results are limited, some programming language features have been found to be particularly prone to error—among them pointers, control transfers of various kinds, defaults and implicit type conversions, and global variables [128, 92 and 91]. Overloading variable names so that they are not unique and do not have a single purpose is also dangerous. On the other hand, the use of languages with static type checking and the use of guarded commands (ensuring that all possible conditions are accounted for in conditional statements and that each branch is fully specified as to the conditions under which it is taken) seem to help eliminate potential programming errors. Some of the most frequently used languages (such as C) are also those that, according to what is known about language design, are the most error prone.

Another way to reduce potential human error is to write specifications and programs that are easily understood. Many languages produce or encourage specifications and programs that are not very readable and thus are subject to misinterpretation or misunderstanding.

16.3.5 Reduction of Hazardous Materials or Conditions

Even if completely eliminating a dangerous material or substituting a safer one is not possible, it may still be possible to reduce the amount of the material to a level where the system operates properly but the hazard is eliminated or significantly reduced. Thus, a plant can be made safer by reducing inventories of hazardous materials in process or storage.

The chemical industry started paying attention to this principle after the Flixborough accident in England in 1974 (Appendix C), in which the large scale of the losses was due to the presence of large amounts of flammable liquid in the reactors at high pressure and temperature. The MIC in the Bhopal accident was also an intermediate that was convenient but not essential to store.

The success of this approach in the chemical industry has been striking. For example, inventories have been reduced by factors of up to 1,000 or more by redesigning separation equipment and heat exchangers, improving mixing, and replacing batch reactors with continuous ones.

A reduction in inventory is sometimes achievable only as a result of *intensification*, that is, by an increase in the pressure or temperature of the reaction. Thus, some of the advantage of less material in the process is offset by the additional energy available to expel the contents of the vessel [291]. The advantage of intensification (and one reason for its rapid acceptance) is that it reduces cost, since smaller vessels, pipes, valves, and so on are needed.

Another way to eliminate or reduce hazards is to change the conditions under which the hazardous material is handled—that is, to use hazardous materials under the least hazardous conditions possible while achieving the system goals. Equipment is often oversized to allow for future increases in throughput, but the tradeoff may be greater risk. For example, potential leak rates can be reduced by reducing the size of pipes—a severed three-inch pipe will produce more than twice the release rate of a severed two-inch pipe.

Other hazards can be eliminated or reduced by processing the hazardous materials at lower temperatures or pressures. In the chemical industry, this approach, which is the opposite of intensification, is called *attenuation*. As an example, the manufacture of phenol traditionally has been carried out close to the temperature at which a runaway reaction can occur. Automatic equipment has to be (or should be) provided to dump the contents of the reactor into a large tank of water if the temperature gets too high. In more recent designs, the operating temperature is lower, and the dump facilities may not be necessary [152]. Again, significant cost savings can be achieved.

The principle of reduction of hazardous materials or conditions can also be applied to software. For example, software should contain only the code that is absolutely necessary to achieve the desired functionality: Operational software should not contain unused executable code. Unused code should be removed and the program recompiled without it. Eliminating unused code has important implications for the use of commercial off-the-shelf (COTS) software in safety-critical systems. Usually, code that is written to be reused or that is general enough to be reused contains features that are not necessary for every system. Although there is a tradeoff here, the assumed increased reliability of COTS software may not have any effect on safety (it may even increase risk, as discussed in Chapter 2), while the extra functionality and code may lead to hazards and may make software hazard analysis more difficult and perhaps impractical.

Because of the possibility of inadvertent jumps to undesired locations in memory (perhaps due to electromagnetic radiation or electrostatic interference), processor memory not used by the program should be initialized to a pattern that will cause the system to revert to a safe state if executed. All overlays should occupy the same amount of memory, and again any unused memory for a particular overlay should be filled such that a safe state will result if it is inadvertently executed.

16.4 Hazard Reduction

Even if hazards cannot be eliminated, in many cases they can be reduced. Most of the general approaches described in the previous section apply. For example, even if a perfectly safe material cannot be substituted, there may be one available with a much lower probability (but still within the realm of reason) of leading to the hazard. In addition, the duration of conditions that can lead to an accident can often be reduced. Hazard reduction may also involve lessening the possibility for human error in design, operation, and maintenance, or reducing the severity of the possible consequences of a hazard (for example, low-voltage circuitry can be used to avoid lethal shocks).

Various types of safeguards can be used to limit hazards. Such safeguards may be *passive* or *active*. Passive safety devices either (1) maintain safety by their presence (for example, shields and barriers such as containment vessels, safety harnesses, hardhats, passive restraint systems in vehicles, and fences) or (2) fail into safe states (such as weight-operated railroad semaphores that drop into a STOP position if a cable breaks, relays or valves designed to fail open or shut, and retractable landing gear for aircraft in which the wheels drop and lock in the landing position if the pressure system that raises and lowers them fails). Passive protection does not require any special action or cooperation to be effective and therefore is preferable to active protection (which requires that a hazard or condition be detected and corrected). Passive safety devices are not perfect, however—for example, snow and ice may jam weighted railroad semaphores so they do not fail safe.

Active safeguards require some actions to provide protection: detecting a condition (monitoring), measuring some variable(s), interpreting the measurement (diagnosis), and responding. Thus, they require a control system of some sort. More and more often these control systems involve a computer.

There are tradeoffs between these two approaches. Whereas passive devices rely on physical principles such as gravity, active devices depend on less reliable detection and recovery mechanisms. On the other hand, passive devices tend to restrict human activity and design freedom more and are not always feasible to implement.

16.4.1 Design for Controllability

One way to reduce hazards is to make the system easier to control, for both humans and computers. Some processes are inherently more "operable" than others [172]. For example, some processes have an extreme reaction to changes while others are more gradual and take more time. Time pressures increase stress, which in turn increases the probability of making a mistake.

Nuclear reactors provide an example of designs that can differ greatly in their ease of control and their dependence on added-on control and trip systems. Compared to other designs, gas-cooled nuclear reactors give the operator more time in which to react to problems and thus more time to reflect on the consequences of an action before needing to intervene. At the other extreme, Chernobyl-style boiling-water reactors (which have a positive power coefficient at low output rates rather than the negative power coefficients of other commercial designs) are more difficult to control. As Kletz says, "It is easier to keep a marble on a concave-up saucer than on a convex saucer. Chernobyl was a marble on a convex surface" [191].

Incremental Control

One important aspect of controllability is incremental control, that is, allowing critical actions to be performed incrementally rather than as a single step [98]. With incremental control, the controller can (1) use feedback from the behavior of the controlled process to test the validity of the models upon which the decisions were made, and (2) take corrective action before significant damage is done.

Intermediate States

Ease of control also results from a design that gives the operator more options than just continuing to run under the given conditions or shutting down the process completely. Various types of fall-back or intermediate states can often be designed into the process. In some software-controlled systems, for example, multiple levels of functionality are defined, including a minimal set of functions required for safety. If a problem occurs in the noncritical functions, the system control can be backed up to a lower level of functionality. Levels may exist for full functionality, reduced capability, and emergency mode. The software must be designed to handle the multiple control modes and the transitions between them.

As an example, air traffic control (ATC) can be continued safely, although at the expense of efficiency, with a small subset of essential ATC functions. To protect against massive system failures, the specification for the new U.S. ATC system requires a mode of operation, called emergency mode, where only that subset of essential functions is provided. The ATC system can enter this mode whenever the controller or performance monitor judges that the essential functions have degraded to a performance threshold below which ATC safety would be compromised. Of course, great care needs to be taken in implementing this design, given the large number of problems and accidents that occur when changing modes.

Decision Aids

Computers can also be provided to operators to assist in controlling the plant, including alarm analysis, disturbance analysis, and valve sequencing. Normally, one of the primary functions of a process control computer is checking if process measurements have exceeded their limits and an alarm needs to be raised. In large, complex plants, a great many alarms may be raised at the same time, and operators may have difficulty sorting the alarms and diagnosing faults. The problem is most acute in the nuclear industry, which has, as a result, taken the lead in developing automated alarm analysis [10]. The computer may structure the alarms as trees or networks showing the interconnections between the various alarms in the plant to help the operator diagnose the problem (see Chapter 17).

A second type of aid is used to analyze process disturbances. Instrumentation collects information, which is preprocessed to check limits, validate the data, filter and derive process variables from measured variables, and separate noise from true deviations. To detect disturbances, the software uses disturbance models (such as cause–consequence diagrams) to represent the anticipated flow of events. These models are then compared with the actual plant data; consequences are predicted, and, if possible and feasible, corrective actions and primary causes are suggested to the operator [21]. This type of analysis is quite difficult to perform reliably and is fairly controversial from a safety standpoint. The implications of using such aids from a human–machine interaction standpoint is described further in the next chapter.

Valve sequencing programs are a third type of computer aid used in process control. Incorrect sequencing of valve operations is a potential cause of accidents in process plants. Two types of computer assistance in the safe sequencing of valves have been proposed: (1) analyzing a valve sequence proposed by an operator to determine whether it is hazardous and (2) synthesizing safe valve sequences [172]. The latter is much more difficult and potentially error prone.

Monitoring

Detecting a problem requires some form of monitoring, which involves both (1) checking conditions that are assumed to indicate a potential problem in the process and (2) validating or refuting assumptions made during design and analysis. As an example of validating assumptions, a simulation of the controlled process used to validate the software requirements during development might be executed in parallel with the control software during operations and compared with the actual process measurements. If discrepancies occur, the requirements validation process may have been flawed.

Monitoring can be used to indicate

□ Whether a specific condition exists.

□ Whether a device is ready for operation or is operating satisfactorily.

□ Whether required input is being provided.

□ Whether a desired or undesired output is being generated.

□ Whether a specified limit is being exceeded, or whether a measured parameter is abnormal [108].

In general, there are two ways to detect equipment malfunction: (1) by monitoring equipment performance, and (2) by monitoring equipment condition [172]. Condition monitoring usually requires the operator to check the equipment physically; performance checks can be made from the control room using instrument displays. Performance checks compare redundant information, where the redundant information may be provided by expected values, prior signals, duplicate identical instruments, other types of instruments, and so on.

Monitors, in general, should (1) detect problems as soon as possible after they arise and at a level low enough to ensure that effective action can be taken before hazardous states are reached; (2) be independent from the devices they are monitoring; (3) add as little complexity to the system as possible; and (4) be easy to maintain, check, and calibrate.

Independence is always limited [9]. Checks require access to the information to be checked. In most cases, providing access introduces the possibility of corrupting the information. In addition, monitoring depends on assumptions about the structure of the system and about the types of faults and errors that may (or may not) occur. These assumptions may be invalid under certain circumstances. Common (and incorrect) assumptions may be reflected both in the design of the monitor and in the devices being monitored. In fact, the success of monitoring depends on how good these assumptions are—that is, how well they reflect the assumptions of the monitored device or program.

A monitoring system provides feedback to an automatic device or the operators (or both) so that they can take remedial action. Measurement should, as much as possible, be made directly on the critical variables or on closely related functions. The monitor must be capable of detecting critical parameters in the presence of environmental stresses that may degrade performance, such as vibration, temperature variations, moisture, and pressure changes. The feedback must be timely, easily recognizable, and easily interpreted as to whether a normal or unusual condition exists. For example, a simple way to provide feedback is to mark a display, such as a dial, with a predetermined limit where an indicator points to the existing level. An automobile gauge to monitor engine oil pressure may show the current level and indicate a limit that signifies an abnormality. A less effective type of feedback is a light that goes on to warn the driver when the oil pressure is less than a preset level—by that time, the driver may be in trouble [108].

Monitoring is especially important when performing functions known to be particularly hazardous, such as startup and shutdown or any non-normal operating mode. The monitor should ensure that the system powers up in a safe state and that safety-critical circuits and components are operating correctly. Similar tests should be performed in the event of power loss or intermittent power failures. Periodic tests should then be run to ensure that the system is operating safely. When computers are involved, checks might include periodic tests of memory, the data bus, data transmission, and inter-CPU communication.

Monitoring should be capable not only of detecting out-of-limit parameters (limit-level sensing control) in the process but also of detecting problems in the instrumentation system itself. Sometimes, distinguishing exactly where the problem arose—in the instrumentation or in the process—is difficult. Instrumentation error should not be assumed automatically. Chapter 15 contains an example of the delayed detection of the ozone hole over the Antarctic because a computer was programmed to assume extreme deviations were sensor faults and to ignore them.

In extremely critical applications, monitors must be designed to indicate any failures of their own circuits or, in the case of computer monitors, any software errors. Detecting circuit failures is much easier (in general) than detecting software errors; for this reason (and others), hardware monitors may be safer than software monitors in extremely critical situations where an indication of a monitor failure or error is critical.

Monitoring Computers

Computers can be used to monitor external devices and processes, or they may be the focus of the monitoring. In the latter case, checks can be classified in a hierarchy (Figure 16.2). At the lowest level, *hardware checks* are used to detect computer hardware failures or individual instruction errors, such as attempts to violate memory protection schemes, execute privileged instructions, or divide

Fail

not detected

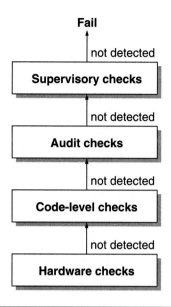

FIGURE 16.2
A hierarchy of software checking.

by zero. Checksums are commonly used to make sure the program is loaded in memory correctly or that data that should not change has not been altered. A checksum is a numerical value that is a function of the binary patterns that make up the program code or memory locations, such as the value produced by adding together all words of the program as if they were integer binary numbers. Self-checking is often built into computer hardware (such as parity checks), and facilities for additional checks are included in or can be added to operating systems.

At the code module level, coding errors and implementation errors can be detected. *Assertions* are statements (Boolean expressions on the system state) about the expected state of the module at different points in its execution or about the expected value of parameters passed to the module. Assertions may take the form of range checks (values of internal variables lie within a particular range during execution), state checks (specific relationships hold among the program variables), and reasonableness checks (values of inputs and outputs from modules are possible or likely).

Auditing (independent monitoring) is performed by a process separate from that being checked. Audits may check the data passed between modules, the consistency of global data structures, or the expected timing of modules or processes.

In system level checking, a *supervisory system* observes the computer externally in order to provide a viewpoint that is totally detached from the observed system. Additional hardware or completely separate hardware may be used, and the observer will often observe both the controlled system and the controller for unexpected behavior.

In general, the farther down in the hierarchy the check can be made, the better in terms of (1) detecting the error closer to the time it occurred and before erroneous data is used, (2) being able to isolate and diagnose the problem, and (3) being able to fix the erroneous state rather than having to recover to a safe state. Higher-level checks detect errors by observing external behavior or the side effects of errors; therefore, they may take longer to discover that something has gone wrong. Some errors, however, cannot be detected except at a high level of abstraction. In all cases, information about the errors that were encountered should be stored for later analysis.

Unfortunately, writing effective code-level checks for software errors is very hard [181], and practicality usually limits the number of checks that can be made in a system constrained by time and memory. By limiting the checks to those that are safety-critical (as determined by the hazard analysis), cost-effective in-line software monitoring may be possible. Special software design and code analysis procedures can be used to guide in the content and placement of the checks, as described in Chapter 18 [184].

Care needs to be taken to ensure that the added monitoring and checks do not cause failures themselves. In a study of self-checks added to detect software errors [181], the self-checks added more errors than they detected. Recovery mechanisms may also be complex or error prone. In fact, a large percentage of the errors found in production software are located in the error-detection or error-handling routines, perhaps because they get the least use and testing.

One way of dealing with these problems is to use a safety kernel or safety executive [184, 185] that coordinates the various monitoring mechanisms. A safety executive allows centralization and encapsulation of safety mechanisms with the concomitant advantages of reusability and possible formal verification of the operations of the executive. In the design shown in Figure 16.3, the detection of unsafe conditions, external to the executive, is achieved through in-line safety assertions [184] and auditing and watchdog processes. Upon detection of an unsafe software state, the executive is passed control and becomes responsible for enforcing safety policy and deciding on the appropriate mechanisms to be used for recovery.

One of the tasks of the safety executive is to communicate with the scheduler. In real-time systems, the criticality of tasks may change during processing and may depend upon runtime environmental conditions. For example, if peak system load increases the computer response time above some critical threshold, runtime reconfiguration of the software may be achieved by delaying or temporarily eliminating noncritical functions. Another important task of the safety executive is to provide information to human operators about the state of the computer and the state of the recovery actions.

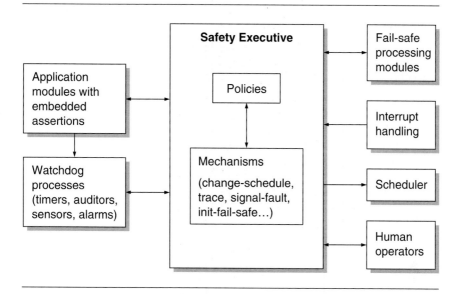

FIGURE 16.3
A design for a safety executive.

An advantage of using a safety kernel or executive is that the monitoring and recovery features of the design become visible and consistent, and safety issues are brought to the forefront, where more informed decisions can be made. Ensuring that safety has been adequately handled is difficult if these features are spread throughout a large program. Also, because of the separation of mechanism from policy in the kernel, modifications and improvements can be made to safety decisions without seriously impacting the entire system. Finally, the potential reuse of safety kernels or executives makes the application of sophisticated and comprehensive verification and validation techniques more practical.

16.4.2 Barriers

One way to reduce the probability of the system getting into hazardous states is to erect barriers, either physical or logical, between physical objects, incompatible materials, system states, or events. A barrier may make access to a dangerous process or state impossible or difficult (a *lockout*), may make it difficult or impossible to leave a safe state or location (a *lockin*), or may enforce a sequence of actions or events (an *interlock*). Barriers may be applied redundantly (in serial or parallel) and may have passages (such as gates or channels) between them whose use is controlled.

Lockouts

A lockout prevents a dangerous event from occurring or prevents someone or something from entering a dangerous area or state. The simplest type of lockout is a wall or fence or some type of physical barrier used to block access to a dangerous condition (such as sharp blades, heated surfaces, or high-voltage equipment).

Lockouts are useful when electrical or magnetic signals can interfere with programmable devices. This phenomenon is called *electromagnetic interference*, or EMI. Examples of EMI include radio signals, electrostatic discharges, or electromagnetic particles (such as alpha or gamma rays).

EMI can be especially difficult to diagnose because of its transient nature. In one case, a programmable device in a ship's crane was intermittently behaving strangely. It turned out that the radio officer was stringing an aerial between the jibs of the cranes in order to increase the range of the ship's transmitter. The crane's cables became receiving antennas [358].

EMI is a major problem for sophisticated military aircraft. In the UH-60 Black Hawk helicopter, for example, radio waves caused complete hydraulic failure, effectively generating false electronic commands. Twenty-two people were killed in five Black Hawk crashes before shielding was added to the electronic controls. After the problem was discovered, the Black Hawk was not permitted to fly near about 100 transmitters throughout the world [235].

A study by Ziegler and Lanford showed that densities in current computer chip technologies are such that about one computer hardware error a week could be attributable to cosmic ray interference at the electron level. As microminiaturization increases, so does the probability of this interference [235]. Electronic components, including computers, need to be protected in some way against electromagnetic radiation, electrostatic interference, power interrupts and surges, stray voltages, and gradual depletion of power supplies.

Electrical interference can be eliminated or minimized in three ways [358]: (1) it can be reduced at its source (for example, suppressing arcing at switch contacts with capacitors), (2) the source and the electronic device can be separated as much as possible (for example, providing an independent electrical supply to the system), or (3) a barrier can be erected around the programmable device (for example, installing shielding or an interference filter).

Authority limiting is a type of lockout that prevents actions that could cause the system to enter a hazardous state. As an example, the control surfaces on an aircraft (or the mechanisms that drive them) may be designed so that an autopilot hardover command causes a worst-case maneuver that is still within the aircraft maneuvering envelope; no matter what the autopilot does, the aircraft structure cannot be compromised. Such authority limitations have to be carefully analyzed to make sure they do not prohibit maneuvers that may be needed in extreme situations.

Lockouts in software include design techniques to control access to and modification of safety-critical code and variables. Safety-critical software often has a few modules or data items that must be carefully protected because their execution (or, in the case of data, their destruction or change) at the wrong time can be catastrophic: an insulin pump administering insulin when the blood sugar is low or a missile launch routine activated inadvertently are two examples. Landwehr has suggested that security techniques involving authority limitation be used to protect safety-critical routines and data [170]. For example, the ability of the software to arm and detonate a weapon might be severely limited and carefully controlled by requiring multiple confirmations. Here again there is a conflict between reliability and safety: To maximize reliability, errors should be unable to disrupt the operation of a weapon, while for safety, errors should often lead to nonoperation. In other words, reliability requires multipoint failure modes, while safety may, in some cases, be enhanced by a single-point failure mode.

Authority limitation with regard to inadvertent activation may be implemented by retaining a human controller in the loop and requiring a positive input by that controller before execution of hazardous commands. The human will obviously require some independent source of information on which to base the decision besides the information provided by the computer.

Various software design techniques developed to provide security may also be applicable to this type of authority limiting. Basically, these techniques control access by associating access rights to modules or users [64]. The access rights may be in the form of general access modes (*read, write, execute*) associated with the protected object or with access control lists that list the authorized users and the rights of each (Figure 16.4a). Alternatively, capabilities [65, 188] may be associated with the user of the protected component (Figure 16.4b). Capabilities are like a ticket in that their possession authorizes the holder to access the object. Access control lists are essentially equivalent to having a guard at a door with a list of all who are permitted to enter; capabilities can be compared to passing out keys to a door and allowing entry to everyone with a key.

More elaborate protection schemes can be built using a *reference monitor* that controls all access to protected data. Only authorized accesses are allowed. Interlocks, such as batons, may also be useful in providing protection (see page 428).

A solution to the more general problem of restricting communication (rather than just data access) is a protected subsystem that performs authorization checks before allowing communication between modules. Secure software systems are often built around a "security kernel"—a relatively small and simple component whose correctness is sufficient to ensure the security of the software (see Section 16.3.3). Rushby has suggested that the security kernel approach is an appropriate way to ensure "negative" properties or things that must not happen [304]—for example, the requirement that a weapon not be armed until it has been readied for firing. Security kernels reside at the lowest levels of a hierarchical system and can influence the higher levels of the system by *not* providing facilities—if the kernel does not provide mechanisms for achieving certain behavior and if no other mechanisms are available, then no layers above the kernel can exhibit that behavior.

A specific type of kernel, called a *separation* or *encapsulation kernel*, can

File MB

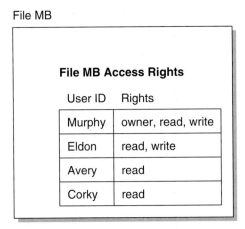

(a) Access Rights: Each file has an associated
list of authorized users and their rights.

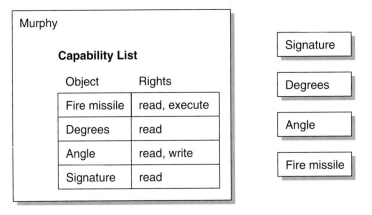

(b) Capabilities: Each user has a list of objects and rights.

FIGURE 16.4
Access rights and capabilities.

be used to enforce a lockout or firewall. It controls all communication and interaction between components and can eliminate some errors of commission. In a missile control system, for example, if the kernel provides no paths for information, control, or data flow between any software component and the warhead arming mechanism—except that intended to trigger the arming function—then no errors except in those two components can cause the warhead to be armed prematurely. In general, an encapsulation kernel can be used to control communication and enforce separation, to ensure sequencing, and to maintain an invariant stating that a component is within its safe operating envelope [304].

All of these lockout designs must be kept very simple or the extra protection features may only add to the software error problem.

Lockins

Lockins maintain a condition. They may be used

- ☐ To keep humans within an enclosure, where leaving under certain conditions would involve proximity with dangerous objects or not allow them to continue to control the system—for example, seat belts and shoulder harnesses in vehicles, safety bars in Ferris wheels and roller coasters, and doors on elevators.
- ☐ To contain harmful products or byproducts, such as electromagnetic radiation, pressure, noise, toxins, or ionizing radiation and radioactive materials.
- ☐ To contain potentially harmful objects—for example, cages around an industrial robot to protect anyone in the vicinity in case the robot throws something.
- ☐ To maintain a controlled environment—for example, buildings, spacecraft, space suits, and diving suits.
- ☐ To constrain a particular sequence of states or events—for example, using speed governors on moving objects (such as on industrial robots or other machinery) to eliminate damage in case of collision or to allow people to get out of the way if the objects move unexpectedly. Slowing operation speed when a human approaches allows workers to know that their presence has been detected. Safety valves, relief valves, and other devices maintain pressure below dangerous levels.

Software needs to be protected against failures and other events in its environment—including erroneous operator inputs, such as inputs that arrive out of order—and it must be designed to stay in a safe state (and to keep the system in a safe state) despite these events. Chapter 15 defined software requirements criteria to ensure that the software is robust against mistaken environmental assumptions. Specifying them is not enough, however; the code must implement these robustness requirements.

Interlocks

Often, the sequence of events is critical. Interlocks are commonly used to enforce correct sequencing or to isolate two events in time. An interlock ensures

- That event A does not occur inadvertently (for example, by requiring two separate events such as pushing buttons A and B).
- That event A does not occur while condition C exists (for example, by putting an access door over high-voltage equipment so that if the door is opened, the circuit is broken).
- That event A occurs before event D (for example, by ensuring that a tank will fill only if a vent valve is opened).

The first two types of interlocks are *inhibits*; the third is a *sequencer*. Examples of interlocks include

- A pressure-sensitive mat or light curtain that shuts off an industrial robot if someone comes within reach.
- A deadman switch that must be held to permit some device to operate— when released, the power is cut off and the device stops.
- Guard gates and signals at railroad crossings to ensure that cars and trains are not in the intersection at the same time. Traffic signals are a similar example.
- A device on machinery that ensures that all prestart conditions are met before startup is allowed, that the correct startup sequence is followed, and that the process conditions for transition from stage to stage are met.
- Pressure relief valves equipped with interlocks to prevent all the valves from being shut off simultaneously.
- A device to prevent the disarming of a trip system or a protection system unless certain conditions are met first and to prevent the system from being left in a disabled state after testing or maintenance.
- Devices to disable a car's ignition unless the automatic shift is in PARK.
- The freeze plug in an automobile engine cooling system whose expansion will force the plug out rather than crack the cylinder if the water in the block freezes. Similarly, to protect against excessive heat, a fusible plug in a boiler becomes exposed when the water level drops below a predetermined level and the heat is not conducted away from the plug, which then melts. The opening permits the steam to escape, reduces the pressure in the boiler, and eliminates the possibility of an explosion.

The system should be designed so that hazardous functions will stop if the interlocks fail. In addition, if an interlock brings something to a halt, adequate status and alarm information must be provided to indicate which interlock was responsible [172].

People have been killed or endangered when the equipment they had de-energized to repair was inadvertently activated by other personnel. One way to avoid such accidents is to install an interlock that only the person making the repairs can operate. The possibility still exists, however, that the interlock can be inadvertently bypassed. In one incident, the doors to a weapons bay on an aircraft were held open by compressed air. An airman working on the system accidentally released the pressure by loosening a fitting while standing between the doors; the doors caught and crushed him [106]. Physically blocking open the doors so that motion is locked out is an alternative in this case. When computers are introduced, complexity may be increased, and physical interlocks may be defeated or omitted. In Chapter 15, an incident was described where a computer unexpectedly closed the bomb bay door on an aircraft after a maintenance interlock was removed.

Engineers are now often removing physical interlocks and safety features in systems and replacing them with software. That was a disastrous mistake in the Therac-25 design, but they are not alone in making it. Most weapon systems now have either replaced hardware interlocks and safety features with software or use software to control them. Other types of systems are quickly following suit. Not only does software control or implementation of interlocks introduce a more complex design, but the procedures for enhancing safety that have been built up over the years in engineering have not yet been developed for software.

In fact, hardware interlocks may be important in systems with computer control in order to protect the system against software errors. Examples of circuitry or other hardware independent of the computer and software include hardwired deadman switches to permit termination of computer-controlled X-ray exposures, electrical interlocks for collision avoidance when motions are computer-controlled, and hardwired electrical sensors to assess the status of critical software-controlled system elements.

If facilities must be provided to override interlocks during maintenance or testing, the design must preclude any possibility of inadvertent interlock overrides or of the interlocks being left in an inoperative state once the system becomes operational again. If software is used to monitor hardware interlocks, it should verify before resuming normal operation that the interlocks have been restored after completion of any tests that remove, disable, or bypass them. While the interlocks are being overridden, information about their state should be made available to any person who might be endangered. In general, if humans are interacting with dangerous equipment, the software controller or physical interlocks or both should ensure that no inadvertent machine movement is possible.

The software also may need to assure that proper sequences are followed and that proper authority has been given to initiate hazardous actions. For example, before firing a weapon, the software may be required to receive separate arm and fire commands to avoid inadvertent firing. Similarly, after an emergency stop of some kind, the operator or the software should be required to go through a restart sequence to assure that the machine is in the assumed proper state before it is activated: The equipment should not simply go to the next operation.

Programming language concurrency and synchronization features are used to order events, but they do not necessarily protect against inadvertent branches caused either by a software error (in fact, they are often so complex as to be error prone themselves) or by a computer hardware fault. Partial protection can be afforded by the use of a *baton*, a simple software device to ensure proper control flow to safety-critical routines. Basically, a baton is a variable that is passed to a routine and checked before the routine is executed to determine whether the required prerequisite tasks have entered their signature. The baton may consist simply of a unique numerical value passed to a subroutine or checked at the beginning of a block of safety-critical code; if the variable does not contain a required value, then the branch to this code was illegal. A *come-from* check is a type of baton that is used in multiple message structures to ensure that data is filtered and that the process receives data only from a valid source.

More elaborate handshaking procedures are possible, but the more complex the design, the more likely that errors will be introduced by the protection devices.

Example: Nuclear Detonation Systems

The approach to safety in nuclear weapon systems in the United States illustrates the use of several types of barriers. The nuclear detonation safety problem is somewhat unique in that safety, in this case, depends on the system *not* working. The goals in a nuclear system are (1) to provide detonation when authorized, and (2) to preclude inadvertent or unauthorized detonation under normal and abnormal conditions. Thus, the concern here is with unintended operation.

Three basic techniques (called *positive measures*) are employed: (1) *isolation* (separating critical elements whose association could lead to an undesired result), (2) *incompatibility* (using unique signals), and (3) *inoperability* (keeping the system in a state that is incapable of detonation) [316].

Figure 16.5 shows a general view of these systems. The nuclear device itself is kept in an inoperable state, perhaps with the ignition device removed or without an arming pin: Positive action has to be taken to make the device operable. The device is also protected by various types of barriers (isolation).

Nuclear detonation requires an unambiguous indication of human intent to be communicated to the weapon. Trying to physically protect the entire communication system from all credible abnormal environments (including sabotage) is not practical. Instead, nuclear systems use a signal pattern of sufficient information complexity that it is unlikely to be generated by an abnormal environment. Not needing to protect the communication (unique signal) lines minimizes or eliminates many design, analysis, testing, and software–computer vulnerability problems. However, the unique signal discriminators (1) must accept the proper unique signal while rejecting spurious inputs, (2) must have rejection logic that is highly immune to abnormal environments, (3) must provide predictably safe response to abnormal environments, and (4) must be analyzable and testable.

The unique signal sources are protected by barriers, and a removable barrier is placed between these sources and the communication channels. Multiple

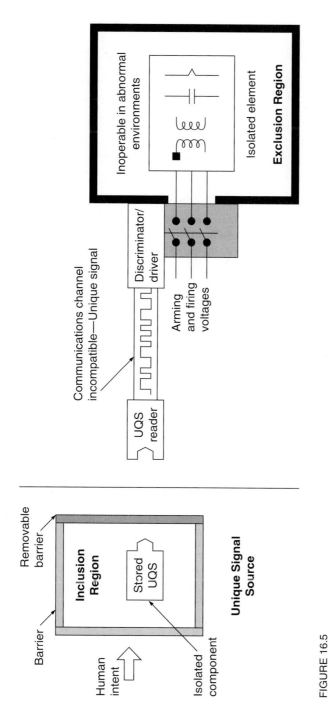

FIGURE 16.5
Subsystem using a un que signal, barriers, and inoperability for nuclear detonation safety. (Source: Stanley D. Spray. Principle-based passive safety in nuclear weapon systems, *High Consequence Operations Safety Symposium*, Sandia National Laboratories, Albuquerque, July 13, 1994.)

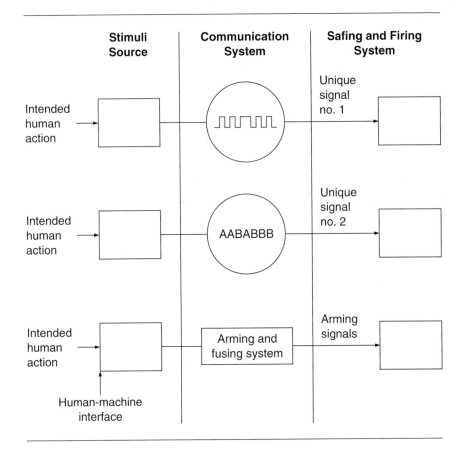

FIGURE 16.6
The use of multiple safety subsystems requiring unique signals (double direct intent with arming) to ensure proper intent. (Source: Stanley D. Spray. Principle-based passive safety in nuclear weapon systems, *High Consequence Operations Safety Symposium*, Sandia National Laboratories, Albuquerque, July 13, 1994.)

unique signals may be required from different individuals along various communication channels, using different types of signals (energy and information), to ensure proper intent to detonate the weapon (Figure 16.6). While this approach enhances safety, it most likely reduces the probability that nuclear detonation will take place when desired (reliability).

Nuclear experts are proud of the fact that no inadvertent nuclear detonation of U.S. weapons has ever occurred. Accidents have happened, however, in which planes carrying these weapons crashed and conventional explosive materials in the bombs went off on impact, dispersing radioactive material around the crash site.[1] Sagan and others have expressed concern about whether organizational and management factors, as described in Chapter 4, might override the technical safeguards [307].

16.4.3 Failure Minimization

Although many hazards are not the result of individual component failures, some hazards *are,* and reducing the failure rate will reduce the probability of those hazards. Section 8.5.2 briefly described several of these reliability-enhancing techniques; the three most applicable to complex systems are safety margins, redundancy, and error recovery.

Safety Factors and Margins

Engineered devices and systems have many uncertainties associated with them: the materials from which they are made; the skill that goes into designing and manufacturing them; their behavior in extreme environmental conditions such as very low or high temperature; and incomplete knowledge about the actual operating conditions, including unexpected stresses, to which they are exposed. Engineering handbooks contain failure rates for standard components, but these rates are subject to implied limits under different conditions and are statistical averages only: Failure rates of individual components may vary considerably from the mean [214].

To cope with these uncertainties, engineers have used safety factors or safety margins, which involve designing a component to withstand greater stresses than are anticipated to occur (see Figure 16.7). A safety factor is expressed as the ratio of nominal or expected strength to nominal stress (load): A part with a

---

[1] In January 1966, a Strategic Air Command (SAC) B-52 and a KC-135 tanker collided during an airborne alert refueling mission near Palomares, Spain. The bomber exploded in mid-air and four hydrogen bombs fell to the earth. There was no nuclear detonation, but the conventional explosive materials from two of the bombs exploded when they hit the ground, spreading considerable radioactive material. One hydrogen bomb was lost at sea for almost three months. As a result, the U.S. Secretary of Defense, Robert McNamara, argued for eliminating the SAC airborne alert program, but was overruled [307].

In January 1968, a similar accident occurred when a Strategic Air Command B-52 bomber was on an airborne alert mission over Thule, Greenland. The co-pilot turned the cabin heater to its maximum heat to combat the cold, and a few minutes later a crew member detected the smell of burning rubber. A search found a small fire in the rear of the lower cabin. The flames grew out of control, the flight instruments became unreadable because of the smoke, and all electrical power was lost. Six of the seven crew members ejected successfully and landed safely in the snow. The plane crashed with a speed at impact of five hundred miles per hour, and the jet fuel exploded. Again, no nuclear detonation occurred; as in Palomares, however, the conventional high explosives in the thermonuclear bombs on board went off, dispersing radioactive debris over a wide expanse of ice. The international protests against American nuclear weapons policy eventually resulted in the termination of nuclear-armed airborne alert flights [307].

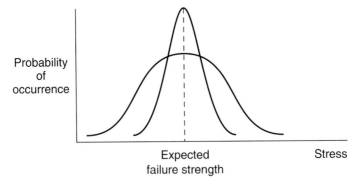

(a) Probability density function of failure for two parts with same expected failure strength.

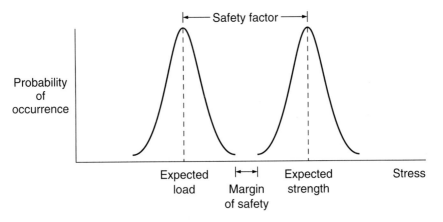

(b) A relatively safe case.

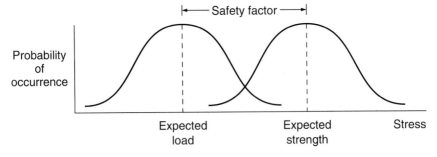

(c) A dangerous overlap but the safety factor is the same as in (b).

FIGURE 16.7
Safety margins. (Adapted from Willie Hammer. *Handbook of System and Product Safety,* 1972, p. 274. Prentice-Hall, Englewood Cliffs, New Jersey.)

safety factor of two, for example, is theoretically able to stand twice the expected stress. The problem with this concept is that the strength of a specific material will vary because of differences in its composition, manufacturing, assembly, handling, environment, or usage. Therefore, a calculated safety factor of two for a component *in general* may be much less for a *particular* component: Averages imply a range of values over which a particular characteristic may vary.

The problem is alleviated somewhat by the use of measures other than expected value or mean in the calculations—such as comparing minimum probable strength and maximum probable stress (called the *safety margin*) or computing the ratio at specified standard deviations from the mean—but the problem is not eliminated. Most solutions involve increased cost for individual components: (1) increase the nominal strength, (2) decrease the nominal stress that will be imposed, or (3) reduce the variations in strength or stress. Even then, computing the margin of safety is difficult for ordinary, stable stresses and even more difficult when continually changing stresses must be considered.

Redundancy

Redundancy involves deliberate duplication to improve reliability. Functional redundancy duplicates function, but may do it with different designs. One of the redundant components should be able to achieve the functional goals regardless of the operational state of the other components. Redundancy may be achieved (1) through standby spares (switching in a spare device when a failure is detected in the one currently being used) or (2) by concurrent use of multiple devices to duplicate a function and voting on the results (with the majority result being used). If only two devices are used in parallel, then fault detection—but not fault correction—is possible. Complex failure detection and comparison voting schemes may be required in some situations. In addition, reconfiguration may be required to switch out failed parts and switch in spares.

The use of this approach in nuclear power plants has resulted in a large number of spurious scrams [349]. To avoid this problem, the redundancy may instead involve independent channels, all carrying the same kind of information and connected so that no protection action will be taken unless a certain number of these channels trip simultaneously. This approach results in some reduction in system reliability (compared with alternative redundant designs), but reduces spurious shutdowns.

Another example of a conflict between safety and reliability can be seen here. Often, redundancy used to increase reliability will at the same time decrease safety and vice versa. The use of two redundant components is much better for error detection than the use of three, but reliability is reduced over that of a single component or of more than two components. Reliability is enhanced when more than two components are used, but error detection is poorer than when only two components check each other.

The more reliable a component, the more likely it is to operate spuriously [349]. In some cases, spurious operation may be as or more hazardous than the failure of the system to function at all. The problems with Ranger 6, described in Section 8.5.2, is an example of redundancy causing spurious activation that ruined a mission. In describing this incident, Weaver concludes, "redundancy is not always the correct design option to use."

Functional redundancy may be accomplished through identical designs (design redundancy) or through intentionally different designs (design diversity). Diversity is used to try to avoid common-cause and common-mode failures, but providing complete diversity is difficult. Weaver, after examining diversity in nuclear power plant designs, concludes that "diversity must be carefully planned and applied. The probability that diversity will prevent an accident may not be very good if such diversity is not expressly designed for that purpose."

Finding and eliminating all potential dependencies in redundant or diverse systems can be extremely difficult. Examples include the following:

- □ A military aircraft was lost when supposedly diverse components, made from titanium, all failed at the same vibration level [32].

- □ A fire in the cable-spreading room of the Browns Ferry nuclear power plant (described in Chapter 4) disabled many electrical and control circuits, which resulted in the loss of the redundant protection systems. Before the accident, common-cause failure of all the protection systems had been deemed not "credible." Harry Green, the superintendent at Browns Ferry, said after the fire: "We had lost redundant components that we didn't think you could lose" [350].

- □ The Turkish Airlines DC-10 crash outside Paris resulted from the cargo door of the baggage hold, which was underneath the passenger compartment, opening at altitude. This event caused the baggage hold to depressurize, which in turn caused the collapse of the cabin floor. The triplicated control lines were all under the floor, so when it collapsed all control of the aircraft was lost.

- □ The simultaneous failure of the auxiliary feedwater valves was instrumental in initiating the loss-of-coolant accident at Three Mile Island. Moreover, the common-cause failure of the high-pressure injection system resulted in the uncovering of the core. Weaver believes that additional diversity in the feedwater system probably would not have prevented the accident [104].

- □ Just when *Challenger's* primary O-ring gasket failed, allowing hot gases to escape, a second adjacent O-ring, designed originally for redundancy, was unseated from its groove by the movement of the rocket casing under pressure [295].

Dependencies may be introduced between redundant or diverse components not only through design but during routine maintenance, testing, and repair. If maintainers perform a task incorrectly on one piece of equipment, they are likely to do it incorrectly on all pieces of equipment [189]. In addition, functional redundancy tends to instill false confidence, which leads to the relaxing of test regimes and schedules and the care with which independent checks are made by inspectors or maintenance personnel.

A vicious circle begins to appear as redundant components introduce more complexity, which adds to the problem of common-cause failures, which leads to more equipment being installed:

> The defense most often advocated for protection against common-mode/common-cause failures has been diversity. However, while diversity in instrumentation has been used for a long time, failures have still occurred. Conditions develop that cannot be anticipated by the designer, with the result that the improvement gained through diversity is limited. Then, too, diversity defeats attempts at standardization and may even result in increased random failures as well as increased plant costs. With functionally designed and periodically tested diverse and redundant systems, the real concerns are those caused by common external influences and inadvertent human responses.

> The pattern is recognizable. Systematic common-mode/common-cause failures are the result of adding complexity to system design. They are the product of a philosophy that has become circular. To date, all proposed "fixes" are for more of the same—more components and more complexity in system design [104, p.191].

Redundancy appears to be most effective against random failures and less effective against design errors. It has been applied to software (which, of course, has only design errors) in an attempt to make it fault tolerant. Software can contain two types of redundancy: data and control.

In data redundancy, data structures or messages used in one program or exchanged between computers include extra data for detecting errors, such as parity bits and other error-detecting and error-correcting codes, checksums, cyclic redundancy check characters, message sequence numbers, sender and receiver addresses, and duplicate pointers or other structural information.

Control or algorithmic redundancy has also been proposed (and used) for software. This type of redundancy involves either (1) built-in reasonableness checks on the computations of the computer and the execution of alternative routines if the test is not passed or (2) writing multiple versions of the algorithms and voting on the result.

The problem with reasonableness checks is the difficulty in writing them. For some limited types of mathematical computations (such as matrix inversion), there are reverse operations that, when applied to the results of a computation, should produce the inputs. In general, this type of reverse operation does not exist. Instead, the outputs or intermediate results are checked to see if they are reasonable given the type of operation being performed. Reasonableness checks are difficult to formulate in general and writing them may be as error prone as writing the original algorithm [181].

An alternative is to write multiple versions of the software and vote on the results during operation. If multiple algorithms for a particular computation are known to have singularities in different parts of their input space, then this approach might be useful. Here, the multiple algorithms used can be carefully planned, as Weaver suggests is necessary for the effective use of diversity in hardware design.

The most common application of the multiple version idea, however, is to use separate teams to write versions of the software, assuming that different people are likely to make different mistakes and design different algorithms. This assumption has not been supported by experimentation. In fact, every experiment with this approach that has checked for dependencies between software failures has found that independently written software routines do not fail in a statistically independent way [39, 38, 73, 163, 181, 164]. This result is not surprising: People tend to make mistakes in the harder parts of the problem and in handling nonstandard and boundary cases in the input space—they do not make mistakes randomly.

The problem of common-cause failures between independently developed software routines is not easily solved. Any shared specifications can lead to common-cause failures. The same problem exists in developing test data to check the software—the testers may omit the same off-nominal or unusual cases that the developers overlooked.

These drawbacks do not mean that multiple versions should not be used, but users should have realistic expectations of the benefits to be derived along with the costs involved. Claims that ultrahigh software reliability will be achieved are just not supported by the empirical and experimental evidence [164]. In fact, the added complexity of providing fault tolerance in this fashion may itself cause runtime failures, just as it can in hardware redundancy. Examples include the synchronization problems arising from software backup redundancy on the first Space Shuttle flight and the NASA experiences (Chapter 4) where all the digital control system failures during flight testing of an experimental aircraft were traced to errors in the redundancy management system. In addition, mathematical models have shown there are limits in the potential software reliability increases possible using this approach [74].

The cost of multiversion programming is not only at least n times the cost of producing one version—where n is the number of versions to be produced—but also n times the cost of maintenance, which is already high for software. Although arguments have been advanced that the increase in cost will be less than n, these arguments rest on the assumption that some aspects of the software development process will not have to be duplicated. Anything not duplicated, however, can potentially contribute to common-cause errors. Furthermore, in experiments with this technique, Knight and Leveson found that in order to get the versions to vote correctly, the specifications had to be much more complete than usually necessary. In other words, many aspects of the processing and outputs (about which nobody really cared) had to be specified in greater detail than usual to make the results comparable. In the end, the specification phase took more time and effort than would normally have been required.

Certainly, some benefits can be derived from this approach, but the real question is whether the limited resources of any project should be spent in producing multiple versions of the software, or whether it would be more cost effective to spend the resources on techniques to avoid or eliminate software errors. Spending more on producing multiple versions of the software usually means that costs must be cut somewhere else. Some people have suggested saving costs by simply testing the multiple versions against each other. This type of testing allows large numbers of test cases to be executed, but it is dangerous because it ensures that the errors that will not be tolerated during operational use (the errors that cause identical incorrect results) will not be found during testing.

In practice, the users of this approach end up with a great deal of similarity in the designs of the multiple versions of the software. In order to get versions to vote in a real-time environment (or to be able to compare intermediate results), the designs for the independent teams are often overspecified and constrained and result in little real software design diversity. Thus, the safety of the system depends on the existence of a quality that has been inadvertently eliminated by the development process.

There is no way to determine how different two software designs are in their failure behavior (which is all that counts in this case). Even when very different algorithms are used, the differences may not help because the problem may not be in the algorithm but in the handling of difficult input cases: The dependencies usually arise from the difficulty of the common problem being solved, not from dependencies in the solution techniques. In one experimental evaluation of this technique, the algorithms used in most of the versions were very different, as were the programming errors made, yet the programs failed on the same inputs [39, 163].

The primary problem with attempts to tolerate software errors using redundancy is that they may not be directed to where the safety problem lies. Multiple versions of the software written from the same requirements specification are effective only against coding errors (and sometimes only a limited set of these), while, as stated earlier, empirical evidence suggests that most safety problems stem from errors in the software requirements, especially misunderstandings about the required operation of the software. Any redundancy, then, will simply duplicate the misunderstandings.

Recovery

If errors are detected by the monitoring and checking procedures described earlier, then failures can be reduced if successful recovery from the error occurs before the component or system fails. Recovery can be performed by humans, or it can be automated: Comparisons between these two approaches are complex and are left for Chapter 17.

Recovery from software errors is sometimes possible. In general, software error recovery can be forward or backward. In *backward recovery*, the computer returns to a previous state (hopefully one that preceded the creation of the erroneous state) and continues computation using an alternate piece of code. No attempt is made to diagnose the particular software error that caused the erroneous state or to assess the extent of any other damage that may have been caused. Multiversion software, as described earlier, is merely a special case of backward recovery where the versions are run in parallel so that state restoration is not necessary. In *forward recovery*, the erroneous part of the state is repaired, and processing continues without rolling back the state of the machine.

Backward recovery procedures assume that the alternate code will work better than the original code. There is, of course, a possibility that the alternate code will work no better than the original code, particularly if the error originated from flawed specifications and misunderstandings about the required operation of the software.

Backward recovery may be adequate if it can be guaranteed that an erroneous computer state will be detected and fixed before any other part of the system is affected. Unfortunately, this property usually cannot be guaranteed. An error may not be readily or immediately apparent: A small error may require hours to build up to a value that exceeds a prescribed safety tolerance limit. Forward recovery relies, on the other hand, on being able to locate and fix the erroneous state, which can be difficult.

In practice, forward and backward recovery are not necessarily alternatives; the need for forward recovery is not precluded by the use of backward recovery. For example, containment of any possible radiation or chemical leaks may be necessary at the same time software recovery is being attempted. In such instances, forward recovery to repair any system damage or minimize hazards will be required [179].

Forward recovery is needed when

- ☐ Backward recovery procedures fail.
- ☐ Redoing the computation means that the output cannot be produced in time.
- ☐ The software control actions depend on the incremental state of the system (such as torquing a gyro or using a stepping motor) and cannot be recovered by a simple software checkpoint and rollback [297].
- ☐ The software error is not immediately apparent and incorrect outputs have already occurred.

Not only is it difficult to roll back the state of mechanical devices that have been affected by undetected erroneous outputs, but an erroneous software module may have passed information to other modules, which then must also be rolled back. Procedures to avoid domino effects in backward recovery are complex and thus error prone, or they require performance penalties such as limiting the amount of concurrency that is possible. In distributed systems, erroneous information may propagate to other nodes and processors before the error is detected.

Forward recovery techniques attempt to repair the erroneous state, which may simply be an internal computer state or the state of the controlled process. Examples of forward recovery techniques include using robust data structures, dynamically altering the flow of control, and ignoring single cycle errors.

Robust data structures use redundancy in the structure (such as extra pointers) or data (such as extra stored information about the structure) to allow reconstruction if the data structure is corrupted [330]. Linked lists with backward as well as forward pointers, for example, allow the list to be constructed if only one pointer is lost or incorrectly changed.

Reconfiguration or dynamic alteration of the control flow is a form of partial shutdown that allows critical tasks to be continued while noncritical functions are delayed or temporarily eliminated. Such reconfiguration may be required because of temporary overload, perhaps caused by peak system usage or by internal conditions, such as excessive attempts to perform backward recovery.

Real-time control systems usually have tasks that are iterated many times per second. In general, this type of software is insensitive to single-cycle errors, which are corrected on the next iteration. Single-cycle errors may originate from bad input data (which is fixed in the next sensor reading) or simply from a singularity in the algorithm or code (which will produce correct results for slightly different input data). The rate at which new data is received may make it possible to ignore single-cycle errors and simply "coast" (that is, repeat the last output or produce a safe output) until new data is received.

Again, the problem with both forward and backward recovery procedures is that they usually depend on assumptions about the state of the system and the correct operation of the software (software requirements specifications) that may be flawed.

Many mechanisms have been proposed for implementing these procedures in software. The real problem is in detecting errors and figuring out how to recover from them, not in devising programming language mechanisms to implement the detection procedures. Some programming languages contain special exception-handling mechanisms that reduce the implementation effort. Many of these language features for error and exception handling, however, are so complex that they may cause the introduction of errors in the error-handling routines and create more problems than they solve. In general, error-handling mechanisms, like everything else, should be as simple as possible.

16.5 Hazard Control

Even if hazards cannot be eliminated, accidents can sometimes still be prevented by detecting the hazard and controlling it before damage occurs. For example, even with the use of a relief valve to maintain pressure below a particular level, a boiler may have a defect that allows it to burst at a pressure less than the relief valve setting. For this reason, building codes often limit the steam boiler pressure that can be used in densely populated areas, or they may require the use of hazard control devices.

Since, by definition, there must be other conditions in the environment that combine with the hazard to cause an accident, reducing the level or the duration of the hazard may increase the probability that the hazardous condition is reversed before all the necessary preconditions for an accident occur. For example, keeping hazardous materials under lower pressure or transporting them in smaller amounts or through smaller pipes will reduce the rate at which they are ejected or lost from the system: The basic design can help in making the hazards controllable.

Resources, both physical and information (such as diagnostics and status information), may be needed to control hazards in an emergency, and therefore these resources need to be managed so that an adequate amount will be available when an emergency arises. As discussed in Chapter 6, too many alarms or too much information may hinder hazard control. Warning signals should not be present for long periods or be too frequent, as people quickly become insensitive to constant stimuli. An operator was killed in an automated factory, for example, when a 2,500 pound robot came up behind him suddenly. The robots had red rotating warning lights to show they were "armed," but the lights shone continually and indicated only that the robots were *capable* of starting up—no real warning of movement was provided [90]. The reason that the designers had failed to include an audible warning when the robot was about to move may have been an incorrect assumption that humans would never have to enter the production area while the robots were operational.

Hazard control measures include limiting exposure, isolation and containment, protection systems, and fail-safe design.

16.5.1 Limiting Exposure

In some systems, it is impossible to stay only in safe states. In fact, increased risk states may be required for the system to accomplish its functions. A general design goal for safety is to stay in a safe state as long and as much as possible. For example, nitroglycerine used to be manufactured in a large batch reactor. Now it is made in a small continuous reactor, and the residence time has been reduced from two hours to two minutes [154].

Another way to reduce exposure is to start out in a safe state and require a change to a higher risk state. The command to arm a missile, for example, might not be issued until the missile is near its target. In the computer shutdown system at the Darlington Nuclear Power Generating Station, the software contains some variables that are used to determine (on the basis of sensor inputs) whether to shut down the plant. Each time through the code, the software initializes these internal variables to the *tripped* value. If a software control flow or other error occurs that results in the omission of some or all of the checks on the sensor inputs, the plant will be tripped. Basically, the safe state for the software in this instance is for the variables to contain a value that will result in plant shutdown; therefore, the variables are assigned this value at all times except right after a check has been made that determines that the condition of the plant is safe.

In general, critical flags and conditions in software should be set or checked as close as possible to the code that they protect. In addition, critical conditions should not be complementary: The absence of an arm condition, for example, should not be used to indicate that the system is unarmed.

16.5.2 Isolation and Containment

Protection may take the form of barriers between the system and the environment, such as containment vessels and shields, which isolate hazardous materials, operations, or equipment away from humans or the conditions that can cause the hazards to lead to an accident.

The proximity of a hazard to an unprotected population will influence the severity of its consequences. The explosion of a chemical plant at Flixborough (which was relatively isolated from an urban population) caused 28 deaths, while the chemical release at Bhopal (which was located in the midst of a crowded residential area) involved over 2,000 deaths and 200,000 injuries. Even if plants are located in an isolated area, the transport of dangerous materials can bring them into contact with large populations: The explosion of a road tanker in San Carlos, Spain, in 1978 killed over 200 people.

16.5.3 Protection Systems and Fail-Safe Design

Hazard control may also take the form of moving the system from a hazardous state to a safe or safer state. The feasibility of building effective fail-safe protection systems[2] depends upon the existence of a safe state to which the system can be brought and the availability of early warning, which in turn requires a suitable delay in the course of events between the warning and an accident. A system may not have a single safe state—what is safe may depend on the conditions in the process and the current system operating mode. A general design rule is that hazardous states should be difficult to get into, while the procedures for switching to safe states should be simple.

Typical protective equipment includes gas detectors, emergency isolation valves, trips and alarms, relief valves and flarestacks, steam and water curtains, flame traps, nitrogen blanketing, fire protection equipment such as insulation and water sprays, and firefighting equipment.

For example, a *panic button* stops a device quickly, perhaps by cutting off power. This feature might be useful when an operator has to enter an unsafe area containing equipment that moves. One of the problems with a panic button is making sure it is within reach when needed; sometimes, a rope is strung around an industrial robot work area and a pull anywhere on the rope will operate the

---

[2] In the nuclear industry, the term "protection system" typically refers only to the electronic systems that detect conditions necessitating some type of safeguarding action but not the equipment that performs the action; the latter are called safety systems or engineered safety features. Protection system is used here to mean both.

panic button. Operators need to be trained to exhibit the correct panic reaction in response to an unexpected event.

Again, passive devices are safer than active devices. Some equipment can be designed to fail into a safe state: Pneumatic control valves, for example, are available as "open-to-air" (open upon air failure) or "close-to-air" (close on air failure), or a mechanical relay can be designed to fail with its contacts open, shutting down a dangerous machine. Occasionally, programmable electronic systems can be designed to fail into a safe state. If not, then designers must add control components (an operator or an automatic system) that will detect a hazardous state and provide an independent way of moving the equipment into a safe state. Any shutdowns by a computer, including shutting itself down, must ensure that no potentially unsafe states are created in the process.

One example of a simple protection device is a watchdog timer—that is, a timer that the system must keep restarting. If the system fails to restart the timer within a given period, the watchdog initiates some type of protection action. Care must be taken to eliminate the possibility of common-cause failures of the watchdog and the thing being monitored. For example, if a watchdog timer is used to check software, the software should not be responsible for initializing the watchdog, and protection should be provided against the software incorrectly resetting it. An infinite loop in the software routine that resets the watchdog, for example, could destroy the watchdog's ability to detect the software error.

Wray relates a case of a common-cause failure of a watchdog and the computer it was monitoring:

> It happened recently to a system that was operating a network of relays, known as "output contactors," which controlled the power supply of some electrical equipment. The user had, unwittingly, fitted the system with a mains transformer that was too small for the job. There were no problems during the first 18 months of operation because no one had used more than two of the contactors at the same time. One day, however, the system's microcomputer called for all of the contactors to operate simultaneously. This overloaded the transformer, whose output voltage dropped and reduced the electrical supply to the microcomputer. The microcomputer stopped working—and it did so before switching off the contactors and closing down the machine. The result was some expensive damage as the machine continued working longer than it was supposed to. Although there was a watchdog on the system, it too was affected by the low supply voltage and failed to cut out the primary contactor [358].

In general, a device (such as a watchdog) at the interface between a computer and the process it is controlling can use timeouts to detect a total computer failure and bring the system to a safe state. If the computer fails to send the interface device a signal at the end of a time interval, such as every 100 milliseconds, the device assumes that the computer has failed and initiates fail-safe action. The interface device might be another computer: A multiprocessing system, for example, might require regular transmissions between the computers. Such transmissions can simply be interrupts, since they need not convey any other information. These checks have been given various names: keep-alive signals, health checks, and sanity checks. Sanity checks can also be performed by the computer on other devices to determine whether input data from that device or information about the status of the device is self-consistent and reasonable.

The protection system itself should provide information about its status and control actions to the operator or bystander. For example, a light might flash or a warning might sound if a person enters a hazardous zone to indicate that the protection system is working and has noticed the intrusion. The status of various sensors and actuators involved in the control system might also be displayed for the operator. Whenever a system is powered up, a signal or warning should be provided to operators and bystanders. Conversely, if the software or other controller has to shut down the system or revert to a safe state, the operator should be informed about the anomaly detected, any action taken, and the current system configuration and status. Before shutting down, the controller may need to recover or undo some damage.

A common design goal is to control the hazard while causing the least damage or interruption to the system. Achieving this goal requires making tradeoffs between safety and interrupting production or damaging equipment. Stressing equipment beyond normal loads (and thus increasing equipment damage or required maintenance actions) may be necessary to reduce the risk of human injuries.

Besides shutting down, some action may be necessary to avoid harm, such as blowing up an errant rocket. At the same time, such safety devices may themselves cause harm, as in the case of the emergency destruct facility that accidentally blew up 72 French weather balloons.

The designer also has to consider how to return the system to an operational state from a fail-safe state. The easier and faster it is to do this, the less likely it is that the safety system will be purposely bypassed or turned off.

Because of these requirements and because some systems must continue to operate at a minimum level in order to maintain safety, various types of fallback states may be designed into a system. For example, traffic lights are safer if they fail into a blinking red or yellow state rather than fail completely. The X-29 is an experimental, unstable aircraft that cannot be flown safely by human control alone. If its digital computers fail, control is switched to an analog backup device that provides less functionality than the computers but at least allows the plane to land safely.

Fallback states might include

- *Partial shutdown:* The system has partial or degraded functionality.
- *Hold:* No functionality is provided, but steps are taken to maintain safety or limit the amount of damage.
- *Emergency shutdown:* The system is shut down completely.
- *Manually or externally controlled:* The system continues to function, but control is switched to a source external to the computer; the computer may

be responsible for a smooth transition, which can be problematic if the fall-back is due to computer malfunction.

□ *Restart:* The system is in a transitional state from non-normal to normal.

The conditions under which each of the control modes should be invoked must be determined, along with how the transitions between states will be implemented and controlled.

There may also be requirements for multiple types of shutdown procedures, for example:

□ *Normal emergency stop:* Cut the power from all the circuits.

□ *Production stop:* Stop as soon as the current task is completed. This facility is useful if shutting down under certain conditions, such as mid-cycle, could cause damage or problems in restarting.

□ *Protection stop:* Shut down the machine immediately, but not necessarily by cutting the power from all the circuits (which could result in damage in some cases). The protection stop command may be monitored to make sure it is obeyed, and there may be a provision to implement an emergency stop if it is not.

If the system cannot be designed to fail into a safe state or to passively change to a safe state in the event of a failure, then the hazard detectors must be of ultra-high reliability, be designed to fail safe themselves, or be designed so that a failure can be detected. For example, equipment can be added to test the detection subsystem periodically by simulating the condition that a sensor is supposed to detect [252]. If the sensor fails to respond to a challenge or if it responds when no challenge is present, then a warning signal is generated. Park provides an example of such a design for an industrial robot:

> For example, an appropriate challenge to a light barrier used as an intru-sion detector would be a small motor-driven vane which repeatedly passes through the light curtain. If the sensor fails to respond when the vane is sup-posed to be in the path of the light beam, then either the sensor or the barrier have [sic] failed, or the motion of the vane has been interfered with. If the sensor shows that an object is present in the sensing area when the vane is not supposed to be, then either a real intrusion has occurred, or the vane is stuck, or the sensor has failed. Only if the signal from the sensor changes from "safe" to "unsafe" in step with the motion of the vane can we be cer-tain that no obstruction is present and that the safety device itself is operating properly.

Park sees three design criteria as important in such safety devices. First, the challenge must not obscure a real hazard. In the light curtain example, the vane must pass through the light beam many times per second, because a real object intruding into the protected space might be undetected for as long as one entire challenge interval. Second, the sensor and challenge subsystems must be highly reliable—Park suggests using redundancy. Third, the sensor and challenge subsystems must be as independent as possible from the monitor subsystem.

Thus, a hazard detection system may consist of three subsystems: (1) a sensor to detect the hazardous condition, (2) a challenge subsystem to exercise and test the sensor, and (3) a monitor subsystem to watch for any interruption of the challenge-and-response sequence [252].

The astute reader may notice that the complexity level is creeping up and that these protection systems are starting to resemble the Rube Goldberg design of a pencil sharpener in Chapter 2, thus decreasing the probability that they will work when needed. This complexity is one reason why safe design features higher up in the levels of precedence are preferable.

16.6 Damage Reduction

Designing to reduce damage in the event of an accident is required because it may not be possible to reduce risk to zero, and the analysts and designers may fail to foresee all hazards. In particular, they may fail to foresee the consequences of modifications: Changes to plant and methods of operation often have unforeseen side effects. Furthermore, humans will make occasional mistakes, and our dependence on them is not eliminated by installing automatic devices. Finally, resources are usually limited: Designers need to determine which hazards should be dealt with immediately and which can be left, at least for the time being.

In an emergency, there probably will be no time to assess the situation, diagnose what is wrong, determine the correct action, and then carry out that action [5]. Therefore, emergency procedures need to be prepared and practiced so that crises can be handled effectively. Contingency planning usually involves determining a "point of no return," when recovery is no longer possible or likely and damage minimization measures should be started. Without predetermining this point, people involved in the emergency may become so wrapped up in attempts to save the system that they wait too long to abandon the recovery efforts or may abandon them prematurely.

Warning systems, like any alarm system, should not be on continuously or frequently because people quickly become insensitive to constant stimuli, as noted earlier. A distinction might be made between warnings used for drills and those used for real emergencies.

Damage minimization techniques include providing escape routes (such as lifeboats, fire escapes, and community evacuation), safe abandonment of products and materials (such as hazardous waste disposal), and devices for limiting physical damage to equipment or people. Some examples of the latter are

□ Providing oil and gas furnaces with blowout panels that give way if overpressurization results from delayed ignition of accumulations of fuel vapors and gases. This feature prevents or reduces damage to furnace walls, boiler tubes, and other critical parts of the equipment and structure. Blowout panels or frangible walls are also used in explosives-processing plants, where an explosion could destroy a structure completely [172].

☐ Collapsible steering columns on automobiles or signposts on highways: if an accident occurs, the steering column or signpost collapses and the possibility of injury is minimized.

☐ Shear pins in motor-driven equipment: If there is an overload, the torque causes shearing of the pin, thus preventing damage to the drive shaft.

16.7 Design Modification and Maintenance

Designs must be maintained, just as physical devices are. Change may be necessary because of changes in the environment or workplace, changes in procedures, changes in requirements and needs, the introduction of new technology, experience that shows that the design does not satisfy the requirements adequately or that assumptions upon which the design was analyzed or implemented do not hold, or the occurrence of accidents or incidents.

Many accidents can be attributed to the fact that the system did not operate as intended because of changes that were not fully coordinated or fully analyzed to determine their effect on the system [264]. Flixborough and the Hyatt-Regency walkway collapse are classic examples.[3] For this reason, reanalysis of the safety features of the design must occur periodically and must always be performed when some known change occurs or when new information is obtained that brings the safety of the design into doubt.

To make design changes safely, the design rationale—why particular design features were included—is needed. Changes can inadvertently eliminate important safety features or diminish the effectiveness of hazard controls. Such design rationale documentation must be updated and compared to accident and incident reports to ensure that the underlying assumptions are correct and have not been invalidated by changes in the system or the environment.

---

[3] In 1981, a walkway at the Kansas City Hyatt-Regency Hotel collapsed, killing 114 people and injuring 200. Investigation showed that the design was changed during construction without an appropriate structural analysis of the new design. After a partial roof collapse during construction, the owner requested an analysis of the redesign, but it was never done [127].

Chapter

17

Design of the Human–Machine Interface

The problem, I suggest, is that the automation is at an intermediate level of intelligence, powerful enough to take over control that used to be done by people, but not powerful enough to handle all abnormalities. Moreover, its level of intelligence is insufficient to provide the continual, appropriate feedback that occurs naturally among human operators. To solve this problem, the automation should either be made less intelligent or more so, but the current level is quite inappropriate. . . . Problems result from inappropriate application, not overautomation.

—Donald Norman
The Problem with Automation

[The designers] had no intention of ignoring the human factor. . . . But the mechanical and technological questions became so overwhelming that they commanded the most attention.

—John Fuller
Death by Robot

Although traditional human–machine interface (HMI) design has a long history of experience and investigation, the introduction of computers has invalidated much of what was known. Digital computers were introduced into control rooms in the 1960s. They were used mostly for data acquisition, but limited uses for control also started at this time. Since then, computers gradually have replaced conventional instrumentation until many systems today use only computer

447

displays. During the past decade, pressures have increased to improve the efficiency of process operations, driven by management's demands for more and better process information, energy conservation, and higher productivity and product quality [329]. Computers have been employed to try to meet these goals.

The new designs have increased complexity, coupling, and probably risk, and have drastically changed the operator's job. The HMI is almost completely computer-based, and operators are responsible for many more control loops than before. Disturbances often have a much greater effect, as they no longer occur in isolation; the effects of a disturbance can spread rapidly over a larger number of processes than in the older, more decoupled systems [329].

The trends are not all negative. Computers provide the flexibility to shape the HMI in ways that were once impossible. They also allow the designer to add new functions, to remove some functions from the operator, and to present a vast array of information in many new ways. New possibilities now exist for allocating tasks and decision-making between humans and machines, with varying degrees of automation of formerly human tasks. Sheridan [311] suggests the range of possibilities:

1. Human does everything.
2. Computer tells human the options available.
3. Computer tells human the options available and suggests one.
4. Computer suggests an action and implements it if asked.
5. Computer suggests action, informs human, and implements it if not stopped in time.
6. Computer selects and implements action if not stopped in time and then informs human.
7. Computer selects and implements action and tells human if asked.
8. Computer selects and implements action and tells human if designer decides human should be told.
9. Computer selects and implements action without any human involvement.

The simplest approach to design is just to automate as much as possible, but the simplest approach is not necessarily the best one. Hirschhorn describes a Canadian chemical plant where computers are used to aid humans rather than to replace them [123]. Chemical plants often need to have their production process continually adjusted to fit varied specifications for different products. As a result, the plants often operate below their potential capacity. A new plant was built to manufacture alcohol for use in carpets, soaps, containers, and so on. The necessary customizing process could have been programmed into a computer and the production automated. Instead, the computer was used to help workers become technologically sophisticated and inventive enough to solve the problems created by the need to customize. Rather than having the computer control production, it was instead used to teach workers by providing them with technical and economic data and allowing them to test their own production decisions. The experience they got could then be used to develop new ways of controlling production:

> Because workers make experimental decisions rather than routine ones, the production process is being continually upgraded, even as workers become more knowledgeable. For this to happen, of course, entails a fundamentally different conception of the interaction of worker and machine [123, p.46].

The designer needs to remember that different is not necessarily better, however, and many changes to traditional work practices do not necessarily represent progress. A negative effect was achieved when a major airline, known for having one of the best maintenance programs in the industry, introduced an expert system to aid their maintenance staff. The quality of maintenance fell: The staff began to depend on the computer decision making and stopped taking responsibility and making their own decisions. When the software was changed to provide only information and only when requested, quality again rose.

We need to determine how best to integrate computers into operations and what HMI principles and designs we should be using to enhance safety. According to Norman,

> The overall message is that it is possible to reduce error through appropriate design considerations. Appropriate design should assume the existence of error, it should continually provide feedback, it should continually interact with the operators in an effective manner, and it should allow for the worst situation possible [242, p.137].

This chapter outlines some traditional HMI design principles and some of the new principles that come with the introduction of computers. Currently, little is known about the human–computer interface in terms of safety. Although many proposals have been made and computers are now being used extensively, little scientific validation of general design principles has been done and experimental results often are conflicting.

17.1 General Process Considerations

In the standard process, human factors engineers first do a task analysis and then often use simulation to evaluate and refine the human–computer interface design. Assessments of the interface design are based on simulation and other test and evaluation procedures.

In safety-critical systems, system hazard analysis can be used to identify high-risk tasks and potentially safety-critical operator errors. This information can then be used in the design of the HMI. Hazard analysis can also be applied to the HMI design itself. Too often, an operational hazard analysis is performed *after* the HMI design is complete in order to evaluate residual risk and to design operational procedures. Instead, this analysis should be done before the interface design is finished, and the results should be used in the design of the system components, including software.

In addition, the results from subsystem hazard analysis, including software hazard analysis, should be used to design HMI features and operational procedures that can respond to computer faults and failures. Later, feedback from incident and accident reports can be used to modify the design. Specific information sources and feedback loops need to be established to validate or refute the assumptions made during design about the human interface with the other subsystems and the system as a whole [223]. Figure 17.1 shows this process.

Hazard analysis results should also be used in operator training to point out the potential accidents that could happen and how they are controlled in the design or operational procedures. The goal is to help the operator understand and appreciate the potential consequences of removing protection features or of inattention to safety-critical operations [95].

Including operators in the HMI design and safety analysis process can result in a better design and safer operations. Experienced operators, such as pilots and nuclear reactor control room operators, can provide invaluable information on which features would be helpful and which would be distracting or useless. The design of a modern, computer-based HMI is such a complex process that the only hope of succeeding is for human factors experts, software engineers, application engineers, and operators to cooperate in the conception and design phase.

Although some general principles and issues for safe HMI design are presented in this chapter, the reader should not apply them uncritically. Guidelines and design principles need to be examined for their applicability to the system under development. Differences in basic system design and use along with differences in the social and educational backgrounds of operators and users may invalidate for one system what is appropriate for another. In addition, information obtained by laboratory experimentation may not apply to a real system. Each system needs to be analyzed to determine what type of HMI will be most effective for that particular situation.

Care needs to be taken especially when applying general HMI guidelines to safety-critical systems; the qualities they enhance may not necessarily be related to safety. Smith and Mosler [317], for example, compiled 944 guidelines, broken down into six functional areas: data entry, data display, sequence control, user guidance, data transmission, and data protection. The only way such lists could be useful is if all qualities desired in a system were complementary and could be achieved in exactly the same way, which, unfortunately, is rarely the case. More often, qualities are conflicting and require tradeoffs and decisions about priorities. An interface that is easy to use may not necessarily be safe.

As an example, one of the guidelines on the Smith and Mosler list is "Ensure that a user need enter any particular data only once, and that the computer can access those data if needed thereafter for the same task or for different tasks." The argument presented for this guideline is that requiring duplicate entry of data creates extra work for users and increases the possibility of entry errors. However, without duplicate entry, the computer is unable to monitor for entry errors unless

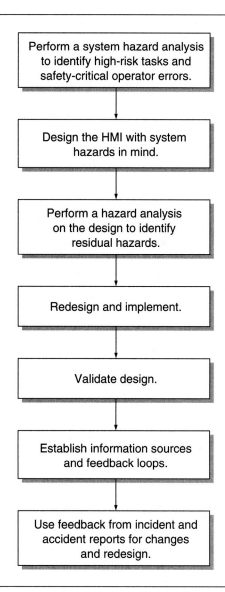

FIGURE 17.1
The process for designing a safer HMI.

the errors are so extreme that they violate reasonableness criteria. A small slip usually cannot be detected. As a result, many hazardous systems require multiple entry of critical data.

Usability and safety frequently conflict. For example, a design that involves displaying data or instructions on a screen for an operator to check and verify by pressing the *enter* button will, over time and after few errors, get the operator in the habit of pressing the enter key multiple times in rapid succession. In the Therac-25 console display, although the operators originally were required to enter the treatment parameters at the treatment site as well as on the computer console, they complained about the duplication. As a result, it was changed so that the parameters were displayed and the operator only needed to press the *return* key if they were correct. Operators quickly became accustomed to pushing the *return* key quickly the required number of times without checking the parameters carefully. As has been stressed repeatedly in this book, conflicts between various design qualities often exist, but they are especially visible in HMI design.

Four sections follow that provide specific design approaches for the issues raised in Chapters 5 and 6. The first section describes an approach to human–machine interaction that emphasizes matching operator tasks to human characteristics. The second section presents some approaches to reducing specific human errors in situations where they could be dangerous. The next two sections discuss providing appropriate information and feedback to humans, including both what information to provide and how to provide it. Next, some suggestions related to training and maintaining skills are presented. Finally, principles for the design of safer HMIs are summarized.

17.2 Matching Tasks to Human Characteristics

One approach to HMI design is to take account of human characteristics and variability rather than try to change humans (perhaps losing much of their power in the process) or to eliminate them. If designers want to take advantage of human problem-solving ability and reduce the number of human actions that cause accidents, then they need to match the task to the human instead of the other way around. Designers should not assume that the systems they build will be operated by perfect humans who never take shortcuts or break the rules [154]. Instead, they should assume that people will behave as they have in the past, and the designs should be able to withstand, without serious accidents, the sort of behavior that experience and psychology show will occur. Systems should be designed so that they do not need perfect decisions.

When computers are used to automate everything that can be automated, the human can be left with a miscellaneous set of tasks, which then become more difficult to execute without error. This approach can degrade the work environment for human operators while depriving the system of the benefits of human flexibility, creativity, and discretion [210, 40].

In fact, we now have the tools, including computers and better human error models, to create better environments for humans to work in than the manual environments we are replacing. The power of computers provides more design flexibility than has been available previously to tailor our systems to human requirements instead of vice versa. As Green says about aircraft, "this means that the onus has moved from training the pilot to cope with what is practically achievable to designing a system that matches the human's capabilities" [101].

Three basic issues in designing for human characteristics are alertness, error tolerance, and task allocation.

17.2.1 Combatting Lack of Alertness

Routine tasks tend to degenerate. "There is not enough 'motivational capital' to go around, to cover the multitude of boring, repetitive tasks on the diligent accomplishment of which all monitoring—and hence safety-engineering—depends" [282]. Ravetz argues that automation is not the solution: It can only reduce the quantity of tasks, not their quality. Also, it does not eliminate the perhaps even more boring tasks of monitoring the system of automatic control.

As awareness increases, accident potential decreases [66]. DeVille, a safety specialist for the U.S. Air Force, hypothesizes that awareness of the elevated risks associated with a particular operation or procedure provides a better measure of accident potential than does an evaluation of the risk level itself. In a mature system that has been refined through experience, he finds that a distraction or unplanned event has little effect when a person is operating at a high level of awareness. Normally, this level of awareness is typical of the more difficult operations—those that require planning and preparation and usually have high visibility with top management. In his experience, these are performed extremely well and, in the vast majority of cases, are accident free.

When performing the normal or routine elements of a job with standard levels of visibility and interest, the identical unplanned event that causes loss of the same level of awareness leads to a high accident potential. Complacency, according to DeVille, moves us rapidly into the danger zone. This happens when people simply do not believe it could or will ever happen to them.

One of the ways to combat complacency and maintain adequate awareness and interest is to introduce a challenge into the routine phases of a job. A challenge can maintain operator involvement and resistance to distraction.

> It may be a single, well-defined goal or some sort of individual or team competition. When a proper challenge is introduced, it increases the individual's awareness. It is surprising at times how small the challenge may be compared to how effective it is in reducing complacency [66].

DeVille recommends that workers themselves help develop or select a challenge. Venda and Lomov [343] suggest modeling predetermined machine malfunctions that are not expected by the operator, and displaying these imitations of emergency situations on a special data display unit. They contend that solving such problems will increase operator preparedness and also act as a monitor of the operator's condition.

Better than making up challenges, of course, would be to provide real challenges in the form of new tasks to fill out periods of passive monitoring. These tasks might be aimed at creating and improving skills and qualifications and maintaining mental models of the system and might be found in mechanical and electronic maintenance, in production planning and management, in quality control, and in system development [246]. The duties should be meaningful (not "make work") and should be directed to the primary task itself [354].

Another way to keep operators challenged is to allow them latitude in deciding how they will accomplish tasks. Most tasks can be accomplished by different strategies with identical efficiency. The HMI can be designed to enforce "one best way" to do a job or it can broaden and enhance the range of options offered to each individual [210].

By leaving the choice of problem-solving strategy up to the individual, monotony and error proneness can be reduced. This approach often has the additional advantage, in terms of safety, of introducing enough flexibility that operators can improvise when a problem cannot be solved by the limited set of behaviors allowed. Many accidents have been avoided when operators jury-rigged devices or procedures to cope with unexpected events.

In Chapter 6, an experiment was described that studied the effects of sleep deprivation. Results showed that alertness and performance held up remarkably well on a simulator where the tasks were stimulating, varied, provided good feedback, and required the active involvement of the subjects in most operations. Relatively few tasks involved either passive or repetitive action; the designers deliberately resisted the pressures to automate (and thereby "remove human error") except to help overcome operator load [8].

17.2.2 Designing for Error Tolerance

As argued in Chapter 5, what is called human "error" is a necessary condition for successful problem solving and decision making in the control of complex systems, in which adaptation to unfamiliar situations is crucial and cannot be avoided. As Reason has said: "Systematic error and correct performance are two sides of the same coin" [287]. Not only do humans use experimentation to solve problems and learn about the system in order to maintain a mental model of its current status, but they also try to get rid of routine decision making and choice by establishing rules for behavior; errors are an inevitable result of the experimentation necessary to establish and update these rules.

Under manual control, human operators often obtain enough feedback about the results of their actions within a few seconds to correct their own errors [17]. Only when the results of human action are irreversible (and therefore have to be reported or result in an accident or incident) or nonobservable (and thus are not corrected in time) do we say that an error has occurred.

By this argument, which has been most eloquently presented by Rasmussen, the aim of the designer should be to build *error-tolerant* systems, in which errors are observable (within an appropriate time limit) and can be reversed before unacceptable consequences develop. In other words, design so that operators can recognize that they have made an error and correct it. The same argument applies to computer errors: The software and the system should be designed such that computer errors are observable by operators and reversible. In essence, this design criterion is just the application of Perrow's argument about tight coupling—making an HMI design error tolerant is equivalent to making it more loosely coupled.

Providing Feedback about Errors.   The key to making errors observable is to provide feedback about them. The feedback might be information about the effects of operator actions or may simply be information about the action that the operator took on the chance that it was inadvertent (such as echoing back operator inputs and requiring confirmation). Note that this requirement is merely the same feedback principle that is applied to the design of process control, but here it is applied to human behavior [270].

Humans might monitor themselves, or computers might monitor humans, or there may be a combination of both. Humans are often capable of monitoring themselves given an appropriate system design—if they are provided with the right type of information and feedback. Rasmussen says that "if the possibility of operators to monitor their own performance were considered explicitly during task design in an ordinary engineering way of thinking, a large fraction of reported cases [of human errors] would not reach the printed page" [270, p.165]. Humans can also monitor each other—one person can perform the procedure while the other checks the actions to make sure each step is accomplished correctly.

Combined human and machine monitoring may be more effective than unaided monitoring by a human, but implementing this monitoring effectively may be difficult. One experiment demonstrating this difficulty involved the use of electronic checklists for pilots [251]. Electronic checklists provide a memory of pending, completed, and skipped steps, and they can guard against pilots perceiving the expected value of a display rather than the actual value. Also, a touch-operated checklist can use direct-manipulation techniques to aid the pilot in switching from one procedure to another without losing track of partially completed checklists and without getting lost in a bulky paper procedures manual. The electronic checklist can provide feedback that guards against four errors associated with conventional paper checklists: (1) forgetting what the current item is and thereby inadvertently skipping an item, (2) skipping items because of interruptions and distractions, (3) intentionally skipping an item and then forgetting to return to it, and (4) stating that an item has been accomplished when it was not.

In the experiment, one version of the automated checklist (manual-sensed)

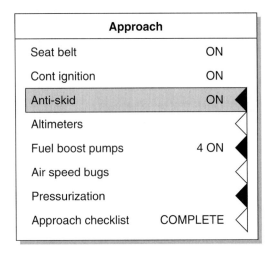

Approach	
Seat belt	ON
Cont ignition	ON
Anti-skid	ON ◀
Altimeters	◁
Fuel boost pumps	4 ON ◀
Air speed bugs	◁
Pressurization	◀
Approach checklist	COMPLETE ◁

FIGURE 17.2
The manual-sensed APPROACH checklist partway through execution. The first two items are colored green and the triangle symbols removed to indicate their completion. The third item has been manually acknowledged by the pilot, but the checklist software has sensed it *not* to have been accomplished. The item has been marked as skipped (amber) and the current-item-box has not advanced to the next item. The checklist will sense the state of the item only after the pilot touches the display to acknowledge completion. The pilot can either complete the item or skip it by moving the current-item-box to the next item. On touching the last item "Checklist . . . Complete," all skipped or uncompleted checklist items are displayed [251].

required the crew to acknowledge the completion of each item manually (Figure 17.2). The other version (automatic-sensed) automatically indicated completed items without requiring pilot acknowledgment. The primary difference between the two checklists was whether the electronic system or the human checked the system state first. The hypothesis was that even though the manual-sensed checklist was more time-consuming, human-monitoring behavior would be less affected by the presence of machine monitoring. A standard paper checklist was used as a control. Small problems or potential pitfalls (which they called *probes*) were introduced to test if the pilots were continuing to monitor the system state manually when the automatic-sensed checklist was also monitoring it.

Three probes were used. The first was detected by all four crews with the paper checklist, by two of the four crews with the manual-sensed checklist, and by none of the crews with the automatic-sensed checklist. The second was detected by three of the four crews with the paper checklist, by one of the crews with the manual-sensed checklist, and by none of the crews with the automatic-sensed checklist. The third was detected by all twelve crews.

The experimenters concluded from the results and from their observation of crew behavior during the experiment that both forms of electronic checklist encouraged flight crews *not* to conduct their own checks—manual checking was largely replaced by machine checking. There was no evidence that the manual-sensed checklist was any more successful in promoting human checking than the automatic-sensed checklist. What appeared to help maintain pilot monitoring was conducting the procedure using two pilots in the usual challenge–response mode. This experiment, although only one, suggests that machine monitoring of the system state will largely *replace*, not add to, human monitoring. Designers cannot assume that machine monitoring provides true redundancy to human monitoring [251].

It would have been interesting to see if a different behavior resulted in this experiment if the automated checklist software had merely aided the human in preventing typical errors (such as by reminding the human that an item had been skipped but never finished) and had not performed the checks itself. Computer performance of the task was not necessary to eliminate the first three of the four manual checklist errors. It seems reasonable that simply providing automated assistance to the manual checklist process could reduce pilot error without the pilots starting to depend on the computer to perform the function itself. Designers commonly overautomate simply because the computer allows us the possibility of doing so. Introducing a powerful new technology often leads to overuse until enough information is available to determine just how much and what use is optimal.

One related and very much open design issue has to do with providing the right type of information to operators about the boundaries of safe operation. Humans need to learn where the boundaries are, but to do so they must sometimes step over them:

> It appears to be essential that actors maintain 'contact' with hazards in such a way that they will be familiar with the boundary to loss of control and will learn to recover. In 'safe' systems in which the margins between normal operation and loss of control are made as wide as possible, the odds are that the actors will not be able to sense the boundaries and, frequently, the boundaries will then be more abrupt and irreversible. Will anti-locking car brakes increase safety or give more efficient transport together with more abrupt and irreversible boundaries to loss of control? A basic design question is: how can boundaries of acceptable performance be established that will give feedback to a learning mode in a reversible way, i.e., absorb violations in a mode of graceful degradation of the opportunity for recovery? [271, p.10]

Allowing for Recovery. Besides providing feedback, error-tolerant designs must allow for recovery from actions. Operators must have adequate flexibility to cope with undesired system behavior and not be constrained by inadequate control options, and there must be enough time for these recovery actions to be taken. In Chapter 16, incremental control was described. By performing critical actions incrementally rather than as a single step, the human controller can observe the controlled process and get feedback about previous steps, and then modify or abort control actions before significant damage is done. For this approach to error tolerance to work, the operator must be provided with compensating actions for incremental actions that have undesired effects.

Hazard Analysis.   According to Rasmussen, the error characteristics of a new system interface can be identified by an error-mode-and-effects analysis based on a taxonomy of human errors and formulated in terms of psychological mechanisms [274]. The practicality of such an approach is based on an assumption that most errors are caused by a fairly small number of psychological mechanisms. The results of the error-mode-and-effects analysis can be used to determine the type of information and procedures needed to detect and recover from errors (to make the system error tolerant) or to break the course of events by protection devices. Other types of hazard analysis might also be applicable.

Unforeseen Hazards.   The concept of error tolerance implies that the solution to the human-error problem is not to replace operator functions by computers, but to *increase* the operators' options for monitoring themselves and recovering from their own errors. But what about extremely hazardous situations? The usual way to cope with the problem of variability in human actions under hazardous conditions is to issue mandatory emergency procedures for predicted scenarios. The fact that accidents result from a confluence of several unusual conditions that cannot be adequately foreseen, however, implies that this approach will not be successful because the predicted scenarios are not likely to fit the actual situation. It is difficult to anticipate everything that can go wrong and to predetermine how to respond. But note that this is exactly what has to be done when writing a computer program to handle emergency situations. Dealing with rare and unforeseen hazards requires human problem solving—automatic recovery eliminates the flexibility of on-the-spot diagnosis. Computer response under these conditions will be less effective than human response, since the computer can only blindly follow the predetermined procedures.

   The conclusion that humans will likely handle unexpected hazards better than computers, however, rests on the assumption that error tolerance can be effectively designed into the system and that the operators will have adequate time and feedback to cope with the situation. If these conditions cannot be fulfilled or if the consequences of an accident are so great that any possibility of human failure to deal with the hazard adequately is unacceptable, then the system must be made fail-safe. Under these conditions, however, the designs cannot assume that humans will be able to monitor computer operations adequately: If operators do not have adequate time and feedback to cope with the situation, they most likely will not have the time and feedback necessary to monitor the computer's attempts to cope with it.

17.2.3 Task Allocation

Even if processes can be made error tolerant, there are strong incentives to automate in order to enhance system productivity or capacity. Computers can provide enhanced control possibilities, if only because of their speed. Whether this should be done strays, once again, into the trans-scientific realm, but designers should recognize that these are not simply engineering decisions and that they have far-reaching implications and results.

If humans are to be included in the control loop in any capacity, a general principle agreed on by almost everyone is that manual involvement must be maintained at some level in order to update the operator's mental model of the system. The controversy begins when considering how much and what type of involvement that should be. If the operator simply acts as an unintelligent actuator for computer-generated commands, the computer could equally well issue the commands directly—and should. The available evidence seems to confirm that humans are unlikely to provide any additional benefit, such as monitoring or error detection, in these circumstances.

At the other extreme, where humans maintain primary control responsibilities, computers can be used to maintain or increase operator effectiveness by supporting human skills and motivation. They can, for example, instruct or advise operators, mitigate errors, provide sophisticated displays, and assist when task loads are high.

Computers have complicated task allocation decisions by introducing the possibility of their taking over much, if not all, of the operator's functions. The question then becomes: How should tasks be allocated between computers and humans, and who should do this allocation?

Design Considerations.   All evidence seems to point to the conclusion that using computers to make decisions or to simplify the operator's decisions is dangerous unless carefully done. Simplifying too much of the operator's task, as shown in Chapter 6, may simply lead to more errors. Automating solely on the basis of the relative abilities of humans and computers may not result in an optimal mix. Performance on a task may depend not only on current conditions, but also on what the operator has just finished doing [229]. In addition, Morris and colleagues point out that aptitudes, cognitive styles, and attitudes differ among individuals. Human performance also varies within individuals over time. It may improve with practice and may degrade when the human becomes tired. Task demands may change over time, and the quality of human performance may reflect changes in the nature or difficulty of the tasks that must be performed concurrently [229]. All of this complicates task allocation strategies.

Some differences between computers and humans, such as perceptual abilities, are universal. Humans readily impart meaning into what is seen, and they are excellent at perceptual organization. Computers, on the other hand, have a great deal of difficulty analyzing scenes, but excel at figure rotation and template matching. Morris and colleagues suggest that these differences can be capitalized upon by using them dynamically for task allocation as the character of a visual display changes over time.

When the total workload requires a high level of automation, some tasks may be easily automated while others may require human support. To reduce risk, operator decision making and input may be required for hazardous operations, such as target selection and launch decisions in a weapon system. Other tasks might be designed for varying levels of human–computer interaction, depending on the current workload.

Multiple tasks may interact and substantially affect human performance. Tasks can be complementary in that they provide important information about each other, and performing one makes it easier to perform the other. Alternatively, they may be mutually incompatible in that responsibility for all of them degrades performance on each [301]. Obviously, the goal is to allocate a set of complementary tasks to the operators that will adequately update their mental models, keep them alert and aware, and optimize system safety. This obvious goal is very difficult to achieve, though.

Failure Detection. When humans are assigned monitoring and error detection tasks, then the relationship of human participation in the control activities and human failure-detection performance is important from a safety standpoint. Results from a relatively large number of experimental studies are conflicting [301]: Some researchers have found that error detection is enhanced if the human continuously controls the system, while others have found the exact opposite.

Different explanations have been advanced for these contradictory results. Ephrath and Young conclude that total workload is the key. In tasks involving low workload, failure detection is better when the operator is kept in the control loop. On the other hand, if the workload is high, failure detection is decreased [79]. Rouse suggests that performing control tasks while monitoring for failures is beneficial if it provides cues that directly help to detect failures and if the workload is low enough to allow the human to utilize these cues. Otherwise, the control tasks simply increase workload and decrease the amount of attention that can be devoted to failure detection [301].

Others believe that the important issue is not just workload but type of workload. Johannsen and Rouse found that pilots reported less depth of planning under autopilot mode in abnormal environmental conditions, presumably because the autopilot was dealing with the abnormal conditions [139]. In contrast, pilots reported more planning under emergency conditions where the autopilot frees the pilots from on-line control so they can think about other things.

Sugiyama and colleagues conclude from their studies that the important variable is intermittency of visual information—in other words, whether the operator is monitoring a single instrument or many instruments. They found that a human controller needed longer detection time than a human monitor when the intermittency rate was high [321].

The jury is obviously still out here, as it is for so many aspects of HMI design. Even if, for various reasons, humans must play only the role of supervisor or monitor, studies have shown that a major benefit can be obtained from allowing them first to interact manually with the system for a while [356]. In all cases, human operators need sufficient practice in controlling the system (preferably not just in a simulator but under normal conditions) to maintain skills and self-confidence if they are expected to take over under abnormal conditions.

Making Allocation Decisions.   Besides the question of what tasks the human and computer should perform, there is also the question of who does the allocation and when. Several approaches are possible. In one, the human is in charge and requests help when desired; the computer is assigned only those tasks that the operator chooses not to perform. One drawback here is the extra operator workload in terms of making allocation decisions and issuing commands to the computer. Alternatively, the human might still make the final decision about task allocation, but the computer could make suggestions.

A second approach is to put the computer in charge of task allocation, perhaps giving the human operator an override or input into the process. Various schemes can then be used by the computer to allocate tasks. In one dynamic allocation scheme, a particular task is allocated according to whether the human or computer has the most resources available to perform it. Rouse and Chu experimented with a scheme whereby the computer only performed tasks when the pilot's workload was excessive. They report substantial improvements in system performance, as well as high pilot opinion ratings [301].

Unless one of these default options for task allocator is used, Enstrom and Rouse suggest that the human can become confused about who is supposed to be performing a task at a particular time. Avoiding this problem, when the computer is in charge, requires displaying the results of the computer's inferences in terms of the allocation of tasks at any particular instant while at the same time not overloading the human with status information [301].

Emergency Shutdown.   A final question arises as to whether a human or an automated system should take over in an emergency when shutdown or stabilization of a process is necessary. This issue was discussed briefly in the previous section for the case where the human operator is controlling the process. Bainbridge says that when the operator is not involved in on-line control, he or she may not be capable of taking over control in an emergency and that automatic control is appropriate when shutdown is simple and inexpensive [17]. Manual shutdown is feasible when there is time for the operator to work out what to do. Overlearned responses (acquired through frequent practice on a simulator) will work for some systems requiring medium response time. When a large number of separate actions must be made in a limited amount of time, some might be made by the automatic system and the remainder by a highly practiced operator.

Finally, for systems where the operator has very little time to act, completely automatic response may be necessary. If reliable automatic response is not feasible for these systems, then Bainbridge says the process should not be built if the costs of failure are unacceptable [17].

17.3 Reducing Safety-Critical Human Errors

Although much of the behavior called operator error is necessary for the successful control of complex systems, some errors have such negative consequences that, rather than tolerate them, an attempt must be made to reduce or eliminate them. Doing so involves either removing or reducing the opportunities for error or changing the work situation so that errors are less likely. As Rasmussen [277] says, "Nobody would accept the design of a fifth floor balcony without a handrail."

The basic concept here is to make safety-enhancing actions easy and robust and to make dangerous actions difficult or impossible. In general, the design should make it more difficult for the operator to operate unsafely than safely.

If safety-enhancing actions are easy, they are less likely to be bypassed intentionally or accidentally. If the safe method of operation is difficult or time-consuming, an unsafe method is likely to be substituted. Shortcuts taken while entering the takeoff longitude of the Korean Air Lines plane shot down by the Russians in 1983 have been hypothesized as the cause of the plane being off-course [12].

A protection system that shuts down the plant should not slow down work or make it more difficult; if it does, humans will try to bypass or disconnect it. Restarting the process after a stop command from the protection system should be easy and fast.

Stopping an unsafe action or leaving an unsafe state should be possible with a single keystroke that moves the system into a safe state. The design should make fail-safe actions easy and natural, and difficult to avoid, omit, or do wrong.

Actions required to maintain safety must also be robust. Multiple physical devices and logical paths should be provided so that a single hardware failure or system error cannot prevent the operator from taking action to maintain a safe system state and avoid hazards.

At the same time, two or more unique operator actions should be required to initiate any potentially hazardous function or sequence of functions. In general, potentially hazardous actions should require fairly complicated procedures, so that if any of a sequence of steps is violated, the system will remain in a safe state. Hazardous actions should be designed to minimize the potential for inadvertent activation of a function; they should not be initiated by pushing a single button, for example. In a cyclotron facility, designers found that a touch computer screen was being accidentally activated by operators when they leaned against the panel while chatting in the control room of a nuclear facility. A button was subsequently installed that had to be pushed at the same time the screen was touched to activate dangerous commands.

Initiating a launch sequence should require multiple keystrokes or actions while stopping a launch should require only one. In general, the design goal should be to preserve the ability to intervene positively, while deliberately making harmful intervention as difficult as possible.

Safety may be enhanced by using procedural safeguards (the operator is instructed to take or avoid specific actions) or by designing safeguards into the system. The latter is much more effective. For example, if the potential error involves leaving out a critical action, either the operator can be instructed to always take that action or it can be made an integral part of the process.

A typical error during maintenance is not to return equipment to the operational mode. The accident sequence at Three Mile Island was initiated by such an error. An action that is isolated and has no immediate relation to the "gestalt" of the repair or testing task is easily forgotten. Instead of stressing the need to be careful (the usual approach), change the system by integrating the act physically into the task, make detection a physical consequence of the tool design, or change operations planning or review. That is, change design or management rather than trying to change the human [274].

On the other hand, sometimes it is important to separate critical functions, such as ARM and FIRE commands for weapon operation. If the operator must be able to halt a sequence when new information is received, conditions change, or monitoring reveals that an error has been made, the operational steps need to be separated and made incremental.

To make decisions easier, references can be provided for making judgments, such as marking meters with safe or unsafe limits. Because humans often revert to stereotype, stereotypes should be followed in design. This criterion includes making computer displays look similar to the analog displays they are replacing. Controls should be placed in the sequence in which they are to be used; similarity, proximity, interference, or awkward location of critical controls should be avoided [106]. Similarly, where operators have to perform different classes or types of action, sequences should be made as dissimilar as possible. Keeping things simple, natural, and similar to what has been done before (not making gratuitous design changes) is a good way to avoid errors when humans are working under stress, are distracted, or are performing tasks while thinking about something else.

One of the most effective design techniques for reducing human error is to design so that the error is not physically possible or so that errors are obvious. For example, valves can be designed so they cannot be interchanged because the connections are different sizes, or connections can be made asymmetric or male and female so that they can be assembled in only one way. Connection errors can be made obvious by color coding. Equivalent techniques can be used in the design of the operator–computer interface.

Finally, physical interlocks can be used to preclude human error. For example, if the operator is not to proceed with startup until a particular valve has been opened, an interlock can be installed to prevent this sequence. An example is an interlock that prevents the operation of switch B when switch A is set to the ON position.

Although most of the examples here involve physical devices, there are direct counterparts in the design of the operator–computer interface, and the same principles apply.

17.4 Providing Appropriate Information and Feedback

The HMI is a communication process—a social interaction between the operator and the machine's designer [267]. As such, it is prone to the same misunderstandings and communication problems of any social interaction. The HMI has the additional problem, however, of being indirect: The nonverbal cues and body language that assist human–human communication are not present. These same issues often arise in electronic mail communication, but misunderstandings are mitigated by the possibility of feedback and followup queries, both of which are less feasible and more complicated with the HMI: The entire interaction and all possible miscommunications and requests for additional information must be anticipated before the interaction occurs.

Even when carefully designed, the HMI may have the effect of dictating the communication process—the operator must conform to the specific structure incorporated in the HMI by the designer. Therefore, the designer must try to anticipate the form of communication that the operator will require and want. There are two aspects of this problem: what information needs to be presented and how this information should be provided.

17.4.1 What Information?

The HMI needs to be carefully tailored to provide an appropriate type and amount of information. This process in turn depends upon the nature of the task being performed. Tasks impose different psychological demands and require different skills. Analyzing the tasks first will help to determine what information is needed.

Tailoring the Display to Cognitive Processing

The increasing use of computer-generated displays raises the possibility of tailoring a display to the cognitive processes used for a task. For example, human decision making might be improved if the HMI presents information that is relevant to the decision-makers' mental model or representation of the controlled process. This approach presupposes that the designer has an idea of the form and content of this model.

The information provided may also depend upon the underlying human error model that is assumed. For example, using the Rasmussen three-level human behavior model suggests that a variety of displays and information is needed to provide the different types of information required for a human to perform effectively on each of the three levels [301]. Rasmussen suggests that even within the same task, the operator has to move between different levels of behavior and process different types of information (signals, signs, or symbols).

Besides the differences in underlying models of human behavior, the information to be displayed at any time may depend upon the level of abstraction at which the operator is thinking about the process [272]. A variety of displays may be needed that provide different types of information to support these various levels.

Bainbridge [17] urges caution in tailoring displays to what is assumed to be the current mode of human cognitive processing:

- □ An interface may be designed that is ideal for normal conditions but hides the development of abnormal ones—for example, displaying only the data relevant to a particular mode of operation such as start-up, routine operations, or maintenance.

- □ The use of different skills is partly a function of the operator's experience. With new technology, there is a tendency to reduce the redundancy of information available, but this reduction is likely to cause problems for the novice user [256]. Goodstein discusses how displays may be designed to be compatible with different levels of operator skill using Rasmussen's three levels of behavior [99].

- □ Interaction under time pressure raises problems. The change between behavior levels (such as between knowledge-based and skill-based behavior) not only is a function of practice, but also depends on the uncertainty of the environment: The same task elements may be performed using different skills at different times [17]. The operator may be confused rather than helped by a display based solely on overall skill level. If not under time stress, the operator may be able to request the information or type of display needed, but this request adds to the workload. Under time stress, operators might not be able to choose or use different displays effectively. Rouse has suggested that the computer might identify what type of skill the operator is using and change the displays [301]. This identification seems difficult and dangerous, however, because it requires information about the current behavior of the operator, which is not easy or perhaps even impossible for the computer or the computer programmer to ascertain.

- □ Operators might be confused by display changes that are not under their control. They may need time to accommodate to shifts between different display modes, just as they need time to shift between activity modes (such as monitoring and control), even when these are under their control [79]. At the least, a great deal of care is needed to make sure that the different displays are compatible.

Feedback

The widespread use of automatic control has shifted the operator's job primarily to monitoring, diagnosis, the handling of emergencies or nonnormal control modes, and problem solving. The tasks performed will affect the type of information that the operator needs. In all of these tasks, however, feedback is essential.

Norman discusses the need for feedback to keep pilots in the loop in modern automated aircraft:

> Although the human operators are indeed no longer in the loop, the culprit is not automation, it is the lack of continual feedback and interaction. . . . The informal chatter that normally accompanies an experienced, socialized crew tends to keep everyone informed of the complete state of the system, allowing for the early detection of anomalies. Hutchins has shown how this continual verbal interaction in a system with highly socialized crews serves to keep everyone attentive and informed, helps the continual training of new members of the crew, and serves as natural monitors for error [242, p.140].

The automated HMI must be designed to give operators the appropriate feedback to keep them in the loop. In a position statement of the Airline Pilot's Association, Hoagland says that pilots do not object to the monitor role; what concerns them is the inadequacy of the means provided for them to fulfill that role. They contend that there is no difference between the information required to perform a task manually and the information necessary to determine that an automatic system is satisfactorily performing that task:

> The pilot must at all times be able to assess airplane performance. If the airplane is being controlled automatically, he must be able to resume manual control at any time, and he must at all times be able to recover from any situation the automatics may get him into. This means that for flight-critical systems, the pilot requires timely and adequate information for the control of those systems. The fact that a system or process is being controlled automatically does not mean that the pilot's information needs are any different than if being controlled manually. The pilot needs the same quality of information for assessing the output of an automatic system as he does for assessing the output of manual operation. Automation is not a substitute for information [124].

There is an added issue involving the independence of the information provided. If the instruments and computers being monitored provide the only information about the system state, the human monitor is providing little, if any, additional assistance. The operator must have access to independent sources of information in order to monitor performance, except in the case of a few extreme failure modes (such as total inactivity). In the command and control warning system computer errors described in Chapter 16, NORAD officers at Cheyenne Mountain were able to determine, through direct contact with the warning sensors (satellites and radars), that the computer displays indicating that the United States was under nuclear attack were incorrect. The direct contact showed that the sensors were operating and had received no evidence of incoming missiles [307]. This error detection would not have been possible if the humans could only get information about the sensors from the computer (which had the wrong information).

Lucas [199] notes that automated control systems impoverish the cognitive coupling between the operator and the process. There is no longer direct sensory feedback between the operator and the task—the computer intervenes and mediates the interaction. The HMI needs to provide feedback of two types:

1. The effect of the operator's actions
2. The state of the system, in order to
   a. Update the operator's mental model so that correct actions can be taken when required.
   b. Provide the information necessary to detect faults in the automated system.

Feedback about the Effects of Actions. Without feedback, operators do not know whether their requests or instructions were received and performed properly or whether these instructions were effective in achieving the operators' goals. Feedback is essential to monitor the effects of operator actions, to allow for the detection and correction of errors, and to maintain alertness. The HMI should provide confirmation of valid data entry and the acceptance and processing of operator-entered commands. Feedback is also important for learning about the system and how it will respond to a variety of situations [242]. Care must be taken, however, not to overwhelm operators with a large amount of marginally relevant or irrelevant information [329].

Feedback to Update Mental Models. The HMI must provide operators with information about the state of the system and feedback about any changes that may occur so that their mental models can be updated. For example, an avionics system during an automatic approach may display an enlarged runway while obliterating the rest of the scene. In case something goes wrong, the image is dislocated and the pilot takes over manual control. The assumption here is that the pilot will take over having already analyzed the situation [168].

Another example of the use of feedback to update user models is signaling bystanders when a machine is powered up so that they will know that it has power and can move. A continuous signal (such as a light), however, is easily ignored. Light or sound could also be used to warn people about proximity to a hazardous zone. For some machines, it is possible to slow the operation speed when humans enter a hazardous area so they know their arrival has been observed [328].

More generally, an automated control system used to maintain safety should provide real-time indication to operators or other appropriate people that it is functioning, and it should also provide information about its internal state (such as the status of the sensors and actuators), its control actions, and its assumptions about the state of the system. Any processing that requires several seconds should provide a status indicator so the operator can distinguish processing from failure [45]. In a system where rapid response by operators is necessary, timing requirements must be placed on the feedback information that the operator uses to make decisions.

The status of safety-critical components or variables should be highlighted in some way and presented unambiguously and completely. If an unsafe condition is detected by the automated system, the operator should be told what anomaly was detected, what action was taken, and the current system configuration. Overrides of potentially safety-critical failures or any clearing of the status data should not be permitted until all of the data has been displayed and perhaps not until the operator has acknowledged seeing it. For example, a system may have a series of faults that can be overridden safely if they occur singly, but multiple faults could result in a hazard. In this case, the operator should be made aware of all safety-critical faults prior to issuing an override command or resetting a status display. After an emergency stop, Askren and Howard suggest the operator should be required to complete a restart sequence before any machinery is activated; the machines should not simply go to the next operation after activation [14].

When safety interlocks have been removed or bypassed for tests or maintenance, as stated in Chapter 15, the computer (or operator) should verify that the interlocks have been restored prior to resumption of normal operation. While the overlocks are being overridden, their status should be displayed on the operator's or tester's console [45].

Feedback to Detect Faults.   Appropriately presented feedback is also necessary for the operator to monitor for faults and errors. If a human operator must monitor computer decision making, then the computer must make decisions in a manner and at a rate that the operator can follow [17]. If this constraint is not enforced, the operator will not be able to follow the system's decision sequence to detect disagreements and trace them back through the sequence to determine their origin. This result has important implications for maintaining operator confidence in the automated system. A loss of confidence may lead to the operator disconnecting the automatic system, perhaps under conditions where that could be hazardous (such as during certain critical points in an automatic landing of an airplane). When the operator can observe on the displays that proper corrections are being made by the automated system, he or she is less likely to intervene inappropriately, even in the presence of disturbances that cause large control actions.

Some human factors experts warn against forcing operators to adopt a management-by-exception strategy, where the operator waits for alarm signals before taking action. This strategy does not allow operators to prevent disturbances by looking for early warnings and trends in the process state. Also, according to experimental studies by Swaanenburg and colleagues, it is not the strategy adopted by operators as their normal supervisory mode [329]. For operators to anticipate undesired events, they need to be continuously updated about the process state so that the system progress and dynamic state can be monitored. A display that provides only an overview and no detailed information about the state may not provide the information necessary for detecting imminent alarm conditions. The problem of feedback in emergencies is complicated by the fact that disturbances may lead to the failure of sensors, and thus the information available to the operator (or to an automated system) becomes increasingly unreliable as the disturbance progresses.

Ease of Interpretation

Although it seems intuitively correct that information should be provided to the operator in a form that can be quickly and easily interpreted, this assumption may not always be true. If rapid reactions are needed, an easily interpreted display is best; however, some psychological research shows that cognitive processing for meaning leads to better information retention. A display that requires little thought and work on the part of the operator may not support acquisition of the knowledge and thinking skills needed in abnormal conditions [278].

Preparing for Failure

Once operators have learned to work with computer displays, serious problems can arise when these displays fail or are not available during abnormal conditions and emergencies. Humans become dependent on automated systems, although training and practice for equipment failure can reduce this problem. This dependence has two implications for the HMI designer.

First, alternative sources of information need to be provided in case the computer-based system fails. For example, manual stations might be provided that allow the operator to manipulate control valves in situations such as the failure of the automatic controls [172]. It has even been suggested that direct wired displays be used for the main process information and computer displays for quantitative detail [17]. In addition, alternative sources of information provide the operator with a way to detect measuring errors. Displays that provide more detailed or extra data about individual process units, for example, can help in this task.

Second, care should be taken that instrumentation meant to help the operator deal with a malfunction is not disabled by the malfunction itself. This is the familiar common-mode failure problem rearing its head again. As an example of this problem, an engine and pylon came off the wing of a DC-10, severing cables that controlled the leading edge flaps and also four hydraulic lines, which disabled several warning signals, including a flap mismatch signal and a stall warning light [259]. If the crew had known the slats were retracted and had been warned of a potential stall, they might have been able to save the plane.

Alarms

When the automated system detects an anomalous condition or event, the operator should be informed of the current system state, the anomaly that occurred, and any action that might have been taken in response to it [45]. As discussed previously, automatic control can hide failures and errors until they are beyond the operator's ability to recover. Therefore, an automated system should monitor for any unusual events or recovery actions and either fail obviously or make any graceful degradation visible to the operator.

Alarms are used in control systems to alert operators to events or conditions in the system or controlled process. They are especially important in systems where operators must respond quickly to low-probability events for which they may not be watching. In complex systems, more devices or conditions may need to be monitored than is practical:

> It has been stated that man is a poor monitor, yet for detecting some situations, man is clearly superior to any automatic monitor. If he does have monitoring difficulty in large transport aircraft, it would appear to arise from the requirement that he monitor a large number of systems and perform other duties at the same time. In spite of many laboratory studies showing the parallel processing capabilities of the human, pilots generally perform many of their tasks as single-channel processors, especially when a task is somewhat out of the ordinary. It is not uncommon, for example, to see pilots concentrate on lateral navigation during a difficult intercept maneuver, to the exclusion of airspeed control [354, p.1007].

Alarms and warnings allow a large number of variables to be monitored at the same time.

Designing good alarm systems is difficult. Lees believes that the alarm system should have a properly thought out philosophy that relates the variable alarmed; the number, types, and degrees of alarm; and the alarm displays and priorities to factors such as instrument failure and operator confidence, the information load on the operator, the distinction between alarms and statuses, and the action that the operator has to take [172].

The "green board" is a human factors ideal denoting a control panel that produces a signal only when it communicates significant information. This ideal is seldom reached:

> At any given time, dozens of enunciator lights may be lit, all of them signaling conditions that are expected and are of no particular consequence to the operation of the plant; these lights can mask the signals from a few indicators that show something is awry . . . To make a perfect green board is difficult because a condition that is normal at one stage of operation may be a symptom of malfunction at another time. Nevertheless, there is room for much improvement in the signal lights that are designed to alert the operators, but that, like the boy who cried wolf, may be ignored because they so often proclaim there is a problem when none exists [19, p.169].

Lewis describes an *incredulity response* where, in the rare event of a major accident, it is common for an operator not to believe that an accident is taking place: The operator is more likely to think that a problem with the instruments or alarms has caused a spurious signal. When the operators have been subjected to a substantial number of false alarms, a real one may very well not be believed [189].

Systems should be designed to keep spurious alarms to a minimum and straightforward checks provided to allow operators to distinguish accidents from faulty instrument performance. In order to issue alarms early enough to avoid drastic countermeasures, the alarm limits must be set close to the desired operating point. This goal is difficult to achieve for some dynamic processes that have fairly wide operating ranges, and it also adds to the problem of spurious alarms. In addition, measurements of variables that indicate the status of the process always contain some statistical and measurement errors.

When response time is not critical, most operators will attempt to check the validity of the alarm [354]. Providing information in a form such that this validity check can be made quickly and accurately, and not become a source of distraction, increases the probability of the operator acting properly. Validity checks must also be possible on the alarm system itself—for example, quick checks of sensors and indicators such as a simple "press to test" for smoke detectors. Lewis argues that, in some situations, safety actions should be mandated even though the operator may believe that malfunctioning instruments are the cause of the problem.

Alarms certainly have an important part to play in alerting an operator to a problem, but too many alarms may have just the opposite effect. The ease with which alarms can be added and the number of parameters that can be checked in automated systems encourages installing them in large numbers in order to produce a feeling of safety. A study of two refineries between 1983 and 1986 found that alarms were not rare [329]; in fact, most operators considered a rate of five to seven per hour as normal. A shift supervisor testified at the TMI hearings that the control room never had less than 52 alarms lit [143]. Swaanenburg and colleagues note that having to push an ALARMS ACKNOWLEDGE button one to five times per minute leaves an operator with little time to do anything else [329]. In addition, too many alarms will cause confusion and lack of confidence.

Although the TMI accident is widely believed to have been the result of operator error, the control room design is just as likely a reason for the operator problems, as discussed in previous chapters. Patrick Haggerty, a member of the commission that investigated the accident, concluded: "What was apparent about the accident was that if a hundred alarms go off in the first two minutes and they all look alike, and some of them are important and some are not, then there's something wrong with the control room" (quoted in [193, p. 52]).

In fact, too many alarms can elicit exactly the wrong response and interfere with operator action to rectify the problems that caused the alarms. This phenomenon is demonstrated by the CHIRP report in Chapter 6 of a pilot who, during an emergency, was so overwhelmed by all the alarms and their verbal assault that he could not talk to his copilot and was tempted to try to eliminate the cacophony first rather than focus on the main problem.

Patterson [257] notes further that a review of the existing situation showed that this pilot's complaints were justified: Some of the aircraft had as many as 15 auditory warnings, they were not conceived as a set, and there was no internal structure to assist the learning and retention of the warnings. A number of the warnings produced sound levels over 100 dB at the pilot's ear and virtually all of them came on instantaneously at their full intensity. In addition, if two of the warnings came on simultaneously, they produced a combined sound that made it difficult to identify either of the conditions involved. From his experiments on aural warnings, Patterson concludes that the number of immediate-action warning sounds should not exceed about six, and each sound should have a distinct melody and temporal pattern.

There are some other general principles for the design of alarm systems. First, routine alarms should be easily distinguishable from safety-critical alarms. Often, it is important to ensure that the operator cannot clear a safety-critical alert without taking corrective action or performing subsequent actions required to complete an interrupted operation [44]. The Therac-25 human–computer interface allowed operators to proceed with treatment five times after error messages simply by pressing one key on their keyboard. No distinction was made between errors that could be safety critical (such as the one indicated by the MALFUNC-TION 54 message that resulted in the accidents) and those that were not. More generally, alarms might be categorized as to which are of the highest priority. The format of the alarm (such as auditory cues or message highlighting) should indicate the degree of urgency.

In addition, alarms with more than one mode, or more than one condition that can trigger the alarm for the mode, must clearly indicate which condition is responsible for the alarm display [354]. Again, with the Therac-25, one message—MALFUNCTION 54—meant that the dosage given was either too low or too high, without providing information to the operator about which had occurred. In general, determining the cause of an alarm may be difficult. In complex, tightly coupled plants, the point where the alarm is first triggered may be far away from where the fault actually occurred.

Proper decision making often requires knowledge about the timing and sequencing of events. However, because of system complexity and built-in time delays due to sampling intervals, information about conditions and events is not always timely or even presented in the sequence in which the events actually occurred. Complex systems are often designed such that monitored variables are sampled at a frequency appropriate for their expected response to events and state changes. Some variables may be sampled every few seconds; for others the intervals may be measured in minutes. Therefore, changes of state variables are not necessarily recorded at the time or in the sequence when they occur. In addition, changes that are negated within the sampling period may not be recorded at all. Thus, events become separated from their circumstances, both in sequence and time [41].

At Three Mile Island, more than a hundred different alarm lights were lit on the control board, each signaling a different malfunction, but providing little information about sequencing and timing. Brookes [41] claims that it is common for operators to suppress alarms in order to destroy historical information whenever they need real-time alarm information for current decisions. So many alarms occurred at TMI that the computer printouts were running hours behind the events and at one point jammed, losing valuable information.

Although the problem of sampling intervals is not entirely solvable (except by not using sampling), as much temporal information as possible about the events and state changes occurring in the system should be provided to operators.

The proliferation of alarms and the problems of false alarms have led to the development of sophisticated disturbance and alarm analysis systems. The problem is most serious in nuclear power plants, and alarm analysis was pioneered by the nuclear energy industry [172]. At the Wylfa Nuclear Power Station, for example, there are two reactors, each with approximately 6,000 fuel channels, 2,700 mixed analog inputs, and 1,900 contacts. Alarm analysis essentially involves identifying and displaying a *prime cause* alarm along with associated *effect* alarms. Determining such a relationship between alarms is difficult: A team of engineers studies the various situations that can occur in the plant and the alarms to which these give rise. Incompleteness in this analysis can lead to serious problems. Rasmussen says that it may be extremely difficult, if not impossible, for the designers of the plant to conduct an analysis that considers not only all possible failures in the plant and in the instrumentation, but also all combinations of failures. If the analysis is to be useful and not mislead the operator, thus causing even more problems than it attempts to solve, it must be comprehensive and include low probability hazardous conditions.

Weiner and Curry [354] ask whether the necessarily complex logic in automated alarm analysis is too complex for operators to perform validity checks and thus leads to overreliance on the system. They also worry that the priorities might not always be appropriate and that operators might not recognize this fact.

Alarm analysis, furthermore, does not solve the potential problem of operators relying on alerting and warning systems as primary rather than back-up devices. After studying thousands of near accidents reported voluntarily by aircraft crews and ground support personnel, one U.S. government report recommended that the altitude alert system (an aural signal) be disabled for all but a few long-distance flights. Investigators found that this signal had caused decreased altitude awareness in the flight crew, resulting in more frequent overshoots—instead of leveling off at 10,000 feet, for example, the craft continues to climb or descend. A study of such overshoots noted that they rarely occur in bad weather, when the crew is most attentive [259, 233].

Norman contends that alarms have been overused. Instead, he suggests

> What is needed is continual feedback about the state of the system, in a normal natural way, much in the manner that human participants in a joint problem-solving activity will discuss the issues among themselves. This means designing systems that are informative, yet non-intrusive, so that interactions are done normally and continually, where the amount and form of feedback adapts to the interactive style of the participants and the nature of

the problem. We don't know how to do this with automatic devices: Current attempts tend to irritate as much as inform, either failing to present enough information or presenting so much that it becomes an irritant [242, p.143].

Feedforward Assistance and Decision Aids

An automated system may provide feedforward information as well as feedback. Predictor displays show the operator one or more future states of process parameters, as well as their present state or value, through a fast-time simulation of a mathematical model or through a cause–consequence diagram that projects forward the progression of a disturbance if nothing is done about it. Such displays can also provide information about the future effects of a particular control action.

The goal of the predictor display is to provide information to operators rather than to tell them what to do. Moray [228] argues that by getting an estimate of the future states of the system, operators can use their time better since they can detect situations when certain variables are likely to be in a normal state and thus need not be observed. This approach seems rather dangerous because it puts a great deal of reliance for safety on the accuracy of the predictor displays and may lull the operators into complacency about the operation of the system.

Predictions can only deal with predetermined sequences, some of which had to be determined even before the system or plant was built and commissioned. Humans can vary their mental models of the system state through feedback about changing conditions or about errors in the original models. But prediction software cannot do this without some special effort and without providing feedback about their performance to the designers.

For these reasons, predictor displays may be most useful in training environments, but Banks and Cerven [18] claim that an operator's performance under stress may be less affected by predictor displays than by conventional displays.

Automated assistance can also be provided in the form of procedural checklists and guides for operations, especially nonroutine operations such as startup, shutdown, and various types of emergency operations that are often associated with accidents. In addition, decision aids may (1) diagnose underlying causes of events and their importance to safe continued operation, (2) outline alternative actions available and provide additional information such as how changes in important variables affect these actions, and (3) suggest an optimal solution.

While this type of information is useful for novice operators, overreliance is also possible. From a performance standpoint, if the steps can be prespecified with exactitude, they can and should just be automated. From a safety standpoint, automation might not be the best approach because of the problems that arise when humans act as monitors: If there are few failures, they will lose vigilance; if there are many failures, they will lose confidence.

Even if some human input is required so that the procedures are not totally automatic but require some thought, reliance on computer guidance may still reduce operator vigilance. Sometimes, steps that can be automated are not, in order to provide the human supervisor with "some room for interpretation in light of his knowledge about the process or objectives that are not shared by the computer" [312]. The question is whether this interpretation will actually be done. An assumption often made in the design and use of decision aids is that operators will continue to perform an internal simulation using their own mental models and will compare this result with the computer simulation and suggested control actions. This assumption is not realistic if few discrepancies are found over time between the computer simulation and the operator's mental simulation, and the operator then starts to rely on the decision aid.

Again, care must be taken to distinguish between providing help and taking over or so simplifying the operator's job that the risk of human error is increased. Automated advice might best be provided only when requested, and serious consideration should be given to designing in ways that keep humans from becoming overly dependent. Operators need to feel they are in charge of the overall system. According to Rouse and Morris, achieving this goal requires that outputs be expressed in terms of advice or suggestions rather than as commands or strict procedures. "By avoiding outputs that are dictatorial, in practice or even only in spirit, the operator can still be innovative when necessary" [300, p.282].

Another problem with decision aids is that, when following advice, an operator's reactions are slower and less integrated than when the operator generates the sequence of activity [17]. In addition, the operator is not getting practice in making decisions. Without this practice, humans often lack the confidence or skills to intervene when the automation fails or errors are detected. Finally, decision aids may increase the load on the operator without providing equivalent help. Ephrath reported a study in which system performance got worse with computer aids because the operator made the decision anyway; checking the computer merely added to the operator workload [17].

17.4.2 Information Presentation

Most systems built today use computer displays in the HMI, which expands the possibilities for data presentation to the operator. Advanced types of displays are under development. An experimental U.S. Army project, called the Light Experimental Helicopter (LHX), illustrates some of the changes that are occurring:

> Instead of facing rows of gauges, the pilot will have two or three CRT monitors displaying only cautions and warnings or specifically requested information. . . . Designers have learned that pilot's CRT menu should be simple and limited to a couple of pages. Other interfaces are likely to include a limited voice-recognition control system that can handle between 20 and 200 spoken commands, and a helmet-mounted display conveying pictorial and digital information—all the information needed to fly the plane. These systems and their characteristics are driven by pilot workload [317].

While computer displays allow (and require) many new ways of displaying information to operators, to optimize safety the displays should reflect what is known about how information is used and what kinds of displays are likely to cause human error. The computer displays mediate the HMI, and even slight changes in the way information is presented can have dramatic effects on performance.

For example, Lees [172] describes several ways in which humans perform diagnostic tasks. Frequently, an operator responds only to the first alarm generated. This response utilizes a simple rule-based strategy (in Rasmussen's terms) where the alarm is associated with a particular fault and the operator responds using a rule of thumb. Although incomplete, this strategy may be successful in a large proportion of cases, especially where a particular fault occurs frequently.

A second diagnosis strategy is to apply static or dynamic pattern recognition to the control panel displays. Static pattern recognition uses instantaneous observation of the displays and matches the pattern to model patterns or templates for different faults. More complex pattern recognition matches the development of the fault over time with dynamic patterns.

A third diagnosis strategy is to use some type of mental decision tree, where particular branches of the tree are taken depending on instrument readings. A fourth and final strategy described by Lees is for the operator to manipulate the controls and to observe the effect on the plant.

The diagnostic strategy used has an effect on both training (Duncan has developed training methods for fault diagnosis that reflect different diagnostic strategies [70]) and display design. For example, the conventional control panel assists in the recognition of static patterns, but computer consoles do not. Chart recorders aid the recognition of dynamic patterns and instrument faults [172]. When monitoring complicated processes, good operators will scan the displays in order to anticipate undesirable events as much as possible instead of waiting for alarm signals [138]. Conventional rows of recorders and indicators (with normal values aligned horizontally) are appropriate for this purpose. In contrast, computer consoles require selection of screen, variable identification and requests, and more detailed mental models [138]. Johannsen and colleagues report rumors of critical incidents that occurred because operators missed important information that did not happen to be on the screen.

Sequential vs. Parallel Presentation

Richardson [291] argues that there is a limit to how much information operators can absorb at any one time and that the display of too much information can be counterproductive. He concludes that there are advantages to systems in which operators have to call for the particular information they think they need. However, such arguments have to be carefully evaluated. A great deal of information can be absorbed relatively easily when it is presented in the form of patterns. Requiring operators to request information specifically, besides the obvious time delay problems, has serious negative implications in terms of missing important information and reducing the possibility of detecting important patterns. Herry warns of the danger in replacing traditional control panels in which a range of information is presented in a way that may help operators to update their mental models of the state of the plant.

In addition, computer displays typically have to be requested and accessed sequentially by the user, a procedure that Bainbridge has noted makes greater memory demands upon the operator, negatively affecting difficult decision-making tasks [17]. With conventional instrumentation, all process information is constantly available to the operator, and an overall view of the process state can be obtained by a glance at the console. Detailed readings are needed only if some deviation from normal conditions is found. The process overview display on a computer console, where only certain variables are displayed and in a digital format, is not equivalent [246]: The overview is more time-consuming and strenuous to read and remember. To obtain additional information about a limited part of the process, the operator has to select consciously among displays.

In a study of HMIs in the process industry, Swaanenburg and colleagues found that most operators considered a computer display more difficult to work with than conventional parallel interfaces, especially with respect to getting an overview of the process state. In addition, operators felt the computer overview displays were of limited use in keeping them updated on task changes; instead, operators tended to rely to a large extent on group displays for their supervisory tasks. Swaanenburg and colleagues conclude that a group display, showing different process variables in reasonable detail (such as measured value, set point, and valve position), clearly provided the type of data operators preferred.

Operators were able to do their job using computer consoles, but they tended to feel less confident using them when they were working under pressure during process disturbances. They stressed the advantage of parallel information presentation on multiple screens under these conditions, instead of on a single screen. Keeping track of the progress of a disturbance is very difficult with sequentially presented information [329]; overview displays provided too low a resolution level to be useful. Bainbridge suggests that operators should not have to page between displays to obtain information about abnormal states in the parts of the process other than the one they are currently thinking about; nor should they have to page between displays that provide the information needed for a single decision process.

Flexibility

A positive aspect of computer displays is that they are flexible: The information shown can be adapted to the current task and process conditions [138]. Moreover, dialog between humans and computers can be designed in many different ways. At one extreme, the human can select from menus; at the other extreme, the computer can react to commands initiated by the human. In between these two extremes are mixed-initiative dialogues in which both the human and computer initiate prompts for each other. For controlling dynamic systems, Rouse suggests that command-driven dialogues are best, with a mixed-initiative alternative for special situations, such as when the human has made a mistake [301].

Interpretation of Displayed Information

The format of information is sometimes changed by computer displays in a way that creates problems for operators. An assumption seems to be common that humans are able to process and react to absolute values. Psychological evidence, however, suggests that human operators are more likely to react to change and will tend to process patterns of events, either visual, conceptual, temporal, or strategic [256].

Increasing the amount of internal processing can increase the amount of time it takes for operators to interpret displays and it can also lead to interpretation errors. Almost everyone is familiar with the increased difficulty of determining how much time is left before some deadline using the digital displays on new watches as opposed to watches with analog displays. At the same time, the digital displays make it easier to evaluate absolute time. Determining which activities are most common, most important in terms of safety, and most error prone can help in deciding on the proper format of displays. Digital displays are not necessarily better than their analog counterparts.

Moray recommends directly displaying the probability of normality rather than the values of the state variables themselves [228]. But while this display might reduce workload, it might also reduce the operators' ability to detect errors in displays by reducing information that enhances error-checking.

Since reaction to displays can be influenced by expectations and assumptions, designs should reflect normal tendencies and expectations. For example, people expect that on a vertically numbered instrument, the higher value numbers will be at the top, and they expect values to increase clockwise. These expectations may change with culture—Americans expect that moving a light switch upward will turn on the light while Europeans expect just the opposite. When under stress and in emergency situations, humans tend to revert to stereotype and react in ways that are consistent with their normal expectations even when recent training has been to the contrary. Figure 17.3 shows some examples of confusing design taken from real control panels in nuclear power plants [127].

Icons with a standard interpretation should be used. Researchers have found that icons often pleased system designers but irritated users [138]. Air traffic controllers, for example, found arrow icons for directions useless and preferred numbers. Whenever possible, software designers should mimic the standard displays with which operators have become familiar instead of trying to be creative or unique.

Norman's concept of *semantic distance*—which he divides into semantic directness and articulatory distance—is a variant of this rule. *Semantic directness* requires matching the level of description required in an interface language to the level at which the person thinks of the task. Users must always do some information processing to span the gulf; semantic distance reflects how much of the required processing is provided by the system and how much by the user. The more the user must provide, the greater the distance to be bridged [131]. For example, suppose a operator's intent is to control how fast the water level in a

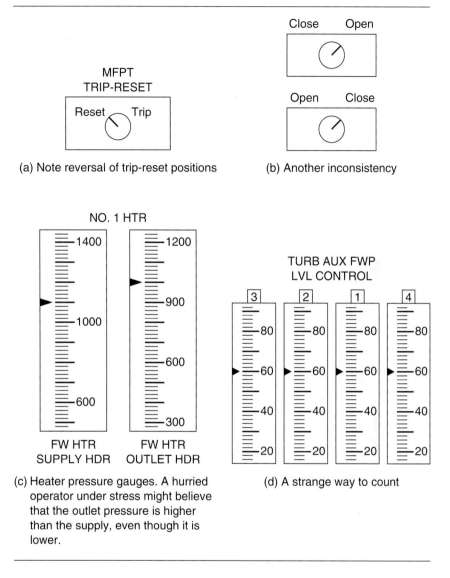

(a) Note reversal of trip-reset positions   (b) Another inconsistency

(c) Heater pressure gauges. A hurried
operator under stress might believe
that the outlet pressure is higher
than the supply, even though it is
lower.

(d) A strange way to count

FIGURE 17.3
Examples of poor designs seen in real control rooms.

tank rises. The operator issues some controlling action and observes the result. If the output shows only the current value, the operator has to observe the value over time and mentally compare the values at different times to determine the rate of change. Displaying the rate of change directly would reduce the mental workload.

Either (1) the designer can design an interface that moves toward the user's mental model, making the semantics of the input and output languages match that of the user or (2) the user can develop competence by building new mental structures to bridge the gulf. The latter requires that the user automate the response sequence and learn to think in the same language as that required by the system [131]. It seems reasonable to assume that minimizing semantic distance and designing to minimize the amount of learning and change required on the part of the user will reduce the potential for human error.

Norman also defines the concept of *articulatory distance*, which has to do with the relationship between the user's intentions and the meanings of expressions. Interface languages should be designed such that the physical form of the vocabulary items is structurally similar to their meanings. The goal of articulatory directness is to couple the perceived form of action and meaning so naturally that the relationships between intentions and actions and between actions and output seem straightforward and obvious. An example is using a moving graphical display rather than a table of numbers.

Layouts

Obviously, operator displays and interactions should be clear, concise, and unambiguous. At Three Mile Island, red lights sometimes indicated a satisfactory state of affairs and at other times that something was wrong. Some control panels use the color red to signify three different states: emergency, warning, and normal [127].

In general, the relative position of controls is a stronger cue than shape, which is stronger than color. Labels are the least perceptive [192], and, when used, they should be brief, bold, simple, and clear. Some labels may need to be repeated. The design should make use of color-coding, highlighting (such as blinking), and other attention-demanding devices for safety-critical information. Bilcliffe comments that some designers seem oversold on uniformity, using row upon row of identical switches, lamps, gauges, and meters, which invite human errors [27]. Displays that are used a relatively large fraction of time should be centrally placed, and displays that are often used together should be placed near each other or integrated into a single display [301].

For easy identification, a particular system variable should be allocated to a specific area of the computer screen (spatial coding) using windowing or other presentation devices. Johannsen and colleagues suggest that within the window, different types of information can be displayed about the relevant process variables corresponding to different operational tasks [138].

Warning displays should be simple and brief. Dramatic warning devices, such as flashing lights and loud sounds, are often used to indicate potential problems, but too many attention-grabbing signals can be distracting and have a negative effect, as discussed earlier. In general, designs should be avoided that place undue stress on the operator and cause fatigue, such as glare, inadequate lighting, vibration, or noise.

Bainbridge [17] also suggests that designers of sophisticated displays should concentrate on making them compatible rather than attempting to display independently what is best for each individual function without considering its relation to information for other functions. All the controls on a panel or screens on a computer display may be well chosen for their intended individual functions, but their arrangement or use together may increase errors or operator reaction times.

Many of the design principles described in this section stress the disadvantages (in terms of safety) of computer displays. Indeed, Lees notes that the transition from the conventional control panel to the computer console involves some serious human factors losses [172]. On the positive side, however, a standard principle of human factors design is that an operator is aided by a control panel that mimics the physical layout of the plant. The flexibility and graphics capabilities of computer displays allow them to achieve this goal much better than do standard displays, and they create exciting possibilities for displaying information in a way that greatly helps the operator diagnose malfunctions and their likely effects. For example, graphical displays allow the status of valves to be shown within the context of piping diagrams, and perhaps even allow the display of the flows of materials. Plots of variables may be shown, highlighting important relationships. The use of graphics in pilot displays of runways in automated approaches, described earlier in this chapter, is another example. Operators can get a much better picture of the state of the plant or system in this way. Lees issues a warning, however:

> Computer graphics now make it possible to create displays which previously could not be contemplated. It is to be hoped that engineers will exploit these possibilities to the full. It is emphasized again, however, that the starting point should be consideration of the operator's tasks and problems, and that a display should evolve as a solution to these. Otherwise, there is the danger that the display will be a solution looking for a problem [172, p.384].

Much still needs to be learned about the best way to display information in the HMI. Computer displays enlarge the possibilities, but mindlessly replacing standard displays with computer displays is likely to decrease safety. There may be good reasons to retain some analog information displays. A mixture of the two, with each being used to its best advantage, will probably turn out to be the safest approach.

17.5 Training and Maintaining Skills

As the role of operators changes, training must also change. Training for operators working with automated systems has to be more extensive and deep; the theory of the control system and the control and design models must be taught if the operator is to be expected to detect anomalies and then diagnose and treat them.

When software is involved, operators must also be taught the way the software operates in process terms [345]. The skill levels, in fact, go up with automated systems, not down, since the operator must have a much better understanding of the process and perhaps the underlying physics.

17.5.1 Teaching Operators about Safety Features

To enhance safety, operators must understand the safety aspects of the design, including the hazards and what has been done to mitigate them. Information about the hazard analysis can highlight for the operator the potential accidents that might occur and how they are controlled so that the operator will understand and appreciate the potential result of removing or overriding controls, changing prescribed procedures, and inattention to safety-critical features or operations [95].

Reviewing past accidents is crucial in preventing future ones. Kletz has written a series of books on accidents in the chemical process industry that analyze their causes and how similar accidents can be prevented in the future. Similar documentation should be provided for other industries. For it to be useful, the accidents cannot just be listed and superficially described: They must be carefully analyzed in depth and organized according to their causal factors and appropriate countermeasures.

Maintainers must also be taught the basic safety features of the design so that they do not accidently undo them during maintenance. Recording these features in the basic documentation is not enough; they must be translated into operational terms and integrated into training programs for both operators and maintainers.

17.5.2 Training for Emergencies

An in-depth understanding of the design and process will help the operator make correct decisions when unexpected events occur and the operator must devise creative solutions to problems that were not anticipated. Simple recognition training will not suffice to develop skills for dealing with unanticipated faults or for choosing corrective action [70]: Operators will have to be trained for general strategies rather than specific responses. Expecting the operators of complex systems to react to unfamiliar events only by consulting predetermined operational procedures is unrealistic: Standard procedures cannot cover all the possibilities, and operators will often have to improvise in emergencies. Bainbridge [17] points out the drawbacks of training operators to follow instructions and then putting them in systems to provide intelligence and problem solving. In addition to training in the control system interface commands and in the way information is obtained, operators need training in systematically looking for information to test hypotheses on possible causes of any disturbance that might arise [329].

It is not enough merely to train operators to react to a single alert or anomaly: Emergency situations usually involve a sequence of events and multiple interdependent failures (where one failure increases the probability that another will occur). Procedures for all anticipated situations must be readily understandable, and operators should be exposed to and drilled on all types of alerts and alert combinations to make sure they know how to deal with them.

Refresher courses and practice are important, not only because humans forget with disuse, but also to maintain self-confidence and eliminate the fear of intervening. Sten and colleagues, in interviews and questionnaires administered to operators in the petroleum industry, found that even experienced operators had a perceived need for training and strongly believed that training in the handling of critical situations was important [318].

Training on procedures to deal with emergency situations may need to be repeated frequently. The same applies to basic manual control skills in an automated system where the operator is expected to act as backup. In such systems, diagnosis and intervention by an operator will probably be a rare and stressful event. Under stress, humans tend to limit the alternatives they consider and to revert to habitual modes of thought and action. Thus, emergency procedures must be overlearned and continually practiced. Bainbridge [17] notes the irony that the most successfully automated systems may provide the operators with the least experience in dealing with alerts and emergencies during normal work and thus may need the greatest investment in operator training.

One of the difficulties of training for emergencies is simulating such emergencies and creating the same motivational and stressful atmosphere. While studying the handling of process disturbances in petroleum production, Sten and colleagues found that the startup period for a plant was a crucial time for acquiring high proficiency in handling process deviations and problems [318]. Operators recruited after the startup period did not get sufficient experience in managing crisis situations through daily work alone.

In some systems, operators can get hands-on practice for a short time during each shift or during an operational period (such as during flight for aircraft), and if possible, the system should be designed to allow for this practice. In other systems, hands-on control may not be possible, and the only alternative for the type of in-depth training required is to use simulators. For training in emergency response, simulators are required.

17.5.3 Simulators

Simulators allow practice with rare and unexpected events and emergencies. As noted several times, errors often occur during startup and other infrequently performed control sequences.

A nuclear-power plant may run for months with one startup and one shutdown, and during this time the operators generally perform only routine sequences of operations involving only a narrow range of power-plant operations. By contrast, the simulator can be programmed to duplicate—quite accurately—virtually any set of conditions that the plant designers can anticipate. Operators can practice the entire plant startup procedures or may begin at any point chosen by the instructor to rehearse those skills in which the operator may be deficient or out of practice. Instrument and equipment failures can be introduced [19, p.164].

Information obtained during simulator training can be used to improve the simulators and the training programs. In addition, records of the actions of the operators and the errors they make provides important information for improving the system design itself.

Simulators are also better than simple pictorial representations in training for fault detection when faults cannot be identified by the steady-state appearance of the control panel or when waiting for the steady state is not acceptable [17]. Dynamic simulators can be used to train operators to identify changes over time.

Simulators need to be realistic, of course, and to adhere to real plant performance. Before startup on some plants, simulations of real inputs to the actual control room and normal displays can be used, but mockups may become necessary after the plant goes online [6].

Simulators and training programs in general may require different facilities than those in the normal control room; the software used to aid performance will be useful for training but probably not without changes or augmentation. Duncan [70] has identified some of the unique requirements of the training environment: provision of advance information, practice accompanied by feedback, different amounts and levels of remedial help, breakdown of the task into smaller subtasks to achieve mastery, and development of appropriate learning strategies.

During the early familiarization phases of operation, performing only a subset of the tasks (while the other tasks are automated) may be an effective way to acquire operational skill in complex situations [354]. Weiner and Curry suggest that automating some of the normal operator subtasks may increase the rate of learning and the ability of operators to detect anomalies in other parts of the process, but warn that the effort required to learn to operate the automatic equipment (which may be a complex process itself) may negate some of the gains from this approach.

Specifying the requirements for simulation facilities calls for careful evaluation of the necessary conditions for acquiring different skills [278]. Learning the perceptual–motor skills of tracking plant responses to restore stability, for example, requires different simulation facilities than learning the cognitive skills of fault diagnosis. It is not at all obvious what constitutes effective simulation facilities for these and other skills in industrial process control [278].

Finally, there are problems in using simulators to train for extreme situations. Unknown faults cannot be simulated, and the system response to faults that have been predicted but never experienced may not be known [17]. But simulators can provide experience with low-probability events that may be known to the trainer but not to the trainee. In addition, although operators cannot be taught about unknown properties of the system, they *can* practice general problem solving using the information available to them.

Because the plant as built may not completely match the plant as designed and changes are inevitable with time, simulators will have to be modified and maintained, just as regular systems are. Feedback from operational experience should be continually employed to check the simulation and adjust it to reality. Because incidents and accidents often involve unexpected events, they will often require changes to the simulator. Two-way tracing between incident information systems and simulators and other training programs is important (1) to get feedback from the simulator about operator performance in order to enhance system design and (2) to get information about the system design in order to improve the simulator.

17.6 Guidelines for Safe HMI Design

Design of the HMI is discussed throughout this book. As an aid to readers, some guidelines for safer HMI design are summarized below. These guidelines are not complete, but are simply some things to think about when designing the HMI and operator training facilities for safety-critical systems.

1. Design the HMI to augment human abilities, not replace them.
2. Begin the design process by considering the operator and continue that perspective throughout.
3. Involve operators in design decisions and safety analysis throughout development.
4. Allow latitude in how tasks are accomplished.
5. Distinguish between providing help and taking over. Do not oversimplify the operator's task.
6. Design for error tolerance: (a) make errors observable (provide feedback about actions and the state of system), (b) provide time to reverse them, and (c) provide compensating (reversing) actions.
7. Maintain manual involvement or ways to update mental models.
8. Make safety-enhancing actions easy and robust. Stopping an unsafe event should be possible with a single keystroke.
9. Make potentially dangerous actions difficult or impossible.
10. Integrate critical actions into the task.
11. Make safety-critical operational steps incremental.
12. Design to stereotypes and cultural norms.
13. Provide adequate feedback to keep operators in the loop.
14. If the operator is to monitor automatic systems, provide independent information.

15. Distinguish processing from failure. Provide real-time indication that the automated control system is functioning, along with information about its internal state (such as the status of sensors and actuators), its control actions, and its assumptions about the system state.

16. Provide facilities for operators to experiment, to update their mental models, and to learn about the system. Design to enhance the operator's ability to make decisions and to intervene when required in emergencies.

17. Do not overload the operator with too much information. Provide ways for the operator to get additional information that the designer did not foresee would be needed in a particular situation.

18. Allow the operator to maintain manual involvement and to update mental models, maintain skills, and preserve self-confidence.

19. Design to aid the operator, not take over.

20. Provide feedback and interaction with the system.

21. Design tasks to be stimulating and varied, to provide good feedback, and to require active involvement of the operators in most operations.

22. Minimize activities requiring passive or repetitive action.

23. Provide multiple ways to change from an unsafe to a safe state.

24. Provide interlocks to prevent inadvertent, potentially dangerous human actions.

25. Provide error messages that distinguish safety-critical states or errors from non-safety-critical ones.

26. Distinguish the override of safety-critical and non-safety-critical error or hazard indications.

27. Provide operators with feedback if commands are canceled (not executed) because of timeouts or for other reasons.

28. Flag rather than remove obsolete information from computer displays. Require the operator to clear it explicitly or implicitly.

29. If important information changes in a very short interval before or after the operator issues a command, make sure the operator is aware of the changes.

30. Highlight the status of safety-critical components or variables and present information about the complete state in an unambiguous manner.

31. For robot systems, signal bystanders when the machine is powered up. Provide warnings when a hazardous zone is entered. Do not assume that humans will not have to enter the robot's area.

32. If the automatic system detects an unsafe condition, inform the operator of the anomaly detected, the action taken, and the current system configuration.

33. Do not permit overrides of potentially safety-critical failures or clearing of status data until all data has been displayed and perhaps not until the operator has acknowledged seeing it.

34. After an emergency stop, require the operator to go through the complete restart sequence.

35. While safety interlocks are being overridden, their status should be displayed. The design should require confirmation that the interlocks have been restored before allowing resumption of normal operation.

36. Avoid designs that require or encourage management by exception.

37. Continually update operators on the current process state.

38. Provide alternative sources of critical information in case the computer display fails.

39. Provide independent means for operators to check safety-critical information.

40. Provide multiple physical devices and logical paths to ensure that a single hardware failure or software error cannot prevent the operator from taking action to maintain a safe system state and avoid hazards.

41. Instrumentation meant to help operators deal with a malfunction should not be able to be disabled by the malfunction itself.

42. Minimize spurious signals and alarms. Provide operators with straightforward checks to distinguish hazards from faulty instruments.

43. Safety-critical alarms should be distinguishable from routine alarms. The form of the alarm should indicate the degree of urgency.

44. Clearly indicate which condition is responsible for the alarm display.

45. Provide the operator with as much temporal information about events and state changes as possible.

46. Provide scannable displays that allow operators to diagnose using pattern recognition. Provide information, if appropriate, in a form in which patterns can be easily recognized.

47. Use group displays rather than overviews. Consider using parallel information presentation on multiple screens.

48. Make all information needed for a single decision process visible at the same time (for example, put it on one display).

49. Avoid displaying absolute values: Show changes and use analog instead of digital displays when they are more appropriate. Provide references for judgment.

50. Designs should reflect normal tendencies and expectations. Use icons with a standard interpretation. Choose icons that are meaningful to users, not necessarily to designers.

51. Minimize the semantic distance between interface displays and mental models.

52. Make the physical form of the vocabulary components structurally similar to their meanings (minimize articulatory distance).

53. Apply the following precedence: (1) relative position, (2) shape, (3) color, and (4) labels.

54. Make labels brief, bold, simple, and clear.

55. Use color coding, highlighting, and other attention-demanding devices for safety-critical information.

56. Use uniformity when helpful, but don't overuse it.

57. Place frequently used displays centrally and group displays of information used together.

58. Make warning displays brief and simple.

59. Design the control panel to mimic the physical layout of the plant or system.

60. Training:
    a. Train operators to understand how the system functions and to think flexibly when solving problems. Explain hazards and the reason behind safety-critical procedures and operational rules. Introduce operators to basic system design principles and train them to think conceptually.
    b. Make sure operators understand the safety aspects of the design, including the hazards and what has been done to mitigate them.
    c. Use hazard analysis information to inform the operator about the potential result of removing or overriding controls, changing prescribed procedures, and inattention to safety-critical features or operations. Review past accidents and their causes.
    d. Provide in-depth understanding of the design of the process.
    e. Train for general strategies (rather than specific responses) to develop skills for dealing with unanticipated events.
    f. Train operators to test hypotheses in appropriate ways.
    g. Train operators in different combinations of alerts and sequences of events and not just single events.
    h. Allow for overlearning emergency procedures and for continued practice.
    i. Provide practice in problem solving.

Chapter

18

Verification of Safety

Unlike the fairy tale Rumplestiltskin, do not think that by having named the devil that you have destroyed him. Positive verification of his demise is required.

—*System Safety Handbook for the Acquisition Manager,*
U.S. Air Force

Once the hazards have been identified through hazard analysis and controlled through design, it is still necessary to determine if any mistakes were made in these processes or in the construction of the system.

For safety verification to be practical, the software must be designed to be verifiable. Chapters 15 and 16 discussed such features as (1) deterministic design to limit necessary testing and to allow reproducing test conditions and replicating the events that occur during operation, (2) identification and separation of safety-critical items and functions, (3) simplicity, and (4) decoupling. Although software can be developed and verified without these features, it will almost certainly be impossible or impractical to assure with high confidence that such software will be safe.

Most verification techniques focus on showing consistency between the code and the specification, but for safety this procedure is not enough. If a computer is treated only as a stimulus-response system, then a system quality such as safety cannot be verified. The need here is to examine not only the relationship between the computer inputs and outputs but also that between the inputs and the effect of the outputs on system behavior. Both the experience of safety engineers and empirical data suggest that errors in the design of the software–system interface rather than coding errors have the greatest impact on safety.

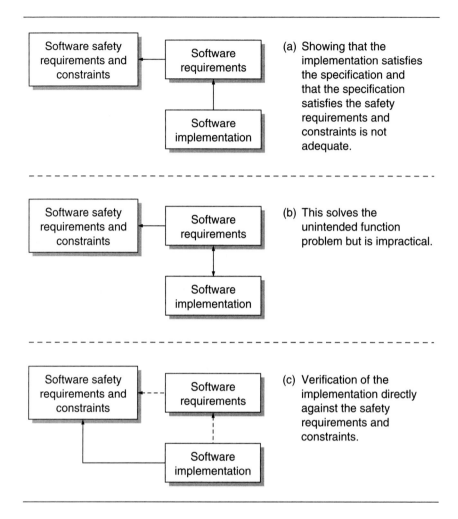

FIGURE 18.1
Alternative strategies.

Not all software errors cause hazards, and not all software that functions according to specification is safe. The goal of verification is to verify that the thing being evaluated satisfies or is consistent with some criteria. In the case of safety, the criteria are the system safety constraints and the safety-related functional requirements. These are derived in earlier steps during the hazard analysis.

It may seem that safety can be verified by showing that the functional requirements specification is consistent with the safety criteria and then just following the normal software development process to guarantee that the implementation satisfies the functional requirements. Unfortunately, this procedure is not adequate. The implementation can do *more* than what is required—it has *unintended function*—and some of that may be hazardous. Unintended function will not be caught by the usual one-way verification process (see Figure 18.1a), where the implementation is shown to satisfy the functional specification. What is needed is a two-way process to show that the implementation is identical to the requirements (Figure 18.1b). This process is much more time-consuming and difficult than the verification that is currently done and probably impractical for any but the simplest systems. In addition, it assumes that all safety-relevant software behavior is embodied in the specification, which is unrealistic.

Alternatively, the consistency between the system safety criteria and the implementation can be shown directly (Figure 18.1c). This approach also has limitations in that the identified safety criteria may be incomplete and the implementation may have behaviors that are hazardous but not restricted by the specified safety criteria. There is, unfortunately, no solution to this problem. However, this alternative approach does guarantee that at least the *identified* hazards and design features to control them are considered while the approaches in Figures 18.1(a) and 18.1(b) do not do even that much. It also has the advantage of being independent of the software requirements and design specifications and thus able to detect errors in them, such as incomplete or omitted specification of safety-critical behavior.

Hazard analysis serves as the basis for this approach to safety verification. Planning for safety verification, then, should begin early in the software development process and use the results of the hazard analysis, which will have identified the software-related system hazards and the safety-critical software modules and variables. Planning for safety verification includes devising test and verification requirements, a test recommendations report listing the items recommended for testing and the test conditions, and information for quality assurance planning about the safety-critical functions and items in the software.

As with hazard analysis, verification of safety is a continuous process. The earlier that problems are found, the easier they are to fix. Thus, the simple model in Figure 18.1(c) can be modified to allow verification to proceed as the software product develops.

The tracing of hazards should be two-way: Not only are hazards traced to the software, but during and after the verification process, the system and software hazard analyses need to be examined in light of the results from software test and analysis, human-factors analyses, reliability analyses, and other subsystem and system analyses. Both the effect of the software on the rest of the system and the effect of the rest of the system on the software need to be considered.

Two types of analysis—dynamic and static—can be used for verification of safety. In dynamic analysis, the code or a model of the code is executed and its performance is evaluated. In static analysis, the code or model is examined without being executed. In either case, remember that evaluating a representation of the code (such as a specification or other type of model) is not equivalent to evaluating the code itself. There is always the possibility that an abstraction or model has inadvertently omitted an important safety factor. In the end, high assurance can only be provided by evaluating the code running on the actual computer hardware that will be used.

18.1 Dynamic Analysis

A great deal has been written about testing. In order to limit this discussion to what is practical to include here, this chapter will focus on software and safety only. The reader is referred to any of dozens of excellent books and papers on the testing of hardware and software in general.

18.1.1 Process Considerations

Testing for safety starts with the software-related system hazards. The goal is to show that the computer will not do anything hazardous from a system standpoint. This goal requires not only testing for hazardous outputs, but testing the effectiveness of any specific (1) safety design features added to the software to eliminate or control potentially hazardous computer behavior and (2) system design features to mitigate this behavior.

Testing often is success oriented: It focuses on doing what the software is supposed to do (providing required outputs) rather than on what it is not supposed to do or on the effects of failures and errors on safety-related behavior. Erroneous inputs are often not tested, and response to hardware failures is almost never tested. Stress testing and off-nominal test cases (such as operator error, hardware failures, and software error conditions) are especially important for safety, but too often testing concentrates only on the nominal or expected situations. A study for NASA of a large sample of the software errors (discrepancy reports) in the operational Shuttle software found that problems associated with rare conditions were the leading cause of software discrepancies during the late testing stage in the sample evaluated. A better methodology for testing rare conditions during the earlier stages could have avoided half of all failures and over two-thirds of the most critical errors [115].

Although the system nature of safety implies that integration testing will be more relevant to safety, unit testing can also involve safety considerations when the safety-critical functions and constraints have been traced to individual modules and variables. Integration testing, however, is the first chance to verify the interface between the hardware and the software.

As with any testing, the requirements for safety testing should be specified early in the development cycle and should evolve as the design and hazard analysis evolves and more is learned about the system design and its hazards. Whenever possible, software safety testing should be integrated into the normal testing process. In some special cases, safety-testing facilities may be needed or may be desirable.

The tests necessary to evaluate safety are identified using information from the various safety analyses that have been performed. If a formal model of the system has been generated, test cases can perhaps be generated automatically from the model using the known hazards. In general, the following aspects of the system need to be considered:

- ☐ Critical functions and variables
- ☐ Boundary conditions
- ☐ Special features such as firewalls or safety kernels upon which the protection of the safety-critical features is based
- ☐ Incorrect and unexpected inputs and input sequences and timing (minimum, maximum, and outside the expected range)
- ☐ Reaction of the software to system faults and failures (environmental stress testing)
- ☐ Go/No-Go and fail-safe modes
- ☐ The model of the system environment that guides critical control and safety decisions
- ☐ The operator interface

Error-handling software often has errors itself because it is less likely to be exercised during testing than is the rest of the software. This problem is exacerbated when testing is used for reliability modeling and measurement because most of the test cases will deal with normal situations.

The increased probability of errors in error-handling software may be related to the reported correlation between high hardware and software failure rates [54, 134]. Connet and colleagues, for example, report that telephone switching systems with high hardware trouble rates usually also experience high software trouble rates [54]. They explain this phenomenon as most likely due to the strain placed on the software to maintain service in spite of hardware problems. The software branches and paths designed to handle these conditions are usually not as well debugged or tested as the main software paths. A partial solution to this problem is to write the error-handling software first. Often, error-handling facilities are added to the software after the main functions are coded, but by writing them first, they will be exercised frequently during the early stages of software construction when many errors are found.

Almost all real-time software is tested with environment simulators. These and other testing tools must themselves undergo a rigorous verification process. In recent testing of the first computer-based shutdown system for a nuclear power plant in Britain, the software failed almost half of the 50,000 test runs over a nine-month period [13]. The utility blamed most of the problems on errors in the test harness.

Simulators allow inducing hardware failure modes or human errors and testing the computer response to them and their effect on the system. The results of this stress testing can be used to improve the software and also to evaluate whether the computer and system response to these problems is that predicted by the analysis. Information about what hardware faults and human errors to induce might be obtained in part from built-in test results and from various types of hazard and reliability analyses.

The identification of safety-critical software modules and variables not only provides input to the test requirements, but this information can be used to trigger reviews by safety personnel. If errors are found to be related to any of the safety-critical modules or variables, a safety review should be performed. In general, any potentially hazardous output by the software during test, especially integration test, is an indication of a failure in the software development process (as it relates to safety) that needs to be investigated. Such errors may point to flaws in the process and therefore to other potential safety problems.

Whenever changes are made to the software or to the system design, complete regression testing usually is required. In addition, safety analyses of the changes must be performed, and special unit and integration tests may be necessary. If special safety testing is required, every effort should be made to integrate it into the regular testing for the change.

Safety engineering personnel should be active in the testing phase of development and directly involved in developing tests and test plans, scheduling tests, conducting tests, reviewing test results, and analyzing data. In general, safety engineers

1. Review test plans.
2. Recommend tests based on the hazard analyses, safety standards and checklists, previous accidents and incidents, interface analyses, and so on.
3. Specify the conditions under which the test is to be conducted.
4. Review the test results for any safety-related problems that were missed in the analysis or in other testing.
5. Ensure that testing feedback is integrated into the safety reviews and analyses that will be used in design modifications.

18.1.2 Limitations of Testing

Hamlet [105] and others have shown mathematically that testing for trustworthiness is an intractable task. There are so many software paths, possible inputs, and hardware failure modes that testing for all of them is not feasible. Testing may chance upon a few hazardous software errors or behaviors, but it is far from a rigorous way to identify them.

Not only is exhaustive testing impossible for most nontrivial software, but it is difficult to provide realistic test conditions. Operating conditions often differ from test conditions because testing in a real setting (such as a nuclear power plant or an aircraft that has not been built yet) is impossible. Thus, most testing must be done in a simulation mode, and there is no way to guarantee that the simulation is accurate. Assumptions must always be made about the controlled process and its environment. To complicate things further, the introduction of an automated system often changes the environment itself. Operators start to act differently than they did before they had the automated equipment. Also, testing with humans is always difficult because human reaction may differ in real emergencies due to increased stress and other factors.

In general, events may be omitted, combinations of events may not be considered or may be unknown, or probabilities of events may be estimated to be so low that they are not programmed into the simulator or test harness. Since at least half of all errors or omissions found in operational software (not just safety-critical ones) can be traced to the specification and since testing is carried out using the specification as a standard, no amount of testing can reveal these faults.

Moreover, catastrophic events happen only very rarely, when the equipment has shortcomings or is used in unanticipated environments or for inappropriate purposes. Rare events that are not anticipated by the designer are equally likely to be unanticipated by the tester.

As argued earlier, using testing to measure safety is futile. Reliability assessment of software does not assess safety. In addition, there are few if any statistics on the probabilities of events and combinations of events in systems as a whole, and reliability assessment by testing at the system level is impractical in any complex system. Accidents are rarely the result of component failure of a type that would be easy to predict through such reliability testing. Rather, the events leading to an accident are usually a complex combination of equipment failure, faulty maintenance, instrumentation and control problems, management errors, design errors, and operator errors. In fact, it may not even be possible to determine whether a particular software test result is safe or not.

These limitations of testing do not mean that we should not test or include testing in a safety program. It merely means that there is a limit to the confidence that can be acquired through dynamic analysis and that testing may have to be augmented with static analysis if that limit is less than what is required. On the other hand, static analysis is not sufficient either because it depends on mathematical analysis of models: The accuracy of the model with respect to the constructed system must be verified along with the satisfaction of the assumptions underlying the mathematical techniques.

When they are used to augment each other, dynamic analysis should focus on the things that are not covered adequately by the static analysis. For example, performance requirements, such as those involving timing and overload, are difficult to verify in a static analysis. Test planning can use the results of static analysis to determine how the testing resources should be used.

18.2 Static Analysis

Static analysis evaluates the software without executing it. Instead, it examines a representation of the software. In some ways, static analysis is more complete than dynamic analysis, since general conclusions can be drawn and not just conclusions limited to the particular test cases that were selected. On the other hand, static analysis necessarily is limited to evaluating a *representation* of a behavior rather than examining the behavior itself. Static analysis may be formal or informal.

18.2.1 Formal Verification

Formality provides the ability to reason about, analyze, and mathematically manipulate system descriptions. Just writing something down in a mathematical language, however, especially one that is not readable by engineers and application experts, will probably not have any effect on safety (as some have claimed). Proving properties, especially safety properties, about the system does have the potential for increasing assurance.

Formal verification essentially provides a proof of consistency between two formal (mathematically rigorous) specifications of a system. If one contains the safety-related properties of the system, then the other can be shown to be consistent with those safety properties. "Proof" here is used somewhat loosely—the goal is to apply careful, analytical thinking about the system description in order to convince ourselves (and others) that the description has the desired properties.

Showing consistency between the requirements and the code is not adequate to raise confidence in safety, since most safety problems stem from flaws in the requirements. Verifying the specifications and code for particular system safety properties may be possible, however. Unfortunately, we are still very limited in the properties that can be verified formally and in the size of the software that can be analyzed; the few formal verifications applied to real programs have required massive effort for relatively small software [93]. In addition, the size and difficulty of the proofs are such that they are likely to contain errors. Even published proofs of small algorithms have been found to be flawed [94, 305].

Formal verification has been applied to security properties, and some of the same techniques can be adapted to aspects of safety [180]. For example, security uses formal models and definitions of security properties along with security policies. Policy statements are rules for determining action. In safety, a safety constraint defines what constitutes a safe state in terms of system hazards and acceptable behavior. A safety policy would describe the rules for determining whether a system is safe and would use the safety constraints as a basis for decision making. An example of such a safety policy can be found in Section 15.5.

In general, the discipline required to make a careful, analytical argument about the software is probably helpful in finding problems and in raising confidence. The major drawbacks to static analysis arise simply from practicality and feasibility concerns. With advances in technology, what is possible to formally verify will surely increase. In the meantime, we need to make sure that we do not waste time and resources applying formal methods to problems that can just as easily be solved with less costly informal techniques, and that we do not overemphasize the parts of the problem that these formal techniques can handle at the expense of those parts that may be more relevant to safety. What *can* be done is much more limited than what *needs* to be done.

18.2.2 Software Fault Tree Analysis

Although mathematical proofs provide confidence, much of the benefit of formal methods can be achieved by applying an analytical process to the problem without actually generating formal proofs. Basically, this approach suggests that much can be gained by disciplined, focused, and careful thought about the process—exactly what is done in most of the hazard analysis techniques described in Chapter 14.

Unless these informal techniques are focused on safety properties, however, they are not likely to have much effect on the safety of the system. Some static analysis techniques have been promoted for software safety that are unlikely to accomplish anything more than waste resources. For example, some companies sell Software Sneak Analysis, which is a standard hardware error-detection technique (Sneak Circuit Analysis) applied to software. The software is first rewritten as "network trees" using circuit diagram symbols. Rewriting software this way seems rather strange, as much better representations exist, and most of this type of static analysis can be performed directly on the code, anyway. The network trees are then analyzed using a checklist of "clues." It appears that this procedure is merely the same type of static analysis provided by many software development environments and tools and often provided free by commercial compilers. In practice, neither Software Sneak Analysis nor the same analyses using standard software tools find many errors [313].

Looking randomly for software errors is somewhat akin to searching for a needle in a haystack, and unless the errors are related to hazards and requirements errors, it may be equivalent to searching for that needle across the street where the light is better rather than where the needle was dropped. Several people have suggested that Fault Tree Analysis, which focuses on hazards rather than on software errors in general, may be useful in analyzing software for safety. McIntee has shown how it can be applied to assembly language programs [218], while Taylor [334] and Leveson and Harvey [183] have demonstrated the technique on software written in higher-level languages.

In all of these approaches, the system fault tree process starts out in the normal way. When a leaf node describes a behavior of the computer, Software Fault Tree Analysis (SFTA) traces that behavior into the logic of the code and determines whether a path exists through the code that could cause the hazardous output. The technique does not provide a quantitative assessment; if a path to the output is found, it should be eliminated, not quantified.

SFTA uses the same backward reasoning (weakest precondition) approach used in formal axiomatic verification [67, 125], but applied slightly differently. The analytical process involves determining what must be true of the state of the

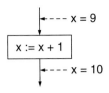

FIGURE 18.2
An example of backward reasoning about variable values.

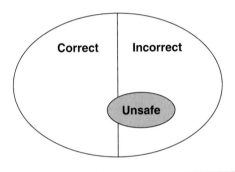

FIGURE 18.3
The relationship between correctness and safety.

computer before a statement is executed given that the state has certain properties after the statement is executed. For example, if a variable contains the value 10 after an instruction adds one to that variable, then the variable must have held the value 9 before the instruction was executed (Figure 18.2).

SFTA, in essence, follows the paths backward through the program from the hazardous outputs to identify any inputs that might cause that output (that is, it finds any legal paths through the code that produce the output). Either paths are found or, hopefully, logical contradictions are found demonstrating that the software logic cannot produce the hazardous result.

The set of states or results of a program can be divided into two sets: *Correct* and *Incorrect* (Figure 18.3). Formal proofs of correctness attempt to verify that given a precondition for the inputs and an initial computer state (before the program begins to execute), the program will halt and a postcondition (representing the desired result) will be true. In other words, they attempt to show that the program results in correct states (produces a result in set *Correct* rather than in set *Incorrect* in Figure 18.3). For continuous, purposely nonhalting (cyclic) programs, intermediate states that create output may need to be considered instead.

The basic goal of safety verification is more limited. The final states are divided into safe and unsafe rather than correct and incorrect. Unsafe states may be "correct" if the specification is flawed and includes behavior that happens to be unsafe or does not specify anything about a particular hazardous behavior—in other words, when there are specification errors or incompleteness. SFTA attempts to verify that the program will never allow an unsafe state to be reached—that is, the result is *not* in set *Unsafe*. It does not determine if program execution results in incorrect (but safe) states. One advantage of the technique is that specification flaws can be identified because the verification is against the system hazard analysis and not against the requirements or design specification.

Because the goal in safety verification is to prove that something will *not* happen, it is helpful to use proof by contradiction. This proof technique assumes that the software has produced a hazardous output and shows that this assumption leads to a logical contradiction and thus cannot happen (is contrary to the logic specified in the code). The generation of any branch in the tree can stop as soon as a contradiction is located. If a path is found through the software and out into the controlled system or its environment that does not contain a logical contradiction, SFTA reveals the input conditions necessary for this software-related hazard to occur.

As an example, SFTA of a scientific satellite control program [183] uncovered the fact that the satellite could be destroyed if the software received input from two solar pulses within 64 ms of each other. The designers and programmers had been entirely unaware that the correct operation of the software interrupt handler was based on an assumption about the minimum timing interval of the solar pulse interrupts. Although it is nearly impossible for real sun pulses to occur so close together, one of them need only be a spike induced by a gamma ray, which is a common occurrence in space electronics.

An appropriate action in this case is to add runtime assertions to detect such conditions and simply to reject incorrect or unsafe input. This check would have been trivial to add to the software if the condition had been known. In other cases, it might be most appropriate to redesign the program, to add code to initiate software recovery routines upon detection of the condition, or to redesign the noncomputer parts of the system to avoid or mitigate the effects of the hazard.

Description of the Procedure

SFTA uses fault tree templates to generate the software fault tree. The process of defining the templates is equivalent to defining the semantics of the programming language statements. Because the technique depends on the semantics of the language in which the algorithm is specified, the templates may be different for each language. A typical structured programming language is assumed in the examples presented here.

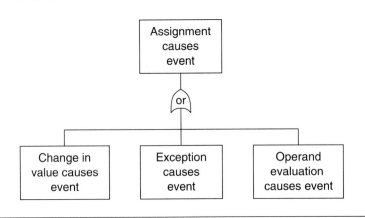

FIGURE 18.4
Template for assignment.

In each template, the statement is assumed to cause the critical event (computer state), and the tree is constructed by considering how this event might occur. As mentioned, the process is the same as that used in formal axiomatic verification, in which the weakest precondition necessary to satisfy the given postconditions is derived. In fact, SFTA is a graphical application of axiomatic verification where the postconditions describe the hazardous conditions rather than the correctness conditions. If the weakest precondition of a statement is *false*, the postcondition can never be satisfied. In SFTA, this result corresponds to a contradiction in the tree, and the analysis along that branch can be stopped. If the weakest precondition is *true*, the program will always cause the hazard to occur (given the appropriate inputs), which means that the program is inherently unsafe and must be changed. Under all other conditions, the analysis must be continued until either a *true* or a *false* is obtained or an input statement has been reached.

Consider the assignment statement template in Figure 18.4. We assume that the event has occurred within the bounds of the statement. In other words, executing the statement in some environment caused the event, so we wish to build the tree that describes that environment. The assignment statement can cause the current state to have a particular unsafe value if either the unsafe value was assigned or the evaluation of the operand caused it (such as during a function call). The template also includes a branch to examine whether an exception raised during execution of the assignment statement caused the unsafe condition or event, if the language has such a feature. Figure 18.5 shows the fault tree generated for a simple sequence of assignment statements.

Figure 18.6 shows how the analysis proceeds back through an *if* statement, and Figure 18.7 shows the fault tree for the simple statement "if $a > b$ then $x := f(x)$ else $x := 10$" when analyzed for the unsafe condition "$x > 100$". The

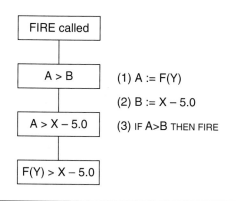

FIGURE 18.5
Example of assignment statements and simple IF.

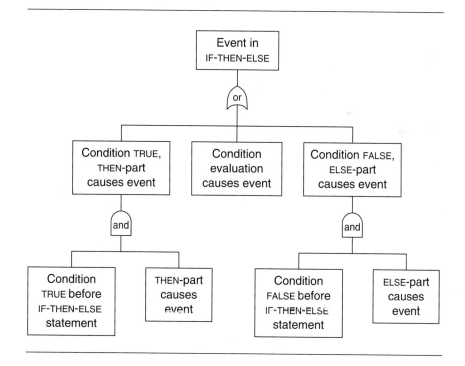

FIGURE 18.6
Template for IF statement.

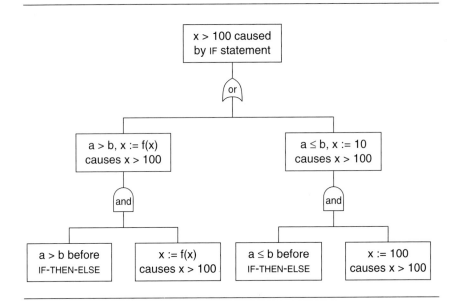

FIGURE 18.7
Example for IF statement.

right subtree describes an impossible situation and can immediately be pruned from the tree. The fault tree for this statement has essentially transformed the problem of analyzing the unsafe event or conditions into three subproblems. The analysis can stop here and assertions can be placed in the code to detect the hazardous state (in this case, $a > b$ and $f(x) > 100$), or the software prior to this *if* statement can be analyzed for ways it can generate this condition.

Fault tree templates for *while* statements and *procedure calls* are shown in Figures 18.8 and 18.9. An example of the *while* loop is shown in Figure 18.10. For the *while* statement:

> **while** $b > x$ do
>   **begin** $b := b - 1$;
> $z := z + 10$;
> **end**

and the unsafe condition "$z > 100$". The left subtree of the figure assumes that the *while* statement never executed. For this to have happened, z had to be greater than 100 initially and b less than or equal to x. The right subtree examines the modification of z within the body of the *while* statement. Letting n represent the unknown number of times the loop will execute and letting z_n be the value of z on the nth iteration, then $z_n > 100$ is the event to be analyzed within the loop. It is now necessary to find an expression for n and z_n in terms of z_0 (the original

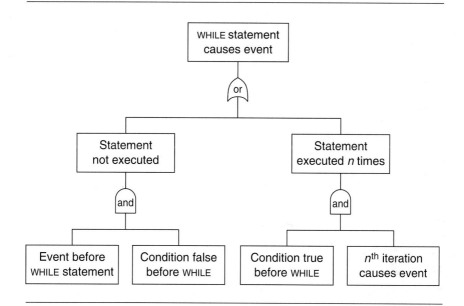

FIGURE 18.8
Template for WHILE statement.

value of z before the loop). In examining the second assignment statement of the loop, it can be seen that the loop invariant (statement always true at the beginning of each loop iteration) with respect to z is

$$z_n = z_0 + 10n \tag{18.1}$$

and after n iterations of the loop, $b_n = b_0 - n$. But $b_n = x$, since iteration stopped after n times, and hence

$$b_0 - n = x$$
$$b_0 - x = n \tag{18.2}$$

Combining (1) and (2), we get

$$100 < z_n \le z_0 + 10(b_0 - x)$$

Leveson and colleagues [182] have generated fault tree templates for Ada and have shown how they can be applied to a multitasking program.

Control is difficult to predict in a real-time system, which affects the analysis by invalidating assumptions about order of processing. For example, in an interrupt-driven system, no assumptions are made about which interrupt normally occurs before another, and so on. In the analysis, therefore, if it is determined that a particular value for x is unsafe in routine F, then all places where x is set must be analyzed for their ability to set x to that value. In effect, if a variable is ever

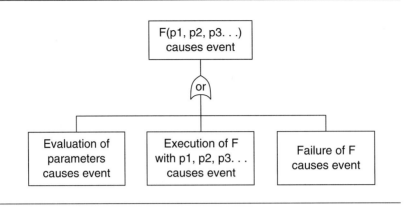

FIGURE 18.9
Template for procedure call statement.

set to an unsafe value, then the system has a hazardous scenario and that scenario must be considered.

Uses for SFTA

SFTA has been applied primarily to software code, but it could also be used for software design if the design was specified using an appropriate language. In this case, any unintended functionality added in later stages of the development process must be detected by further analyses.

In addition to finding software paths leading to hazardous outputs, SFTA can determine the conditions under which fail-safe procedures should be initiated, guide in the placement and content of runtime checks to detect hazardous software states, and facilitate effective safety testing by pinpointing critical functions and test cases. If SFTA is used with a system simulator, the critical software interfaces with the rest of the system can be identified and used to determine appropriate simulation states and events.

SFTA has been used on real software projects for each of these purposes. One example is the verification of the safety of some nuclear power plant shutdown software [34]. During the process of generating the software fault trees for this system, various internal conditions were detected that could lead to the software untripping the trip variables when they should stay tripped. These internal conditions, such as a particular variable at a certain point assuming a negative value, can be shown to be unachievable according to the logic of the code. However, the checks for such conditions were so simple (such as a change to the type definition or the use of a simple *if* statement) that it was decided to include them in the code in case (1) the SFTA process was flawed (as well as the formal verification procedure applied to the complete functionality of the software), (2) com-

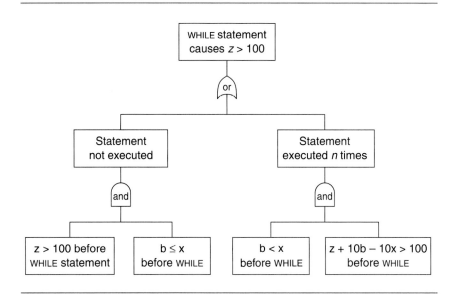

FIGURE 18.10
Example of WHILE statement.

puter hardware failures or environmental factors cause these memory locations to become negative despite the "correctness" of the software logic, or (3) the hazardous internal state is caused by other unexpected factors that never seem to be identified until after they occur and occasionally never are diagnosed. Note that the possible causes of the hazardous internal state do not need to be identified in order to identify the states themselves and to add protection.

Evaluation of SFTA

SFTA has been applied to assembly language programs as well as to software written in higher-level languages. Although SFTA appears to be practical for relatively small, industrial software at a reasonable cost, the practicality of its use on large-scale software has not been demonstrated.

Because SFTA is basically a structured walkthrough of the code with an emphasis on hazardous behavior, its practicality should be similar to that of other structured walkthough techniques. However, because the entire code is not usually safety critical, only a relatively small percentage of it may need to be examined in SFTA. If care is taken to separate and minimize critical code during the design process (as discussed in Chapter 16), the process may be simplified further.

For the scientific satellite software mentioned earlier, only 12 percent of the code needed to be examined and the analysis was completed in two days.

SFTA performed during the development of a nuclear power plant shutdown system (which has about 3,000 lines of code written in Fortran and Pascal) took about three person-months, which included the time required to become familiar with the technique. In contrast, a full formal verification of the same software using functional abstraction took 30 person-years. The engineers involved in this project concluded that SFTA was useful and easy to learn and that they would use it again. The same conclusion might not be reached for a larger project, however.

Another factor that must be considered in determining practicality is that the software fault tree need not be completed to be useful. In many cases, generation of the tree can stop before a contradiction is reached. Instead, assertions or exception conditions can be added to the code at a particular point to detect the unsafe conditions that the analysis showed could lead to the hazard if they occurred at that point in the software execution.

Adding runtime software checks is particularly useful in those applications for which procedures to fail soft or fail safe are feasible. The software fault tree provides the information necessary to determine which assertions and exception conditions are most critical, what their content should be, and where they should be placed. Because runtime checking is expensive in time and other resources, this information is extremely useful.

Even if SFTA shows that a path to a hazardous output does not exist, as stated earlier, it might be wise to include such runtime checks because they can catch errors or failures in the underlying hardware and support software (such as operating system problems). SFTA is concerned only with the safety of the code's logic and assumes that the underlying virtual machine (compiler) and hardware both operate correctly. Assertions and checks generated from the software fault tree will be directed at the runtime conditions that are the most safety critical.

In the nuclear power plant shutdown software mentioned, no hazardous paths through the software were identified, but 42 checks were added to the software where the fault tree showed that a particular state was critical (the software could fail to detect a problem and not trip the reactor when required), and the software was reorganized somewhat to make it more fault tolerant as a result of the information obtained during SFTA. If one of the runtime checks detects an unsafe state, a fail-safe hardware backup system is initiated.

The success of SFTA appears to be related to the fact that the analyst is forced to view the program in a different way than is common during development, increasing the chance for finding errors. Programmers tend to concentrate on what they want the program to do; SFTA requires consideration of what the program must *not* do. The more different ways a program is examined, the more likely that errors will be found.

SFTA also starts from a separate specification (the system fault tree) and therefore can find errors in the software requirements specification. In addition, the process of working backward through the software and out into the environment allows identification of safety-critical assumptions about the environment.

On the negative side, the analysis depends on the analyst's abilities. Much— but not all—of the analysis can be automated, and human involvement will still be required. Industrial users of the technique have commented that having people examine the code thoroughly is crucial to its effectiveness and may actually be its most important benefit. This means that completely automating the generation of the trees may not be a worthwhile goal, anyway. The process, like any walk-though, requires careful thought about the code, which may be its most important benefit.

In addition, SFTA is only a complement to and not a substitute for other verification procedures. It provides extra assurance by focusing on hazards, by forcing a different view of the software, and by starting from a different specification. Also, it usually costs much less than a complete static analysis of the code. But SFTA is no less error prone than other static-analysis techniques, and it focuses only on particular aspects of the code while not handling others very well. The size and complexity of the code for which it is practical are still unknown.

18.3 Independent Verification and Validation

Independent verification and validation (IV&V) is a process in which the products of development are reviewed by an organization that is financially, technically, and managerially independent from the developers. Often, the IV&V process and techniques differ only from regular V&V by being performed by an independent organization. The review might involve examining either the process, the product, or both.

For some special systems regulated by government agencies, hazards or hazard categories are mandated—such as the four nuclear hazards of the U.S. Department of Defense—as well as the form of IV&V. Nuclear Safety Cross Check Analysis (NSCCA) and Software Nuclear Safety Analysis (SNSA) are rigorous independent verification and validation (IV&V) procedures developed for and sometimes required on nuclear systems.

NSCCA is an adjunct to normal IV&V rather than a replacement: IV&V usually tries to show that the system does what it *is* supposed to do, while NSCCA tries to show that the system cannot do what it *is not* supposed to do.

NSCCA has procedural and technical components. The procedural component implements security and control measures to protect against sabotage, collusion, compromise, or alteration of critical software components, tools, or NSCCA results. The technical component evaluates the software using analysis and testing to ensure that it satisfies the system's nuclear safety objectives.

The first step in the technical component is a criticality analysis that maps the four nuclear safety hazards against the discrete functions of the software. Qualitative judgments are made to assess the degree to which each function affects the hazard. The program manager uses the criticality assessment to decide where to allocate resources most effectively to meet the requirements.

The criticality assessment is also used to devise an NSCCA program plan, which establishes in advance the evaluation criteria, purpose, objectives, and expected results for specific NSCCA analyses and tests, including the tools and facilities requirements, analyses requirements, test requirements, test planning, and test procedures. Then, the four nuclear hazards are broken down into specific requirements that represent the minimum positive measures necessary to demonstrate that nuclear weapon system software is predictably safe. The rest of the NSCCA technical procedure is similar to a standard IV&V, where the requirements are traced to the modules and various types of analysis and testing are performed.

SNSA is a similar iterative analysis and test process used to evaluate nuclear weapon software for its compliance with the DoD nuclear safety standards. Most of the emphasis is on testing the software and evaluating covert threats, operations, and abnormal environments.

The effectiveness of any IV&V program is determined by the specific techniques applied and the competence of those applying them. Any such after-the-fact, independent evaluation is limited usually by being applied late in the development process and by those not actually developing the software. Early feedback is crucial to building safe software.

18.4 Conclusions

Those using computers for safety-critical functions should be wary of relying too heavily on the techniques described in this chapter. All are severely limited in their ability to provide adequate assurance of safety. They are *necessary* but not *sufficient*.

It is tempting just to develop software in the usual way and then try to assure that the finished product is safe. This approach is akin to relying on downstream protection systems—the cost can be exorbitant and the assurance limited. The most practical and effective way to enhance software system safety is to follow a complete Safeware program that applies safety enhancing techniques throughout software development and maintenance.

EPILOGUE:
THE WAY FORWARD

In theory, software development should be identical to other engineering processes—we would examine known and relevant risks, and restrict our ambitions to what we knew we could handle. In practice, software invites fiendish complexity.

. . . There will be no breakthrough, indeed can be none. . . . Lacking a set of inviolable natural laws to govern what software can and cannot do, we must learn to play God. Managers and engineers must substitute their own judgment for nature's rules. The intellectual rigor applied should be as consistent and as ruthless as Newton's Second Law.

[Software] developers have always had to explain relationships within and between their systems. If they can explain those relationships with the simplicity and consistency demanded of other engineering disciplines, they will succeed. If not, it probably means that a dash for novelty has sprinted too far, too fast, and too soon.

—G. F. McCormick
When Reach Exceeds Grasp

Safety is a complex, socio-technological problem for which there will be no simple solutions. Unlike the happy endings in fairy tales, the simple, cheap, effective, and magic potion for our problems does not exist. Our solutions will require difficult and costly procedures that in turn require special knowledge and experience on the part of system developers and maintainers. Unfortunately, we have no other choice if we want to use computers to control safety-critical systems without introducing unacceptable risk.

In this book, I have tried to describe the problem and the tools and approaches at hand for solving it and to suggest ways to build safety-critical systems that include computers as an integral component. The basic approach is that used in system safety, which attempts to anticipate hazards and prevent accidents before they occur. It requires establishing appropriate managerial and organizational structures and applying safety-enhancing techniques throughout the entire software development, maintenance, and evolution process.

Certain themes run throughout the book:

- ☐ Our most effective tool in making things safer is simplicity and building systems that are intellectually manageable.

- ☐ Safety and reliability are different and must not be confused.

- ☐ Placing too much reliance on probabilistic risk assessment is unwise.

- ☐ Building safety into a system will be much more effective than adding protection devices onto a completed design. The earlier safety is considered in the development process, the better will be the results.

- ☐ To make progress, we must stop oversimplifying accidents and recognize their complex, multifactorial nature. Fixing only symptoms while leaving root (level three) causes intact will not prevent the repetition of most accidents. Concentrating on only one or a few aspects of the problem will probably not have the desired effect. In particular, concentrating only on technical issues and ignoring managerial and organizational deficiencies will not result in effective safety programs.

- ☐ Simply replacing humans with computers will not solve the safety problem. Human "error" is integrally related to human flexibility and creativity. We should be working on ways to augment human abilities with computers rather than on ways to replace them.

- ☐ Safety is a system problem and can only be solved by experts in different disciplines working together. In particular, software cannot be developed effectively in isolation from the rest of the system. Software engineers must understand system safety concepts and techniques. At the same time, system safety personnel must be more involved in software development and include software in the system safety process.

- ☐ The safety of software can only be evaluated in the context of the system within which it operates. The safety of a piece of software cannot be evaluated by looking at the software alone.

- ☐ Complacency is perhaps the most important risk factor in a system, and a safety culture must be established that minimizes it.

- ☐ Just because the events leading to an accident are not foreseen does not mean the accident is not preventable. The hazard is usually known and often can be eliminated or reduced significantly. Often a decision is made to try to eliminate the preceding events (rather than the hazards) because that would require the fewest tradeoffs with other goals, such as desired functionality or lower cost. The decisions involved are trans-scientific. But engineers have a duty to clarify the risks for decision makers and to make sure that complacency or other factors or pressures do not interfere with the engineering issues or risks being given due consideration in decision making.

- ☐ We must learn from the past so that we do not repeat the same mistakes.

Much progress in system safety is currently being made, and new editions of this book will surely be required in the future. I have attempted to describe what is currently known and practiced and to outline a Safeware program that incorporates the most promising approaches. Although the use of such a program cannot and will not eliminate all accidents, it is the best we can do with current knowledge. Hopefully, the information provided will encourage others to develop new and better approaches to reducing accidents.

APPENDICES

Medical Devices: The Therac-25 Story

A.1 Introduction

Between June 1985 and January 1987, a computer-controlled radiation therapy machine, called the Therac-25, massively overdosed six people. These accidents have been described as the worst in the 35-year history of medical accelerators [284].

A detailed accident investigation, drawn from publicly available documents, can be found in Leveson and Turner [187]. The following account is taken from this report and includes both the factors involved in the overdoses themselves and the attempts by the users, manufacturers, and governments to deal with them. Because this accident was never officially investigated, only partial information on the Therac-25 software development, management, and quality control procedures is available. What is included below has been gleaned from law suits and depositions, government records, and copies of correspondence and other material obtained from the U.S. Food and Drug Administration (FDA), which regulates these devices.

A.2 Background

Medical linear accelerators (linacs) accelerate electrons to create high-energy beams that can destroy tumors with minimal impact on the surrounding healthy tissue. Relatively shallow tissue is treated with the accelerated electrons; to reach deeper tissue, the electron beam is converted into X-ray photons.

In the early 1970s, Atomic Energy of Canada Limited (AECL)[1] and a French company called CGR went into business together building linear accelerators. The products of this cooperation were (1) the Therac-6, a 6 million electron volt (MeV) accelerator capable of producing X-rays only and later (2) the Therac-20, a 20 MeV, dual-mode (X-rays or electrons) accelerator. Both were versions of older CGR machines, the Neptune and Sagittaire, respectively, which were augmented with computer control using a DEC PDP-11 minicomputer. We know that some of the old Therac-6 software routines were reused in the Therac-20 and that CGR developed the initial software.

Software functionality was limited in both machines: The computer merely added convenience to the existing hardware, which was capable of standing alone. Industry-standard hardware safety features and interlocks in the underlying machines were retained.

The business relationship between AECL and CGR faltered after the Therac-20 effort. Citing competitive pressures, the two companies did not renew their cooperative agreement when scheduled in 1981.

In the mid-1970s, AECL had developed a radical new "double pass" concept for electron acceleration. A double-pass accelerator needs much less space to develop comparable energy levels because it folds the long physical mechanism required to accelerate the electrons, and it is more economical to produce. Using this double-pass concept, AECL designed the Therac-25, a dual-mode linear accelerator that can deliver either photons at 25 MeV or electrons at various energy levels.

Compared with the Therac-20, the Therac-25 is notably more compact, more versatile, and arguably easier to use. The higher energy takes advantage of the phenomenon of *depth dose*: As the energy increases, the depth in the body at which maximum dose build-up occurs also increases, sparing the tissue above the target area. Economic advantages also come into play for the customer, since only one machine is required for both treatment modalities (electrons and photons).

Several features of the Therac-25 are important in understanding the accidents. First, like the Therac-6 and the Therac-20, the Therac-25 is controlled by a PDP-11 computer. However, AECL designed the Therac-25 to take advantage of computer control from the outset; they did not build on a stand-alone machine. The Therac-6 and Therac-20 had been designed around machines that already had histories of clinical use without computer control.

In addition, the Therac-25 software has more responsibility for maintaining safety than the software in the previous machines. The Therac-20 has independent protective circuits for monitoring the electron-beam scanning plus mechanical interlocks for policing the machine and ensuring safe operation. The Therac-25 relies more on software for these functions. AECL took advantage of the com-

---

[1] AECL was an arms-length entity, called a crown corporation, of the Canadian government. Since the time of the incidents related in this paper, AECL Medical, a division of AECL, was privatized and is now called Theratronics International, Ltd. Currently, the primary business of AECL is the design and installation of nuclear reactors.

puter's abilities to control and monitor the hardware and decided not to duplicate all the existing hardware safety mechanisms and interlocks.

Some software for the machines was interrelated or reused. In a letter to a Therac-25 user, the AECL quality assurance manager said, "The same Therac-6 package was used by the AECL software people when they started the Therac-25 software. The Therac-20 and Therac-25 software programs were done independently starting from a common base" [187]. The reuse of Therac-6 design features or modules may explain some of the problematic aspects of the Therac-25 software design. The quality assurance manager was apparently unaware that some Therac-20 routines were also used in the Therac-25; this was discovered after a bug related to one of the Therac-25 accidents was found in the Therac-20 software.

AECL produced the first hardwired prototype of the Therac-25 in 1976, and the completely computer-controlled commercial version was available in late 1982.

Turntable Positioning. The Therac-25 turntable design plays an important role in the accidents. The upper turntable (see Figure A.1) rotates accessory equipment into the beam path to produce two therapeutic modes: electron mode and photon mode. A third position (called the field light position) involves no beam at all, but rather is used to facilitate correct positioning of the patient. Because the accessories appropriate to each mode are physically attached to the turntable, proper operation of the Therac-25 is heavily dependent on the turntable position, which is monitored by three microswitches.

The raw, highly concentrated accelerator beam is dangerous to living tissue. In electron therapy, the computer controls the beam energy (from 5 to 25 MeV) and current, while scanning magnets are used to spread the beam to a safe, therapeutic concentration. These scanning magnets are mounted on the turntable and moved into proper position by the computer. Similarly, an ion chamber to measure electrons is mounted on the turntable and also moved into position by the computer. In addition, operator-mounted electron trimmers can be used to shape the beam if necessary.

For X-ray (or photon) therapy, only one energy level is available: 25 MeV. Much greater electron-beam current is required for X-ray mode (some 100 times greater than that for electron therapy) [284] to produce comparable output. Such a high dose-rate capability is required because a "beam flattener" is used to produce a uniform treatment field. This flattener, which resembles an inverted ice cream cone, is a very efficient attenuator; thus, to get a reasonable treatment dose rate out of the flattener, a very high input dose rate is required. If the machine should produce a photon beam with the beam flattener not in position, a high output dose to the patient results. This is the basic hazard of dual-mode machines: If the turntable is in the wrong position, the beam flattener will not be in place.

In the Therac-25, the computer is responsible for positioning the turntable

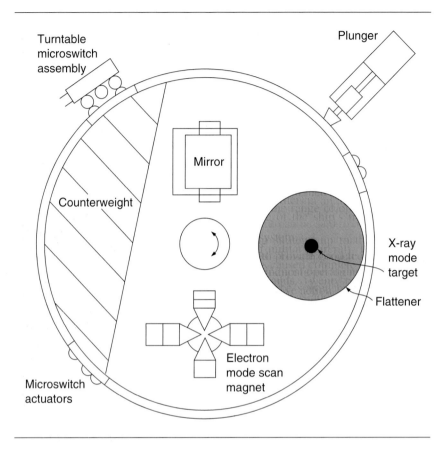

FIGURE A.1
Upper turntable assembly.

(and for checking the turntable position) so that a target, flattening filter, and X-ray ion chamber are directly in the beam path. With the target in place, electron bombardment produces X-rays. The X-ray beam is shaped by the flattening filter and measured by the X-ray ion chamber.

No accelerator beam is expected in the third or field light turntable position. A stainless steel mirror is placed in the beam path and a light simulates the beam. This lets the operator see precisely where the beam will strike the patient and make necessary adjustments before treatment starts. There is no ion chamber in place at this turntable position, since no beam is expected.

Traditionally, electromechanical interlocks have been used on these types of equipment to ensure safety—in this case, to ensure that the turntable and attached equipment are in the correct position when treatment is started. In the Therac-25, software checks were substituted for many of the traditional hardware interlocks.

```
PATIENT NAME     : TEST
TREATMENT MODE  : FIX        BEAM TYPE: X     ENERGY (MeV): 25

                             ACTUAL      PRESCRIBED
        UNIT RATE/MINUTE        0           200
        MONITOR UNITS          50    50     200
        TIME (MIN)             0.27        1.00

GANTRY ROTATION (DEG)              0.0         0      VERIFIED
COLLIMATOR ROTATION (DEG)        359.2       359      VERIFIED
COLLIMATOR X (CM)                 14.2        14.3    VERIFIED
COLLIMATOR Y (CM)                 27.2        27.3    VERIFIED
WEDGE NUMBER                         1           1    VERIFIED
ACCESSORY NUMBER                     0           0    VERIFIED

DATE  : 84-OCT-26   SYSTEM : BEAM READY   OP.MODE  : TREAT    AUTO
TIME  : 12:55:8     TREAT  : TREAT PAUSE           : X-RAY    173777
OPR ID : T25V02-R03  REASON : OPERATOR    COMMAND:
```

FIGURE A.2
Operator interface screen layout.

The Operator Interface.   The description of the operator interface here applies to the version of the software used during the accidents. Changes made as a result of an FDA recall are described later.

The Therac-25 operator controls the machine through a DEC VT100 terminal. In the general case, the operator positions the patient on the treatment table, manually sets the treatment field sizes and gantry rotation, and attaches accessories to the machine. Leaving the treatment room, the operator returns to the console to enter the patient identification, treatment prescription (including mode or beam type, energy level, dose, dose rate, and time), field sizing, gantry rotation, and accessory data. The system then compares the manually set values with those entered at the console. If they match, a *verified* message is displayed and treatment is permitted. If they do not match, treatment is not allowed to proceed until the mismatch is corrected. Figure A.2 shows the screen layout.

When the system was first built, operators complained that it took too long to enter the treatment plan. In response, AECL modified the software before the first unit was installed: Instead of reentering the data at the keyboard, operators could simply use a carriage return to copy the treatment site data [225]. A quick series of carriage returns would thus complete the data entry. This modification was to figure in several of the accidents.

The Therac-25 could shut down in two ways after it detected an error condition. One was a *treatment suspend*, which required a complete machine reset to restart. The other, not so serious, was a *treatment pause*, which only required a single key command to restart the machine. If a *treatment pause* occurred, the operator could press the Ⓟ key to "proceed" and resume treatment quickly and conveniently. The previous treatment parameters remained in effect, and no reset was required. This feature could be invoked a maximum of five times before the machine automatically suspended treatment and required the operator to perform a system reset.

Error messages provided to the operator were cryptic, and some merely consisted of the word MALFUNCTION followed by a number from 1 to 64 denoting an analog/digital channel number. According to an FDA memorandum written after one accident:

> The operator's manual supplied with the machine does not explain nor even address the malfunction codes. The Maintance [sic] Manual lists the various malfunction numbers but gives no explanation. The materials provided give <u>no</u> indication that these malfunctions could place a patient at risk.
>
> The program does not advise the operator if a situation exists wherein the ion chambers used to monitor the patient are saturated, thus are beyond the measurement limits of the instrument. This software package does not appear to contain a safety system to prevent parameters being entered and intermixed that would result in excessive radiation being delivered to the patient under treatment.

An operator involved in one of the accidents testified that she had become insensitive to machine malfunctions. Malfunction messages were commonplace and most did not involve patient safety. Service technicians would fix the problems or the hospital physicist would realign the machine and make it operable again. She said,

> It was not out of the ordinary for something to stop the machine. . . . It would often give a low dose rate in which you would turn the machine back on. . . . They would give messages of low dose rate, V-tilt, H-tilt, and other things; I can't remember all the reasons it would stop, but there was a lot of them.

A radiation therapist at another clinic reported that an average of 40 dose-rate malfunctions, attributed to underdoses, occurred on some days.

The operator further testified that during instruction she had been taught that there were "so many safety mechanisms" that she understood it was virtually impossible to overdose a patient.

Hazard Analysis. In March 1983, AECL performed a safety analysis on the Therac-25. This analysis was in the form of a fault tree and apparently excluded the software. According to the final report, the analysis made several assumptions about the computer and its software:

1. Programming errors have been reduced by extensive testing on a hardware simulator and under field conditions on teletherapy units. Any residual software errors are not included in the analysis.
2. Program software does not degrade due to wear, fatigue, or reproduction process.
3. Computer execution errors are caused by faulty hardware components and by "soft" (random) errors induced by alpha particles and electromagnetic noise.

The fault tree resulting from this analysis does appear to include computer failure, although apparently, judging from the basic assumptions above, it considers hardware failures only. For example, in one OR gate leading to the event of getting the wrong energy, a box contains "Computer selects wrong energy," and a probability of 10^{-11} is assigned to this event. For "Computer selects wrong mode," a probability of 4×10^{-9} is given. The report provides no justification of either number.

A.3 Events

Eleven Therac-25s were installed: five in the United States and six in Canada. Six accidents occurred between 1985 and 1987, when the machine was finally recalled to make extensive design changes. These changes include adding hardware safeguards against software errors.

Related problems were found in the Therac-20 software, but they were not recognized until after the Therac-25 accidents because the Therac-20 includes hardware safety interlocks. Thus, no injuries resulted.

A.3.1 Kennestone Regional Oncology Center, June 1985

Details of this accident in Marietta, Georgia, are sketchy because it was never investigated. There was no admission that the injury was caused by the Therac-25 until long after the occurrence, despite claims by the patient that she had been injured during treatment, the obvious and severe radiation burns the patient suffered, and the suspicions of the radiation physicist involved.

After undergoing a lumpectomy to remove a malignant breast tumor, a 61-year-old woman was receiving follow-up radiation treatment to nearby lymph nodes on a Therac-25 at the Kennestone facility in Marietta. The Therac-25 had been operating at Kennestone for about six months; other Therac-25s had been operating, apparently without incident, since 1983.

On June 3, 1985, the patient was set up for a 10 MeV electron treatment to the clavicle area. When the machine turned on, she felt a "tremendous force of heat . . . this red-hot sensation." When the technician came in, she said, "You burned me." The technician replied that that was impossible. Although there were no marks on the patient at the time, the treatment area felt "warm to the touch."

It is unclear exactly when AECL learned about this incident. Tim Still, the Kennestone physicist, said that he contacted AECL to ask if the Therac-25 could operate in electron mode without scanning to spread the beam. Three days later the engineers at AECL called the physicist back to explain that improper scanning was not possible.

In an August 19, 1986 letter from AECL to the FDA, the AECL quality assurance manager said, "In March of 1986 AECL received a lawsuit from the patient involved . . . This incident was never reported to AECL prior to this date, although some rather odd questions had been posed by Tim Still, the hospital physicist." The physicist at a hospital in Tyler, Texas, where a later accident occurred, reported, "According to Tim Still, the patient filed suit in October 1985 listing the hospital, manufacturer and service organization responsible for the machine. AECL was notified informally about the suit by the hospital, and AECL received official notification of a lawsuit in November 1985."

Because of the lawsuit (filed November 13, 1985), someone at AECL must have known about the Marietta accident—although no investigation occurred at this time. FDA memos point to the lack of a mechanism in AECL to follow up reports of suspected accidents [187].

The patient went home, but shortly afterward she developed a reddening and swelling in the center of the treatment area. Her pain had increased to the point that her shoulder "froze," and she experienced spasms. She was admitted to a hospital in Atlanta, but her oncologists continued to send her to Kennestone for Therac-25 treatments. Clinical explanation was sought for the reddening of the skin, which at first her oncologist attributed to her disease or to normal treatment reaction.

About two weeks later, the Kennestone physicist noticed that the patient had a matching reddening on her back as though a burn had gone right through her body, and the swollen area had begun to slough off layers of skin. Her shoulder was immobile, and she was apparently in great pain. It was now obvious that she had a radiation burn, but the hospital and her doctors could provide no satisfactory explanation.

The Kennestone physicist later estimated that the patient received one or two doses of radiation in the 15,000 to 20,000 rad (radiation absorbed dose) range. He did not believe her injury could have been caused by less than 8,000 rads. To understand the magnitude of this, consider that typical single therapeutic doses are in the 200 rad range. Doses of 1,000 rads can be fatal if delivered to the whole body; in fact, 500 rads is the accepted figure for whole-body radiation that will cause death in 50 percent of the cases. The consequences of an overdose to a smaller part of the body depend on the tissue's radio-sensitivity. The director of radiation oncology at the Kennestone facility explained their confusion about the accident as due to the fact that they had never seen an overtreatment of that magnitude before [308].

Eventually, the patient's breast had to be removed because of the radiation burns. Her shoulder and arm were paralyzed, and she was in constant pain. She had suffered a serious radiation burn, but the manufacturer and operators of the machine refused to believe that it could have been caused by the Therac-25. The treatment prescription printout feature of the computer was disabled at the time of the accident, so there was no hardcopy of the treatment data. The lawsuit was eventually settled out of court.

From what we can determine, the accident was not reported to the FDA until *after* further accidents in 1986. The reporting requirements for medical device incidents at that time applied only to equipment manufacturers and importers, not users. The regulations required that manufacturers and importers report deaths, serious injuries, or malfunctions that could result in those consequences, but health-care professionals and institutions were not required to report incidents to manufacturers. The comptroller general of the U.S. Government Accounting Office (GAO), in testimony before Congress on November 6, 1989, expressed great concern about the viability of the incident-reporting regulations in preventing or spotting medical device problems. According to a 1990 GAO study, the FDA knew of less than 1 percent of deaths, serious injuries, or equipment malfunctions that occurred in hospitals [36]. The law was amended in 1990 to require health-care facilities to report incidents to the manufacturer and to the FDA.

At this point, the other Therac-25 users were also unaware that anything untoward had occurred and did not learn about any problems with the machine until after subsequent accidents. Even then, most of their information came through personal communication among themselves.

A.3.2 Ontario Cancer Foundation, July 1985

The second in this series of accidents occurred about seven weeks after the Kennestone patient was overdosed. At that time, the Therac-25 at the Ontario Cancer Foundation in Hamilton, Ontario (Canada), had been in use for more than six months. On July 26, 1985, a forty-year-old patient came to the clinic for her twenty-fourth Therac-25 treatment for carcinoma of the cervix. The operator activated the machine, but the Therac shut down after five seconds with an HTILT error message. The Therac-25's console display read NO DOSE and indicated a TREATMENT PAUSE.

Since the machine did not suspend and the control display indicated no dose was delivered to the patient, the operator went ahead with a second attempt at treatment by pressing the ⓟ key (the *proceed* command), expecting the machine to deliver the proper dose this time. This was standard operating procedure, and Therac-25 operators had become accustomed to frequent malfunctions that had no untoward consequences for the patient. Again, the machine shut down in the same manner. The operator repeated this process four times after the original attempt—the display showing NO DOSE delivered to the patient each time. After the fifth pause, the machine went into treatment suspend, and a hospital service technician was called. The technician found nothing wrong with the machine. According to a Therac-25 operator, this scenario also was not unusual.

After the treatment, the patient complained of a burning sensation, described as an "electric tingling shock" to the treatment area in her hip. Six other patients were treated later that day without incident. She came back for further treatment on July 29 and complained of burning, hip pain, and excessive swelling in the region of treatment. The patient was hospitalized for the condition on July 30, and the machine was taken out of service.

AECL was informed of the apparent radiation injury and sent a service engineer to investigate. The U.S. FDA, the then Canadian Radiation Protection Bureau (RPB),[2] and users were informed that there was a problem, although the users claim that they were never informed that a patient injury had occurred. Users were told that they should visually confirm the proper turntable alignment until further notice (which occurred three months later).

The patient died on November 3, 1985, of an extremely virulent cancer. An autopsy revealed the cause of death as the cancer, but it was noted that had she not died, a total hip replacement would have been necessary as a result of the radiation overexposure. An AECL technician later estimated the patient had received between 13,000 and 17,000 rads.

Manufacturer's Response

AECL could not reproduce the malfunction that had occurred, but suspected a transient failure in the microswitch used to determine the turntable position. During the investigation of the accident, AECL hardwired the error conditions they assumed were necessary for the malfunction and, as a result, found some turntable positioning design weaknesses and potential mechanical problems.

The computer senses and controls turntable position by reading a 3-bit signal about the status of three microswitches in the turntable switch assembly. Essentially, AECL determined that a 1-bit error in the microswitch codes (which could be caused by a single open-circuit fault on the switch lines) could produce an ambiguous position message to the computer. The problem was exacerbated by the design of the mechanism that extends a plunger to lock the turntable when it is in one of the three cardinal positions: The plunger could be extended when the turntable was way out of position, thus giving a second false position indication. AECL devised a method to indicate turntable position that tolerated a 1-bit error so that the code would still unambiguously reveal correct position with any one microswitch failure.

In addition, AECL altered the software so that the computer checked for "in transit" status of the switches to keep further track of the switch operation and turntable position and to give additional assurance that the switches were working and the turntable was moving.

---

[2] On April 1, 1986, the Radiation Protection Bureau and the Bureau of Medical Devices were merged to form the Bureau of Radiation and Medical Devices (BRMD).

As a result of these improvements, AECL claimed in its report and correspondence with hospitals that "analysis of the hazard rate of the new solution indicates an improvement over the old system by at least *5 orders of magnitude* [emphasis added]." However, in its final incident report to the FDA, AECL concluded that they "cannot be firm on the exact cause of the accident but can only suspect . . . ," which underscored their inability to determine the cause of the accident with any certainty. The AECL quality assurance manager testified that they could not reproduce the switch malfunction and that testing of the microswitch was "inconclusive." The similarity of the errant behavior and the patient injuries in this accident and a later one in Yakima, Washington, provide good reason to believe that the Hamilton overdose was probably related to software error rather than to a microswitch failure.

Government and User Response

The Hamilton accident resulted in a voluntary recall by AECL, and the FDA termed it a Class II recall. Class II means "a situation in which the use of, or exposure to, a violative product may cause temporary or medically reversible adverse health consequences or where the probability of serious adverse health consequences is remote." The FDA audited AECL's subsequent modifications, and after the modifications were made, the users were told they could return to normal operating procedures.

As a result of the Hamilton accident, the head of advanced X-ray systems in the Canadian RPB, Gordon Symonds, wrote a report that analyzed the design and performance characteristics of the Therac-25 with respect to radiation safety. Besides citing the flawed microswitch, the report faulted both hardware and software components of the Therac's design. It concluded with a list of four modifications to the Therac-25 necessary for compliance with Canada's Radiation Emitting Devices (RED) Act. The RED law, enacted in 1971, gives government officials power to ensure the safety of radiation-emitting devices.

The modifications specified in the Symonds report included redesigning the microswitch and changing the way the computer handled malfunction conditions. In particular, treatment was to be terminated in the event of a dose-rate malfunction, giving a treatment "suspend." This change would have removed the option to proceed simply by pressing the Ⓟ key. The report also made recommendations regarding collimator test procedures and message and command formats. A November 8, 1985 letter, signed by the director of the Canadian RPB, asked that AECL make changes to the Therac-25 based on the Symonds report "to be in compliance with the RED act."

Although, as noted above, AECL did make the microswitch changes, they did not comply with the directive to change the malfunction pause behavior into treatment suspends, instead reducing the maximum number of retries from five to three. According to Symonds, the deficiencies outlined in the RPB letter of November 8 were still pending when the next accident happened five months later.

Immediately after the Hamilton accident, the Ontario Cancer Foundation hired an independent consultant to investigate. He concluded in a September 1985 report that an independent system (beside the computer) was needed to verify the turntable position and suggested the use of a potentiometer. The RPB wrote a letter to AECL in November 1985 requesting that AECL install such an independent interlock on the Therac-25. Also, in January 1986, AECL received a letter from the attorney representing the Hamilton clinic. The letter said that there had been continuing problems with the turntable, including four incidents at Hamilton, and requested the installation of an independent system (potentiometer) to verify the turntable position. AECL did not comply: No independent interlock was installed by AECL on the Therac-25s at this time. The Hamilton clinic, however, decided to install one themselves on their machine.

A.3.3 Yakima Valley Memorial Hospital, December 1985

In this accident, as in the Kennestone overdose, machine malfunction was not acknowledged until after later accidents were understood.

The Therac-25 at Yakima, Washington, had been modified by AECL in September 1985 in response to the overdose at Hamilton. During December 1985, a woman treated with the Therac-25 developed erythema (excessive reddening of the skin) in a parallel striped pattern on her right hip. Despite this, she continued to be treated by the Therac-25, as the cause of her reaction was not determined to be abnormal until January 1986. On January 6, her treatments were completed.

The staff monitored the skin reaction closely and attempted to find possible causes. The open slots in the blocking trays in the Therac-25 could have produced such a striped pattern, but by the time the skin reaction was determined to be abnormal, the blocking trays had been discarded, so the blocking arrangement and tray striping orientation could not be reproduced. A reaction to chemotherapy was ruled out because that should have produced reactions at the other treatment sites and would not have produced stripes. When the doctors discovered that the woman slept with a heating pad, they thought maybe the burn pattern had been caused by the parallel wires that deliver the heat in such pads. The staff X-rayed the heating pad, but discovered that the wire pattern did not correspond to the erythema pattern on the patient's hip.

The hospital staff sent a letter to AECL on January 31, and they also spoke on the phone with the AECL technical support supervisor. On February 24, the AECL technical support supervisor sent a written response to the director of radiation therapy at Yakima saying, "After careful consideration we are of the opinion that this damage could not have been produced by any malfunction of the Therac-25 or by any operator error." The letter goes on to support this opinion by listing two pages of technical reasons why an overdose by the Therac-25 was impossible, along with the additional argument that there have "apparently been no other instances of similar damage to this or other patients." The letter ends, "In closing, I wish to advise that this matter has been brought to the attention of our Hazards Committee as is normal practice."

The hospital staff eventually ascribed the patient's skin reaction to "cause unknown." In a report written on this first Yakima incident after another Yakima overdose a year later, the medical physicist involved wrote:

> At that time, we did not believe that [the patient] was overdosed because the manufacturer had installed additional hardware and software safety devices to the accelerator.
>
> In a letter from the manufacturer dated 16-Sep-85, it is stated that "Analysis of the hazard rate resulting from these modifications indicates an improvement of at least five orders of magnitude"! With such an improvement in safety (10,000,000%) we did not believe that there could have been any accelerator malfunction. These modifications to the accelerator were completed on 5,6-Sep-85.

Even with fairly sophisticated physics support, the hospital staff, as users, did not have the ability to investigate the possibility of machine malfunction further. They were not aware of any other incidents and, in fact, were told that there had been none, so there was no reason for them to pursue the matter. No further investigation of this incident was done by the manufacturer or by any government agencies (who did not know about it).

About a year later (February 1987), after the second Yakima overdose led the hospital staff to suspect that this first injury had been due to a Therac-25 fault, the staff investigated and found that the first overdose victim had a chronic skin ulcer, tissue necrosis (death) under the skin, and was in continual pain. The damage was surgically repaired, skin grafts were made, and the symptoms relieved. The patient is alive today with minor disability and some scarring related to the overdose. The hospital staff concluded that the dose accidentally delivered in the first accident must have been much lower than in the second, as the reaction was significantly less intense and necrosis did not develop until six or eight months after exposure. Some other factors related to the place on the body where the overdose occurred also kept her from having more significant problems.

A.3.4 East Texas Cancer Center, March 1986

More is known about the Tyler, Texas, accidents than the others because of the diligence of the Tyler hospital physicist, Fritz Hager, without whose efforts the understanding of the software problems may have been delayed even further.

The Therac-25 had been at the East Texas Cancer Center (ETCC) for two years before the first serious accident, and more than 500 patients had been treated. On March 21, 1986, a male patient came into ETCC for his ninth treatment on the Therac-25, one of a series prescribed as followup to the removal of a tumor from his back.

This treatment was to be a 22 MeV electron beam treatment of 180 rads on the upper back and a little to the left of his spine, for a total of 6,000 rads over six and a half weeks. He was taken into the treatment room and placed face down on the treatment table. The operator then left the treatment room, closed the door, and sat at the control terminal.

The operator had held this job for some time, and her typing efficiency had increased with experience. She could quickly enter prescription data and change it conveniently with the Therac's editing features. She entered the patient's prescription data quickly, then noticed that she had typed "x" (for X-ray) when she had intended "e" (for electron) mode. This was a common mistake as most of the treatments involved X-rays, and she had gotten used to typing this. The mistake was easy to fix; she merely used the ⬆ key to edit the mode entry.

Because the other parameters she had entered were correct, she hit the return key several times and left their values unchanged. She reached the bottom of the screen, where it was indicated that the parameters had been VERIFIED and the terminal displayed BEAM READY, as expected. She hit the one-key command, ⓑ for *beam on*, to begin the treatment. After a moment, the machine shut down and the console displayed the message MALFUNCTION 54. The machine also displayed a TREATMENT PAUSE, indicating a problem of low priority. The sheet on the side of the machine explained that this malfunction was a "dose input 2" error. The ETCC did not have any other information available in its instruction manual or other Therac-25 documentation to explain the meaning of MALFUNCTION 54. An AECL technician later testified that "dose input 2" meant that a dose had been delivered that was either too high or too low. The messages had been expected to be used only during internal company development.

The machine showed a substantial underdose on its dose monitor display— 6 monitor units delivered whereas the operator had requested 202 monitor units. She was accustomed to the quirks of the machine, which would frequently stop or delay treatment; in the past, the only consequences had been inconvenience. She immediately took the normal action when the machine merely paused, which was to hit the ⓟ key to proceed with the treatment. The machine promptly shut down with the same MALFUNCTION 54 error and the same underdose shown by the dosimetry.

The operator was isolated from the patient, since the machine apparatus was inside a shielded room of its own. The only way that the operator could be alerted to patient difficulty was through audio and video monitors. On this day, the video display was unplugged and the audio monitor was broken.

After the first attempt to treat him, the patient said that he felt as if he had received an electric shock or that someone had poured hot coffee on his back: He felt a thump and heat and heard a buzzing sound from the equipment. Since this was his ninth treatment, he knew that this was not normal. He began to get up from the treatment table to go for help. It was at this moment that the operator hit the ⓟ key to proceed with the treatment. The patient said that he felt like his arm was being shocked by electricity and that his hand was leaving his body. He went to the treatment room door and pounded on it. The operator was shocked and immediately opened the door for him. He appeared visibly shaken and upset.

The patient was immediately examined by a physician, who observed intense reddening of the treatment area, but suspected nothing more serious than electric shock. The patient was discharged and sent home with instructions to return if he suffered any further reactions. The hospital physicist was called in, and he found the machine calibration within specifications. The meaning of the malfunction message was not understood. The machine was then used to treat patients for the rest of the day.

In actuality, but unknown to anyone at that time, the patient had received a massive overdose, concentrated in the center of the treatment location. After-the-fact simulations of the accident revealed possible doses of 16,500 to 25,000 rads in less than 1 second over an area of about 1 cm.

Over the weeks following the accident, the patient continued to have pain in his neck and shoulder. He lost the function of his left arm and had periodic bouts of nausea and vomiting. He was eventually hospitalized for radiation-induced myelitis of the cervical cord causing paralysis of his left arm and both legs, left vocal cord paralysis (which left him unable to speak), neurogenic bowel and bladder, and paralysis of the left diaphragm. He also had a lesion on his left lung and recurrent herpes simplex skin infections. He died from complications of the overdose five months after the accident.

User and Manufacturer Response

The Therac-25 was shut down for testing the day after this accident. One local AECL engineer and one from the home office in Canada came to ETCC to investigate. They spent a day running the machine through tests, but could not reproduce a Malfunction 54. The AECL engineer from the home office reportedly explained that it was not possible for the Therac-25 to overdose a patient. The ETCC physicist claims that he asked AECL at this time if there were any other reports of radiation overexposure and that AECL personnel (including the quality assurance manager) told him that AECL knew of no accidents involving radiation overexposure by the Therac-25. This seems odd since AECL was surely at least aware of the Hamilton accident that had occurred seven months before and the Yakima accident, and, even by their account, learned of the Georgia lawsuit around this time (which had been filed four months earlier). The AECL engineers then suggested that an electrical problem might have caused the burn.

The electric shock theory was checked out thoroughly by an independent engineering firm. The final report indicated that there was no electrical grounding problem in the machine, and it did not appear capable of giving a patient an electrical shock. The ETCC physicist checked the calibration of the Therac-25 and found it to be satisfactory. He put the machine back into service on April 7, 1986, convinced that it was performing properly.

A.3.5 East Texas Cancer Center, April 1986

Three weeks later, on April 11, 1986, another male patient was scheduled to receive an electron treatment at ETCC for a skin cancer on the side of his face. The prescription was for 10 MeV. The same technician who had treated the first Tyler accident victim prepared this patient for treatment. Much of what follows is from the operator's deposition.

As with her former patient, she entered the prescription data and then noticed an error in the mode. Again she used the edit ⑴ key to change the mode from X-ray to electron. After she finished editing, she pressed the RETURN key several times to place the cursor on the bottom of the screen. She saw the BEAM READY message displayed and turned the beam on.

Within a few seconds the machine shut down, making a loud noise audible via the (now working) intercom. The display showed MALFUNCTION 54 again. The operator rushed into the treatment room, hearing her patient moaning for help. He began to remove the tape that had held his head in position and said something was wrong. She asked him what he felt, and he replied, "fire" on the side of his face. She immediately went to the hospital physicist and told him that another patient appeared to have been burned. Asked by the physicist to described what had happened, the patient explained that something had hit him on the side of the face, he saw a flash of light, and he heard a sizzling sound reminiscent of frying eggs. He was very agitated and asked, "What happened to me, what happened to me?"

This patient died from the overdose on May 1, 1986, three weeks after the accident. He had disorientation, which progressed to coma, fever to 104°F, and neurological damage. An autopsy showed an acute high-dose radiation injury to the right temporal lobe of the brain and the brain stem.

User and Manufacturer Response

After this second Tyler accident, the ETCC physicist immediately took the machine out of service and called AECL to alert them to this second apparent overexposure. The physicist then began a careful investigation of his own. He worked with the operator, who remembered exactly what she had done on this occasion. After a great deal of effort, they were eventually able to elicit the MALFUNCTION 54 message. They determined that data entry speed during editing was the key factor in producing the error condition: If the prescription data was edited at a fast pace (as is natural for someone who has repeated the procedure a large number of times), the overdose occurred. It took some practice before the physicist could repeat the procedure rapidly enough to elicit the MALFUNCTION 54 message at will.

The next day, an engineer from AECL called and said that he could not reproduce the error. After the ETCC physicist explained that the procedure had to be performed quite rapidly, AECL could finally produce a similar malfunction on its own machine. Two days after the accident, AECL said it had measured the dosage (at the center of the field) to be 25,000 rads. An AECL engineer explained that the frying sound heard by the patients was the ion chambers being saturated.

In one lawsuit that resulted from the Tyler accidents, the AECL quality control manager testified that a "cursor up" problem had been found in the service (maintenance) mode at other clinics in February or March of 1985 and also in the summer of 1985. Both times, AECL thought that the software problems had been fixed. There is no way to determine whether there is any relationship between these problems and the Tyler accidents.

Related Therac-20 Problems

The software for both the Therac-25 and Therac-20 "evolved" from the Therac-6 software. Additional functions had to be added because the Therac-20 (and Therac-25) operate in both X-ray and electron mode, while the Therac-6 has only X-ray mode. CGR modified the software for the Therac-20 to handle the dual modes. When the Therac-25 development began, AECL engineers adapted the software from the Therac-6, but they also borrowed software routines from the Therac-20 to handle electron mode, which was allowed under their cooperative agreements.

After the second Tyler, Texas, accident, a physicist at the University of Chicago Joint Center for Radiation Therapy heard about the Therac-25 software problem and decided to find out whether the same thing could happen with the Therac-20. At first, the physicist was unable to reproduce the error on his machine, but two months later he found the link.

The Therac-20 at the University of Chicago is used to teach students in a radiation therapy school conducted by the center. The center's physicist, Frank Borger, noticed that whenever a new class of students started using the Therac-20, fuses and breakers on the machine tripped, shutting down the unit. These failures, which had been occurring ever since the school had acquired the machine, might happen three times a week while new students operated the machine and then disappear for months. Borger determined that new students make many different types of mistakes and use "creative methods" of editing parameters on the console. Through experimentation, he found that certain editing sequences correlated with blown fuses and determined that the same computer bug (as in the Therac-25 software) was responsible. The physicist notified the FDA, which notified Therac-20 users [148].

The software error is just a nuisance on the Therac-20 because this machine has independent hardware protective circuits for monitoring the electron beam scanning. The protective circuits do not allow the beam to turn on, so there is no danger of radiation exposure to a patient. While the Therac-20 relies on mechanical interlocks for monitoring the machine, the Therac-25 relies largely on software.

The Software "Bug"

A lesson to be learned from the Therac-25 story is that focusing on particular software "bugs" is not the way to make a safe system. Virtually all complex software can be made to behave in an unexpected fashion under some conditions. The basic mistakes here involved poor software engineering practices and building a machine that relies on the software for safe operation. Furthermore, the particular coding error is not as important as the general unsafe design of the software overall. Examining the part of the code blamed for the Tyler accidents is instructive, however, in demonstrating the overall software design flaws. First the software design is described and then the errors believed to be involved in the Tyler accidents and perhaps others.

Therac-25 Software Development and Design.   AECL claims proprietary rights to its software design. However, from voluminous documentation regarding the accidents, the repairs, and the eventual design changes, we can build a rough picture of it.

The software is responsible for monitoring the machine status, accepting input about the treatment desired, and setting the machine up for this treatment. It turns the beam on in response to an operator command (assuming that certain operational checks on the status of the physical machine are satisfied) and also turns the beam off when treatment is completed, when an operator commands it, or when a malfunction is detected. The operator can print out hardcopy versions of the CRT display or machine setup parameters.

The treatment unit has an interlock system designed to remove power to the unit when there is a hardware malfunction. The computer monitors this interlock system and provides diagnostic messages. Depending on the fault, the computer either prevents a treatment from being started or, if the treatment is in progress, creates a pause or a suspension of the treatment.

There are two basic operational modes: treatment mode and service mode. Treatment mode controls the normal treatment process. In service mode, the unit can be operated with some of the operational and treatment interlocks bypassed, and additional operational commands and characteristics may be selected. Service mode is entered only through the use of a password at the service keyboard.

The manufacturer describes the Therac-25 software as having a stand-alone, real-time treatment operating system. The system does not use a standard operating system or executive. Rather, the real-time executive was written especially for the Therac-25 and runs on a 32K PDP-11/23. Cycles are allocated to the critical and noncritical tasks using a preemptive scheduler.

The software, written in PDP-11 assembly language, has four major components: stored data, a scheduler, a set of critical and noncritical tasks, and interrupt services. The stored data includes calibration parameters for the accelerator setup as well as patient-treatment data. The interrupt routines include

- A clock interrupt service routine
- A scanning interrupt service routine

- Traps (for software overflow and computer hardware generated interrupts)
- Power up (initiated at power up to initialize the system and pass control to the scheduler)
- Treatment console screen interrupt handler
- Treatment console keyboard interrupt handler
- Service printer interrupt handler
- Service keyboard interrupt handler

The scheduler controls the sequencing of all noninterrupt events and coordinates all concurrent processes. Tasks are initiated every 0.1 second, with the critical tasks executed first and the noncritical tasks executed in any remaining cycle time. Critical tasks include the following:

- The treatment monitor (Treat) directs and monitors patient setup and treatment via eight operating phases. These are called as subroutines, depending on the value of the Tphase control variable. Following the execution of a particular subroutine, Treat reschedules itself. Treat interacts with the keyboard processing task, which handles operator console communication. The prescription data is cross-checked and verified by other tasks (such as keyboard processor or parameter setup sensor) that inform the treatment task of the verification status via shared variables.
- The servo task controls gun emission, dose rate (pulse repetition frequency), symmetry (beam steering), and machine motions. The servo task also sets up the machine parameters and monitors the beam-tilt-error and the flatness-error interlocks.
- The housekeeper task takes care of system status interlocks and limit checks and displays appropriate messages on the CRT display. It decodes some information and checks the setup verification.

Noncritical tasks include

- Checksum processor (scheduled to run periodically)
- Treatment console keyboard processor (scheduled to run only if it is called by other tasks or by keyboard interrupts). This task acts as the communication interface between the other software and the operator.
- Treatment console screen processor (run periodically). This task lays out appropriate record formats for either CRT displays or hard copies.
- Service keyboard processor (run on demand). This task arbitrates non-treatment-related communication between the therapy system and the operator.
- Snapshot (run periodically by the scheduler). Snapshot captures preselected parameter values and is called by the treatment task at the end of a treatment.
- Hand control processor (run periodically).
- Calibration processor. This task is responsible for a package of tasks that

let the operator examine and change system setup parameters and interlock limits.

It is clear from the AECL documentation on the modifications that the software allows concurrent access to shared memory, that there is no real synchronization aside from data that are stored in shared variables, and that the "test" and "set" for such variables are not indivisible operations. Race conditions resulting from this implementation of multitasking played an important part in the accidents.

Specific Design Errors. The following explanation of the specific software problems found at this time is taken from the description AECL provided to the FDA, but clarified somewhat. The description leaves some unanswered questions, but it is the best that can be done with the information available.

The treatment monitor task (Treat) controls the various phases of treatment by executing its eight subroutines. The treatment phase indicator variable (Tphase) is used to determine which subroutine should be executed (Figure A.3). Following the execution of a particular subroutine, Treat reschedules itself.

One of Treat's subroutines, called Datent (data entry), communicates with the keyboard handler task (a task that runs concurrently with Treat) via a shared variable (Data Entry Complete flag) to determine whether the prescription data has been entered. The keyboard handler recognizes the completion of data entry and changes the Data Entry Complete variable to denote this. Once this variable is set, the Datent subroutine detects the variable's change in status and changes the value of Tphase from 1 (Datent) to 3 (Set Up Test). In this case, the Datent subroutine exits back to the Treat subroutine, which will reschedule itself and begin execution of the Set Up Test subroutine. If the Data Entry Complete variable has not been set, Datent leaves the value of Tphase unchanged and exits back to Treat's mainline. Treat will then reschedule itself, essentially rescheduling the Datent subroutine.

The command line at the lower right-hand corner of the screen (see Figure A.2) is the cursor's normal position when the operator has completed all the necessary changes to the prescription. Prescription editing is signified by moving the cursor off the command line. As the program was originally designed, the Data Entry Complete variable by itself is not sufficient because it does not ensure that the cursor is located on the command line; under the right circumstances, the data entry phase can be exited before all edit changes are made on the screen.

The keyboard handler parses the mode and energy level specified by the operator and places an encoded result in another shared variable, the 2-byte Mode/Energy Offset variable (MEOS). The low-order byte of this variable is used by another task (Hand) to set the collimator/turntable to the proper position for the selected mode and energy. The high-order byte of the MEOS variable is used by Datent to set several operating parameters.

Initially, the data-entry process forces the operator to enter the mode and

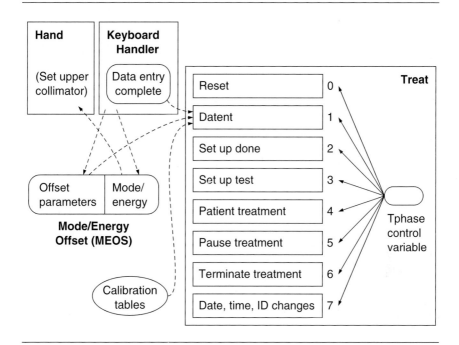

FIGURE A.3
Tasks and subroutines in the code blamed for the Tyler accidents.

energy except when the photon mode is selected, in which case the energy defaults to 25 MeV. The operator can later edit the mode and energy separately.
If the keyboard handler sets the Data Entry Complete flag before the operator
changes the data in MEOS, Datent will not detect the changes because it has already exited and will not be reentered again. The upper collimator (turntable), on
the other hand, is set to the position dictated by the low-order byte of MEOS by
another concurrently running task (Hand) and can therefore be inconsistent with
the parameters set in accordance with the information in the high-order byte. The
software appears to contain no checks to detect such an incompatibility.

The first thing Datent does when it is entered is to check whether the key
board handler has set the mode and energy in MEOS. If so, it uses the high-order
byte to index into a table of preset operating parameters and places them in the
digital-to-analog output table. The contents of this output table are transferred to
the digital-to-analog converter during the next clock cycle. Once the parameters
are all set, Datent calls the subroutine Magnet, which sets the bending magnets.
The following shows a simplified pseudocode description of relevant parts of the
software:

Datent:
    if mode/energy specified **then**
        begin
            calculate table index
            repeat
                fetch parameter
                output parameter
                point to next parameter
            until all parameters set
            call Magnet
            if mode/energy changed **then return**
        end
    if data entry is complete **then** set Tphase to 3
    if data entry is not complete **then**
        if reset command entered **then** set Tphase to 0
    return

Magnet:
    Set bending magnet flag
    repeat
        Set next magnet
        call Ptime
        if mode/energy has changed, **then** exit
    until all magnets are set
    return

Ptime:
    repeat
        if bending magnet flag is set **then**
            if editing taking place **then**
                if mode/energy has changed **then** exit
    until hysteresis delay has expired
    Clear bending magnet flag
    return

Setting the bending magnets takes about eight seconds. Magnet calls a subroutine called Ptime to introduce a time delay. Since several magnets need to be set, Ptime is entered and exited several times. A flag to indicate that the bending magnets are being set is initialized upon entry to the Magnet subroutine and cleared at the end of Ptime. Furthermore, Ptime checks a shared variable, set by the keyboard handler, that indicates the presence of any editing requests. If there are edits, then Ptime clears the bending magnet variable and exits to Magnet, which then exits to Datent. But the edit change variable is checked by Ptime only if the bending magnet flag is set. Because Ptime clears it during its first execution, any edits performed during each succeeding pass through Ptime will not be recognized. Thus, an edit change of the mode or energy, although reflected on the operator's screen and the mode/energy offset variable, will not be sensed by Datent so it can index the appropriate calibration tables for the machine parameters.

Recall that the Tyler error occurred when the operator made an entry indicating the mode and energy, went to the command line, then moved the cursor up to change the mode or energy and returned to the command line all within eight seconds. Because the magnet setting takes about eight seconds and Magnet does not recognize edits after the first execution of Ptime, the editing had been completed by the return to Datent, which never detected that it had occurred. Part of the problem was fixed after the accident by clearing the bending magnet variable at the end of Magnet (after *all* the magnets have been set) instead of at the end of Ptime.

But this is not the only problem. Upon exit from the Magnet subroutine, the data entry subroutine (Datent) checks the Data Entry Complete variable. If it indicates that data entry is complete, Datent sets Tphase to 3 and Datent is not entered again. If it is not set, Datent leaves Tphase unchanged, which means it will eventually be rescheduled. But the Data Entry Complete variable only indicates that the cursor has been down to the command line, not that it is still there. A potential race condition is set up. To fix this, AECL introduced another shared variable controlled by the keyboard handler task that indicates the cursor is not positioned on the command line. If this variable is set, then prescription entry is still in progress and the value of Tphase is left unchanged.

The Government and User Response

The FDA does not approve each new medical device on the market: All medical devices go through a classification process that determines the level of FDA approval necessary. Medical accelerators follow a procedure called pre-market notification before commercial distribution. In this process, the firm must establish that the product is substantially equivalent in safety and effectiveness to a product already on the market. If that cannot be done to the FDA's satisfaction, a pre-market approval is required. For the Therac-25, the FDA required only a pre-market notification. After the Therac-25 accidents, new procedures for approval of software-controlled devices were adopted.

The agency is basically reactive to problems and requires manufacturers to report serious ones. Once a problem is identified in a radiation-emitting product, the FDA is responsible for approving the corrective action plan (CAP)

The first reports of the Tyler incidents came to the FDA from the State of Texas Health Department, and this triggered FDA action. The FDA investigation was well under way when AECL produced a medical device report to discuss the details of the radiation overexposures at Tyler. The FDA declared the Therac-25 defective under the Radiation Control for Health and Safety Act and ordered the firm to notify all purchasers, investigate the problem, determine a solution, and submit a corrective action plan for FDA approval.

The final CAP consisted of more than twenty changes to the system hardware and software, plus modifications to the system documentation and manuals. Some of these changes were unrelated to the specific accidents, but were improvements to the general safety of the machine. The full CAP implementation, including an extensive safety analysis, was not complete until more than two years after the Tyler accidents.

AECL made their accident report to the FDA on April 15, 1986. On that same date, AECL sent out a letter to each Therac user recommending a temporary "fix" to the machine that would allow continued clinical use. The letter (shown in its complete form) stated:

> SUBJECT: CHANGE IN OPERATING PROCEDURES FOR THE THERAC 25 LINEAR ACCELERATOR
>
> Effective immediately, and until further notice, the key used for moving the cursor back through the prescription sequence (i.e., cursor 'UP' inscribed with an upward pointing arrow) must not be used for editing or any other purpose.
>
> To avoid accidental use of this key, the key cap must be removed and the switch contacts fixed in the open position with electrical tape or other insulating material. For assistance with the latter you should contact your local AECL service representative.
>
> Disabling this key means that if any prescription data entered is incorrect then a 'R' reset command must be used and the whole prescription re-entered.
>
> For those users of the Multiport option it also means that editing of dose rate, dose and time will not be possible between ports.

On May 2, 1986, the FDA declared the Therac defective, demanded a CAP, and required renotification of all the Therac customers. In the letter from the FDA to AECL, the Director of Compliance, Center for Devices and Radiological Health, wrote:

> We have reviewed [AECL's] April 15 letter to purchasers and have concluded that it does not satisfy the requirements for notification to purchasers of a defect in an electronic product. Specifically, it does not describe the defect nor the hazards associated with it. The letter does not provide any reason for disabling the cursor key and the tone is not commensurate with the urgency for doing so. In fact, the letter implies the inconvenience to operators outweighs the need to disable the key. We request that you immediately renotify purchasers.

AECL promptly made a new notice to users and also requested an extension to produce a CAP. The FDA granted this request.

About this time, the Therac-25 users created a user's group and held their first meeting at the annual conference of the American Association of Physicists in Medicine. At the meeting, users discussed the Tyler accident and heard an

AECL representative present the company's plans for responding to it. AECL promised to send a letter to all users detailing the CAP.

Several users described additional hardware safety features that they had added to their own machines to provide additional protection. An interlock (that checked gun current values), which the Vancouver clinic had previously added to their Therac-25, was labeled as redundant by AECL; the users disagreed. There were further discussions of poor design and other problems that caused a 10- to 30-percent underdosing in both modes.

The meeting notes said

There was a general complaint by all users present about the lack of information propagation. The users were not happy about receiving incomplete information. The AECL representative countered by stating that AECL does not wish to spread rumors and that AECL has no policy to 'keep things quiet.' The consensus among the users was that an improvement was necessary.

After the first user's group meeting, there were two user's group newsletters. The first, dated fall 1986, contained letters from Tim Still, the Kennestone physicist, who complained about what he considered to be eight major problems he had experienced with the Therac-25. These problems included poor screen-refresh subroutines that leave trash and erroneous information on the operator console and some tape-loading problems upon startup that he discovered involved the use of "phantom tables" to trigger the interlock system in the event of a load failure instead of using a checksum. He asked the question, "Is programming safety relying too much on the software interlock routines?" The second user's group newsletter, in December 1986, further discussed the implications of the phantom table problem.

AECL produced its first CAP on June 13, 1986. The FDA asked for changes and additional information about the software, including a software test plan. AECL responded on September 26 with several documents describing the software and its modifications but no test plan. They explained how the Therac-25 software evolved from the Therac-6 software and stated that "no single test plan and report exists for the software since both hardware and software were tested and exercised separately and together over many years." AECL concluded that the current CAP improved "machine safety by many orders of magnitude and virtually eliminates the possibility of lethal doses as delivered in the Tyler incident."

An FDA internal memo dated October 20 commented on these AECL submissions, raising several concerns:

Unfortunately, the AECL response also seems to point out an apparent lack of documentation on software specifications and a software test plan.

. . . concerns include the question of previous knowledge of problems by

AECL, the apparent paucity of software quality assurance at the manufacturing facility, and possible warnings and information dissemination to others of the generic type problems.

. . . As mentioned in my first review, there is some confusion on whether the manufacturer should have been aware of the software problems prior to the ARO's [Accidental Radiation Overdoses] in Texas. AECL had received official notification of a law suit in November 1985 from a patient claiming accidental over-exposure from a Therac-25 in Marietta, Georgia. . . . If knowledge of these software deficiencies were known beforehand, what would be the FDA's posture in this case?

. . . The materials submitted by the manufacturer have not been in sufficient detail and clarity to ensure an adequate software quality assurance program currently exists. For example, a response has not been provided with respect to the software part of the CAP to the CDRH's [FDA Center for Devices and Radiological Health] request for documentation on the revised requirements and specifications for the new software. In addition, an analysis has not been provided, as requested, on the interaction with other portions of the software to demonstrate the corrected software does not adversely affect other software functions.

The July 23 letter from the CDRH requested a documented test plan including several specific pieces of information identified in the letter. This request has been ignored up to this point by the manufacturer. Considering the ramifications of the current software problem, changes in software QA attitudes are needed at AECL.

AECL also planned to retain the malfunction codes, but the FDA required better warnings for the operators. Furthermore, AECL had not planned on any quality assurance testing to ensure exact copying of software, but the FDA insisted on it. The FDA further requested assurances that rigorous testing would become a standard part of AECL's software modification procedures.

We also expressed our concern that you did not intend to perform the protocol to future modifications to software. We believe that the rigorous testing must be performed each time a modification is made in order to ensure the modification does not adversely affect the safety of the system.

AECL was also asked to draw up an installation test plan to ensure that both hardware and software changes perform as designed when installed.

AECL submitted CAP Revision 2 and supporting documentation on December 22, 1986. They changed the CAP to have dose malfunctions suspend treatment and included a plan for meaningful error messages and highlighted dose error messages. They also expanded their diagrams of software modifications and expanded their test plan to cover hardware and software.

A.3.6 Yakima Valley Memorial Hospital, January 1987

On Saturday, January 17, 1987, the second patient of the day was to be treated for a carcinoma. This patient was to receive two film verification exposures of 4 and 3 rads plus a 79-rad photon treatment (for a total exposure of 86 rads.)

Film was placed under the patient and 4 rads were administered. After the machine paused to open the collimator jaws further, the second exposure of 3 rads was administered. The machine paused again.

The operator entered the treatment room to remove the film and verify the patient's precise position. He used the hand control in the treatment room to rotate the turntable to the field light position, which allowed him to check the alignment of the machine with respect to the patient's body in order to verify proper beam position. He then either pressed the *set* button on the hand control or left the room and typed a SET command at the console to return the turntable to the proper position for treatment; there is some confusion as to exactly what transpired. When he left the room, he forgot to remove the film from underneath the patient. The console displayed "beam ready," and the operator hit the Ⓑ key to turn the beam on.

The beam came on, but the console displayed no dose or dose rate. After five or six seconds, the unit shut down with a pause and displayed a message. The message "may have disappeared quickly"; the operator was unclear on this point. However, since the machine merely paused, he was able to push the Ⓟ key to proceed with treatment.

The machine paused again, this time displaying FLATNESS on the reason line. The operator heard the patient say something over the intercom, but could not understand him. He went into the room to speak with the patient, who reported "feeling a burning sensation" in the chest. The console displayed only the total dose of the two film exposures (7 rads) and nothing more.

Later in the day, the patient developed a skin burn over the entire treatment area. Four days later, the redness developed a striped pattern matching the slots in the blocking tray. The striped pattern was similar to the burn a year earlier at this same hospital, which had first been ascribed to a heating pad and later officially labeled by the hospital as "cause unknown."

AECL began an investigation, and users were told to confirm the turntable position visually before turning on the beam. All tests run by the AECL engineers indicated that the machine was working perfectly. From the information that had been gathered to that point, it was suspected that the electron beam had come on when the turntable was in the field light position. But the investigators could not reproduce the fault condition.

On the following Thursday, AECL sent in an engineer from Ottawa to investigate. The hospital physicist had, in the meantime, run some tests himself. He placed a film in the Therac's beam and then ran two exposures of X-ray parameters with the turntable in field light position. The film appeared to match the film that was left (by mistake) under the patient during the accident.

After a week of checking the hardware, AECL determined that the "incorrect machine operation was probably not caused by hardware alone." After checking the software, AECL engineers discovered a flaw (described below) that could explain the erroneous behavior. The coding problems explaining this accident are completely different from those associated with the Tyler accidents.

Preliminary dose measurements by AECL indicated that the dose delivered under these conditions—that is, when the turntable is in the field light position—is on the order of 4,000 to 5,000 rads. After two attempts, the patient could have received 8,000 to 10,000 instead of the 86 rads prescribed. AECL again called users on January 26 (nine days after the accident) and gave them detailed instructions on how to avoid this problem. In an FDA internal report on the accident, the AECL quality assurance manager investigating the problem is quoted as saying that the software and hardware changes to be retrofitted following the Tyler accident nine months earlier (but which had not yet been installed) would have prevented the Yakima accident.

The patient died in April from complications related to the overdose. He had a terminal form of cancer, but a lawsuit was initiated by his survivors alleging that he died sooner than he would have and endured unnecessary pain and suffering due to the radiation overdose. The suit, like all the others, was settled out of court.

The Yakima Software "Bug"

The software problem for the second Yakima accident is fairly well-established and different from that implicated in the Tyler accidents. There is no way to determine what particular software design errors were related to the Kennestone, Hamilton, and first Yakima accidents. Given the unsafe programming practices exhibited in the code, unknown race conditions or errors could have been responsible for them. There is speculation, however, that the Hamilton accident was the same as this second Yakima overdose. In a report of a conference call on January 26, 1987, between the AECL quality assurance manager and Ed Miller of the FDA discussing the Yakima accident, Miller notes,

> This situation probably occurred in the Hamilton, Ontario accident a couple of years ago. It was not discovered at that time and the cause was attributed to intermittent interlock failure. The subsequent recall of the multiple microswitch logic network did not really solve the problem.

The second Yakima accident was again attributed to a type of race condition in the software—this one allowed the device to be activated in an error setting (a "failure" of a software interlock). The Tyler accidents were related to problems in the data-entry routines that allowed the code to proceed to Set Up Test before the full prescription had been entered and acted upon. The Yakima accident involved problems encountered later in the logic after the treatment monitor Treat reaches Set Up Test.

The Therac-25's field light feature allows very precise positioning of the patient for treatment. The operator can control the machine right at the treatment

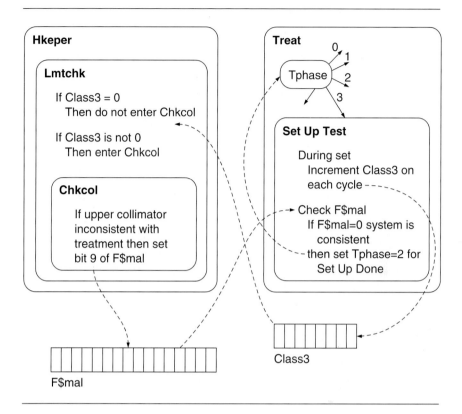

FIGURE A.4
The Yakima software flaw.

site using a small hand control that offers certain limited functions for patient setup, including setting gantry, collimator, and table motions.

Normally, the operator enters all the prescription data at the console (outside the treatment room) before the final setup of all machine parameters is completed in the treatment room. This gives rise to an UNVERIFIED condition at the console. The operator then completes patient setup in the treatment room, and all relevant parameters now VERIFY. The console displays a message to PRESS SET BUTTON while the turntable is in the field light position. The operator now presses the *set* button on the hand control or types "set" at the console. That should set the collimator to the proper position for treatment.

In the software, after the prescription is entered and verified by the Datent routine, the control variable Tphase is changed so that the Set Up Test routine is entered (Figure A.4). Every pass through the Set Up Test routine increments the upper collimator position check, a shared variable called Class3. If Class3 is nonzero, there is an inconsistency and treatment should not proceed. A zero value for Class3 indicates that the relevant parameters are consistent with treatment, and the software does not inhibit the beam.

After setting the Class3 variable, Set Up Test next checks for any malfunctions in the system by checking another shared variable (set by a routine that actually handles the interlock checking) called F$mal to see if it has a nonzero value. A nonzero value in F$mal indicates that the machine is not ready for treatment, and the Set Up Test subroutine is rescheduled. When F$mal is zero (indicating that everything is ready for treatment), the Set Up Test subroutine sets the Tphase variable equal to 2, which results in next scheduling the Set Up Done subroutine and the treatment is allowed to continue.

The actual interlock checking is performed by a concurrent Housekeeper task (Hkeper). The upper collimator position check is performed by a subroutine of Hkeper called Lmtchk (analog-to-digital limit checking). Lmtchk first checks the Class3 variable. If Class3 contains a nonzero value, Lmtchk calls the Check Collimator (Chkcol) subroutine. If Class3 contains zero, Chkcol is bypassed and the upper collimator position check is not performed. The Chkcol subroutine sets or resets bit 9 of the F$mal shared variable, depending on the position of the upper collimator—which in turn is checked by the Set Up Test subroutine of Treat to decide whether to reschedule itself or to proceed to Set Up Done.

During machine setup, Set Up Test will be executed several hundred times because it reschedules itself waiting for other events to occur. In the code, the Class3 variable is incremented by one in each pass through Set Up Test. Since the Class3 variable is one byte, it can only contain a maximum value of 255 decimal. Thus, on every 256th pass through the Set Up Test code, the variable will overflow and have a zero value. That means that on every 256th pass through Set Up Test, the upper collimator will not be checked and an upper collimator fault will not be detected.

The overexposure occurred when the operator hit the "set" button at the precise moment that Class3 rolled over to zero. Thus, Chkcol was not executed and F$mal was not set to indicate that the upper collimator was still in the field-light position. The software turned on the full 25 MeV without the target in place and without scanning. A highly concentrated electron beam resulted, which was scattered and deflected by the stainless steel mirror that was in the path.

The technical "fix" implemented for this particular software flaw is described by AECL as simple: the program is changed so that the Class3 variable is set to some fixed nonzero value each time through Set Up Test instead of being incremented.

Manufacturer, Government, and User Response

On February 3, 1987, after interaction with the FDA and others, including the user's group, AECL announced to its customers

1. A new software release to correct both the Tyler and Yakima software problems

2. A hardware single-pulse shutdown circuit

3. A turntable potentiometer to independently monitor turntable position

4. A hardware turntable interlock circuit

The second item, a hardware single-pulse shutdown circuit, essentially acts as a hardware interlock to prevent overdosing by detecting an unsafe level of radiation and halting beam output after one pulse of high energy and current. This interlock effectively provides an independent way to protect against a wide range of potential hardware failures and software errors. The third item, a turntable potentiometer, was the safety device recommended by several groups after the Hamilton accident.

After the second Yakima accident, the FDA became concerned that the use of the Therac-25 during the CAP process, even with AECL's interim operating instructions, involved too much risk to patients. The FDA concluded that the accidents demonstrated that the software alone could not be relied upon to assure safe operation of the machine. In a February 18, 1987, internal FDA memorandum, the Director of the Division of Radiological Products wrote:

> It is impossible for CDRH to find all potential failure modes and conditions of the software. AECL has indicated the "simple software fix" will correct the turntable position problem displayed at Yakima. We have not yet had the opportunity to evaluate that modification. Even if it does, based upon past history, I am not convinced that there are not other software glitches that could result in serious injury.
>
> . . . We are in the position of saying that the proposed CAP can reasonably be expected to correct the deficiencies for which they were developed (Tyler). We cannot say that we are reasonable [sic] confident about the safety of the entire <u>system</u> to prevent or minimize exposure from other fault conditions.

On February 6, 1987, Ed Miller of the FDA called Pavel Dvorak of Canada's Health and Welfare to advise him that the FDA would recommend that all Therac-25s be shut down until permanent modifications could be made. According to Miller's notes on the phone call, Dvorak agreed and indicated that Health and Welfare would coordinate their actions with the FDA.

AECL responded on April 13 with an update on the Therac-25 CAP status and a schedule of the nine action items pressed by the users at a user's group meeting in March. This unique and highly productive meeting provided an unusual opportunity to involve the users in the CAP evaluation process. It brought together all concerned parties in one place and at one time so that a course of action could be decided upon and approved as quickly as possible. The attendees included representatives from

- The manufacturer (AECL)
- All users, including their technical and legal staffs
- The FDA and the Canadian Bureau of Radiation and Medical Devices

□ the Canadian Atomic Energy Control Board

□ the Province of Ontario

□ the Radiation Regulations Committee of the Canadian Association of Physicists

According to Gordon Symonds, from the Canadian BRMD, this meeting was very important to the resolution of the problems, since the regulators, users, and manufacturer arrived at a consensus in one day.

At this second user's meeting, the participants carefully reviewed all the six known major Therac-25 accidents to that date and discussed the elements of the CAP along with possible additional modifications. They came up with a prioritized list of modifications they wanted included in the CAP and expressed concerns about the lack of independent evaluation of the software and the lack of a hardcopy audit trail to assist in diagnosing faults.

The AECL representative, who was the quality assurance manager, responded that tests had been done on the CAP changes, but that the tests were not documented and that independent evaluation of the software "might not be possible." He claimed that two outside experts had reviewed the software, but he could not provide their names. In response to user requests for a hardcopy audit trail and access to source code, he explained that memory limitations would not permit including such options and that source code would not be made available to users.

On May 1, AECL issued CAP Revision 4 as a result of the FDA comments and the user's meeting input. The FDA response on May 26 approved the CAP subject to submission of the final test plan results and an independent safety analysis, distribution of the draft revised manual to customers, and completion of the CAP by June 30, 1987. The FDA concluded by rating this a Class I recall: a recall in which there is a reasonable probability that the use of, or exposure to, a violative product will cause serious adverse health consequences or death [35].

AECL sent more supporting documentation to the FDA on June 5, 1987, including the CAP test plan, a draft operator's manual, and the draft of the new safety analysis. This time the analysis included the software in the fault trees but used a "generic failure rate" of 10^{-4} for software events. This number was justified as being based on the historical performance of the Therac-25 software. The final report on the safety analysis states that many of the fault trees had a computer malfunction as a causative event, and the outcome for quantification was therefore dependent on the failure rate chosen for the software. Assuming that all software errors are equally likely seems rather strange.

A close inspection of the code was also conducted during this safety analysis to "obtain more information on which to base decisions." An outside consultant performed the inspection, which included a detailed examination of the implementation of each function, a search for coding errors, and a qualitative assessment of the software's reliability. No information is provided in the final safety report about whether any particular methodology or tools were used in the software inspection or whether someone just read the code looking for errors.

AECL planned a fifth revision of the CAP to include the testing and final safety analysis results. Referring to the test plan at this, the final stage of the CAP process, an FDA reviewer said,

> Amazingly, the test data presented to show that the software changes to handle the edit problems in the Therac-25 are appropriate prove the exact opposite result. A review of the data table in the test results indicates that the final beam type and energy (edit change) has no effect on the initial beam type and energy. I can only assume that either the fix is not right or the data was entered incorrectly. The manufacturer should be admonished for this error. Where is the QC [Quality Control] review for the test program? AECL must: (1) clarify this situation, (2) change the test protocol to prevent this type of error from occurring, and (3) set up appropriate QC control on data review.

A further FDA memo indicated:

> [The AECL quality assurance manager] could not give an explanation and will check into the circumstances. He subsequently called back and verified that the technician completed the form incorrectly. Correct operation was witnessed by himself and others. They will repeat and send us the correct data sheet.

At the American Association of Physicists in Medicine meeting in July 1987, a third user's meeting was held. The AECL representative described the status of the latest CAP and explained that the FDA had given verbal approval and that he expected full implementation by the end of August 1987. He went on to review and comment on the prioritized concerns of the last meeting. Three of the user-requested hardware changes had been included in the CAP. Changes to tape load error messages and checksums on the load data would wait until after the CAP was done. Software documentation was described as a lower priority task that needed definition and would not be available to the FDA in any form for over a year.

On July 6, 1987, AECL sent a letter to all users to update them on the FDA's verbal approval of the CAP and to delineate how AECL would proceed. Finally, on July 21, 1987, AECL issued the final and fifth CAP revision. The major features of the final CAP are these:

- All interruptions related to the dosimetry system will go to a treatment suspend, not a treatment pause. Operators will not be allowed to restart the machine without reentering all parameters.
- A software single-pulse shutdown will be added.
- An independent hardware single-pulse shutdown will be added.
- Monitoring logic for turntable position will be improved to ensure that the turntable is in one of the three legal positions.
- A potentiometer will be added to the turntable. The output is used to monitor exact turntable location and provide a visible position signal to the operator.

- ❑ Interlocking with the 270-degree bending magnet will be added to ensure that the target and beam flattener are in position if the X-ray mode is selected.

- ❑ Beam-on will be prevented if the turntable is in the field light or any intermediate position.

- ❑ Cryptic malfunction messages will be replaced with meaningful messages and highlighted dose-rate messages.

- ❑ Editing keys will be limited to *cursor up*, *backspace*, and *return*. All other keys will be inoperative.

- ❑ A motion-enable footswitch (a type of deadman switch) will be added. The operator will be required to hold this switch closed during movement of certain parts of the machine to prevent unwanted motions when the operator is not in control.

- ❑ Twenty-three other changes will be made to the software to improve its operation, including disabling of unused keys, changing the operation of the *set* and *reset* commands, preventing copying of the control program on site, changing the way various detected hardware faults are handled, eliminating errors in the software that were detected during the review process, adding several additional software interlocks, disallowing changes in the service mode while a treatment is in progress, and adding meaningful error messages.

- ❑ The known software problems associated with the Tyler and Yakima accidents will be fixed.

- ❑ The manuals will be fixed to reflect the changes.

Figure A.5 shows a typical Therac-25 installation after the CAP changes were made.

Ed Miller, the director of the Division of Standards Enforcement, Center for Devices and Radiological Health at the FDA, wrote in 1987:

> FDA has performed extensive review of the Therac-25 software and hardware safety systems. We cannot say with absolute certainty that all software problems that might result in improper dose have been found and eliminated. However, we are confident that the hardware and software safety features recently added will prevent future catastrophic consequences of failure.

No Therac-25 accidents have been reported since the final corrective action plan was implemented.

A.4 Causal Factors

Many lessons can be learned from this series of accidents. A few are considered here.

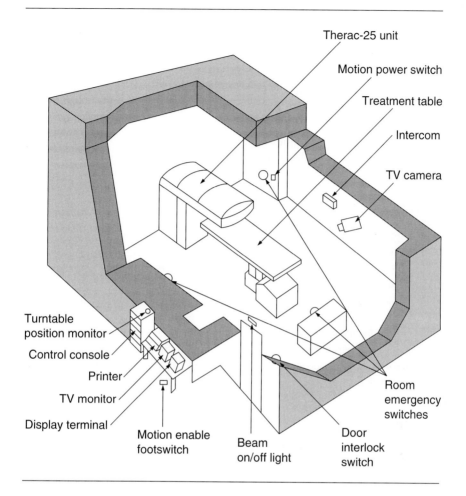

FIGURE A.5
A typical Therac-25 facility after the final CAP.

Overconfidence in Software.   A common mistake in engineering, in this case and in many others, is to put too much confidence in software. There seems to be a feeling among nonsoftware professionals that software will not or cannot fail, which leads to complacency and overreliance on computer functions.

A related tendency among engineers is to ignore software. The first safety analysis on the Therac-25 did not include software—although nearly full responsibility for safety rested on it. When problems started occurring, it was assumed that hardware had caused them, and the investigation looked only at the hardware.

Confusing Reliability with Safety. This software was highly reliable. It worked tens of thousands of times before overdosing anyone, and occurrences of erroneous behavior were few and far between. AECL assumed that their software was safe because it was reliable, and this led to complacency.

Lack of Defensive Design. The software did not contain self-checks or other error-detection and error-handling features that would have detected the inconsistencies and coding errors. Audit trails were limited because of a lack of memory. However, today larger memories are available and audit trails and other design techniques must be given high priority in making tradeoff decisions.

Patient reactions were the only real indications of the seriousness of the problems with the Therac-25; there were no independent checks that the machine and its software were operating correctly. Such verification cannot be assigned to operators without providing them with some means of detecting errors: The Therac-25 software "lied" to the operators, and the machine itself was not capable of detecting that a massive overdose had occurred. The ion chambers on the Therac-25 could not handle the high density of ionization from the unscanned electron beam at high beam current; they thus became saturated and gave an indication of a low dosage. Engineers need to design for the worst case.

Failure to Eliminate Root Causes. One of the lessons to be learned from the Therac-25 experiences is that focusing on particular software design errors is not the way to make a system safe. Virtually all complex software can be made to behave in an unexpected fashion under some conditions: There will always be another software bug. Just as engineers would not rely on a design with a hardware single point of failure that could lead to catastrophe, they should not do so if that single point of failure is software.

The Therac-20 contained the same software error implicated in the Tyler deaths, but this machine included hardware interlocks that mitigated the consequences of the error. Protection against software errors can and should be built into both the system and the software itself. We cannot eliminate all software errors, but we can often protect against their worst effects, and we can recognize their likelihood in our decision making.

One of the serious mistakes that led to the multiple Therac-25 accidents was the tendency to believe that the cause of an accident had been determined (e.g., a microswitch failure in the case of Hamilton) without adequate evidence to come to this conclusion and without looking at all possible contributing factors. Without a thorough investigation, it is not possible to determine whether a sensor provided the wrong information, the software provided an incorrect command, or the actuator had a transient failure and did the wrong thing on its own. In the case of the Hamilton accident, a transient microswitch failure was assumed to be the cause even though the engineers were unable to reproduce the failure or to find anything wrong with the microswitch.

In general, it is a mistake to patch just one causal factor (such as the software) and assume that future accidents will be eliminated. Accidents are unlikely to occur in exactly the same way again. If we patch only the symptoms and ignore the deeper underlying causes, or if we fix only the specific cause of one accident, we are unlikely to have much effect on future accidents. The series of accidents involving the Therac-25 is a good example of exactly this problem: Fixing each individual software flaw as it was found did not solve the safety problems of the device.

Complacency.   Often it takes an accident to alert people to the dangers involved in technology. A medical physicist wrote about the Therac-25 accidents:

> In the past decade or two, the medical accelerator "industry" has become perhaps a little complacent about safety. We have assumed that the manufacturers have all kinds of safety design experience since they've been in the business a long time. We know that there are many safety codes, guides, and regulations to guide them and we have been reassured by the hitherto excellent record of these machines. Except for a few incidents in the 1960's (e.g., at Hammersmith, Hamburg) the use of medical accelerators has been remarkably free of serious radiation accidents until now. Perhaps, though we have been spoiled by this success [284].

This problem seems to be common in all fields.

Unrealistic Risk Assessments.   The first hazard analyses initially ignored software, and then they treated it superficially by assuming that all software errors were equally likely. The probabilistic risk assessments generated undue confidence in the machine and in the results of the risk assessment themselves. When the first Yakima accident was reported to AECL, the company did not investigate. Their evidence for their belief that the radiation burn could not have been caused by their machine included a probabilistic risk assessment showing that safety had increased by five orders of magnitude as a result of the microswitch fix.

The belief that safety had been increased by such a large amount seems hard to justify. Perhaps it was based on the probability of failure of the microswitch (typically 10^{-5}) AND-ed with the other interlocks. The problem with all such analyses is that they typically make many independence assumptions and exclude aspects of the problem—in this case, software—that are difficult to quantify but which may have a larger impact on safety than the quantifiable factors that are included.

Inadequate Investigation or Followup on Accident Reports.   Every company building safety-critical systems should have audit trails and incident analysis procedures that are applied whenever any hint of a problem is found that might lead to an accident. The first phone call by Tim Still should have led to an extensive investigation of the events at Kennestone. Certainly, learning about the first lawsuit should have triggered an immediate response.

Inadequate Software Engineering Practices. Some basic software engineering principles that apparently were violated in the case of the Therac-25 include the following:

- ☐ Software specifications and documentation should not be an afterthought.
- ☐ Rigorous software quality assurance practices and standards should be established.
- ☐ Designs should be kept simple and dangerous coding practices avoided.
- ☐ Ways to detect errors and get information about them, such as software audit trails, should be designed into the software from the beginning.
- ☐ The software should be subjected to extensive testing and formal analysis at the module and software level; system testing alone is not adequate. Regression testing should be performed on all software changes.
- ☐ Computer displays and the presentation of information to the operators, such as error messages, along with user manuals and other documentation need to be carefully designed.

The manufacturer said that the hardware and software were "tested and exercised separately or together over many years." In his deposition for one of the lawsuits, the quality assurance manager explained that testing was done in two parts. A "small amount" of software testing was done on a simulator, but most of the testing was done as a system. It appears that unit and software testing was minimal, with most of the effort directed at the integrated system test. At a Therac-25 user's meeting, the same man stated that the Therac-25 software was tested for 2,700 hours. Under questioning by the users, he clarified this as meaning "2700 hours of use." The FDA difficulty in getting an adequate test plan out of the company and the lack of regression testing are evidence that testing was not done well.

The design is unnecessarily complex for such critical software. It is untestable in the sense that the design ensured that the known errors (there may very well be more that have just not been found) would most likely not have been found using standard testing and verification techniques. This does not mean that software testing is not important, only that software must be designed to be testable and that simple designs may prevent errors in the first place.

Software Reuse. Important lessons about software reuse can be found in these accidents. A naive assumption is often made that reusing software or using commercial off-the-shelf software will increase safety because the software will have been exercised extensively. Reusing software modules does not guarantee safety in the new system to which they are transferred and sometimes leads to awkward and dangerous designs. Safety is a quality of the system in which the software is used; it is not a quality of the software itself. Rewriting the entire software in order to get a clean and simple design may be safer in many cases.

Safe versus Friendly User Interfaces. Making the machine as easy as possible to use may conflict with safety goals. Certainly, the user interface design left much to be desired, but eliminating multiple data entry and assuming that operators would check the values carefully before pressing the return key was unrealistic.

User and Government Oversight and Standards. Once the FDA got involved in the Therac-25, their response was impressive, especially considering how little experience they had with similar problems in computer-controlled medical devices. Since the Therac-25 events, the FDA has moved to improve the reporting system and to augment their procedures and guidelines to include software. The input and pressure from the user group was also important in getting the machine fixed and provides an important lesson to users in other industries.

Aerospace: Apollo 13, the DC-10, and Challenger

B.1 The Approach to Safety in Civil Aviation

The approach to safety used by the space industry and NASA has been described throughout the book. The civil aviation industry's approach has developed in parallel but with some distinct features.

Unlike other parts of the aerospace industry, commercial aviation technology, at least until recently, has progressed very slowly and with only a few major changes. The current high level of safety has been reached and maintained by careful analysis of accidents and immediate feedback of experience to design and operation. As O'Neill says, "Nearly every successful aircraft type has had one or more crashes in its early period and has subsequently been improved and redesigned to fly successfully for many years" (quoted in [145]).

The present approach to safety in commercial aviation has developed throughout the industry's relatively short history and has differed somewhat in Europe and the United States. The earliest approach to safety was to build each component so that it would not fail. The Wright brothers were aware that every major experimenter before them had been killed, so they built every part of their early aircraft with as high integrity as possible. In 1927, Charles Lindbergh, in the *Spirit of St. Louis*, also depended on high integrity of the parts. He designed his aircraft for one flight only and did not want a lot of redundancy because of the weight. The Ford Tri-motor in the 1930s again depended on high integrity in the parts.

The single-element integrity approach was adequate for limited flight operations, but it did not work for extensive commercial operations—sooner or later, something would fail. The 1930s saw a rash of Tri-motor crashes on takeoff when the aircraft lost an engine.

According to Follensbee, 1930 to 1945 was a transition period in which high integrity was still the primary goal, but selective redundancy was introduced along with efforts to design for failures [86]. For example, TWA insisted that their planes be able to take off with the failure of an engine, and a requirement for at least two engines was introduced.

Despite these hints of things to come, the dominant design philosophy was still based on single-element integrity. In addition, the Europeans, led by ICAO and the British Air Registration Board (predecessor to the present Civil Aviation Authority, or CAA), were strong advocates of *defined risk* or *acceptable risk*. This approach, emphasizing a calculated failure probability, matched a mathematically expressed level of risk to a design-failure risk number. The Americans during this period avoided the use of mathematical risk models and stayed with the qualitative techniques of design integrity.

The high activity in the post–World War II era marked the beginning of the current *fail-safe* concept in commercial aviation, designed to get the public on airplanes: In the 1950s, only 20 percent of the public was willing to fly. The lack of public confidence was well founded: Safety problems were experienced with flight controls, propellers, engine fires, and environmental conditions (such as heavy icing).

In this period, American planes started to be built according to the *single failure concept*, which specified that planes must be safe upon the occurrence of one failure. The adoption of this concept represented a major change in philosophy: The result was a decrease in accidents, an increase in public confidence, and an expansion of air travel.

While single-failure accidents were reduced by this new approach, multiple-failure accidents were still occurring. For example, an American Airlines Convair 240 accident in 1955 resulted from an engine fire and an independent fuel valve failure. During 1955, 18 air carrier accidents occurred in the United States. Although that year was worse than normal, it was not that unusual—in most years, there were 14 or 15 accidents.

To reduce accidents caused by failure combinations, fail-safe design was expanded beyond the single-failure concept to include any single failure plus any foreseeable combination of failures. The concept was continually developed and refined as experience with aircraft grew. By 1979, accidents had been reduced to half the number experienced in the 1950s, and by 1991 the number was reduced to approximately four or five accidents a year—one-fourth the number experienced in the 1950s—despite a ten- to twentyfold increase in airline operations between 1955 and 1991.

Follensbee believes that fail-safe design, which was increasingly built into the U.S. regulatory codes, has contributed greatly (along with advancing technology) to these impressive results. The reduction of accidents, however, cannot all be attributed to fail-safe design. Other factors may have been as or more important. In particular, the introduction of gas turbine engines (jets) had a tremendous influence on the overall safety record. Jet engines are much simpler than other engines in terms of needing fewer controls and fewer components, and they can sustain large amounts of damage before complete failure. In addition, improved cockpit interfaces and standardized training practices had major influences on safety.

The basic fail-safe design concept is that "no single failure or probable combination of failures during any one flight shall jeopardize the continued safe flight and landing of the airplane" [86]. This concept has been incorporated in the air worthiness codes along with additional safety considerations such as crashworthiness requirements for the entire airplane, aircraft performance requirements after loss of engine power, engine rotor-burst protection, performance requirements after total loss of electrical power, water flotation requirements, airplane controllability requirements, and fire-protection systems. Many of these requirements are the result of findings from accident investigations.

The use of the fail-safe concept is dependent on the definition of foreseeable catastrophic failures. Follensbee defines a failure as *foreseeable* if, on the basis of current scientific knowledge, logical analysis, or historical experience, it is judged likely to occur sometime in the lifetime of the fleet.

A variety of techniques are used to implement fail-safe design. These include

- Design integrity and quality
- Redundancy
- Isolation (so that a failure in one component does not affect another component)
- Reliability enhancement (high component reliability)
- Failure indications (the pilot needs to know that a failure has occurred since it might require flying the plane differently)
- Specified flight crew procedures
- Design for checkability and inspectability
- Damage tolerance (systems surrounding failures should be able to tolerate them in case the failures cannot be contained; this criterion is especially important for structures)
- Failure containment
- Designed failure paths (high energy failure sometimes cannot be contained or tolerated, but it can be directed to a safe path; an example is the use of structural "fuses" in pylons so that the engine will fall off before it damages the structure)
- Safety margins or factors
- Error tolerance (a design in which a human cannot make errors or in which errors are tolerated—for example, in the careful design of cockpit layouts and switches or the use of color coding or different shape connectors in wiring)

Fail-safe design does exact penalties in terms of weight, cost, and performance, and the U.S. aircraft industry relied heavily on advancing technology to reduce this impact. The introduction of the turbine engine and transonic speed technology in the 1950s greatly mitigated the penalties of fail-safe design and increased safety directly by the use of the safer jet technology. U.S. designers of that period assessed the fail-safe structural weight penalty at 7 percent, but felt the benefits exceeded the cost. The 1960s saw an explosion in the growth of air transport, largely because of improved jet aircraft technology that provided increased speed, efficiency, and safety. This improvement allowed and encouraged acceptance and expansion of fail-safe design requirements, and by 1970, the fail-safe design concept had been made the basis and primary criterion of U.S. transport certification rules [86].

The fail-safe concept never caught on in Europe, where integrity plus numerical probability (the 10^{-9} approach) was preferred. However, U.S. FAA Type Certification became the preferred standard of international carriers, and so the European manufacturers were forced to satisfy the U.S. airworthiness regulations.

This approach to safety, as we have seen, has been very effective in the aircraft industry. Some of this success is attributable to the relatively slow pace of basic design change and the ability to learn from experience. The aircraft industry has relied on conservatism and on the use of well-understood and "debugged" designs to maintain and enhance safety. As with other industries, however, the pace of technological change is increasing and new design features are being employed, such as the use of fly-by-wire systems, automated flight controls, and some unstable aircraft features. The increased pace is partially due to competitive pressures to introduce advanced control features and reduce fuel consumption. The impact on safety of these new factors is still unknown.

B.2 Apollo 13

Only a very brief description of this accident is included here. A more detailed description can be found in Bond [31], which was the source for much of the information below.

B.2.1 Background

By the time Apollo 13 was launched on April 11, 1970, much of the public and government excitement over the moon program had ebbed. Although the later Apollo missions carried a larger variety of scientific equipment and were scheduled to explore new and wider areas, government budget cuts forced two Apollo flights to be cancelled. There was an air of despondency among NASA staff [31].

Apollo was composed of three modules: a service module, a command module, and a lunar module. The lunar module, named *Aquarius*, was designed only for transport to the moon from the command module and back. The command module was located between the other two modules.

B.2.2 Events

The preparations for the Apollo 13 mission were not incident-free. During a test, liquid oxygen drained from the rocket, causing sparks from car ignition systems to set the vehicles on fire. A helium tank on the lunar module repeatedly had a higher pressure than expected. Most important with respect to the upcoming events, one of the two tanks that supplied oxygen for the command module's fuel cells and cabin air would not drain properly. To empty the tanks, personnel had to turn on the internal heaters and carry out the operation several times. Because of pressure to meet the launch schedule, the engineers decided to keep the tank since the drainage problem did not seem to affect its performance. This decision turned out to be a mistake. Later investigations suggested that the wires in one of the oxygen tanks were almost devoid of insulation as a result of accidental overheating and the extended process of emptying the tank.

The crew for the mission was originally supposed to be James Lovell, Fred Haise, and Thomas Mattingly. Just five days before launch, Mattingly had to be replaced because he had been exposed to German measles by one of the backup crew (Charles Duke). Since the backup crew could not simply be switched for the primary crew, Jack Swigert was tapped as a last-minute replacement as command module pilot. This switch meant that the crew would not have a chance to gain experience working together in critical situations.

Apollo 13 was launched on schedule with a destination of the Fra Mauro uplands. A problem with the Saturn V rocket—the second-stage engines cut off two minutes early—required the remaining engines to fire longer than planned, but the spacecraft reached Earth orbit successfully. Despite the extra burn, there was still enough fuel for the mission.

Everything was working perfectly, and the flight director at ground control told the press, "We've had no hardware problems at all." There were minor problems, though. Swigert had problems reading the gauge for one of the oxygen tanks; the reading had gone off the scale, and ground control asked for several "cryogenic stirs" to stir up the oxygen. They also were having problems with the helium pressure in the lunar module descent stage and low pressure in one of the hydrogen tanks.

About 56 hours after launch, the real problems began. Lovell later described what happened:

> Fred was still in the lunar module, Jack was back in the command module in the left-hand seat, and I was halfway in between the lower equipment bay wrestling with TV wires and a camera—watching Fred come on down—when all three of us heard a rather large bang—just one bang. Now before that . . . Fred had actuated a valve which normally gives us that sound. Since he didn't tell us about it, we all rather jumped up and were sort of worried about it; but it was his joke and we thought it was a lot of fun at the time. So when this bang came, we really didn't get concerned right away . . . but then I looked up at Fred . . . and Fred had that expression like it wasn't

his fault. We suddenly realized that something else had occurred . . . but exactly what we didn't know (quoted in [31, p.229–230]).

The crisis had begun five minutes earlier when an amber warning light indicated low pressure again in a hydrogen tank in the service module. As before, Swigert was told to stir the tank. He threw four switches that turned on fans in the tanks. Sixteen seconds later, an arc of electricity jumped across two wires, causing a fire in the oxygen tank. A rapid increase in the pressure of the oxygen was unnoticed for a while because the hydrogen pressure warning light overrode the warning light system for oxygen pressure. The escaping oxygen spread the fire through a service module bay. Combined with the gases from burning insulation, the oxygen blew out the weakest part of the bay—a panel on the craft's outer surface—causing the loud bang the astronauts heard. Swigert heard a master power alarm over his earphones and saw an amber warning light that signaled a power drop in main electrical bus B (one of two buses). He closed the hatch to the lunar module, returned to his seat, and told Mission Control, "OK, Houston, we've had a problem."

The explosion had closed the oxygen supply lines to fuel cells 1 and 3, which had then stopped working. Oxygen is critical both for the fuel cells to make electricity and as a source of nearly all the water and cabin oxygen for the astronauts. Because the instrumentation and telemetry could not directly relay the fact that an oxygen tank had exploded, the astronauts and ground control saw only a confusing pattern of pressure and temperature readings. The seriousness of the situation became apparent as Lovell reported that the oxygen pressure in tank 2 was reading zero, and the pressure in tank 1 was dropping.

Lovell looked out the window, saw a white cloud surrounding the service module, and calmly reported, "It looks to me that we are venting something. We are venting something out into space." One immediate problem was that the venting was pushing the spacecraft off course, which could have put it into an attitude that would have caused the guidance system to lock. Communications with mission control were poor and sometimes stopped completely as the spacecraft began to wobble.

At this point, the situation was serious. Two of the three fuel cells were dead, and the power output from the third cell was dropping rapidly. One oxygen tank was registering zero, and the oxygen in the second tank was also falling. If the third fuel cell died, the command module would have no electricity. The astronauts had only two hours of oxygen left in the command module, and the water supply was critical. At first, mission control didn't realize the extent of the emergency. There had been a quadruple failure, but nobody believed this was possible and so they assumed it had to be an instrumentation failure. Fred Haise later said:

> The ground may not have believed what it was seeing, but we did. It's like blowing a fuse in a house—the loss is a lot more real if you're in it. Things turn off. We believed that the oxygen situation was disastrous, because we could see it venting. The ground may have been hoping there

was an instrumentation problem, but on our gauges we could see that the pressure was gone in one tank and going down in the other, and it doesn't take you long to figure out what happened (quoted in [31, p.232]).

The astronauts had connected the reentry battery to main bus A, but they were told to disconnect it as the power drain continued. This backup battery would be their only source of power during reentry. The same was true for an oxygen tank in the command module, which was needed to ensure adequate oxygen during reentry. Ground control then ordered the valves closed that linked fuel cell 3 to the oxygen tanks, hoping that it was the fuel cell, not the tanks, that was leaking, but closing the valves made no difference. Once the valves were shut, they could not be opened again. The mission control engineers were first hopeful that the moon landing could be salvaged, but these thoughts were put aside when they realized that they were very likely to lose the spacecraft and the astronauts.

The lunar module has its own supply of oxygen and water, and it would have to act as a "life raft" until ground control could get the astronauts back to Earth. At the same time, the astronauts would also need the command module because it was the only part of the spacecraft that could survive reentry. In order to save enough battery power for reentry, the command module batteries were shut down. But without power, the command module became very cold: Nobody was sure that the instruments could take the cold and still work later when needed.

For the next four days, the astronauts lived in *Aquarius*. The lunar module was designed to keep two men alive for up to 50 hours, but it now had to provide life support for three men for 84 hours. There had never been a practice or simulation of this emergency, but contingency plans had been drawn up previously by NASA engineers and these were now dusted off. With just 15 minutes of power left in the command module, the crew charged up the reentry battery so it would be ready when they needed it and prepared to move into the lunar module.

Aquarius had no seats and had standing room only for two men. So while two men stayed in the lunar module, the third astronaut went into the cold and dark command module to try to get some sleep. To get them home, there were two choices. One was to try to reverse course, but the lunar module's descent engine did not have the power for this maneuver, and a failure would cause the spacecraft to crash on the moon. The alternative was to continue around the moon and use the moon's gravity to get back to Earth. The problem with this latter plan was that it would take 100 hours. So some means had to be found to reduce this time while at the same time stretching the remaining water and oxygen on the craft.

There were many dramatic moments and events over the next four days, and the astronauts were required to make difficult corrective maneuvers without the usual instruments. During this time, the crew coasted home in cold (below 10°C) and darkness while operating under the effects of fatigue, stress, lack of food (there was no means of heating water and the food packs did not mix well with cold water), and dehydration (they were drinking only 6 ounces of liquid per day, less than one-fifth the normal minimum). A deadly CO_2 buildup in the lunar module became a problem when they ran out of CO_2 filters. The lunar module required round canisters, but the command module used square filters. Using only the materials they could find on the spacecraft, the astronauts jury-rigged a way to connect the square filters and solved the problem.

The astronauts got less than 12 hours of sleep during the three and a half days between the explosion and splashdown. Haise was coming down with a bladder infection from the lack of water. At the same time, if the crucial maneuvers were not done right, the astronauts would either burn up in reentry or carom off into space forever.

Calculations had to be done on Earth—the lunar module had less computing power than the average PC today. NASA engineers worked out a reentry procedure that they hoped would work with the remaining equipment. The checklist took two hours to read up to the astronauts and required the use of every scrap of paper they could find in the spacecraft. Right before reentry, the astronauts moved back to the command module and powered up the backup battery, main bus B, and the other equipment, hoping that the freezing cold had not damaged them. To everyone's relief, everything seemed to work.

There was also worry about whether the heat shield was still intact, as the explosion had been in the same area of the spacecraft, but there was no way to check this. The lunar and service modules were jettisoned, and as the service module floated by, the astronauts could see the extensive damage caused by the explosion.

Radio contact is not possible for three minutes during reentry. That time passed and then another 30 seconds without any reply from the spacecraft. Everyone on the ground began to despair:

> Then came the sound of Jack Swigert's voice: "OK, Joe." In full view of the cameras on board the carrier *Iwo Jima*, first the drogues and then the three main parachutes opened. It was one of the most accurate splashdowns of all time, and the fastest recovery. The clapping and cheering in Mission Control were echoed all over the world [31, p.241].

A review panel investigated the accident and recommended modifications to the command and service modules that would eliminate the dangers associated with the use of pure oxygen. All Teflon insulation was replaced by stainless steel, and a fourth oxygen tank, located apart and isolated from the others, was added to the service module [31]. After five months, the improved spacecraft was put back into service.

B.2.3 Causal Factors

Many of the same general factors appear here that are found in most serious accidents. NASA was under budget pressures and had morale problems. Schedule pressures may have contributed to the engineers deciding to use the damaged oxygen tank despite the warning signs.

Nobody believed such a quadruple failure could occur—independence had been assumed incorrectly. This belief lead to a failure to take account of what was considered a low-probability event: Nobody thought the spacecraft could lose two fuel cells and two oxygen tanks. In addition, contingency plans had been drawn up for using the lunar module in an emergency, but had never been practiced in the simulator.

B.3 The DC-10 Cargo Door Saga

One of the worst accidents in aviation history occurred near Paris in March 1974, when a Turkish Airline DC-10 crashed, resulting in 346 deaths. A very detailed account of this accident and its precursors can be found in Eddy, Potter, and Page [75].

B.3.1 Background

To understand the accident, some background information about the DC-10 design is needed. During much of an airplane's flight regime, the air pressure outside is significantly less than that inside the cabin, resulting in a high pressure differential. Structural failure of the cabin hull, therefore, can lead to explosive decompression. The door design is particularly critical as the doors represent a potential weak point in the structural integrity of the plane.

The DC-10 was designed such that the flight controls for the number-2 engine, the elevators, the mechanically controlled trim, and the rudder are routed under the cabin floor, which has considerably less strength than the external parts of the airframe. If the cargo hold becomes depressurized, the higher pressure in the passenger compartment above can cause the cabin floor to collapse (which is what happened in the Paris crash), potentially severing the flight control cables.

B.3.2 Events

In 1968, while the DC-10 was still being designed, engineers from Rijksluchtvaartdienst (RLD), the Dutch equivalent of the FAA, issued repeated warnings about the integrity of the passenger compartment floors in jumbo jets. In the same year, American Airlines asked Douglas to change the hydraulic actuators for closing the cargo doors on the DC-10 to electrical ones. The Douglas engineers had proposed hydraulic actuators because they were highly familiar with this technology and so were their subcontractors. The American Airlines engineers, however, thought that a hydraulically operated door would have too many working parts, and electrically operated actuators would be lighter and thus save money in fuel costs. Because the electric actuators would have fewer parts, the door would also be easier to maintain. Douglas agreed to the American Airlines request.

In 1969, Douglas asked Convair, the firm developing the fuselage of the plane under a subcontract, to draft a failure modes and effects analysis (FMEA) for the lower cargo door system. Convair found nine potential failure sequences that could lead to a Class IV hazard (one involving danger to life); four failure modes involved explosive decompression in flight. The exact problem that eventually led to the accidents was not identified by the FMEA, but the analysis did demonstrate the danger of the door design without a totally reliable fail-safe locking system: A scenario very similar to what actually happened later in the Windsor and Paris accidents was identified. According to the FMEA, little reliance was to be given to warning lights on the flight deck because "failures in the indicator circuit, which result in incorrect indication of door locked and/or closed, may not be discovered during the checkout prior to takeoff" (quoted in [75]). Convair also concluded that even less reliance should be placed on warning systems that depended on the alertness of ground crews.

Before FAA certification, manufacturers are required to provide a FMEA for those systems critical to safety. However, the DC-10 FMEAs submitted by Douglas to the FAA did not include any mention of the possibility of a Class IV hazard related to a malfunction of the lower cargo doors.

The RLD concern continued, and they explicitly warned about the cargo-door danger at an ICAO meeting in Montreal. In 1970, a prototype DC-10 was unveiled, and on May 29, the passenger floor did collapse after the cargo door blew out during a static ground test of the air conditioning system. The test involved building up a pressure differential of four to five pounds per square inch, which caused a large section of the cabin floor to collapse into the hold.

The Douglas response to this event was similar to their response to later events—they blamed it on human error on the part of the mechanic who was responsible for closing the door. They did, however, modify the door to add what they assumed were extra safeguards. In fact, the new vent door system contributed little or no extra safety [75].

In 1971, the aircraft was certified despite reports of problems with the rear cargo door and the floor collapse during test. The RLD complained directly to Douglas about the design when KLM decided to buy the plane, but no changes were made. The FAA was not informed about these discussions.

After the plane became operational, the warnings about the cargo-door design turned out to be correct. There were 11 entries in maintenance logs up to June 1972 concerning difficulties with locking the door. Then, on June 12, 1972, an American Airlines DC-10 lost part of its passenger floor when a cargo door failed over Windsor, Ontario. Catastrophe was averted only by the extraordinary poise and skill of the pilot, Bryce McCormick. He had trained himself to fly the plane using only the engines because he was concerned about a decompression-caused loss of the control cables.

McCormick was a conservative pilot and had been worried from the beginning about the absence of any mechanical way to operate the control surfaces on the DC-10. In most smaller jets at the time, there was a manual backup system to operate the flaps, rudder, and elevator if the hydraulic systems should fail. The jumbo jets, however, relied on hydraulics without a manual backup.

To prepare himself for an emergency, McCormick experimented with a DC-10 simulator in Texas. He figured out what would happen in the event of total hydraulic failure and how to fly the DC-10 "on its engines" by using differential engine power to steer.

By chance, McCormick was the pilot when this emergency first occurred. The hydraulic lines survived the explosive decompression and partial floor collapse, but the wire cables that send signals from the cockpit to the tail were severed or jammed. McCormick was able to land the plane, using the differential engine power technique he had devised in the simulator.

After his near catastrophe, McCormick recommended that every DC-10 pilot be informed of the consequences of explosive decompression and trained in the flying techniques that he and his crew had used to save their passengers and plane. McDonnell-Douglas never did this. Instead, they attributed the Windsor incident to human failure on the part of the baggage handler and not to any error on the part of their designers and engineers. McDonnell-Douglas decided that all they had to do was to come up with a fix that would prevent baggage handlers from forcing the door.

One of the discoveries after this accident was that the door could be improperly closed, but the external signs, such as the position of the external handle, made it appear to be closed properly. In addition, this incident proved that the cockpit warning system could fail, and the crew would then not know that they were taking off without a properly closed door.

> The aviation industry does not normally receive such manifest warnings of basic design flaws in an aircraft without cost to human life. Windsor deserved to be celebrated as an exceptional case when every life was saved through a combination of crew skill and the sheer luck that the plane was so lightly loaded. If there had been more passengers and thus more weight, damage to the control cables would undoubtedly have been more severe, and it is highly questionable if any amount of skill could have saved the plane [75].

The regional branch of the FAA, headed by a man named Basnight, started to investigate the Windsor incident and asked the Douglas company if there had been any previous problems with DC-10 cargo doors. The company admitted only that there had been a few "minor problems," but did not provide the operating reports filed by the airlines using DC-10s. A highly experienced test pilot, Dick Sliff, who worked for Basnight, knew that airplane systems usually give some warning before they fail. He was disturbed by Douglas' attitude and "raised a fuss" to get the airline reports [75]. Examining the records, Sliff found that there had been about one hundred reports of the door failing to close properly during the ten months of DC-10 service and that Douglas had already recommended modifications to the system.

The National Transportation Safety Board recommended that the FAA issue an Airworthiness Directive requiring (1) the redesign of the door so that it was physically impossible for the door to be improperly closed and (2) the modification and strengthening of the cabin floor to prevent its collapse after a sudden decompression.

The FAA Western Regional Office, under Basnight's supervision, wrote a draft Airworthiness Directive for the problem, but it was never issued. Instead, a nonmandatory agreement was made between Douglas and the head of the FAA, which later became known as the "Gentleman's Agreement," simply to add a metal plate rather than redesign the door to eliminate the hazard. Basnight wrote a memo expressing his outrage at this arrangement.

Fifteen days after the Windsor incident, the senior Convair engineer directing the DC-10 fuselage development, Dan Applegate, wrote and filed away his own memo expressing his shock and dismay at the agreement (quotations from this latter memo can be found in Chapter 3). Applegate's memo, directed to the vice president of Convair, detailed the ways that cargo doors could open during flight, the history of the cargo door design changes, and the inevitability of future accidents unless the door design was changed and the cabin floor was strengthened.

In their response to Applegate, Convair management denied neither the technical assessment nor the predictions, but argued that the potential Convair financial liabilities involved in grounding the plane (which would be high and would place McDonnell-Douglas at a competitive disadvantage) prohibited them from passing on the contents of the Applegate memo to McDonnell-Douglas [238]. Applegate was told by his management that no additional effort would be made to correct the problem. The FAA was never notified about this memo; in fact, under Convair's contract with McDonnell-Douglas, Convair was prohibited from contacting the FAA directly about the issue [147].

The plate added to the door might have been sufficient, but first it had to be added. There were 39 DC-10s in service when Douglas proposed the changes. Five planes were modified within 90 days, 18 were not modified until 1973, and one not until a year and a half after the bulletin was issued. In Long Beach, the required changes also were not made to some new aircraft still at the factory, including one destined for Turkish Airlines (THY), but this omission was not discovered until later.

After the Windsor incident, in September 1972, the Dutch RLD again sent a delegation to Los Angeles, this time to meet with both the FAA and McDonnell-Douglas in order to discuss their concerns about the DC-10 design. McDonnell-Douglas took the position that the DC-10 floor met all of the FAA air worthiness directives. The RLD replied that the directives were inadequate. In a formal reply to the RLD, the FAA said, "We do not concur with RLD views concerning the inadequacy of FAA requirements" [75]. The RLD certified the DC-10, but placed on record their reluctance in doing so.

By February 1973, the FAA had changed their minds and decided that something needed to be done about jumbo jet floors. McDonnell-Douglas insisted that the chances of a cargo door opening in flight were "extremely remote" and that a reassessment of the DC-10 design showed that the current standard was adequate.

In 1973, DC-10 number 29 was delivered to Turkish Airlines, whose ground crews were presumably trained in all aspects of the maintenance of the aircraft.

Records hint that this was not necessarily the case, perhaps because of national pride or attempts by Turkish Airlines to limit expenses [309].

On the day of the crash, a strike in London grounded all British European Airways (BEA) flights. Demand for flights to London was high because a rugby match had just been played in Paris, and the Turkish Airlines plane filled quickly. Many flights had to be canceled because of the strike, but the Turkish plane could get out if they hurried, and the departure was rushed.

Ground support for Turkish Airlines aircraft at Orly was sublet to a private company called SAMOR. The person doing the work was a 39-year-old Algerian immigrant named Mahmoudi, who had worked for SAMOR since 1968. He was not familiar with this version of the DC-10 cargo door, but was given instructions about how to close the door and told that if for any reason the latches did not go home, the locking handle would encounter resistance and the vent door would refuse to close. He was warned against trying to force the handle. However, for various controversial reasons, the locking pins in the door had been adjusted so that only 13 pounds of pressure was required to operate the locking handle successfully and to close the vent door even if the latches were actually only partially closed.

Instructions for locking the door were printed in English next to it, but although Mahmoudi spoke several languages, English was not one of them. The procedure was complicated and difficult. When he closed the door, the handle appeared to seat and the vent door to close.

The final check on the door was not Mahmoudi's job. SAMOR's contract said that the airline was responsible for ensuring that every plane was safe before it took off, and someone from Turkish Airlines was supposed to check the cargo door peephole. Usually this task was done by Osman Zeytin, the Turkish Airlines' head mechanic at Orly, but he was away on vacation. Sometimes Turkish Airlines flight engineers would leave the cockpit to peer through the peepholes, and there was also a Turkish Airlines ground mechanic, Hasan Engin Uzok, on board the DC-10. None of the airport workers saw him or the flight engineer check the door.

A safety device, added by McDonnell-Douglas after the failure of the cabin floor during the air conditioning tests, should not have allowed the cabin to be pressurized when the door was not properly locked. Apparently this device failed, as it had in the 1972 Windsor accident. An annunciator light on the flight engineer's panel should have warned that the cargo door was not properly closed. The light was designed to remain on until the cargo door had been fully closed, but when Mahmoudi pulled the locking handle down, the light in the cockpit went off. There have been allegations that the light had been tampered with, perhaps to make maintenance easier.

The Turkish Airlines plane took off carrying 353 passengers, 11 crew members, and a full cargo compartment. It climbed to 13,000 feet—approximately the same altitude as the Windsor accident—and headed for London. Eight minutes later, the cargo door blew out and the cabin floor buckled. Six passengers, still in their seats, were sucked down and out of the plane. The control cables to the rudder and stabilizer were severed, and the pilots could not recover. If the plane had not been so full (and had less pressure been on the floor), enough of the controls might have survived the floor collapse to avoid the accident.

After the crash, Sanford McDonnell expressed the McDonnell-Douglas position by placing the blame on Mahmoudi—whom he called an "illiterate" baggage handler—and the other ground personnel, just as the company had blamed the Windsor accident on the baggage handler. Later, the company shifted the blame to Convair and Turkish Airlines, both of which it accused of negligence [75].

An FAA investigation showed that the cargo door support plate, stipulated in the Gentleman's Agreement, was never added to the door of the Turkish Airlines DC-10 (number 29) in the factory before being delivered. Laker Airlines also found that the modification was missing on two planes it received after the change was agreed upon.

The president of Douglas Aircraft claimed that the records showed that the factory modifications had been made, and the aircraft was stamped by its inspectors as having been modified. The inspectors were questioned under oath after the accident, and none could recall having worked on the cargo door of any DC-10 at any time during 1972 nor could they recall any occasion on which they had worked together. They were certain they had not inspected the doors of number 29 on July 18, as the records showed, and had no idea how their stamps could have gotten on the maintenance records. McDonnell-Douglas' position was that the falsification of manufacturing records was an isolated and totally mysterious failure in an otherwise excellent system [75].

The FAA also discovered, after an examination of the records of every U.S. airline that owned DC-10s for the six-month period between October 1973 and March 1974, that there had been 1,000 cargo-door incidents in less than 100 DC-10s—an average of more than ten cargo door incidents for every DC-10 operating in the United States. Airlines routinely submit these maintenance reliability reports to the manufacturers [75].

The FAA finally ordered modifications on all DC-10s that eliminated the hazard and made mandatory the modifications that were supposed to have been made 20 months before. In addition, an FAA regulation introduced in July 1975 required all wide-bodied jet floors to be able to tolerate a hole in the fuselage of 20 square feet.

B.3.3 Causal Factors

The DC-10's manufacturer, McDonnell-Douglas—with the FAA's apparent acquiescence—had ignored the clear warning in the Windsor accident. They had also failed to modify the door on the plane sold to Turkish Airlines.

Again, we find failure to heed warnings, failure to eliminate root causes, irregularities in the certification procedures, and blaming accidents on human error instead of eliminating the design problem.

B.4 The Space Shuttle Challenger Accident

The report of the Presidential Commission on the Space Shuttle *Challenger* Accident [295] should be read by anyone interested in the engineering of safe systems: It provides an excellent example of a well-researched and comprehensive accident report that does not stop with a superficial treatment of the accident causes but goes beyond the easy attribution of "technical failure" or "human error." The problems the Rogers Commission found were not unique to NASA, but are common in many industries and organizations. Unless otherwise noted, the information about the accident provided in this appendix is from the Rogers Commission report.

B.4.1 Background

The Space Shuttle is part of a larger Space Transportation System (STS) concept that arose in the 1960s when Apollo was in development. The concept originally included a manned Mars expedition, a space station in lunar orbit, and an Earth-orbiting station serviced by a reusable ferry, or Space Shuttle. Funding for this large an effort, on the order of that provided for Apollo, never materialized, and the concept was scaled back until the reusable Space Shuttle, earlier considered only the transport element of a broad transportation system, became the focus of NASA's efforts.

The Shuttle concept itself was scaled back, because of cost considerations, to a three-part system consisting of the orbiter, an expendable external fuel tank containing liquid propellants for the orbiter's engines, and two recoverable solid rocket boosters (SRBs). Contracts were awarded in 1972: Rockwell was responsible for the design and development of the orbiter, Martin Marietta was assigned the development and fabrication of the external tank, Morton Thiokol was awarded the contract for the SRBs, and Rocketdyne (a division of Rockwell) was selected to develop the orbiter main engines.

Three NASA field centers were given responsibility for the program. Johnson Space Center in Houston, Texas, was to manage the orbiter, while Marshall Space Flight Center in Huntsville, Alabama, was assigned responsibility for the orbiter's main engines, the external tank, and the SRBs. Kennedy Space Center in Merritt Island, Florida, would assemble the Shuttle components, check them out, and conduct launches. The management structure in NASA is fairly complex (see Chapter 12 for a broad outline). Basically there are four management levels, with Level I being the highest.

Because of continual budget cuts and constraints, the original fleet of five Shuttle orbiters was reduced to four. The orbital test flight program began in early 1981, and, after the landing of STS4 in July 1982, NASA declared that the Shuttle was "operational." Including the initial orbital tests, the Shuttle flew 24 successful missions over a 57-month period before the *Challenger* accident.

An important factor in this accident was the pressures exerted on NASA by an unrealistic flight schedule with inadequate resources and by commitments to customers. The nation's reliance on the Shuttle as its principal space launch capability created a relentless pressure on NASA to increase the flight rate. The attempt to build up to 24 missions a year brought problems such as compression of training schedules, a lack of spare parts, the focusing of resources on near-term projects, and a dilution of the human and material resources that could be applied to any particular flight. In addition, customer commitments may occasionally have obscured engineering concerns.

The Rogers Commission report notes that at the same time the flight rate was increasing, a variety of factors reduced the number of skilled personnel available to deal with it: retirements, hiring freezes, transfers to other programs like the Space Station, and changing to a single contractor for operations support (a significant number of employees elected not to change, which resulted in the need to hire and qualify new personnel).

NASA had a perception that less safety, reliability, and quality assurance activity would be required during routine Shuttle operations. Therefore, after the successful completion of the orbital test phase and the declaration of the Shuttle as "operational," several safety, reliability, and quality assurance organizations were reorganized and reduced in size. The Chief Engineer at NASA headquarters had overall responsibility for safety, reliability, and quality assurance. To carry out this responsibility, he had a staff of 20 people, only two of whom spent 10 percent and 25 percent of their time, respectively, on these issues. Moreover, some safety panels, which were providing safety review, went out of existence or were merged.

> The unrelenting pressure to meet the demands of an accelerating flight schedule might have been adequately handled by NASA if it had insisted upon the exactingly thorough procedures that were its hallmark during the Apollo program. An extensive and redundant safety program comprising interdependent safety, reliability, and quality assurance functions existed during and after the lunar program to discover any potential safety problems. Between that period and 1986, however, the program became ineffective. This loss of effectiveness seriously degraded the checks and balances essential for maintaining flight safety [295, p.152].

The Rogers Commission concluded that the technical cause of the accident was a failure of a pressure seal in the aft field joint of the right solid rocket motor. The solid rocket motor is assembled from four large cylindrical segments—each over 25 feet long, 12 feet in diameter, and containing more than 100 tons of fuel; the resulting four joints are called field joints. These joints are sealed by two rubber O-rings that are installed when the motor is assembled (see Figure B.1). The primary O-ring and its backup, the secondary O-ring, were designed to seal a tiny gap in the joints that is created by pressure at ignition. The O-ring seal must be pressure actuated very early in the solid rocket motor ignition. If this actuation is delayed, the rocket's combustion gases may blow by the O-ring and damage or destroy the seals.

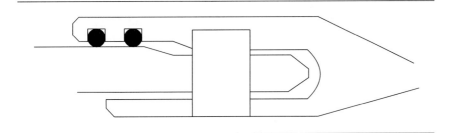

FIGURE B.1
Shuttle SRB joint with two O-rings.

O-ring resiliancy is directly related to temperature. If the temperature is low, resiliancy is reduced, and the O-ring is very slow to return to its normal rounded shape. If the O-ring remains in its compressed position too long, then the gap between the O-ring and the upstream channel wall may not be sealed in time to prevent joint failure.

The design of the Shuttle SRB was based on the U.S. Air Force Titan III, one of the most reliable ever produced. Significant design changes were made, however, including changes in the placement of the O-rings. The shuttle solid rocket motor had two O-rings—the second was intended to provide backup: If the primary O-ring did not seal, then the secondary one was supposed to pressurize and seal the joint. Part of the Shuttle joint was longer than in the Titan in order to accommodate two O-rings instead of one. The longer length made the joint more susceptible to bending under combustion pressure than the Titan joint.

B.4.2 Events

The Rogers Commission found that the Space Shuttle's SRB problem began with a faulty design of its joint and increased as both NASA and the Thiokol management first failed to recognize the problem, then failed to fix it when it was recognized, and finally treated it as an acceptable risk.

Leon Ray (an engineer at Marshall) first concluded after tests in 1977 and 1978 that rotation of the SRB field joint under pressure caused the loss of the secondary O-ring as a backup seal. Nevertheless, in November 1980, the SRB joint was classified on the NASA Shuttle Critical Items List (CIL) as Criticality 1R.[1] The use of R, representing redundancy, signifies that NASA believed that the secondary O-ring would pressurize and seal if the primary O-ring failed to do so. The 1980 CIL does express doubt about the secondary O-ring successfully sealing if

---

[1] Criticality 1 means that failure could cause the loss of life or vehicle. Criticality 1R means that the component contains redundant hardware. Over 700 pieces of the Shuttle hardware were listed as Criticality 1 [215].

the primary should fail under certain conditions—when the motor case pressure reaches or exceeds 40 percent of maximum expected operating pressure—but the joint was assigned a 1R classification from November 1980 through the flight of STS-5 in November 1982.

O-ring anomalies were found during the initial flights, but the O-ring erosion problem was not reported in the Marshall problem assessment system and given a tracking number, as were other flight anomalies. After tests in May 1982, Marshall management finally accepted the conclusion that the secondary O-ring was no longer functional after the joints rotated under 40 percent of the SRB maximum operating pressure, and the criticality was changed to Criticality 1 on December 17, 1982.

Testimony at the Rogers Commission hearings supported the conclusion that, despite the change in criticality from 1R to 1, NASA and Thiokol management still considered the joint to be a redundant seal in all but a few exceptional cases. The disagreement went to a "referee" for testing, which was not concluded until after the *Challenger* accident. Since the design was now rated Criticality 1, a waiver was required to allow it to be used. However, most of the problem reporting paperwork tracking the O-ring erosion problem that was generated by Thiokol and Marshall still listed the SRB field joint seal as Criticality 1R long after the status had been changed to Criticality 1. The Rogers Commission suggested that this misrepresentation of criticality may have led some managers to believe—wrongly—that redundancy existed. The problem assessment system operated by Rockwell contractors at Marshall still listed the field joint as 1R on March 7, 1986, more than five weeks after the accident. The Commission concluded that, as a result, informed decision making by key managers was impossible.

Before STS flight 41-B in January 1984, the O-ring erosion and blow-by problem occurred infrequently. STS 41-B had extensive erosion, but Thiokol filed a problem report concluding that the secondary O-ring was an adequate backup according to the tests they had made. Some engineers at Marshall and Thiokol disagreed with the Thiokol numbers, but approval to fly 41-C was given. After more erosion and blow-by was found on 41-C, NASA asked Thiokol for a formal review of the SRB joint-sealing procedures. Thiokol was asked to identify the cause of the erosion, determine whether it was acceptable, define any necessary changes, and reevaluate the putty then being used.[2]

A letter in 1984 from Thiokol suggested that the chance of O-ring erosion had increased because of a change (higher pressure) made after STS-9 in the procedures used to check for leaks in the joint seal. The increased air pressure forced through the joint during the O-ring leak check was creating more putty blow holes, allowing more focused jets on the primary O-ring, and thereby increasing the frequency of erosion. The flight experiences supported this conclusion. During the first nine flights (before flight 41-B in January 1984), when the leak check

---

[2] Asbestos-filled putty was used to pack the space in the joint and prevent O-ring damage from the heat of combustion gases. Problems with the putty can lead to the burning of both O-rings and thus to an explosion.

pressure was lower, only one field joint anomaly had been found. When the leak-test pressure was increased for STS 41-B and later flights, over half the Shuttle missions experienced field joint O-ring blow-by erosion of some kind. The same experience was found with the nozzle O-ring.

Thiokol and NASA witnesses at the Rogers Commission hearings agreed that they were aware that the increase in leak-test blow holes in the putty could contribute to O-ring erosion. Nevertheless, Thiokol recommended and NASA accepted the increased pressure to ensure that the joint passed the integrity tests. Thiokol did establish plans for putty tests to determine how the putty was affected by the leak check after the 41-C experience, but their progress in completing the tests was slow.

On January 24, 1985, STS 51-C was launched at the coldest temperature to that date—53 degrees. O-ring erosion occurred in both solid boosters, and blow-by was more significant than had been experienced before. The problem assessment report (which was started to track field joint erosion after 41-B) described the O-ring anomaly after 51-C as "as bad or worse than previously experienced. . . . Design changes are pending test results" [295, p.136]. The design changes being considered included modifying the O-rings and adding grease around them to fill the void left by the putty blow holes created by the leak tests.

Thiokol presented an analysis of the problem on February 8, 1985 that noted a concern that the seal could be lost, but it concluded that the risk of primary O-ring damage should be accepted. Risk acceptance was justified, in part, on the assumption that the secondary O-ring would work even with erosion. During the flight readiness assessment at Marshall for 51-D, Thiokol mentioned temperature, for the first time, as a factor in O-ring erosion and blow-by. Thiokol concluded that "low temperature enhanced probability of blow-by—51-C experienced worst case temperature change in Florida history" [295, p.136].

The joint seal problem occurred in each of the next four Shuttle flights. Thiokol conducted O-ring resiliency tests in response to the extensive O-ring problems found on flight 51-C in January and found that the key variable was temperature.

STS 51-B was launched on April 29, 1985. Inspection of the O-rings after the flight revealed a more serious problem than they had previously experienced: The primary nozzle O-ring never sealed at all, and the secondary O-ring was eroded. The erosion was greater than that predicted as the maximum possible by the model they were using. As a result, the Marshall Problem Assessment Committee (a Level III committee) placed a launch constraint on the Shuttle system that applied to flight 51-F and all subsequent flights (including the fatal 51-L *Challenger* flight). Thiokol officials testified at the Rogers Commission hearings that they were unaware of this launch constraint, but Thiokol letters referenced the report containing the constraint.

A launch constraint means that the problem has to be addressed during the flight readiness cycle to ensure that NASA is staying within the "test experience base"—that is, the suspect element is operated only within the parameters for which it has worked successfully before. Although launch constraints are required to be reported to Level II, this was not done. After the launch constraint was imposed, it was waived for each shuttle flight thereafter, including the fatal *Challenger* flight. The Rogers Commission was told that two entries on the O-ring erosion nozzle problem report had erroneously stated that the O-ring erosion problem had been resolved or closed.

After the 51-B erosion problems became known, Roger Boisjoly (an engineer at Thiokol) wrote a memo on July 31, 1985, recommending that a team be set up to solve the O-ring problem. The memo concluded that a catastrophe could occur if immediate action was not taken. On August 19, Thiokol and Marshall program managers briefed NASA Headquarters on the seal erosion problem and concluded that the O-ring seal was a critical matter but that it was safe to fly. An "accelerated pace" was recommended for the effort to eliminate seal erosion. Thiokol's Vice President for Engineering, noting that "the result of a leak at any of the joints would be catastrophic," announced on August 20 the establishment of a Thiokol task force to recommend short-term and long-term solutions.

Early in October, Thiokol management received two separate memos from the O-ring task force describing administrative delays and lack of cooperation. One was written by Roger Boisjoly and warned about lack of management support for the O-ring team's efforts. The other memo started with the word "HELP!" and complained about the seal task force being "constantly delayed by every possible means"; the memo ended with the words "This is a red flag."

Shuttle flight 61-A was launched on October 30, 1985, and experienced both nozzle O-ring erosion and field joint O-ring blow-by. These anomalies were not mentioned at the Flight Readiness Review for the next flight. Flight 61-B was launched on November 26, 1985; it also sustained nozzle O-ring erosion and blow-by.

In December, R. V. Ebeling (manager of Thiokol's solid rocket motor ignition system) became so concerned about the seriousness of the O-ring problem that he told the other members of the seal task force that he believed Thiokol should not ship any more motors until the problem was fixed.

On December 10, Thiokol wrote a memo to NASA suggesting that the O-ring problem be closed with respect to the problem-tracking process. Thiokol officials testified at the Rogers Commission hearings that this was in response to a request from the Director of Engineering at Marshall. Having the problem listed as closed meant that it would not be involved in the flight readiness reviews, although it could still be worked on. The letter was still in the review cycle at the time of flight 51-L (*Challenger*), but entries were placed on all Marshall problem reports (the closed-loop tracking system) indicating that the problem was considered closed. The Commission heard testimony that these entries were "in error."

Flight 51-L was originally scheduled for July 1985, but by January 1985 the flight had been postponed to late November to accommodate changes in payloads. The launch was later delayed further and finally rescheduled for January 22, 1986. The launch was further delayed three times and scrubbed once. The first of these last three postponements was announced on December 23, 1985, in order to accommodate a slip in the launch date of mission 61-L. On January 22, the launch was changed from January 23 to January 25 because of problems caused by the late launch of flight 61-C.

The third postponement occurred on January 25: Because of an unacceptable weather forecast for the Kennedy area, the launch was rescheduled for January 27. But the January 27 launch countdown had to be halted when the crew entry and exit hatch handle jammed. By the time the hatch handle was fixed, the crosswinds at Kennedy exceeded the maximum allowable for a return-to-launch abort, and the launch was canceled at 12:26 P.M. and rescheduled for January 28.

At 2 P.M. on February 27, the mission management team met again. At that time, the weather was expected to clear, but temperatures were to be in the low twenties overnight and a temperature of 26 degrees was predicted at the intended time of launch (9:38 A.M.).

Robert Ebeling, at the Thiokol plant, heard about the predicted low temperatures and called a meeting at 2:30 P.M. with Roger Boisjoly and the other Thiokol engineers. The engineers expressed great concern about launching in such low temperatures, since this was far below previous experience and below the temperatures for which the SRBs had been qualified.

A teleconference was set up for 5:45 P.M. with the Thiokol engineering people in Utah, the Thiokol people at Marshall, and the Thiokol representative at Kennedy. NASA participants were all from Marshall.[3] Concerns about the effect of low temperature on the O-rings and joint seal were presented by Thiokol, along with an opinion that the launch should be delayed. A recommendation was also made that Arnold Aldrich, the Program Manager at Johnson (Level II), be informed about the concerns, but this was never done. The Rogers Commission report criticized the propensity at Marshall to contain potentially serious problems and to attempt to resolve them internally rather than communicate them forward. It also noted that the project managers for the various elements of the Shuttle program felt more accountable to their center management than to the Shuttle program organization. Vital program information frequently bypassed the NSTS Program Manager.

The Marshall and Thiokol personnel decided to schedule a second teleconference later in the day, after data could be faxed to the various locations. The Thiokol charts and written data were faxed to Kennedy, and the second phase of the teleconference started at 8:45 P.M. with additional personnel involved. The history of the O-ring erosion and blow-by in the SRB joints of previous flights was presented along with the test results at Thiokol. Bob Lund, Thiokol Vice President of Engineering, presented the conclusion of the Thiokol engineers that the O-ring temperature must be at or greater than 53 degrees at launch, which

---

[3] These NASA participants included the Marshall Deputy Director of Science and Engineering, the Marshall Shuttle Project Manager, and the Marshall Deputy Shuttle Project Manager.

was the previous lowest launch temperature. Boisjoly testified at the Commission hearings that no pro-launch statement was made by anyone in the room.

During this conference, the Marshall Deputy Director of Science and Engineering is reported to have said that he was "appalled" by Thiokol's recommendation. The manager of the SRB project at Marshall suggested that Thiokol was using different launch criteria than in the previous 24 flights and that under those criteria, they would not be able to launch until April. After protesting that Thiokol was changing the launch criteria on the night before a scheduled mission, he reportedly exclaimed, "You can't do that." The NASA personnel challenged the Thiokol conclusions and recommendations, stressing that the secondary O-ring would seal if the primary one did not. Some Thiokol engineers testified that usually in reviews, the engineers were required to prove that they were ready to launch. In this discussion, however, they felt that the roles had been reversed and that the engineers were required to prove that the launch would *not* be successful.

The teleconference was recessed at about 10:30 P.M. for an off-the-air caucus of Thiokol personnel. This recess lasted for about 30 minutes. During this time, the Thiokol manager of the Space Booster Project at Kennedy continued to argue against the launch. He testified that he said, "If we are wrong and something goes wrong on this flight, I wouldn't want to have to be the person to stand up in front of a board of inquiry and say that I went ahead and told them to go ahead and fly this thing outside what the motor was qualified to" [295, p.95].

At Thiokol in Utah, about ten engineers participated in the discussion, and very strong objections to the launch were voiced. After the discussion between Thiokol management and engineers was completed, a final management review began. The Thiokol Senior Vice President said that a management decision had to be made, turned to the Thiokol Vice President of Science and Engineering, and asked him to take off his engineering hat and to put on his management hat.

The teleconference was reconvened at 11:00 P.M., at which time Thiokol management stated that they had reassessed the problem and were withdrawing their opposition to the launch—the temperature was a concern, but the data was inconclusive.[4] They concluded that (1) there was a substantial margin to erode the primary O-ring by a factor of three times the previous worst case and (2) the "harder" O-rings would take longer to seat, but that if the primary seal did not seat, the secondary seal would. They therefore recommended that launch proceed. NASA Level I and II management and the Launch Director for 51-L were never

---

[4] The Commission report noted that a careful analysis of the flight history of O-ring performance would have revealed the correlation of O-ring damage and low temperature, but neither NASA nor Thiokol carried out such an analysis. Instead, they considered only the flights in which thermal distress had been observed and not the frequency of occurrence in all flights. When all flights are included, only three incidents of O-ring thermal distress occurred out of 20 flights with O-ring temperatures at 66°F or above, while all four flights at 63°F or below experienced it. "Consideration of the entire launch temperature history indicates that the probability of O-ring distress is increased to almost a certainty if the temperature of the joint is less than 65" [295].

told about the initial Thiokol concerns and opposition to the launch—all the discussions and conferences had included only Marshall and Thiokol personnel. The Rogers Commission concluded that the Thiokol management reversed its position and recommended the launch of 51-L, at the urging of Marshall and contrary to the views of its engineers, in order to accommodate a major customer.

There had been heavy rain since *Challenger* had been rolled out to the launch pad, approximately 7 inches compared with the 2.5 inches that would have been normal for that season. The Rogers Commission report notes that water may have gotten into the joints, and at the time of launch, it was cold enough that water present in the joint would freeze. Tests showed that ice in the joint could inhibit proper secondary seal performance.

Ice accumulated on the launch pad during the night. At the weather briefing for the Shuttle crew, the temperature and ice on the pad were discussed, but the crew was not informed of any concern about the effects of low temperature. After an ice inspection, the launch was delayed to allow more time for the ice to melt. After consultation with senior advisors and without having been told about the O-ring discussions at Marshall or about the doubts of the Thiokol engineers concerning flight safety at those low temperatures, Shuttle Director Jesse Moore gave the permission to launch. The ambient temperature at launch was 36 degrees measured at ground level, 15 degrees colder than that of any previous launch.

The flight began at 11:39 A.M. on January 28, 1986. Analysis of photographs taken immediately after ignition showed a puff of black smoke coming from the after section of the right SRB. As *Challenger* cleared the tower, gas was already blowing by the rings, although the gap was temporarily plugged by burning rubber and putty. *Challenger* experienced the worst vibrations of any flight to date as it was buffeted by gusts of wind for almost 30 seconds. At 58.7 seconds after ignition, a small flame like a blowtorch appeared at the side of the SRB, unnoticed by anyone on the ground or in the shuttle. It began to burn through the main fuel tank as well as one of the struts that held the rocket to the tank. Less than 14 seconds later, the strut gave way and the pointed nose of the SRB swiveled inward to pierce the fuel tank.

Seventy three seconds after the flight had begun, it ended with the hydrogen and oxygen propellants igniting in a huge ball of flame that destroyed the external tank and exposed the orbiter to severe aerodynamic loads that caused complete structural breakup. All seven crew members died. The two SRBs flew out of the fireball and were destroyed by the Air Force range safety officer 110 seconds after launch. It was the worst accident in the history of manned spaceflight and the first time any American astronauts were lost during a mission.

The Rogers Commission concluded that the loss was caused by a failure in the joint between the two lower segments of the right solid rocket motor. The failure was the result of the destruction of the seals that are intended to prevent hot gases from leaking through the joint during the propellant burn of the rocket motor. Although the exact cause of the O-ring failure cannot be determined with certainty, the Commission suggested:

A likely cause of the O-ring erosion appears to have been the increased leak check pressure that caused hazardous blow holes in the putty. Such holes at booster ignition provide a ready path for combustion gases directly to the O-ring. The blow holes were known to be created by the higher pressure used in the leak check [295, p.156].

B.4.3 Causal Factors

The Rogers Commission report describes in detail what it called NASA's Silent Safety Program. It concludes that a properly staffed, supported, and robust safety organization might well have avoided the communication and organizational failures that influenced the launch decision on January 28, 1986.

Lack of Trend Analysis

The Commission noted several significant trends in the flight readiness reviews. First, O-ring erosion was not considered early in the program when it first occurred. Then, when the problem grew worse after STS 41-B, there was an early acceptance of the phenomenon without much analysis or research. Later flight readiness reviews gave the problem only a cursory review and often dismissed it as within "acceptable" or "allowable" limits because it was "within the database" of prior experience.

Both Thiokol and Marshall continued to rely on the redundancy of the secondary O-ring long after NASA had officially declared that the seal was a nonredundant single point of failure. In 1985, when temperature became a major concern after STS 51-C and the launch constraint was imposed, higher management levels (I and II) were never informed.

At no time was a trend analysis conducted to observe and perhaps trace to a root cause the increase in O-ring anomalies that had started in January 1984. Several changes at that time might have been the cause of the problems and might have been detected in time to avoid the accident if adequate attention had been paid to the problem. These changes to SRB procedures at Kennedy include discontinuation of on-site O-ring inspections; an increase in the leak check pressure on the field joint, which sometimes blew holes through the protective putty; a change in the type of putty used; changes in the patterns for positioning the putty; increased reuse of motor segment casings; and a change in the government contractor who managed the SRB assembly.

Management Structure

The organizational structures at Kennedy placed the safety, reliability, and quality assurance offices under the supervision of the very organizations and activities they were to check. In addition, they were dependent on the NASA management structure to get information and recommendations about safety problems and for implementing suggested changes. But these structures and communication lines were flawed.

At the same time, the organizational responsibility for system safety was not adequately integrated and available to decision-making levels. In the absence of a structured process to integrate safety-related analyses and conformance to specifications, information about safety issues was several interfaces removed from the people involved in the decisions on schedules and launch.

In the testimony to the Commission, NASA's safety staff, curiously, was never mentioned. No one thought to invite a safety representative to the hearings or to the January 27 teleconference between Marshall and Thiokol. No representative of safety was on the mission management team that made key decisions during the countdown on January 28. Safety was originally identified as a separate responsibility by the Air Force during the ballistic missile programs to solve exactly the problems seen here—to make sure that safety is given due consideration in decision making involving conflicting pressures and that safety issues are visible at all levels of decision making. Having an effective safety program cannot prevent errors in judgment in balancing conflicting requirements of safety and schedule or cost, but it can at least make sure that decisions are informed and that safety is given due consideration.

The lack of an independent role for the safety engineers and their effectively low-level status undoubtedly contributed to the *Challenger* accident. The Rogers Commission report recommended that NASA establish an Office of Safety, Reliability, and Quality Assurance reporting directly to the NASA administrator and having direct authority for these functions throughout the agency. Such an office was later established.

Problem Reporting and Tracking

After 1983, problem reporting requirements were reduced, and management lost insight into flight safety problems, flight schedule problems, and problem trends. This change represented a breakdown in what had been considered in the system safety business as an outstanding hazard analysis and follow-up program [224]. The new problem-reporting requirements failed to get critical information (such as anomalous events, the status of safety-critical items, criticality levels of components, and launch constraints) to the proper levels of management and engineering.

Complacency

Complacency was rampant in the program. Morton Thiokol did not accept the implication of tests early in the program that the design had a serious and unanticipated flaw. NASA did not accept the judgment of its engineers that the design was unacceptable, and as the joint problems grew in number and severity, NASA minimized them in management briefings and reports. Thiokol's stated position was that "the condition is not desirable, but is acceptable." Both groups ignored warnings and overrelied on redundancy.

Neither Thiokol nor NASA expected the rubber O-rings sealing the joints to be touched by hot gases during motor ignition, much less to be partially burned. However, as tests and then flights confirmed damage to the sealing rings, the reaction by both NASA and Thiokol was to increase the amount of damage considered "acceptable." At no time did management either recommend a redesign of the joint or call for the Shuttle's grounding until the problem was solved.

NASA and Thiokol accepted escalating risk apparently because they "got away with it last time." As Commissioner Feynman observed, the decision making was

> a kind of Russian roulette . . . [The Shuttle] flies [with O-ring erosion] and nothing happens. Then it is suggested, therefore, that the risk is no longer so high for the next flights. We can lower our standards a little bit because we got away with it last time [295, p.148].

Communication Lines

The Commission report found miscommunication of technical uncertainties and failure to use information from past near-misses. Relevant concerns were not being reported to management. For example, NASA Level I and II management responsible for the launch of 51-L never heard about the concerns raised by the Morton Thiokol engineers about the detrimental effects of cold temperatures on the performance of the SRB joint seal, nor did they know about the degree of concern raised by the erosion of the joint seals in prior flights.

Memoranda and analyses expressing concerns about performance and safety were subject to many delays in transmission up the organizational chain, as well as subject to numerous stages of editing and potential vetoes on further transmittals.

Appendix

The Chemical Industry: Seveso, Flixborough, Bhopal

C.1 Safety in the Chemical Process Industry

The chemical industry is relatively young, having started with the synthesis of the first organic compound (urea) by the German chemist Fredrich Wohler in 1828. This research changed fundamental thought about the nature of chemical reactions, and by 1920 the chemical industry had become an important factor in industrial development in the West. After 1940, the rate of growth was tremendous; today the chemical process industry involves the manufacture of tens of thousands of chemical substances throughout the world [30].

The process and materials in the chemical process industry are inherently hazardous, and the approach to safety was driven by insurance needs. Thus, an actuarial approach to safety was adopted, and the term commonly used in the industry, *loss prevention*, reflects these origins. Loss, in this case, refers to the financial loss of damaged plant, third party claims, and lost production [172].

In the chemical and petrochemical industries, the three major hazards are fire, explosion, and toxic release. Toxic release occurs when a loss of containment allows a dangerous material to escape from a plant in sufficient quantity that its inherent nature (such as toxicity) or subsequent behavior (such as mixing with air and igniting) leads to casualties, property damage, or environmental harm. A *vapor cloud* is a bubble of explosive or toxic gas that drifts in the atmosphere and may explode if it comes upon a source of ignition. Vapor cloud explosions thus usually refer to those explosions that occur in the open air. In recent years, increased environmental concerns have added such hazards as thermal radiation (flares), noise, asphyxiation, and chronic environmental pollution to the list of hazards considered [249].

Of the three traditional hazards (fire, explosion, and toxic release), fire is the most common, explosions are less common but cause greater losses, and toxic release is relatively rare but has been the cause of the largest losses. Since loss of containment is a precursor for all of these hazards, much of the emphasis in loss prevention is on avoiding an escape of explosive or toxic materials through leaks, ruptures, explosions, and so on.

Risk is influenced by several factors [172]:

- *Size of inventory*: As plants have grown in size and output, so has the amount of materials being processed and stored.
- *Energy*: Energy is required for a hazardous material to explode inside the plant or to disperse in the form of a flammable or toxic vapor cloud. In most cases, this energy is found in the material itself, either in its basic state or in a potential chemical reaction.
- *Time*: Time is involved in both the rate of release and the warning time available to take emergency countermeasures and to reduce the number of people exposed.
- *Intensity/distance relationship*: The area over which a hazard may cause injury or damage will vary. In general, fire has a relatively short range, explosion a greater range, and toxic release a potentially unlimited range, in terms of both distance and time.
- *Exposure*: The number of people or the amount of property exposed to the hazard will obviously affect the amount of loss.

The three major hazards related to the chemical industry have remained virtually unchanged in their nature for many years. Design and operating procedures to eliminate or control these hazards have evolved and been incorporated into codes and standards. This approach sufficed before World War II because the industry operated on a relatively small scale and development was slow enough to allow learning by experience. After World War II, however, the chemical and petrochemical industries began to grow in complexity, size, and new technology at a tremendous rate. The potential for major hazards grew at a corresponding rate. Plants have increased in size, typically by a factor of ten, and they are often single-stream in order to realize economies of scale. Huge pieces of equipment and inventory are now found in these plants, and the processes contain greater stored energy than previously.

The operation of chemical plants also has increased in difficulty, and startup and shutdown have become complex and expensive. Process operating conditions, such as pressure and temperature, have increased, exacerbating the problems of process control and plant construction. Profitability concerns have led to plants being operated under extreme conditions and close to their limits of safety, using relatively sophisticated protection systems. At the same time, the reliability of large plants has often decreased because of such factors as an increase in maintenance difficulty as layouts become more compact and equipment more sophisticated; increased interdependence and coupling in the plant; and increased economies in capital costs in aspects such as construction and duplication of equipment [172]. Moreover, chemical and petrochemical plants are becoming less isolated from urban environments, and growing quantities of chemicals are being transported over long distances.

The effect of these changes has been to increase the consequences of accidents, to increase environmental concerns such as pollution and noise, to make the control of hazards more difficult, and to reduce the opportunity to learn by trial and error. Although there have always been more injuries and as many deaths in these industries resulting from mundane work-related accidents as from high technology, and the safety records of the past are relatively good, the number of major accidents appears to be increasing along with loss. For example, the frequency and severity of vapor cloud explosions (the most potentially destructive hazard in this industry) have increased worldwide [172]. Toxic exposures, such as the accidental release of methyl isocyanate at Bhopal, have caused losses of unprecedented scale.

At the same time, the social context has been changing. In the past, safety efforts in these industries were primarily voluntary and based on self-interest and economic considerations. However, pollution has become of increasing concern to the public and to government. Major accidents, such as Flixborough (in England) and Seveso (in Italy), have drawn enormous publicity and have generated political pressure for legislation to prevent similar accidents in the future. Most of this legislation requires a qualitative hazard analysis, including identification of the most serious hazards and their contributing factors and modeling of the most significant accident potentials [299].

These factors have caused the industry to increase its proactive efforts to analyze potential hazards more carefully and to reduce emissions and noise. The result of the increased application of hazard analysis has been a 50-percent reduction in human injuries, reduced absence, increased ease of operations, and decreased production stoppages [299]. The accident at Bhopal (where supposedly a hazard analysis was done) demonstrates that hazard analysis by itself is not enough, however; management practices may be even more important.

Applying hazard analysis in the chemical process industry has special complications compared to other industries that make the modeling of accidents and event sequences especially difficult [325]. The chemical industry has a large number and variety of processes: The number of chemicals is large (and growing daily), each chemical may be produced in a variety of ways, and many of the reactions are not well understood. Thus, experience gained in one study may not be applicable in another.

Although the chemical industry does use some standard reliability and hazard analysis techniques, the unique aspects of the application have led to the development of industry-specific techniques. The hazardous features of many chemicals, for example, are well understood and have been catalogued. Indexes such as the *Dow Chemical Company Fire and Explosion Index Hazard Classification Guide* (usually called the *Dow Index*) and the *Mond Fire, Explosion, and Toxicity Index* (the *Mond Index*) were originally used to select fire protection methods, but they have been expanded to allow for more general hazard identification and evaluation.

Another technique developed for and used primarily in the chemical and petrochemical industries, is called Hazards and Operability Analysis (HAZOP). This technique, described in Chapter 14, is a systematic approach for examining each item in a plant to determine the causes and consequences of deviations from normal plant operating conditions. The information about hazards obtained in this study is used to make changes in design, operating, and maintenance procedures.

Hazard analyses on chemical plants are often done late in the design process or on existing plants or designs where the only alternative for controlling hazards without costly design changes or retrofits is to add on protective devices. Along with the introduction of new technology and new plants, however, has come more attention in the early design stages to finding ways of avoiding hazards. Hazard analyses performed early in the design process can be used to help build simpler, cheaper, and safer plants by avoiding the use of hazardous materials, using less of them, or using them at lower temperatures or pressures [152]. Thus, there are some attempts to move the chemical industry from a downstream approach to safety toward a more upstream, system safety approach.

These new trends are especially relevant as computers replace equipment that is well understood and for which standards and codes have been developed through extensive experience. Automated, computer-based control and safety devices are now widely used in the chemical and petrochemical industries. Building inherently safe plants may be even more relevant for this new technology.

C.2 Seveso

A detailed description of this accident can be found in Lagadec [168]. Most of the information included here is summarized from that description.

C.2.1 Background

The Icmesa Chemical Company is located in Meda, northern Italy, a town of 17,000 residents about 15 miles from Milan. The adjoining community of Seveso was more severely affected by the accident, and thus has given its name to it. The Icmesa plant is owned by the Swiss company Givaudan, which is a subsidiary of the Swiss pharmaceutical giant Hoffman–LaRoche.

The chemical being produced at the time of the accident was trichlorophenol, which is used to make the bactericide hexachlorophene and a herbicide. When the factory was first established, Icmesa had told the authorities that it was to be used for the manufacture of pharmaceutical products. Local law required notification of the mayor and other parties 15 days before the start of any new production. But when the plant was later modified for the manufacture of trichlorophenol, no notification was given to the mayor or any other government regulatory authorities, nor were any of the required certificates obtained [168].

Lawsuits after the accident claimed that some public officials had known since 1972 that the chemical was being produced at Meda but that they had ignored what was happening there. Because no indication of the manufacturing of trichlorophenol had been given, the housing plan of Icmesa was approved in 1973 without inspection of the factory. In 1972, the mayor had requested a report on atmospheric pollution following concerns about the function of the plant, but Icmesa made no mention in the report of the manufacture of the chemical [168].

There have been charges that Givaudan chose Italy in which to manufacture trichlorophenol because of the absence of restrictive regulations and the weakness of the controls on production of dangerous substances compared to those in Switzerland. In addition, salaries were low and the trade unions were understanding [168]. The company claims that fewer restrictions in terms of safety and the environment played no part in the siting decision.

The trichlorophenol is not itself dangerous, but during processing a hydrocarbon called tetrachlorodibenzodioxine (TCDD), or dioxin for short, can be produced as an unwanted byproduct [172]. Normally, dioxin is created only in trace amounts in the reaction that produces trichlorophenol. An accidental increase of temperature and pressure in the reactor, however, can result in large amounts of it. An estimated 2 kg of dioxin was released in this accident.

Dioxin is one of the most poisonous substances known: 500 times more toxic than strychnine and 10,000 times more than cyanide [168]. It can enter the body by ingestion, inhalation, or skin contact. A major symptom of dioxin poisoning is an acne-like skin condition called chloracne, which involves cysts, boils, and inflammation of the sebacious glands of the skin. A mild case of chloracne usually clears up within a year, but a severe case can last several years [172]. Other effects include skin burns and rashes; gastrointestinal lesions; reduction of sexual potency and libido; and damage to the liver, kidneys, urinary system, thyroid, and nervous system. Nervous system changes may express themselves as memory problems, personality changes, sleep problems, emotional instability, and so on. The chemical is remarkably stable and can be eliminated only in negligible quantities: It accumulates in the liver, nerves, and fatty tissue. The initial appearance of dioxin poisoning symptoms is usually delayed until several days after exposure, when skin lesions (the most obvious symptom) appear.

Dioxin seems to have an unusual ability to interfere with the metabolic processes and is fatal to laboratory animals. No experiments have been done on primates because of the toxicity. Some evidence suggests dioxin is immunosuppressant, carcinogenic, mutagenic, and teratogenic (causing fetal malformations), but these properties are still a matter of controversy.

C.2.2 Safety Features

Process control in this plant was manual, and therefore operators had to be present to operate the controls. An automatic system was in the process of being installed. Temperature was critical: The optimal temperature for the reaction was 170°, and the heating device could not cause it to go above 190°, which was well below the critical temperature of 230°. No high temperature alarm or automatic shutdown switch was installed.

The cooling system was also operated manually, so again operators needed to be present to open the valves of this subsystem. An automatic relief valve was installed on the reactor, but it was designed not to control a possible exothermic reaction but rather as protection for an operation at the start of the reaction [168]. A sudden increase in temperature during the reaction was not anticipated.

Changes had been made in the production process to save money, but at the increased risk of exothermic reaction and dioxin forming. These changes allowed a reduction of staff, time, energy, and other costs, but differed from the original patented Givaudan process [168]. Apparently, no review of the safety features of the new process took place when the changes were made.

C.2.3 Events

At 7 P.M. on July 9, 1976, the workers at the Icmesa plant were told to start a new reaction and distillation cycle, ten hours later than normal. This cycle usually lasted for 15 hours. The night workers left at 6 A.M., and the plant was unattended for the weekend. When the night shift workers left, they cut off all energy supply to the system, leaving the reactor to cool off.

At 12:37 P.M. on Saturday, the relief valve lifted after a sudden increase in temperature and pressure, releasing dioxin into the atmosphere. An Icmesa technician later told the investigating commission that the reactor temperature at the time of the accident was between 450° and 500° and that conditions for the formation of a significant amount of dioxin had developed. The reasons for the sudden increase in temperature and pressure are, according to Givaudan and Icmesa official statements, unknown and unexplainable [168].

A toxic cloud drifted over part of the town. Heavy rain fell and brought the toxic material down to the ground. Some children reported seeing the cloud, but then it disappeared. A plant manager happened to be in the vicinity when the release occurred and took steps to stop it. He notified the man who was taking the place of the man in charge of production (who was on vacation). The commission inquiring into the accident could find no other actions that were taken that day.

On Sunday, the first effects of the accident were noticed: vegetation was burned; animals became ill; and about 20 children had sores on their arms, red spots on their faces, burns on their bodies, high fever, and intestinal problems. An Icmesa engineer sent samples of the burned vegetation to the Givaudan laboratories in Switzerland for analysis. The police launched an inquiry and were told by the company that a cloud of herbicide had spread over the area around the factory—no mention was made of dioxin. The technical director of Givaudan said in a deposition that he had heard of similar dioxin accidents, and he did think of that possibility. But he thought a very high concentration of dioxin would be located only near the relief valve and small concentrations elsewhere. "I could not think at that time that the dioxin could have expanded over a very large area" (translated in Lagadec [168, p.50]).

On Monday, the factory was open, and normal work resumed. Icmesa sent a letter to the local health authorities that confirmed that an incident had occurred at the factory, but, again, they mentioned only herbicides. "Not being able to evaluate the nature of the substances carried by those vapors and their exact effects, we have intervened with neighbors asking them not to consume garden products, knowing that the final product is also used in herbicides" [168, 51].

Tuesday, July 13: Health authorities sent a letter to the mayors of Meda and Seveso assuring them that there was no danger to people living in the surrounding areas.

Wednesday, July 14: Analyses at the Givaudan Laboratories in Switzerland confirmed that dioxin was present. Near the factory, the deaths of a large number of animals were reported.

Thursday, July 15: Serious cases of poisoning began to be reported among the population. The mayors announced that precautions should be taken by the residents, such as not eating vegetables grown in area gardens. The mayors met with the Icmesa plant owners, who made no mention of dioxin.

Friday, July 16: Fifteen children, four of whom were in grave condition, were admitted to the hospital, but nobody knew what treatment to give. The residents called for a strike and insisted that the authorities give them accurate information. The Italians authorities took samples for analysis.

Saturday, July 17: The mayors of Seveso and Meda added extra instructions for the residents around the factory, now ordering the burning of polluted garden vegetables and the killing and burning of affected animals. The director of the provincial chemical laboratory established that there could have been a release of dioxin.

Sunday, July 18: The mayor of Meda ordered the factory closed.

Monday, July 19: Five more children were hospitalized while the director of the provincial chemical laboratory learned during a visit to Givaudan that the industrial owners knew that a cloud of dioxin had been released during the accident.

Tuesday, July 20: The local health director returned from Switzerland and informed the mayors. Animals died within a 3-km radius outside the area originally considered endangered.

Wednesday, July 21: More meetings of local authorities were held to decide what to do. Additional protective measures were announced that included not eating meat from animals within the area, closing some establishments, and medical checks of residents.

Friday, July 23: A large meeting of medical experts took place at the police commissioner's office in Milan. They concluded that it was not necessary to take any civil defense actions. The university representatives at the meeting unanimously agreed that further measures were not necessary or urgent. The director general of the Health Service confirmed on the television news that everything was under control.

At the same time, the director of Hoffmann–LaRoche's medical center in Basel declared that the situation was very serious, that draconian measures were necessary, and that 20 cm of the ground surface had to be removed, the factory buried, and the houses destroyed.

Saturday, July 24: The regional health director castigated the Hoffmann–LaRoche medical director:

> This person was dumped on us; nobody expected him, and nobody expected such severe statements. To my knowledge, he is not an official representative of the company and I shall today request to know on whose behalf he speaks. I have made clear to him the seriousness of what he says. I have the impression that this person is bluffing. And this person will have to answer for his statements [168, p.53].

Later that afternoon the official position changed, and a decision was made to evacuate 179 people who lived in an area of two square miles. They were told not to eat any produce or meat from the area (which, except for the immediate neighbors of the factory, they had eaten for the previous two weeks). The contaminated area was not closed completely, however; a road passing through it continued to be used [172]. The mayors left the meeting and found the populace in an uproar.

July 25–30: The first evacuation of 250 people took place, and the army enclosed the evacuated area with barbed wire. They worked with their bare hands, and no special provisions were taken [168]. Eventually they were given rubber boots. Amazingly, the evacuated residents were allowed to take their clothes, food, and other potentially contaminated objects.

New contaminated areas were detected and subsequently evacuated and cordoned off. Deaths of chickens, rabbits, and dogs began in an area several miles from the company and with a population of 15,000. Women and children were removed from this area, and people were asked not to procreate during the following months. A British expert arrived and suggested that the estimated 2 kg of dioxin released was greatly understated; he warned that there could have been 130 kg.

By the end of July, about 250 cases of skin infection had been diagnosed, 50 people had been admitted to a hospital, 600 people had been told to evacuate their homes, and 2,000 people had been given blood tests. There was fear of outside contamination from people who came from the evacuated area: Some hotels refused to provide them with accommodation [172] and, ironically, Switzerland temporarily closed its border to Italian food products and took air samples along the border in order to detect any contamination that might reach Swiss territory. Some businesses refused to take shipments of furniture coming from the Seveso area. In Italy, an argument ensued about whether therapeutic abortions should be allowed for pregnant women exposed to the dioxin.

In early August, the authorities found that the contaminated area was five times as large as originally thought. This larger area contained 40 factories. The mayor of a local town, who had been one of the first people to visit the contaminated area, was found to have an excessive number of white blood cells. Controversy reigned about what to do, which resulted in delays in taking any action. Eventually, decontamination of the area was started.

By the beginning of the next year (1977), cases of chloracne were still being discovered in areas not thought to be contaminated, and many births of malformed children occurred in the second quarter of that year. Whether the percentage of birth defects was greater than normal depends on whose figures are used and which areas are included. More than a year after the release, the first 120 people (out of a total of 800 evacuees) were allowed to return to their homes. Others were readmitted to the area later. A recent report found that cancer rates have increased in the area.

C.2.4 Causal Factors

As with most serious accidents, extraneous factors combined either to mitigate or to increase the consequences. In this case, a heavy rain brought the toxic cloud down to earth, and later heavy rains raised fears that the dioxin would be further dispersed. The fact that it was a weekend made it difficult to contact authorities immediately to warn the public and take emergency action. Being a weekend also meant that the factory operators had gone home and nobody was around to stop the release. Of course, this latter factor was not just random chance, but reflects the management decision to leave the reactor unattended during a cycle. By chance, an employee was in the area, saw the toxic cloud, and was able to take action to avert an even worse accident.

Other factors were not so random.

Complacency and Discounting Risk. The possibility of high temperature and high pressure in the reactor was discounted, and no preparation was taken for this event. After the accident, management at Givaudan and at Icmesa argued that foreseeing such an event was impossible and cited a lack of scientific information. Lagadec points out, however, that the scientific literature between 1971 and 1974 includes descriptions of other accidents where dioxin was formed during the production of trichlorophenol [168]. Milnes had pointed out in 1971 the conditions under which an out-of-control exothermic reaction could develop rapidly and generate temperatures up to 410°, causing the release of large quantities of gaseous products [226]. The commission investigating the Seveso accident concluded that it was improbable that the technical directors of Givaudan and Icmesa could have been unaware of this possibility. The directors confirmed to the commission that they knew before the accident of Milnes' results [168].

During a press conference in Basel, the director of Givaudan indicated that he knew in advance of the risk of toxic products at the Icmesa factory, but that he had never imagined that "such a disaster" could occur. He explained that that was the reason no emergency plans had been worked out with the local authorities [168].

The workers were told to start a new cycle of reaction and distillation on Friday evening, even though it could not have been finished by the time the workers would leave for the weekend and the process control and cooling systems were manual. The director of Givaudan testified to the commission of enquiry that the manual controls were adequate. The commission concluded, "This logic renders the responsibility even heavier because it is quite evident that if the merely manual controls were considered adequate, the continuous presence of people who are capable of applying them is an absolute necessity" (translated in Lagadec [168, p.44]).

Uncommunicated and Unreviewed Changes.   Changes were made, without adequate review, both in the chemical being manufactured and in the production process. These changes violated local regulations and the original patented process.

Training.   The staff was not qualified to deal with these products and were not aware of the risks connected with the manufacture of trichlorophenol. The risks involved not only a major release to the surrounding community but small releases within the plant. On several occasions, production residues had escaped from containers or pipes [168].

Competing Priorities.   Local authorities reportedly had difficulty in getting information from the company about the chemicals involved in the release and about the appropriate countermeasures [168]. Doctors at first did not know what treatment to prescribe. Perrow suggests that plant officials tried to avoid a panic simply by not informing the public about what had happened [259]. Lagadec points out that there was silence at the start of the affair, later denials to reassure others and themselves that dioxin was not dangerous, and refusal by both the manufacturers and the local officials to follow up seriously on the effects of the poison.

Superficial and Ineffective Safety Measures.   Inadequate alarms and interlocks were installed on the reactor: There was no warning of high temperature or other type of signaling or shutdown equipment, perhaps because a sudden increase in temperature was not anticipated. In addition, the reactor was operated while no operator was present to work the primarily manual controls.

Analysis of the released material could not be done on short notice locally. Samples had to be sent to Givaudan in Switzerland to determine the composition of the materials released. The government agencies, not knowing that a dangerous chemical was being produced, might have had justification for this deficiency, but the company did not.

Finally, the lesson was learned that a pressure relief valve on a plant handling highly toxic substances should not discharge to the atmosphere but instead into a closed system.

C.3 Flixborough

The Flixborough accident was investigated by a British Court of Inquiry, and much of the following information comes from this report [245]. The court's investigation was severely limited in its viewpoint and focused primarily on narrow technical issues. Other committees and reports of the British government in the wake of the accident, however, considered additional factors. The accident itself raised the general awareness of *major hazards*—where an accident could threaten the lives of thousands of people—and focused attention on the inadequacy of the precautions and controls used.

The Advisory Committee on Major Hazards was established shortly after the accident to consider the safety problems associated with large-scale industrial facilities (other than nuclear installations) that conduct potentially hazardous operations. The reports that resulted were highly influential in establishing new research and regulatory initiatives. A Health and Safety Commission was established to propose draft regulations governing the operations of installations where hazardous materials are handled in large quantities. As a result, the Health and Safety at Work Act was passed on July 31, 1974, and a Health and Safety Executive was created to enforce the new regulations.

C.3.1 Background

The explosion occurred in 1974 at the Nypro Ltd. chemical works at Flixborough, a small rural community near Scunthorpe, 160 miles north of London. The plant had been built in 1938 as a subsidiary of Fisons, Ltd., to manufacture fertilizer. In 1964, it was passed to Nypro to produce caprolactum, an intermediary product in the manufacture of nylon.

Nypro was reorganized in 1967 with the participation of Dutch State Mines, the British National Coal Board, and Fisons, Ltd. In August, the company started producing caprolactum from phenol at a rate of 20,000 tons per year. In 1972, the caprolactum capacity was increased to 70,000 tons a year by adding a new unit that used a process based on cyclohexane. The use of cyclohexane introduced a new dimension into the safety problem. When the changes were made, local authorities were not notified.

Nypro was under financial pressure. Instead of the 70,000 tons it was supposed to be producing, output was only 47,000 tons per year at the time of the accident, and the owners were losing money in the operation. They had requested the government's price commission to authorize a 48-percent increase in the price of caprolactum, but this request was refused.

Nypro was the only manufacturer of caprolactum in Great Britain at that time. The factory supplied it to two fiber manufacturers, Courtauld and British Enkalon. These companies were in direct competition with the other big nylon manufacturers, ICI and Dupont, who held patents on a process for the manufacture of caprolactum that most experts agreed was safer.

Cyclohexane has many properties similar to gasoline; it is highly inflammable and dilutes quickly in the air and in the temperature near a hot spot. To make caprolactum, cyclohexane is oxidized by passing it through a set of six reactors. Air and catalysts act on the heated cyclohexane, and the desired product is distilled out. In this process, large quantities of cyclohexane have to be circulated through the plant under pressure and at a temperature of 155°C. Loss of containment can release flashed liquid, which produces a large flammable vapor cloud. During the oxidation process, compressed air is injected into the reactors, creating an exothermic reaction. In contrast, the process for making caprolactum involving the hydrogenation of phenol, which Nypro could not use because the patent was held by its customers' competitors, is not exothermic.

On the day of the accident, Nypro had in stock 330,000 gallons of cyclohexane, 66,000 gallons of naphtha, 11,000 gallons of methyl benzene, 26,400 gallons of benzene, and 450 gallons of gasoline. The Petroleum Act of 1928 put the licensing and control of these potentially dangerous substances under the control of the local government. At the time of the explosion, the only licenses that had been issued authorized only 7,000 gallons of naphtha and 1,500 gallons of gasoline. Thus, the facility stocked over 400,000 gallons of dangerous products while being licensed for only 8,700 gallons.

C.3.2 Events

At the beginning of 1974, the maintenance engineer at the Flixborough plant left for personal reasons and by June 1974 (when the plant was destroyed by the explosion) had not been replaced. None of the other engineers had special competence in mechanical engineering.

The plant had a series of six reactors, each slightly lower than the one before. Gravity caused cyclohexane to flow from reactor 1 to reactor 6 through short 28-inch-diameter connecting pipes. To allow for expansion, each 28-inch pipe contained a bellows (see Figure 4.3).

A small escape of cyclohexane from reactor 5 was discovered on the morning of March 27, 1974. An investigation found a vertical crack in the outer casing of the reactor, which indicated that the internal casing was also defective. The production engineer called the director for that zone of the plant, and they agreed that the installation would have to be closed down, depressurized, and cooled while a complete inspection took place.

The following morning (March 28), the director inspected the crack and found it was about six and a half feet long. This situation was serious, and the morning was spent deciding what to do. The director wanted to restart production as soon as possible, so a temporary fix was proposed: Reactor 5 would be shut down for inspection, and oxidation would continue using the remaining five reactors by building a bypass to link reactors 4 and 6. Once the bypass was in place, the factory would go back on stream. Nobody at the meeting considered the difficult technical problems involved in constructing a bypass: Possible design problems and alternatives were not discussed. Nobody (with perhaps the exception of the area engineer) thought there was a need to inspect the other reactors to find out if any of them had a similar defect that had not yet developed to the point where it could cause an escape. The main goal of the meeting was to restart the oxidation process with a minimum of delay.

The original crack in reactor 5 is now thought to have been caused by the corrosion resulting from past sprinkling of small escapes of cyclohexane with water. Plant cooling water, which contained nitrates, was used as it was convenient and available. The water had penetrated the insulation, and when it evaporated had deposited nitrates on the steel lining. Nitrate-induced cracking was well known to metallurgists at the time but not to other engineers [154].

The openings to be connected between reactors 4 and 6 were 28 inches in diameter, but the largest pipe available on site that could be used for the bypass was 20 inches in diameter. Because the two flanges were at different heights, the connection had to be built in the form of a dogleg of three lengths of pipe welded together and bolted to the flanges at each end (Figure 4.3).

After the modifications, the plant was started up again without anyone trying to understand the cause of the crack in reactor 5 or to make sure that the other reactors were in good condition. No calculation was made to check whether the bypass could take the load. No reference was made to British standards or to the guidelines published by the manufacturer of the bellows—both of which were violated by the bypass assembly. No piping layout was made besides a full-scale chalk drawing on the workshop floor. And no safety pressure test, either of the piping or of the whole unit, was made before the bypass was installed—such a test would almost certainly have caused the rupture of the bypass assembly. The tests that were made were for leaks and not for the strength of the assembly. No means was used to support the piping from underneath or to prevent lateral movement. The scaffolding constructed was meant as a support during assembly to prevent the weight of the assembly from pulling out the bellows, and it was inadequate for operating conditions. The maintenance manager had given his assistant a sketch of supports for the assembly, but these supports were never erected and the maintenance manager never insisted that they be installed.

The bypass was completed on the evening of March 29, after two days of work. Once in place, it was tested for leaks. A leak was found, so the plant was depressurized. They forgot to mark the leak, however, and had to pressurize the plant again, find the leak, and repair it after depressurizing. Pressurizing a plant is not a simple task—it can take several hours and require thousands of steps. Once the leak was repaired, the plant was repressurized to test again for leaks, but none were found. The pressure was increased for further tests, the plant was depressurized again, and finally startup procedures were carried out.

The bypass assembly was set up by April 1 and appeared to work, but an unusually large use of nitrogen was detected and investigated. The repair held up from April 1 to May 29, even though the bellows were subjected to forces for which they were not designed, and the assembly was not held in place from above nor adequately secured from below. The bypass assembly was not checked closely during this period, but it was looked at in passing by a large number of people. Some observed that under pressure the pipe seemed to lift slightly off the support pipes, but no one noticed anything "amiss." The report states, "It must therefore be taken that albeit there may have been some displacement of the assembly during the period, it cannot have been great enough to attract attention" [245].

The plant was shut down only for short periods twice in May. The four days preceding the accident, however, were filled with problems. On May 29, a valve was found to be leaking, and the plant was shut down to repair the leak. On the morning of June 1, startup began after repairing the leak and performing escape tests. At 4 A.M., a new leak occurred, others were discovered, and the process was stopped again. They later determined that the leaks had "righted themselves," and at about 5 A.M. operations were restarted. At this point, pressure went up at an abnormal rate, requiring substantial venting. Shortly thereafter, the process was stopped again because of another leak. This time repairs could not be carried out immediately because the necessary spark-proof tools were not available—they were locked in a shed for the weekend. The process was restarted at 7 A.M. on Saturday morning and continued until 3 P.M. Temperature and pressure problems began again, the pressures being high enough to be disquieting without being alarming.

The precise sequence of events at this point is complex and uncertain, because the explosion killed everyone in the control room and destroyed all the instruments. The report is careful to point out that no operator errors were involved. A crucial feature of the situation was that the reactors were subjected to a slightly higher than normal pressure. Pressure would normally be controlled by venting, but this procedure involved the loss of considerable quantities of nitrogen. A number of anomalies were unexplained at this point, especially the fast rise in pressure and the excessive consumption of nitrogen, both of which, according to the report, appear to be independent of the condition of the bypass pipe.

Shortly after the final warmup started, they discovered that they did not have enough nitrogen to begin oxidation and additional supplies would not arrive until after midnight. Although all records of what exactly happened were destroyed in the explosion and ensuing fires, the need to conserve nitrogen would tend to inhibit their use of venting to reduce pressure [172]. Several theories are advanced in the report, but none can be proven.

During the late afternoon, something happened that resulted in the escape of large quantities of cyclohexane. Most people now believe that this event was the rupture of the 20-inch bypass pipe, perhaps accompanied by a fire in a nearby 8-inch pipe. Through the two 28-inch openings from reactors 4 and 6, hot cyclohexane escaped under pressure in massive quantities. Some evidence points to the possibility of two explosions rather than one. Within 30 seconds, the cyclohexane formed a vapor cloud 700 feet in diameter and 350 feet in height that was composed of 40 to 50 tons of the chemical. A wind of 15 miles per hour drove the mixture 300 feet to the discharge tower of the hydrogen unit, which acted as a source of ignition. At about 4:53 P.M., a massive unconfined vapor cloud explosion occurred, estimated to be equivalent to the force of 15 to 45 tons of TNT. The explosion was heard 30 miles away and devastated the 60-acre factory site. All buildings within a radius of a third of a mile were destroyed, and more than 2,450 houses were damaged in the vicinity. Windows were shattered in houses up to eight miles away.

The blast from the explosion shattered the windows of the control room and caused the roof to collapse, killing everyone inside. Of the 28 people who died in the explosion, 18 of them were in the control room. Some of the victims were killed by flying glass while others were crushed by the roof. A total of 72 people were present at the site when the explosion occurred; on a regular working day there would have been 550 present and presumably a great many more deaths and injuries. Off site, 53 people were injured and hundreds more suffered minor injuries that were not officially recorded.

The flames from the fires on the site rose 250 to 350 feet high and burned for many days. Even after 10 days, the fires were still hindering rescue work at the site. All the fire extinguishing facilities in the plant were immediately destroyed, and it took two and a half days for the firefighters to get to the main sources of the fire.

The material damages from this accident were estimated at $60 million: more than $48 million for the reconstruction of the factory, $10 million for interruption of operations, and $2 million for third-party liability.

C.3.3 Causal Factors

Several conditions combined to mitigate the potential consequences of this accident. First, the site was rural and far from any major population centers: Casualties might have been much greater in a more densely populated area. Second, the wind was light. If it had been stronger, a larger plume might have been created and the explosion could have come later, extending the damage. Daylight and good weather increased the effectiveness of the fire brigades. Finally, the explosion occurred on a weekend when there was a skeletal crew at the plant, so casualties were lower than they might have been.

Other causal factors again show the pattern to be found in most serious accidents.

Complacency and Lack of Forethought.   The report by the Court of Inquiry concludes that nobody among those in charge of the design or the construction of the factory foresaw the possibility of a major accident. No disaster plan had been drawn up.

Although large quantities of unlicensed fluids were stored at the plant, notifying the authorities about them would have made no difference because licensing practices at the time would have allowed the increased storage without requiring additional constraints [172]. However, the accident did reveal the need for better methods of notifying local planning authorities about major hazards and the need for greater guidance in safety matters for these local authorities and for the installations themselves.

Although other vapor cloud explosions had occurred elsewhere in the world, this one was unique in that it provided British industry, the British public, and the rescue squads with the first direct experience of the consequences of such an event. They could no longer ignore the danger [168].

Unheeded Warnings.   The crack in one reactor did not lead them to inspect the other ones. In addition, the bypass pipe had been noted to move slightly during operation, and there had been unexplained anomalies in pressure, temperature, and hydrogen consumption. Yet no thorough investigation was done.

In a broader scope, the Chief Inspector of Factories had been warning, first in 1967 and later from 1970 to 1972, of the problems arising from the use of large quantities of dangerous materials [113].

Conflicting Priorities.   The decisions leading to the accident reflect a conflict of priorities between safety and production. The report said,

> We entirely absolve all persons from any suggestion that their desire to resume production caused them knowingly to embark on a hazardous course in disregard of the safety of those operating the Works. We have no doubt, however, that it was this desire which led them to overlook the fact that it was potentially hazardous to resume production without examining the remaining reactors and ascertaining the cause of the failure of the fifth reactor. We have equally no doubt that the failure to appreciate that the connection of Reactor No. 4 to Reactor No. 6 involved engineering problems was largely due to the same desire. . . . The design and the construction of the whole link should not have been carried out in a hurry as it was in this case. There should have been time to consider what problems would arise and how they could be suitably dealt with [245].

The report recommended that more attention be devoted to the cost-effectiveness of designing continuous process plants so that they could be repaired without shutdown, thus avoiding the need for pragmatic management decisions under competing priorities.

Although the storage of such flammable materials as naphtha, benzene, and gasoline was not involved in the initial explosion, these substances made a major contribution to the heat, flames, and smoke when they ignited, and they also hindered rescue operations. Kletz observes that before the Flixborough explosion, little conscious thought was given to the possibility of increasing safety by reducing inventories of hazardous materials in process and in storage. Up to then, engineers usually designed a plant and accepted whatever inventory was called for by the design.[1] Hazards were controlled by adding protective equipment such as trips, alarms, fire protection, and fire fighting. In fact, a great deal can be done to reduce inventories without reducing production. As a result of Flixborough, many companies have reduced their stocks of hazardous intermediates, and there has been renewed interest in intensification (see Chapter 16) [159].

Organizational Structure. The installation did not have a sufficient complement of qualified and experienced people. There was no works manager and no adequately qualified mechanical engineer on site. As a result, some engineers had been asked to assume responsibilities for which they were not qualified. In addition, the engineers who were there were overworked.

With the departure of the maintenance engineer, there was no mechanical engineer on site having sufficient qualifications to deal with complex or novel engineering problems or having the status and authority to enforce necessary safety measures. The maintenance engineer's duties were assigned temporarily to a subordinate whose qualifications were not sufficient for the job. The personnel that remained at the plant did not seem to realize that they lacked important knowledge to carry out their assigned duties.

The problems were exacerbated by the fact that the director and technical director were both chemical engineers with no training in mechanics. The company had recognized that the structure of the engineering section was weak, and a consultant from the National Coal Board had been called on in 1974 for advice about reorganization.

There was also no engineering organization independent of production-line management that was responsible for assessing the overall system and ensuring that proper controls were exercised. The role of safety officer at the Flixborough plant was poorly defined. He considered himself responsible to the personnel director although he had direct access to the director general. Kletz has suggested that the accident demonstrated the need for higher status of safety advisors. "In highly technical industries like the process industries, it is not sufficient to employ as safety advisor only an elderly foreman who sees his job as taking statements from men who fall off bicycles" [153, p.109].

Superficial Safety Activities. Anomalies were not carefully reviewed, and the stress testing and safety analysis of the effects of the bypass were insufficient. No safety organization was responsible for such analyses and reviews. More specifically,

---

[1] The MIC at Bhopal was an intermediate that was convenient but not essential to store.

□ Nobody was familiar with the British standard then in existence for piping in petrochemical plants, which specifically prohibited the type of bypass pipe that had been installed between the reactors.

□ No calculations were made that took into account the forces arising from the dogleg shape of the connecting pipe between reactors 4 and 6. No drawing of the bypass pipe was made other than in chalk on the workshop floor. No calculations were done to check whether the bellows would withstand the forces caused by the dogleg-shaped pipe connection. No pressure testing was carried out either on the pipe or on the complete assembly before it was fitted. The pressure testing done on the plant was not up to the safety valve pressure. In addition, the test was pneumatic, not hydraulic.

□ The scaffolding to support the pipe was intended only for use during construction. It was not suitable as a permanent support for the bypass assembly during normal operation.

□ The 20-inch bypass pipe was not constructed and installed in accordance with the current standards and codes of practice. The bellows manufacturer produced a guide for their use that made it clear that two such bellows should not be used out of line in the same pipe without adequate support for the pipe.

The explosion occurred during plant startup. The report suggests that special attention should be given to factors that necessitate the shutdown of a chemical plant so as to minimize the number of shutdown–startup sequences and to reduce the frequency of critical management decisions. After a defect was discovered, the plant was restarted, but the remaining reactors were not examined nor was the cause of the failure of the fifth reactor determined.

Unreviewed Changes.   The process was changed and the capacity was tripled, but safety questions were not rethought. The court's report on the accident recommended that existing regulations for modifying steam boilers be extended to apply to pressure systems containing hazardous materials.

C.4 Bhopal

The Bhopal accident has been widely investigated in newspapers, scientific articles, and books. Several good references exist for further information and are listed in the bibliography. A book by Bogard [30] and an article by Ayres and Rohatgi [15] are especially helpful in understanding this accident, and much of the information below comes from these sources.

C.4.1 Background

The accident at Bhopal, 10 years after Flixborough, involved the release of methyl isocyanate (MIC), a highly reactive, toxic, volatile, flammable, and unstable chemical. This substance is unusually dangerous, both to store and to handle. Union Carbide is one of two major U.S. producers; Bayer makes the chemical in Europe. Most of Union Carbide's production of MIC is at its plant in Institute, West Virginia, which began to produce it in 1967. Production in India by Union Carbide India, Ltd., began on a small scale in 1977.

Demand for MIC dropped sharply after 1981, leading to reductions in production and pressure on the company to cut costs: The Bhopal plant was operating at less than half its capacity when the accident occurred. Union Carbide put pressure on its Indian subsidiary to reduce losses, but no specific details were given about how this was to be done [15].

In response, the maintenance and operating personnel were cut in half [30]. As the plant lost money, many of its skilled workers left for more secure jobs and either were not replaced or were replaced by unskilled workers. Maintenance procedures were severely cut back, and the shift-relieving system was suspended: If no replacement showed up at the end of a shift, the following shift went unmanned. "Despite the minimal training of many of these workers in how to handle nonroutine emergencies at the plant, no consideration was seriously given to the idea of shutting the facility down" [30, p.29].

C.4.2 Safety Features

MIC is used in the production of a number of pesticides and in the production of polyurethanes (which are used in plastics, varnishes, and foams). It is highly volatile, and the vapor is heavier than air. One of the major hazards in handling MIC is contact with water, which results in large amounts of heat. The concentrated gas burns any moist part of the body, including the throat, nasal passages, eyes, and lungs. The hazardous and toxic nature of MIC was described in the Union Carbide operating manual, along with the chemical's ability to cause fatal pulmonary edema.

Union Carbide specified requirements for operating procedures, storage facilities, and safeguards to reduce the hazards of producing MIC. The chemical was to be stored in underground tanks encased in concrete. The Bhopal facility used three double-walled, stainless steel tanks, each with a capacity of 60 tons. The operating manual specified that the tanks were never to contain more than half their maximum volume or a standby tank was to be available to which some of the chemical could be transferred in case of trouble. The Bhopal tanks were interconnected so that the MIC in one tank could be bled into another tank. As specified in the operating manual, the tanks were embedded in concrete.

The chemical was also to be stored in an inert atmosphere of nitrogen gas at 2 to 10 psi over atmospheric pressure. Regular, scheduled inspection and cleaning of valves and piping was specified as imperative, and storage time was limited to

12 months maximum. If staff were doing sampling, testing, or maintenance at a time when there was a possibility of a leak or a spill, the Union Carbide operating manual specified that they were to use protective rubber suits and airbreathing equipment.

In order to limit its reactivity, MIC was supposed to be maintained at a temperature near 0°C. A refrigeration unit was provided for this purpose. In addition to the refrigeration system and standby tank, the plant had several backup protection systems and lines of defense [15]:

1. A vent gas scrubber was designed to neutralize any escaping gas with caustic soda. The scrubber was capable of neutralizing about 8 tons of MIC per hour at full capacity.

2. The flare tower was supposed to burn off any escaping gas missed by the scrubber; the toxic gases would be burned high in the air, making them harmless.

3. Small amounts of gas missed by the scrubber and the flare tower were to be knocked down by a water curtain that reached 40 to 50 feet above the ground. The water jets could reach as high as 115 feet, but only if operated individually.

4. In case of an uncontrolled leak, a siren was installed to warn the workers and the surrounding community.

C.4.3 Events

The Indian government required the Bhopal plant to be operated completely by Indians [214]. At first, Union Carbide flew plant personnel to West Virginia for intensive training and had teams of U.S. engineers make regular on-site safety inspections. But by 1982, financial pressures had led Union Carbide to give up direct supervision of safety at the plant, even though it retained general financial and technical control [214]. No American advisors were resident at Bhopal after 1982.

Several Indian staff who were trained in the United States resigned and were replaced by less experienced technicians. When the plant was first built, the operators and technicians had the equivalent of two years of college education in chemistry or chemical engineering. In addition, Union Carbide provided them with six months of training. When the plant began to lose money, educational standards and staffing levels were reportedly reduced [15].

In 1983, the chemical engineer managing the MIC plant resigned because he disapproved of falling safety standards and was replaced by an electrical engineer. A significant number of operating staff had been turned over in the previous three years, and the new employees lacked safety training [191]. Morale at the plant was low, and management and labor problems followed the financial losses [191]. "There was widespread belief among employees that the management had taken drastic and imprudent measures to cut costs and that attention to the details that ensure safe operation were absent" [191].

These are just some examples of the unsafe conditions that were permitted:

- At the time of the accident, it was estimated that the chloroform contamination of the MIC was four to five times higher than specified in the operating manual, but no corrective action was taken [360].
- The MIC tanks were not leaktight to a required pressure test.
- Workers at Bhopal regularly did not wear safety equipment, such as gloves or masks—even after suffering adverse symptoms like chest pains and vomiting—because of high temperatures in the plant. There was no air conditioning [214].
- Inspections and safety audits at the plant were few and superficial [15].

Prior warnings and events presaging the accident were ignored. The Bhopal plant had six minor accidents between 1981 and 1984, several of which involved MIC. One worker was killed in 1981, but official inquiries required by law were often shelved or tended to minimize the government's or the company's role [30]. A leak similar to the one involved in the events described below had occurred the year before [15].

Within the government, at least one person tried to bring up questions of hazards to those inside and in the immediate area of the plant. He was forced to resign [30].

The local press had published articles criticizing the safety practices at the plant in detail, including one that virtually predicted the accident [15]. Local authorities appear to have done nothing in response. The articles, titled "Please save our city" and "Bhopal sitting on the mouth of a volcano," were part of Rajukman Kesmani's crusade to get the authorities to recognize the potential danger. He had even posted warnings: "Poison gas. Thousands of workers and millions of citizens are in danger" [214]. The crusade was unsuccessful, although it was mentioned in debates in the state legislature [167].

Five months before the accident, local Union Carbide India management decided to shut down the refrigeration system. Refrigeration is important in MIC storage in order to control dangerous chemical reactions (exothermic degradation). The most commonly advanced explanation for why the refrigeration system was turned off is cost cutting. The local management claimed that the unit was too small and never worked satisfactorily. There is disagreement about whether Union Carbide in the United States approved this measure.

Because the chemical had a higher temperature without the refrigeration than that allowed by the alarm system, the set point of the temperature alarms on the MIC tanks was raised from $11°$ to $20°C$ and logging of tank temperatures was halted.

Six weeks before the accident, production of MIC had been halted because of an oversupply of the pesticides the chemical was used to make. Workers performed routine maintenance while production was stopped.

At about 10:30 P.M. on December 2, 1984, a relatively new worker was assigned to wash out some pipes and filters, which were clogged. The pipes being cleaned were connected to the MIC tanks by a relief valve vent header, which was normally closed. The worker properly closed the valves to isolate the tanks from the pipes and filters being washed, but nobody inserted a required safety disk (called a slip blind) to back up the valves in case they leaked. The maintenance sheet contained no instruction to insert this disk, although there was a note to the night shift to wash the pipe [15]. The worker who had been assigned this task did not check to see whether the pipe was properly isolated because, he said, it was not his job to do so. Reportedly, he knew that the valves leaked, but the safety disks were the job of the maintenance department. The pipe-washing operation should have been supervised by the second shift supervisor, but that position had been eliminated in the cost cutting.

At the time of the accident, tank 610 (from which the MIC escaped) contained 40 to 50 tons out of the total capacity of 60 tons, which violated the safety requirements: The tanks were not to be more than half-filled with MIC, and a spare tank was to be available to take any excess. The adjacent tank, 611, was thought to contain 15 tons on the basis of shipping records, but actually contained nearer to 21 tons. Tank 619, the spare tank, contained less than 1 ton, although the level gauge showed that it was about 20-percent full [15]. Many of the gauges were not working properly or were improperly set. This fact may reflect design flaws in the equipment, although operation and maintenance errors also played a part.

When the night shift came on duty at 11 P.M., the first sign of trouble was detected. The pressure gauge indicated that pressure was rising (10 psi instead of the recommended 2 to 3 psi) but was at the upper end of the normal range. The temperature in the tank was above 20°C. Both instruments were ignored because they were believed to be inaccurate.

The instrumentation for detecting pressure and temperature levels of the chemicals at the plant was faulty and unreliable; workers did not trust the information it provided. They were told to use eye irritation as the first sign of exposure in the absence of reliable detection mechanisms to gauge threshold levels accurately. The plant had few automatic shutoffs or alarm systems that might have detected and stopped the gas leak before it spread beyond the facility.

The leak of liquid from an overhead line was first discovered around 11:30 P.M., after some workers noticed slight eye irritation. Leaky valves were common—small leaks occurred from time and time and were not considered to be significant [15]. The workers looked for the leak, and one saw a continuous drip on the outside of the MIC unit. He reported it to the MIC supervisor, but the shift supervisor did not consider it urgent and decided to postpone an investigation until after the tea break.

At 12:40 P.M. on December 3, the control room operator noticed that the pressure gauge on tank 610 was approaching 40 psi and the temperature was at the top of the scale (25°C). At about 12:45 A.M., loud rumbling noises were heard from the tank. The concrete around the tank cracked.

The temperature in the tank rose to 400°C, causing an increase in pressure that ruptured the relief valve. The pressurized gas escaped in a fountain from the top of the vent stack and continued to escape until 2:30 A.M. The MIC was vented from the stack 108 feet above the ground, well above the height of the water curtain. A safety audit two years earlier had recommended increasing the capacity of the water curtain system, but this had not been done. Eventually 50,000 pounds of MIC gas would escape.

The operator turned off the water-washing line when he first heard the loud noises at 12:45 A.M. and turned on the vent scrubber system, but the flow meter showed no circulation of caustic soda. He was unsure whether the meter was working. To verify that the flow had started, the operator would have had to check the pump visually, which he refused to do unless accompanied by the supervisor; the supervisor declined to go with him.

The vent scrubber was not kept operational because it was presumed not to be necessary when production was suspended. By the time it was turned on, it was too late to help. Allegedly, there was not enough caustic soda to neutralize the MIC, anyway [167]. The vent scrubber was designed to neutralize only small quantities of gas at relatively low pressure and temperature. The pressure of the escaping gas during the accident exceeded the scrubber's design by two and a half times, and the temperature was at least 100°C more than the scrubber could handle. There is speculation that had the vent scrubber been in operation, the reaction of MIC with caustic soda would have caused further release of heat and still greater pressures [15]. If this had happened, much of the MIC would have ultimately escaped, anyway.

The operator never opened the valve connecting tank 610 to the spare tank 619 because the level gauge erroneously showed it to be partially full. The assistant plant manager was called at home at 1 A.M. and ordered the vent flare turned on. He was told that it was not operable. At the time of the accident, the flare tower was out of service for maintenance: A section of the pipe connecting it to the tank was being repaired. In any case, the design of the flare tower was inadequate to handle the 50 tons of MIC that escaped during the accident. Ayres and Rohatgi claim that had it been turned on, the result would have been a violent explosion [15].

The plant manager learned of the leak at 1:45 A.M., when he was called by the city magistrate. When the leak of MIC was serious enough to cause physical discomfort to the workers, they panicked and fled, ignoring the four buses that were intended to be used to evacuate employees and nearby residents. A system of walkie-talkies, kept for such emergencies, was never used. The MIC supervisor could not find his oxygen mask and ran to the boundary fence, where he broke his leg attempting to climb over it. The control room supervisor stayed in the control room until the next afternoon, when he emerged unharmed.

The toxic gas warning siren was not activated until 12:50 A.M., when MIC was seen escaping from the vent stack. It was turned off after only five minutes, which was Union Carbide policy. It remained off until turned on again at 2:30

A.M. The police were not notified, and when they called between 1 and 2 A.M., they were given no useful information.

A large number of squatters had settled in the vacant areas surrounding the plant. Such settlements of desperately poor migrant workers, in search of any form of employment, are common in India. They also take advantage of whatever water and electricity are available. The plant was located by the railway station, bus station, hospitals, and so on; settlements are also common near such facilities. The railway station in India is a community center.

No information had been provided to the public about protective measures in case of an emergency or other information on hazards. The siren sounded so many times a week (estimates range from 20 to 30) that there was no way for people living near the plant to know what the siren signified; the emergency signal was identical to that used for other purposes, including practice drills. If the people had known to stay home, close their eyes, and breathe through a wet cloth, the deaths could have been prevented.

Eventually the army came and tried to help by transporting people out of the area and to medical facilities. This help was delayed by the fact that nobody at the plant notified authorities about the release.

Agnees Chisti, a journalist who was in a small hotel visiting the city, described the events outside the plant after the release:

> I was trying to get one of the foreign stations on the radio at about 2:30 A.M. when I felt some choking in my throat and I thought it was some ordinary case of bad throat or something. I tried to get some cough syrup, but then I realized that it was something much more than that. There was a burning sensation in the eye. I somehow opened the door of my room. First I thought it was a hotel problem. I went out. I was running for some open space where I could get relief but I could get relief nowhere. . . .
>
> When I came out, I saw hordes of people moving towards some direction. I was new to Bhopal City, I didn't know all the routes. . . . Anyway, I walked. And that was a ghastly experience. I saw ladies, almost undressed, straight out of bed in petticoats, children clinging to their breasts, all wailing, weeping, some of them vomiting, some falling down. I now presume falling down dead . . . they were falling dead, family members were leaving their own family members behind and running for safety . . .
>
> Fifteen months later, the area resonates with the coughs and groans of perpetually sick passengers. Deaths due to the aftereffects of exposure to gas are even now not infrequent although medical records no longer mention 'MIC poisoning' as the cause of the ailments as was done before [52, p.7–8].

The result was the worst industrial accident in history. The weather and wind direction contributed to the consequences. In addition, because the release took place in the middle of the night, most people were asleep, and it was difficult to see what was happening.

Infants and children under the age of 12 as well as elderly people were the most likely to die from exposure to the chemical. The victims were primarily local residents but also included 87 railway employees and the superintendent of the Bhopal railway station. Large numbers of animals also died. The exact number of fatalities and injuries is a matter of controversy. Estimates of deaths range from 1,750 up to 10,000. Many deaths occurred among refugees who escaped from Bhopal into the surrounding areas, where no systematic count was possible, and deaths continued over a long period and thus were not attributed directly to the accident.

By two days after the accident, Prime Minister Gandhi said that 20,000 victims had received treatment at various hospitals in the city. Eventually there were 232,691 victim claims for compensation. A house-to-house survey of about 25,000 families found that one out of 25 families affected by the gas leakage experienced blindness or partial blindness of one of its members [52].

Nobody knows for sure what caused the runaway reaction. Experiments attempting to reproduce the accident conditions determined that there must have been at least 45 tons of MIC, one half to one ton of water, and one to one and a half tons of chloroform in the tank for the reaction to have occurred.

The most likely cause was water getting into the tank, but a possibility exists that another contaminant entered the tank through the nitrogen line or the scrubber and catalized the reaction [15]. One widely accepted hypothesis is that a small amount of water got into the storage tank through leaky valves during or after the cleaning of the pipes and filters earlier in the day. The cleaning itself had been necessary because two of four valves that should have been open to allow water flow were clogged. The extra pressure from the clogged pipes is an alternative hypothesis for the leak of water into the tank [214]. A further hypothesis implicates slow chemical reactions of the MIC with the stainless steel walls of the storage tank itself [30]. Union Carbide claimed that the amount of water in the tank may have been very large (up to 240 gallons of water) and suggested the possibility of deliberate sabotage.

C.4.4 Causal Factors

Most of the level three conditions and constraints described in Chapter 4 were involved in this accident.

Discounting Risk. Union Carbide went into large-scale production of MIC without having performed adequate research on the stability of the chemical. After the accident, when there was serious concern about the other MIC tanks at the plant, neither Union Carbide nor Bayer knew of an effective inhibitor for the type of reaction that occurred [15].

The accident came as a complete surprise to almost everyone, including the Union Carbide scientists and risk assessors.

> The belief that such a catastrophe could not happen with such modern technology, that so many safety systems could not fail simultaneously, that the

Bhopal plant was a "model" facility, etc., directed necessary attention away from the overall production process and its possible worst consequences and fostered a general atmosphere of safety [30, p.24].

In addition, contrary to official government policy, the plant was located in a highly populated area.

Assuming Risk Decreases over Time.   Not having accidents in the past led to complacency. Union Carbide and the Indian government pointed to the relatively minor nature of chemical accidents at the plant to support their refusal to install backup safety equipment or to move the plant away from populated areas:

The extrapolation from the past safety record of the plant, which in reality was not all that good but was presented as such, was in essence an excuse or alibi for failing to deal squarely with the potential, however small, of a catastrophic accident. The assurance that past performance is an adequate guide in the assessment of hazards is itself an incentive for maintaining the status quo [30, p.19].

Ignoring Warning Signs.   The management and the state government ignored the risk and warning signs before the accident and then made the consequences of the leak worse by repeated denials of the urgency and magnitude of the disaster [167].

According to Bogard, the significance of early warning signs was muted by several factors: (1) the reluctance of the company to become involved in the day to day affairs of the plant's safety and maintenance routines, despite the control it exercised over high-level decisions and budgetary matters; (2) the cost of new equipment and training; and (3) the importance of pesticides to the region's farmers [30].

Ignoring Low-Probability, High-Consequence Events.   There was a failure to imagine a worst-case scenario and to take it seriously [15]. Designers did not anticipate an MIC release of anywhere near the magnitude that occurred. Emergency equipment was inadequate for the job, and the plant was not designed to cope with a major leak. Emergency training and procedures were also inadequate, such as the policy of turning off the warning siren after five minutes. Ayres and Rohatgi suggest that those who framed such a policy never conceived of an accident of this magnitude [15].

There was systematic analysis and training for serious events to some extent, but it was not comprehensive. For the most part, workers did not have adequate training on what to do about nonroutine events and conditions. Emergency procedures and drills were held, but there was no systematic analysis of low-probability and high-consequence conditions that could lead to a major accident [360]. The procedures and training, accordingly, did not sensitize plant personnel to the "importance of various seemingly minor deficiencies that could combine to produce a major disaster" [360, p.446].

Ayres and Rohatgi note that none of the parties—plant designers, operators, company management, and responsible public officials—anticipated the possibility of an accident the size of the one that happened [15]. However, all the significant components had occurred repeatedly, including corroded pipes, pump failures, leaky valves, staff failures to follow procedures specified in the operating manual, systems down for maintenance, and even the major leaks of MIC and phosgene, which had happened previously one or more times. The adverse weather conditions (an atmospheric inversion) were unusual but by no means unprecedented. The only new factor was the combination of all of these things at one point in time.

Low Priority Assigned to Safety.   All levels of management were lax in enforcing safety-related policies [15]. The Indian government inspection agencies were understaffed and uninformed about the safety problems related to MIC. "Safety was given a low priority by all the parties involved" [167].

Inadequate training was provided for emergencies. Even the supervisors forgot what they had been taught when the emergency occurred. There appeared to be no real evacuation plans. The scope of the disaster was thus greatly increased because of total unpreparedness [214].

Flawed Resolution of Conflicts between Safety and Other Goals.   The safety equipment was inadequate, and much of what was there was shut down to save money. Cutbacks in staff, training, and maintenance to reduce costs undoubtedly also contributed to the accident.

Company policy was to turn off the siren and not to report minor leaks or accidents. The typical excuse for such secrecy is that the company does not want to create "unnecessary" alarm and fear [15]. Even the local Bhopal community was uninformed about what was going on in the plant. An effective public information program would have been relatively inexpensive. Even simply sending a sound truck through the streets telling people to breathe through wet cloths would have saved thousands of lives [15].

Ineffective Organizational Structure.   Union Carbide had transferred legal responsibility for safety inspections to overseas operators even though it retained general management, technical, and financial control [214], creating divided responsibilities.

The organizational structure involved a complicated relationship between Union Carbide and Union Carbide India, which was mostly under the supervision of Indian managers carrying out general directives from the parent company [167]. The directives issued from the parent company and the Indian government were not implemented in the actual practices and everyday operations at the plant, including the behavior of plant operators, managers, and government bureaucrats [167].

Superficial Safety Activities. Leaks were routine occurrences and the reasons for them were seldom investigated: Problems were either fixed without further examination or ignored. While the initial design of the plant included many safety features, there was an absence of an ongoing review and audit process. The scenario assumptions for the protection systems were obviously incomplete, and, as noted earlier, inspections by outside authorities were few and superficial [15].

A safety audit in 1982 by a team from Union Carbide noted several safety problems at the plant, including several involved in the accident. There is debate about whether the information was fully shared with the Union Carbide India subsidiary and about who was responsible for making sure changes were made. However, no follow-up seems to have occurred to make sure that the problems had been corrected. The report noted such things as filter-cleaning operations without using slip blinds, leaking valves, the possibility of contaminating the tank with material from the vent gas scrubber, and bad pressure gauges. The audit recommended raising the capacity of the water curtain and pointed out that the alarm at the flare tower from where the MIC leaked was nonoperational and thus any leakage could go unnoticed for a long time. According to the Bhopal manager, all the improvements called for in the report had been taken care of, but that was obviously untrue [15].

Ineffective Risk Control. Many of the safety devices were inadequately designed. Ayres and Rohatgi describe several improvements that could have been incorporated into the system design, some of which are on the Bayer plant in Germany.

Moreover, MIC was an intermediary that was convenient but not necessary to store. Since Bhopal, many companies have reduced their stocks of hazardous intermediates [159].

Nuclear Power: Windscale, Three Mile Island, and Chernobyl

D.1 Background

A brief introduction to nuclear power plants is provided to help the reader understand the accidents. An introduction to safety in nuclear power is also provided.

D.1.1 How a Nuclear Power Plant Works

A nuclear reactor generates heat as a result of the splitting apart of an atomic nucleus (most often that of the heavy atom uranium). This process is called nuclear fission. The nucleus at the core of each atom contains two types of particles tightly bound together: protons, which carry a positive charge, and neutrons, which have no charge. When a free neutron strikes the nucleus of a uranium atom, the nucleus splits apart, producing two smaller radioactive atoms, energy, and free neutrons. Most of the energy is immediately converted to heat. The new free neutrons can now strike other nuclei, producing a chain reaction and continuing the fission process. Free neutrons can be captured by the atomic nuclei of some elements, such as boron or cadmium, which stops them from continuing the fission process. Thus, elements that are strong absorbers of neutrons can be used to control the rate of fission and to shut off a chain reaction almost instantaneously [230, 143].

Other radioactive materials are products of the fission of uranium. They are almost all unstable and hence radioactive, with half-lives ranging from millionths

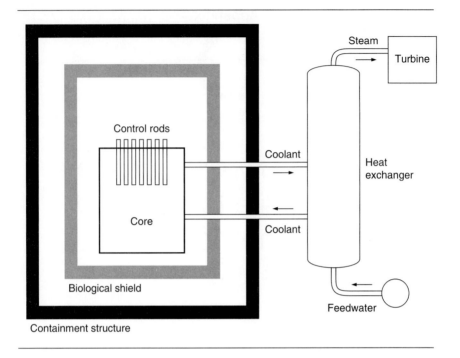

FIGURE D.1
Generic nuclear power plant components.

of a second to hundreds of years. They decay by emitting gamma or beta radiation. While the reactor is working, new fission products are constantly being formed, while those formed earlier are constantly decaying.

The free neutrons produced by nuclear fission are inefficient producers of further energy at the high energy at which they were originally emitted. Essentially, they move too fast and miss the uranium atoms too easily. So they must be slowed down to induce additional fissions efficiently and to sustain the chain reaction. A *moderator* is used to slow down the neutrons, but it should not capture them or the reaction will stop. The particular moderator used is one of the main differences between different types of nuclear power plant. Other differences arise in the layout of the various components, the canning material (the material in which the core is held), the coolant, the pressure under which the coolant operates, and whether the reactor uses natural or enriched uranium as fuel.

Nearly every reactor has the following components [219] (see Figure D.1):

□ The *core* consists of the fuel elements and moderator.
□ The *control rods* contain elements that absorb free neutrons and thus control the speed of the reaction.

- The *coolant* carries away the heat generated in the core. The coolant, by removing heat, also keeps the fuel rods from becoming overheated.
- The *heat exchanger* transfers the heat carried by the coolant to water in a secondary circuit, which boils and creates steam.
- The *turbine(s)* converts steam to rotational energy, which powers a generator that creates electricity.
- The water in a secondary circuit, called *feedwater,* transfers the heat from the steam generators to the turbine.
- A *biological shield* absorbs any neutrons produced in fission that escape from the core.
- A *containment vessel* contains any radioactivity that escapes from the core or coolant system.

In the 1950s, when nuclear power and energy plant designs were first being conceived by the five nuclear powers—the United States, Russia, Britain, France and Canada—only Canada had no interest in building nuclear weapons. The rest wanted to manufacture plutonium as well as generate electricity [219]. To accomplish both requires different reactors or limits the design options to rather unsatisfactory compromises.

For commercial power generation, the United States chose light water reactors, of which there are more operating in the world than any other kind. In these reactors, ordinary "light" water is used for both the moderator and the coolant. Because of the high absorption of neutrons by water, the fuel must be considerably enriched (the uranium content is 3 percent instead of the 0.7 percent of natural uranium). The United States already had a large fuel-enrichment program, so getting the enriched fuel was not a great problem. The disadvantages of this design are that the fuel cycle is more expensive and the compact size of the core may lead to control problems. On the other hand, the compact size makes for easier export sales, and the need for enriched uranium leads to the possibility of future business in the reprocessing and enrichment of fuel because most countries buying reactors do not have this capability. The first reactor, built under the direction of Admiral Hyman Rickover, was a power unit for the submarine USS *Nautilus*, launched in 1954. The submarine design influenced the land-based versions, the first of which was installed at Shippingport, Pennsylvania, and became the first nuclear power plant in the United States.

The reactor core in these reactors is contained in a thick-walled pressure vessel made of welded steel. The water acts as both a moderator and a coolant. At the top of the core, the hot water (about 320°C) is piped through the side of the pressure vessel to a heat exchanger, in which it is forced through thousands of small pipes immersed in a secondary water circuit. This secondary water is heated by contact. The water in the primary circuit is under high pressure, but the lower pressure of the secondary circuit water allows it to turn to steam when it is heated, and this steam is fed to the steam turbine. The primary coolant water is then pumped back to the reactor to be heated again. A *pressure equalizer* maintains the coolant at the correct pressure (as the reactor power is changed) by allowing some of the water to evaporate or condense. The control and shutoff rods are generally suspended above the core inside the pressure vessel and are controlled through the lid of this vessel.

This type of reactor is refueled only when it is shut down. To accomplish this, the core is first allowed to cool down and then a large tank on top of the core is filled with water to provide shielding and also to provide cooling water to remove the fission-produced heat. The lid of the pressure vessel is then removed and the fuel replaced. Because of the time required for this process, the reactor is usually shut down for refueling once per year, and a large percentage of the fuel is replaced at that time.

For safety, the pressure vessel, the core, and the primary coolant circuit are contained in a biological shield of concrete about seven feet thick. In case a malfunction occurs in the cooling system, an emergency cooling system is provided. Additional safety features of the *defense-in-depth* approach are described later in this appendix.

The light water reactor described is called a pressurized water reactor (PWR). In a boiling water reactor (BWR), the water is allowed to boil within the core and the resulting steam is piped directly to the turbine. Thus, no secondary coolant circuit is needed. However, something has to be done with the steam in case a malfunction makes the turbine unable to accept it. The reactor is therefore enclosed inside a second vessel, this one made of reinforced concrete, which acts as the biological shield and from which the steam can be channeled into a pool of water under the reactor. The BWR is also refueled when shut down.

The second type of reactor involved in the events described in this appendix is graphite-moderated and water-cooled. The first American reactor of this type was built at Hanford, Washington, in 1944 for the military production of plutonium. The British also built a graphite-moderated reactor at Windscale at about the same time and for the same purpose. The Soviets chose this type of reactor for civilian use for reasons discussed later.

The Soviet version of this reactor type, called the RBMK (a Russian acronym that roughly translates as "reactor cooled by water and moderated by graphite"), uses low-enriched uranium. Water is boiled directly within the core of the reactor and led off to drive the turbines.

Instead of using a single large pressure vessel to contain both fuel and coolant, the fuel elements are contained in more than 1,600 separate pressure tubes. Water is allowed to boil in the pressure tubes. The resulting steam contains many water droplets (which have to be removed before entering the turbine), so the steam is collected and dried in four huge drums. Each drum contains more than 400 welds, which must be pressure tight. There has been some criticism within the Soviet Union about shortcuts taken in the haste of building the Chernobyl reactors (and others) and thus accusations of substandard construction and quality problems [219]. The graphite temperature is about 700°C under normal conditions in the RBMK reactor, which is above its ignition temperature in air. Therefore, the graphite is blanketed in an inert mixture of helium and nitrogen.

Although other types of reactors are not involved in these events, they are described briefly for comparison. Graphite-moderated, gas-cooled reactors use enriched uranium and are cooled with carbon dioxide. The carbon dioxide, like the water circulating in a PWR, is used to carry heat to heat exchangers, which change it to steam to drive the turbines. One advantage of this design is that it does not have to be shut down to be refueled. A new design of this type, the advanced gas-cooled reactor (AGR), uses enriched uranium and increases the potential power output of the reactor.

Canada uses heavy-water moderated and cooled reactors called CANDU (CANadian Deuterium Uranium) reactors. The heavy-water moderator is contained in a cylindrical stainless steel tank (called a calandria), below which is an empty tank into which the moderator can be dumped in case of an emergency. There is also a large building next to the reactor, which is leaktight, and kept empty and under continual vacuum; this structure is to be used to contain any vaporized heavy water and volatile fission products released in a severe reactor accident. CANDU reactors can be refueled without being shut down.

A final type of reactor, called a fast reactor, does not require a moderator, but does need a highly enriched fuel and uses liquid metals as coolant. The advantages of this type of reactor are the small size of its core and the possibility of "breeding" more fissile material. Removing heat requires the use of liquid metals, which are circulated through the core by the use of electromagnetic pumps having no moving parts (the liquid metal itself is the only part that moves). These liquid metals react explosively with water, and any accidental leaks of coolant will ignite spontaneously with the moisture in the air. Of course, an accidental fire cannot be put out with water but must be smothered with sodium chloride particles.

D.1.2 Safety Features

Nuclear power not only has the same type of safety engineering problems being faced by other new and potentially dangerous technologies, but, in addition, it has a relatively unique problem with public relations and has had to put a great deal of energy into convincing government regulators and the public that the plants are safe. This requirement, in turn, has resulted in a greater emphasis in some countries on probabilistic methods of risk assessment; the time required for empirical evaluation and measurement of safety is orders of magnitude greater than the pace of technological development [274] and also greater than what the public is willing to accept.

In an effort to promote the development of nuclear power and also partly because the associated hazards were not entirely understood, the industry was exempted from the requirements of full third-party insurance in some countries (for example, by the Price-Anderson Act in the United States) [337]. Instead, government regulation and certification were substituted as a means of enforcing safety practices in the industry. The first nuclear power plant designs and sizes were also limited, although this has changed somewhat over the years as confidence in the designs and protection mechanisms has grown. In general, the nuclear industry and its regulators have taken a relatively conservative approach to risk issues.

The nuclear industry uses *defense in depth*, which includes [234]

- A succession of barriers to a propagation of malfunctions, including the fuel itself, the cladding in which the fuel is contained, the closed reactor coolant system, the reactor vessel, any additional biological shield, and the containment building (including elaborate spray and filter systems).
- Primary engineered safety features to prevent any adverse consequence in the event of malfunction.
- Careful design and construction, involving review and licensing at many stages.
- Training and licensing of operating personnel.
- Assurance that ultimate safety does not depend on correct personnel conduct in case of an accident.
- Secondary safety measures designed to mitigate the consequences of conceivable accidents.

Licensing is based upon an identification of the hazards, design to control these hazards under normal circumstances, and backup or shutdown systems that function in abnormal circumstances to further control the hazards. The backup system designs are based upon the use of multiple, independent barriers, a high degree of single element integrity for passive features, and the provision that no single failure of any active component will disable any barrier.

Siting nuclear power plants in remote locations is a form of barrier in which the separation is enforced through isolation. Perrow argues the impracticality of isolation:

> The ideal spot for a nuclear plant cannot exist. It should be far from any population concentration in case of an accident, but close to one because of transmission economies; it has to be near a large supply of water, but that is also where people like to live; it should be far from any earthquake faults, but these tend to be near coastlines or rivers or other desirable features; it should be far from agricultural activities, but that also puts it far from the places that need its power. The result has been that most of our plants are near population concentrations, but in farming or resort areas just outside of them [259, p.41].

Because of the difficulty in isolating plants, emergency planning has gotten more attention since the Three Mile Island accident.

With the nuclear power defense-in-depth approach to safety, an accident requires a disturbance in the process, a protection system that fails, and inadequate or failing physical barriers. These events are assumed to be statistically independent because of differences in their underlying physical principles: A very low calculated probability of an accident can be obtained as a result of this independence assumption [274].

Recovery after a problem has occurred depends on the reliability and availability of the shutdown systems and the physical barriers. A major emphasis in building such systems, then, is on how to increase this reliability, usually through redundancy of some sort.

Probabilistic risk assessment has been proposed for and occasionally used in the nuclear industry. Risk assessments include estimating the reliability of the barriers and protection systems. In Britain, the worst possible accident that could occur, even if all the protection systems and barriers worked within their proper margins of tolerance following a disturbance, is called a *design basis accident* [114]. Any event bigger than a design basis release is an *uncontrolled release* [114]. (In the United States, design basis accidents usually refer to a set of disturbances against which the design is evaluated, including foreseeable failures of barriers.)

Early risk assessments involved developing scenarios of *credible* or worst-case accident sequences that were still considered within the realm of possibility. These event sequences were called *maximum credible accidents,* and the design was evaluated against them. The probability of the maximum credible accident might be very low, but not so low as to make it impractical to incorporate safeguards. Hammer [106] illustrates this concept with the following simple example, framed in a slightly different context:

> An aircraft is to be developed to carry a thermal device using a radioactive isotope as the source of energy. The device is nonexplosive; the principal danger is the possibility that a fire could cause dispersion of the radioactive material in airborne products of combustion. The Maximum Credible Accident would be an aircraft crash severe enough to rupture the device and then a fire that would cause isotope dispersion. Since aircraft crashes and fires do occur, it is necessary to provide a container that will not rupture should the Maximum Credible Accident occur [106, p.67].

A possible criticism of the maximum credible accident approach is that the definition of what is credible is subjective. Farmer, in 1967, proposed a more rigorous approach to the assessment of nuclear plant safety that uses probability. He claimed that for any given factory or other industrial installation, the acceptable frequency of accidents that may harm third parties varies inversely with the magnitude of the consequences of those accidents. He suggested that nuclear power plants be required to meet a safety criterion expressed in terms of consequence and probability.

Since empirical measurement of probability is not practical for nuclear plant designs, most approaches to probabilistic risk assessment build a model of accident events and construct an analytical risk assessment based upon this model. Such models include the events leading up to the uncontrolled release as well as probability data on factors relating to the potential consequences of the release, such as weather conditions and population density.

The use of probabilistic risk assessment has been quite controversial. The arguments in favor are usually based on the ability of the technique to provide input to decision making. Identifying hazards alone does not help in determining how funds should be allocated in reducing them. Comparative probability data can be useful in such decision making. Decision making in the certification of plant designs is also eased by the use of such numbers, and probabilistic risk assessment has been advocated for use by government agencies in decision making about nuclear energy and other potentially hazardous plants.

One recent trend in Britain is the substitution of *tolerable* risk for *acceptable* risk. If emphasis is placed on probabilistic risk assessment and other quantitative measures, then a need arises to determine how to make decisions based on those numbers (as discussed in Chapter 1). The concept of *acceptable* risk has been used in this decision-making process; however, objections have been raised to labeling something with such serious consequences as a nuclear accident as "acceptable." As defined in a recent publication of the British Health and Safety Executive about risk from nuclear power stations,

> 'Tolerability' does not mean 'acceptability.' It refers to a willingness to live with a risk so as to secure certain benefits and in the confidence that it is being properly controlled. To tolerate a risk means that we do not regard it as negligible or something we might ignore, but rather as something we need to keep under review and reduce further if and as we can [114].

This change in terminology may reflect a change in philosophy, or it may simply be an attempt at better public relations.

Although the introduction of computers into protection systems started only very recently, most government regulatory agencies are now being faced with certifying such systems. Emphasis in this certification activity in some countries is placed on the reliability of the operational software and, sometimes, on analytical assessments of this reliability.

The first computer-based shutdown systems were quite simple and small, but more recent designs have been enormously more complex and have raised concerns in the software engineering community about whether such complex software designs can ever be assured or trusted to have the reliability required for nuclear installations.

D.2 Windscale

D.2.1 Background

The Windscale reactor was located on the Cumberland coast of Britain and was the first British production reactor. The reactor was designed for the production of plutonium and thus was different from reactors used for civilian production of electricity. Windscale was graphite-moderated and air-cooled. This type of reactor is called "straight through" or "once through" because the air coolant is not recirculated but instead is blown straight out into the atmosphere. Because any particulates in the air would become radioactive, inlet filters were installed to remove these particulates. (Civilian reactors to produce electricity have closed cooling loops, and fission products cannot escape directly to the atmosphere.)

The original design did not include filtering the air again before release, but exhaust filters were added during construction. Megaw tells of a rumor that John Cockcroft, in a visit to Hanford in the United States, saw a big hole being dug beside the construction site of a similar reactor [219]. When he asked the purpose, he was told that it was for the exhaust filters. Supposedly, he then made a surreptitious visit to the post office at lunch to send a cable to the man in charge of the Windscale reactor construction, Christopher Hinton, saying "put exhaust filters on the Windscale reactors." By this time, the only way to add the filters was to put them at the top of the stacks (400 feet above ground level) and to add an elevator and staircase to the stack so the filters could be serviced. The story might be true because, according to Megaw, there was little reason to put the filters in such an inconvenient place unless they were added at the last moment. The filters became known as Cockcroft's Folly because they were thought to be superfluous.

When graphite slows down neutrons, some of the energy of the neutrons appears directly as heat while some of the energy is stored in the graphite. This phenomenon was not known when the Windscale reactors were designed, although it was predicted soon afterwards by Wigner and became known as Wigner energy. The energy accumulates in the graphite until eventually, if nothing is done, the stored energy is released as heat. If this release happens unexpectedly or in an uncontrolled way, it can cause the graphite temperature to rise to unacceptable levels and even trigger the melting of some fuel cans.

D.2.2 Events

The following account of events is taken primarily from Megaw [219]. In September 1952, a spontaneous release of Wigner energy occurred at Windscale while the reactor was shut down. The temperature of the graphite rose, but not to dangerous levels, and no harmful effects resulted. Because of this incident, periodic controlled releases were instituted for the reactors. Megaw describes this procedure as triggering the Wigner energy release by raising the graphite operating temperature above normal by running the reactor without coolant air flow. Once the release was started, the reaction was self-sustaining, and the reactor was shut down. The procedure needed to be delicately balanced because of the time lag in the temperature response of the graphite: If the reactor was shut down too soon, the graphite temperature would not rise sufficiently, but if too much nuclear heating was applied, some fuel elements might overheat and the cans leak. By 1957, the procedure had been performed more than a dozen times and was regarded as fairly routine.

On October 7, 1957, a Wigner energy release was started on a Windscale reactor. The engineer in charge of the operation thought that the release was dying away too soon. What he did not know was that the thermocouples used to measure the heat had not been installed in the hottest part of the core. A second nuclear heating was applied at too fast a rate and probably caused one or more fuel cans to fail; the contents quietly oxidized away. The instruments did not indicate that anything untoward had happened until the afternoon of October 10, when a radioactivity alarm went off. Visual inspection at 4:30 P.M. through one plug hole showed glowing fuel elements and, through another one, flames shooting out of the discharge face of the reactor.

Every means they could think of was used to extinguish the fire, but nothing worked. By midnight, they decided to try water, since everything else had failed. In order to minimize the possibility of a steam explosion, a veritable "tidal wave" of water was used [214]. The water was turned on at 8:55 A.M. on Friday, October 11, and off at 3:10 P.M. on October 12. By this time the pile was cold, but various types of radioactive elements had been released to the atmosphere and were being carried by the wind and deposited on the ground. The radioactive material (by then at low concentration) reached Belgium late on October 11 and Frankfurt late on October 12. By October 15, it had eventually circled back to Norway.

The immediate problems were to control the dose received by the workers on the reactor and to protect public health in the vicinity of the station. Men working on the reactors wore protective clothing and respirators, and their length of exposure was controlled. Because the major risk was to small children who drank milk from cows grazing on grass contaminated by iodine 131, milk from an area 200 miles downwind of the plant was destroyed. The milk would not have been medically harmful if it had been processed into dried milk, cheese, or chocolate and then the products stored for three months until the iodine had decayed, but the Ministry of Agriculture decided that the public relations problems were too great to make that worthwhile.

In total, 2 million liters of milk were destroyed. The farmers were compensated for their losses, and Megaw says that it was rumored that once the farmers realized what was happening to their milk, the output of milk from the cows in the affected area increased dramatically. Water samples and other products were examined, but none were found to pose a significant risk.

There is some controversy about whether Cockcroft's filters were effective or not. Some people contend that the filters retained large amounts of iodine 131 and kept a major accident from becoming a catastrophe. Others claim that the stack filters retained only small amounts. The effects of the low-level radiation on people is also unknown. With the benefit of 25 years of extra research on the effects of radiation, a report of the British Nuclear Radiation Protection Board in 1982 estimated the eventual additional deaths from thyroid cancer (most cases of thyroid cancer are cured) to be 20 as a result of the accident. An addendum was later issued that, because of additional information about the materials that were released, raised the estimate to 33. This number is an upper estimate, and the actual number is likely to be lower, perhaps even zero [219].

More clear results of the accident were a death of public naivete about the potential danger of nuclear power and the belief prevalent at the time that technology could conquer all. A committee of inquiry was established to investigate, although official reports of the inquiry were not released to the public for over 20 years in order to protect the nuclear industry [214]. In response to public concerns, a new branch of the British Atomic Energy Authority was established (now known as the Safety and Reliability Directorate), which was to be responsible for reactor safety [102]. It was years before the events at Windscale were referred to as an accident (before that it was called the Windscale Incident) [219], and the name of the plant was changed to Sellafield to deflect attention [214]. In the United States, of course, the former AEC also kept embarrassing events of their own secret at that time.

After the accident, both reactors at Windscale were permanently shut down and sealed off because it was decided that adding the required safety features would be too expensive. It took over 10 years before dismantling of the reactor could begin [214].

D.2.3 Causal Factors

Certainly, lack of knowledge about nuclear reactors played a part along with complacency about their safety. After a dozen years of practically trouble-free reactor operations, many operators and others had become complacent [219]. More detailed analysis of the causal factors is not possible because of the lack of public information about the accident.

D.3 Three Mile Island

D.3.1 Background

On Wednesday, March 28, 1979, at 4 A.M., several water pumps stopped working at a nuclear power plant at Three Mile Island (TMI) in Pennsylvania. The Kemeny Commission, which investigated the accident, concluded that "a series of events—compounded by equipment failures, inappropriate procedures, and human errors and ignorance—escalated into the worst crisis yet experienced by the nation's nuclear power industry" [143, p.81].

TMI, located 10 miles southeast of Harrisburg, has two nuclear power plants, TMI-1 and TMI-2. Together they have a capacity of 1,700 megawatts— enough electricity to supply 300,000 homes. The two plants are owned jointly by Pennsylvania Electric Company, Jersey Central Power & Light Company, and Metropolitan Edison Company, and are operated by the latter (Met Ed). These three companies are subsidiaries of General Public Utilities Corporation, an electric utility holding company headquartered in New Jersey.

At TMI-2, the reactor core holds some 100 tons of uranium. The uranium, in the form of uranium oxide, is molded into cylindrical pellets, each about an inch tall and less than a half-inch wide. The pellets are stacked one on top of another inside fuel rods. These thin tubes, each about 12 feet long, are made of Zircaloy-4, a zirconium alloy. This alloy shell—called the "cladding"—transfers heat well and allows most neutrons to pass through. TMI-2's reactor contains 36,816 fuel rods.

TMI-2's reactor has 69 control rods. Control rods contain materials called "poisons" because they are strong absorbers of neutrons and shut off chain reactions. The absorbing materials in TMI's control rods are 80-percent silver, 15-percent indium, and 5-percent cadmium. When the control rods are all inserted in the core, fission is effectively blocked, as explained earlier. Withdrawing them starts a chain reaction. By varying the number of and the length to which they are withdrawn, operators can control how much power a plant produces. The control rods are held up by magnetic clamps: In an emergency, the magnetic field is broken and the control rods, responding to gravity, drop immediately into the core to halt fission. This is called a "scram."

The primary hazard from nuclear power plants is the potential for the release of radioactive materials produced in the reactor core as the result of fission. These materials are normally contained within the fuel rods. Damage to these fuel rods can release radioactive material into the reactor's cooling water, and this radioactive water might be released to the environment if the other barriers—the reactor coolant system and containment building barriers—are also breached.

A nuclear power plant has three basic safety barriers, each designed to prevent the release of radiation. The first line of defense is the fuel rods themselves, which trap and hold radioactive materials produced in the uranium fuel pellets. The second barrier consists of the reactor vessel and the closed reactor coolant system loop. The TMI-2 reactor vessel, which holds the reactor core and its control rods, is a 40-foot-high steel tank with walls eight and a half inches thick. This tank, in turn, is surrounded by two separated concrete and steel shields, with a total thickness of up to nine and a half feet, which absorb radiation and neutrons emitted from the reactor core. Finally, all this is set inside the containment building, a 193-foot-high, reinforced-concrete structure with walls four feet thick.

In the normal operation of a pressurized-water reactor, it is important that the water heated in the core remain below "saturation"—that is, the temperature and pressure combination at which water boils and turns to steam. In an accident, steam formation itself is not a danger, because it too can help cool the fuel rods, although not as effectively as the coolant water. But problems can occur if enough of the core's coolant water boils away that the core becomes uncovered.

An uncovered core can lead to two problems. The first is that the temperature may rise to a point, roughly 2200°F, where a reaction of water and the cladding could begin to damage the fuel rods and also produce hydrogen. The second problem is that the temperature might rise above the melting point of the uranium fuel, which is about 5200°F. Either poses a potential danger. Damage to the zirconium cladding releases some radioactive materials trapped inside the fuel rods into the core's cooling water. A melting of the fuel itself could release far more radioactive materials. If a significant portion of the fuel should melt,

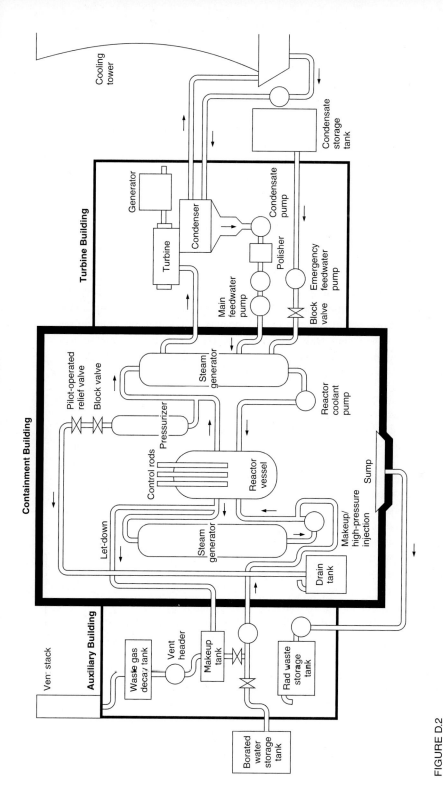

FIGURE D.2
The Three Mile Island nuclear power plant. (Source: John G. Kemeny. *Report of the President's Commission on the Accident at Three Mile Island*, U.S. Government Accounting Office, Washington, D.C., 1979.)

the molten fuel could melt through the reactor vessel itself and release large quantities of radioactive materials into the containment building.

The essential elements of the TMI-2 system during normal operations (Figure D.2) include

- The reactor (fuel and control rods).
- Water, which is heated by the fission process going on inside the fuel rods to ultimately produce steam to run the turbine. This water, by removing heat, also keeps the fuel rods from becoming overheated.
- Two steam generators, through which the heated water passes and gives up its heat to convert cooler water in another closed system to steam.
- A steam turbine that drives a generator to produce electricity.
- Pumps to circulate water through the various systems.
- A pressurizer, which is a large tank that maintains the reactor water at a pressure high enough to prevent boiling. At TMI-2, the pressurizer tank usually holds 800 cubic feet of water and 700 cubic feet of steam above it. The steam pressure is controlled by heating or cooling the water in the pressurizer. The steam pressure, in turn, is used to control the pressure of the water cooling the reactor.

Normally, water to the TMI-2 reactor flows through a closed system of pipes called the "reactor coolant system" or "primary loop." The water is pushed through the reactor by four reactor coolant pumps, each powered by a 9,000 horsepower electric motor. In the reactor, the water picks up heat as it flows around each fuel rod. Then it travels through 36-inch diameter stainless steel pipes, shaped like and called "candy canes," and into the steam generators.

In the steam generators, a transfer of heat takes place. The very hot water from the reactor coolant system travels down through the steam generators in a series of corrosion-resistant tubes. Meanwhile, water from another closed system—the feedwater or "secondary loop"—is forced into the steam generator.

The feedwater in the steam generators flows around the tubes that contain the hot water from the reactor coolant system. Some of this heat is transferred to the cooler feedwater, which boils and becomes steam. Just as in a coal- or oil-fired generating plant, the steam is carried from the two steam generators to turn the steam turbine, which runs the electricity-producing generator.

The water from the reactor coolant system, which has now lost some of its heat, is pumped back to the reactor to pass around the fuel rods, pick up more heat, and begin its cycle again.

The water from the feedwater system, which has turned to steam to drive the turbine, passes through devices called condensers. Here, the steam is condensed back to water and is forced back to the steam generators again.

The condenser water is cooled in the cooling towers. The water that cools the condensers is also in a closed system or loop. It cools the condensers, picks up heat, and is pumped to the cooling towers, where it cascades along a series of steps. As it does, it releases its heat to the outside air, creating the white vapor plumes that drift skyward from the towers. Then the water is pumped back to the condensers to begin its cooling process over again.

Neither the water that cools the condensers, the vapor plumes that rise from the cooling towers, nor any of the water that runs through the feedwater system is radioactive under normal conditions. The water that runs through the reactor coolant system is radioactive, of course, since it has been exposed to the radioactive materials in the core.

The turbine, the electric generator it powers, and most of the feedwater system piping are outside the containment building in other structures. The steam generators, however, which must be fed by water from both the reactor coolant and feedwater systems, are inside the containment building with the reactor and the pressurizer tank.

A nuclear power facility is designed with many ways to protect against system failure. Each of its major systems has an automatic backup system to replace it in the event of a failure. For example, in a loss-of-coolant accident— that is, an accident in which there is a loss of the reactor's cooling water—the emergency core cooling system automatically uses existing plant equipment to ensure that cooling water covers the core.

In a loss-of-coolant accident such as occurred at TMI-2, the vital part of the emergency core cooling system is the high pressure injection pumps, which can pour about 1,000 gallons a minute into the core to replace cooling water being lost through a stuck-open valve, broken pipe, or other type of leak. But the emergency core cooling system can be effective only if plant operators allow it to keep running and functioning as designed. At Three Mile Island, they did not.

D.3.2 Events

On the morning of March 28, 1979, a series of feedwater system pumps supplying water to TMI's steam generators tripped.[1] The plant was operating at 97-percent capacity at the time. Without the feedwater pumps, the flow of water to the steam generators stopped, which meant that soon there would be no steam. The steam turbine and the generator it powered were automatically shut down. This all occurred in the first two seconds of the accident.

Steam not only runs the generator to produce electricity, but it removes some of the intense heat the reactor water carries. When the feedwater flow stopped, the temperature of the reactor coolant increased and the rapidly heating water expanded. The pressurizer level (the level of the water inside the pressurizer tank) rose, and the steam in the top of the tank compressed. Pressure inside the pressurizer built to 2250 psi, 100 psi more than normal. A valve on top of the pressurizer, called a pilot-operated relief valve, or PORV, is designed to relieve excess pressure. The PORV opened correctly, and steam and water began flowing out of the reactor coolant system through a drain pipe to a tank on the

---

[1] In the electric industry, a *trip* means a piece of equipment stops operating.

floor of the containment building. Pressure continued to rise, however, and eight seconds after the first pump tripped, the reactor scrammed—that is, the control rods automatically dropped down into the reactor core to halt its nuclear fission.

The heat generated by fission was essentially zero less than a second later. In any reactor, decaying radioactive materials left from the fission process continue to heat the reactor's coolant water. Although this heat is just 6 percent of that released during fission, it has to be removed to keep the core from overheating. When the pumps that normally supply the steam generator with water shut down, three emergency feedwater pumps started automatically. Fourteen seconds into the emergency, an operator in the control room noticed that the emergency feedwater pumps were running. He did not notice two lights that indicated that a valve was closed on each of the two emergency feedwater lines and thus no water could reach the steam generators. One light was covered by a yellow maintenance tag. Nobody knows why the second light was missed.

With the reactor scrammed and the PORV open, pressure in the reactor coolant system fell. The PORV should have closed 13 seconds into the accident, when the pressure dropped to 2205 psi, but it stuck open. A light on the control room panel indicated that the electric power that opened the PORV had gone off (the solenoid was deenergized), misleading the operators into assuming that the valve had shut. The PORV would remain open for 2 hours and 22 minutes, draining needed coolant water and starting a loss-of-coolant accident.

In the first 100 minutes of the accident, over one-third of the entire capacity of the reactor coolant system—32,000 gallons—escaped through the PORV and out the reactor's let-down system.[2] If the valve had closed as it was designed to do, or if the control room operators had realized that the valve was stuck open and closed a backup valve to stem the flow of coolant water, or if they had simply left on the plant's high pressure injection pumps, the accident at TMI would have been only a minor event.

Reactor operators are trained to respond quickly in emergencies, with the initial actions ingrained and almost automatic and unthinking. The first alarm in the control room was followed by a cascade of 100 alarms within minutes. The operators reacted quickly as trained to counter the turbine trip and reactor scram. Later, one operator told the commission about his reaction to the incessant alarms, "I would have liked to have thrown away the alarm panel. It wasn't giving us any useful information."

The shift foreman was called back to the control room. He had been overseeing maintenance on one of the plant's polishers—a machine that uses resin beads to remove dissolved minerals from the feedwater system. They were using a mixture of air and water to break up resin that had clogged a pipe that transfers resin from a polisher (demineralizer) to a tank in which the resin is regenerated. Later investigation revealed that a faulty valve in one of the polishers allowed some

---

[2] The *let-down system* is the means by which water is removed from the reactor coolant system. The *make-up system* adds water. Piping from both runs through the auxiliary building.

water to leak into the air-controlled system that opens and closes the polishers' valves. This malfunctioning valve probably triggered the initial pump trip that led to the accident. The same problem of water leaking into the polishers' valve control system had occurred at least twice before at TMI-2. "Had Met Ed corrected the earlier polisher problem, the March 28 sequence of events may never have begun" [143].

With the PORV stuck open and heat being removed by the steam generators, the pressure and temperature of the reactor coolant system dropped, and the water level in the pressurizer fell. Thirteen seconds into the accident, the operators turned on a water pump. The water in the system was shrinking as it cooled, and therefore more water was needed to fill the system. Forty-eight seconds into the accident, while pressure continued falling, the water in the pressurizer began to rise again because the amount of water being pumped into the system was greater than that being lost through the PORV.

A minute and 45 seconds into the accident, the steam generators boiled dry because their emergency water lines were blocked. The reactor coolant heated up again, expanded, and helped send the pressurizer level up further.

Two minutes into the incident, with the pressurizer level still rising, pressure in the reactor coolant system dropped sharply. Two large pumps, called high pressure injection pumps, that are part of the emergency core cooling system, automatically began pouring about 1,000 gallons a minute into the system. The level of water in the pressurizer continued to rise, and the operators, conditioned to maintain a certain level in the pressurizer, took this to mean that the system had plenty of water in it. However, the pressure of the reactor coolant system water was falling, and its temperature became constant.

About two and a half minutes after the high pressure injection pumps began working, an operator shut down one and reduced the flow of the second to less than 100 gallons per minute. The reactor operators had been taught to keep the system from "going solid"—a condition in which the entire reactor and its cooling system, including the pressurizer, are filled with water. A solid system makes controlling the pressure within the reactor coolant system more difficult and can damage the system.

The Kemeny Commission concluded that the falling pressure, coupled with a constant reactor coolant temperature after high-pressure injection came on, should have alerted the operators that a loss-of-coolant accident had occurred and that safety required that they maintain high-pressure injection. An operator told the commission, however, "The rapidly increasing pressurizer level at the onset of the accident led me to believe that the high pressure injection was excessive, and that we were soon going to have a solid system" [143, p.94].

The saturation point was reached five and a half minutes into the accident. Steam bubbles began forming in the reactor coolant system, displacing the coolant water in the reactor itself. The displaced water moved into the pressurizer, sending its level even higher. Again, this suggested to the operators that there was still plenty of water in the system. They did not realize that water was actually flashing into steam in the reactor. With more water leaving the system than being added, the core was on its way to being uncovered. And so the operators began draining off the reactor's cooling water through the let-down system piping.

Eight minutes into the accident, someone discovered that no emergency feedwater was reaching the steam generators. An operator scanned the light on the control panel that indicates whether the emergency feedwater valves are open or closed. One pair of emergency feedwater valves designed to open after the pumps reach full speed were open. But a second pair, called the "twelve-valves," which are always supposed to be open except during a specific test of the emergency feedwater pumps, were closed. The operator opened the two twelve-valves and water rushed into the steam generators.

The twelve-valves were known to have been closed two days earlier, on March 26, as part of a routine test of the emergency feedwater pumps. The Kemeny Commission investigation did not identify a reason why the valves were in a closed position at eight minutes into the accident. They concluded that the most likely explanations were (1) the valves were never reopened after the March 26 test, (2) the valves were reopened after the test but the control room operators mistakenly closed them during the very first part of the accident, or (3) the valves were closed mistakenly from control points outside the control room after the test. The loss of emergency feedwater for eight minutes had no significant effect on the outcome of the accident, but it did add to the confusion that distracted the operators as they tried to understand the cause of their primary problem.

The Kemeny Commission noted that during the first two hours of the accident, the operators ignored or failed to recognize the significance of several things that should have warned them that they had an open PORV and a loss-of-coolant accident. One of these was the high temperatures at the drain pipe that led from the PORV to the reactor coolant drain tank. One emergency procedure states that a pipe temperature of 200°F indicates an open PORV. Another states that when the drain pipe temperature reaches 130°F, the block valve beneath it should be closed. But the operators testified that the pipe temperature normally registered high because either the PORV or some other valve was leaking slightly. "I have seen, in reviewing logs since the accident, approximately 198 degrees," the shift supervisor told the Commission. "But I can remember instances before . . . just over 200 degrees" [143, p.96]. So they dismissed the significance of the temperature readings, which the supervisor recalled as being in the range of 230°F (the top value was recorded as 285°F). He told the Commission that he thought the high temperature on the drainpipe represented residual heat: "Knowing that the relief valve had lifted, the downstream temperature I would expect to be high and that it would take some time for the pipe to cool down below the 200-degree set point" [143, p.96].

At 4:11 A.M., an alarm signaled that there was high water in the containment building's sump, an indication of a leak or break in the system. The water, mixed with steam, had come from the open PORV, first falling to the drain tank on the containment building floor. That tank was eventually filled, and the water flowed into the sump. At 4:15 A.M., a rupture disc on the drain tank burst as pressure in the tank rose. This break sent more slightly radioactive water onto the floor and into the sump. From the sump it was pumped to a tank in the nearby auxiliary building.

Five minutes later, instruments showed a higher than normal count of the neutrons inside the core, another indication that steam bubbles were present in the core and were forcing cooling water away from the fuel rods. During this time, the temperature and pressure inside the containment building rose rapidly because of the heat and steam escaping through the PORV and drain tank. The operators turned on the cooling equipment and fans inside the building. The Kemeny Commission concluded that the fact that they did not know that these conditions resulted from a loss-of-coolant accident indicated a severe deficiency in their training to identify the symptoms of such an accident.

At about this time, one of the operators got a call from the auxiliary building saying that an instrument there showed more than six feet of water in the containment building sump. When the operator queried the control room computer about this, he got the same answer. He then recommended shutting off the two sump pumps in the containment building. He did not know where the water was coming from and did not want to pump water that might be radioactive outside the containment building. Both sump pumps were stopped at about 4:39 A.M., but as much as 8,000 gallons of slightly radioactive water might already have been pumped into the auxiliary building. Only 39 minutes had passed since the start of the accident.

By this time, managers and experts had arrived at TMI-2. The superintendent of technical support testified that what he found was not what he expected. "I felt we were experiencing a very unusual situation, because I had never seen pressurizer level go high and peg in the high range, and at the same time, pressure being low. They have always performed consistently" [143, p.99]. The control room staff agreed. They later described the accident as a combination of events they had never experienced, either in operating the plant or in their training simulation.

Shortly after 5 A.M., the four reactor coolant pumps began vibrating severely. The vibration was a result of pumping steam as well as water, and it was another unrecognized indication that the reactor's water was boiling into steam. The operators were afraid that the violent shaking would damage the pumps or the coolant piping. The control room supervisor and his operators followed their training: At 5:14 A.M., they shut down two of the pumps and 27 minutes later the other two remaining pumps, stopping the forced flow of cooling water through the core.

By approximately 6 A.M., radiation alarms inside the containment building provided evidence that at least a few of the fuel rod claddings had ruptured from the high gas pressures inside them and allowed radioactive gases within the rods to escape into the coolant water. With coolant continuing to stream out the open PORV and little water being added, the top of the core became uncovered and heated to the point where the zirconium alloy of the fuel rod cladding reacted with steam to produce hydrogen. Some of this hydrogen escaped into the containment building through the open PORV and drain tank, while some remained within the reactor.

At 6:22 A.M., the open block valve was closed, 2 hours and 22 minutes after the PORV had opened. The loss of coolant was stopped and pressure began to rise, but the damage continued. For some unexplained reason, high pressure injection to replace the water lost through the PORV and let-down system was not started for almost another hour. Before that time, rising radiation levels were detected in the containment and auxiliary buildings, and evidence indicates that as much as two-thirds of the 12-foot-high core was uncovered, with temperatures as high as 3,500 to 4,000°F in parts of the core. At 6:54 A.M., the operators turned on one of the reactor coolant pumps, but shut it down 19 minutes later because of high vibrations. More radiation alarms went off, and a site emergency[3] was declared. This declaration initiated a series of actions required by the emergency plan, including notifying state authorities. Later, after more alarms sounded, a general emergency was declared.[4]

Four hours after the accident began, the containment building isolated, an automatic procedure to help prevent radioactive material from escaping into the environment. Pipes carrying coolant run between the containment building and auxiliary buildings. These pipes close off when the containment building isolates, but the operators can open them. They were opened in this case and some of this piping leaked radioactive material into the auxiliary building, some of which escaped from there into the atmosphere outside.

In the TMI-2 design, isolation occurs only when pressure in the containment building reaches a certain point. Although large amounts of steam entered the containment building early in the accident through the open PORV, the operators had kept pressure there low by using the building's cooling and ventilation system. The NRC had instituted new criteria for isolation in 1975, but TMI-2 was grandfathered under the old criteria. The Kemeny Commission concluded, however, that the failure to isolate early made little difference in the accident; some of the radioactivity ultimately released into the atmosphere occurred from leaks in the let-down system that continued to carry radioactive water out of the containment building and into the auxiliary building after isolation.

At 8:26 A.M., the operators once again turned on the emergency core cooling system's high pressure injection pumps and maintained a relatively high rate of flow. The core was still uncovered at this time, and evidence indicates that it took until about 10:30 A.M. for the pumps to cover the core again fully.

Many off-site emergency procedures were initiated at this time, which will not be detailed here. Activities in the control room became even more difficult as workers had to put on protective face masks with filters to screen out any airborne radioactive particles, making communication among those managing the accident difficult.

At 1:50 P.M. on Wednesday, a "thud" was heard in the control room. It was

---

[3] Declared when some event threatens an uncontrolled release of radioactivity to the immediate environment.

[4] An incident that has "potential for serious radiological consequences to the health and safety of the general public."

the sound of a hydrogen explosion inside the containment building, but nobody recognized this until late Thursday. The noise was dismissed at the time as the slamming of a ventilation damper. A pressure spike on a computer strip chart was written off as possible instrument malfunction.

By Friday, the nuclear industry had become deeply involved in the accident, sending experts from around the country. It was also on Friday that concern arose about a hydrogen bubble in the reactor possibly exploding if sufficient oxygen should enter the bubble. Someone in the NRC provided a theory (which turned out to be wrong) that the radiation in the reactor could cause decomposition of water into hydrogen and oxygen, leading to an explosion that might blow the pressure vessel apart. The concern turned out to be unfounded, but it continued through the weekend, with laboratories and scientists outside the NRC providing advice.

The cost of the accident, including cleanup of the buildings and disposal of approximately one million gallons of radioactive water, a substantial amount of radioactive gases, and solid radioactive debris, was estimated between $1 billion and $1.86 billion, not counting the loss of the plant itself.

The public health effects of the accident were negligible; very little radioactive material was released outside the plant. The maximum whole-body dose that could have been received by those outside was about the same dose as a person receives in a year from natural radiation. Plant personnel had slightly greater exposure. At one point in the crisis, on March 30, the governor of Pennsylvania advised that children and pregnant women living in the vicinity of TMI should leave, and many did so. An evacuation center at Hershey, about 15 miles away, only attracted about 200 people; the rest made their own arrangements. The Kemeny Commission report concludes that the major health effect of the accident was found to be mental stress. The public relations consequences for the nuclear industry were much more serious, including a lowering of public confidence in the industry and in its regulatory agencies.

D.3.3 Causal Factors

Because of the complexity of this accident, the hierarchical model described in Chapter 3 is used in trying to understand it. This model separates the events (level 1), the conditions that allow those events (level 2), and the constraints and conditions (root causes) at level 3 that account for the level 2 conditions. The events have been presented already.

Level 2 Conditions

On the positive side, the containment building at TMI remained intact, despite a hydrogen explosion within it, and kept most of the radioactive material from escaping. The building at Chernobyl was destroyed by a hydrogen explosion. Some reactors in the United States also lack strong containment systems, such as the ones producing weapons-grade plutonium for the Department of Energy and early versions of boiling-water reactors.

On the other hand, many of the operators' actions contributed to the accident sequence. The TMI-2 operators had never been trained for the sequence of the stuck-open PORV, and instructions on how to handle it were not included in their emergency procedures. They also had never had specific training about the danger of saturation conditions in the core, although they were generally familiar with the concept. Although Met Ed believed that saturation (which could have led to the core being uncovered) had occurred in an incident a year before the accident, the hazards of the problem were not emphasized to the operators. When saturation occurred during the accident, the operators did not recognize its significance and take corrective action quickly. In addition, the operators were not given adequate information about the temperatures to be expected in the PORV tailpipe after the PORV opened.

In general, the Kemeny Commission concluded that most of the operators and others involved in the accident did not fully understand the operating principles of the plant equipment. Their training gave insufficient emphasis to a fundamental understanding of the reactor and to the principles of reactor safety.

In particular, the simulator training of operators at Babcock and Wilcox (B&W) did not prepare operators for multiple-failure accidents. In fact, the simulator was not programmed to reproduce the conditions that the operators faced during the accident. It was unable to simulate increasing pressurizer level at the same time that reactor coolant pressure was dropping.

Some of the key written operating and emergency procedures in use at TMI were inadequate, including the procedures for a loss-of-coolant accident and for pressurizer operation. The Kemeny report notes that the deficiencies in these procedures could cause operator confusion or incorrect action. For example, a 1978 B&W analysis of a certain type of small-break loss-of-coolant accident was misinterpreted by Met Ed. That misinterpretation was incorporated into the loss-of-coolant accident emergency procedures available at the time of the accident.

Operating and emergency procedures that had been approved by Met Ed and were in use contained many minor substantive errors, typographical errors, and imprecise or sloppy terminology. Some were inadequate. For example, a 1978 revision in the TMI-2 surveillance procedure for the emergency feedwater block valves violated TMI-2's technical specifications, but no one realized it at the time. The approval of the revision was not done according to Met Ed's own administrative procedures.

The Kemeny Commission staff noted that pipe and valve identification practices were significantly below industrial standards. Eight hours into the accident, Met Ed personnel spent 10 minutes trying unsuccessfully to locate three decay heat valves in a high radiation field in the auxiliary building.

TMI-2 had repeated problems with the condensate polishers. During the 18-month period before the accident, no effective steps were taken to correct these problems. These polishers probably initiated the March 28 sequence of events. At the time of the accident, Met Ed also had not corrected deficiencies in radiation monitoring equipment pointed out by an NRC audit months before.

The TMI-2 control room was not adequately designed with the management of an accident in mind: The designers had never systematically evaluated the design to see how well it would serve in emergency conditions. The design problems ranged from the details of the control-board layout and the positioning of controls and displays, to larger-scale problems of system design that lead to human errors in the interpretation of data. "It is not surprising that the operators made errors, because the design of the control-room details was such as to enhance, not to minimize, errors" [41, p.157]. Some examples of control room design and information presentation that confused the operators follow:

- The operators were faced with over 100 alarms within 10 seconds of the first one. There was no way to suppress the unimportant signals so that the operators could concentrate on the important ones.
- The arrangement of controls and indicators was not well thought out. Some key indicators relevant to the accident were on the back of the control panel. Information was not presented in a clear and sufficiently understandable form. For example, although the pressure and temperature within the reactor coolant system were shown, there was no direct indication that the combination of pressure and temperature meant that the cooling water was turning into steam. Patrick Haggerty (a member of the Kemeny Commission) was appalled by this deficiency:

  > It's inconceivable to me that the really serious accident parameters are not grouped together instead of being scattered all over the control room—and even then not very well portrayed. It's inconceivable that somebody hadn't grouped those few indicators that absolutely would have shown the operator what counted—that the core was or was not covered. I just can't believe it. . . . If you take the simplest kind of microcomputer . . . it would probably be competent to provide information and plot out saturation so that it is always visible (quoted in [193, p.54]).

  A B&W official testified that a direct reading of the level of coolant in the core would be difficult to provide and too expensive, and would create other complications. Although there were several indirect indications, each proved to be faulty or ambiguous.
- Operators were unable to determine the water pressure in the core because engineers had not anticipated this need [123].
- The manual control station of the polisher bypass valve was nearly inaccessible and took great effort, in a physically awkward position, to operate.
- Several instruments went off scale during the course of the events, so the operators lacked some highly significant diagnostic information. These instruments were not designed to follow the course of an accident.
- The computer printer registering alarms was running more than two and

a half hours behind the events and at one point jammed, losing valuable information.

John Kemeny, after a tour of the TMI-1 control room, remarked in the presence of journalists that he did not think that it was a masterpiece of modern technology.

> In fact, I said that it was at least twenty years behind the times. I was heavily criticized for this. And with good reason, because my statement proved to be wrong: we discovered later, in the documents of the NRC, a report written ten years earlier in which an expert had said that the control rooms were, then, twenty years behind the times [144, p.66].

A large number of control room instruments were out of calibration, and many tags were hanging on the instrument panel indicating equipment out of service. One of those tags obscured the emergency feedwater block control valve indicator lights.

In general, plant procedures were deficient. For example,

- When shifts changed in the control room, there was no systematic check required on the status of the plant and the line-up of valves.
- Although Met Ed procedures required closing the PORV block valve when temperatures in the tailpipe exceeded 130°F, the block valve had not been closed at the time of the accident even though temperatures had been well above 130°F for weeks.
- Performance of surveillance tests was not adequately verified to be sure that the procedures were followed correctly. The emergency feedwater valves that, during the accident, should have been open but were closed may have been left closed during a surveillance test two days earlier.
- The iodine filters in the auxiliary and fuel handling buildings were left in continuous use rather than being preserved to filter air in the event of radioactive contamination. Thus, on the day of the accident, their charcoal filtering capacity was partially expended and they did not perform as designed. The NRC had waived testing requirements to verify the filter effectiveness.
- After the accident, radiological control practices were observed to be deficient. Contaminated and potentially contaminated equipment was found in uncontrolled areas of the auxiliary building.

Finally, the maintenance force was overworked at the time of the accident and had been reduced in size to save money. There were many shutdowns, and a variety of equipment was out of order.

Review of equipment history for the six months prior to the accident showed that a number of equipment items that were involved in the accident had had a poor maintenance history without adequate corrective action. These included the pressurizer level transmitter, the hydrogen recombiner, pressurizer heaters, make-up pump switches, and the condensate polishers. Despite a history of problems with these polishers, procedures were not changed to ensure that operators would bypass the polishers during maintenance operations to protect the plant from a possible malfunction of the polisher. Inspection of the valves in the TMI-1 containment building after the accident showed long-term lack of maintenance. Boron stalactites more than a foot long hung from the valves and stalagmites had built up from the floor.

Level 3 Conditions and Constraints

Ignoring Warnings.   Similar incidents in other plants demonstrated the incipient problems and the operators' need for clear instructions to deal with events like those that happened. Some of these warnings, including a similar incident at the Davis-Besse nuclear power plant a year before, were detailed in Chapter 4. In addition, after an April 1978 incident at TMI, a control room operator had complained to his management about problems with the control room, but no corrective action was taken by the utility [143].

Design for Controllability.   Both the RBMK reactor at Chernobyl and the TMI PWR reactor are sensitive to perturbations. The B&W reactor at TMI has a once-through cooling system, with a small volume of water compared to other U.S. reactors and an undersized pressurizer [4]. This design makes it respond more to disturbances, and thus it is more difficult for the operators to control.

> For water-cooled systems, the drive for economy leads to high fuel ratings and therefore to an extremely rapid sequence of accident events given an initiation due, for example, to the loss of coolant. The times available for intervention are such that the reactor has essentially become a "fly-by-wire" device rather than a piloted one.
>
> To give sufficient statistical assurance that such a device will "fly" without crashing, large degrees of redundancy in safety systems have to be provided. The consequent increase in complexity makes it even more likely that the operator, if he intervenes, will do something counterproductive [87, p.22].

Franklin suggests that it is worth giving up a few percent of capital cost-effectiveness for reactors that provide the operator with a half-hour to reflect upon the consequences of actions before needing to intervene [87].

Lack of Attention to Human Factors.   The designers paid little attention to the interaction between humans and machines under the rapidly changing and confusing conditions of an accident. The design ignored the needs of operators during a slowly developing small-break accident, perhaps because of a concentration on large-break accidents, which do not allow time for significant operator action.

While acknowledging the role the operators played in the accident events, the Kemeny Commission refrained from simply blaming them for the accident but noted that "many factors contributed to the action of the operators, such as deficiencies in their training, lack of clarity in their operating procedures, failure of organizations to learn the proper lessons from previous incidents, and deficiencies in the control room" [143, p.11].

As discussed in Chapter 6, more attention is now being given to human factors by the nuclear power industry. Barrett says, "The industry now appears to recognize the importance of operator selection, training, motivation, and licensing, and the need to design a system from the point of view of communication, information retrieval, record keeping, and human factors psychology" [19, p.170]. Hornick, on the other hand, has argued that little has really changed: "Unfortunately, there is not much to suggest that this attitude has changed significantly. Some believe that the status of human factors is nearly as bad as it was before TMI" [127, p.113]. Perhaps the problem is just that, as Wahlstrom and Swaton suggest, the diffusion of new knowledge takes time [346].

Complacency. The Kemeny report points out that a feeling had pervaded the entire U.S. nuclear power industry, and even the government oversight committees, that a major accident could not happen in the United States.

> After many years of operation of nuclear power plants, with no evidence that any member of the general public had been hurt, the belief that nuclear power plants are sufficiently safe grew into a conviction. One must recognize this to understand why many key steps that could have prevented the accident at TMI were not taken. The Commission is convinced that this attitude must be changed to one that says nuclear power is by its very nature potentially dangerous, and, therefore, one must continually question whether the safeguards already in place are sufficient to prevent major accidents. A comprehensive system is required in which equipment and human beings are treated with equal importance [143, p.9].

As another aspect of complacency and discounting risk, the plant was inadequately designed to cope with the cleanup of a damaged plant [143].

Management. The Kemeny report notes significant deficiencies in the management of TMI-2. Shift foremen could not adequately fulfill their supervisory roles because of excessive paperwork not related to supervision. There was no systematic check on the status of the plant and the lineup of valves when shifts changed. Surveillance procedures were not adequately supervised. And there were weaknesses in the program of quality assurance and control. A review of TMI-2's licensee event reports (required by the NRC) disclosed repeated omissions, inadequate failure analyses, and inadequate corrective actions. There was also no group with special responsibility for receiving and acting upon potential safety concerns raised by employees. Finally, the report notes that management allowed operation of the plant with a number of poor control room practices.

The GPU Service Corporation (GPUSC) had final responsibility for design of the plant. However, by its own admission, it lacked the staff or expertise in certain areas. Once construction was complete, GPUSC turned the plant over to Met Ed to run, but Met Ed did not have sufficient knowledge, expertise, and personnel to operate the plant or to maintain it adequately.

Responsibility for management decisions was divided among the TMI site, Met Ed, and GPU. GPU recognized in early 1977 that integration of operating responsibility into one organization was desirable. An outside management audit, completed in the spring of 1977, recommended clarifying and reevaluating the roles of GPUSC and Met Ed in the design and construction of new facilities; strengthening communications between the two; and establishing minimum standards for the safe operation of GPU's nuclear plants. However, integration of management did not occur until after the accident.

Quality Assurance. Met Ed had a quality assurance plan that met NRC requirements. But the Kemeny report notes that the NRC requirements at that time were inadequate—they did not require that quality assurance programs be applied to the plant as a whole, but rather only to systems classified as "safety-related." Neither the PORV nor the condensate polishers were placed in this category. In addition, according to the Kemeny report, the NRC did not require the level of independent review (outside of line management) normally found in the quality assurance programs of safety-critical industries.

Met Ed's implementation of its quality assurance plan was also found to have significant deficiencies by the Kemeny Commission staff and in an NRC post-accident audit. Independent audit of the performance of surveillance procedures was required only every two years. There was no plan for such a review and, in fact, no review had been made of those TMI-2 procedures that were more than two years old. There were deficiencies in the reporting, analysis, and resolution of problems in "safety-related" equipment and other events required to be reported to the NRC. Independent assessment of general plant operations was minimal.

Weaknesses in the Approval of Operating Procedures. Operating procedures were not thoroughly reviewed by experts. After the accident, the NRC started to require that plant safety committees review the procedures, but this was not standard before the accident [4]. Met Ed had no requirement for an independent (outside of line management) safety assessment of operating procedures.

Training. The Kemeny report concluded that the training of TMI operators was greatly deficient. While it might have been adequate for the operation of a plant under normal circumstances, insufficient attention was paid to possible serious accidents and to accident sequences involving more than one failure. The content of the operator instructional program did not lead to sufficient understanding of reactor systems.

The person responsible for training at B&W was a witness at the hearings. He was very proud of the last five years of his company's program. When asked what he considered his most important achievement, he replied, "When I arrived many courses had been given by engineers. But the engineers don't know how to talk in a way which people can understand. Consequently, the first rule I introduced was that no engineer was authorized to participate in the training of operators" (quoted in [144, p.65]). The Kemeny Commission found that all theory had been taken out of the operator training program and that they were trained to be button pushers. The training was adequate for normal conditions, but the operators had not been prepared for a serious situation [144]. This satisfied NRC requirements and had become standard practice: The operators were only trained for an accident in the course of which only *one* thing went wrong. "They were never trained for a situation in which *two* independent things could go wrong. And in this particular accident *three* independent things went wrong" [144, p.66].

Note, however, that this problem did not exist just for the operators: The TMI emergency and engineering personnel also had difficulty in analyzing events, and the hydrogen bubble issues confused even outside experts. Even after supervisory personnel took charge, significant delays occurred before the full amount of core damage was recognized and stable cooling of the core was achieved. Of the people on duty at the plant when the accident started, none were nuclear engineers, none were even college graduates, and none were trained to handle complex reactor emergencies.

Most of the operators and others involved in the accident did not fully understand the operating principles of the plant equipment. The lack of depth in this understanding, even by senior reactor operators, left them unprepared to deal with something as confusing as the situation in which they found themselves.

The TMI training program, however, did conform to the NRC standard for training at that time. Moreover, TMI operator candidates had higher scores than the national average on NRC licensing examinations and operating tests.

The Kemeny Commission concluded that NRC standards allowed a shallow level of operator training and prescribed only minimum training requirements. There were no minimal educational requirements for operators and no requirements for checks on psychological fitness or criminal records. In addition, an individual could fail parts of the licensing examination, including sections on emergency procedures and equipment, and still pass the overall examination by getting a passing average score.

The NRC also had no criteria for the qualification of those people who conduct the operator training programs and did not regularly conduct in-depth reviews of the training programs.

Information Collection and Use.   The lessons from previous accidents and incidents did not result in new, clear instructions being passed on to the operators. The NRC accumulates an enormous amount of information on the operating experience of plants (2,000 to 3,000 reports a year). However, before the TMI accident, systematic methods were lacking for evaluating these experiences and looking for danger signals of possible generic safety problems. In 1978, the General Accounting Office had criticized the NRC for this failure, but no corrective action had been taken as of the TMI-2 accident.

> In a number of important cases, General Public Utilities Corporation, Met Ed, and B&W failed to acquire enough information about safety problems, failed to analyze adequately what information they did acquire, or failed to act on that information. Thus, there was a serious lack of communication about several critical safety matters within and among the companies involved in the building and operation of the TMI-2 plant. A similar problem existed in the NRC [143, p.43].

There also seems to have been a lack of closure in the system: Important safety issues were raised and studied to some degree, but were not carried through to resolution. According to the Kemeny Commission report, the lessons learned from these studies did not reach those people and organizations that most needed to know about them.

Licensing and Regulation. Licensing deficiencies occupied a major place in the Kemeny report. Most of these have been fixed since the accident. It is important to understand them, however, because many of these same deficiencies can be found in the licensing procedures for other industries, and some of the same mistakes are being repeated with respect to the introduction of computers into the control of nuclear power plants and other hazardous processes and industries.

The Kemeny Commission report concluded that prior to TMI, the NRC paid insufficient attention in licensing reviews to loss-of-coolant accidents of this size (such as might be caused by a stuck-open valve). Instead, the NRC focused most of its attention on large-break loss-of-coolant accidents. Those managing the TMI accident were unprepared for the significant amount of hydrogen generated. TMI illustrates a situation where the NRC emphasis on large breaks did not cover the effects observed in a smaller accident.

The licensing process also concentrated on equipment, assuming that the presence of operators would only improve the situation—they would not be part of the problem. The Kemeny Commission noted a persistent assumption that plants could be made sufficiently safe to be "people-proof." Thus, not enough attention in the licensing process was devoted to the training of operating personnel and to operator procedures.

Moreover, at that time, license applicants were only required to analyze single-failure accidents. They were not required to analyze what happens when two or more systems fail independently of each other (as happened at TMI) or to provide emergency operating procedures for such events.

There was also a sharp delineation between those components in systems that are "safety-related" and those that are not. Strict reviews and requirements applied to the former; the latter were exempt from most requirements—even though they can have an effect on the safety of the plant. Items not labeled "safety-related" did not need to be reviewed in the licensing process, were not required to meet NRC design criteria, did not need to be testable, did not require redundancy, and were ordinarily not subject to NRC inspection. "We feel that this sharp either/or definition is inappropriate. Instead, there should be a system of priorities as to how significant various components and systems are for the overall safety of the plant."

The Kemeny Commission also noted that there were no precise criteria as to which components and systems were to be labeled safety-related; the utility made the initial determination subject to NRC approval. For example, at TMI-2, the PORV was not a safety-related item because it had a block valve behind it. On the other hand, the block valve was not safety-related because it had a PORV in front of it.

> The NRC's reliance upon artificial categories of "safety-related" items has caused it to miss important safety issues and has led the nuclear industry to merely comply with NRC regulations and to equate that compliance with operational safety. Thus, over-emphasis by the NRC process on specific categories of items labeled "safety-related" appears to interfere with the development, throughout the nuclear industry, of a comprehensive safety consciousness, that is, a dynamic day-to-day process for operating safely [143, p.53].

At that time, plants could receive an operating license with several safety issues still unresolved. This placed such a plant in a regulatory "limbo," with jurisdiction divided between two different offices within the NRC. TMI-2 had this status at the time of the accident, 13 months after it had received its operating license.

The report noted more generally that there was no identifiable office within the NRC responsible for systems engineering examination of overall plant design and performance, including interaction between major systems, and also no office to examine the interface between machines and humans:

> There seems to be a persistent assumption that plant safety is assured by engineered equipment, and a concomitant neglect of the human beings who could defeat it if they do not have adequate training, operating procedures, information about plant conditions, and manageable monitors and controls. Problems with the control room contributed to the confusion during the TMI accident [143, 53].

A further problem noted was the NRC's primary focus on licensing and insufficient attention to the process of assuring nuclear safety in operating plants. The labeling of a problem as *generic* (applying to a number of different nuclear power plants) provided a convenient way to postpone decisions on a difficult problem. Once an issue was labeled generic, the individual plant being licensed was not responsible for resolving the issue prior to licensing. There was a reluctance to apply new safety standards to previously licensed plants.

Finally, the existence of a vast body of NRC regulations tended to focus industry attention narrowly on the meeting of regulations rather than on a systematic concern for safety. For example, because the licensing process concentrated on the consequences of single failures, there was no attempt to prepare operators for accidents in which two systems failed independently of each other.

Emergency Preparedness. In the approval process for reactor sites, the NRC at that time required licensees to plan for off-site consequences only in the "area of residents"—about a two-mile radius for TMI. The existence of a state emergency or evacuation plan was also not required. In general, emergency planning had a low priority in the NRC (and the AEC before it) prior to the TMI accident. The Kemeny Commission report suggests that the reasons for this included the agency's confidence in design reactor safeguards and their desire to avoid raising public concern about the safety of nuclear power. The report also suggests that the attitude fostered by the NRC regulatory approach and by Met Ed at the local level was that radiological accidents having off-site consequences beyond the two-mile radius were so unlikely as not to be of serious concern.

The TMI emergency plan did not require the utility to notify state or local authorities in the event of a radiological accident, and delays occurred in doing this. Met Ed also did not notify its physicians under contract, who would have been responsible for the on-site treatment of injured and contaminated workers, and the emergency medical care training given to these physicians was inadequate. Moreover, the emergency control center for health physics operations and the analytical laboratory to be used in emergencies were located in an area that became uninhabitable in the early hours of the accident; there was a shortage of respirators; and there was an inadequate supply of uncontaminated air [143].

The response to the emergency was characterized by an atmosphere of almost total confusion and a lack of communication at all levels. Almost all the local communities around TMI lacked detailed emergency plans. Many key recommendations were made by people who did not have accurate information, and those who managed the accident were slow to realize the significance and implications of the events that had taken place. "The fact that too many individuals and organizations were not aware of the dimensions of serious accidents at nuclear power plants accounts for a great deal of the lack of preparedness and the poor quality of the response" [143].

The Kemeny Commission recommended centralization of emergency planning and response in a single agency at the federal level, with close coordination between it and state and local agencies. This agency would have responsibility both for ensuring that adequate planning takes place and for taking charge of the response to the emergency. They also recommended that siting rules for plants be changed.

D.4 Chernobyl

In August 1986, representatives from the Soviet Union presented a 382-page report at the IAEA Expert Conference on the Chernobyl Accident held in Vienna. The report provides an account of the shortcomings in design and reactor operation that led to the accident. Later analyses by others filled in missing pieces, including one by Atomic Energy of Canada, Ltd (AECL) [211].

D.4.1 Background

As described earlier, the Chernobyl reactor design, called the RBMK, is graphite moderated and water cooled. Shields on the side of the RBMK reactor are made of water, sand, and concrete. The bottom and the top both have concrete shields. All the pressure tubes and control rods are attached to this top shield, and the entire reactor and shield complex is inside a confinement building.

The pipes below the reactor core were inside boxes that were connected to a huge pool of water under the entire building. If one of the pipes in the boxes broke, the steam would be forced into the pool, where it and any radioactive particles it contained would be trapped in the water. But all the steam pipes above the core were inside ordinary industrial buildings. Thus, if one of these pipes broke, a release of radioactive steam would occur. The Russians at the time relied on accident prevention and mitigation and provided only partial containment. After TMI, they started to add containment to their reactors.

The reactor is controlled by 211 control rods. The large number of rods is meant to compensate for their relatively slow speed. The effectiveness of a control rod varies with the stage of insertion: A rod is not as marginally effective in the early or late stages of insertion as in the intermediate stages [4]. It takes about 20 seconds for the rods to be fully inserted.

An important aspect of this reactor, with respect to safety, is that it has a *positive void coefficient*. Briefly, the power increases as water flowing through the core decreases—the opposite of most reactors. In a PWR, water is used as a moderator and without it, fissioning stops. However, fuel elements may still melt from the heat generated by decaying fission products. This is what happened in part of the TMI core.

Water in the RBMK is used only for transferring heat. The water does capture some neutrons, however, preventing them from producing further fissions. If the water boils and becomes less dense, the neutrons it would have captured instead go into the graphite, where they cause more fissioning. The absence of water thus increases the reactivity and the rate of fissioning. To handle this positive void coefficient, the RBMK reactors depend on a complex, computer-run control system [4]. There are four main water circulating pumps: three used in normal operation and a fourth as standby. Emergency feedwater pumps and pressurized accumulators switch on in an emergency between 10 and 20 seconds after the main feedwater stops.

An experiment had been planned while the reactor was being shut down for "medium repair" on April 25, 1986. The purpose of the experiment was to determine whether, after steam had been shut off from the turbo-generator, the inertia of the still rotating generator would be sufficient to generate enough electricity to operate auxiliary motors that were part of the reactor emergency cooling system.

The operation of a nuclear power plant does not rely on the electricity it generates, which is sent out to distribution centers. Lines from other power stations provide electric power to run the essential parts of the plant. The systems requiring off-site electricity include instrumentation, control, and some of the pumps. Other pumps are run by steam generated by the plant. Because of the positive void coefficient in the RBMK, the emergency feedwater pumps must be kept running at all times to circulate water through the reactor.

The Russians design their plants to withstand both an accident and a simultaneous loss of electrical power. Because the reactor is shut down immediately, it cannot generate its own power directly. Normally, electricity would be obtained from the electrical supply to the station or from other reactors at the same site. An extra level of protection is provided, however, in case either of these sources also fail. The normal backup is to provide diesel engines to drive emergency generators. U.S. plants are required to have emergency batteries for instantaneous response and diesel generators that go from cold start to full power in 10 seconds [4]. The Russians have said that their diesel run-up time is 15 seconds, but the report released in Vienna indicated they need other sources of power for at least 45 seconds. They decided to tap the energy of the spinning turbine—which is so heavy it takes a while to slow down—to generate electricity for the few seconds before their diesels start. The experiment was to see how long this electricity would power the main pumps that keep the cooling water flowing over the fuel.

The experiment had been done before at other plants with no problems, but they found that the voltage from the generator dropped sharply long before the generator stopped rotating. In the new test, they planned to try to eliminate this problem by using a special system to regulate the magnetic field of the generator. The Vienna report said that the test procedure was not prepared or approved in the proper way and was of low quality. In addition, personnel deviated from the plan, which created the emergency conditions.

The basic plan was to reduce reactor power to less than half its normal output, so that all the steam could be put into one turbine. This remaining turbine was then to be disconnected and its spinning energy used to run the main pumps for a short while.

D.4.2 Events

The reactor was operated normally until 1 A.M. on April 25, when the operators started to reduce reactor power in preparation for the test. This operation was done slowly, with the reactor reaching 50-percent power 12 hours later. Only one of the two turbines was needed at this point to take the steam from the reactor, so the second turbine was disconnected at 1:05 P.M. to simulate the loss of off-site power.

At this point, the electrical supply for the four main cooling pumps and two feedwater pumps (which were normally powered from the switched-off generator) were transferred to the operational generator. The emergency cooling system was disconnected from the pipelines at 2 P.M. according to plan, so that its power consumption would not affect the test results. Normally, the test would have continued with the power being reduced to about 30 percent. However, further shutdown of the reactor was delayed because of a request from the grid distribution center at Kiev. The controller at Kiev asked that output be maintained to satisfy an unexpected demand. The continued operation of the reactor for another nine hours, without its emergency cooling system, was a gross breach of operating regulations, although it did not affect the accident.

The test finally began at 11:10 P.M. The test procedures called for the test to be carried out at a reactor power between 700 and 1000 Mw. To enable the reactor to operate at this low power, the local automatic control system had to be switched off. The global (or average power) control system is meant to be used primarily as a backup to the local control system; the local system is more accurate and smooths out the effects of perturbations. Local control is required during transitions from one operating regime to another [340].

A sudden power reduction causes a quick buildup of xenon in uranium fuel. Xenon is a radioactive gas that readily absorbs neutrons and tends to hasten the reactor shutdown. At this point, sustaining a chain reaction became difficult because many of the neutrons needed for fission were being absorbed by the xenon. In addition, the core was at such low power that the water in the pressure tubes was not boiling, as it normally does, but was liquid. Liquid water absorbs like xenon. The operators continued inserting control rods in order to continue shutting the plant down. As a result, the reactor power dropped to below 30 Mw. The reactor was almost shut down, and the power was too low for the test.

The operators saw the drastic undershoot and tried to increase power by pulling out control rods. By 1 A.M., they managed to get the reactor back to 200 Mw. This was below the power level specified for the test (which was 700 Mw), but it was as high as they could go because of the xenon and water, and they decided to proceed anyway.

By this time, both the automatic regulator rods (inserted from the bottom of the reactor) and the control rods (inserted from the top of the reactor) had been withdrawn almost to their fullest extent. Snell describes this as rather like "driving a car with the accelerator floored and the brakes on—it was abnormal and unstable" [211, p.15]. Running this type of reactor with all the control rods withdrawn is a very serious error because some of them are needed for emergency shutdown. If they are all pulled out well above the core, it takes too long for them to move back into the high-power part of the reactor in an emergency, and the shutdown is very slow. A minimum of 30 rods is considered minimal for safety, but only 6 to 8 were in the core at this time.

At 1:03 and 1:07 A.M., two more cooling pumps (the normal reserve pumps) were switched on, in addition to the six pumps that were operating. This was done to ensure that at the end of the experiment (during which four of the pumps were required to be shut down), four pumps would remain operating to provide reliable cooling of the reactor core. Under normal levels of power output, adding the pumps would not have been been a problem, but at 200 Mw, the reactor required many manual adjustments to maintain a safe balance of steam and water.

One explanation for the following events is that the operation of these pumps greatly increased the flow of cold water into the reactor, decreased the rate of steam generation, and reduced the level of water in the steam separator below the emergency level. An emergency shutdown would normally have occurred automatically at this point.

The AECL explanation suggests that the operator had to take over manual flow of water returning from the turbine, as the automatic controls were not operating well—the plant was never intended to operate at such low power. Controlling the flow of water is a complex task to carry out manually, and the operator did not succeed in getting the flow correct. The reactor was so unstable it was close to being shut down by the emergency rods.

In either case, because a shutdown would abort the test, the operators short-circuited the emergency protection signals. At 1:23 A.M., the shut-down control valves of the second generator were closed, and the reactor continued to operate at a power of 200 Mw. They decided to start the test.

Normally, the reactor would shut down automatically if the remaining turbine was disconnected, as was planned for the test. However, they wanted a chance to repeat the test immediately if it were not done correctly, which they could not do if the reactor were shut-down. Therefore, an operator disabled this shutdown signal also. The remaining automatic shutdown signals would go off on abnormal power levels, but would not react immediately to the test conditions. The second turbine was then tripped.

At this point, the reactor was operating at 200 Mw and still producing steam. Because both generators were turned off, there was no place for the steam to go, and steam pressure began to rise. At the same time, the flow of water through the reactor began to decrease, since four of the eight pumps were working off the generator, which was deprived of steam and running down. Further steam generation resulted and, since steam absorbs neutrons much less effectively than water does, there was a rapid rise of reactivity and the reactor power increased to more than 530 Mw in less than three seconds. At this point (1:23.40 A.M.), the operator pushed the emergency SCRAM button which inserted all control and shutdown rods into the reactor.

By this time, as noted earlier, the automatic control rods were at the bottom of the core (where they had been withdrawn in order to get the reactor power up to 200 Mw), and the manual adjustments by the operators in their attempts to achieve the test conditions had resulted in practically all the other control rods being withdrawn to the top of the core. When the SCRAM button was pressed, the rods went down, but the operator saw that they stopped before they reached the correct depth. He then cut off the drive couplings so that they fell into the core under their own weight.

People outside the reactor building reported that they heard two explosions, one after the other, at 1:24 A.M. Hot fragments and sparks flew up above the reactor building and some of them started a fire on the roof of the turbine room.

Total agreement is lacking about the detailed cause of each of these explosions. There is consensus, however, that the first was caused by the great amount of heat produced by the increased rate of fissioning. This heat production occurred over too short a time for heat transfer to occur. Enormous pressure built up in the vertical pressure pipes, which lifted the concrete slab above the reactor, took off the roof of the building above the concrete slab, and blew the fuel out.

Experts also differ about the cause of the reported second explosion. Some believe it was a hydrogen explosion, while others believe it was caused by an additional fuel excursion [4]. Megaw explains it as resulting from the sharp temperature increase in the reactor core, the rupture of the cooling channels (releasing steam onto the hot graphite moderator and producing water gas), and the chemical reaction between the overheated zirconium canning and water [219].

The initial fires were started by the burning debris that was expelled after the second explosion. The core graphite also caught on fire. As the fission products were expelled from the reactor, they were carried aloft by the heat released from the fire and, because of local weather conditions, were pushed high into the atmosphere, where they were subject to various wind patterns.

The first hint outside the Soviet Union that anything was wrong came from Sweden [219]. At the Forsmark nuclear generating station just north of Stockholm, a worker arriving for the morning shift on Monday, April 28, set off an alarm on a radiation detector. Assuming that the leak was from their own reactor, the operators shut it down and closed the plant. Later tests showed that the radiation was not from Forsmark or any other Swedish reactor.

The Swedes alerted the Americans, who first thought that the radioactivity was the result of a Russian underground weapons test that accidentally leaked to the atmosphere. By the afternoon, Swedish scientists had identified the radioactive components and determined that they must have come from a reactor and not from a weapons test. Radioactive atoms are unstable, continually trying to change themselves into a more stable configuration [219]. The greater the instability, the faster they change. The rate of decay is measured by the *half-life*—decay time for half of the atoms in a particular sample. The radioactive products formed in fission all have different half-lives and decay at different rates. Since in a weapons test they are all formed at the same time, they start to decay at the same time. But in a reactor, they are formed over a long period and start to decay at different times. From an examination of the proportions of various fission products present in a sample, Swedish scientists were able to determine that the radioactivity came from at least a partial meltdown of a reactor. Using the time that the radioactive cloud first appeared on their coast and known wind speeds and directions, they were able to trace the cloud backwards over Latvia and Minsk to Kiev.

Swedish diplomats asked the Russians for an explanation, but were told that there was no information. At 9 P.M., an announcement was made on Soviet television: "An accident has occurred at the Chernobyl Nuclear Power Plant and one of the reactors has been damaged. Measures are being taken to eliminate the consequences of the accident. Aid is being given to those affected. A Government Commission has been set up" [219, p.19]. Little additional information was provided for a while, but this has been true of many nuclear incidents around the world; some countries with more open news organizations have been able to withhold information for shorter times, but rarely has information immediately after the incident been very forthcoming and sometimes not even later.

At 8 A.M. on the morning of Tuesday, April 29, a scientific attache from the Soviet Embassy in Bonn went to Atomforum, a non-government agency representing West Germany's nuclear power industry and asked if the Germans knew anyone who could advice them about how to put out a graphite fire in a reactor. The Germans gave some advise and suggested they ask the British, who had experience with the graphite fire at Windscale. The Russians also asked the Swedish nuclear authority for advice. The American government offered various types of assistance, but the offer was politely refused. The Russians did invite an American bone-marrow specialist, Dr. Robert Gale, to provide medical assistance. By this time, satellite photos of the damaged reactor had appeared in the western press.

By April 30, other countries became aware that a radioactive cloud from the accident was depositing radioactive materials on their territory. Some countries banned the sale of milk, advised the population against drinking water, and gave out potassium iodide (to counteract the effects of iodine on the thyroid).

Thirty-one plant workers and firefighters died from acute radiation sickness and burns. The thousand families living in a workers' town one mile from the plant were evacuated 12 hours after the explosion. The evacuation of nearby Pripyat and 71 villages within 18 miles of the plant started the next day [214]. To date, the official death tally is 42. The number of deaths or cancers attributable to the accident that have occurred already or to be expected in the future is unknown and probably unknowable.

D.4.3 Level 2 Conditions

At the meeting in Vienna, the Soviets pointed out the following:

- □ Because the test was scheduled to be carried out just before a planned shutdown for routine maintenance, the operators were under extra pressure. If the test could not be performed successfully this time, then they would have to wait for another year for the next shutdown [211].
- □ Chernobyl-4 was a model plant. Of all the RBMK type plants, it ran the best. Its operators felt they were an elite crew, and they had become overconfident.
- □ The test was perceived as an electrical test only and had been conducted uneventfully before. Thus, the operators did not think carefully enough about

the effects on the reactor. There is a strong possibility, in fact, that the test was being supervised by representatives of the turbine manufacturer instead of the normal operators.

The positive coefficient of the RBMK reactor makes it very difficult to control, and safety is dependent on the water supply. Supposedly, the British had previously warned the Soviet Union that the RBMK design had serious defects and that the design gave the operators too difficult a job. The RBMK operators had minutes, and maybe only seconds, to react to an emergency.

The Soviets most likely built RBMK reactors, instead of the safer PWR reactor, for several reasons. For one, they wanted to produce plutonium and electricity in the same plants [219], and they did not have the resources of other countries to build separate reactors for these two goals. They also did not have the ability (at the time the RBMK reactors were built) to make the large pressure vessels or steam generators required by the PWR design [4]. The RBMK requires neither of these, and the graphite core comes in easy-to-construct modules. The Soviets later built PWRs, after they had developed the necessary manufacturing capability.

The Chernobyl reactor had no containment structure but rather a "confinement building," which had fans and filters. In the case of a release of radioactive gases, the filters would remove the radioactivity before it was vented outside. But the building was not designed to withstand much overpressure [4].

The test procedures had been developed by a station electrical engineer, and the operators thought it was an electrical test. They did not conceive of it as a nuclear test.

D.4.4 Level 3 Factors

Design for Controllability.   As noted in the section on Three Mile Island, nuclear reactor designs differ greatly in their ease of control and their dependence on added-on control and trip systems that may fail or may be neglected.

The official Russian position was that the operators were to blame for the accident. Scientists from other countries who attended the Vienna meeting did not entirely accept this argument. They agreed that the immediate cause was the operators' actions, but they argued strongly that a prime factor was also the basic design of the reactor (the positive void coefficient), which made the reactor difficult to control [219]. Lord Marshall (Chairman of the British Central Electricity Generating Board) said that his government had warned the Soviets nine years earlier of the defects in the RBMK reactor design. "You can make any design safe by having clever enough operators," he said, "but the designers of Chernobyl gave the operators too difficult a task" [219, p.65]. Lord Marshall claimed that the Soviets chose this design because it would save money. They knew it had defects, but they thought they could compensate. He added, "We are not talking about hindsight here. This was a judgment made in advance."

The head of the Russian delegation replied that he did not know about any British warnings in 1977. "He declined to compare the quality of the Chernobyl reactors with western ones and said that the accident was caused by a series of awkward and silly mistakes by the operators" [219, p.65].

When serious accidents happen, they usually occur in ways not foreseen—which is what makes them serious. But the fact that the exact events leading to an accident are not foreseen does not mean the accident is not preventable. The hazard is usually known, and measures can be often be taken to eliminate or reduce it. The exact events at Chernobyl did not have to be predicted to know that the reactor design made the operators' job too difficult: *Some* events would occur during the life of the reactor that would require manual control under stress. Similarly, Applegate warned that some events would occur during the life of the DC-10 that would lead to a cabin floor collapse. In both cases, the decisions were made to try to eliminate the preceding events because that would require the fewest tradeoffs with other goals such as lower cost or desired functionality. The necessity to make such tradeoff decisions leads to most of the difficulties in dealing with safety issues.

Training.   Operators and other staff were not trained in the technological processes in a nuclear reactor. They had also "lost any feeling for the hazards involved" [340]. In addition, as at TMI, the operators at Chernobyl had no simulator training for the accident sequence that occurred.

Approval of Operating Procedures.   The Soviet report said that neither the plant's chief engineer nor the resident representative of the atomic safety committee was consulted in the test design, and the test procedures were not reviewed by safety personnel, nuclear engineers, or physicists.

Complacency.   The Soviets admitted that the operators at the Chernobyl plant had become complacent. The plant had run so well that they began to be too relaxed—they slipped into the dangerous attitude that an accident could never happen [4]. A U.S. observer in Vienna noted that the Soviets were still incredulous that the accident could have happened.

In Vienna, the Soviets admitted that they were learning many of the lessons the United States had learned after TMI: the need for better training of operators and for simulator training, including that focused on accident sequences; the necessity to have procedures checked by a safety committee before tests are performed; and the danger of complacency. Much of the damage at Chernobyl could have been avoided had the Soviets paid more attention to the TMI investigations [4]. Unfortunately, this is true for most industries and most major accidents. Learning from the errors of others seems to be difficult.

REFERENCES

1. Russell L. Ackoff. Towards a system of systems concepts. *Management Science*, 17(11):661–671, July 1971.

2. E.E. Adams. Accident causation and the management system. *Professional Safety*, October 1976.

3. Michelle Adato, James MacKenzie, Robert Pollard, and Ellyn Weiss. *Safety Second: The NRC and American's Nuclear Power Plants*. Indiana University Press, Bloomington, Ind., 1987.

4. John F. Ahearne. Nuclear power after Chernobyl. *Science*, 236:673–679, May 8, 1987.

5. Air Force Space Division. *System Safety Handbook for the Acquisition Manager*, SDP 127-1, January 12, 1987.

6. A. Aitken. Fault analysis. In A.E. Green, editor, *High Risk Safety Technology*, pages 67–72, John Wiley & Sons, New York, 1982.

7. David J. Allen. Digraphs and fault trees. *Hazard Prevention*, pages 22–25, January/February 1983.

8. M.F. Allnutt, D.R. Haslam, M.H. Rejman, and S. Green. Sustained performance and some effects on the design and operation of complex systems. In D.E. Broadbent, J. Reason, and A. Baddeley, editors, *Human Factors in Hazardous Situations*, pages 81–93, Clarendon Press, Oxford, United Kingdom, 1990.

9. Tom Anderson and Peter A. Lee. *Fault Tolerance: Principles and Practice*. Prentice-Hall, Englewood Cliffs, N.J., 1981.

10. P.K. Andow, F.P. Lees, and C.P. Murphy. The propagation of faults in process plants: A state of the art review. In *7th International Symposium on Chemical Process Hazards*, pages 225–237. University of Manchester, Institute of Science and Technology, United Kingdom, April 1980.

11. Anonymous. Blown balloons. *Aviation Week and Space Technology*, page 17, September 20, 1971.

12. Anonymous. Doomed journey: Tracking the KAL tragedy. *Time Magazine*, 128(9):18, September 1, 1986.

13. Charles Arthur. Extra tests forced on Sizewell's safety software. *New Scientist*, pages 6 7, November 6, 1993.

14. William B. Askren and John M. Howard. Software safety lessons learned from computer-aided industrial machine accidents. In *Compass '87*, Washington, D.C., June 1987.

15. Robert U. Ayres and Pradeep K. Rohatgi. Bhopal: Lessons for technological decision-makers. *Technology in Society*, 9:19–45, 1987.

16. D. Bahn. Reliance on computers. In Peter G. Neumann, editor, *Forum on Risks to the*

Public in Computer Systems, Volume 6, Issue 40, ACM Committee on Computers and Public Policy, March 9, 1988.

17. Lisanne Bainbridge. Ironies of automation. In Jens Rasmussen, Keith Duncan, and Jacques Leplat, editors, *New Technology and Human Error*, pages 271–283, John Wiley & Sons, New York, 1987.

18. W.W. Banks and F. Cerven. Predictor displays: The application of human engineering in process control systems. *Hazard Prevention*, pages 26–32, January/February 1985.

19. Richard S. Barrett. The human equation in operating a nuclear power plant. In David L. Sills, C.P. Wolf, and Vivien B. Shelanski, editors, *Accident at Three Mile Island: The Human Dimensions*, pages 161–171, Westview Press, Boulder, Colo., 1982.

20. H. Bassen, J. Silberberg, F. Houston, W. Knight, C. Christman, and M. Greberman. Computerized medical devices: Usage, trends, problems, and safety technology. In *7th Annual Conference on IEEE Engineering in Medicine and Biology Society*, Chicago, September 1986.

21. W. Bastl and L. Felkel. Disturbance analysis systems. In Jens Rasmussen and William B. Rouse, editors, *Human Detection and Diagnosis of System Failures*, pages 451–473, Plenum Press, New York, 1981.

22. B.J. Bell and A.D. Swain. Overview of a procedure for human reliability analysis. *Hazard Prevention*, pages 22–25, January/February 1985.

23. Leo Beltracchi. Personal communication.

24. Ludwig Benner, Jr. Accident investigations: Multilinear events sequencing methods. *Journal of Safety Research*, 7(2):67–73, June 1975.

25. Ludwig Benner, Jr. Accident perceptions: Their implications for accident investigators. In Ted S. Ferry, editor, *Readings in Accident Investigation: Examples of the Scope, Depth, and Source*, pages 265–276, Charles C. Thomas Publisher, Springfield, Ill., 1984.

26. Ludwig Benner, Jr. Generating hypotheses to explain accidents and other rare events. In Ted S. Ferry, editor, *Readings in Accident Investigation: Examples of the Scope, Depth, and Source*, pages 3–6, Charles C. Thomas Publisher, Springfield, Ill., 1984.

27. Denis S.C. Bilcliffe. Human error causal factors in man–machine systems. *Hazard Prevention*, pages 26–31, January/February 1986.

28. Frank E. Bird and Robert G. Loftus. *Loss Control Management*. Institute Press, Loganville, GA., 1976.

29. Earl Boebert. Personal communication.

30. William Bogard. *The Bhopal Tragedy*. Westview Press, Boulder, Colo., 1989.

31. Peter Bond. *Heroes in Space*. Basil Blackwell Ltd., New York, 1987.

32. B.J. Bonnett. Position paper on software safety and security critical systems. In *Proceedings of IEEE Compcon '84*, page 191, September 1984.

33. Richard C. Booten Jr. and Simon Ramo. The development of systems engineering. *IEEE Transactions on Aerospace and Electronic Systems*, AES-20(4):306–309, July 1984.

34. W.C. Bowman, G.H. Archinoff, V.M Raina, D.R. Tremaine, and N.G. Leveson. An application of fault tree analysis to safety-critical software at Ontario Hydro.

In *Conference on Probabilistic Safety Assessment and Management (PSAM)*, April 1991.

35. C.A. Bowsher. Medical device recalls: Examination of selected cases. Technical Report GAO Report GAO/PEMD-90-6, U.S. Government Accounting Organization, October 1990.

36. C.A. Bowsher. Medical devices: The public health at risk. Technical Report GAO Report GAO/T-PEMD-90-2, U.S. Government Accounting Organization, 1990.

37. Berndt Brehmer. Development of mental models for decision in technological systems. In Jens Rasmussen, Keith Duncan, and Jacques Leplat, editors, *New Technology and Human Error*, pages 111–120, John Wiley & Sons, New York, 1987.

38. Susan Brilliant, John C. Knight, and Nancy G. Leveson. The consistent comparison problem in N-version programming. *IEEE Transactions on Software Engineering*, SE-15(11), November 1989.

39. Susan Brilliant, John C. Knight, and Nancy G. Leveson. Analysis of faults in an N-version software experiment. *IEEE Transations on Software Engineering*, SE-16(2), February 1990.

40. P. Brodner. Qualification based production—The superior choice to the "unmanned factory." In G. Mancini, G. Johannsen, and L. Martensson, editors, *Analysis, Design, and Evaluation of Man–Machine Systems*, pages 15–19, Pergamon Press, New York, 1986.

41. Malcolm J. Brookes. Human factors in the design and operation of reactor safety systems. In David L. Sills, C.P. Wolf, and Vivien B. Shelanski, editors, *Accident at Three Mile Island: The Human Dimensions*, pages 155–160, Westview Press, Boulder, Colo., 1982.

42. Michael L. Brown. Personal communication from comments on an early version of this manuscript.

43. Michael L. Brown. Software safety for complex systems. In *IEEE Conference on Computers in Medicine*, Chicago, September 1985.

44. Michael L. Brown. Software systems safety and human errors. Transparencies.

45. Michael L. Brown. Software systems safety design guidelines and recommendations. Technical Report NSWCTR 89-33, Naval Surface Warfare Center, Dahlgren, Va., March 1989.

46. Irvin C. Bupp and Jean-Claude Derian. *Light Water: How the Nuclear Dream Dissolved*. Basic Books, New York, 1978.

47. J. Calder. Scientific accident prevention. *American Labor Legislative Review*, 1:14–24, January 1911.

48. Stephen S. Cha. *Safety Analysis Applied to Software Design*. PhD thesis, University of California, Irvine, Calif., June 1991.

49. Peter Checkland. *Systems Thinking, Systems Practice*. John Wiley & Sons, New York, 1981.

50. Harold Chestnut. Information requirements for systems understanding. *IEEE Transactions on Systems Science and Cybernetics*, SSC-6(1):3–12, January 1970.

51. Charles W. Childs. Cosmetic system safety. *Hazard Prevention*, May/June 1979.

52. Agnees Chisti. *Dateline Bhopal*. Concept Publishing Company, New Delhi, India, 1986.

53. Committee for Review of Oversight Mechanisms for Space Shuttle Flight Software Development Processes. An assessment of Space Shuttle flight software development processes, National Research Council, 1993.

54. John R. Connet, Edward J. Pasternak, and Bruce D. Wagner. Software defenses in real-time control systems. In *Real-Time Software*, pages 181–193, Prentice Hall, Englewood Cliffs, N.J., 1983.

55. J.H. Cooper. Accident-prevention devices applied to machines. *Transactions of the ASME*, 12:249–264, 1891.

56. Stephen Cotgrove. Risk, value conflict, and political legitimacy. In Richard F. Griffiths, editor, *Dealing with Risk: The Planning, Management and Acceptability of Technological Risk*, pages 122–140, Manchester University Press, Manchester, United Kingdom, 1981.

57. Council for Science and Society. *The Acceptability of Risks (The Logic and Social Dynamics of Fair Decisions and Effective Controls)*. Barry Rose Publishers Ltd., London, 1977.

58. A. Cross. Fault trees and event trees. In A.E. Green, editor, *High Risk Safety Technology*, pages 49–65, John Wiley & Sons, New York, 1982.

59. W.J. Cullyer. Invited presentation at Compass '90, June 1990.

60. James W. Danaher. Human error in ATC system operations. *Human Factors*, 22(5):535–545, May 1980.

61. B.K. Daniels, R. Bell, and R.I. Wright. Safety integrity assessment of programmable electronic systems. In *Proceedings Third International Workshop on Achieving Safe Real Time Systems*, pages 1–12, Queen's College, Cambridge, United Kingdom, Pergamon Press, September 1983.

62. J.T. Daniels and P.L. Holden. Quantification of risk. In *Loss Prevention and Safety Promotion in the Process Industries*, pages G33–G45, Institution of Chemical Engineers, Rugby, United Kingdom, 1983.

63. E.S. Dean. Software system safety. In *Proceedings Fifth International System Safety Conference*. System Safety Society, 1981.

64. Dorothy E. R. Denning. *Cryptography and Data Security*. Addison-Wesley Publishing Co., Reading, Mass., 1982.

65. J.B. Dennis and E.C. VanHorn. Programming semantics for multiprogrammed computations. *Communications of the ACM*, 9(3):143–155, March 1966.

66. Edsel DeVille. Mishap potential versus risk: A cumulative viewpoint. *Hazard Prevention*, pages 12–15, January/February 1988.

67. Edsgar Dijkstra. *A Discipline of Programming*. Prentice Hall, Englewood Cliffs, N.J. 1976.

68. Paul Williams, Don Page, and Dennis Boyd. Report of the Inquiry into the London Ambulance Service. Communications Directorate, South West Thames Regional Health Authority, 40 Eastbourne Terrace, London W2 3QR, February 1993.

69. Boyce W. Duke. Program manager's handbook for system safety and military standard 882B. *Hazard Prevention*, pages 15–21, March/April 1986.

70. K.D. Duncan. Fault diagnosis training for advanced continuous process installations. In Jens Rasmussen, Keith Duncan, and Jacques Leplat, editors, *New Technology and Human Error*, pages 209–221, John Wiley & Sons, New York, 1987.

71. K.D. Duncan. Reflections on fault diagnostic expertise. In Jens Rasmussen, Keith

Duncan, and Jacques Leplat, editors, *New Technology and Human Error*, pages 261–269, John Wiley & Sons, New York, 1987.

72. John P. Eaton and Charles A. Haas. *Titanic: Triumph and Tragedy*. P. Stephens Publishers, Wellingborough, Great Britain, 1987.

73. D.E. Eckhardt, A.K. Caglayan, J.C. Knight, L.D. Lee, D.F. McAllister, M.A. Vouk, and J.P.J. Kelly. An experimental evaluation of software redundancy as a strategy for improving software reliability. *IEEE Transactions on Software Engineering*, SE-17(7):692–702, July 1991.

74. D.E. Eckhardt and L. Lee. A theoretical basis for the analysis of multiversion software subject to coincident errors. *IEEE Transactions on Software Engineering*, SE-11(12):1511–1516, December 1985.

75. Paul Eddy, Elaine Potter, and Bruce Page. *Destination Disaster*. Quandrangle/N.Y. Times Book Co., New York, 1976.

76. M. Edwards. The design of an accident investigation procedure. *Applied Ergonomics*, 12:111–115, 1981.

77. D.E. Embrey. A new approach to the evaluation and quantification of human reliability in systems assessment. In *Third National Reliability Conference*, 1981.

78. D.E. Embrey. Modelling and assisting the operator's diagnostic strategies in accident sequences. In G. Mancini, G. Johannsen, and L. Martensson, editors, *Analysis, Design, and Evaluation of Man–Machine Systems*, pages 219–224, Pergamon Press, New York, 1986.

79. A.R. Ephrath and L.R. Young. Monitoring vs. man-in-the-loop detection of aircraft control failures. In Jens Rasmussen and William B. Rouse, editors, *Human Detection and Diagnosis of System Failures*, pages 143–154, Plenum Press, New York, 1981.

80. C.A. Ericson. Software and system safety. In *5th International System Safety Conference*, pages III–B–1 to III–B–11, Denver, System Safety Society, July 1981.

81. F.R. Farmer. Quantification, experience, and judgement. In B.H. Harvey, editor, *European Major Hazards*, pages 51–59, Oyez Scientific and Technical Services, Ltd., London, 1984.

82. Ted S. Ferry. *Safety Program Administration for Engineers and Manager*. Charles C. Thomas Publisher, Springfield, Ill., 1984.

83. Baruch Fischhoff, Christoph Hohenemser, Roger Kasperson, and Robert Kates. Handling hazards. In Jack Dowie and Paul Lefrere, editors, *Risk and Chance*, pages 161–179, Open University Press, Milton Keynes, United Kingdom, 1980.

84. J.D. Foley and A. Van Dam. *Fundamentals of Interactive Computer Graphics*. Addison-Wesley, Reading, Mass., 1982.

85. S. Folkard. Circadian performance rhythms: Some practical and theoretical implications. In D.E. Broadbent, J. Reason, and A. Baddeley, editors, *Human Factors in Hazardous Situations*, pages 95–105, Clarendon Press, Oxford, United Kingdom, 1990.

86. R.E. Follensbee. The fail-safe concept. In *FAA Seattle Aircraft Certification Office Systems Designated Engineering Representative Workshop*, September 14, 1993.

87. Ned Franklin. The accident at Chernobyl. *The Chemical Engineer*, pages 17–22, November 1986.

88. F. Ronald Frola and C.O. Miller. System safety in aircraft acquisition. Technical report, Logistics Management Institute, Washington, D.C., January 1984.

89. J.G. Fuller. We almost lost Detroit. In Peter Faulkner, editor, *The Silent Bomb*, pages 46–59, Random House, New York, 1977.

90. J.G. Fuller. Death by robot. *Omni*, 6(6):45–46, 97–102, March 1984.

91. John Gannon. An experimental evaluation of data type conventions. *Communications of the ACM*, 20(8):584–595, August 1977.

92. John D. Gannon and J.J. Horning. Language design for programming reliability. *IEEE Transactions on Software Engineering*, SE-1(2):179–191, June 1975.

93. Susan Gerhart, Dan Craigen, and Ted Ralston. Experience with formal methods in critical systems. *IEEE Software*, 11(1):21–28, January 1994.

94. Susan L. Gerhart and Lawrence Yelowitz. Observations of fallibility in applications of modern programming methodologies. *IEEE Transactions on Software Engineering*, 2(3), September 1976.

95. Carol S. Giffen. Operations hazard analysis. *Hazard Prevention*, pages 23–25, May/June 1987.

96. James Gleick. Hole in ozone over South Pole worries scientists. *New York Times*, page C1, Times Science Section, July 29, 1986.

97. David S. Gloss and Miriam Gayle Wardle. *Introduction to Safety Engineering*. John Wiley & Sons, New York, 1984.

98. Jack Goldberg. Some principles and techniques for designing safe systems. *Software Engineering Notes*, 12(3):17–19, July 1987.

99. L.P. Goodstein. Discriminative display support for process operators. In Jens Rasmussen and William B. Rouse, editors, *Human Detection and Diagnosis of System Failures*, pages 185–198, Plenum Press, New York, 1981.

100. M. Granger-Morgan. Choosing and managing technology-induced risk. *IEEE Spectrum*, pages 53–60, December 1981.

101. R. Green. Human error on the flight deck. In D.E. Broadbent, J. Reason, and A. Baddeley, editors, *Human Factors in Hazardous Situations*, pages 55–64, Clarendon Press, Oxford, United Kingdom, 1990.

102. Richard F. Griffiths, editor. *Dealing with Risk: The Planning, Management and Acceptability of Technological Risk*. Manchester University Press, Manchester, United Kingdom, 1981.

103. William Haddon, Jr. The prevention of accidents. In Duncan W. Clark and Brian MacMahon, editors, *Preventive Medicine*, page 595, Little, Brown, and Company, Boston, 1967.

104. E.W. Hagen. Common-mode/common-cause failure: A review. *Nuclear Safety*, 21(2):184–191, March-April 1980.

105. Richard Hamlet. Testing for trustworthiness. In J.P. Jacky and D. Schuler, editors, *Directions and Implications of Advanced Computing*, pages 97–104, Ablex Publishing Company, 1989.

106. Willie Hammer. *Handbook of System and Product Safety*. Prentice-Hall, Inc., Englewood Cliffs, N.J., 1972.

107. Willie Hammer. *Occupational Safety Management and Engineering*. Prentice-Hall, Englewood Cliffs, N.J., 1976.

108. Willie Hammer. *Product Safety Management and Engineering*. Prentice-Hall, Inc., Englewood Cliffs, N.J., 1980.

109. Carl M. Hansen. *Universal Safety Standards*. Universal Safety Standards Publishing Company, New York, 1914.

110. Carl M. Hansen. Standardization of safeguards. In *Proceedings Fourth Safety Congress*, pages 139–146, 1915.

111. David Harel. Statecharts: A visual formalism for complex systems. *Science of Computer Programming*, 8:231–274, 1987.

112. R.C. Harriss, C. Hohenemser, and R.W. Kates. The burden of technological hazards. In G.T. Goodman and W.D. Rowe, editors, *Energy Risk Management*, pages 103–138, Academic Press, New York, 1979.

113. B.H. Harvey, editor. *European Major Hazards*. Oyez Scientific and Technical Services, Ltd., London, 1984.

114. Health and Safety Executive. *The Tolerability of Risk from Nuclear Power Stations*. Her Majesty's Stationery Office, London, 1988.

115. Herbert Hecht. Investigation of Shuttle software errors. Technical report, Sohar, Inc., Beverly Hills, Calif., 1992.

116. Mat P.E. Heimdahl. *Static Analysis of State-Based Requirements: Analysis for Completeness and Consistency*. PhD thesis, University of California, Irvine, Calif., 1994.

117. Mats P.E. Heimdahl and Nancy G. Leveson. Completeness and consistency checking of software requirements. In *Proceedings of the International Conference on Software Engineering*, IEEE Computer Society, Los Alamitos, Calif., April 1995.

118. H.W. Heinrich. *Industrial Accident Prevention: A Scientific Approach*. McGraw-Hill, New York, 1931.

119. H.W. Heinrich, Dan Petersen, and Nestor Roos. *Industrial Accident Prevention*. McGraw-Hill Book Company, New York, 1980.

120. N. Herry. Errors in the execution of prescribed instructions: Design of process control work aids. In Jens Rasmussen, Keith Duncan, and Jacques Leplat, editors, *New Technology and Human Error*, pages 239–245, John Wiley & Sons, New York, 1987.

121. Anthony Hidden. *Investigation into the Clapham Junction Railway Accident*. Department of Transport, Her Majesty's Stationary Office (HMSO), PO Box 276, London SW8 5DT, 1990.

122. J.C. Higgs. A high integrity software based turbine governing system. In *Safecomp '83*, pages 207–218, Pergamon Press, Elmsford, New York, 1983.

123. Larry Hirschhorn. The soul of a new worker. *Working Papers*, pages 42–47, January/February 1982.

124. Mel Hoagland. The pilot's role in automation. In *Proceedings of the ALPA Air Safety Workshop*, Airline Pilots Association, 1982.

125. C.A.R. Hoare. An axiomatic basis for computer programming. *Communications of the ACM*, 12:576–580, 1969.

126. S. Hope, et.al. Methodologies for hazard analysis and risk assessment in the petroleum refining and storage industry. *Hazard Prevention*, pages 24–32, July/August 1983.

127. Richard J. Hornick. Dreams—Design and destiny. *Human Factors*, 29(1):111–121, 1987.

128. J.J. Horning. Programming languages for reliable computing systems. In F.L. Bauer

and M. Broy, editors, *Lecture Notes in Computer Science, Vol. 69*, pages 494–530, Springer-Verlag, 1979.

129. Walter B. Howard. Efficient time use to achieve safety of processes, or "How many angels can stand on the head of a pin?". In *Loss Prevention and Safety Promotion in the Process Industries*, pages A11–A19, Institution of Chemical Engineers. Rugby, United Kingdom, 1983.

130. D.M. Hunns. Discussions around a human factors data base. In A.E. Green, editor, *High Risk Safety Technology*, pages 181–215, John Wiley & Sons, New York, 1982.

131. Edwin L. Hutchins, James D. Hollan, and Donald A. Norman. Direct manipulation interfaces. *Human–Computer Interaction*, 1:311–338, 1985.

132. Andrey Illesh. *Chernobyl*. Richardson and Steirman, Inc., New York, 1987.

133. Floyd Isley and John Wick. Unique signal message format. Technical Report DNA-TR-92-7, Defense Nuclear Agency, September 1992.

134. R.K. Iyer and P. Velardi. Hardware related software errors: Measurement and analysis. *IEEE Transactions on Software Engineering*, SE-11(2):223–231, February 1985.

135. Matthew S. Jaffe. *Completeness, Robustness, and Safety of Real-Time Requirements Specification*. PhD thesis, University of California, Irvine, Calif., 1988.

136. Matthew S. Jaffe, Nancy G. Leveson, Mats P.E. Heimdahl, and Bonnie E. Melhart. Software requirements analysis for real-time process-control systems. *IEEE Transations on Software Engineering*, SE-17(3):241–258, March 1991.

137. F. Jahanian and A.K. Mok. Safety analysis of timing properties in real-time systems. *IEEE Transactions of Software Engineering*, SE-12(9):890–904, September 1986.

138. G. Johannsen, J.E. Rijndorp, and H. Tamura. Matching user needs and technologies of displays and graphics. In G. Mancini, G. Johannsen, and L. Martensson, editors, *Analysis, Design, and Evaluation of Man–Machine Systems*, pages 51–61, Pergamon Press, New York, 1986.

139. G. Johannsen and W.B. Rouse. Problem solving behavior of pilots in abnormal and emergency situations. In *1st European Annual Conference on Human Decision Making and Manual Control*, pages 142–150, Delft University, Netherlands, 1981.

140. William G. Johnson. *MORT Safety Assurance Systems*. Marcel Dekker, Inc., New York, 1980.

141. Joseph Jorgens. The purpose of software quality assurance: A means to an end. In *Developing, Purchasing, and Using Safe, Effective, and Reliable Medical Software*, pages 5–9, Association for the Advancement of Medical Instrumentation, Arlington, Virginia, October 1990.

142. J.S. Juechter. Guarding: The keystone of system safety. In *Proc. Fifth International System Safety Conference*, pages V–B–1 – V–B–21, System Safety Society, July 1981.

143. John G. Kemeny. *Report of the President's Commission on Three Mile Island (The Need for Change: The Legacy of TMI)*. U.S. Government Accounting Office, Washington, D.C., 1979.

144. John G. Kemeny. Saving American democracy: The lessons of Three Mile Island. *Technology Review*, pages 65–75, June–July 1980.

145. Emory Kemp. Calamities of technology. *Science Digest*, pages 50–59, July 1986.

146. P. Kinnersly. *The Hazards of Work: How to Fight Them*. Pluto Press, London, 1973.

147. Kenneth Kipnis. Engineers who kill: Professional ethics and the paramountcy of public safety. *Business & Professional Ethics Journal*, 1(1):77–91, 1981.

148. M. Kivel, editor. *Radiological Health Bulletin*, volume XX:8. Center for Devices and Radiological Health, Food and Drug Administration, Rockville, Maryland, December 1986.

149. Urban Kjellen. An evaluation of safety information systems at six medium-sized and large firms. *Journal of Occupational Accidents*, 3:273–288, 1982.

150. Urban Kjellen. A changing role of human actors in accident control—Implications for new technology systems. In Jens Rasmussen, Keith Duncan, and Jacques Leplat, editors, *New Technology and Human Error*, pages 169–175, John Wiley & Sons, New York, 1987.

151. Urban Kjellen. Deviations and the feedback control of accidents. In Jens Rasmussen, Keith Duncan, and Jacques Leplat, editors, *New Technology and Human Error*, pages 143–156, John Wiley & Sons, New York, 1987.

152. T.A. Kletz. Simpler, cheaper plants or wealth and safety at work. In B.H. Harvey, editor, *European Major Hazards*, pages 33–41, Oyez Scientific and Technical Services, Ltd., London, 1984.

153. Trevor Kletz. The Flixborough cyclohexane disaster. *Loss Prevention*, 9, 1975.

154. Trevor Kletz. *Myths of the Chemical Industry*. The Institution of Chemical Engineers, Rugby, Warwickshire, United Kingdom, 1984.

155. Trevor Kletz. Eliminating potential process hazards, part i. *Hazard Prevention*, pages 4–15, September/October 1985.

156. Trevor Kletz. Eliminating potential process hazards, part ii. *Hazard Prevention*, pages 6–11, November/December 1985.

157. Trevor Kletz, editor. *What Went Wrong?: Case Histories from Process Plant Disasters*. Gulf Publishing Company, Houston,1988.

158. Trevor Kletz. Wise after the event. *Control and Instrumentation*, 20(10):57–59, October 1988.

159. Trevor Kletz. Plants should be friendly. In *Safety and Loss Prevention in the Chemical and Oil Processing Industries*, pages 423–433, The Institution of Chemical Engineers, Rugby, United Kingdom, 1990.

160. Trevor Kletz. *An Engineer's View of Human Error*. Institution of Chemical Engineers, Rugby, Warwickshire, United Kingdom, 1991.

161. Trevor Kletz, editor. *Lessons from Disaster*. Gulf Publishing Company, Houston, 1993.

162. Trevor Kletz. Human problems with computer control. *Plant/Operations Progress*, 1(4), October 1982.

163. John C. Knight and Nancy G. Leveson. An experimental evaluation of the assumption of independence in multi-version programming. *IEEE Transations on Software Engineering*, SE-12(1):96–109, January 1986.

164. John C. Knight and Nancy G. Leveson. A reply to the criticisms of the Knight and Leveson experiment. *ACM Software Engineering Notes*, January 1990.

165. H. Kopetz and W. Merker. The architecture of MARS. In *Proceedings International Symposium on Fault Tolerant Computing Systems*, pages 274–279, June 1985.

166. Thomas S. Kuhn, editor. *The Structure of Scientific Revolution*. The University of Chicago Press, Chicago, 1962.

167. John Ladd. Bhopal: An essay on moral responsibility and civic virtue. Department of Philosophy, Brown University, Rhode Island, January 1987.

168. Patrick Lagadec. *Major Technological Risk: An Assessment of Industrial Disasters.* Pergamon Press, New York, 1982.

169. Patrick Lagadec. *States of Emergency.* Butterworth-Heinemann, London, 1990.

170. Carl Landwehr. Security and safety. In *Workshop on Software Safety*, Naval Intelligence Center, Washington, D.C., 1993.

171. Jerome Lederer. How far have we come? A look back at the leading edge of system safety eighteen years ago. *Hazard Prevention*, pages 8–10, May/June 1986.

172. Frank P. Lees. *Loss Prevention in the Process Industries, Vol. 1 and 2.* Butterworths, London, 1980.

173. M. Lehtela. Computer-aided failure mode and effect analysis of electronic circuits. *Microelectronic Reliability*, 30(4):761–773, 1990.

174. Jacques Leplat. Accidents and incidents production: Methods of analysis. In Jens Rasmussen, Keith Duncan, and Jacques Leplat, editors, *New Technology and Human Error*, pages 133–142, John Wiley & Sons, New York, 1987.

175. Jacques Leplat. Occupational accident research and systems approach. In Jens Rasmussen, Keith Duncan, and Jacques Leplat, editors, *New Technology and Human Error*, pages 181–191, John Wiley & Sons, New York, 1987.

176. Jacques Leplat. Some observations on error analysis. In Jens Rasmussen, Keith Duncan, and Jacques Leplat, editors, *New Technology and Human Error*, pages 311–316, John Wiley & Sons, New York, 1987.

177. Jacques Leplat and Jens Rasmussen. Analysis of human errors in industrial incidents and accidents for improvement of work safety. In Jens Rasmussen, Keith Duncan, and Jacques Leplat, editors, *New Technology and Human Error*, pages 157–168, John Wiley & Sons, New York, 1987.

178. Eric Lerner. Automating U.S. air lanes: A review. *IEEE Spectrum*, pages 46–51, November 1982.

179. Nancy G. Leveson. Software fault tolerance: The case for forward recovery. In *Proceedings of the AIAA Conference on Computers in Aerospace*, AIAA, Hartford, Connecticut, 1983.

180. Nancy G. Leveson. Verification of safety. In *Proceedings Third International Workshop on Achieving Safe Real Time Systems*, Queen's College, Cambridge, United Kingdom, September 1983.

181. Nancy G. Leveson, Stephen S. Cha, John C. Knight, and T.J. Shimeall. The use of self checks and voting in software error detection: An empirical study. *IEEE Transactions on Software Engineering*, SE-16(4), April 1990.

182. Nancy G. Leveson, Stephen S. Cha, and Timothy J. Shimeall. Safety verification of Ada programs using software fault trees. *IEEE Software*, 8(7):48–59, July 1991.

183. Nancy G. Leveson and Peter R. Harvey. Analyzing software safety. *IEEE Transations on Software Engineering*, SE-9(5):569–579, September 1983.

184. Nancy G. Leveson and Timothy J. Shimeall. Safety assertions for process control systems. In *Proceedings 13th International Symposium on Fault Tolerant Computing*, Milan, July 1983. IEEE.

185. Nancy G. Leveson, Timothy J. Shimeall, Janice L. Stolzy, and Jeffrey Thomas.

Design for safe software. In *Proceedings of the American Institutue for Astronautics and Aeronautics Space Sciences Meeting*, AIAA, Reno, Nev., 1983.

186. Nancy G. Leveson and Janice L. Stolzy. Safety analysis using Petri nets. *IEEE Transations on Software Engineering*, SE-13(3):386–397, March 1987.

187. Nancy G. Leveson and Clark S. Turner. An investigation of the Therac-25 accidents. *IEEE Computer*, 26(7):18–41, July 1993.

188. Hank Levy. *Capability-Based Computer Systems*. Digital Press, 1983.

189. E.E. Lewis. *Introduction to Reliability Engineering*. John Wiley & Sons, New York, 1987.

190. Peter Lewycky. Notes toward an understanding of accident causes. *Hazard Prevention*, pages 6–8, March/April 1987.

191. David A. Lihou. Management styles—The effects on loss prevention. In *Safety and Loss Prevention in the Chemical and Oil Processing Industries*, pages 147–156. The Institution of Chemical Engineers, Rugby, United Kingdom, 1990.

192. David A. Lihou. Case studies of inadequate instrumentation. *The Chemical Engineer*, page 41, November 1986.

193. Thomas G. Lombardo. TMI: An insider's viewpoint. *IEEE Spectrum*, pages 52–55, May 1980.

194. E.S. London. Operational safety. In A.E. Green, editor, *High Risk Safety Technology*, pages 111–127. John Wiley & Sons, New York, 1982.

195. D.R.T. Lowe. The hazards of risk analysis. *Reliability Engineering*, 9:243–256, 1984.

196. D.R.T. Lowe and C.H. Solomon. Hazard identification procedures. In *Loss Prevention and Safety Promotion in the Process Industries*, pages G8–G24, Institution of Chemical Engineers, Rugby, United Kingdom, 1983.

197. William W. Lowrance. *Of Acceptable Risk: Science and the Determination of Safety*. William Kaufman, Inc., Los Altos, Calif., 1976.

198. Deborah A. Lucas. Mentals models and new technology. In Jens Rasmussen, Keith Duncan, and Jacques Leplat, editors, *New Technology and Human Error*, pages 321–325. John Wiley & Sons, New York, 1987.

199. Deborah A. Lucas. New technology and decision making. In Jens Rasmussen, Keith Duncan, and Jacques Leplat, editors, *New Technology and Human Error*, pages 337–340, John Wiley & Sons, New York, 1987.

200. Robyn R. Lutz. Analyzing software requirements errors in safety-critical, embedded systems. In *Software Requirements Conference*, IEEE, January 1992.

201. Robyn R. Lutz. Targeting safety-related errors during software requirements analysis. In *Proceedings SIGSOFT '93: Foundations of Software Engineering*, 1993.

202. Robert E. Machol. The Titanic coincidence. *Interfaces*, 5(5):53–54, May 1975.

203. Robert E. Machol and Ralph M. Miles, Jr. The engineering of large-scale systems. In Ralph M. Miles Jr., editor, *Systems Concepts: Lectures on Contemporary Approaches to Systems*, pages 33–50, John F. Wiley & Sons, New York, 1973.

204. Dale A. Mackall. Development and flight test experiences with a flight-crucial digital control system. Technical Report NASA Technical Paper 2857, National Aeronautics and Space Administration, Dryden Flight Research Facility, November 1988.

205. James J. Mackenzie. Nuclear power: A skeptic's view. *IEEE Technology and Society Magazine*, pages 9–15, 18–21, March 1984.

206. William B. Mackley. Aftermath of Mount Erebus. *Flight Safety Digest*, pages 1–5, September 1982.

207. Thomas Mahon. *Report of the Royal Commission to Inquire into the Crash on Mount Erebus, Antarctica of a DC-10 Aircraft Operated by Air New Zealand Limited*. P.D. Hasselberg, Wellington, New Zealand, 1981.

208. Sol W. Malasky. *System Safety*. Hayden Book Company, Inc., Rochelle Park, N.J., 1974.

209. Fred A. Manuele. Accident investigation and analysis. In Ted S. Ferry, editor, *Readings in Accident Investigation: Examples of the Scope, Depth, and Source*, pages 201–211, Charles C. Thomas Publisher, Springfield, Ill., 1984.

210. F. Margulies. Flexible automation—new options for men, economy, and society. In G. Mancini, G. Johannsen, and L. Martensson, editors, *Analysis, Design, and Evaluation of Man–Machine Systems*, pages 11–14, Pergamon Press, New York, 1986.

211. David R. Marples. *The Social Impact of the Chernobyl Disaster*. St. Martin's Press, New York, 1988.

212. Cora Bagley Marrett. The President's Commission: Its analysis of the human equation. In David L. Sills, C.P. Wolf, and Vivien B. Shelanski, editors, *Accident at Three Mile Island: The Human Dimensions*, pages 203–214, Westview Press, Boulder, Colo., 1982.

213. Eliot Marshall. NRC takes a second look at reactor design. *Science*, 207:1445–1448, March 28, 1980.

214. Mike W. Martin and Roland Schinzinger. *Ethics in Engineering*. McGraw-Hill Book Company, New York, 1989.

215. Malcolm McConnell. *Challenger: A Major Malfunction*. Doubleday and Company, Inc., Garden City, N.J., 1987.

216. G.F. McCormick. When reach exceeds grasp. Unpublished essay.

217. Norman J. McCormick. *Reliability and Risk Analysis*. Academic Press, New York, 1981.

218. James W. McIntee. *Fault Tree Techniques as Applied to Software (Soft Tree)*. Dept. of Air Force.

219. James Megaw. *How Safe?: Three Mile Island, Chernobyl, and Beyond*. Stoddard Publishing Company, Toronto, Ontario, 1987.

220. G. Arthur Mihram. The modeling process. *IEEE Transactions on System, Man, and Cybernetics*, SMC-2(5):621–629, November 1972.

221. Ralph M. Miles, Jr. Introduction. In Ralph M. Miles, Jr., editor, *Systems Concepts: Lectures on Contemporary Approaches to Systems*, pages 1–12, John F. Wiley & Sons, New York, 1973.

222. John Stuart Mill. *A system of logic, ratiocinative, and inductive: Being a connected view of the principle of evidence, and methods of scientific inquiry*. J.W. Parker, London, 1843.

223. C.O. Miller. A comparison of military and civil approaches to aviation system safety. *Hazard Prevention*, pages 29–34, May/June 1985.

224. C.O. Miller. The broader lesson from the Challenger. *Hazard Prevention*, pages 5–7, January/February 1987.

225. Ed Miller. The Therac-25 experience. In *Conference of State Radiation Control Program Directors*, 1987.

226. M.H. Milnes. Formation of tetracholorodibenzodioxin by thermal decomposition of sodium tricholophenate. *Nature*, 232:395–396, 1971.

227. RCA Missile and Surface Radar Division. *DDG51 Combat System Safety Program Plan*. AEGIS Shipbuilding Program, DDG CDRL C048, Dept. of Navy, July 15, 1986.

228. N. Moray. The role of attention in the detection of errors and the diagnosis of failures in man–machine systems. In Jens Rasmussen and William B. Rouse, editors, *Human Detection and Diagnosis of System Failures*, pages 185–198, Plenum Press, New York, 1981.

229. N.M. Morris, W.B. Rouse, and S.L. Ward. Experimental evaluation of adaptive task allocation in an aerial search environment. In G. Mancini, G. Johannsen, and L. Martensson, editors, *Analysis, Design, and Evaluation of Man–Machine Systems*, pages 67–72, Pergamon Press, New York, 1986.

230. Thomas H. Moss and David L. Sills, editors. *Safety Considerations in the Design of Light Water Nuclear Power Plants*, Annals of the New York Academy of Sciences, New York, 1981.

231. Noel Mostert. *Supership*. Alfred A. Knopf, New York, 1974.

232. NASA. *Methodology for the Conduct of NSTS Hazard Analysis*. National Space Transportation System, NSTS 22254 edition, May 1987.

233. NASA Aviation Safety Reporting System Staff. Human factors associated with altitude alert systems. NASA ASRS Sixth Quarterly Report, NASA TM-78511, July 1978.

234. National Nuclear Energy Policy Group. *Nuclear Power Issues and Choices*. Ballinger, Cambridge, Mass., 1977.

235. Peter G. Neumann. Some computer-related disasters and other egregious horrors. *ACM Software Engineering Notes*, 11(5), October 1986.

236. Peter G. Neumann. *Computer-Related Risks*. ACM Press, 1994.

237. Allen Newell and Herbert A. Simon. *Human Problem Solving*. Prentice-Hall, Englewood Cliffs, N.J., 1972.

238. John Newhouse. *The Sporty Game*. Alfred A. Knopf, New York, 1982.

239. T. Nichols and P. Armstrong. *Safety or Profit: Industrial Accidents and Conventional Wisdom*. Falling Wall Press, London, 1973.

240. Dan Nielsen. Use of cause–consequence charts in practical systems analysis. In *Theoretical and Applied Aspects of System Reliability and Safety Assessment*, pages 849–880, SIAM, Philadelphia, 1975.

241. William B. Noble. Developing safe software for critical airborne applications. In *Proceedings of IEEE 6th Digital Conference*, pages 1–5, Baltimore, December 1984.

242. Donald A. Norman. The 'problem' with automation: Inappropriate feedback and interaction, not 'over-automation'. In D.E. Broadbent, J. Reason, and A. Baddeley, editors, *Human Factors in Hazardous Situations*, pages 137–145, Clarendon Press, Oxford, United Kingdom 1990.

243. Donald A. Norman. Categorization of action slips. *Psychological Review*, 88(1):1–15, January 1981.

244. Donald A. Norman. Design rules based on analyses of human error. *Communications of the ACM*, 26(4):254–258, April 1983.

245. Department of Employment. *The Flixborough Disaster: Report of the Court of Inquiry*. Her Majesty's Stationery Office, London, 1975.

246. G. Olsson. Job design in complex man–machine systems. In J. Ranta, editor, *Analysis, Design, and Evaluation of Man-Machine Systems*, pages 313–318. Pergamon Press, New York, 1989.

247. Committee on Shuttle Criticality Review and Hazard Analysis Audit. *Post-Challenger Evaluation of Space Shuttle Risk Assessment and Management*. National Research Council, National Academy Press, Washington D.C., January 1988.

248. C. O'Reilly. Control of industrial major accident hazards—Off-site planning by local authorities. In B.H. Harvey, editor, *European Major Hazards*, pages 107–123. Oyez Scientific and Technical Services, Ltd., London, 1984.

249. Henry Ozog. Hazard identification, analysis, and control. *Hazard Prevention*, pages 11–17, May/June 1985.

250. Henry Ozog and Lisa M. Bendixen. Hazard identification and quantification. *Hazard Prevention*, pages 6–13, September/October 1987.

251. Everett Palmer and Asaf Degani. Electronic checklists: Evaluation of two levels of automation. In *Sixth Symposium on Aviation Psychology*, Columbus, Ohio, 1991.

252. William T. Park. Robot safety suggestions. Technical Report Technical Note No. 159, SRI International, April 29, 1978.

253. David Lorge Parnas. Software aspects of strategic defense systems. *Communications of the ACM*, 28(12):1326–1335, December 1985.

254. Elisabeth Pate-Cornell. Organizational aspects of engineering system safety: The case of offshore platforms. *Science*, 250:1210–1217, 30 November 1990.

255. Elisabeth Pate-Cornell. Fault trees vs. event trees in reliability analysis. *Risk Analysis*, 4(3):177–186, 1984.

256. J. Patrick. Information at the human–machine interface. In Jens Rasmussen, Keith Duncan, and Jacques Leplat, editors, *New Technology and Human Error*, pages 341–345, John Wiley & Sons, New York, 1987.

257. R.D. Patterson. Auditory warning sounds in the work environment. In D.E. Broadbent, J. Reason, and A. Baddeley, editors, *Human Factors in Hazardous Situations*, pages 37–44, Clarendon Press, Oxford, United Kingdom, 1990.

258. Charles Perrow. The President's Commission and the normal accident. In David L. Sills, C.P. Wolf, and Vivien B. Shelanski, editors, *Accident at Three Mile Island: The Human Dimensions*, pages 173–184, Westview Press, Boulder, Colo., 1982.

259. Charles Perrow. *Normal Accidents: Living with High-Risk Technology*. Basic Books, Inc., New York, 1984.

260. Charles Perrow. The habit of courting disaster. *The Nation*, pages 346–356, October 1986.

261. Dan Petersen. *Techniques of Safety Management*. McGraw-Hill Book Company, New York, 1971.

262. J.L. Peterson. *Petri Net Theory and the Modeling of Systems*. Prentice-Hall, Englewood Cliffs, N.J., 1981.

263. Henry Petroski. *To Engineer is Human: The Role of Failure in Successful Design.* St. Martin's Press, New York, 1985.

264. Ted A. Pettit, Sergio R. Concha, and Herb Linn. Application and use of interlock safety devices. *Hazard Prevention*, 19(6):4–9, November/December 1983.

265. William H. Pickering. Systems engineering at the Jet Propulsion Laboratory. In Ralph M. Miles, Jr., editor, *Systems Concepts: Lectures on Contemporary Approaches to Systems*, pages 125–150, John F. Wiley & Sons, New York, 1973.

266. D. Purdue. Australian ATMs . . . . In Peter G. Neumann, editor, *Forum on Risks to the Public in Computer Systems*, ACM Committee on Computers and Public Policy, Volume 5, Issue 3, June 18, 1987.

267. S. Antonio Ruiz Quintanilla. New technologies and human error: Social and organizational factors. In Jens Rasmussen, Keith Duncan, and Jacques Leplat, editors, *New Technology and Human Error*, pages 125–128, John Wiley & Sons, New York, 1987.

268. Simon Ramo. The systems approach. In Ralph M. Miles, Jr., editor, *Systems Concepts: Lectures on Contemporary Approaches to Systems*, pages 13–32, John F. Wiley & Sons, New York, 1973.

269. Jens Rasmussen. Some remarks on mental load. In N. Moray, editor, *Mental Workload: Its Theory and Measurement*, Plenum Press, New York, 1979.

270. Jens Rasmussen. Human factors in high risk technology. In A.E. Green, editor, *High Risk Safety Technology*, pages 143–169, John Wiley & Sons, New York, 1982.

271. Jens Rasmussen. Human error and the problem of causality in analysis of accidents. In D.E. Broadbent, J. Reason, and A. Baddeley, editors, *Human Factors in Hazardous Situations*, pages 1–12, Clarendon Press, Oxford, United Kingdom, 1990.

272. Jens Rasmussen. Models of mental strategies in process plant diagnosis. In Jens Rasmussen and William B. Rouse, editors, *Human Detection and Diagnosis of System Failures*, pages 241–258, Plenum Press, New York, 1981.

273. Jens Rasmussen. Human errors, a taxonomy for describing human malfunction in industrial installations. *Journal of Occupational Accidents*, 4:311–333, 1982.

274. Jens Rasmussen. Approaches to the control of the effects of human error on chemical plant safety. In *International Symposium on Preventing Major Chemical Accidents*, American Inst. of Chemical Engineers, February 1987.

275. Jens Rasmussen. Cognitive control and human error mechanisms. In Jens Rasmussen, Keith Duncan, and Jacques Leplat, editors, *New Technology and Human Error*, pages 53–61, John Wiley & Sons, New York, 1987.

276. Jens Rasmussen. The definition of human error and a taxonomy for technical system design. In Jens Rasmussen, Keith Duncan, and Jacques Leplat, editors, *New Technology and Human Error*, pages 23–30, John Wiley & Sons, New York, 1987.

277. Jens Rasmussen. Reasons, causes, and human error. In Jens Rasmussen, Keith Duncan, and Jacques Leplat, editors, *New Technology and Human Error*, pages 293–301, John Wiley & Sons, New York, 1987.

278. Jens Rasmussen, Keith Duncan, and Jacques Leplat. *New Technology and Human Error*. John Wiley & Sons, New York, 1987.

279. Jens Rasmussen and William B. Rouse, editors. *Human Detection and Diagnosis of System Failures*, Plenum Press, New York, 1981.

280. Norman C. Rasmussen. Methods of hazard analysis and nuclear safety engineering.

In Thomas H. Moss and David L. Sills, editors, *The Three Mile Island Nuclear Accident: Lessons and Implications*, pages 20–36, Annals of the New York Academy of Science, Volume 365, New York, 1981.

281. Norman C. Rasmussen. The application of probabilistic risk assessment techniques to energy technologies. In Theodore S. Glickman and Michael Gough, editors, *Readings in Risk*, pages 195–205, Resources for the Future, New York, 1990.

282. Jerome R. Ravetz. The safety of safeguards. *Minerva*, 12(3):323–325, July 1974.

283. Anders P. Ravn and Hans Rischel. Specifying and verifying requirements of real-time systems. *IEEE Transactions on Software Engineering*, SE-19(1):41–55, January 1993.

284. J.A. Rawlinson. Report on the Therac-25. In *OCTRF/OCI Physicists Meeting*, Kingston, Ontario, May 1987.

285. James Reason. The contribution of latent human failures to the breakdown of complex systems. In D.E. Broadbent, J. Reason, and A. Baddeley, editors, *Human Factors in Hazardous Situations*, pages 27–36, Clarendon Press, Oxford, United Kingdom, 1990.

286. James Reason. A framework for classifying errors. In Jens Rasmussen, Keith Duncan, and Jacques Leplat, editors, *New Technology and Human Error*, pages 5–14, John Wiley & Sons, New York, 1987.

287. James Reason. General error-modelling system (GEMS: A cognitive framework for locating common human error forms. In Jens Rasmussen, Keith Duncan, and Jacques Leplat, editors, *New Technology and Human Error*, pages 63–83, John Wiley & Sons, New York, 1987.

288. James Reason. A preliminary classification of mistakes. In Jens Rasmussen, Keith Duncan, and Jacques Leplat, editors, *New Technology and Human Error*, pages 15–22, John Wiley & Sons, New York, 1987.

289. James Reason. The psychology of mistakes: A brief review of planning failures. In Jens Rasmussen, Keith Duncan, and Jacques Leplat, editors, *New Technology and Human Error*, pages 45–52, John Wiley & Sons, New York, 1987.

290. Jon Damon Reese. *Software Deviation Analysis*. PhD thesis, University of California, Irvine, Calif., 1995.

291. J.F. Richardson. Major hazards research. In B.H. Harvey, editor, *European Major Hazards*, pages 79–88. Oyez Scientific and Technical Services, Ltd., London, 1984.

292. J.-M. Robert. Learning by exploration. In G. Mancini, G. Johannsen, and L. Martensson, editors, *Analysis, Design, and Evaluation of Man–Machine Systems*, pages 189–193, Pergamon Press, New York, 1986.

293. Verne L. Roberts. Defensive design. *Mechanical Engineering*, pages 88–93, September 1984.

294. William P. Rogers. *Introduction to System Safety Engineering*. John Wiley & Sons, New York, 1971.

295. William P. Rogers. *Report of the Presidential Commission on the Space Shuttle Challenger Accident*. U.S. Government Accounting Office, Washington, D.C., 1986.

296. Harold E. Roland and Brian Moriarty. *System Safety Engineering and Management*. John Wiley & Sons, New York, 1983.

297. C.W. Rose. The contribution of operating systems to reliability and safety in real-time systems. In *Proceedings of IFAC Safecomp '82*, Pergamon Press, Elmsford, New York, 1982.

298. Gilbert L. Roth. Aerospace Safety Advisory Panel: Added safety through independence. In *Proc. Fifth International System Safety Conference*, pages IX–C–2 to IX–C–12, System Safety Society, July 1981.

299. Veikko Rouhiainen. The quality assessment of safety analysis. Technical Report Publications 61, Technical Research Center of Finland, Espoo, Finland, 1990.

300. W.B. Rouse and N.M. Morris. Conceptual design of a human error tolerant interface for complex engineering systems. In G. Mancini, G. Johannsen, and L. Martensson, editors, *Analysis, Design, and Evaluation of Man-Machine Systems*, pages 281–286, Pergamon Press, New York, 1986.

301. William B. Rouse. Human–computer interaction in the control of dynamic systems. *Computing Surveys*, 13(1):71–99, March 1981.

302. William D. Ruckelshaus. Risk in a free society. *Risk Analysis*, 4(3):157–162, 1984.

303. William D. Ruckelshaus. Risk, science, and democracy. In Theodore S. Glickman and Michael Gough, editors, *Readings in Risk*, pages 105–118, Resources for the Future, New York, 1990.

304. John Rushby. Kernels for safety. In T. Anderson, editor, *Safe and Secure Computing Systems*, pages 210–220. Blackwell Scientific Publications, 1989. (Proceedings of a symposium held in Glascow, Scotland, October 1986.)

305. John Rushby. Formal verification of algorithms for critical systems). *IEEE Transactions on Software Engineering*, SE-19(1):13–23, January 1993.

306. E.A. Ryder. The control of major hazards—The advisory committee's third and final report. In B.H. Harvey, editor, *European Major Hazards*, pages 5–16, Oyez Scientific and Technical Services, Ltd., London, 1984.

307. Scott D. Sagan. *The Limits of Safety: Organizations, Accidents, and Nuclear Weapons*. Princeton University Press, Princeton, N.J., 1993.

308. R. Saltos. Man killed by accident with medical radiation. *Boston Globe*, June 20, 1986.

309. Fay Sawyier. The case of the DC-10. In Martin Curd and Larry May, editors, *Professional Responsibility for Harmful Actions*, pages 388–401, Kendall Hunt, Dubuque, Iowa, 1984.

310. Roland Schinzinger. Technological hazards and the engineer. *IEEE Technology and Society Magazine*, pages 12–16, June 1986.

311. T.B. Sheridan. Trustworthiness of command and control systems. In J. Ranta, editor, *Analysis, Design, and Evaluation of Man-Machine Systems*, pages 427–431, Pergamon Press, New York, 1989.

312. T.B. Sheridan, L. Charny, M.B. Mendel, and J.B. Roseborough. Supervisory control, mental models and decision aids. In J. Ranta, editor, *Analysis, Design, and Evaluation of Man-Machine Systems*, pages 175–181, Pergamon Press, New York, 1989.

313. Timothy J. Shimeall and N. G. Leveson. An empirical comparison of software fault tolerance and fault elimination. *IEEE Transactions on Software Engineering*, SE-17(2):173–183, February 1991.

314. John Shore. *The Sachertorte Algorithm and Other Antidotes to Computer Anxiety*. Penguin Books, New York, 1986.

315. Society for the Prevention of Accidents in Factories, Mulhouse, Alsace-Lorraine. *Collection of Applicances and Apparatus for the Prevention of Accidents in Factories*, 1895.

316. Stanley D. Spray. Principle-based passive safety in nuclear weapon systems. In *High Consequence Operations Safety Symposium*, July 13 1994, Sandia National Laboratories, Albuquerque, N.M.

317. Spectrum Staff. Too much, too soon: Information overload. *IEEE Spectrum*, pages 51–55, June 1987.

318. T. Sten, L. Bodsberg, O. Ingstad, and T. Ulleberg. Handling process disturbances in petroleum production. In J. Ranta, editor, *Analysis, Design, and Evaluation of Man-Machine Systems*, pages 127–131, Pergamon Press, New York, 1989.

319. William I. Stieglitz. Engineering for safety. *Aeronautical Engineering Review*, February 1948.

320. Robert Sugarman. Nuclear power and the public risk. *IEEE Spectrum*, pages 59–111, November 1979.

321. S. Sugiyama, N. Yuhara, and S. Horiuchi. The effects of participatory mode on the detection of dynamic system failure. In J. Ranta, editor, *Analysis, Design, and Evaluation of Man-Machine Systems*, pages 279–283, Pergamon Press, New York, 1989.

322. J. Suokas and R. Kakko. On the problems and future of safety and risk analysis. *Journal of Hazardous Materials*, 21:105–124, 1989.

323. Jouko Suokas. On the reliability and validity of safety analysis. Technical Report Publications 25, Technical Research Center of Finland, Espoo, Finland, September 1985.

324. Juoko Suokas. The role of management in accident prevention. In *First International Congress on Industrial Engineering and Management*, Paris, June 11–13 1986.

325. Juoko Suokas. Evaluation of the quality of safety and risk analysis in the chemical industry. *Risk Analysis*, 8(4):581–591, 1988.

326. Juoko Suokas. The role of safety analysis in accident prevention. *Accident Analysis and Prevention*, 20(1):67–85, 1988.

327. Juoko Suokas and Veikko Rouhiainen. Quality control in safety and risk analysis. *Journal of Loss Prevention in Process Industry*, 2:67–77, April 1989.

328. J. Suominen and T. Malm. Intelligent safety systems provide production adapted safety strategies for occupational accident prevention. In W. Karwowski, editor, *Ergonomics of Hybrid Automated Systems II*, pages 889–896, Elsevier Science Publishers B.V., New York, 1990.

329. H.A.C. Swaanenburg, H.J. Zwaga, and F. Duijnhouwer. The evaluation of VDU-based man–machine interfaces in process industry. In J. Ranta, editor, *Analysis, Design, and Evaluation of Man-Machine Systems*, pages 71–76, Pergamon Press, New York, 1989.

330. D.J. Taylor, D.E. Morgan, and J.P. Black. Redundancy in data structures: Improving software fault tolerance. *IEEE Transactions on Software Engineering*, SE-6(6):585–594, November 1980.

331. Donald H. Taylor. The hermeneutics of accidents and safety. In Jens Rasmussen, Keith Duncan, and Jacques Leplat, editors, *New Technology and Human Error*, pages 31–41, John Wiley & Sons, New York, 1987.

332. Donald H. Taylor. The role of human action in man–machine system errors. In Jens Rasmussen, Keith Duncan, and Jacques Leplat, editors, *New Technology and Human Error*, pages 287–292, John Wiley & Sons, New York, 1987.

333. J.R. Taylor. Sequential effects in failure mode analysis. In *Theoretical and Applied*

Aspects of System Reliability and Safety Assessment, pages 881–894, SIAM, Phildelphia, 1975.

334. J.R. Taylor. Fault tree and cause–consequence analysis for control software validation. Technical Report RISO-M-2326, Riso National Laboratory, Roskilde, Denmark, January 1982.

335. J.R. Taylor. An integrated approach to the treatment of design and specification errors in electronic systems and software. In E. Lauger and J. Moltoft, editors, *Electronic Components and Systems*, North-Holland Publishing Co., 1982.

336. K.E. Ternham. Automatic complacency. *Flight Crew*, pages 34–35, Winter 1981.

337. J.R. Thomson. *Engineering Safety Assessment: An Introduction*. John Wiley & Sons, New York, 1987.

338. Alton L. Thygerson. *Accidents and Disasters: Causes and Countermeasures*. Prentice-Hall, Englewood Cliffs, N.J., 1977.

339. Barry A. Turner. *Man-Made Disasters*. Wykeham Publications Ltd., London, 1978.

340. U.S.S.R. State Committee on the Utilization of Atomic Energy. The accident at the Chernobyl nuclear power plant and its consequences. Report presented at the AIEA Experts Meeting, Vienna, Austria, August 25–29, 1986.

341. T. van de Putte. Purpose and framework of a safety study in the process industry. *Hazard Prevention*, pages 18–21, January/February 1983.

342. David J. van Horn. Risk assessment techniques for experimentalists. In John M. Hoffmann and Daniel C. Maser, editors, *Chemical Process Hazard Review*, pages 23–29, American Chemical Society, Washington, D.C., 1985.

343. V.F. Venda and B.F. Lomov. Human factors leading to engineering safety systems. *Hazard Prevention*, pages 6–13, March/April 1980.

344. W.E. Vesely, F.F. Goldberg, N.H. Roberts, and D.F. Haasl. Fault tree handbook. Technical Report NUREG-0492, U.S. Nuclear Regulatory Commission, Washington, D.C., 1981.

345. Hedley Voysey. Problems of mingling men and machines. *New Scientist*, pages 416–417, August 1977.

346. B. Wahlstrom and E. Swaton. Influence of organization and management on industrial safety. Technical report, International Institute for Applied Systems Analysis, 1991.

347. Frederick Warner. Foreward: The foundations of risk assessment. In Richard F. Griffiths, editor, *Dealing with Risk: The Planning, Management and Acceptability of Technological Risk*, pages ix–xxii, Manchester University Press, Manchester, England, 1981.

348. Kenneth E.F. Watt. *The Titanic Effect*. Sinauer Associates, Inc., Stamford, Conn., 1974.

349. W.W. Weaver. Pitfalls in current design requirements. *Nuclear Safety*, 22(3), May-June 1981.

350. Vivien Weil. Browns Ferry Case. In Martin Curd and Larry May, editors, *Professional Responsibility for Harmful Actions*, pages 402–411, Kendall Hunt, Dubuque, Iowa, 1984.

351. Alvin M. Weinberg. Science and trans-science. *Minerva*, 10:209–222, 1972.

352. Gerald Weinberg. *An Introduction to General Systems Thinking*. John Wiley & Sons, New York, 1975.

353. Earl L. Weiner. Controlled flight into terrain accidents: System-induced errors. *Human Factors*, 22(5):170–177, May 1980.

354. Earl L. Weiner and Renwick E. Curry. Flight-deck automation: Promises and problems. *Ergonomics*, 23(10):995–1011, 1980.

355. D. Whitfield and G. Ord. Some human factors aspects of computer aiding concepts for ATCOs. *Human Factors*, 22(5):569–580.

356. C.D. Wickens and C. Kessel. Failure detection in dynamic systems. In Jens Rasmussen and William B. Rouse, editors, *Human Detection and Diagnosis of System Failures*, pages 155–170, Plenum Press, New York, 1981.

357. C.P. Wolf. Some lessons learned. In David L. Sills, C.P. Wolf, and Vivien B. Shelanski, editors, *Accident at Three Mile Island: The Human Dimensions*, pages 215–232, Westview Press, Boulder, Colo., 1982.

358. Tony Wray. The everyday risks of playing safe. *New Scientist*, pages 61–65, September 8, 1988.

359. E. Yourdon and L. Constantine. *Structured Design*. Prentice-Hall, Englewood Cliffs, N.J., 1979.

360. Edwin L. Zebroski. Sources of common cause failures in decision making involved in man-made catastrophes. In James J. Bonin and Donald E. Stevenson, editors, *Risk Assessment in Setting National Priorities*, pages 443–454, Plenum Press, New York, 1989.

361. H.A. Zogg. System safety methodology and applied to an underground rail station. *Hazard Prevention*, pages 16–18, November/December 1985.

CREDITS

Epigraph Credits

Dedication. From Samuel C. Florman, *The Civilized Engineer*, pp. 149–150. New York: St. Martin's Press, 1987. Reprinted with permission.

Preface. Patrick Lagadec. *Major Technological Risk: An Assessment of Industrial Disasters.* Pergamon Press, New York, 1982.

Chapter 1. William D. Ruckelshaus. Risk in a free society. *Risk Analysis*, 4(3):157–162, 1984. Reprinted with permission of Plenum Publishing Corp.

Chapter 2. G. Frank McCormick, Flight Contols Software Specialist and FAA Designated Engineering Representative Boeing Commercial Airplane Group. "When reach exceeds grasp." Unpublished essay.

Chapter 2. T. B. Sheridan. Trustworthiness of command and control systems. In J. Ranta, editor, *Analysis, Design, and Evaluation of Man-Machine Systems*, pages 427–431, Pergamon Press, New York, 1989.

Chapter 4. C. O. Miller. A comparison of military and civil approaches to aviation system safety. *Hazard Prevention*, pages 29–34, May/June 1985.

Chapter 4. Richard J. Hornick, "Dreams—Design and destiny." *Human Factors*, 29(1):111–121, 1987.

Chapter 5. Earl L. Weiner and Renwick E. Curry, "Flight-deck automation: Promises and problems." *Ergonomics*, 23(10):995–1011, 1980. Reprinted with permission of Taylor & Francis Groups Ltd.

Chapter 6. From Ralph M. Miles, Jr., *Systems Concepts: Lectures on Contemporary Approaches to Systems*, p. 5, John F. Wiley & Sons, New York, 1973. Reprinted with permission.

Chapter 9. Russell L. Ackoff, "Towards a system of systems concepts." *Management Science*, 17(11):661–671, July 1971. Copyright 1971, The Institute of Management Sciences, 290 Westminster Street, Providence, R.I. 02903.

Part IV. From *What Went Wrong?* by Trevor A. Kletz. Copyright ©1988 by Gulf Publishing Co., Houston, Tex. Used with permission. All rights reserved.

Chapter 11. Anthony Hidden. *Investigation into the Clapham Junction Railway Accident.* Department of Transport, Her Majesty's Stationary Office (HMSO), PO Box 276, London SW8 5DT, 1990. Crown copyright is reproduced with the permission of the Controller of HMSO.

Chapter 13. From *What Went Wrong?* by Trevor A. Kletz. Copyright ©1988 by Gulf Publishing Co., Houston, Tex. Used with permission. All rights reserved.

Chapter 15. Trevor Kletz. "Wise after the event." *Control and Instrumentation*, (UK), Morgan Grampian P.L.C., 20(10):57–59, October 1988. Reprinted with permission.

Chapter 16. From Mike W. Martin and Roland Schinzinger. *Ethics in Engineering*, p. 139. N.Y.: McGraw-Hill Book Company, 1989. Reprinted with permission of the McGraw-Hill, Inc.

Chapter 16. G. Frank McCormick, Flight Contols Software Specialist and FAA Designated Engineering Representative Boeing Commercial Airplane Group. "When reach exceeds grasp." Unpublished essay.

Chapter 17. From John Fuller, "Death by robot," *Omni*, March 1984. Reprinted by permission of Roberta Pryor, Inc.

Chapter 17. Donald A. Norman, "The 'problem' with automation: Inappropriate feedback and interaction, not 'over-automation.' " In D.E. Broadbent, J. Reason, and A. Baddeley, editors, *Human Factors in Hazardous Situations*, pages 137–145, Clarendon Press, Oxford, 1990. By permission of Oxford University Press.

Epilogue. G. Frank McCormick, Flight Contols Software Specialist and FAA Designated Engineering Representative Boeing Commercial Airplane Group. "When reach exceeds grasp." Unpublished essay.

Text Credits

15. Robert U. Ayres and Pradeep K. Rohatgi, "Bhopal: Lessons for technological decision-makers." *Technology in Society*, 9:p.36, 1987. Copyright 1987 with kind permission from Elsevier Science Ltd., the Boulevard, Langford Lane, Kidlingt6on, OX 5 1GB UK.

19. Richard S. Barrett. "The human equation in operating a nuclear power plant." In David L. Sills, C.P. Wolf, and Vivien B. Shelanski, eds. *Accident at Three Mile Island: The Human Dimensions*, pages 164, 169. Westview Press, Boulder, Colo., 1982. Reprinted with permission of the Social Science Research Council, New York.

71. From K. D. Duncan, "Reflections on fault diagnostic expertise." In Jens Rasmussen, et al., eds. *New Technology and Human Error*, pages 261–269. Chichester, UK: John Wiley & Sons, Ltd., 1987. Reprinted with permission.

83. Baruch Fischhoff, Christoph Hohenemser, Roger Kasperson, and Robert Kates. Handling hazards. In Jack Dowie and Paul Lefrere, editors, *Risk and Chance*, page 168, Open University Press, Milton Keynes, United Kingdom, 1980.

121. Anthony Hidden, *Investigation into the Clapham Junction Railway Accident*. Department of Transport, Her Majesty's Stationary Office (HMSO), PO Box 276, London SW8 5DT, 1990. Crown copyright is reproduced with the permission of the Controller of HMSO.

127. Richard J. Hornick, "Dreams—Design and destiny." *Human Factors*, 29(1):113; 114; 111–121, 1987.

160. Trevor Kletz, *An Engineer's View of Human Error*. Institution of Chemical Engineers, Rugby, Warwickshire, United Kingdom, 1991. Reprinted with permission.

193. Thomas G. Lombardo, "TMI: An insider's viewpoint." *IEEE Spectrum*, page 55, May 1980, ©1980 IEEE.

216. G. Frank McCormick, Flight Control Software Specialist and FAA Designated Engineering Representative, Boeing Commercial Airplane Group, "When reach exceeds grasp." Unpublished essay.

242. Donald A. Norman. The 'problem' with automation: Inappropriate feedback and interaction, not 'over-automation.' In D.E. Broadbent, J. Reason, and A. Baddeley, editors, *Human Factors in Hazardous Situations*, pages 137, 138, 140, 143. Clarendon Press, Oxford, United Kingdom 1990. By permission of Oxford University Press.

252. William T. Park, "Robot safety suggestions." Technical Report Technical Note No. 159, SRI International, April 29, 1978. Reprinted with permission.

254. Excerpted with permission from Elisabeth Pate-Cornell, "Organizational aspects of engineering system safety: The case of offshore platforms." *Science*, 250:1215, 11/30/90. Copyright 1990 American Association for the Advancement of Science.

259. From *Normal Accidents: Living with High-Risk Technology*. by Charles Perrow. Copyright ©1984 by Basic Books, Inc. Reprinted by permission of Basic Books, a division of Harper Collins Publisher, Inc.

354. Earl L. Weiner and Renwick E. Curry, "Flight-deck automation: Promises and problems." *Ergonomics*, 23(10):1007, 1980. Reprinted with permission of Taylor & Francis Group Ltd.

358. Tony Wray, "The everyday risks of playing safe." *New Scientist*, pages 61–65, September 8, 1988. Reprinted with permission.

INDEX

A320 accidents, 93
Acceptable risk, 15, 55, 181, 556, 616
Access control, 411–412, 423, 425
Access rights, 423, 424
Accident, definition, 175–176
Accident investigation, 83–86, 551
Accident reports, 243-244
  bias, 43–44
Accountability, 230–231
Action Error Analysis (AEA), 350, 357–358
Activation Trigger Schema Model
    (Norman), 210–213
Active control, 154–155, 414–415, 442
Active failures, 204
Aerospace industry, 127,405
Aerospace Safety Advisory Panel, 228–229
Air Traffic Control (ATC), 30, 114, 119,
    124–125, 416
Air Force, 145–149, 579
Air Safety Reporting System (ASRS),
    245–246
Alarms, 122–123, 440, 445, 469–474
  alarm analysis, 416, 473
  Bhopal, 40, 42, 119
  false alarms, 119, 471
  Seveso, 590
  Three Mile Island, 114, 471, 472–473
  validity checks, 548
Alert queue, 367. *See also* Event queue.
Alertness, 118–120, 453–454
Ambiguity in requirements. 363. *See also*
    Completeness.
Apollo, 62, 140, 149, 166, 228
Apollo 13 accident, 61, 72, 404, 558–563
Applegate memo, 50–51, 566
Articulatory distance, 480
ASRS. *See* Air Safety Reporting System.
Assertions, software, 419, 504–505, 506
Atomic Energy Authority (Britain), 619

Atomic Energy Commission (AEC), 54,
    66, 619
Attenuation, 414
Audits, 161–162, 260, 608
Audit trail, 242, 246, 252, 551
  software, 255, 546, 550
Auditing, software, 419–420
Authority for safety, 74, 230–231
Authority limiting, 422–423
Autopilot, 11, 117, 407
Aviation, civil. *See* Civil aviation.

B-52 accidents, 160, 161, 432
Babcock and Wilcox reactors, 64, 65, 87,
    96
Backward recovery, 437–439
Backward search, 308–309, 332, 347
Baltic Star accident, 39–40
Barriers, 183, 421–431
Baton, 423, 428
Bhopal, 3, 5, 6, 40-42, 55, 58, 59–60, 64,
    69, 74, 77, 119, 413, 441, 583,
    598–608
Boeing 767 incidents, 99, 101
Bottom-up search, 165–166, 309, 361
Bravo oil rig, 48
British Health and Safety Executive, 67
British Health and Safety at Work Act, 67,
    229
Browns Ferry, 12, 57–58, 65–67, 434

Capabilities, 423
Capacity, 30, 375, 376–379, 379–382
  environmental (output), 379–382
Capture errors, 211, 212–213, 219
Causal factors, 43
Cause (causality)
  definition, 43
  filtering, 43–44
  hierarchical model, 48–51, 138, 197